COLLEGE LIBRARY

**Please return this book by the date stamped below
- if recalled, the loan is reduced to 10 days**

Fines are payable for late return

Published by A & C Black Publishers Ltd
37 Soho Square, London W1D 3QZ
www.acblack.com

Seventh edition 2002
Reprinted 2000
Sixth edition 1998
Fifth edition 1994
Fourth edition 1990
Third edition 1986
Second edition 1982
First edition 1980

First and second editions published by
Greenaway, Surrey

ISBN 0 7136 6096 1

A CIP catalogue record for this book is
available from the British Library.

A & C Black uses paper produced with
elemental chlorine-free pulp, harvested from
managed sustainable forests.

Acknowledgements
Cover photography © Collections

Maps by ML Design (www.ml-design.co.uk)

Printed and bound in Great Britain by
Creative Print & Design (Wales), Ebbw Vale

CONTENTS

FOREWORD

Many may like to walk out into the prime countryside with a map or a guidebook. I am lucky enough to be able to do that from my door. But if you are looking for a clear, and proven, walking route, turn to this Handbook. It is the only publication that records all the long distance paths in the United Kingdom and points you to the detailed information on them.

The origin of these paths is diverse – a geological line like the Greensand Ridge Walk in Bedfordshire; a geographical feature like the Cumbria Coastal Way; a historical theme along St Cuthbert's Way across the Borders; and many others. Whether you are looking for a week of walking in our finest landscapes, or a well-marked route for a day, you can find it easily.

For full enjoyment you should combine the Handbook with the new Long Distance Path Chart to be published by Harvey Maps. This will show you the wide range of walks available to everyone's taste. The LDWA has done a superb compilation job. It is absorbing reading and will lead to days, weeks, and years of pleasure and discovery.

Sir John Johnson
President, Long Distance Walkers Association

ACKNOWLEDGEMENTS

The Long Distance Walkers Association is most grateful to all those who have contributed to this Handbook, all of whom have worked on a voluntary basis. A team, comprised of Sue Hazell, Paul Lawrence, Les Maple and Brian Smith, completed the bulk of the work, with Ann Sayer producing the maps. Thanks are due to many members of the LDWA who have contributed information or helped in other ways, along with individuals or organizations who have provided information or responded to enquiries about particular paths.

INTRODUCTION

Walking a long distance path is a fulfilling experience: a fine route through attractive countryside, with the route planning taken care of, and, at the end, the satisfaction of having achieved an objective, perhaps commemorated by a badge or certificate.

The first long distance path to catch the public imagination was the Pennine Way, conceived by Tom Stephenson in 1935 and eventually opened in 1965 as Great Britain's first official long distance route. A trickle and then a flood of other paths followed, providing many attractive ways through the varied British countryside. Such routes vary enormously, from those that simply follow the banks of a river to those that cross open moorland or mountain ridges where navigation skills are essential. Some routes are semi-urban, but nevertheless manage to find delightful back-ways. Books or leaflets have been written about many routes, usually with a route description or sketch map, and perhaps with notes on local history and wildlife. The attention given to the development and documentation gives walkers confidence in the quality of a route and thus enhances enjoyment.

Now in its seventh edition the Directory has been fully updated throughout. Well over 600 main walks are covered – many new routes and linking walks have been added and the regional maps expanded.

An up-to-date summary of each walk describes its special character and distinctive features. To help in finding and planning a route, the locations of all main paths are indicated on easy-to-read regional maps.

Routes range from National Trails, such as the South West Coast Path, paths developed by local authorities, such as the Fife Coastal Path, and routes developed by enthusiastic individuals, such as the London Countryway. This Handbook is not itself a guidebook, but gives an overview of the network of long distance paths to give ideas on where to wander. For each route there is an outline of the places visited, the terrain, linking routes, and, most importantly, a list of publications where further details can be obtained, to follow the route in detail.

The Handbook attempts to include routes of 20 miles or more that are mainly off-road, for which some form of route description publication is readily available. Some shorter routes are included, where, for example, they provide useful links between longer routes. Also included are some challenges for which the detailed route is self-devised and for which navigational skills are required.

The Long Distance Walkers Association (LDWA), who have compiled this Handbook, hope that you will find the information useful, and above all that you will take great pleasure from walking the routes and discovering attractive and interesting parts of Britain.

The addresses and websites of organisations and companies mentioned in the Handbook are gathered at the back of the book. For those mentioned in the introductory sections, the telephone numbers and, where available, e-mail addresses are given within these sections.

ROUTE DETAILS

Information on each route is presented in a standard format. The header gives the regional area of the route, and the route length in miles and kilometres. A brief description indicates towns and villages en route, the terrain, linking routes including some shorter local paths, and any special features. The locations of the start and finish of the paths are stated, with full grid references. The relevant Ordnance Survey (OS) maps, both 1:50,000 and 1:25,000 scales, which cover the routes are listed, along with an indication of whether the routes are named on OS maps. The nature of waymarks, if any, is indicated, as is any user group (e.g. Pennine Way Association), along with any website address for the path itself. Publications pertaining to the paths are listed and, where available, details of badges and certificates available to those who complete the route.

MAPS

The number against each route entry is used to identify the route on the maps at the back of the Handbook. A coloured map showing the LDP path network, available folded or as a wallchart, is to be published by Harvey Maps (01786 841202) in conjunction with this Handbook and is obtainable through the LDWA (Merchandise 0115 992 1849) or from booksellers.

A large-scale map should be carried when walking any LDP. Each route entry includes its Ordnance Survey map numbers (Ordnance Survey: tel 08456 050505). The Landranger 1:50,000 scale maps are good for initial planning and adequate for most route-finding purposes. For those who like more detail, including field boundaries, etc, the Ordnance Survey Outdoor Leisure and Explorer 1:25,000 series now cover all of England and Wales and parts of Scotland. The routes of many major LDPs are marked on these maps. Official guidebooks to the English National Trails contain extracts from OS maps and these may suffice if detours from the route are not contemplated. Other publishers, in particular Harvey Maps, have produced dedicated maps for certain LDPs.

Maps are widely available through local book and outdoor shops. Major stockists include Cordee Ltd (0116 254 3579), Guidepost (0115 937 6716), The Map Shop (0800 08454080), National Map Centre (020 7222 2466), Northern Map Distributors (0800 834920) and Stanfords (020 7836 1321).

PUBLICATIONS

A criterion for a route to be included in this Handbook is that there is a current source of information that enables it to be followed. Usually this is a publication describing the path, but these vary enormously, from leaflets to guidebooks, and from a bare route outline to a full description with details of transport and accommodation. A few routes are marked only on OS maps, and one has only a website, each without a supporting paper publication. In some cases, the detailed route is self-devised. For books, publication details and costs are given. Many books are available through booksellers or from Internet sales outlets, but privately published books may have to be obtained from the author or distributor. Leaflets may often be obtained on request by sending an SAE, or there may be a small charge. Full addresses of publishers and distributors are listed at the back of the Handbook. Tourist Information Centres often stock publications relating to local paths.

Publication information is believed to be correct at the time of going to press, but it should be remembered that books go out of print, costs change, and some leaflets are revised regularly.

WALKING LONG DISTANCE PATHS (LDPs)

There are many approaches to walking LDPs, depending on time available, fitness, whether the walk is to be combined with other local sightseeing, etc. The most popular approach is to walk a path over several consecutive days, covering 10–20 miles each day and stopping at bed and breakfast accommodation en route, or perhaps camping. A number of organisations offer led holidays along LDPs, with accommodation and meals arranged. For some paths there is a central booking service that will arrange nightly accommodation along the route, and sometimes arrangements can be made to transport luggage between overnight stops. Longer paths can be completed in sections over several holidays or weekends. Some walkers cover a route in a number of day walks, though transport back to the starting point each time can be difficult. A shorter LDP can be an exhilarating challenge to complete in a single long day, and walking groups sometimes include a 20-mile path in their programme.

Careful planning is essential for any long distance route and for this the publications listed in this Handbook should prove helpful. The distance to be walked each day requires thought: trying to walk too far carrying a heavy rucksack will detract from the enjoyment! Advice on safe walking may be found in many books, and specific local advice is contained in many of the publications cited. Particular attention should be given to equipment, clothing and food to be carried, which will depend on the remoteness and terrain of the route.

ACCOMMODATION

Some publications include accommodation information, and the route entries indicate where a dedicated accommodation list is published. The value of Local Tourist Information Centres (TICs), who have extensive accommodation lists, should not be underestimated. Contact details of all British TICs are included in the special '*Visitor Map*' publication – telephone numbers can also be found in *Yellow Pages*. There are many other rural 'bed and breakfasts' that simply display a sign or rely on word of mouth. An Internet search can lead quickly to accommodation in many areas.

Visitor Map of Britain's Tourist Information Centres, published by Visitmap Limited (01342 825999 and fax 01342 825666), cost £1.50 (incs p&p).

The Rambler's Yearbook and Accommodation Guide, ISBN 1901184382 (2002) published annually by the Ramblers' Association (RA Central Office – London, 020 7339 8500), £5.99 but distributed free to members, is a valuable source for walkers, which includes B&B, camping barns, bunkhouses and hostels.

The various Youth Hostels Associations maintain networks of youth hostels and camping barns, and in some cases provide a booking service: in England and Wales, The Youth Hostels Association (01629 825850, fax 01629 581062); the Scottish Youth Hostels Association (01786 451181) and for Northern Ireland, Hostelling International (028 9032 4733).

The Backpackers Press (01629 580427 and e-mail DaveDalley@aol.com) publish two guides by Sam Dalley, the *Independent Hostel Guide*, ISBN 0953618501, £4.95, and *Accommodation for Groups*, ISBN 0952338165, £2.95.

Stilwell (020 7739 7179, fax 020 7739 7191 and e-mail info@stilwell.co.uk) publish B&B information, in *Stilwell's National Trail Companion*, ISBN 1900861259, £9.95 (+ £1.00 p&p) for 46 major LDPs, and in *Stilwell's Britain: Bed and Breakfast 2002*, ISBN 1900861283, £10.95 (+£2.00 p+p) and its companion *Scotland* guide, ISBN 1900861291, £7.95 (+ £1.00 p&p).

UP TO DATE INFORMATION

With ever increasing outdoor activity, long distance paths are being developed all the time, some cease to be maintained, new books and leaflets are written whilst others go out of print. The LDWA journal *Strider* has a regular column 'News of Long Distance Paths' which keeps readers up to date with developments.

The Worldwide Web (or Internet) has become a standard source of information. Many long distance paths, including national trails, have their own web pages. Whilst most web pages are well maintained, users should be aware that not all information is regularly updated. There are links to many paths from the LDWA pages: www.ldwa.org.uk

The LDWA maintains a comprehensive record of LDP information, and receives regular information from many sources. Information on new routes or publications is always welcome, and should be sent to the LDWA LDP Information Officer, 21 Upcroft, Windsor, Berks, SL4 3NH.

SCOTLAND AND IRELAND

As a result of different walking traditions, relatively few long distance routes have been developed in Scotland and Ireland. This does not mirror the tremendous walking opportunities to be found, but rather a reluctance to emphasise particular routes through true wilderness areas.

In Scotland there is a fine network of hill paths that can be combined into all manner of long distance expeditions. *Scottish Hill Tracks*, ISBN 0950281182, costing £16.00 (including map), published by the Scottish Rights of Way and Access Society (0131 558 1222), describes 330 routes across hills and moors and through glens and passes in all areas from the Cheviots to the Highlands.

This Handbook includes waymarked routes in Northern Ireland. An increasing number of walking routes, with route guides and waymarking, are being developed in the Republic of Ireland, which is outside the scope of this Handbook. Details are available from the Irish Tourist Board (08000 397000) and from EastWest Mapping (00353 54 77835, e-mail: eastwest@eircom.net). Hostel accommodation is listed in the publication *Ireland: All the Hostels* (0121 449 0298 and listed in the address index).

CANAL ROUTES

Canal towpaths offer opportunities for long distance routes. Several are described in this Handbook. More information on canals is available from British Waterways (01923 226422).

E-ROUTES: UK AND EUROPE

Over the past 10 years and more a number of European Long Distance Paths that cross several countries have been established. Currently, two of these, E2 and E8, go through Britain, with a proposed third, E9, being finalised. The E2 runs from Galway to Nice. The 3030 miles (4850 kilometres) route starts in Stranraer, then goes through Southern Scotland, with variants through Eastern England and the Netherlands or Central and Southern England and Flanders to Antwerp, then Ardennes, Luxembourg, Vosges, Jura, Grande Traversée des Alpes (this is the well-known GR5) to Nice. The E8 is a 2740 miles (4390 kilometres) route from East Cork in Ireland to Istanbul, crossing England from Liverpool to Hull along the Trans-Pennine Way, then via Rotterdam, Aachen, Regensburg, Vienna, Bratislava, through Southern Bulgaria to the Turkish Border. The E9, the 'European Coast Path' from France to Estonia, is currently being extended along the South Coast of England.

Details of these E-routes may be reached through the LDPs section of the LDWA web pages: www.ldwa.org.uk

Many European countries have their own LDP networks, which in some cases are highly structured. Details may be obtained through the European Ramblers Association: www.era-ewv-ferp.org.

The paths included in the E2, E8 and E9 routes comprise:

E2   (Eastern Variant: Dover – Stranraer)
North Downs Way National Trail, Dover to Guildford; **Wey-South Path/Wey Navigation**, Guildford to Weybridge; **Thames Path National Trail**, Weybridge to Oxford; **Oxford Canal**, Oxford to Kirtlington; **Oxfordshire Way**, Kirtlington to Bourton on the Water; **Heart of England Way**, Bourton on the Water to Cannock Chase; **Staffordshire Way**, Cannock Chase to Rushton Spencer; **Gritstone Trail**, Rushton Spencer to Disley; **Goyt Way**, Disley to Compstall; **Etherow/Goyt Valley Way**, Compstall to Broadbottom; **Tameside Trail**, Broadbottom to Mossley; **Oldham Way**, Mossley to Standedge; **Pennine Way National Trail**, Standedge, via Middleton in Teesdale where the Central/Southern variant joins, to Kirk Yetholm; **St Cuthbert's Way**, Kirk Yetholm to Melrose; **Southern Upland Way**, Melrose to Stranraer.

E2   (Central/Southern Variant: Harwich – Stranraer)
Essex Way, Harwich to Dedham; **Stour Valley Path**, Dedham (via link path) to Stetchworth; **Icknield Way**, Stetchworth to Linton; **(Roman road link not included in the Handbook**, Linton to Cambridge); **Fen Rivers Way**, Cambridge to Ely; **Hereward Way**, Ely to Rutland Water; **Viking Way**, Rutland Water to Barton-upon-Humber; **(Humber Bridge**, Barton-upon-Humber to Hessle); **Wolds Way National Trail**, Hessle to Filey; **Cleveland Way National Trail**, Filey to Guisborough; **Tees Link**, Guisborough to Middlesbrough; **Teesdale Way**, Middlesbrough to Middleton in Teesdale; joint section **Pennine Way National Trail**, Middleton in Teesdale to Kirk Yetholm; **St Cuthbert's Way and Southern Upland Way** (as above).

E8   Trans Pennine Trail, section from Hull to Liverpool.

E9 – Proposed   Dover to Plymouth
Saxon Shore Way, Dover to Rye; **1066 Country Walk**, Rye to Jevington; **South Downs Way National Trail**, Jevington to Queen Elizabeth Country Park (QECP); **Staunton Way**, QECP to Broadmarsh; **Solent Way**, Broadmarsh to Portsmouth. From Portsmouth there are mainland and Isle of Wight (IoW) variants.

Mainland variant: Solent Way, Portsmouth to Lymington on Sea and Milford on Sea; (**Local routes**, not yet finalised, Milford on Sea to Poole); **Sandbanks Ferry** to Studland; **South West Coast Path National Trail**, Studland to Plymouth.

IoW variant: Ferry, Portsmouth to Ryde; **Isle of Wight Coastal Path (IoWCP)**, Ryde to Bembridge; **Bembridge Trail**, Bembridge to Newport; (**Local route**, Newport to Carisbrooke); **Tennyson Trail**, Carisbrooke to The Needles; **IoWCP**, Needles to Yarmouth; **Ferry**, Yarmouth to Lymington; then as the mainland variant to Plymouth.

THE LONG DISTANCE WALKERS ASSOCIATION

The LDWA's aim is *to further the interests of those who enjoy long distance walking*, with a particular emphasis on non-competitive walking in rural, mountainous and moorland areas. The LDWA disseminates information on long distance paths, and also promotes 'challenge walks', that is cross-country walks undertaken by many walkers on the same occasion aiming to complete a route within a given time limit. Sometimes LDPs are used for challenge events; indeed the South Downs Way National Trail has been the basis for the LDWA's annual 100-miles event on six occasions.

The LDWA was founded in 1972, becoming the Sports Council governing body for Long Distance Walking in 1985 and a company limited by guarantee in 1999. The Association now has over 6000 members and 40 local groups across Britain each with programmes of regular walks. The magazine *Strider*, sent to LDWA members three times a year, contains articles on all aspects of long distance walking, including information on long distance paths, details and reports of challenge walks, and local group programmes. The LDWA maintains the 'Hillwalkers' Register' of those who have completed ascents of hills in various categories.

A membership application form may be obtained from the LDWA Membership Secretary, 63 Yockley Close, The Maultway, Camberley, Surrey GU15 1QQ, or from the Web page: www.ldwa.org.uk, where further information on the LDWA may be found. The annual subscription for 2002 is £7.00 for individual membership and £10.50 for family membership.

DISCLAIMER

Whilst every effort has been made to ensure that the information in this Handbook is accurate and expedient, no responsibility whatsoever can be accepted by the Long Distance Walkers Association Limited, its directors, officers or authors, or the publishers, for any consequences arising from the contents of the Handbook.

Inclusion of a route in this Handbook is in no way an indication of its quality in terms of scenery, attraction, usability or safety. Whilst care has been taken to include routes that are on rights of way, or paths or access areas where permission exists, inclusion of a route is no evidence of a right of way or permissive access.

The content of this Handbook depends on information obtained from well over 2000 enquiries and from many publications and reliance has had to be placed on the information providers. Whilst every effort has been made to ensure correctness of detail, errors or omissions may have escaped notice.

This Handbook does not attempt to provide advice on safety aspects of walking. There are inherent risks in any outdoor activity, and walkers should note the specific safety advice offered in the various publications.

HOW TO USE THIS HANDBOOK

The Handbook recognises two categories of routes: main routes (numbered 1–638) and sub-routes (mentioned within main route entries). Sub-routes are usually local, shorter or linking routes. Use the maps in conjunction with the text – many queries can be answered via the maps.

The Handbook has six main parts:
- Introduction, including background for maps, accommodation, E-Routes etc.
- Details of Routes – gives detailed information for each main, numbered path, including maps, waymarks, publications, badges and certificates.
- Routes by Distance – lists main and sub-routes in order of distance down to 10 miles (16 km).
- Addresses list – lists sources of publications and other useful addresses and websites.
- Index – the alphabetical index of main routes, with route (not page) numbers, and sub-routes.
- Map Section – comprises overall UK and detailed regional maps showing route locations and numbers.

How to find a named route/path
- Use the Details of Routes (alphabetical order) to find it, if it is a main route.
- Use the Index to find it as a sub-route, or look for similar names. Then follow the cross-references to main route numbers. Read descriptions for nearby routes if this fails.
- Use the Map Section showing waymarked routes and selected unwaymarked routes, if you are unsure of the name but know the area.
- Use the list at the end of the Map Section, listing by area unwaymarked routes not shown on the maps.

How to find information on routes in an area where you plan to walk
- Use the Map Section maps to find waymarked and selected unwaymarked routes.
- For other unwaymarked routes not on the maps, find the area name from the overall UK map and use the listing by area at the end to find the path numbers in that area.
- Then go to the relevant Details of Routes to find information on sub-routes.

How to use the route details and obtain a publication, badge or certificate
- Use the Key Page for a quick guide to a route entry: there is more background in the Introduction.
- Use the route website address that may provide more, or updated information and contact any user group.
- Identify the publication, badge or certificate and the source of supply given in parentheses – ( ).
- Write to the address of the source given in the Address List, enclosing an SAE and payment. Bookshops will supply many publications but publishers' addresses are included in case of difficulty or to obtain their book lists.

Please provide feedback, updates and new information to the LDWA – address in the Introduction under 'Up to date information'.

KEY TO ROUTE ENTRIES

Path name and areas

Path number and distance

Description and links to main and local paths

Wolds Way National Trail   624

E Yorks, N Yorks   *127 km / 79 miles*

This National Trail goes west along the River Humber and then north around the western edge of the Yorkshire Wolds, through woods and across arable land through Thixendale, and along the northern escarpment of the Wolds through dry valleys and sheep pasture to the coast and the Cleveland Way National Trail at Filey. See Centenary Way (North Yorkshire), East Riding Heritage Way, High Hunsley Circuit, Humber Bridge Link Walk, Minster Way. See also E-Routes (E2).

Start:	Hessle (Haven), E Yorks	TA035256
Finish:	Filey Brigg, N Yorks	TA126817
Landranger Maps:	100, 101, 106, 107	✔
1 : 25,000 Maps:	Ex 281, 300, 301	
Waymark:	National Trail Acorn	
Path website:	www.woldsway.gov.uk	

Publications, badges and certificates:
Softback: *Wolds Way* (Official Guide) by Roger Ratcliffe (Aurum Press) 1992. ISBN 1854101897. 210 x 130. £9.99.
Leaflet: *Wolds Way* (Countryside Agency Publications) 1992. A4/3. Free.
Booklet: *Wolds Way Accommodation and Information Guide* (North York Moors National Park) Annual. 30pp. £0.95 (+ 55p p&p).
Badge: (RA East Yorkshire & Derwent Area). £1.00 (+ SAE).

Start/finish and OS Grid References

Indicates by ✔ if path is named on OS maps

OS maps: Explorer (Ex) & Outdoor Leisure (OL)

Waymarking symbol

Path website

Pages and size

Publication type

Source of Supply – in ( )

Price including post and packing and envelope size

- Paths named on OS maps may not yet be marked on all OS maps.
- Sources of Supply for publications, addresses and websites are tabulated in the index section.
- Books can usually be obtained through high street booksellers
- Sizes follow standard paper sizes (e.g., A5) or are in millimetres; SAE sizes include some inch sizes.
- A4/3 means an A4 trifold, etc. Items may be further folded for posting.

Abbreviations

AONB	Area of Outstanding Beauty	**RA**	Ramblers' Association
ISBN	International Standard Book Number	**SAE**	stamped addressed envelope
		SSSI	Site of Special Scientific Interest
LDP	Long Distance Path	**TBA**	to be announced
LDWA	Long Distance Walkers Association Ltd	**TIC**	Tourist Information Centre
		YHA	Youth Hostels Association
OS	Ordnance Survey		

DETAILS OF ROUTES

1 to 15 Link   1

Beds, Cambs, Northants, Suffolk   *120 km / 75 miles*

A challenge walk designed jointly by the Waendel and HavAC Walkers and split into 13 sections. St Neots and Cambridge are visited en route.

Start:	Wellingborough, Northants	SP888683
Finish:	Haverhill, Suffolk	TL675455
Landranger maps:	152, 153, 154	
1 : 25,000 maps:	Ex 208, 209, 210, 224, 225	
Path website:	www.bwf-ivv.org.uk/1to15.htm	

Publications, badges and certificates:
Leaflets: *The 1 to 15 Link* (Waendel Walkers Club). 13 route leaflets; A5. £5.00 (+ 30p p&p).
Badge: (Waendel Walkers Club). Free on completion of entire walk.
Certificates: available for each section of the walk (Waendel Walkers Club). Free.

1066 Country Walk   2

E Sussex   *50 km / 31 miles*

A route taking in topics of historical interest with links from the main route between Battle and Hastings and between Doleham and Bexhill. From Pevensey Castle there are further links to two points on the South Downs Way National Trail near to Jevington. In essence a link is created between the Saxon Shore Way (at Rye) and the South Downs Way. See E-Routes (E9).

Start:	Pevensey Castle, Pevensey, E Sussex	TQ646048
Finish:	Rye, E Sussex	TQ918205
Landranger maps:	189, 199	✔
1 : 25,000 maps:	Ex 123, 124, 125	
Waymark:	Red & white named logo	

Publications, badges and certificates:
Paperback: *The 1066 Country Walk* by Brian Smailes (Challenge Publications) 2000. ISBN 1903568005. 57pp; 125 x 185. £4.95 (incs p&p).
Leaflet: *1066 Country Walk* published by Rother District Council (Battle Tourist Information Centre) 2000. A4/3. Free (+ 9 x 4 SAE).
Badge: (Challenge Publications). £3.50 (incs p&p).
Certificate: (Challenge Publications). £0.75 (incs p&p).

Abberley Amble 3
Worcs *32 km / 20 miles*

A route of mixed terrain through woods and valleys it passes a number of points of local interest including Glasshampton Monastery, the Burf (a cider house) and Grubbers Alley.

Start and Finish:	Bewdley, Worcs	SO788754
Landranger maps:	138	
1 : 25,000 maps:	Ex 204, 218	

Publications, badges and certificates:
Looseleaf: Abberley Amble (Eric Perks). 4pp; A4. Free (+ 9 x 6 SAE).
Badge and certificate: (Eric Perks). £2.00 & £1.00 (+ SAE).

Abbeys Amble 4
N Yorks *167 km / 104 miles*

A walk linking three Yorkshire Abbeys (Fountains, Bolton and Jervaulx) and three Yorkshire castles (Ripley, Bolton and Middleham), which uses stretches of some already established routes – Harrogate Ringway, Dales Way, Yoredale Way and Ripon Rowel. Profits from sales are donated to Christian Aid.

Start and Finish:	Ripon, N Yorks	SE315710
Landranger maps:	98, 99, 104	
1 : 25,000 maps:	Ex 297, 298, 302 OL 10, 30	

Publications, badges and certificates:
Paperback: *Abbeys Amble* (John Eckersley) 1999. ISBN 0953586200. 88pp; 248 x 170. £7.99 (+ £1.00 p&p).
Certificate: (John Eckersley). £1.00 (incs p&p).

Abbott's Hike 5
Cumbria, N Yorks, W Yorks *172 km / 107 miles*

The Hike, named after its originator, links 25 miles of the Dales Way, 14 miles of the Three Peaks Walk and three miles of the Pennine Way National Trail to provide a route from Yorkshire to the Lake District.

Start:	Ilkley, W Yorks	SE117476
Finish:	Pooley Bridge, Cumbria	NY470247
Landranger maps:	90, 91, 97, 98, 104	
1 : 25,000 maps:	Ex 297 OL 2, 5, 7, 19, 30	

Publications, badges and certificates:
Paperback: *Abbott's Hike* by Peter Abbott (Peter Abbott) 1980. 64pp; 210 x 149. £2.00 (incs p&p).

Aiggin Stone Ramble   6
Lancs, W Yorks   *45 km / 28 miles*

The route is mainly over the moorland of the Lancashire/Yorkshire border visiting Shore, Littleborough, Hollingworth, Blackstone Edge and Withens Clough Reservoir as well as passing the Aiggin Stone, an ancient waymarker on the Roman road at Blackstone Edge Moor.

Start and Finish:	Todmorden, W Yorks	SD934245
Landranger maps:	103, 104, 109, 110	
1 : 25,000 maps:	OL 21	

Publications, badges and certificates:
Leaflet: *The Aiggin Stone Ramble* (LDWA Calderdale Group). 2pp; A4. Free (+ 9 x 4 SAE).
Badge & certificate: (LDWA Calderdale Group). £1.50 & £1.00 (+ SAE).

Ainsty Bounds Walk   7
N Yorks   *71 km / 44 miles*

A walk through the area of Ainsty which is bounded by the Rivers Wharf, Nidd and Ouse. As far as is possible the route is along river banks passing through Boston Spa, Wetherby, Moor Monkton, the outskirts of York and Bolton Percy. Proceeds from the sales of the publication are donated to a local hospice. It is coincident in parts with the Jorvic Way.

Start and Finish:	Tadcaster, N Yorks	SE488434
Landranger maps:	105	
1 : 25,000 maps:	Ex 289, 290	

Publications, badges and certificates:
Looseleaf: *Ainsty Bounds Walk* (Simon Townson). 4pp; A4. £1.50 (incs p&p).

Airedale Way   8
N Yorks, W Yorks   *80 km / 50 miles*

The Way provides a natural route from Leeds to the heart of the Yorkshire Dales, by following as far as possible paths by the River Aire and, in spite of passing through such small industrial towns as Shipley, Bingley and Keighley, is very largely rural. There are links with the Bradford-Dales Way at Shipley and the Pennine Way National Trail at Gargrave and Malham.

Start:	Leeds, W Yorks	SE298333
Finish:	Malham Tarn, N Yorks	SD894661
Landranger maps:	98, 103, 104	
1 : 25,000 maps:	Ex 288, 289 OL 2, 21	

Publications, badges and certificates:
Paperback: *The Airedale Way* by Douglas Cossar (RA West Riding Area) 1996. ISBN 0900613955. 80pp; A5. £4.50 (+ 80p p&p).
Badge: (RA West Riding Area). £1.50.

Allerdale Ramble   9

Cumbria   *87 km / 54 miles*

From central Lakeland the route heads northwards along the western side of
Borrowdale and Derwent Water to Keswick. Here there is a choice of route, either
across the foothills of Skiddaw or over its summit, before heading along the
Derwent valley to Cockermouth. The Ramble then crosses the agricultural land of
mid-Allerdale to reach the coast at Maryport, where it turns along the flat coastline
providing extensive views across the Solway Firth.

Start:	Seathwaite, Cumbria	NY235119
Finish:	Grune Point, Cumbria	NY145571
Landranger maps:	85, 89, 90	✔
1 : 25,000 maps:	Ex 314 OL4	
Waymark:	Named posts	

Publications, badges and certificates:
Paperback: *The Cumbria Way and the Allerdale Ramble* by Jim Watson (Cicerone Press) 1997.
ISBN 1852842423. 144pp. £6.99.

Almscliff Amble   10

N Yorks, W Yorks   *48 km / 30 miles*

A route visiting Otley Chevin, Bramhope, Harewood House, Almscliff Crag and
Farnley. A 20-miles alternative route is available.

Start and Finish:	Otley, W Yorks	SE217457
Landranger maps:	104	
1 : 25,000 maps:	Ex 297	

Publications, badges and certificates:
Looseleaf: *Almscliff Amble* (Louise Mallinson). Free (+ 9 x 4 SAE).
Badge and certificate: (Louise Mallinson). £1.50 (+ SAE).

Altrincham Circular   11

Cheshire, Gtr Man   *27 km / 17 miles*

A route around the town of Altrincham, passing along the district boundary to
Davenport Green, through Halebarns to the Bollin and Ashley Heath, Bow Green
and Little Bollington, returning via Dunham and Oldfield Brow.

Start and Finish:	W Timperley, Gtr Man	SJ771901
Landranger maps:	109	
1 : 25,000 maps:	Ex 277	

Publications, badges and certificates:
Paperback: *The Altrincham Circular* by Altrincham WEA (Willow Publishing) 1989. ISBN
0946361282. 56pp; A5. £3.75 (+ 80p p&p).

Angles Way 12

Norfolk, Suffolk   *126 km / 78 miles*

The Way was devised by the RA, and together with the Peddars Way, Norfolk Coast Path and Weavers Way, forms the 227-mile Around Norfolk Walk. From Great Yarmouth the route goes by Breydon Water, along the River Waveney to its source, and by the Little Ouse through heathland and marsh to Knettishall Heath. See Mid Suffolk Footpath and Waveney Way. At Bungay, there is a link into the waymarked Bigod Way (10 miles) which is a circular route around the town, the site of Bigod's Castle. See Iceni Way.

Start:	Great Yarmouth, Norfolk	TG522081
Finish:	Knettishall Heath, Suffolk	TL944807
Landranger maps:	134, 144, 156	✔
1 : 25,000 maps:	Ex 230, 231 OL 40	
Waymark:	Named discs	

Publications, badges and certificates:
Paperback: *The Angles Way – Walking in an Historic Landscape* by Kate Skipper and Tom Williamson (Suffolk County Council) 1993. ISBN 0906219345. 132pp. £5.00 (+ £2.00 p&p).
Paperback: *Angles Way* (includes accomodation & public transport details) (RA Norfolk Area) 2001. ISBN 1901184498. 28pp; 210 x 143. £2.70 (+ 30p p&p).
Paperback: *Langton's Guide to the Weavers Way and Angles Way* by Andrew Durham (Andrew Durham) 1995. ISBN 1899242015. 144pp; 210 x 130. £6.95 (incs p&p).
Leaflet: *Angles Way* (Norfolk County Council). A5. £0.70 (+ SAE).
Leaflet: *Bigod Way* (Bungay Tourist Information Centre). A4/3. Free (+ 9 x 4 SAE).

Anglesey Coast Path 13

Anglesey   *195 km / 121 miles*

First created by the Ynys Mon (Anglesey) Group of the RA, this circuit around the island uses existing rights of way, linked by roads which form about a quarter of the route, to follow the coastline as closely as possible. It passes attractive bays, fine cliff scenery, marshes and sands.

Start and Finish:	Menai Bridge, Anglesey	SH556716
Landranger maps:	114	
1 : 25,000 maps:	Ex 262, 263	

Publications, badges and certificates:
Booklet: *Walking the Isle of Anglesey Coastline* by John Merrill (Walk & Write Ltd). ISBN 1874754136. 60pp; A5. £4.50 (+ 75p p&p).
Badge and certificate: (Walk & Write Ltd). £3.50 (incs p&p).

Anglezarke Amble 14

Lancs   *34 km / 21 miles*

Devised by the West Lancs group of the LDWA, this route is over Rivington Pike, Winter Hill and passes several reservoirs across moor and farmland.

Start and Finish:	Rivington Hall Barn, Lancs	SD633144
Landranger maps:	109	
1 : 25,000 maps:	Ex 287	

Publications, badges and certificates:
Looseleaf: *Anglezarke Amble* (LDWA West Lancashire Group). Free (+ 9 x 4 SAE).
Badge and certificate: (LDWA West Lancashire Group). £1.50 (+ A4 SAE).

Anglezarke Anguish 15

Lancs *32 km / 20 miles*

The walk is in the West Pennine Moors Country Park, taking in Leverhulme Park and the seven-arched Romanesque style bridge. It passes Pidgeon Tower, Rivington Pike and three reservoirs, over rough moorland to the village of White Coppice. There is an alternative 10-mile route.

Start and Finish:	Rivington Hall Barn, Lancs	SD633144
Landranger maps:	109	
1 : 25,000 maps:	Ex 287	

Publications, badges and certificates:
Looseleaf: *Anglezarke Anguish Walk* (Norman Thomas). Free (+ SAE).
Badge and certificate: (Norman Thomas). £1.50 (+ SAE).

Anita's Mucking Ugley Ways Through Messing, Essex 16

Essex *200 km / 125 miles*

A route devised by the late Anita Totham which, as well as visiting Mucking, Ugley and Messing, takes in other quaint sounding localities such as Herongate, Stanford Rivers, Birchanger, Stisted and South Woodham Ferrers. The British Heart Foundation benefits from sales.

Start and Finish:	Mucking Creek Footbridge, Essex	TQ688815
Landranger maps:	167, 168, 177	
1 : 25,000 maps:	Ex 175, 183, 184, 195	

Publications, badges and certificates:
Softback: *Anita's Mucking Ugley Ways Through Messing, Essex* by PC Wood (British Heart Foundation) 1998. 96pp; 215 x 152. £3.75 (+ 50p p&p).

Arden Way 17

Warks *42 km / 26 miles*

A route with an historic theme in the Forest of Arden passing through Henley in Arden, Alcester, Ullenhall and other villages/places of interest. It is coincident in parts with the Heart of England Way between Henley and south of Alcester.

Start and Finish:	Henley-in-Arden, Warks	SP151658
Landranger maps:	150, 151	✔

1 : 25,000 maps:	Ex 205, 220
Waymark:	Name encircled with a chain of leaves
User group:	Heart of England Way Association

Publications, badges and certificates:
Leaflet: *The Arden Way* (Heart of England Way Association). £1.25 (+ 40p p&p).
Certificate: (Heart of England Way Association). £1.00 (+ A5 SAE).

Around the Carneddau   18

Conwy   *64 km / 40 miles*

A circuit around the edge of the Carneddau visiting the lakes of Llyn Crafnant, Llyn Cowlyd, Melynnllyn and Llyn Dulyn. It descends to the Aber Falls via the Roman Road over Bwlch y Ddeufaen, traverses Moel Wnion to Gerlon and Ogwen then skirts Llyn Ogwen.

Start and Finish:	Capel Curig, Conwy	SH721583
Landranger maps:	115	
1 : 25,000 maps:	OL 17	

Publications, badges and certificates:
Looseleaf: *Around the Carneddau* (Dave Irons) 1994. 5pp; A4. £1.00 (incs p&p).

Around the Lakes   19

Cumbria   *233 km / 145 miles*

Based on the Bob Graham Round, a circular route primarily for fell-runners, this route also includes Kentmere, the Far Eastern and Coniston Fells, and provides a circuit taking in all the peaks of the Lake District, involving 50,000ft of ascent.

Start and Finish:	Grasmere, Cumbria	NY339072
Landranger maps:	89, 90, 96, 97	
1 : 25,000 maps:	OL 4, 5, 6, 7	

Publications, badges and certificates:
Paperback: *Walking Round the Lakes* by John and Anne Nuttall (Cicerone Press). ISBN 1852840994. 240pp; 116 x 176. £6.99.

Arun Way   20

W Sussex   *35 km / 22 miles*

A route along the Lower Arun Valley through a varied landscape of beach, remote villages, riverside meadows and the South Downs, inhabited at various times by Romans, Saxons and Normans. The Way crosses the South Downs Way National Trail and the Monarch's Way and is partly coincident with the Wey-South Path.

Start:	Littlehampton, W Sussex	TQ024022
Finish:	Pulborough, W Sussex	TQ042187
Landranger maps:	197	
1 : 25,000 maps:	Ex 121	

Publications, badges and certificates:
Paperback: *Along the Arun* by John Adamson (Alexius Press) 1994. ISBN 0951988611. 114pp; A5. £7.95 (incs p&p).

Ashford on Foot   21

Kent   *35 km / 22 miles*

Partly coincident with the Stour Valley Walk (Kent) and the Greensand and North Downs Ways, this route around Ashford visits a number of villages including Huthfield, Mersham and Wye. Links into the Town and the International Station are included.

Start and Finish:	Wye, Kent	TR051462
Landranger maps:	189	
1 : 25,000 maps:	Ex 137	

Publications, badges and certificates:
Leaflet: *Ashford on Foot – No 2 (Longer Walks)* (Ashford Tourist Information Centre). A4/3. Free (+ 9 x 4 SAE).

Avon Valley Path   22

Dorset, Hants, Wilts   *55 km / 34 miles*

The Path follows the lower reaches of one of England's best-known chalk rivers, through a valley much of which is designated as an SSSI and of great botanical interest, besides being known for its salmon. Though much of the Path does not follow the riverbank, it aims to keep as close to it as possible through Downton, Fordingbridge and Ringwood. See Sarum Way.

Start:	Salisbury, Wilts	SU142295
Finish:	Christchurch, Dorset	SZ160925
Landranger maps:	184, 195	✔
1 : 25,000 maps:	Ex 130 OL 22	
Waymark:	Green and beige with bridge	

Publications, badges and certificates:
Paperback: *The Avon Valley Path* (RA New Forest Group) 1994. ISBN 086146088X. 64pp; A5. £4.00 (incs p&p).
Paperback: *A Guide to the Avon Valley Footpath* by Sarah Moxey (Halsgrove Press) 1998. ISBN 1874448264. 96pp; A5. £2.99 (incs p&p).
Leaflet: *Avon Valley Path* (Hampshire County Council). A4/3. Free (+ SAE).

Aylesbury Ring   23

Bucks, Herts   *50 km / 31 miles*

Originally created by the Aylesbury and District group of the RA, the route is never more than 5 miles from the centre of Aylesbury, encompassing some of the remoter areas of the Vale and passing through Great Kimble, Dinton, Waddesdon, Hardwick, Rowsham, Hulcott and Aston Clinton. Much of the western route is coincident with the North Bucks Way. See Oxfordshire Way.

Start and Finish:	Wendover, Bucks	SP869078
Landranger maps:	165	✔
1 : 25,000 maps:	Ex 181	
Waymark:	Aylesbury duck	

Publications, badges and certificates:
Leaflet: *The Aylesbury Ring* (Buckinghamshire County Council) 1993. A4/3. Free (+ SAE).

Back o' Skidda   24
Cumbria   *45 km / 28 miles*

A high-level circuit, with over 7,600ft of ascent, across the relatively unfrequented mountains of the northern Lake District, including the summits of High Pike, Calva, Skiddaw, Blencathra and Bannerdale Crags.

Start and Finish:	Mosedale, Cumbria	NX357323
Landranger maps:	90	
1 : 25,000 maps:	OL 4, 5	

Publications, badges and certificates:
Looseleaf: *Back o' Skidda* (Joyce Sidebottom). Free (+ 9 x 4 SAE).
Badge and certificate: (Joyce Sidebottom). £2.50 (+ 9 x 7 SAE).

Barnsley Boundary Walk   25
S Yorks, W Yorks   *119 km / 74 miles*

Created by Barnsley Borough Council in association with the publishing arm of the Barnsley Chronicle, the Walk aims to provide a view of the varied countryside, industrial heritage and other points of interest in the Borough. Included are Langsett Reservoir, the former salt road to Dunford Bridge, several reservoirs and the Country Parks at Cannon and Bretton Halls.

Start and Finish:	Flouch Inn, S Yorks	SE197016
Landranger maps:	110, 111	✔
1 : 25,000 maps:	Ex 278, 288 OL 1	
Waymark:	Named posts	

Publications, badges and certificates: No publications: on OS mapping.

Basingstoke Canal Walk   26
Hants, Surrey   *60 km / 37 miles*

A route through the Surrey and Hampshire countryside along the tree-lined towpath of the recently restored 200 years old canal and through woodland, heathland, wetland and pasture. See Blackwater Valley Footpath.

Start:	Byfleet, Surrey	TQ070630
Finish:	Basingstoke, Hants	SU640527
Landranger maps:	186	
1 : 25,000 maps:	Ex 144, 145, 161	

Publications, badges and certificates:
Booklet: *Guide to the Basingstoke Canal* by Dieter Jebens (Basingstoke Canal Authority) 1996.
28pp; A5. £3.50 (+ 45p p&p).
Stripmap (folded): *Basingstoke Canal Map* (GEOprojects) 1995. ISBN 0863510205. 135 x 213.
£4.00 (+ 50p p&p).

Beacon Banks Challenge   27
N Yorks   *40 km / 25 miles*

A route through a scenic and little walked area offering views of the Howardian Hills, the White Horse, passing Byland Abbey and visiting Husthwaite and Kilburn.

Start and Finish:	Easingwold, N Yorks	SE528696
Landranger maps:	100	
1 : 25,000 maps:	Ex 300	

Publications, badges and certificates:
Looseleaf: *The Beacon Banks Challenge* (Ben Booth). 5pp. Free (+ 9 x 4 SAE).
Badge and certificate: (Ben Booth). £2.00 (+ 9 x 6 SAE).

Beacon Way   28
Staffs, W Midlands   *40 km / 25 miles*

This green route is from Sandwell at the heart of the West Midlands conurbation, and goes via the outskirts of Birmingham through the countryside of Walsall and into Staffordshire. The walk takes in the Forest of Mercia, lakes, nature reserves, woods, and the banks of canals. The northern end links with the Heart of England Way on Gentleshaw Common. Only the section from Sandwell to Chasewater is shown on OS maps.

Start:	Sandwell Park Farm, W Midlands	SP019914
Finish:	Gentleshaw Common, Staffs	SK052116
Landranger maps:	139	✔ (part)
1 : 25,000 maps:	Ex 220, 244	
Waymark:	Named posts and standard arrows	

Publications, badges and certificates:
Binder: A ring binder of weatherproof route cards of the Beacon Way and other routes will be available (Walsall Metropolitan Borough Council). Details to be advised.

Beating the Bounds (Cheshire)   29
Cheshire   *74 km / 46 miles*

A route following the boundary of Stockport, devised as part of the Millennium celebrations and visiting Werneth Low, Mellor, Poynton, Woodford and Gatley.

Start and Finish:	Reddish Vale, Cheshire	SJ904923
Landranger maps:	109	
1 : 25,000 maps:	Ex 268, 277 OL 1	

Publications, badges and certificates:
Booklet: *Beating the Bounds – Stockport Millennium Walk* (Stockport Metropolitan Borough Council). 16pp; A5. Free (+ 9 x 6 SAE).

Bell Walk Major 30

Derbys, S Yorks *58 km / 36 miles*

The Bell Walk devised by the Dronfield Parish Church Bellringers links the churches of Dronfield, Old Whittington, Norton, Dore, Hathersage, Totley and Holmesfield, all of which have bells. The route is through woodland, past a little industry, historical sites, parkland, moorland, villages, riverside, into valleys and within easy reach of 50 pubs.

Start and Finish:	Dronfield, Derbys	SK353784
Landranger maps:	110, 119	
1 : 25,000 maps:	Ex 269, 278 OL 1, 24	

Publications, badges and certificates:
Looseleaf: *Bell Walk Major* (Vic Cox). Free (+ 9 x 6 SAE).
Badge and certificate: (Vic Cox). £2.00 (+ 9 x 6 SAE).

Belvoir Witches Challenge Walk 31

Leics, Lincs *40 km / 25 miles*

A walk around the Vale of Belvoir where 17th century witches were in residence. The route takes in part of the Grantham Canal, Denton Reservoir and Belvoir Castle.

Start and Finish:	Bottesford, Leics	SK806392
Landranger maps:	129, 130	
1 : 25,000 maps:	Ex 247	

Publications, badges and certificates:
Booklet: *The Belvoir Witches Challenge Walk* by John Merrill (Walk & Write Ltd) 1994. ISBN 1874754489. A5. £3.95 (+ 75p p&p).
Belvoir Castle Badge and certificate: (Walk & Write Ltd). £3.50 (incs p&p).

Berwickshire Coastal Path 32

Northumberland, Borders *24 km / 15 miles*

The Path crosses farmland and cliff tops as it passes through Burnmouth, Eyemouth and St Abbs. Some of the cliff walking is very exposed and reaches a maximum height of 340ft. A short extension to the route can be gained by taking advantage of the paths of the National Nature Reserve of St Abbs Head.

Start:	Berwick on Tweed, Northumberland	NT996536
Finish:	Coldingham, Borders	NT904660
Landranger maps:	67, 75	✔
1 : 25,000 maps:	Ex 342	
Waymark:	Named 'Scottish Border Walks' signs	

Publications, badges and certificates:
Leaflet: *The Berwickshire Coastal Path* (Berwick-upon-Tweed Tourist Information Centre). A4/3. Free (+ 9 x 4 SAE).

Bilsdale Circuit   33

N Yorks   *48 km / 30 miles*

A strenuous circuit with over 4,000ft of ascent, mainly along tracks and the high moors within sight of the Bilsdale TV mast. The route takes in Roppa Edge and Urra Moor where it is coincident with the Lyke Wake Walk and Cleveland Way National Trail, and West Moor.

Start and Finish:	Newgate Bank Top, N Yorks	SE564890
Landranger maps:	93, 100	
1 : 25,000 maps:	OL 26	

Publications, badges and certificates:
Looseleaf: *Bilsdale Circuit* (LDWA Cleveland Group). Free (+ 9 x 4 SAE).
Badge and certificate: (LDWA Cleveland Group). £1.70 & £0.30 (+ SAE).

Birmingham and Aberystwyth Walk   34

Ceredigion, Herefs, Powys, Shrops,   *238 km / 148 miles*
Staffs, W Midlands, Worcs

The Walk follows canals through the Black Country to Stourbridge and then crosses rural Shropshire via the high point of Titterstone Clee to enter Wales at Knighton. 25 miles of wild hills and tiny villages take the walker to Rhaeadr after which the Elan Valley reservoirs are skirted and desolate moorland crossed to Devil's Bridge. A further fifteen miles brings the walker to the coast and journey's end. The Walk encounters the Staffordshire Way, Worcestershire Way, North Worcestershire Path, Offa's Dyke and the Wye Valley Walk among others.

Start:	Gas Street Canal Basin, Birmingham	SP062866
Finish:	Bridge Street, Aberystwyth	SN583813
Landranger maps:	135, 138, 139, 147, 148	
1 : 25,000 maps:	Ex 187, 200, 201, 203, 213, 218, 219, 220	

Publications, badges and certificates:
Paperback: *The Birmingham & Aberystwyth Walk* by John Roberts (Walkways) 2001. ISBN 0947708375. 128pp; A5. £6.95 (incs p&p).
Looseleaf: The Birmingham & Aberystwyth Walk Accommodation List (Walkways). Free.

Birmingham Greenway   35

W Midlands   *37 km / 23 miles*

The walk crosses Birmingham from the north east boundary to the south western edge and uses many of the city's green spaces. The guidebook contains local information, including public transport availability. The end of the walk is less than half a mile from the North Worcestershire Path.

Start:	Camp Farm, Watford Gap	SK117003
Finish:	Ten Ashes Lane, Cofton Hackett	SP001758
Landranger maps:	139	
1 : 25,000 maps:	Ex 220	

Publications, badges and certificates:
Paperback: *The Birmingham Greenway* by Fred Willits (Meridian Books) 2000. ISBN 1869922409. 64pp; A5. £4.95 (+ £1.00 p&p).

Bishop Bennet Way   36

Cheshire, Shropshire   *55 km / 34 miles*

Named after an 18th Century traveller, the Way was primarily devised for use by horse riders. Whilst part of the route is along minor roads, most of this can be avoided by walkers using other rights of way. The route also takes in green lanes, bridleways and field paths as it passes through Milton Green, Coddington, Shocklach and Grindley Brook.

Start:	Beeston, Cheshire	SJ526596
Finish:	Wirswall, Shropshire	SJ537448
Landranger maps:	117	✔
1 : 25,000 maps:	Ex 257, 266, 267	
Waymark:	Named signs	

Publications, badges and certificates:
Booklet: *The Bishop Bennet Way* (Cheshire County Council). 16pp; A5. Free (+ 9 x 6 SAE).

Black and White Village Trail   37

Herefs   *99 km / 61 miles*

Originally conceived by David Gorvett as a route for car-drivers, the Trail provides a similar route for walkers through the villages between Leominster and Kington, an area characterised by the large number of timbered and half-timbered buildings. The landscape is generally undulating farmland, and provides good views of the surrounding hill ranges.

Start and Finish:	Leominster Station, Herefs	SO502589
Landranger maps:	148, 149	
1 : 25,000 maps:	Ex 201, 202, 203	

Publications, badges and certificates:
Paperback: *The Black and White Village Trail* by David Gorvett and Les Lumsdon (Scarthin Books) 1991. ISBN 0907758479. 64pp; A5. £5.95 (+ £0.60 p&p).

Black Fen Waterway Trail   38

Cambs, Norfolk   *105 km / 65 miles*

A route following the courses of various waterways including the River Great Ouse and the Nene-Ouse Navigation Link passing through Downham Market, Littleport,

Ely and Chatteris. Details of a loop to Flood's Ferry (10 miles) are included. See Brown Fen Waterway Trail.

Start and Finish:	March, Cambs	TL412976
Landranger maps:	143	
1 : 25,000 maps:	Ex 225, 226, 227, 228, 236	
Waymark:	Named signs with land/water/plant life logo	

Publications, badges and certificates:
Leaflet: *Explore the Fens Waterways – Walkers Guide to Black Fen and Brown Fen Waterway Trails* (Spalding Tourist Information Centre). Free (+ 9 x 4 SAE).

Black Mountains Traverse Challenge　　39

Herefs, Powys　　　　　　　　　　*37 km / 23 miles*

An undulating route across the Black Mountain ridge taking in the highest peaks and lowest valley points.

Start:	Llangorse Church, Powys	SO135276
Finish:	Craswall, Herefs	SO278361
Landranger maps:	161	
1 : 25,000 maps:	OL 13	

Publications, badges and certificates:
Looseleaf: *The Black Mountains Traverse Challenge* (Richard Hill). 2pp. Free (+ 9 x 6 SAE). Certificate: (Richard Hill). £3.00 (+ 10 x 8 SAE).

Blackmore Vale Path　　40

Dorset, Somers　　　　　　　　　*114 km / 71 miles*

A route using ancient tracks, it takes in Dorchester and Yeovil, many villages within the Blackmore Vale, Sherborne Abbey, Sturminster Newton, Okeford Hill Ridgeway and the Cerne Giant.

Start and Finish:	Blandford Forum, Dorset	ST886064
Landranger maps:	183, 194	
1 : 25,000 maps:	Ex 117, 118, 129	

Publications, badges and certificates:
Booklet: *The Blackmore Vale Path* by Edward R. Griffiths (Green Fields Books) 1995. ISBN 0951937634. 150pp; A5. £4.95 (+ £1.00 p&p).

Blackwater Valley Footpath　　41

Bracknell For, Hants, Surrey, Wokingham　　*30 km / 19 miles*

This route along the Surrey/Wokingham/Hampshire border via Sandhurst, Farnborough and Aldershot is planned to link eventually to the North Downs Way National Trail at Farnham, and via the Loddon Valley to the Thames between Reading and Henley. It crosses the Basingstoke Canal Walk at the aqueduct near Aldershot.

Start:	Rowhill Nature Reserve, Aldershot, Hants	SU848500
Finish:	Swallowfield, Wokingham	SU727648
Landranger maps:	175	✔
1 : 25,000 maps:	Ex 145, 159, 160	
Waymark:	Named posts and arrows with coot and reed logo	

Publications, badges and certificates:
Booklet: *Discover the Blackwater Valley Footpath* (Blackwater Valley Team) 2001. £2.95 (details TBA).
Looseleaf: *Discover the Blackwater Valley* (Blackwater Valley Team). 4pp; A4. Free.

Blue Man Walk   42

N Yorks   *26 km / 16 miles*

A walk developed and fully waymarked by the Forestry Commission through the upland coniferous forests on the east side of the North York Moors.

Start:	Reasty Bank Top, N Yorks	SE965944
Finish:	Allerston, N Yorks	SE876830
Landranger maps:	101	
1 : 25,000 maps:	OL 27	
Waymark:	Blue man logo	

Publications, badges and certificates:
Looseleaf: *Blue Man Walk Route* (Forest Enterprise North Yorkshire). 1pp; A4. Free (+ 9 x 4 SAE).
Badge: (Forest Enterprise North Yorkshire). £0.75 (+ SAE).

Bog Dodgers Way   43

Lancs, West Yorkshire   *37 km / 23 miles*

A demanding route along a valley, over rough pasture and high open peat moorland, and deep gorges which is partly coincident with the Pennine Way National Trail. Wessenden Moor, Black Hill and Standedge are passed along the Way.

Start and Finish:	Marsden Church, West Yorks	SD047116
Landranger maps:	110	
1 : 25,000 maps:	OL 1, 21	

Publications, badges and certificates:
Looseleaf: *Bog Dodgers Way* (LDWA Vermuyden Group). 1pp. Free (+ 9 x 4 SAE).
Badge and certificate: (LDWA Vermuyden Group). £1.50 & £0.25 (+ 9 x 6 SAE).

Bollin Valley Way   44

Cheshire, Gtr Man   *36 km / 22 miles*

The River Bollin rises in the Pennine Foothills and flows through Macclesfield, Prestbury, Wilmslow, Hale and Bowdon, eventually running into the Manchester Ship Canal (i.e., the Mersey) at Bollin Point. The Way is a spiral route giving access to a wider footpath network.

Start:	Macclesfield, Cheshire	SD915746
Finish:	Partington, Gtr Man	SJ706912
Landranger maps:	109, 118	
1 : 25,000 maps:	Ex 268, 276	
Waymark:	Named discs with river logo	

Publications, badges and certificates:
Folder: *The Bollin Valley Way* (Bollin Valley Project) 1997. 5pp; A4/3. Free (+ 9 x 4 SAE).

Bonnie Prince Charlie Walk 45

Derbys *28 km / 17 miles*

Devised to celebrate the RA Diamond Jubilee, the walk follows the general route taken by Prince Charles Edward Stuart on his march from Ashbourne to Derby in 1745, through woods and farmland. It links with the Centenary Way (Derbyshire) at Ashbourne. Two village walks, the Ednaston Circular Walk (6 miles) and the Osmaston Circular Walk (4 miles) link into the main route providing alternative options.

Start:	Ashbourne, Derbys	SK180467
Finish:	Derby, Derbys	SK353363
Landranger maps:	128	✔
1 : 25,000 maps:	Ex 259	
Waymark:	Named logo – in east to west direction	

Publications, badges and certificates:
Leaflet: *Bonnie Prince Charlie Walk* (John Pritchard-Jones) 1995. A5/4. Free (+ 9 x 4 SAE).
Leaflet: *Circular Walk from Ednaston* (Elvaston Castle Country Park) 2001. A4/3. Free (+ 9 x 6 SAE).
Leaflet: *Circular Walk from Osmaston* (Elvaston Castle Country Park) 2001. A4/3. Free (+ 9 x 6 SAE).

Borders Abbeys Way 46

Borders *105 km / 65 miles*

A route under development, it will ultimately link the ruined Borders Abbeys of Kelso, Jedburgh, Melrose and Dryburgh as well as the towns of Hawick and Selkirk. For the present just the Kelso to Jedburgh section (12 miles) is open and further developments are expected in 2002.

Start and Finish:	Kelso Abbey, Borders	NT727337
Landranger maps:	74	
1 : 25,000 maps:	Ex 331 OL 16, 44	
Waymark:	AW symbol	

Publications, badges and certificates:
Leaflet: *Borders Abbeys Way – Kelso to Jedburgh* (Jedburgh Tourist Information Centre). A4/3. Free (+ 9 x 4 SAE).

Boudica's Way 47
Norfolk *61 km / 38 miles*

Named after the legendary warrior Queen of the Iceni, the route incorporates a strong historical theme with links to Caistor Roman Town and Tasburgh Hill Fort. It connects with the Angles Way at Scole.

Start:	Railway Station, Norwich, Norfolk	TG230080
Finish:	Diss, Norfolk	TM128797
Landranger maps:	134, 156	✔
1 : 25,000 maps:	Ex 230, 237, OL 40	
Waymark:	Yellow & green named discs with sword in centre	

Publications, badges and certificates:
Folder: *Boudica's Way* (South Norfolk Council) 1999. 28pp; A5. £3.50 (incs p&p).

Bourne Blunder 48
Lincs *32 km / 20 miles*

A route to the south of Grantham taking in a sculpture trail, the Grimsthorpe Castle Estate, an 11th century castle mound, a chestnut avenue and lakes at Hollywell Hall.

Start and Finish:	Bourne Woods Car Park, Lincs	TF077202
Landranger maps:	130	
1 : 25,000 maps:	Ex 234, 248	

Publications, badges and certificates:
Looseleaf: *The Bourne Blunder* (Martyn Bishop). Free (+ 9 x 4 SAE).
Badge and certificate: (Martyn Bishop). £1.50 (+ SAE).

Bowland-Dales Traverse 49
Lancs, N Yorks *153 km / 95 miles*

An upland route across the Forest of Bowland and the Yorkshire Dales, contrasting Bowland's heather-clad gritstone hills with the limestone terraces of the Dales. Besides visiting the villages of Slaidburn, Malham, Kettlewell, Aysgarth and Reeth, the route passes Attermire Scar, Malham Cove, Kilnsey Crag and Buckden Pike, the latter being the highest point at 2302ft.

Start:	Garstang, Lancs	SD492450
Finish:	Richmond, N Yorks	NZ171009
Landranger maps:	92, 98, 99, 102, 103	
1 : 25,000 maps:	Ex 304 OL 2, 30, 41	

Publications, badges and certificates:
Paperback: *The Bowland-Dales Traverse* by John Gillham (Grey Stone Books) 1991. ISBN 0951599623. 64pp; 105 x 150. £2.95.

Bradford Ring 50

W Yorks *51 km / 32 miles*

Fourteen walks (each with a return route), forming a chain encircling Bradford, make up the main ring walk, and provide very flexible walking routes. From Cottingley the walk heads along the Aire valley to Shipley and Apperley, where it loops to Pudsey, Birkenshaw, Scholes, Shelf and Thornton.

Start and Finish:	Cottingley Bridge, W Yorks	SE112380
Landranger maps:	104	
1 : 25,000 maps:	Ex 288	

Publications, badges and certificates:
Booklet: *Bradford Ringwalks* by Arthur Gemmell and Paul Sheldon (Stile Publications) 1989. ISBN 0906886449. 128pp; 200 x 120. £1.50 (+ 9 x 6 SAE).
Certificate: (Anthony Wintle). Free (+ 2 x 2nd class stamps).

Brecon Beacons Traverse 51

Carms, Mons, Powys *142 km / 88 miles*

A route through the rolling and wild regions of the Carmarthen Fan, Forest Fawr, Brecon Beacons and the Black Mountains. Included is a 9 miles long road section and 16,000ft of ascent.

Start:	Pen Rhiw-Wen, Carms	SN732184
Finish:	Llanthony Abbey, Mons	SO289278
Landranger maps:	160, 161	
1 : 25,000 maps:	OL 12, 13	

Publications, badges and certificates:
Looseleaf and maps: *Brecon Beacons Traverse* (Derek G. Fisher). 18pp; A4. £2.50 (+ 50p p&p).
Certificate: (Derek G. Fisher). £0.50 (incs p&p).

Brighouse Boundary Walk 52

W Yorks *29 km / 18 miles*

Originally created in 1993 to celebrate the centenary of the former Borough of Brighouse and re-launched in 2001, the Walk encircles the town, gaining access to the moors and crossing the Calder Valley. At Hartshead Moor it links with the Bronte, Calderdale and Kirklees Ways and the Spen Way Heritage Trail.

Start and Finish:	Wellholme Park, Brighouse, W Yorks	SE147237
Landranger maps:	104, 110	
1 : 25,000 maps:	Ex 288	
Waymark:	Letter B with arrow protruding from base	

Publications, badges and certificates:
Folder: *Brighouse Boundary Walk* (Hebden Bridge Tourist Information Centre). 4 leaflets. Cost TBA 2002.

Brighton Way 53
Brighton H, E Sussex, Surrey, W Sussex   *84 km / 52 miles*

A route through farmland, villages and over the South Downs linking with the South Downs Way National Trail at Buckland Bank and the Sussex Border Path near Burgess Hill. Connections with a number of railway stations are included on the route.

Start:	Horley, Surrey	TQ286426
Finish:	Brighton H	TQ313038
Landranger maps:	187, 198	
1 : 25,000 maps:	Ex 122, 134, 135, 146	

Publications, badges and certificates:
Looseleaf: *The Brighton Way* by Norman Willis (Walk and Write Ltd) 2002. £3.95 Details TBA.

Bristol to Lynton Walk 54
Bath NES, Bristol, Devon, N Somers, Somers *161 km / 100 miles*

A route devised to raise funds for the Samaritans through sales of the publication and based on youth hostels along the way. The walk takes in the Chew Valley, the Mendip Hills, the Somerset Levels and Exmoor. There is a suggested extension of 30 miles along the coast path to Croyde from Lynton, and the Avon Walkway could be used to link the Cotswold Way National Trail at Bath with the start of this route.

Start:	Clifton Suspension Bridge, Bristol	ST566732
Finish:	Lynton, Devon	SS721495
Landranger maps:	172, 180, 181, 182	
1 : 25,000 maps:	Ex 139, 140, 141, 154 OL 9	

Publications, badges and certificates:
Softback: *A Walk from Bristol to Lynton* by Graham Hoyle (J. & M. Davis) 2000. ISBN 0953776700. 90pp; 112 x 149. £4.95 (+ 50p p&p).

Bromley Circular Walks 55
Gtr London, Kent   *125 km / 77 miles*

A series of inter-linking circular walks and trails based on (Pack One) Nash (5.2 miles), Leaves Green (6.5 miles), Farnborough (4.5 miles), Cudham (7.5 miles), Berrys Green (7.5 miles), Biggin Hill (7 miles), and Green Street Green (7.5 miles) and (Pack Two) Jubilee Park (1.4 miles), St Mary Cray (2.2 miles), Bromley Common (4 miles), Petts Wood (4 miles), St Pauls Cray (4 miles), Three Commons (5 miles), Chelsfield (5.5 miles) and Cray Riverway (6 miles).

Start and Finish:	Various	Various
Landranger maps:	177, 187, 188	
1 : 25,000 maps:	Ex 147, 148, 162	
Waymark:	Named posts	

Publications, badges and certificates:
Folder: B*romley Circular Walks & Trails – Pack One* (Bromley Countryside Ranger Service) 2000. 7 route cards; A5. £2.50 (+ 50p p&p).
Folder: *Bromley Circular Walks & Trails – Pack Two* (Bromley Countryside Ranger Service) 2000. 8 route cards; A5. £2.50 (+ 50p p&p).

Bronte Round   56

W Yorks   *32 km / 20 miles*

The circuit crosses open moorland to Haworth, passing Top Withins before returning to Hebden Bridge via riverside and farm paths. It links places associated with the Bronte Family.

Start and Finish:	Hebden Bridge, W Yorks	SD992273
Landranger maps:	103, 104	
1 : 25,000 maps:	OL 21	

Publications, badges and certificates:
Booklet: *Bronte Round/Pendle and Ribble Round* by Derek Magnall (Norman Thomas) 1994. 36pp; A5. £1.85 (incs p&p).
Badge and certificate: (Norman Thomas). £2.00 (+ SAE).

Bronte Way   57

Lancs, W Yorks   *64 km / 40 miles*

The Way provides a cross-Pennine route linking various places associated with the lives and works of the Bronte sisters. It takes in the Thursden Valley to link with the Pendle Way at Wycoller Hall (Ferndean Manor in the novel Jane Eyre), the moors to Top Withins (Wuthering Heights), Haworth Parsonage, where the Brontes lived and now a Bronte Museum, the Brontes' birthplace at Thornton, along the hills west of Bradford to the Spen Valley (Shirley country) before finishing at Oakwell Hall (Fieldhead in the novel Shirley). The Worth Way (11 miles circular and on OS mapping) can be linked with the Bronte Way at Haworth. See Brighouse Boundary Walk and Burnley Way.

Start:	Gawthorpe Hall, Lancs	SD805340
Finish:	Oakwell Hall, W Yorks	SE217271
Landranger maps:	103, 104	✔
1 : 25,000 maps:	Ex 288 OL 21	
Waymark:	Named posts	

Publications, badges and certificates:
Paperback: *Bronte Way* by Paul Hannon (Hillside Publications) 2000. ISBN 1870141563. 56pp; 115 x 178. £4.50 (+ 50p p&p).
Paperback: *The Bronte Way* by Marje Wilson (RA West Riding Area) 1997. ISBN 1901184056. 64pp; A5. £4.50 (+ 80p p&p).
Folder: *The Bronte Way* (Haworth Tourist Information Centre) 1997. 4pp; A5. £3.00 (+ 54p p&p).
Leaflet: *The Worth Way* (Haworth Tourist Information Centre). A3/4. £0.30 (+ 9 x 4 SAE).
Badge (Worth Way): (Haworth Tourist Information Centre). £1.20 (+ SAE).

Brown Fen Waterway Trail 58
Lincs, Suffolk *105 km / 65 miles*

A route following the courses of various waterways visiting Surfleet, Spalding, Crowland and Donnington with a spur to Swainshead (10 miles) also described. See Black Fen Waterway Trail.

Start and Finish:	Boston, Lincs	TF332434
Landranger maps:	131	
1 : 25,000 maps:	Ex 235, 248, 249, 261	
Waymark:	Named signs with land/water/plant life logo	

Publications, badges and certificates:
Leaflet: *Explore the Fens Waterways – Walkers Guide to Black Fen and Brown Fen Waterway Trails* (Spalding Tourist Information Centre). Free (+ 9 x 4 SAE).

Burley Bridge Hike 59
W Yorks *34 km / 21 miles*

A route over Ilkley Moor passing the Cow and Calf Rocks, Riddlesden, Crossflatts and Burley Woodhead. Proceeds of sales go towards the costs of a bridge provision over the River Wharfe at Burley.

Start and Finish:	Burley-in-Wharefdale, W Yorks	SE164458
Landranger maps:	104	
1 : 25,000 maps:	Ex 297	

Publications, badges and certificates:
Looseleaf: *Burley Bridge Hike* (John Sparshatt). 2pp; A4. Free (+ 9 x 4 SAE).
Badge and certificate: (John Sparshatt). £2.00 (+ 9 x 6 SAE).

Burnley Way 60
Lancs *64 km / 40 miles*

A route around the Town crossing a wide variety of terrain from moorland to canal towpath and passing a number of reservoirs. There are links to the Bronte, Pendle and Rossendale Ways.

Start and Finish:	Weavers Triangle, Lancs	SD838322
Landranger maps:	103	✔
1 : 25,000 maps:	Ex 277 OL 21	
Waymark:	Stylised B and bird logo	

Publications, badges and certificates:
No publications: on OS mapping.

Calderdale Way 61
W Yorks *80 km / 50 miles*

The Way, a circuit around Calderdale, was pioneered by local civic trusts. The main and link routes to the valley bottom are designed so that they can be completed in short stages. The walk encircles Halifax, Hebden Bridge and Todmorden, following old packhorse ways across the open gritstone hillsides, passing through hillside villages and old mill towns on the banks of the River Calder. See Brighouse Boundary Walk.

Start and Finish:	Greetland, W Yorks	SE097214
Landranger maps:	103, 104, 110	✔
1 : 25,000 maps:	OL 21	
Waymark:	Letters CW/trefoil	

Publications, badges and certificates:
Paperback: *Calderdale Way* by Paul Hannon (Hillside Publications) 2001. ISBN 1870141717. 48pp; 115 x 178. £3.99 (+ 40p p&p).
Paperback: *The Calderdale Way Guide* by the Calderdale Way Association (Hebden Bridge Tourist Information Centre). 72pp; A5. £4.99 (+ 70p p&p).

Cal-Der-Went Walk   62
Derbys, S Yorks, W Yorks   *48 km / 30 miles*

A route taking in Bretton Park, High Hoyland and Penistone crossing the watersheds and valleys of the Calder, Dearne, Don and Derwent. The 'Link Paths' publication describes suggested routes including one to connect the Cal-Der-Went Walk to the Limey Way/Rivers Way.

Start:	Horbury Bridge, W Yorks	SE281179
Finish:	Ladybower Reservoir, Derbys	SK195865
Landranger maps:	110	
1 : 25,000 maps:	Ex 278 OL 1	

Publications, badges and certificates:
Booklet: *The Cal-Der-Went Walk* by Geoffrey Carr (Walk & Write Ltd). ISBN 1874754268. 40pp; A5. £3.75 (+ 75p p&p).
Booklet: *Link Paths* by Geoffrey Carr & John N. Merrill (Walk & Write Ltd). ISBN 1903627158. 44pp; A5. £4.50 (+ 75p p&p).
Looseleaf: *The Cal-Der-Went Walk – walk information* (Geoffrey Carr). Free (+ 9 x 4 SAE).
Badge & certificate: (Geoffrey Carr). £2.00 & 20p (+ SAE).

Cambrian Way   63
Caerphilly, Cardiff, Carms, Ceredigion,   *441 km / 274 miles*
Conwy, Gwynedd, Mons, Powys, Torfaen

Described as the Mountain Connoisseur's Walk, this route through upland Wales involves 61,540ft of ascent and requires much stamina to complete. It is a tough, high-level route which should not be underestimated. From the south coast, it follows a meandering northerly route over the Black Mountains, Brecon Beacons, Carmarthen Fan, Plynlimon, Cadair Idris, the Rhinogs, the Snowdon massif and the Carneddau to reach the north coast. Tony Drake pioneered the route, and his guide includes a comprehensive accommodation and services list (with periodic update inserts). He is willing to give advice and information on the route, and provide and update the accommodation list. Navigational skills are of paramount importance. See also Coast to Coast – Wales and Meirionnydd Coast Walk.

Start:	Cardiff	ST180765
Finish:	Conwy	SH783775
Landranger maps:	115, 124, 135, 147, 160, 161, 171	
1 : 25,000 maps:	Ex 151, 152, 187, 213, 214, 215	
	OL 12, 13, 17, 18, 23	

Publications, badges and certificates:
Paperback: *Cambrian Way: The Mountain Connoisseur's Walk* by A. J. Drake (RA Central Office – London) 2000. ISBN 0950958042. 96pp; 210 x 128. £5.50 (+ £1.50 p&p).
Accommodation list/updates: (A. J. Drake). £0.50 (+ SAE).
Paperback: *A Cambrian Way* by Richard Sale (Gwasg Carreg Gwalch) 2000. ISBN 0863816053. 230pp; 182 x 121. £6.90 (+ £1.00 p&p).

Cape Wrath Trail   64
Highland   *330 km / 205 miles*

Initially following the Great Glen, the route turns north to cross Glen Garry, Glen Loyne and Glenshiel before crossing the wilderness to Strathcarron, continuing north through Torridon, Dundonnell (ferry) and Ullapool, where the coast is followed to Cullnacraig. The Coigach and Assynt Hills are traversed followed by the high moorland to Achfary and then via Foinaven, Rhiconich, Kinlochbervie and Sandwood Bay to the finish. The 'North to the Cape' publication (202 miles) follows a similar route in connecting the extremities.

Start:	Banavie, Highland	NN112769
Finish:	Cape Wrath, Highland	NC269747
Landranger maps:	9, 15, 19, 25, 33, 34, 41	
1 : 25,000 maps:	TBA 2002	

Publications, badges and certificates:
Paperback: *The Cape Wrath Trail* by David Paterson (Peak Publishing Ltd) 1996. ISBN 0952190826. 128pp; 260 x 225. £13.95.
Paperback: *North to the Cape* by Denis Brook and Phil Hinchliffe (Cicerone Press) 1999. ISBN 1852842857. 207pp; 116 x 176. £11.99.

Capital Ring   65
Gtr London   *116 km / 72 miles*

This is an inner London circular route linking parks, commons and open spaces. The Dollis Valley Greenwalk (10 miles and included on OS mapping) provides a link between the London LOOP and the Capital Ring. Individual leaflets for the fifteen sections are/will be available free from London Boroughs. Not all were published at the time of going to press. Check with the London Walking Forum website for availability. The Cicerone book is a comprehensive guide to walking routes in Greater London.

Start and Finish:	Woolwich Foot Tunnel	TQ432793
Landranger maps:	176 ,177	
1 : 25,000 maps:	Ex 161, 162, 173, 174	

Waymark: Named discs with Big Ben picture
Path website: www.londonwalking.com

Publications, badges and certificates:
Leaflets: *Walk the Capital Ring* (London Walking Forum). 15 leaflets; A4/3. Free (+ SAE). See description for availability of leaflets.
Paperback (laminated): *London – the Definitive Walking Guide* by Colin Saunders (Cicerone Press) late 2002. ISBN 185284339X. Price TBA.
Guidebook: *Capital Ring* by Colin Saunders (Aurum Press) 2003. Details TBA.

Capital Walk – Cardiff 66
Caerphilly, Cardiff, Newport, Glamorgan 59 km / 37 miles
A route around Cardiff taking in Dinas Powys, St Fagan's, Taff's Well, Ruperra Castle and Castleton linking with the Taff-Ely Ridgeway Walk and Taff Trail at Taff's Well, and the Rhymney Valley Ridgeway Walk near Caerphilly.

Start:	Swanbridge, Glamorgan	ST174676
Finish:	Peterstone-Wentlooge, Newport	ST292810
Landranger maps:	171	
1 : 25,000 maps:	Ex 151, 152	

Publications, badges and certificates:
Booklet: More Capital Walks (RA Cardiff) 1997. 40pp; A5. Free (+ 41p SAE).

Cardigan Bay Coast Walk 67
Ceredigion 99 km / 62 miles

This Walk keeps as close to the coast as possible avoiding major roads. The terrain is mixed with both cliff top and beach walking. The guidebook advises where walking at high tide must be avoided. There are excellent views and the chance to see much wildlife, including auks, seals and bottle-nosed dolphins.

Start:	Cardigan, Ceredigion	SN174460
Finish:	Ynyslas, Ceredigion (S of Dovey estuary)	SN610941
Landranger maps:	135, 145, 146	
1 : 25,000 maps:	Ex 198, 199, 213	

Publications, badges and certificates:
Booklet: *Walking the Cardigan Bay Coast* by Liz Allan (Kittiwake) 2000. ISBN 1902302095. 32pp; A5. £3.95 (+ 50p p&p).

Carleton Trail 68
Dungannon & Tyrone 48 km / 30 miles
One of the official Waymarked Ways in Northern Ireland, this route is associated with the 19th Century poet and author, William Carleton. It follows lanes and forest tracks in passing Lough More with views of the Clogher Valley. It connects with the Sliabh Beagh Way at Clogher.

Start and Finish:	Clogher, Dungannon	H537515
Landranger maps:	OS(NI) 18, 19	✔
1 : 25,000 maps:	Not applicable in NI	
Waymark:	Route name/walker outline on blue background	

Publications, badges and certificates:
Leaflet: *An Illustrated Guide to the Carleton Trail* (Dungannon & Tyrone Borough Council). £0.50 (+ 9 x 6 SAE).

Carneddau Challenge Walk   69

Conwy, Gwynedd   *32 km / 20 miles*

A route from sea level near Bangor to the summit of Carnedd Llewelyn with 4750ft of ascent.

Start and Finish:	Aber-Ogwen, Gwynedd	SH613721
Landranger maps:	115	
1 : 25,000 maps:	OL 17	

Publications, badges and certificates:
Booklet: *The Carneddau Challenge Walk* by Tony Hill (Walk & Write Ltd) 1994. ISBN 1874754462. A5. £3.95 (+ 75p p&p).
Badge and certificate: (Walk & Write Ltd). £3.50 (incs p&p).

Carpet Baggers 50   70

Shrops, Staffs, Worcs   *80 km / 50 miles*

This route passes through Bewdley, along the Severn Valley, through Seckley Wood, Alverley, and other villages, to Abbot's Hill and along the Staffordshire Way. A climb over Kinver Edge is followed by a return to the Severn.

Start and Finish:	Stourport-on-Severn, Worcs	SO815736
Landranger maps:	138, 139	
1 : 25,000 maps:	Ex 218, 219	

Publications, badges and certificates:
Looseleaf: *Carpet Baggers 50* (Eric Perks). 4pp; A4. Free (+ 9 x 6 SAE).
Badge and certificate: (Eric Perks). £2.00 (+ SAE) & £1.00 (+ 9 x 6 SAE).

Cateran Trail   71

Angus, Perth & Kinross   *101 km / 63 miles*

Basically a circular route based on Bridge of Cally, but including a spur to and from Blairgowrie, through the Perthshire Glens passing close to Kirkmichael, Enochdhu, Spittal of Glenshee, Cray and Alyth. Use is made of very minor roads, tracks and paths and it includes some high level walking.

Start and Finish:	Blairgowrie, Perth	NO178454
Landranger maps:	43, 53	✔
1 : 25,000 maps:	Ex 381, 387	
Waymark:	Red heart with yellow arrow	

Publications, badges and certificates:
Stripmap: *The Cateran Trail* by Nicholson Maps (Cateran Trail Company Ltd) 2000. ISBN 1860970966. £5.75 (incs p&p).
Brochure: Booking and baggage carrying service (Cateran Trail Company Ltd). Free (+ SAE).

Causeway Coast Way 72

Coleraine, Moyle   *53 km / 33 miles*

One of the official Waymarked Ways in Northern Ireland, the Way passes sandy beaches, rocky bays, high cliffs, resorts and villages, offering a great variety of coastal scenery within the Causeway Coast and Glens AONB. Sites of interest include the Giant's Causeway, the ruins of Dunluce, the Carrick-a-rede rope bridge and Dunserverick and Kenbane Castles. It connects with the Moyle Way at Ballycastle.

Start:	Portstewart, Coleraine	C812368
Finish:	Ballycastle, Moyle	D114407
Landranger maps:	OS(NI) 4, 5	✔
1 : 25,000 maps:	Not applicable in NI	
Waymark:	Route name/walker outline on blue background	

Publications, badges and certificates:
Leaflet: *An Illustrated Guide to the Causeway Coast Way* (Moyle District Council). £0.50 (+ 9 x 6 SAE).

Cavendish 27 Circuit 73

N Yorks   *43 km / 27 miles*

A route encircling the Barden Fell, it follows the river Wharfe to Bolton Bridge, and then takes in the villages of Draughton, Eastby, Embsay, Hasby, Rylstone, Cracoe, Thorpe, Burnsall and Howgill before climbing up to Simon's Seat.

Start and Finish:	Bolton Abbey Hall, N Yorks	SE071540
Landranger maps:	98, 103, 104	
1 : 25,000 maps:	OL 2	

Publications, badges and certificates:
Looseleaf: *Cavendish 27 Circuit* (Lawrence Turner). 1pp. 2nd class stamp (+ 9 x 4 2nd class SAE).
Badge and certificate: (Lawrence Turner). £1.00 (+ SAE) & 0.50 (+ 9 x 4 SAE).

Ceiriog Trail 74

Denbighs, Powys, Shrops, Wrexham   *37 km / 23 miles*

The Trail was developed primarily for horse riders and crosses some rugged terrain. The River Ceiriog is crossed at Pandy and Castle Mill. It is coincident with Offa's Dyke Path National Trail in the Bronygarth/Craignant area. The waymarked Upper Ceiriog Trail (14 miles and on OS mapping), takes in Llanarmon Dyffryn Ceiriog to provide a loop to the west of Pandy.

Start and Finish:	Spring Hill Farm, Pandy, Powys	SJ210346
Landranger maps:	117, 125, 126	✔
1 : 25,000 maps:	Ex 240, 255, 256	
Waymark:	Stirrup / 'Llwybr Ceiriog Trail' in black on white	

Publications, badges and certificates:
Leaflet: *The Ceiriog Trail* (Llangollen Tourist Information Centre). A4/3. £1.20 (+ 9 x 4 SAE).
Leaflet: *The Upper Ceiriog Trail* (Llangollen Tourist Information Centre). A4/3. £1.20 (+ 9 x 4 SAE).
Looseleaf: *Accommodation List for each of the Ceiriog Trails* (Llangollen Tourist Information Centre). Free (if ordered with leaflets).

Celtic Way   75

Bridgend, Cardiff, Carms, Cornwall,   *1161 km / 722 miles*
Devon, Glamorgan, Hants, Mons,
Neath PT, Pembs, Powys, Rhondda CT,
S Glos, Somers, Wilts

The route visits more than 100 pre-historic sites through South Wales and the South West peninsula and includes 111 miles of the Land's End Trail. Alternative routes across Exmoor or through Wessex are incorporated.

Start:	Strumble Head, Pembrokes	SM895412
Finish:	St Michael's Mount, Cornwall	SW524299
Landranger maps:	145, 157, 159, 160, 170, 171, 172, 173, 181, 182, 183, 184, 185, 191, 193, 194, 200, 201, 203, 204	
1 : 25,000 maps:	Ex 102, 104, 106, 108–110, 113–117, 129–132, 140–143, 151, 152, 155-157, 165-167, 185, 186 OL 9, 12, 14, 15, 28, 35	
User group:	Celtic Way Project	

Publications, badges and certificates:
Softback: *The Celtic Way* by Val Saunders Evans (Sigma Leisure) 1998. ISBN 1850586187. 270pp; 150 x 210. £9.95.

Centenary Circle   76

Essex   *37 km / 23 miles*

A route around Chelmsford passing via Sandon, Galleywood, Writtle, Broomfield and the River Chelmer.

Start and Finish:	Sandford Mill, Essex	TL740060
Landranger maps:	167	✔
1 : 25,000 maps:	Ex 183	
Waymark:	Profiles of Queens Victoria and Elizabeth II in garland	

Publications, badges and certificates:
No paper publication: See Website (Chelmsford Borough Council). www.chelmsfordbc.gov.uk.

Centenary Way (Derbyshire) 77

Derbys *38 km / 24 miles*

A walk devised by the Derbyshire Footpaths Preservation Society to commemorate their centenary, visiting the lesser known but attractive villages of South Derbyshire. The Way links with the Bonnie Prince Charlie Walk at Ashbourne.

Start:	Ilkeston, Derbys	SK460418
Finish:	Ashbourne, Derbys	SK180470
Landranger maps:	119, 129	✔
1 : 25,000 maps:	Ex 259	
Waymark:	Named signs	

Publications, badges and certificates:
Booklet: Centenary Way – Ilkeston to Ashbourne (Derbyshire Footpaths Preservation Society) 1994. 24pp; A5. £2.50 (incs p&p).

Centenary Way (North Yorkshire) 78

N Yorks *133 km / 83 miles*

A route devised to celebrate the 100th anniversary of Yorkshire County Council. It runs across the Howardian Hills and Yorkshire Wolds via Castle Howard and Wharram Percy, linking York and the Foss Walk with the Wolds Way and Cleveland Way National Trails. It combines riverside walks in deep valleys with forest tracks. See Hovingham Hobble.

Start:	York, N Yorks	SE603522
Finish:	Filey Brigg, N Yorks	TA126817
Landranger maps:	100, 101, 105	✔
1 : 25,000 maps:	Ex 300, 301	
Waymark:	Letters CW on standard waymarks	

Publications, badges and certificates:
No publications: on OS mapping.

Centenary Way (Warwickshire) 79

Warks *158 km / 98 miles*

The Way was devised to celebrate one hundred years of Warwickshire County Council. It passes the Tame Valley, Atherstone Ridge, the George Eliot country around Nuneaton, before passing to the east of Coventry to Kenilworth, Warwick and Leamington Spa. From here it heads to the Burton Dassett Hills, Edge Hill, Shipston-on-Stour and Ilmington Downs. See Coventry and Heart of England Ways, Midland Link and Warwickshire Villages Trail.

Start:	Kingsbury Water Park, Warks	SP204959
Finish:	Upper Quinton, Warks	SP176454
Landranger maps:	139, 140, 151	✔
1 : 25,000 maps:	Ex 191, 205, 206, 221, 222, 232 OL 45	
Waymark:	Bear and ragged staff	

Publications, badges and certificates:
Paperback: *The Centenary Way* by Geoff Allen and John Roberts (Walkways) 1996. ISBN 0947708332. 124pp; 210 x 145. £6.45.
Folder: *Centenary Way* (Warwickshire County Council) 1989. 11 leaflets; A4/3. £4.00 (+ 50p p&p).

Central Sperrins Way 80

Omagh, Strabane   *40 km / 25 miles*

One of the official Waymarked Ways in Northern Ireland, the route is through one of the largest uplands in Ireland. Within the Sperrins AONB, the gentle contours of the Sperrin Hills are followed through villages using country lanes, open moorland, green lanes and farm tracks.

Start and Finish:	Barnes Gap, Plumbridge, Strabane	H550900
Landranger maps:	OS(NI) 13	✔
1 : 25,000 maps:	Not applicable in NI	
Waymark:	Route name/walker outline on blue background	

Publications, badges and certificates:
Leaflet: *An Illustrated Guide to the Central Sperrins Way* (Omagh District Council). £0.50 (+ 9 x 6 SAE).

Centre of The Kingdom Walk 81

Lancs   *75 km / 46 miles*

A route through many of the historical sites of the Borough of Ribble Valley taking in Chatburn, Bolton by Bowland, Slaidburn, Dunsop Bridge, Whitewell, Chipping and Bashall Eaves. The village of Dunsop Bridge has been determined by the Ordnance Survey as the point nearest to the centre of the British Isles, thus the name of the walk.

Start and Finish:	Clitheroe Castle, Lancashire	SD744415
Landranger maps:	103	
1 : 25,000 maps:	OL 41	

Publications, badges and certificates:
Folder: Journey Through the Centre of the Kingdom (Ribble Valley Borough Council). 8 leaflets. £1.00 – with accommodation list.

Chaddesley Chase 82

Worcs   *35 km / 22 miles*

A route taking in Chaddesley, Santery Hill, Pepper Wood and Hillpool Mill making use of open fields and following streams and country lanes.

Start and Finish:	Chaddesley Corbett, Worcs	SO892736
Landranger maps:	138, 139	
1 : 25,000 maps:	Ex 218, 219	

Publications, badges and certificates:
Looseleaf: *Chaddesley Chase* (Eric Perks). 4pp; A4. Free (+ 9 x 6 SAE).
Badge and certificate: (Eric Perks). £2.00 (+ SAE) & £1.00 (+ 9 x 6 SAE).

Chalkland Way 83

E Yorks *64 km / 40 miles*

A tour around the most northerly chalk outcrop in Britain – the Yorkshire Wolds, noted for green, dry valleys. A route taking in the villages of Great Givendale, Bugthorpe, Thixendale, Fimber, Wetwang and Huggate.

Start and Finish:	Pocklington, E Yorks	SE802488
Landranger maps:	100, 101, 106	
1 : 25,000 maps:	Ex 294, 300	

Publications, badges and certificates:
Looseleaf: *The Chalkland Way* (Ray Wallis) 1994. Free (+ 9 x 4 SAE).
Badge: (Ray Wallis). £1.00 (+ SAE).

Channel to Channel (Devon – Somerset) 84

Devon, Somers *80 km / 50 miles*

In linking the English and Bristol Channels this route, initiated and developed by members of the Ramblers' Association, avoids the honey-pot area of the Quantocks as it passes through or close to Axminster, Taunton and Wilton along the narrow waist of the south west peninsula. As well as the connection with the South West Coast Path National Trail at Seaton, it links with the West Deane Way at Taunton and ends at Watchet some 8 miles from the start of the South West Coast Path at Minehead.

Start:	Seaton, Devon	ST245899
Finish:	Watchet, Somers	ST073435
Landranger maps:	181, 193	
1 : 25,000 maps:	Ex 116, 128 OL 9	

Publications, badges and certificates:
Booklet: *Channel to Channel* (Ken Young). 28pp; A5. £2.00 (+ 50p p&p).

Charnwood Forest Challenge Walk 85

Leics *40 km / 25 miles*

A walk around the hill country to the north-east of Leicester passing Newton Lifford, Ulverscroft Priory, Bardon Hill, Mount St Bernard Abbey, Beacon Hill and Woodhouse Eaves.

Start and Finish:	Bradgate Park, Leics	SK543114
Landranger maps:	129	
1 : 25,000 maps:	Ex 246	

Publications, badges and certificates:
Booklet: *Charnwood Forest Challenge Walk* by John Merrill (Walk & Write Ltd) 1992. ISBN 0907496644. 32pp; A5. £3.95 (+ 75p p&p).
Badge and certificate: (Walk & Write Ltd). £3.50 (incs p&p).

Charnwood Round 86

Leics   *53 km / 33 miles*

A walk round the ancient Charnwood Forest which lies on high ground to the north-west of Leicester. Peaceful countryside, once quarried by Romans, settled by monks, criss-crossed with paths and full of interesting relics of the past. Links with the Leicestershire Round.

Start and Finish:	Newtown Linford, Leics	SK521098
Landranger maps:	129, 140	
1 : 25,000 maps:	Ex 233, 246	

Publications, badges and certificates:
Leaflet: *The Charnwood Round* by Heather McDermid (Cordee Ltd). ISBN 1871890128. 10pp; A4. £2.95.

Cheltenham Circular Footpath 87

Glos   *40 km / 25 miles*

A route around Cheltenham with views of the Cotswold escarpment and the Severn Vale.

Start and Finish:	Cheltenham, Glos	SO955237
Landranger maps:	162, 163	
1 : 25,000 maps:	Ex 179	
Waymark:	Walk name under a green tree	

Publications, badges and certificates:
Booklet: *Cheltenham Circular Footpath* by Cheltenham Borough Council and others (Reardon Publishing) 1996. ISBN 187387717X. 40pp; 210 x 150. £3.95 (+ 50p p&p).

Cheshire Ring Canal Walk 88

Cheshire, Gtr Man, Staffs   *158 km / 97 miles*

A route following the towpaths along six historic canals of various ages and character, this Walk offers the solitude of quiet countryside, the hustle and bustle of city streets and views of the Cheshire Plain and Peak District hills. See Dane Valley Way.

Start and Finish:	Marple, Gtr Man	SJ962884
Landranger maps:	108, 109, 117, 118	✔
1 : 25,000 maps:	Ex 257, 258, 267, 275 OL 1, 24	
Waymark:	Metal plaque with bridge and barge	

Publications, badges and certificates:
Booklet: *The Cheshire Ring* by John N. Merrill (Walk & Write Ltd). ISBN 0907496636. 80pp; A5. £4.95 (+ 75p p&p).

Cheshire Ways 89

Cheshire *Various km / Various miles*

These Ways comprise the Baker Way (8 miles) Brines Brow – Christleton; Delamere Way (22 miles) Stockton Heath – Frodsham; Eddisbury Way (18 miles) Frodsham – Burwardsley; Longster Trail (11 miles) Helsby – Pipers Ash. They provide links with the Sandstone Trail at Frodsham.

Start and Finish:	Various	
Landranger maps:	109, 117, 118	✔
1 : 25,000 maps:	Ex 257, 266, 267	
Waymark:	Named discs	

Publications, badges and certificates:

Booklet: *Longer Trails in Vale Royal* – reference included to Delamere Way; Eddisbury Way; Longster Trail: (Vale Royal Borough Council) 1993. 76pp; A5. £1.95 (incs p&p).

Booklet: *Waymarked Walks in Central Cheshire* – Baker Way (Brines Brow – Christleton) (Mid Cheshire Footpath Society). 16pp; 100 x 223. £1.00 (+ 9 x 6 SAE).

Booklet: *Waymarked Walks in Central Cheshire* – *Baker Way* (Christleton – Brines Brow) (Mid Cheshire Footpath Society). 16pp; 100 x 223. £1.00 (+ 9 x 6 SAE).

Booklet: *Waymarked Walks in Central Cheshire* – *Delamere Way* (Frodsham – Stockton Heath) (Mid Cheshire Footpath Society). 16pp; 100 x 223. £1.00 (+ 9 x 6 SAE).

Booklet: *Waymarked Walks in Central Cheshire* – *Delamere Way* (Stockton Heath – Frodsham) (Mid Cheshire Footpath Society). 16pp; 100 x 223. £1.00 (+ 9 x 6 SAE).

Booklet: *Waymarked Walks in Central Cheshire* – *Eddisbury Way* (Frodsham – Burwardsley) (Mid Cheshire Footpath Society). Details TBA.

Booklet: *Waymarked Walks in Central Cheshire* – *Eddisbury Way* (Burwardsley – Frodsham) (Mid Cheshire Footpath Society). Details TBA.

Booklet: *Waymarked Walks in Central Cheshire* – *Longster Trail* (Helsby – Pipers Ash) (Mid Cheshire Footpath Society). 8pp; 100 x 223. £1.00 (+ 9 x 6 SAE).

Booklet: *Waymarked Walks in Central Cheshire* – *Longster Trail* (Pipers Ash – Helsby) (Mid Cheshire Footpath Society). 8pp; 100 x 223. £1.00 (+ 9 x 6 SAE).

Chesterfield Round 90

Derbys *80 km / 50 miles*

A route devised to celebrate the Ramblers' Association Golden Jubilee that is, as the name suggests, a walk through the countryside around the town.

Start and Finish:	Troway, Derbys	SK412792
Landranger maps:	119	
1 : 25,000 maps:	Ex 269 OL 24	

Publications, badges and certificates:

Folder: *Chesterfield Round Walk* (RA Chesterfield & NE Derbyshire). 3pp; A5. £1.00 (+ 9 x 6 SAE).

Cheviot Hills 2,000ft Summits 91

Northumb *40 km / 25 miles*

This upland walk over rough terrain and involving 5,000ft of ascent links the Cheviot, Windy Gyle, Bloodybush Edge, Cushat Law, Comb Fell and Hedgehope, each over 2,000ft. Good navigation skills are required. An alternative route from Wooler, adding 10 miles, is described.

Start and Finish:	Hawsen Burn, Northumb	NT954225
Landranger maps:	75, 80	
1 : 25,000 maps:	OL 16	
Path website:	www.blencathra.demon.co.uk/nldwa	

Publications, badges and certificates:
Looseleaf: *Cheviot Hills 2,000ft Summits Walk* (LDWA Northumbria Group). Free (+ 9 x 4 SAE).
Certificate: (LDWA Northumbria Group). £0.10 (+ A5 SAE).

Chiltern Heritage Trail 92

Bucks   *85 km / 53 miles*

The trail links the towns and parishes of Chiltern District and goes through scenic country and picturesque villages. It is partly coincident with the South Bucks Way and meets the Chiltern Way at Chalfont St Giles.

Start and Finish:	Chesham Town Centre, Bucks	SP960017
Landranger maps:	165, 175	
1 : 25,000 maps:	Ex 172, 181	
Waymark:	Named discs with beech leaf design	

Publications, badges and certificates:
Booklet: *Chiltern Heritage Trail* by Barry Totterdell (Chiltern District Council) 2000. 32pp; A5. £2.99 (incs p&p).
Leaflet: *The Chiltern Heritage Trail* (Chiltern District Council) 2000. A5. Free.

Chiltern Way 93

Beds, Bucks, Herts, Luton, Oxon   *200 km / 125 miles*

Created by the Chiltern Society as its Millennium Project the Way takes in all of the Chilterns in a 125 miles circuit extending from Ewelme in the south west, Chorleywood in the south east and Sharpenhoe Clappers and Great Offley in the north east. Although officially starting at Hemel Hempstead Station, the walk can be started at many other places on the route. The Way passes through some of the most attractive parts of the Chilterns, including the Bovingdon Plateau, the Chess valley, the Misbourne valley, Penn Country, the Hambleden valley, Stonor Park, Ewelme, Swyncombe Down, Bledlow Ridge, Hampden Country, Bulbourne valley and Dunstable Down. The Way also has links with other routes including Chiltern Heritage Trail, Ridgeway National Trail, Icknield Way Path, Oxfordshire, Swan's and South Bucks Ways and Grand Union Canal, Lea Valley and Chess Valley Walks.

Start and Finish:	Hemel Hempstead, Herts	TL043059
Landranger maps:	165, 166, 175, 176	✔
1 : 25,000 maps:	Ex 170, 171, 172, 181, 182, 192, 193	
Waymark:	Named signposts and discs	
User group:	Chiltern Society Office	

Publications, badges and certificates:
Paperback: *The Chiltern Way* by Nick Moon (Book Castle & Chiltern Society Mail Order Bookshop) 2000. ISBN 1871199794. 176pp; A5. £7.99 (p&p £1.60 Book Castle; 85p Chiltern Society Mail Order Bookshop).
Leaflet: *The Chiltern Way* (Chiltern Society Office) 2001. A4/3. Free.

Churnet Valley Challenge Walk 94

Staffs   *39 km / 24 miles*

Set in the Churnet Valley, the route takes in several villages, a section of the Caldon Canal and part of the Staffordshire Way. There is 2,600ft of ascent.

Start and Finish:	Froghall, Staffs	SK027476
Landranger maps:	119	
1 : 25,000 maps:	Ex 259 OL 24	

Publications, badges and certificates:
Looseleaf: *Churnet Valley Challenge Walk* (Alan S. Edwards). 2pp. Free (+ SAE).
Certificate: (Alan S. Edwards). A5. £0.30 (+ A5 SAE).

Cistercian Way 95

Cumbria   *53 km / 33 miles*

A route along the paths, tracks and byways of the low limestone hills that fringe the northern shores of Morecambe Bay via woodlands to Hampsfell and Cartmel Priory to Cark and Holker Hall. The route then continues over the sands of the Leven Estuary, but this is dangerous and should only be attempted with the recognised Sand Pilot. Otherwise the train should be caught to Ulverston where the Way continues by Dalton to Furness Abbey and the coast.

Start:	Grange-over-Sands, Cumbria	SD412781
Finish:	Roa Island, Cumbria	SD232648
Landranger maps:	96, 97	✔
1 : 25,000 maps:	OL 6, 7	
Waymark:	Monk	

Publications, badges and certificates:
Leaflet: Cistercian Way (South Lakeland District Council). A4/3. Free (+ 9 x 4 SAE).

Clarendon Way 96

Hants, Wilts   *39 km / 24 miles*

Named after Clarendon Park on the eastern edge of Salisbury, the Way links that city on the River Avon with Winchester on the River Itchen. Crossing the River Test at Kings Somborne, the scenery ranges from the water meadows of the valleys with their charming villages through woodlands to chalk downs with their fine views. See Sarum Way.

Start:	Salisbury, Wilts	SU143297
Finish:	Winchester, Hants	SU483293

Landranger maps:	184, 185	✔
1 : 25,000 maps:	Ex 130, 131, 132	
Waymark:	Green and white discs with bishop's mitre	

Publications, badges and certificates:
Leaflet: *Test & Clarendon Way* (Hampshire County Council). A4/3. Free (+ SAE).

Cleveland Way National Trail   97
Cleveland, N Yorks   *177 km / 110 miles*

The Way climbs to the North York Moors at Sutton Bank, where there is a short extension to the Kilburn White Horse, and then heads north along the western edge of the high heather moors to Osmotherley from where it follows tracks along the northern escarpment to Greenhow Moor. It turns over Kildale Moor, Roseberry Topping and Guisborough Moor to leave the North York Moors National Park and to reach the coast at Saltburn-by-the-Sea then following a varied and undulating coastal path southwards along clifftops, sands and passing several harbours and resorts. This roughly horse-shoe shaped trail has led to the development of suggested routes linking the start and finish including the waymarked Tabular Hills Link Walk (48 miles). Relevant publications etc. are listed. The waymarked Cleveland Street Walk (11 miles), which is included on OS mapping, connects Guisborough with Loftus (and easy access to the coast/Cleveland Way National Trail), crossing the Cleveland Way National Trail inland at Slapewath to provide alternative options. See Teesdale Way/Tees Link. See Bilsdale Circuit, Centenary Way (North Yorkshire), East Riding Heritage Way, Lyke Wake Walk, Newlands Way, Samaritan Way, White Rose Walk, Wolds Way National Trail. See also E-Routes (E2).

Start:	Helmsley, N Yorks	SE611839
Finish:	Filey Brigg, N Yorks	TA126817
Landranger maps:	93, 94, 99, 100, 101	✔
1 : 25,000 maps:	Ex 301 OL 26, 27	
Waymark:	National Trail Acorn	
Path website:	www.clevelandway.gov.uk	

Publications, badges and certificates:
Softback: *Cleveland Way* (Official Guide) by Ian Sampson (Aurum Press) 1999. ISBN 1854106066. 144pp; 210 x 130. £10.99.
Softback: *Cleveland Way Companion* by Paul Hannon (Hillside Publications) 1992. ISBN 1870141172. 96pp; 175 x 115. £6.50 (+ £0.60 p&p).
Booklet: *The Cleveland Way* by John Merrill (Walk & Write Ltd). ISBN 0907496709. 80pp; A5. £4.95 (+ 75p p&p).
Paperback: *Cleveland Way plus the Tabular Hills Link* by Martin Collins (Dalesman Publishing Co Ltd) 1997. ISBN 1855681137. 224pp; 165 x 100. £4.99.
Leaflet: *Cleveland Way* (Countryside Agency Publications) 1996. A4/3. Free.
Booklet: *Cleveland Way Accommodation and Information Guide* (North York Moors National Park) Annual. £0.50 (+ 55p p&p).
Stripmap: *The Cleveland Way Map and Guide* (Footprint). ISBN 1871149096. £3.50.
Badge and certificate: (Walk & Write Ltd). £3.50 (incs p&p).
Badge: (North York Moors National Park). £0.99 (+ SAE).
Booklet: *The Link Through the Tabular Hills Walk* (North York Moors National Park) 1993. ISBN 0907480446. 44pp; 120 x 170. £3.95 (+ 95p p&p).
Leaflet: *The Cleveland Street Walk* (Redcar & Cleveland Borough Council) 1999. £0.50 (incs p&p).

Clitheroe 60K   98

Lancs   *60 km / 37 miles*

A walk devised to commemorate the RA Diamond Jubilee. From the Ribble Valley the route takes in Longridge Fell, the Hoddle Valley, Newton, then skirting Grindleton Fell to Sawley and Downham, finally traversing Pendle Hill. The route includes almost 5000ft of ascent and links with the Pendle Way (on Pendle Hill) and Ribble Way (at Sawley Bridge).

Start and Finish:	Clitheroe, Lancs	SD742419
Landranger maps:	103	
1 : 25,000 maps:	287 OL 41	

Publications, badges and certificates:
Leaflet: *Clitheroe 60k route card* by Eddie Ross (Ribble Valley Borough Council) 1995. 2pp; A5. Free (+ 9 x 6 SAE).
Certificate: (Ribble Valley Borough Council). Free (+ 9 x 6 SAE).

Cloud 7 Circuit   99

Cheshire, Staffs   *53 km / 33 miles*

Named after the seven Cloud hills, this strenuous route with 5400ft of ascent covers the area between Leek, Buxton, Macclesfield and Congleton. There are shorter route options of 28 and 20 miles.

Start and Finish:	Rushton Spencer, Staffs	SJ935625
Landranger maps:	118, 119	
1 : 25,000 maps:	Ex 268 OL 24	

Publications, badges and certificates:
Leaflet: *Cloud 7 Circuit* (Derek Nash). A4. Free (+ 9 x 4 SAE).
Badge and certificate: (Derek Nash). £1.50 & £0.75 (+ SAE).

Clwydian Way   100

Conwy, Denbighs, Flints   *196 km / 122 miles*

From Prestatyn the route takes the Clwydian Range to Llangollen and then turns west along the Llantysilio Range to Corwen. The return to the start is via Brenig and the Clocaenog Forest. The walk links with Offa's Dyke Path National Trail, the North Wales Path and the Mynydd Hiraethog & Denbigh Moors Footpath amongst others.

Start and Finish:	Prestatyn, Denbighs	SJ061838
Landranger maps:	116, 117, 125	
1 : 25,000 maps:	Ex 255, 256, 264, 265	

Publications, badges and certificates:
Paperback: *The Clwydian Way* by David Hollett (RA North Wales Area) 2000. ISBN 1901184366. 88pp; 239 x 165. £5.95 (+ £1.00 p&p).

Clyde Walkway 101

Glasgow, N Lanark, S Lanark *64 km / 40 miles*

A route under development which will eventually allow for an unhindered way following the course of the River Clyde from the centre of Glasgow through Hamilton, Strathclyde Park and Lanark passing the attractions of Bothwell Castle and woods, the Palace Grounds and Mausoleum at Hamilton, and the Barons Haugh Nature Reserve to the spectacular Falls of Clyde. For the present, there are isolated access difficulties. Details of ongoing route availablity are available from the Access Development Officer (Simon Pilpel on 01698 455938 and email simon.pilpel@southlanarkshire.gov.uk). In Glasgow, the Walkway links in to the numerous pathways of the City. See Edinburgh to Glasgow Canals Walk.

Start:	Central Glasgow	NS584649
Finish:	New Lanark, S Lanark	NS881424
Landranger maps:	64, 72	
1 : 25,000 maps:	Ex 335, 342, 343	
Waymark:	Named signs	

Publications, badges and certificates:
Leaflet: *Welcome to the Clyde Walkway* (South Lanarkshire Council). A4/3. Free (+ 9 x 4 SAE).
Leaflet: *The Clyde Walkway – Crossford to the Falls of Clyde* (South Lanarkshire Council). A4/3. Free (+ 9 x 4 SAE).

Coast to Coast 102

Cumbria, N Yorks *306 km / 190 miles*

The classic route by Alfred Wainwright was intended in part to encourage others to devise their own routes in connecting the Irish and North Seas. This particular route also links three National Parks taking a high level traverse wherever possible. From the west, the coastal plain is crossed to, and through, the Lake District to Shap, followed by the crossing of the Westmorland limestone plateau to Kirkby Stephen, a climb to the Pennine watershed and then through Keld, Reeth and Richmond to the low level Vale of Mowbray before again achieving height across the North York Moors. Details of alternative route publications are listed. See also Cumbria Coastal Way, Falklands Way, Lyke Wake Walk, Swale Way and Stepping over Stone.

Start:	St Bees, Cumbria	NX959119
Finish:	Robin Hood's Bay, N Yorks	NZ953048
Landranger maps:	89, 90, 91, 92, 93, 94, 98, 99, 100	
1 : 25,000 maps:	Ex 303, 304 OL 4, 5, 7, 19, 26, 27, 30	

Publications, badges and certificates:
Paperback: *Coast to Coast Walk* by A. Wainwright (Michael Joseph) 1994. ISBN 0718140729. £11.99.
Paperback: *Wainwright's Coast to Coast Walk* by A. Wainwright (Michael Joseph). ISBN 0718140931. 208pp; 250 x 215. £16.99.
Paperback: *Coast to Coast Walk: St Bees to Robin Hood's Bay* (190 miles) by Paul Hannon (Hillside Publications) 1997. ISBN 1870141555. 152pp; 175 x 115. £8.99 (+ £0.80 p&p).

Stripmap: *Coast to Coast Walk: St Bees Head to Keld* (Ordnance Survey) 1999. ISBN 0319260909. £6.75.

Stripmap: *Coast to Coast Walk: Keld to Robin Hood's Bay* (Ordnance Survey) 1999. ISBN 0319260917. £6.75.

Stripmap: *Coast to Coast: Part 1: St Bees Head to Swaledale* – map & guide (Footprint) 1994. ISBN 1871149118. £3.50.

Stripmap: *Coast to Coast: Part 2: Swaledale to Robin Hood's Bay* – map & guide (Footprint) 1994. ISBN 1871149126. £3.50.

Booklet: *Coast to Coast Accommodation Guide* (Doreen Whitehead) Annual. 72pp; 100 x 150. £3.00 (incs p&p).

Booklet: *Coast to Coast Walk Accommodation Guide* by Ewen Bennett (North York Moors Adventure Centre) Biannual. 36pp; A6. £3.95 (incs p&p).

Booklet: *Booking Bureau – Youth Hostels* (YHA Northern Region) Annual. 20pp; A5. Free.

OTHER ROUTE PUBLICATIONS:

Softback: *The Northern Coast to Coast: St Bees to Robin Hood's Bay* (178 miles) by Terry Marsh (Cicerone Press) 1993. ISBN 1852841265. 280pp; 116 x 176. £7.99.

Paperback: *The Alternate Coast to Coast: Walney Island to Holy Island* (192 miles) by Dennis Brook & Phil Hinchliffe (Cicerone Press). ISBN 1852842024. 272pp; 116 x 176. £9.99.

Paperback: *The Ravenber: Ravenglass to Berwick-upon-Tweed* (210 miles) by Ron Scholes (Pentland Press Ltd) 1997. ISBN 1858213894. 302pp; 121 x 176. £7.50.

Paperback: *Blackpool to Bridlington – The Aerospace Way* (148 miles) by Harry Cadman and Anthony Johnson (British Aerospace Ltd) 1997. ISBN 0952966107. 108pp; A5. £5.95 – cheques payable to RNLI.

Coast to Coast – Scotland   103

Argyll, Fife, Perth, Stirling   *206 km / 129 miles*

The route takes a line through Tyndrum, Crianlarich, St Fillans and passes the Hopetoun Monument. In the Ronald Turnbull publication, no set route is provided – in keeping with the spirit of the annual TGO Challenge which allows for participants to plan their own routes within broad limits – but it details various alternatives.

Start:	Oban, Argyll	NM858299
Finish:	St Andrews, Fife	NO514168
Landranger maps:	49, 50, 51, 57, 58, 59	
1 : 25,000 maps:	Ex 359, 365, 368, 369, 370, 371, & one TBA 2002	
	OL 38	

Publications, badges and certificates:

Paperback: *The Scottish Coast to Coast* by Brian Smailes (Challenge Publications). ISBN 095269008X. 64pp; 125 x 185. £6.50 (incs p&p).

Paperback: *Across Scotland on Foot* by Ronald Turnbull (Grey Stone Books). ISBN 095159964X. 160pp; 205 x 130. £5.95.

Coast to Coast – Southern England   104

Various   *387/456 km / 242/283 miles*

Not necessarily inspired by AW but certainly offering alternative coast to coast routes, the two publications provide details of connecting the Bristol and English Channels by mainly taking advantage of established long distance paths. The first listed publication covers 242 miles to finish at Lydd-on-Sea, the second 283 miles at Dover.

Start:	Weston-super-Mare, N Somers	ST316615
Finish:	See Path Description	
Landranger maps:	Book1: 173, 174, 182, 183, 185, 189, 197, 198, 199	
	Book 2: 179, 182, 183, 184, 185, 186, 187, 188, 189	
1 : 25,000 maps:	Various	

Publications, badges and certificates:
Booklet: *Channel to Channel* by Ian & Kay Sayer (Kimberley Publishing) 1996. 96pp; A5. £3.95.
Paperback: *The Southern Coast-to-Coast Walk* by Ray Quinlan (Cicerone Press) 1993. ISBN 1852841176. 200pp; 116 x 176. £6.99.

Coast to Coast – Wales   105
Carms, Ceredigion, Conwy,   *Max 348 km / 216 miles*
Gwynedd, Powys, Swansea

The walk climbs to and crosses the peaks of the Carneddau and the Glyders before dropping down through the Llanberis Pass then up and over Snowdon, the Moelwyns, the Rhinogs, Cadair Idris and the Tarrens before descending into the Dyfi valley and Machynlleth. The route, by then becoming more wild and remote, passes Bwlch Hyddgen, Plynlimon, Rheidol, and enters the Elan valley. The Carmarthen Fan and the Black Mountain are crossed, continuing over the Lliw Hills, passing to the west of Swansea, on to the Gower and the coast path. See also Cambrian Way.

Start:	Llanfairfechan, Conwy	SH680750
Finish:	Parkmill, Swansea	SS545892
Landranger maps:	115, 124, 135, 136, 147, 159, 160	
1 : 25,000 maps:	Ex 187, 200, 213, 214, 215 OL 12, 17, 18, 23	

Publications, badges and certificates:
Paperback: *A Welsh Coast to Coast Walk – Snowdonia to Gower* by John Gillham (Cicerone Press) 1996. ISBN 1852842180. 152pp; 115 x 174. £7.99.
Paperback: *Snowdonia to Gower* by John Gillham published by Baton Wicks (Cordee Ltd). ISBN 1898573514. 112pp; 265 x 215. £15.99 – to be published 2002.

Coed Morgannwg Way   106
Merthyr T, Neath PT, Rhondda CT   *58 km / 36 miles*

The Way, most of which is on Forestry Commission land, meets the Taff Trail at the finish. It crosses part of the Coed Morgannwg, a complex of four upland forests visiting the Dare Valley and Craig y Llyn, climbing to several more viewpoints, to reach Afan Argoed Country Park. From here the route follows less elevated paths past a number of archaeological remains from prehistoric to industrial times. Near to Bodvic Stone the Way links with the Ogwr Ridgeway Walk. See St Illtyd's Walk.

Start:	Gethin Woodland Park, Merthyr T	SO057032
Finish:	Margam, Neath PT	SS814860
Landranger maps:	170	✔
1 : 25,000 maps:	Ex 165, 166	
Waymark:	White footprint on brown background	

Publications, badges and certificates:
Booklet: *Coed Morgannwg Way* (Neath & Port Talbot County Borough Council) 1995. 10pp; A5. £1.00 (incs p&p).

Colne Valley Circular Walk   ·   107

West Yorks   *21 km / 13 miles*

A route around the area of Kirklees through Slaithwaite and Marsden and over moors, passing mills, canal and other historical sites. There are links to the Kirklees Way at various points.

Start and Finish:	Golcar, West Yorks	SD096158
Landranger maps:	110	
1 : 25,000 maps:	OL 21	
Waymark:	Colne Valley Society logo	

Publications, badges and certificates:
Booklet: *Colne Valley Circular Walk* by J. W. Balmforth (Colne Valley Society). 60pp; A5. £2.50 (+ 40p p&p).

Colne Valley Way, Colne Valley Trail & Ebury Way   108

Bucks, Herts, Gtr London, Slough, Surrey, Windsor M   *32 km / 20 miles*

The Colne Valley Way (10 miles) starts at the Thames Path National Trail and ends at the Grand Union Canal at Cowley Lock near Uxbridge where it connects with the Colne Valley Trail (7 miles) which goes on to Rickmansworth. From here a short link leads to the Ebury Way (3 miles; not on OS maps) to Oxhey Park. From Oxhey Park it is a short distance to the waymarked Ver-Colne Valley Walk (15 miles from Redbourn to Watford and on OS mapping). At Rickmansworth the waymarked Chess Valley Walk (10 miles and on OS mapping) goes to Chesham to join to the Chiltern Link, providing a link to the Ridgeway National Trail.

Start:	Staines, Surrey	TQ029718
Finish:	Oxhey Park, Herts	TQ111953
Landranger maps:	166, 176	✔ (not Ebury)
1 : 25,000 maps:	Ex 160, 172	
Waymark:	Named posts	

Publications, badges and certificates:
Leaflet: *Colne Valley Way* (Groundwork Thames Valley) 1993. Free (+ SAE).
Leaflet: *Colne Valley Trail* (Groundwork Thames Valley) 1996. A4/3. Free (+ SAE).
Leaflet: *Explore the Ebury Way* (Three Rivers District Council) 1996. A4/3. Free (+ SAE).
Leaflet: *Ver-Colne Valley Walk* (Hertfordshire County Council (Hertford)). A4/3. Free (+ SAE).
Leaflet: *Chess Valley Walk* (Buckinghamshire County Council) 1996. A4/3. Free (+ SAE).

Community Forest Path 109
Bath NES, Bristol, N Somers, S Glos   *72 km / 45 miles*

A route around Bristol using footpaths, tracks and some sections of rural lanes providing a variety of landscapes with views of the Mendip Hills, Severn Estuary and the Severn road bridges. It takes in Ashton Court, Blaise Castle and the Clifton Suspension Bridge. It is coincident with the Bristol & Bath Railway Path (16 miles) for two miles at Warmley. It is coincident with part of the Two Rivers Way and links with the Avon Walkway (30 miles and included on OS mapping) at Keynsham.

Start and Finish:	Keynsham, Bath NES	ST659690
Landranger maps:	172	✔
1 : 25,000 maps:	Ex 155, 167	
Waymark:	Named signs and disc with Forest of Avon logo	

Publications, badges and certificates:
Leaflet: *Community Forest Path* (Forest of Avon) 1998. A5. Free.
Leaflet: *Bristol & Bath Railway Path* (Bath & North East Somerset Council). A4/3. Free (+ SAE).

Compo's Way 110
S Yorks, W Yorks   *61 km / 38 miles*

A route over moors and through country associated with the television series – 'Last of the Summer Wine'.

Start:	Hunter's Bar, Sheffield, S Yorks	SK333857
Finish:	Sid's Cafe, Holmfirth, W Yorks	SE145083
Landranger maps:	110	
1 : 25,000 maps:	OL 1	

Publications, badges and certificates:
Booklet: *Compo's Way* by Alan Hiley (Walk & Write Ltd). ISBN 187475473X. 40pp; A5. £4.50 (+ 75p p&p).
Badge and certificate: (Walk & Write Ltd). £3.50 (incs p&p).

Coniston Water Circuit 111
Cumbria   *35 km / 22 miles*

A route around Coniston Water taking in Nibthwaite, Brockbarrow, Tilberthwaite, Coniston and over Beacon Fell. In parts it is coincident with the Cumbria Way.

Start and Finish:	Wateryeat, Cumbria	SD288891
Landranger maps:	96	
1 : 25,000 maps:	OL 6, 7	

Publications, badges and certificates:
Looseleaf: *Coniston Water Circuit* (Brian Richmond). Free (+ 9 x 4 SAE).
Badge and certificate: (Brian Richmond). £1.50 (+ SAE).

Cotswold Canals Walk 112

Glos, Wilts   *76 km / 47 miles*

From the Severn to the Thames the Walk follows the line of old canals through some of the most beautiful parts of the English landscape. Sometimes the towpaths are followed past scenes redolent with industrial archaeology whilst at other times fieldpaths are taken through pastoral countryside.

Start:	Framilode, Glos	SO750104
Finish:	Lechlade, Glos	SU214994
Landranger maps:	162, 163	
1 : 25,000 maps:	Ex 168, 169, 170 OL 14	

Publications, badges and certificates:
Paperback: *The Cotswold Canals Walk* by Gerry Stewart (Countryside Matters) 2000. ISBN 0952787032. 96pp; A5. £5.95 (post free).

Cotswold Ring 113

Glos, Worcs   *89 km / 55 miles*

A route from the spa town of Cheltenham taking in many villages such as Bourton-on-the-Water, Stow-on-the-Wold and Moreton-in-Marsh. Links with the Cotswold Way National Trail, Heart of England Way, Windrush Way and Wardens Way.

Start and Finish:	Cheltenham, Glos	SO237955
Landranger maps:	150, 151, 163	
1 : 25,000 maps:	Ex 179 OL 45	

Publications, badges and certificates:
Booklet: *The Cotswold Ring* by Christopher Knowles (Reardon Publishing) 1996. ISBN 1873877161. 40pp; 210 x 150. £2.95 (+ 50p p&p).

Cotswold Round 114

Bath NES, Glos, Oxon, S Glos, Warks, Worcs   *333 km / 207 miles*

Devised by the Macmillan Way Association for the purpose of raising funds for Macmillan Cancer Relief the Round comprises the Cross Cotswold Pathway (86 miles) from Banbury to Bath, a suggested turn north along the Cotswold Way National Trail to Chipping Campden and then a return to Banbury by way of the Cotswold Link (21 miles). The Pathway is based largely on the Macmillan Way and the Link is coincident in parts with the Heart of England Way.

Start and Finish:	Banbury Cross, Oxon	SP458400
Landranger maps:	150, 151, 162, 163, 172, 173	
1 : 25,000 maps:	Ex 155, 156, 167, 168, 179, 191, 206 OL 45	
Waymark:	Cotswold Way/Macmillan Way marks, these sections only	

Publications, badges and certificates:
Booklet: Cross *Cotswold Pathway* (Macmillan Way Association) 1999. ISBN 0952685116. 49pp; A5. £3.50 (incs p&p).

Booklet: *Cotswold Link* (Macmillan Way Association). 12pp; A5. £1.75 (incs p&p).
Leaflet: *Cotswold Accommodation Guide* (Macmillan Way Association). 4pp; A5. £1.25 (incs p&p).

Cotswold Village Trail   115
Glos   *148 km / 92 miles*

A route through the Cotswolds which complements the Cotswold Way National Trail but avoids the market towns and show piece villages associated with that route. There are links with the Heart of England and Warden's and Windrush Ways (Oxfordshire Way).

Start:	Mickleton, Glos	SP162432
Finish:	Westonbirt, Glos	ST858891
Landranger maps:	151, 163, 173	
1 : 25,000 maps:	Ex 156, 168 OL 45	

Publications, badges and certificates:
Softback: *Cotswold Village Trail* by Nigel Bailey (Reardon Publishing) 1998. ISBN 1873877277. 189pp; 150 x 210. £7.95 (+ 75p p&p).

Cotswold Way National Trail   116
Bath NES, Glos, S Glos, Worcs   *163 km / 102 miles*

The route is being upgraded to National Trail status, which includes some improvements to the current line. The Trail meanders along the western edge of the Cotswold Hills, mainly following the top of this limestone escarpment, from where there are extensive views over the Severn Vale to the Malverns and the distant hills of the Mendips and the Welsh border, but descending from time to time to visit attractive villages nestling under the shelter of the edge. It crosses stone-walled farming countryside, passing villages and country houses built from the local limestone, and many sites of archaeological interest. The waymarked Frome Valley Walkway (18 miles and on OS mapping) provides a link from Old Sodbury to Frenchay. The waymarked Jubilee Way (South Gloucestershire) (16 miles and on OS mapping, publication in preparation and details TBA) is another link from Old Sodbury but ending at the Severn Bridge. See Bristol to Lynton Walk, Cotswold Ring, Round and Walk, Kennet and Avon Walk, Limestone Link (Cotswold to Mendips), Oxfordshire Way and Wychavon Way.

Start:	Chipping Campden, Glos	SP152392
Finish:	Bath, Bath NES	ST751647
Landranger maps:	150, 151, 162, 163, 172	✔
1 : 25,000 maps:	Ex 155, 167, 168, 179 OL 45	
Waymark:	White spot, now being replaced with the National Trail Acorn	

Publications, badges and certificates:
Paperback: *The Cotswold Way* by Anthony Burton (Aurum Press) 1995. ISBN 1854103172. 144pp; 210 x 130. £10.99.

Paperback: *The Cotswold Way* by Kev Reynolds (Cicerone Press) 1994. ISBN 1852830498. 168pp; 116 x 176. £7.99.
Paperback: *The Cotswold Way* by Mark Richards (Reardon Publishing) 1995. ISBN 1873877102. 64pp; A5. £3.95 (+ 50p p&p).
Booklet: *Cotswold Way Handbook & Accommodation List* edited by Joy Sagar and Don Stockwell (RA Gloucestershire Area) Annual. ISBN 1901184439. 28pp; 130 x 225. £2.00 (+ 50p p&p).
Stripmap (folded): *Cotswold Way* (Harvey Maps) 2000. ISBN 185137342X. 240 x 115. £8.95 (+ 80p p&p).
Stripmap: *The Cotswold Way* by Roger Noyce (Reardon Publishing). ISBN 1873888250. £3.95 (+ 50p p&p).
Map (folded): *The Cotswold Way Illustrated Map* by Roger Ellis (Reardon Publishing). ISBN 1873877196. A5. £4.95 (+ 50p p&p).
Video (60 minutes): *The Cotswold Way* (Reardon Publishing). ISBN 187387720X. £12.95 (+ £1.50 p&p).
CD ROM: *The Cotswold Way Interactive Guide Book* (Reardon Publishing). ISBN 1873877382. £12.99 (+ £1.00 p&p).
Badge: (RA Gloucestershire Area). £1.30 (+ 40p p&p).
Postcards: Six Scenes. (Reardon Publishing). ISBN 187387734X. £1.99 (+ 50p p&p).
Booklet: *Frome Valley Walkway* (South Gloucestershire Council) 1999. 34pp; A4/3. Free (+ SAE).

Cotswolds Walk 117
Glos, Warks, Worcs 133 km / 83 miles

Linking many of the north Cotswold villages and other places of interest, this walk, beginning at Shakespeare's birthplace, goes south to Mickleton then on to Chipping Campden. The walk continues to Broadway, Stanton, Blockley, Batsford Arboretum, Stow-on-the-Wold, Upper and Lower Slaughter and Bourton-on-the-Water where it turns to Wood Stanway, Sudeley Castle and Winchcombe.

Start:	Stratford-upon-Avon, Warks	SP204549
Finish:	Cheltenham, Glos	SO947222
Landranger maps:	150, 151, 163	
1 : 25,000 maps:	Ex 179, 205 OL 45	

Publications, badges and certificates:
Paperback: *Footpath Touring: Cotswolds* by Ken Ward (Footpath Touring) 1988. ISBN 0711703426. 64pp; 221 x 114. £4.00.

Coventry Canal Walk 118
Staffs, W Midlands, Warks 61 km / 38 miles

A towpath walk linking the Trent and Mersey Canal Walk at Fradley to Coventry. Both publications show information for the Ashby and Birmingham & Fazeley Canals.

Start:	Fradley Junction, Staffs	SK142140
Finish:	Coventry Basin	SP333796
Landranger maps:	128, 139, 140	
1 : 25,000 maps:	Ex 221, 232, 245	

Publications, badges and certificates:
Leaflet: *Exploring the Canals in the West Midlands* (British Waterways – Sawley). A5. Free.
Stripmap (folded): *Coventry & Ashby Canals* (GEOprojects) 1998. ISBN 0863510450. 135 x 213.
£4.75 (+ 50p p&p).

Coventry Way   119

W Midlands, Warks   *64 km / 40 miles*

Never more than five miles or so from the centre of Coventry, the route is partly coincident with the Heart of England and Centenary (Warwickshire) Ways and visits a number of villages and hamlets including Stoneleigh, Bubbenhall, Ryton, Wolston, Bretford, Brinklow, Ansty, Barnacle and Corley Moor.

Start and Finish:	Queens Head, Old Road, Meriden, Warks	SP252820
Landranger maps:	140	✔
1 : 25,000 maps:	Ex 221, 222	
Waymark:	Named disc with three white spires on green background	
User group:	A Coventry Way Association	

Publications, badges and certificates:
Booklet: *A Coventry Way* by Cyril J. Bean (A Coventry Way Association) 2000. ISBN 0952663104. 20pp; A5. £1.00 (+ 50p p&p) – cheques payable to ACWA.
Certificate: (A Coventry Way Association). Free – includes 40 miler club card.

Cown Edge Way   120

Derbys, Gtr Man   *30 km / 19 miles*

This generally U-shaped route on the eastern edge of Greater Manchester rises to Cown Edge Rocks via Strines and Mellor, returning via Charlesworth and Werneth Low. There is a mixture of terrain from urban to moorland.

Start:	Hazel Grove, Gtr Man	SJ927875
Finish:	Gee Cross, Gtr Man	SJ945930
Landranger maps:	109, 110	✔
1 : 25,000 maps:	Ex 277 OL 1	
Waymark:	Named posts and amber discs and arrows	

Publications, badges and certificates:
Booklet: *The Cown Edge Way* (RA Manchester Area) 1985. 29pp; A5. £1.20 (incs p&p).

Crake Valley Round   121

Cumbria   *37 km / 23 miles*

Over three outlying fells including Brockbarrow, the route passes through the villages of Sparkbridge, Broughton Beck and Nibthwaite and takes in small sections of the Cumbria Way and Furness Way with a circuit of Coniston Water included.

Start and Finish:	Kirkby in Furness, Cumbria	SD235822
Landranger maps:	96	
1 : 25,000 maps:	OL 6, 7	

Publications, badges and certificates:
Looseleaf: *The Crake Valley Round* (Brian Richmond). Free (+ 9 x 4 SAE).
Badge and certificate: (Brian Richmond). £1.50 (+ SAE).

Cranborne Chase Path   122

Dorset, Hants, Wilts   *122 km / 76 miles*

A route taking in Salisbury Cathedral and Shaftesbury Abbey. A long stretch of Roman road and an old drove road are included giving fine high-level views whilst passing ancient barrows, manor houses and many small villages.

Start and Finish:	Wimborne Minster, Dorset	SZ009999
Landranger maps:	183, 184, 195	
1 : 25,000 maps:	Ex 118, 130 OL 22	

Publications, badges and certificates:
Paperback: *Cranborne Chase Path* by Edward Griffiths (Green Fields Books) 1995. ISBN 0951937626. 168pp; A5. £4.95 (+ £1.00 p&p).

Crewe and Nantwich Circular Walk   123

Cheshire   *45 km / 28 miles*

A route around Crewe and Nantwich through Weston and Acton which is split into three sections. Old villages, historical buildings and old battle sites are visited in using ancient paths, a canal towpath and field paths. The Pathways are within reach of Crewe and Nantwich.

Start and Finish:	Coppenhall, Cheshire	SJ706582
Landranger maps:	118	✔
1 : 25,000 maps:	Ex 257, 267	
Waymark:	Crossed swords and wheel within a leaf	

Publications, badges and certificates:
Leaflets: *Pathways within reach of Crewe and Nantwich* (Cheshire County Council). 3 leaflets; A3/4. Free (+ 9 x 6 SAE).

Cromer to the M11   124

Cambs, Essex, Norfolk, Suffolk   *265 km / 165 miles*

Using established trails and ancient trackways, this walk follows closely the lines of communication used since prehistoric times to traverse this region of East Anglia. Passing along the Norfolk Heritage Coast, south to Breckland and on into the chalk hills of Cambridgeshire and north Essex, the walk has the M11 motorway as its modern, symbolic end, close to Saffron Walden. In addition to the Peddars Way & Norfolk Coast Path National Trail, links are made with the Nar Valley Way and Icknield Way Path.

Start:	Cromer, Norfolk	TG219425
Finish:	Audley End, Essex	TL509372
Landranger maps:	132, 133, 144, 154, 155	
1 : 25,000 maps:	Ex 195, 210, 226, 229, 236, 250, 251, 252	

Publications, badges and certificates:
Paperback: *Treading Gently from Cromer to the M11 – Cromer to Wells-next-the-Sea* by C. Andrews & D. Dear (Pathway Publishing) 1996. ISBN 0952662817. 32pp; A5. £2.50 (incs p&p).
Paperback: *Treading Gently from Cromer to the M11 – Wells-next-the-Sea to Hunstanton* by C. Andrews & D. Dear (Pathway Publishing) 1996. ISBN 0952662825. 28pp; A5. £2.50 (incs p&p).
Paperback: *Treading Gently from Cromer to the M11 – Hunstanton to Thetford* by C. Andrews & D. Dear (Pathway Publishing) 1996. ISBN 0952662833. 32pp; A5. £2.50 (incs p&p).
Paperback: *Treading Gently from Cromer to the M11 – Thetford to M11* by C. Andrews & D. Dear (Pathway Publishing) 1997. ISBN 0952662841. 28pp; A5. £2.50 (incs p&p).

Crooked Spire Walk 125

Shrops, Worcs 35 km / 22 miles

A route from Wyre Forest passing through Buckridge, Bayton, Cleobury Mortimer (which has the church with the crooked spire) and Shakenhurst.

Start and Finish:	Bewdley, Worcs	SO752740
Landranger maps:	138	
1 : 25,000 maps:	Ex 218	

Publications, badges and certificates:
Looseleaf: *Crooked Spire Walk* (Eric Perks). 4pp; A4. Free (+9 x 6 SAE).
Certificate: (Eric Perks). £1.00 (+ SAE).

Cross Bucks Way 126

Beds, Bucks 38 km / 24 miles

A route mainly through agricultural land linking with the Oxfordshire Way at Stratton Audley, the North Bucks Way at Addington, the Swan's Way at Swanbourne and the Greensand Ridge Walk at Old Linslade. See Oxbridge Walk.

Start:	Stratton Audley, Bucks	SP609260
Finish:	Linslade, Beds	SP912262
Landranger maps:	164, 165	✔
1 : 25,000 maps:	Ex 192	
Waymark:	Named standard waymarks	

Publications, badges and certificates:
Leaflet: *Cross Bucks Way* (Buckinghamshire County Council). A4/3. Free (+ SAE).

Crowthorn Crawl 127

Lancs 43 km / 27 miles

A walk in the West Pennine Moors skirting the reservoir country north of Bolton taking in Darwen Tower, Snig Hole, Irwell Vale and Stubbins Wood. Proceeds from the badge sales are donated to the National Children's Homes Charity.

Start and Finish:	Clough Head Information Centre, Lancs	SD752232
Landranger maps:	103, 109	
1 : 25,000 maps:	Ex 287	

Publications, badges and certificates:
Looseleaf: *Crowthorn Crawl* (Margaret Griffiths). Free (+ 9 x 4 SAE).
Badge: (Margaret Griffiths). £1.50 (+ SAE).

Crowthorn Rose   128

Lancs   *64 km / 40 miles*

Comprising two separate 20 mile long walks, one based on Crowthorn School and
the other on Baxenden Church, the routes take in reservoirs, moorland and
farmland with some hill walking in the vicinity of Accrington, Haslingden and
Ramsbottom. Both walks link in with the Rossendale Way and one additionally with
the Witton Weavers Way. Proceeds from the badge sales are donated to the
National Children's Homes Charity.

Start and Finish:	First stage: Crowthorn School, Lancs;	SD746183
	Second stage: Baxenden Church, Lancs	SD773265
Landranger maps:	103	
1 : 25,000 maps:	Ex 287 OL 21	

Publications, badges and certificates:
Looseleaf: *Crowthorn Rose* (Margaret Griffiths). 2pp; A4. Free (+ 9 x 4 SAE).
Badge: (Margaret Griffiths). £1.50 (+ SAE).

Crowthorn Star   129

Lancs   *63 km / 39 miles*

A series of five walks varying in distance from 6 to 9 miles based on Crowthorn
School. The walks explore the countryside around the school including a walk
along part of the shore of Wayoh Reservoir. Proceeds from badge sales are donated
to National Children's Homes.

Start and Finish:	Crowthorn School, Lancs	SD746183
Landranger maps:	103	
1 : 25,000 maps:	Ex 287	

Publications, badges and certificates:
Looseleaf: *The Crowthorn Star* (Margaret Griffiths). 2pp; A4. Free (+ 9 x 4 SAE).
Badge: (Margaret Griffiths). £1.50 (+ SAE).

Cuckoo Walk   130

Gtr Man, W Yorks   *29 km / 18 miles*

A strenuous and at times boggy upland circuit via Wessenden Reservoir, Black Hill
and White Moss and is partly coincident with the Pennine Way National Trail and
several of the walks in this area.

Start and Finish:	Marsden, W Yorks	SE049116
Landranger maps:	110	
1 : 25,000 maps:	OL 1, 21	

Publications, badges and certificates:
Looseleaf: *The Cuckoo Walk* (D. E. Wilkins). Free (+ 9 x 4 SAE).
Badge and certificate: (D. E. Wilkins). £1.35 (+ SAE) & £0.15 (+ 9 x 4 SAE).

Cuckoo Way   131
Derbys, Notts, S Yorks   *74 km / 46 miles*

A walk along the 220yrs old Chesterfield Canal, known locally as the Cuckoo Dyke. It ceased to be used commercially in the 1950s. Efforts are being made to restore the canal, but in some places the path is overgrown and occasionally difficult to find on the ground. The path passes through, or close to, Staveley, Worksop and Retford.

Start:	Chesterfield, Derbys	SK338717
Finish:	West Stockwith Lock, Notts	SK786946
Landranger maps:	112, 119, 120	✔
1 : 25,000 maps:	Ex 269, 271, 278, 279, 280	
Waymark:	Canal company plaque	

Publications, badges and certificates:
Paperback: *A Walkers' and Boaters' Guide to the Chesterfield Canal and Cuckoo Way* by Christine Richardson and John Lower (Hallamshire Press) 1994. ISBN 1874718253. £5.95.

Cumberland Way   132
Cumbria   *129 km / 80 miles*

The Way takes a meandering route from the Irish Sea across the historic county of Cumberland and the Lake District National Park to reach the former Westmorland boundary and the old market town of Appleby. It avoids the mountain summits and follows old tracks and footpaths, providing a safe route across the open fells, over passes and along lakesides. The Way visits Strands, Wast Water, Black Sail Pass, Buttermere, Keswick, Castlerigg stone circle, Aira Force, Brougham Castle and Cliburn. See Furness Way.

Start:	Ravenglass, Cumbria	SD083963
Finish:	Appleby-in-Westmorland, Cumbria	NY683203
Landranger maps:	89, 90, 91, 96	
1 : 25,000 maps:	OL 4, 5, 6, 19	

Publications, badges and certificates:
Softback: *Cumberland Way* by Paul Hannon (Hillside Publications). ISBN 1870141113. 88pp; 175 x 115. £6.50 (+ 65p p&p).

Cumbria Coastal Way 133

Cumbria, Lancs *267 km / 167 miles*

The route follows the Cumbrian coast linking the Coast to Coast route at St Bees and Hadrian's Wall Path National Trail at Bowness on Solway.

Start:	Milnthorpe, Lancs	SD497813
Finish:	Carlisle, Cumbria	NY403556
Landranger maps:	85, 89, 96, 97	✔
1 : 25,000 maps:	Ex 314, 323 OL 4, 6, 7	
Waymark:	Named posts (Milnthorpe – Carlisle)	

Publications, badges and certificates:

Leaflet: *The Cumbria Coastal Way – Morecambe Bay estuaries – Milnthorpe to Barrow-in-Furness* (South Lakeland District Council). A4/3. Free (+ 9 x 4 SAE).
Leaflet: *Cumbria Coastal Way – Barrow-in-Furness to Carlisle* (Cumbria County Council) 1993. A5. Free.

Cumbria Way 134

Cumbria *112 km / 70 miles*

The Way provides a relatively low-level crossing of the Lake District National Park, following tracks and paths along valleys and over passes in the midst of splendid and varied scenery. It passes Coniston Water, Tarn Hows and Dungeon Ghyll and crosses the Stake Pass to Borrowdale, Derwent Water and Keswick. The Way continues to Caldbeck either via Dash Falls or over High Pike, and then follows the Caldew valley to Carlisle. See Coniston Water Circuit, Crake Valley Round and Furness Way.

Start:	Ulverston, Cumbria	SD284785
Finish:	Carlisle, Cumbria	NY400554
Landranger maps:	85, 89, 90, 96, 97	✔
1 : 25,000 maps:	OL 4, 5, 6, 7	
Waymark:	Named posts	

Publications, badges and certificates:

Paperback: *The Cumbria Way* by Anthony Burton (Aurum Press) 1999. ISBN 1854106155. 144pp; 210 x 130. £12.99.
Paperback: *The Cumbria Way and the Allerdale Ramble* by Jim Watson (Cicerone Press) 1997. ISBN 1852842423. 144pp. £6.99.
Booklet: *Guide to the Cumbria Way* by Philip Dubock (Miway Publishing) 2000. ISBN 0952915030. 72pp; A5. £5.95 (+ 60p p&p).
Booklet: *Cumbria Way Accommodation Guide* by Philip Dubock (Miway Publishing) 2000. ISBN 0952914049. £1.25 (incs p&p).
Booklet: *Booking Bureau – Youth Hostels* (YHA Northern Region) Annual. 20pp; A5. Free.
Stripmap: *Cumbria Way* (Harvey Maps). ISBN 1851373349. £8.95 (+ 80p p&p).

Daffodil Dawdle 135

Cambs, Suffolk *42 km / 26 miles*

A route of grassy tracks, woods and pasture between Newmarket and the River Stour. There is also an option for an 18 mile route. The walk is coincident in part with the Icknield Way Path and the Stour Valley Path (East Anglia).

Start and Finish:	Stetchworth, Cambs	TL642583
Landranger maps:	154	
1 : 25,000 maps:	Ex 210	

Publications, badges and certificates:
Looseleaf: *Daffodil Dawdle* (Bobbie Sauerzapf) 2001. 2pp; A4. Free (+ SAE).
Badge and certificate: (Bobbie Sauerzapf). £1.50 (+ A4 SAE).

Dales Traverse 136

N Yorks   *40 km / 25 miles*

Based in Upper Wharfedale, the route takes in Kettlewell, Cam Head, Buckden Pike, Litton and Mastiles Lane. Proceeds from sales of badges are donated to a local hospice.

Start and Finish:	Kilnsey, N Yorks	SD974679
Landranger maps:	98	
1 : 25,000 maps:	OL 2, 30	

Publications, badges and certificates:
Looseleaf: *Dales Traverse* (Simon Townson). Free (+ 9 x 4 SAE).
Badge and certificate: (Simon Townson). £2.00 (+ 10 x 7 SAE).

Dales Way 137

Cumbria, N Yorks, W Yorks   *130 km / 81 miles*

The Way mainly follows attractive dales through the Yorkshire and Howgill Fells and the south-eastern part of the Lake District. From Ilkley it heads along Wharfedale passing Bolton Abbey, the Strid, Grassington and Buckden before crossing Cam Fell and the Pennine Way National Trail to descend to Dentdale. From here, the River Dee is followed to Sedbergh, then the Lune to the Crook of Lune. The Way crosses farmland to reach Burneside and the River Kent, which is traced for several miles before the path branches off to the finish. There are three link routes to the Way: from Leeds (Leeds – Dales Way, 19 miles) and Shipley/Bradford (Shipley – Dales Way, 8 miles) each described in the Stile publication, and from Harrogate (Harrogate – Dales Way, 20 miles) for which a publication is listed. All links are included on OS mapping.

Start:	Ilkley, W Yorks	SE117476
Finish:	Bowness-on-Windermere, Cumbria	SD402968
Landranger maps:	96, 97, 98, 104	✔
1 : 25,000 maps:	Ex 288, 297, 298 OL 2, 7, 19, 30	
Waymark:	Named signposts	
User group:	Dales Way Association	

Publications, badges and certificates:
Paperback: *The Dales Way* by Anthony Burton (Aurum Press) 1995. ISBN 1854103148. £12.99.
Paperback: *Dales Way Companion* by Paul Hannon (Hillside Publications) 1997. ISBN 1870141539. 88pp; 175 x 115. £5.99 (+ 60p p&p) – includes details of link routes.
Paperback: *The Dales Way* by Terry Marsh (Cicerone Press) 1992. ISBN 1852841028. 136pp; 116 x176. £6.99.

Paperback: *The Dales Way Walk – Seven Glorious Days* by Alistair Wallace (Jema Publications) 1997. ISBN 1871468531. 96pp; A5. £5.99.
Booklet: *Dales Way Route Guide* by Arthur Gemmell and Colin Speakman (Stile Publications) 1996. ISBN 0906886724. 44pp; 197 x 120. £4.00 (+ 9 x 6 44p SAE).
Booklet: *Dales Way Handbook* – (includes accommodation details) (Dales Way Association) Annual. A5. £1.50 (incs p&p).
Booklet: *Booking Bureau – Youth Hostels* (YHA Northern Region) Annual. 20pp; A5. Free.
Badge and certificate: for Dales Way (Dales Way Association). £1.50 & £1.50 (incs p&p).
Looseleaf: *Harrogate – Dales Way* (RA Harrogate Group) A5. 6pp. £0.30 (+ A5 SAE).
Badge: for Harrogate – Dales Way Section (Joan Clack). £1.50 (+ SAE).

Dam Long Walk · 138

Derbys — *61 km / 38 miles*

A demanding walk around 32 dams/reservoirs in the Black Hill area of the Dark Peak, achieved by combining short sections of the Pennine Way National Trail with lesser-known tracks. A shorter variation of the route is possible by using sections of roads.

Start and Finish:	Crowden Youth Hostel, Derbys	SK073994
Landranger maps:	110	
1 : 25,000 maps:	OL 1	

Publications, badges and certificates:
Booklet: *Dam Long Walk* (Ken Jones). A5. Free (+ 9 x 6 SAE).
Certificate: (Ken Jones). Free (+ strengthened 9 x 6 SAE).

Dane Valley Way · 139

Cheshire, Derby, Staffs — *64 km / 40 miles*

A route which follows, where possible, the course of the River Dane, passing Shires Head, Danebridge, Eaton, Congleton and Holmes Chapel. There are links with the Staffordshire Way, the Gritstone Trail, the South Cheshire Way and the Cheshire Ring Canal Walk.

Start:	Buxton, Derbys	SK056734
Finish:	Middlewich, Cheshire	SJ694670
Landranger maps:	118, 119	✔
1 : 25,000 maps:	Ex 267, 268 OL 24	
Waymark:	Yellow disc with black letters DVW superimposed	

Publications, badges and certificates:
Leaflet: *The Dane Valley Way* by Raymond M. Lloyd (Congleton Tourist Information Centre). Extended A3/5. £1.00 (+ 9 x 4 SAE).

Danum Trail · 140

S Yorks — *113 km / 70 miles*

Devised to celebrate the RA Diamond Jubilee, this walk explores the open countryside in the outer reaches of Doncaster Metropolitan Borough. A combination of woodlands, nature reserves, country parks, farmland and limestone escarpments with views of the North York Moors and Wolds, there is much of historical interest, Saxon, Roman – even prehistoric.

Start and Finish:	Dome Leisure Park, Doncaster, S Yorks	SE598017
Landranger maps:	111	
1 : 25,000 maps:	Ex 278, 279	
Waymark:	Roman centurion	

Publications, badges and certificates:
Paperback: *The Danum Trail* by David C. Ward (RA Doncaster) 1995. ISBN 0900613920. 80pp; 210 x 145. £2.95 (incs p&p).
Badge: (RA Doncaster). £1.50 (incs p&p).

d'Arcy Dalton Way 141

Glos, Oxon, Warks *107 km / 67 miles*

The Way, devised to mark the RA Golden Jubilee, is named after the late Col. W. P. d'Arcy Dalton who worked for over half a century to preserve rights of way in Oxfordshire. The Way takes a meandering route, first crossing ironstone hills to Epwell and Hook Norton, and then following footpaths and tracks across the limestone uplands of the eastern Cotswolds via Great and Little Rollright, Churchill, Fifield, Great Barrington and Holwell. The River Thames is crossed at Radcot Bridge and the Way continues across the flatter farmland of the vale of the White Horse, finally climbing to the crest of the chalk ridge of the Oxfordshire Downs, along which the Ridgeway runs. The guide includes eight circular walks.

Start:	Wormleighton, Warks	SP448518
Finish:	Wayland's Smithy, Oxon	SU281853
Landranger maps:	151, 163, 164, 174	
1 : 25,000 maps:	Ex 170, 191, 206 OL 45	
Waymark:	Named signs	

Publications, badges and certificates:
Softback: *The d'Arcy Dalton Way across the Oxfordshire Cotswolds and Thames Valley* by Nick Moon (Book Castle & Chiltern Society Mail Order Bookshop) 1999. ISBN 1871199344. 128pp; A5. £6.99 (p&p £1.40 Book Castle; 85p Chiltern Society Mail Order Bookshop).

Darent Valley Path 142

Kent *31 km / 19 miles*

The River Darent flows from its source in the Greensand hills, south of Westerham, to join the Thames, north of Dartford. The walk is through a varied landscape of riverside fringed with ancient willows, hop gardens and cornfields, secretive woodlands, downland carpeted with wild flowers and expanses of marshland and has the added attractions of Roman remains, majestic viaducts, historic houses, old mills and picturesque villages with beautiful churches. There is an alternative start point at Chipstead (TQ500561). See also North Downs Way National Trail.

Start:	Sevenoaks, Kent	TQ522554
Finish:	Confluence of Rivers Darent and	
	Thames, Kent	TQ542779

Landranger maps:	177, 188	✔
1 : 25,000 maps:	Ex 147, 162	
Waymark:	Stylised tree and river	

Publications, badges and certificates:
Booklet: *Darent Valley Path* by Lorna Jenner and Elia Lawton (Kent County Council) 1997. ISBN 1873010532. 93pp; 210 x 213. £5.00 post free.

Dark Peak Boundary Walk   143

Derbys, S Yorks, W Yorks   *131 km / 81 miles*

A mainly high-level circuit of the three great moorland masses of Kinder Scout, Bleaklow and Black Hill, the Walk passes Glossop, Marsden, Hathersage and Bradwell, and traverses gritstone edges, moorland, wooded cloughs and stone villages passing numerous reservoirs.

Start and Finish:	Hayfield, Derbys	SK037869
Landranger maps:	110	
1 : 25,000 maps:	OL 1, 21	

Publications, badges and certificates:
Looseleaf: *Dark Peak Boundary Walk* (Dave Irons). 14pp; A4. £2.00 (incs p&p).

Dark Peak Challenge Walk   144

Derbys   *38 km / 24 miles*

This is a demanding high-level walk taking in Stanage Edge, Derwent Edge, Back Tor, Derwent Reservoir, Win Hill and Bamford. There is 3,300ft of ascent.

Start and Finish:	Hathersage, Derbys	SK232815
Landranger maps:	119	
1 : 25,000 maps:	OL 1	

Publications, badges and certificates:
Booklet: *Dark Peak Challenge Walk* by John Merrill (Walk & Write Ltd). ISBN 0907496660. 32pp; A5. £3.95 (+ 75p p&p).
Badge and certificate: (Walk & Write Ltd). £3.50 (incs p&p).

Dark Peak Snake   145

Derbyshire   *28 km / 17 miles*

Following the ridges and high ground encircling the Snake Road, the route includes a variety of terrain and situations. Initially following Blackden Brook, a line is taken to Kinder Edges over Blackden Moor and ends down the wooded Alport valley. Navigational skills are appropriate over Bleaklow.

Start and Finish:	Snake Road, Derbyshire	SK131895
Landranger maps:	110	
1 : 25,000 maps:	OL 1	

Publications, badges and certificates:
Booklet: *Dark Peak Snake* (Ken Jones). A5. Free (+ 9 x 6 SAE).
Certificate: (Ken Jones). Free (+ 9 x 6 strengthened SAE).

Dark Peak Stones   146

Derbys   *32 km / 20 miles*

This high level route across undulating terrain visits 20 of the uniquely eroded stone features of the Dark Peak including Higher Shelf, Bleaklow, Margery and Dove. The route provides an excellent insight into the rugged nature of the area. The route can be extended by another 12 miles to pass other weathered stone features.

Start:	Snake Road Summit, Derbys	SK088929
Finish:	Ladybower Inn, Derbys	SK205865
Landranger maps:	110	
1 : 25,000 maps:	Ex 1	

Publications, badges and certificates:
Booklet: *Dark Peak Stones* (Ken Jones). 12pp; A5. Free (+ 9 x 6 SAE).
Certificate: (Ken Jones). Free (+ 9 x 6 strengthened SAE).

Dartmoor Ramble   147

Devon   *79 km / 49 miles*

This route was devised to take advantage of the youth hostels at Bellever, Okehampton and Steps Bridge and takes in some of the wildest parts of Dartmoor. The walk visits Belstone, Chagford, North Bovey and Post Bridge.

Start and Finish:	Bellever Youth Hostel, Devon	SX651774
Landranger maps:	191	
1 : 25,000 maps:	OL 28	

Publications, badges and certificates:
Booklet: *Dartmoor Ramble* by Martyn Hanks (YHA Northern Region). 16pp; A5. £1.95 (incs p&p).
Booklet: *Booking Bureau – Youth Hostels* (YHA Northern Region) Annual. 20pp; A5. Free.

Dartmoor Way   148

Devon   *138 km / 86 miles*

A route around Dartmoor linking hamlets, villages and towns with a variety of scenery including wild upland, sheltered valleys and quiet lanes. Two routes exist, one for walkers and the other for cyclists. The walkers' route is coincident with the Tarka Trail between Sticklepath and Okehampton and with the West Devon Way between Okehampton and Tavistock and is not shown separately in the Map Section.

Start and Finish:	Buckfastleigh, Devon	SX736661
Landranger maps:	191, 202	
1 : 25,000 maps:	OL 20, 28	
Waymark:	Named signs in some parts. No waymarks on open moorland or where coincident with other routes.	

Publications, badges and certificates:
Folder with booklet, map: *The Dartmoor Way* published by Dartmoor Towns Ltd (Devon County Council) 1999. ISBN 0953587207. 56pp; 132 x 210. £7.95 (incs p&p) – quote ref. DP71; accommodation list included.
Leaflet: *The Dartmoor Way, Escapes on foot* (Ashburton Tourist Information Centre). A4. Free (+ A4 SAE).

Dartmoor's Ancient Boundary Perambulation 149

Devon   *80 km / 50 miles*

The Perambulation marks the boundary of the ancient forest of the moor and is one of the oldest walks on Dartmoor. From Rundlestone, the route heads through Great Mis Tor and Yes Tor, King's Oven, Dartmeet and Ryder's Hill. At Eastern White Barrow the Perambulation reaches its most southerly point and returns to Rundlestone via Siward's Cross.

Start and Finish:	Rundlestone, Devon	SX574750
Landranger maps:	191, 202	
1 : 25,000 maps:	OL 20, 28	

Publications, badges and certificates:
Looseleaf: *Dartmoor's Ancient Boundary Walk* (Ian & Caroline Kirkpatrick). 1pp; A4. Free (+ SAE).
Badge and certificate: (Ian & Caroline Kirkpatrick). £2.00 (+ SAE) & £0.30 (+ A4 SAE).

Dearne Way 150

S Yorks, W Yorks   *48 km / 30 miles*

A route following the River Dearne from the source to the confluence with the River Don passing through and near to a contrasting countryside including Bretton Country Park, Barnsley, canals and riverside.

Start:	Birds Edge, W Yorks	SE202079
Finish:	Mexborough, S Yorks	SE490002
Landranger maps:	110, 111	✔
1 : 25,000 maps:	Ex 278, 288	
Waymark:	Named discs with miners lamp logo	

Publications, badges and certificates:
No publications: on OS mapping.

Denby Way 151

S Yorks, W Yorks   *80 km / 50 miles*

The Way is situated in the area to the west of the M1, bounded by the River Calder to the north and the River Don to the south. The Way takes in Denby Dale, famous for the giant pie, Penistone, Silkstone, Bretton Park and Emley Moor.

Start and Finish:	Denby Dale, W Yorks	SE228084
Landranger maps:	110	
1 : 25,000 maps:	Ex 278	

Publications, badges and certificates:
Folder: *Walking in Pie Country* (Yorkshire Footpath Trust) 1995. ISBN 1898978026. 26pp; 210 x 147. £3.45 (incs p&p).
Certificate: (Yorkshire Footpath Trust). Free (+ 9 x 6 SAE).

Derby Canal Ring   152
Derbys, Notts   *45 km / 28 miles*
A walk taking in the Derby, Erewash and Trent & Mersey canals.

Start and Finish:	Railway Station, Derby	SK362356
Landranger maps:	128	
1 : 25,000 maps:	Ex 245, 259, 260	

Publications, badges and certificates:
Booklet: *Walking the Derby Canal Ring* by John Merrill (Walk & Write Ltd). ISBN 1874754284. A5. £3.50 (+ 75p p&p).
Badge and certificate: (Walk & Write Ltd). £3.50 (incs p&p).

Derbyshire Top Ten   153
Derbyshire   *47 km / 29 miles*
A route visiting the ten highest peaks/moorland fells of Derbyshire, including Crowden Head, Edale Head (the highest at 2087ft), Bleaklow Head and Hartshorn (the lowest at 1982ft).

Start and Finish:	Edale car park, Derbyshire	SK125853
Landranger maps:	110	
1 : 25,000 maps:	OL 1	

Publications, badges and certificates:
Booklet: *The Derbyshire Top Ten* by Brian Smailes (Challenge Publications) 2001. ISBN 190356803X. 40pp; 125 x 185. £3.95 (incs p&p).

Derwent Valley Skyline   154
Derbyshire   *42 km / 26 miles*
From Ladybower Dam, the route intitially follows the Derwent Edges and then takes to the desolate Howden Edge to Bleaklow Stones and the Alport Ridge. The terrain can be difficult and it should not be taken lightly, particularly in winter. Navigational skills are appropriate on some sections.

Start and Finish:	Ladybower Reservoir	SK197864
Landranger maps:	110	
1 : 25,000 maps:	OL 1	

Publications, badges and certificates:
Booklet: *Derwent Valley Skyline* (Ken Jones). A5. Free (+ 9 x 6 SAE).
Certificate: (Ken Jones). Free (+ strengthened 9 x 6 SAE).

Doncastrian Way · 155

S Yorks   *53 km / 33 miles*

A walk around the old County Borough of Doncaster following a route from the urban fringes to open fields, river banks and green lanes towards the settlements of Barnby Dun and Dunsville returning through Sprotbrough and along the River Don.

Start and Finish:	Doncaster, S Yorks	SE566041
Landranger maps:	111	✓
1 : 25,000 maps:	Ex 279	
Waymark:	Named signposts	

Publications, badges and certificates:
Leaflet: *Doncastrian Way* (LDWA Vermuyden Group). A5. Free (+ SAE).
Badge and certificate: (LDWA Vermuyden Group). £1.25 (+ A5 SAE).

Donnington Way · 156

Glos   *99 km / 61 miles*

Based on the Cotswold brewery of Donnington in Stow-on-the-Wold, the Way's theme is the brewery and its 15 pubs. It visits Bourton-on-the-Water, Naunton, Guiting Power, Broadway, Chipping Campden and Moreton-in-Marsh.

Start and Finish:	Stow-on-the-Wold, Glos	SP192258
Landranger maps:	163	
1 : 25,000 maps:	OL 45	
Waymark:	Beer Mug	

Publications, badges and certificates:
Paperback: *The Donnington Way* by Colin Handy (Reardon Publishing) 1991. ISBN 1874192006. 44pp; A5. £3.95 (+ 50p p&p).

Dorset Jubilee Trail · 157

Dorset   *145 km / 90 miles*

A trail created to celebrate the RA Diamond Jubilee crossing Dorset, through quiet villages, passing old churches, historic sites and stately homes, offering extensive views of the rolling downs and secret valleys. Links are made with the South West Coast Path National Trail and Wessex Ridgeway, Monarch's Way, Macmillan Way and Hardy Way.

Start:	Forde Abbey, Dorset	ST362052
Finish:	Bokerley Dyke, Dorset	SU050187
Landranger maps:	183, 184, 193, 194, 195	✓
1 : 25,000 maps:	Ex 116, 117, 118 OL 15	
Waymark:	Combined tree, arrow and name on green background	

Publications, badges and certificates:
Paperback: *Dorset Jubilee Trail* (RA Dorset). ISBN 1901184048. 54pp; A5. £4.50 (+ 50p p&p).
Leaflet: *Dorset Jubilee Trail* (Dorset County Council) 1995. A4/3. Free (+ SAE).
Badge: (RA Dorset). £2.50 (+ SAE).

Downs Link 158

Surrey, W Sussex   *59 km / 37 miles*

A bridleway link between the two Downs National Trails. From St Martha's Hill on the North Downs Way the Link is over wooded heath and farmland to meet and follow the trackbed of the former Horsham and Guildford direct railway through Cranleigh and the former Shoreham to Itchingfield Junction line through Partridge Green and Bramber, crossing farmland to meet the South Downs Way, and then on to Shoreham-by-Sea. See Sussex Diamond Way.

Start:	St Martha's Hill, Surrey	TQ032484
Finish:	Shoreham-by-Sea, W Sussex	TQ208060
Landranger maps:	186, 187, 198	✔
1 : 25,000 maps:	Ex 122, 134, 145	
Waymark:	Green/white disc with bridge	

Publications, badges and certificates:
Folder: *Downs Link* (West Sussex County Council) 1996. 12pp; 210 x 147. £2.00 (+ SAE).

Dronfield 2000 Rotary Walk 159

Derbyshire   *24 km / 15 miles*

Created as a Millennium project, the route is through woodland and farmland visiting Apperknowle and Holmesfield. There are links with the Sheffield Way.

Start and Finish:	Coal Aston, Derby	SK797365
Landranger maps:	110, 119	
1 : 25,000 maps:	Ex 269, 278 OL 24	
Waymark:	Named finger posts/metal signs	

Publications, badges and certificates:
Leaflet: *Dronfield 2000 Rotary Walk* (Dronfield 2000 Rotary Walk). A2/3. £1.50 (+ 50p p&p).

Duddon Horseshoe 160

Cumbria   *32 km / 20 miles*

A hard mountain walk for experienced walkers which follows an undulating route around the Duddon Valley to cross both Hardknott Pass and Wrynose Pass, two of the highest road passes in the Lakeland area.

Start and Finish:	Seathwaite, Cumbria	NY227950
Landranger maps:	96	
1 : 25,000 maps:	OL 6	

Publications, badges and certificates:
Looseleaf: *Duddon Horseshoe* (Brian Richmond). Free (+ 9 x 4 SAE).
Badge and certificate: (Brian Richmond). £1.00 (+ SAE).

Duddon Triangle Walk 161

Cumbria *32 km / 20 miles*

A tough mountain walk encircling Duddon Valley and taking in Whitfell and Harter Fell.

Start and Finish:	Ulpha Bridge, Cumbria	NY196930
Landranger maps:	96	
1 : 25,000 maps:	OL 6	

Publications, badges and certificates:
Looseleaf: *Duddon Triangle Walk* (Brian Richmond). Free (+ 9 x 4 SAE).
Badge and certificate: (Brian Richmond). £1.00 (+ SAE).

Dunford Round 162

S Yorks *37 km / 23 miles*

One of a series of walks, this route crosses Thurlstone Moors and visits Dunford Bridge.

Start and Finish:	Flouch Inn, S Yorks	SE197016
Landranger maps:	110	
1 : 25,000 maps:	OL 1	

Publications, badges and certificates:
Booklet: *Dunford Parish Footpaths* (Allen Pestell) 1997. £1.00 (+ 9 x 6 SAE).

Dunnerdale Horseshoe and Burney Challenge 163

Cumbria *32 km / 20 miles*

Three connecting loops with just a minimum of duplication of path walking through Grizebeck, Broughton Mills, The Knott, Stickle Pike and Thronthwaite, taking in the Dunnerdale Fells.

Start and Finish:	Beckside, Cumbria	SD235822
Landranger maps:	96	
1 : 25,000 maps:	OL 6	

Publications, badges and certificates:
Looseleaf: *Dunnerdale Horseshoe and Burney Challenge* (Brian Richmond). Free (+ 9 x 4 SAE).
Badge and certificate: (Brian Richmond). £1.50 (+ SAE).

Durham Coastal Footpath 164

Durham *18 km / 11 miles*

This stretch of the Durham coastline has seen many changes. The cliff-top land had been subjected to intense farming or used for the tipping of colliery waste whilst the beach itself was also damaged by tipping. However, on the closure of the pits in the early 1990s, a reclamation project and the natural effects of the sea have brought about improvements, with several Sites of Special Scientific Interest. The route passes through or close to Seaham Harbour, Dawdon, Easington, Danemouth and Blackhall.

Start:	Seaham Hall Beach, Durham	NZ422511
Finish:	Crimdon Park, Durham	NZ476384
Landranger maps:	88, 93	✔
1 : 25,000 maps:	Ex 306, 308	
Waymark:	Large circular sculptures (approx 2ft diameter/6ft high) annotated with two sets of hoops	

Publications, badges and certificates:
Booklet: *The Durham Coastal Footpath* (Turning The Tide). 20pp; A5. Free (+ 9 x 6 SAE).

Durham Railway Paths 165
Durham   *92 km / 57 miles*

A network of former railway lines which have been reclaimed for use by walkers, horseriders and cyclists. The network comprises the Derwent Valley Walk (11 miles), Lanchester Valley (12 miles), Waskerley Way (7 miles), Deerness Valley (8 miles), Brandon-Bishop Auckland (9 miles), Tees Rail Way (6 miles) and Auckland Way (4 miles). With the exception of the latter two, they are included on OS mapping and can be linked to provide extended linear walks.

Start and Finish:	Various	Various
Landranger maps:	87, 88, 92, 93	✔ 5 of 7
1 : 25,000 maps:	Ex 308, 316	

Publications, badges and certificates:
Folder: *Railway Paths in County Durham* (Durham County Council) 1997. 16pp; A5. £2.25 (+ 50p p&p).

Durham Round 166
Durham   *250 km / 155 miles*

A route which basically follows the boundary of County Durham and takes in such as the City of Durham, Beamish, Cow Green Reservoir, the River Tees and the coastline.

Start and Finish:	Durham	NZ270426
Landranger maps:	87, 88, 92, 93	
1 : 25,000 maps:	Ex 304, 305, 306, 307, 308 OL 31	

Publications, badges and certificates:
Paperback: *The Durham Round* by Jill Delaney (Printability Publishing Ltd) 1997. ISBN 187223917X. 78pp; A5. £5.95 (+ £1.00 p&p).

Dyfi Valley Way 167
Ceredigion, Gwynedd, Powys   *174 km / 108 miles*

The Dyfi (English Dovey) valley is one of the most beautiful valleys in Wales. This route follows the north side of the Dyfi through Pennal and the centre for Alternative Technology at Llwyngwern Quarry. Across the site of King Arthur's last battle at Camlan, the Way takes in the strenuous climb up to the summit of Aran Fawddwy, which at 2,971ft is the highest peak south of Snowdon. At Llanuwchllyn the route retraces its steps south of the Dyfi through Llanymawddwy and Machynlleth. The walk links with the Meirionnydd Coast Walk at Aberdyfi.

Start:	Aberdyfi, Gwynedd	SN614959
Finish:	Borth, Ceredigion	SN609901
Landranger maps:	124, 125, 135, 136	
1 : 25,000 maps:	Ex 215 OL 18, 23	
Waymark:	Letters DVW in shape of salmon	

Publications, badges and certificates:
Paperback: *A Guide to the Dyfi Valley Way* by Laurence Main (Laurence Main) 1996. ISBN 1900477009. 82pp; 130 x 210. £3.95 (+ £1.00 p&p).

East Devon Way 168
Devon *64 km / 40 miles*

A route that follows the estuary of the River Exe to Lympstone and then turns east over the commons and rolling hills of the East Devon AONB via Harpford, Sidbury, Farway and Colyton. It can be combined with part of the South West Coast Path National Trail to form a circular walk.

Start:	Exmouth, Devon	SX999814
Finish:	Uplyme, Devon	SY333933
Landranger maps:	192, 193	✔
1 : 25,000 maps:	Ex 110, 115, 116	
Waymark:	Foxglove (logo of AONB)	

Publications, badges and certificates:
Booklet: *The East Devon Way* by Norman Barns (Devon County Council) 1993. 60pp. £5.65 (incs p&p) – quote ref. DP17.

East Riding Heritage Way 169
E Yorks, N Yorks *136 km / 84 miles*

This is the overall name given to four linked walks devised by Glen Hood, and now under the auspices of the East Yorkshire Group, LDWA. The walks are: Beverley Twenty – 20 miles from the Humber Bridge car park to the Beverley Minster and shown on OS mapping (see Humber Bridge Link Walk). Initially along the Humber Estuary and then following a meandering north-easterly course (with variations available), on field paths and tracks across flat to gently undulating farmland. Links also with Wolds Way National Trail and Trans-Pennine Trail. Hutton Hike – 23 miles from Beverley Minster to Driffield, along farmland and riverside paths, dykes, and a Yorkshire Water nature reserve, passing through Arram, Cranswick and Hutton to Driffield. Rudston Roam – 21 miles from Driffield to Bridlington following river, beckside and field paths over level to gently undulating farmland, visiting a number of villages with historical interest, including Nafferton, Burton Agnes and the Rudston monolith. Headland Walk – 20 miles from Bridlington to Filey along the chalk cliffs of the Heritage coast to Flamborough Head and the RSPB reserve at Bempton giving spectacular views, before the final promenade along the sea shore at Filey, with an alternative finish at the Brigg where it connects with the Cleveland and Wolds Way National Trails.

Start:	Hessle (Point), E Yorks	TA026253
Finish:	Filey Brigg, N Yorks	TA126817
Landranger maps:	101, 106, 107	✔ Beverley 20
1 : 25,000 maps:	Ex 293, 295, 301	
Waymark:	B. 20 stickers for Beverley 20 only	

Publications, badges and certificates:
Looseleaf: *East Riding Heritage Way* by Glen Hood (Glen Hood) 1993. 9pp; A4. Free (+ SAE).
Badge and certificate: for East Riding Heritage Way (Glen Hood). £1.15 (+ SAE) & £0.15 (+ 9 x 6 SAE).
Individual route badges: (Glen Hood). £0.75 each (+ SAE).

East Thriding Treble Ten 170

E Yorks   *48 km / 30 miles*

A figure-of-eight route over the southern chalk wolds of East Yorkshire, it crosses farmland and mixed woodland, going through attractive dales and visiting Brantingham, South Cave and North Cave.

Start and Finish:	Welton, E Yorks	SE959272
Landranger maps:	106	
1 : 25,000 maps:	Ex 293	

Publications, badges and certificates:
Looseleaf: *East Thriding Treble Ten* (Kim Peacock). Free (+ 9 x 4 SAE).
Badge: (Kim Peacock). £1.00 (+ 9 x 6 SAE).

Ebor Way 171

N Yorks, W Yorks   *112 km / 70 miles*

A relatively gentle walk, taking its name from Eboracum, Roman York. From Helmsley it heads southwards to Hovingham and crosses undulating farmland to Strensall, from where the River Foss is followed to York. The city is crossed on the path along its medieval walls and is left along the banks of the River Ouse. At Tadcaster the route turns west and continues along the Wharfe valley and the Ainsty bounds to Wetherby and Harewood. Here the Way climbs to the gritstone outcrops of the Chevin and Cow and Calf Rocks on the edge of Ilkley Moor before descending to Ilkley in Wharfedale. See Hovingham Hobble.

Start:	Helmsley, N Yorks	SE611839
Finish:	Ilkley, W Yorks	SE117476
Landranger maps:	100, 104, 105	✔
1 : 25,000 maps:	Ex 289, 290, 297, 300 OL 26	
Waymark:	Ebor Way signposts	

Publications, badges and certificates:
Folder: *The Ebor Way* by J. K. E. Piggin (Yorkshire Footpath Trust) 2000. ISBN 1872881009. 22pp; 204 x 117. £4.00 (incs p&p).
Certificate: (Yorkshire Footpath Trust). Free (+ 9 x 6 SAE).

Eden Way   172

Cumbria   *126 km / 78 miles*

The route follows the River Eden from the Solway Firth through quiet countryside to the source on Mallerstang Edge, south of Kirkby Stephen.

Start:	Rockcliffe Marsh, Cumbria	NY333619
Finish:	Black Fell Moss, Cumbria	SD807998
Landranger maps:	85, 86, 90, 91, 98	
1 : 25,000 maps:	Ex 315 OL 5, 19	

Publications, badges and certificates:
Paperback: *Eden Way* by Charlie Emett (Cicerone Press) 1990. ISBN 1852840404. 192pp; 176 x 116. £6.99.

Edinburgh to Glasgow Canals Walk   173

E Dunbarton, Edinburgh, Falkirk, Glasgow,
N Lanark, W Dunbarton, W Lothian   *108 km / 67 miles*

A route following wherever possible the towpaths of the Union and Forth & Clyde Canals through Ratho, Broxburn, Linlithgow, Falkirk and Bonnybridge. In Glasgow the route links in to the city's numerous pathways and cycleways providing access to the start of the West Highland Way at Milngavie and also the Clyde Walkway.

Start:	Haymarket Station, Edinburgh	NT237730
Finish:	Old Kilpatrick, W Dunbarton	NS448736
Landranger maps:	64, 65, 66	
1 : 25,000 maps:	Ex 342, 347, 348, 349, 350	

Publications, badges and certificates:
Paperback: *Exploring the Edinburgh to Glasgow Canals* by Hamish Brown (Mercat Press) 1997. ISBN 0114957355. 120pp; 135 x 220. £8.99.
Leaflet: *Fit for Life – Glasgow Walkways* (Glasgow City Council) 2000. A1 folded to A4. Free.
Stripmap (folded): *Forth & Clyde and Union Canals with the Crinan Canal* (GEOprojects) 2001. ISBN 0863511392. 135 x 213. £4.75.

Elan Valley Way   174

Herefs, Powys, Shrops, Worcs   *206 km / 128 miles*

The Way is loosely based on the Elan Valley aqueduct which, since 1904, has carried the water supply for Birmingham from the Elan Valley. The route keeps within 3 miles of the aqueduct as it passes through Cookley, Bewdley, Ludlow, Knighton and Rhayader.

Start:	Frankley, Worcs	SO999804
Finish:	Elan Valley Visitor Centre, Powys	SN935645
Landranger maps:	138, 139, 147, 148	
1 : 25,000 maps:	Ex 200, 201, 203, 218, 219	

Publications, badges and certificates:
Softback: *The Elan Valley Way* by David Milton (Meridian Books). ISBN 1869922395. 160pp; 232 x 150. £7.95 (+ £1.00 p&p).

Elham Valley Way 175
Kent *37 km / 23 miles*

The Way explores the variety of countryside along and around the unspoilt Elham Valley in East Kent. It is mainly a valley walk through the Kent Downs occasionally affording striking panoramic views from the chalk hills. See Skylark Walk.

Start:	Hythe, Kent	TR165349
Finish:	Canterbury, Kent	TR150578
Landranger maps:	179, 189	✔
1 : 25,000 maps:	Ex 138, 150	
Waymark:	Stylised valley & church spire	

Publications, badges and certificates:
Booklet: *Along and Around the Elham Valley Way* (Kent County Council) 1997. ISBN 1873010958. 108pp; 210 x 210. £5.00 (post free).

Esk Valley Walk 176
N Yorks *56 km / 35 miles*

This route through the North York Moors National Park starts with a circular walk over Danby and Westerdale moors from Castleton to the source of the river at Esklets, and then follows the river valley through Glaisdale and Grosmont to the sea. There is a variety of countryside from open moorland to riverside pastures.

Start:	Castleton Railway Station, N Yorks	NZ683085
Finish:	Whitby, N Yorks	NZ900117
Landranger maps:	94, 100	
1 : 25,000 maps:	OL 27	
Waymark:	Leaping salmon emblem	

Publications, badges and certificates:
Booklet: *Esk Valley Walk* (North York Moors National Park) 1992. ISBN 090748039X. 32pp; 120 x 170. £2.95 (+ 55p p&p).
Booklet: *Moors Visitor Guide including Accommodation Listing* (North York Moors National Park) Annual. £0.50 (+ 55p p&p).
Badge: (North York Moors National Park). £0.99 (+ SAE).

Eskdale Way 177
Cleveland, N Yorks *134 km / 83 miles*

A varied circuit of the fields, woodlands, moors and country lanes of Eskdale, from the fishing port of Whitby along the northern side of the valley via Glaisdale and Commondale and looping over the Guisborough Moors before returning to the valley at Kildale. The return route meanders along or near the south side of the dale, looping south to visit Wheeldale and Goathland before returning to Whitby.

Start and Finish:	Whitby, N Yorks	NZ900117
Landranger maps:	94	
1 : 25,000 maps:	OL 26, 27	

Publications, badges and certificates:
Folder: *Eskdale Way* (Yorkshire Footpath Trust) 1998. ISBN 1898978034. 13 cards; 210 x 147. £3.45 (incs p&p).
Certificate: (Yorkshire Footpath Trust). Free (+ 9 x 6 SAE).

Essex Country to the Coast 178

Essex *45 km / 28 miles*

A walk across the breadth of Essex, taking in many different aspects of the Essex countryside, including farmland, riverside paths, ancient woodlands and a river valley. Attractive buildings along the walk are plentiful. See Three Footpaths Walk.

Start:	Bures, Essex	TL906340
Finish:	West Mersea, Essex	TM001128
Landranger maps:	168	
1 : 25,000 maps:	Ex 184, 196	

Publications, badges and certificates:
Booklet: *The Essex Country to the Coast Walk* by John Edwards (John Edwards Footpath Guides) 2001. 24pp; A5. £2.49 (incs p&p).
Certificate: (John Edwards Footpath Guides). Free (+ SAE).

Essex Way 179

Essex *130 km / 81 miles*

The Way heads across gently undulating agricultural land, passing through or near many attractive old villages including Willingdale, Pleshey, Coggeshall, Dedham, which has connections with the painter John Constable, and Manningtree where it takes to the Stour Estuary. To celebrate the 21st year of the Essex Way the 13 miles long Ridley Round was created which is coincident with six miles of the Essex Way. Beating the Bounds (Essex) is another circular walk (16 miles) and meets the Essex Way at Great Waltham. See Stour Valley Path (East Anglia)/Stour & Orwell Walk/Suffolk Coast and Heaths Path/Three Footpaths Walk. The John Ray Walk (9 miles) crosses the Essex Way between Braintree and Witham. At Epping the Epping Forest Centenary Walk (15 miles and on OS mapping) provides a link to the Forest Way and then goes on to Manor Park. See also E-Routes (E2).

Start:	Epping, Essex	TL465012
Finish:	Harwich, Essex	TM259329
Landranger maps:	155, 167, 168, 169	✔
1 : 25,000 maps:	Ex 174, 183, 184, 195, 196, 197	
Waymark:	Named green discs and posts	

Publications, badges and certificates:
Booklet: *The Essex Way* (includes free accommodation guide) (Essex County Council) 1994. ISBN 1852810874. 32pp; A5. £3.00.
Leaflet: *The Ridley Round* (Essex County Council) 1993. A5. Free (+ SAE).
Leaflet: *Beating the Bounds* (Essex County Council) 1996. A3/6. Free (+ 9 x 4 SAE).
Booklet: *The John Ray Walk* (Essex County Council) 2000. ISBN 185281206. 24pp; A5. £1.00.

Booklet: *Epping Forest Centenary Walk: Manor Park – Epping* by Fred Matthews and Harry Bitten (Epping Forest Information Centre) 1992. ISBN 0852030215.
16pp; A5. £1.00 (+ 30p p&p) – cheques payable to Corporation of London.
Badge (cloth): (Essex County Council). Free.

Etherow – Goyt Valley Way   180

Cheshire, Derbys   *24 km / 15 miles*

A route linking Stockport with Longdendale on the western edge of the Peak District, it follows the River Goyt upstream to the confluence with the River Etherow north of Marple which it then follows to Broadbottom continuing through Woolley Bridge and Hollingworth to Bottoms Reservoir and the Longdendale Trail. There is a link to the Trans Pennine Trail walking route at Bottoms Reservoir. See Midshires Way. See also E-Routes (E2).

Start:	Vernon Park, Stockport, Cheshire	SJ905908
Finish:	Hadfield, Derbys	SK024960
Landranger maps:	109, 110	✔
1 : 25,000 maps:	Ex 277 OL 1	
Waymark:	Stylised heron	

Publications, badges and certificates:
Booklet: *Etherow – Goyt Valley Way* (Tameside Countryside Warden Service). 24pp; A5. £2.00 (incs p&p).

Exe Valley Way   181

Devon, Somers   *72 km / 45 miles*

This route from the Exe Estuary to the steeply wooded valleys on Exmoor follows, for the most part, quiet country lanes and footpaths along the Exe valley through Bickleigh, Tiverton and Bampton. See Two Counties Way.

Start:	Starcross, Devon	SX977817
Finish:	Hawkridge, Somers	SS861307
Landranger maps:	181, 192	✔
1 : 25,000 maps:	Ex 110, 114 OL 9	
Waymark:	Named discs with stylised V symbol (not on moorland section)	

Publications, badges and certificates:
Booklet: *The Exe Valley Way* (Devon County Council). 24pp; 210 x 98. £1.25 (incs p&p) – quote ref. DP14.

Exmoor & Lorna Doone Tour   182

Devon, Somers   *161 km / 100 miles*

A walk taking in some of the most attractive scenery of the National Park and the countryside in which the novel Lorna Doone is set, passing Dunkery Beacon – at 1,703ft, the highest point on Exmoor – then to Dulverton, Withypool via the famous Tarr Steps, Simonsbath and down through the Doone valley.

Start:	Dunster, Somers	SS992437
Finish:	Lynmouth, Devon	SS724494
Landranger maps:	180, 181	
1 : 25,000 maps:	OL 9	

Publications, badges and certificates:
Paperback: *Footpath Touring: Exmoor and Lorna Doone* by Ken Ward (Footpath Touring) 1985.
ISBN 0711701954. 64pp; 224 x 114. £4.00.

Falklands Way   183

Cumbria   *72 km / 45 miles*

A route linking part of the Coast to Coast Walk with the Pennine Way National Trail, which visits Tan Hill, Keld, Muker, Great Shunner Fell, Cotterdale, Swarth Fell Pike and Wild Boar Fell.

Start and Finish:	Kirkby Stephen, Cumbria	NY774082
Landranger maps:	91, 98	
1 : 25,000 maps:	OL 19, 30	

Publications, badges and certificates:
Booklet: *The Falklands Way* by Richard Sewell (Peter Denby). 20pp; 150 x 210. £1.00 (+ 9 x 6 SAE).
Badge and certificate: (Peter Denby). £1.00 & Free (+ A4 SAE).

Famous Highland Drove Walk   184

Highland, Perth   *290 km / 180 miles*

A walk tracing one of the routes taken by the cattle drovers from Skye, through seven mountain ranges, along riversides, quiet glens and wild mountain passes, to the mart at Crieff, Perthshire.

Start:	Glenbrittle, Highland	NG411211
Finish:	Crieff, Perth	NN863218
Landranger maps:	32, 33, 34, 41, 50, 51, 52, 57, 58	
1 : 25,000 maps:	Ex 368, 378, 392 & one TBA 2002, OL 38	

Publications, badges and certificates:
Paperback: *The Famous Highland Drove Walk* by Irving Butterfield (Grey Stone Books) 1996.
ISBN 0951599658. 128pp; A5. £9.95.

Fen Rivers Way   185

Cambs, Norfolk   *80 km / 50 miles*

For much of the route, the Way follows the well-drained floodbanks of the rivers Cam and Great Ouse. At King's Lynn, there is a ferry link with the Peter Scott Walk (10 miles and on OS mapping but no publication) along the western edge of the Great River Ouse to the Wash and along the sea wall to the outfall of the River Nene. See also Nene Way and Iceni Way. See also E-Routes (E2).

Start:	Cambridge, Cambs	TL449592
Finish:	King's Lynn, Norfolk	TF616199
Landranger maps:	131, 132, 143, 154	✔
1 : 25,000 maps:	Ex 209, 226, 228, 236, 250	
Waymark:	Name and eel logo	
User group:	Fen Rivers Way Association	

Publications, badges and certificates:
Booklet: *The Complete Fen Rivers Way and other walks* (Fen Rivers Way Association) 2001. 49pp; A5. £4.00 (incs p&p).
Folder: *The Fen Rivers Way – Cambridge to Ely Section* (Cambridgeshire County Council) 1995. 36pp; A5. £2.50 (incs p&p).
Leaflet: *Fen Rivers Way* (Norfolk County Council). A5. £0.70 (+ SAE).

Fife Coast Path   186
Edin, Fife   *132 km / 82 miles*

The Fife Coast Path keeps faithfully to the shore between the Forth Road Bridge and St Andrews Bay, though, for convenience, this route starts and finishes at railway stations. It includes numerous castles, fishing villages, remarkable rock formations, caves and long sandy beaches. The coast is a haven for bird life and flora. Apart from an exposed chain walk at Kincraig Point, the walking is easy, though times of high tide are best avoided in some places as the walk uses the foreshore. The Kingdom of Fife Council are in the process of developing relevant services for the route.

Start:	Dalmeny Station, Edinburgh	NT139779
Finish:	Leuchars Station, Fife	NO449207
Landranger maps:	59, 65, 66	✔
1 : 25,000 maps:	Ex 367, 371	
Path website:	www.standrews.co.uk	

Publications, badges and certificates:
Hardback: *The Fife Coast* by Hamish Brown (Mainstream Publishing Co Ltd) 1994. ISBN 1851586083. 226pp; 155 x 232. £12.99.
Leaflets: *Fife Coastal Path – North Queensferry to Crail* (Kingdom of Fife). 4 leaflets. Free (+ 9 x 4 SAE).

Flower of Suffolk   187
Suffolk   *42 km / 26 miles*

A route using coastal and heathland paths. There is also a choice of 10 and 17 mile circuits.

Start and Finish:	Walberswick, Suffolk	TM498746
Landranger maps:	156	
1 : 25,000 maps:	Ex 212, 231	

Publications, badges and certificates:
Looseleaf: *Flower of Suffolk* (Bobbie Sauerzapf). 2pp. Free (+ 9 x 4 SAE).
Badge and certificate: (Bobbie Sauerzapf). £1.50 (+ SAE).

Forest of Bowland Challenge Walk 188

Lancs *42 km / 26 miles*

A route to the south of the Forest of Bowland taking in three summits – Beacon Fell, Parlick and Fair Snape. Langden Beck links them together. There are no facilities on the route.

Start and Finish:	Beacon Fell, Lancs	SD565426
Landranger maps:	103	
1 : 25,000 maps:	OL 41	

Publications, badges and certificates:
Booklet: *Forest of Bowland Challenge Walk* by John Merrill (Walk & Write Ltd). ISBN 1874754500. 48pp; A5. £3.95 (+ 75p p&p).
Badge and certificate: (Walk & Write Ltd). £3.50 (incs p&p).

Forest Way 189

Essex *40 km / 25 miles*

The Way links two forests and several open spaces in south-west Essex. From the edge of Epping Forest it runs north over farmland, from where there are views over the Lea valley, and crosses Latton and Harlow Commons to Hatfield Heath, Woodside Green and Hatfield Forest. At the end the walk meets with the waymarked Flitch Way (15 miles and on OS mapping) which follows the track of a former railway between Braintree and Bishops Stortford – see also Mansell Way.

Start:	Loughton Station, Essex	TQ423956
Finish:	Takeley Street, Essex	TL534213
Landranger maps:	167, 177	✔
1 : 25,000 maps:	Ex 174, 183, 194, 195	
Waymark:	Bright green Forest Way signposts & plaques	

Publications, badges and certificates:
Paperback: *The Forest Way* (Essex County Council) 1996. ISBN 1852810238. 14pp; A5. £2.50 – includes free accommodation guide.
Leaflet: *Flitch Way* (Essex County Council). Folded; 118 x 210. Free (+ SAE).
Badge (cloth): (Essex County Council). Free (+ SAE).

Formartine and Buchan Way 190

Aberdeenshire *87 km / 54 miles*

Former railway lines which have been developed for leisure use. The main route links Fraserburgh with Dyce (Aberdeen) – 38 miles. At Maud there is a spur of 16 miles through Mintlaw to Peterhead.

Start:	Parkhill, Dyce, Aberdeenshire	NJ884128
Finish:	Fraserburgh, Aberdeenshire	NJ994667
Landranger maps:	30, 38	✔
1 : 25,000 maps:	Ex TBA 2002	
Waymark:	Initials F & BW	

Publications, badges and certificates:
Leaflet: *The Formartine and Buchan Way* (Aberdeenshire County Council). A4/3. Free (+ SAE).

Foss Walk   191

N Yorks   *45 km / 28 miles*

The Walk follows footpaths along or near the river Foss, from its confluence with the Ouse in the historic city of York to its source at Pond Head, four miles from the finish. The Walk passes through Strensall, Sheriff Hutton, Crayke and Oulston. See Centenary Way (North Yorkshire).

Start:	York, N Yorks	SE603522
Finish:	Easingwold, N Yorks	SE528698
Landranger maps:	100, 105	✔
1 : 25,000 maps:	Ex 290, 299	
Waymark:	Named signposts and named arrows with frog logo	

Publications, badges and certificates:
Booklet: *The Foss Walk* by Mark W. Jones (Maxiprint) 1994. 16pp; 210 x 135. £3.45 (incs p&p).

Founders Footpaths   192

Surrey   *42 km / 26 miles*

A route around the Surrey Hills visiting sites associated with the founding of the LDWA, including Steer's Field and Blatchford Down, both named in memory of the founders of the Association.

Start and Finish:	Steer's Field, Surrey	TQ141504
Landranger maps:	186, 187	
1 : 25,000 maps:	Ex 146	

Publications, badges and certificates:
Booklet: *Founders Footpaths* (Ann Sayer) 1998. 12pp; A5. Free (+ 9 x 6 SAE).
Certificate: (Ann Sayer). £1.00 (incs p&p).

Four Pikes Hike   193

Gtr Man, Lancs, W Yorks   *72 km / 45 miles*

A route over moors and farmland via the Pikes of Rivington, Hoglaw, Thievely and Stoodley.

Start:	Great House Barn, Lancs	SD628139
Finish:	Hebden Bridge, W Yorks	SD992273
Landranger maps:	103, 109	
1 : 25,000 maps:	Ex 287 OL 21	

Publications, badges and certificates:
Looseleaf: *The Four Pikes Hike* (Norman Thomas). Free (+ 9 x 4 SAE).
Badge and certificate: (Norman Thomas). £2.00 (+ SAE).

Furness Five Trigs Walk   194

Cumbria   *40 km / 25 miles*

The Walk visits the trig points at Bank House Moor, High Haume, Yarlside, Birkrigg
Common and the Hoad Monument. It is possible to link the start and finish points.

Start:	Gillbanks, Ulverston, Cumbria	SD285787
Finish:	Hoad Monument, Ulverston, Cumbria	SD294791
Landranger maps:	96, 97	
1 : 25,000 maps:	OL 6, 7	

Publications, badges and certificates:
Looseleaf: *Furness Five Trigs Walk* (Brian Richmond). Free (+ 9 x 4 SAE).
Badge & certificate: (Brian Richmond). £1.00 (+ SAE).

Furness Way   195

Cumbria   *121 km / 75 miles*

A coast to coast route across southern Lakeland linking with the Westmorland Way,
Cumberland Way and Cumbria Way and exploring High Furness, it passes through
the Lyth Valley, Cartmel, Coniston, the Duddon Valley and Eskdale. See Crake Valley
Round.

Start:	Arnside, Cumbria	SD455787
Finish:	Ravenglass, Cumbria	SD083963
Landranger maps:	89, 96, 97	
1 : 25,000 maps:	OL 6, 7	

Publications, badges and certificates:
Paperback: *Furness Way* by Paul Hannon (Hillside Publications) 1994. ISBN 187014127X.
104pp; 175 x 115. £5.99 (+ 60p p&p).

Gallo Way Round   196

Dumfries & Gall, Ayrshire   *80 km / 50 miles*

A high-level route, with 12,500ft of ascent over 30 tops in the three main ranges of
the Galloway Hills. Views are extensive from the route which dips into the skirts of
the forestry plantations three times. The bulk of the way is over the tops with only
odd traces of path, and will test navigation skills. The mixed terrain can be very
tough through heather, bog and rocks with short turf above 2,000ft.

Start and Finish:	Bruce's Stone, L Trool, Dumfries & Gall	NX415803
Landranger maps:	77	
1 : 25,000 maps:	OL 32	

Publications, badges and certificates:
Looseleaf: *Gallo Way Round* (Glyn Jones). Free (+ SAE).
Certificate: (Glyn Jones). £1.00 (+ SAE).

Glevum Way 197

Glos   *42 km / 26 miles*

A route around the outskirts of the City of Gloucester. It was devised by the Gloucester Ramblers Group as part of the RA Diamond Jubilee celebrations.

Start and Finish:	Castle Meads, Glos	SO826185
Landranger maps:	162	
1 : 25,000 maps:	Ex 179	
Waymark:	Named discs with letters GW	

Publications, badges and certificates:
Leaflet: *The Glevum Way* (RA Gloucester) 2001. A3/6. £0.50 (+ 40p p&p).

Gloucestershire Way 198

Glos, Mons   *161 km / 100 miles*

A route through the Forest of Dean, Severn Plain and Cotswolds linking the Wye Valley Walk and Offa's Dyke Path National Trail to the Severn, Cotswold, Oxfordshire and Heart of England Ways. The guide also provides details of a link from Tewksbury to the Worcestershire Way. See also Three Choirs Way.

Start:	Chepstow Castle, Mons	ST534941
Finish:	Tewkesbury, Glos	SO891324
Landranger maps:	150, 162, 163, 172	✔
1 : 25,000 maps:	Ex 167, 179, 190 OL 14, 45	
Waymark:	Gloucester Cathedral, river and tree topped hill	

Publications, badges and certificates:
Paperback: *The Gloucestershire Way* by Gerry Stewart (Countryside Matters) 1996. ISBN 0952787008. 128pp; 210 x 140. £4.95 (incs p&p).
Leaflet: *Walking the Gloucestershire Way* (Gloucestershire County Council) 2000. A4/3. Free.

Glyndwr's Way/Llwybr Glyndwr National Trail 199

Powys   *213 km / 132 miles*

Named after Owain Glyndwr, the 15th century warrior/statesman who attempted to establish an independent Welsh nation, the route is by, or close to, many sites connected with his rebellion. It links with Offa's Dyke Path National Trail at both ends and passes through Abbey Cwmhir, Llanidloes, Machynlleth, Llangadfan and Hope. The Trail has only recently become a National Trail and part of the upgrade has significantly reduced the amount of road walking. The Ann Griffiths Walk (7 miles) between Pont Llogel and Pontrobert along the Afon Efyrnwy links into Glyndwr's Way National Trail at each end catering for a circular route of about 16 miles.

Start:	Knighton, Powys	SO283724
Finish:	Welshpool, Powys	SJ227074
Landranger maps:	125, 126, 135, 136, 137, 148	✔
1 : 25,000 maps:	Ex 201, 214, 215, 216, 239 OL 23	
Waymark:	National Trail Acorn and gold dragon	

Publications, badges and certificates:
Paperback: *Owain Glyndwr's Way* by Richard Sale (Gwasg Carreg Gwalch) 2001. ISBN 0863816908. 148pp; 183 x 121. £4.95 (+ £1.00 p&p).
Paperback: *Owain Glyndwr's Way* by C. & R. Catling (Cicerone Press) 2002. ISBN 1852842997. £7.99 (details TBA).
Leaflet: *Glyndwr's Way/Llwybr Glyndwr* produced by Countryside Council for Wales (Machynlleth Tourist Information Centre) 2000. A4/3. Free (+ SAE).
Leaflets: *Glyndwr's Way/Llwybr Glyndwr* produced by Countryside Council for Wales (Machynlleth Tourist Information Centre) 2001. 16 section leaflets; A4/3. Set £4.00 (+ 80p p&p) – individual leaflets free (+ SAE).
Leaflet: *Glyndwr's Way Accommodation Guide* (Powys County Council) Annual. A4/3. Free (+ SAE).
Booklet: *Ann Griffiths Walk* (Powys County Council). 20pp; A5. £2.20 (incs p&p).
Badge (cloth): for Glyndwr's Way (Offa's Dyke Association). £1.30 (+ 26p p&p).

Gordano Round   200

N Somers   *42 km / 26 miles*

The Round, devised by the Gordano Footpath Group, is a figure-of eight walk initially following the coast path of the Severn Estuary past the Black Nore Lighthouse to Clevedon. Turning inland through the town the walker then follows wooded countryside to Clapton in Gordano. More farmland and woods lead to the eastern limit of the walk at Abbots Leigh where the route circles back to Clapton in Gordano. From here the walk is in open countryside back to the start. The guidebook includes four links which can be used to make short circular walks.

Start and Finish:	Roath Road, Portishead	ST467762
Landranger maps:	171, 172	
1 : 25,000 maps:	Ex 154	
Waymark:	Named discs with lapwing	

Publications, badges and certificates:
Booklet: *The Gordano Round* (Gordano Footpath Group) 2001. 56pp; A5. £3.99 (+ £1.00 p&p).

Gordon Way   201

Aberdeenshire   *34 km / 21 miles*

From Bennachie the route takes in forests, farmland and moorlands across several hills. Currently the available publication covers the route to Suie car park, with the intention to extend to Rhynie in due course.

Start:	Bennachie Centre, Aberdeenshire	NJ700217
Finish:	Rhynie, Aberdeenshire	NJ500270
Landranger maps:	37, 38	✔
1 : 25,000 maps:	Ex TBA 2002	
Waymark:	Hexagonal logo with letter G	

Publications, badges and certificates:
Leaflet: *Bennachie and The Gordon Way* (Bennachie Project) 1996. A4/3. £0.50 (+ 9 x 4 SAE).

Grand Union Canal Walk   202

Bucks, Gtr London, Herts, Northants,   *234 km / 145 miles*
W Midlands, Warks

This first national waterways walk was created as part of the celebrations of the 200th anniversary of the creation of the canal companies that later formed the Grand Union Canal. Being almost entirely towpath it provides much for those interested in canal history. From the centre of London at Little Venice the canal heads to Slough and then through Hertfordshire and the Chilterns to Tring. Apart from the stretch through Milton Keynes the route is then largely rural passing the Canal Museum at Stoke Bruerne to Leamington Spa and Warwick. The final stretch is through the suburbs of Birmingham. From Little Venice the Regent's Canal (8½ miles) takes the walker to Limehouse and the Thames Path National Trail and on the way the Hertford Union Canal (1½ miles) provides a link to the Lea Valley Walk. At Startop's End, near Marsworth, the Aylesbury Arm (6 miles) provides a link to that town. Similarly at Bulbourne the Wendover Arm (6 miles) links to Wendover. The Two Ridges Link (8 miles and on OS mapping) at Leighton Buzzard gives access to the Ridgeway National Trail and the Greensand Ridge Walk. See Leicester Line and Worcester & Birmingham Canal Walks, Leighton – Linslade Loop, Heart of England and Jurassic Ways, Hillingdon Trail and Colne Valley Way, Colne Valley Trail & Ebury Way.

Start:	Little Venice, Paddington, Gtr London	TQ260818
Finish:	Birmingham, Gas Street Basin,	
	W Midlands	SP062867
Landranger maps:	139, 151, 152, 165, 166, 175, 176	✔
1 : 25,000 maps:	Ex 161, 172, 173, 181, 182, 192, 207, 220,	
	221, 222, 223	
Waymark:	Named posts at regular intervals	

Publications, badges and certificates:
Softback: *Grand Union Canal Walk* by Anthony Burton and Neil Curtis (Aurum Press) 1993. ISBN 1854102443. 168pp; 210 x 130. £9.99.
Paperback: *The Grand Union Canal Walk* by Clive Holmes (Cicerone Press) 1996. ISBN 1852842067. 120pp. £5.99.
Leaflet: *Exploring the Grand Union Canal* (British Waterways – Sawley) 2000. A5. Free (+ SAE).
Leaflet: *Exploring the Grand Union Canal – Birmingham to Daventry* (British Waterways – Sawley). A5. Free (+ SAE).
Leaflet: *Services and Attractions on the Grand Union Canal South* (British Waterways – Sawley). A5. Free (+ SAE).
Leaflet: *Explore the Grand Union Canal – Milton Keynes* (British Waterways – Sawley). A5. Free (+ SAE).
Stripmap (folded): *Grand Union Canal map 1: Birmingham to Fenny Stratford* (GEOprojects) 2001. ISBN 0863511414. 135 x 213. £4.75 (+ 50p p&p).
Stripmap (folded): *Grand Union Canal map 2: Braunston to Kings Langley* (GEOprojects) 2001. ISBN 0863511414. 135 x 213. £4.75 (+ 50p p&p).
Stripmap (folded): *Grand Union Canal map 3: Fenny Stratford to the Thames* (GEOprojects) 2001. ISBN 0863511430. 135 x 213. £4.75 (+ 50p p&p).
Paperback: *Exploring the Regent's Canal* by Michael Essex-Lopresti (Brewin Books Ltd) 1994. ISBN 185858017X. 101pp; 148 x 209. £8.95 (+ 90p p&p).
Booklet: *Explore London's Canals* (British Waterways – Enfield). 28pp; A5. Free (+ SAE).

Leaflet: *The Aylesbury Arm* (Buckinghamshire County Council). A4/3. Free (+ SAE).
Leaflet: *The Wendover Arm* (Buckinghamshire County Council). A4/3. Free (+ SAE).
Leaflet: *Two Ridges Link* (Buckinghamshire County Council). A4/3. Free (+ SAE).

Grand Western Canal 203
Devon, Somers 38 km / 24 miles

A route along the course of the Grand Western Canal which is water-filled between Tiverton and Lowdwells. Along the dry section, use is made in parts of the actual canal bed. The area abounds in flora and fauna. See Two Counties Way and West Deane Way.

Start:	Tiverton, Devon	SS963124
Finish:	Taunton, Somers	ST228255
Landranger maps:	181, 192, 193	✔
1 : 25,000 maps:	Ex 114, 128	

Publications, badges and certificates:
Booklet: *Exploring the Grand Western Canal in Somerset* (J. Hall and J. Yeates) 1992. 24pp; A5. £1.50 (incs p&p).
Folder: *In Search of the Grand Western Canal – Somerset Section* (Taunton Deane Borough Council) 1996. 10 cards; 168 x 220. £3.95 (incs p&p).
Leaflet: *Grand Western Canal Country Park – Devon Section* (Devon County Council). A3/4. £0.25 (incs p&p) – quote ref. DP37.

Grantham Canal 204
Leics, Lincs, Notts 53 km / 33 miles

The Grantham Canal was opened in 1797, and was built to link Grantham with the River Trent at Nottingham. Although the canal is no longer navigable the towpath provides an opportunity to enjoy the countryside in the East Midlands, running through the heart of the Vale of Belvoir and passing through many unspoilt villages. Part of the Leicestershire section has been designated an SSSI.

Start:	Nottingham, Notts	SK569392
Finish:	Grantham, Lincs	SK908355
Landranger maps:	129, 130	
1 : 25,000 maps:	Ex 246, 247, 260	

Publications, badges and certificates:
Paperback: *Discover the Grantham Canal in Nottinghamshire* – full route (Nottinghamshire County Council). 84pp; A5. £3.75 (+ 35p p&p).

Grasmere Skyline Classic Walk 205
Cumbria 32 km / 20 miles

A high level route taking in Heton Pike, Fairfield, Calf Crag and Blea Rigg.

Start and Finish:	White Moss Common, Cumbria	NY348065
Landranger maps:	90	
1 : 25,000 maps:	OL 7	

Publications, badges and certificates:
Looseleaf: *Grasmere Skyline Classic Walk* (Brian Richmond). Free (+ 9 x 4 SAE).
Badge and certificate: (Brian Richmond). £1.00 (+ SAE).

Great English Walk   206
Numerous   *1003 km / 623 miles*

A journey across England from south-east Wales to north-east England. The route
takes in the Forest of Dean, Wenlock Edge, the Cheshire Plain, the Peak District, the
lesser used parts of the Yorkshire Dales, Allendale and the Northumbrian towns of
Rothbury and Wooler.

Start:	Chepstow, Monmouth	ST535942
Finish:	Berwick-upon-Tweed, Northumb	NT996533
Landranger maps:	75, 80, 81, 87, 92, 99, 103, 104, 110, 117, 118, 119, 126, 138, 149, 150, 162	
1 : 25,000 maps:	Ex 190, 204, 217, 218, 241, 257, 267, 268, 297, 298, 302, 307, 339, 346 OL 1, 14, 16, 21, 24, 30, 31, 42, 43	

Publications, badges and certificates:
Softback: *The Great English Walk – Volume One. Chepstow to Hathersage* by Margaret & Brian
Nightingale (Nightingale Publications) 1996. ISBN 0952949016. 192pp; 210 x 148. £7.95.
Softback: *The Great English Walk – Volume Two. Hathersage to Berwick-upon-Tweed* by
Margaret & Brian Nightingale (Nightingale Publications) 1997. ISBN 0952949024. 192pp; 210
x 148. £7.95 (both volumes together – £15.00).

Great Glen Way   207
Highland   *117 km / 73 miles*

The fourth and indeed last of the official Long Distance Routes in Scotland will
officially open in 2002. It links the west coast at Fort William, the end of the West
Highland Way, with the east coast at Inverness via the Great Glen and Loch Ness.
Use is made of forestry tracks, the towpath of the Caledonian Canal and various
minor lanes and tracks with very little use made of the main A82.

Start:	Fort William, Highland	NN104743
Finish:	Inverness, Highland	NH667452
Landranger maps:	26, 34, 35, 41	✔
1 : 25,000 maps:	Ex 392 & others TBA 2002	
Waymark:	Thistle within hexagon	
Path website:	www.greatglenway.com	

Publications, badges and certificates:
Paperback (spiral/laminated): *The Great Glen Way & Map – the Official Guide* by Jacquetta
Megarry (Rucksack Readers). ISBN 1898481075. 70pp; 145 x 215. £9.99.
Hardback: *The Great Glen Way* by Heather Connon and Paul Roper (Mainstream Publishing Co
Ltd) 1997. ISBN 1851588647. 192pp; 215 x 125. £9.99.
Paperback: *The Caledonian Canal* by Anthony Burton (Aurum Press) 1998. ISBN 185410554X.
96pp; 210 x 130. £9.99.
Leaflet: *The Great Glen Cycle Route* (Forest Enterprise N Scotland) 1993. A4/3. Free.
Stripmap (folded): *Caledonian Canal & the Great Glen* (GEOprojects) 1997. ISBN 0863510434.
135 x 213. £4.75.

Great North Forest Trail   208

Tyne & Wear   *105 km / 65 miles*

The Trail is part of an initiative to improve the countryside in this former mining area and passes Pelton, Bournmoor, Hetton-le-Hole, the Penshaw Monument and Witherwack. Part of the route connects with the shorter walks: Coalfield Way (10 miles) and Stephenson Trail (10 miles). See Tyne-Wear Trail.

Start and Finish:	Causey Arch, Tyne & Wear	NZ204564
Landranger maps:	88	✔
1 : 25,000 maps:	Ex 308	
Waymark:	Name & leaf	

Publications, badges and certificates:
Folder: *Great North Forest Trail* (Great North Forest). 5 leaflets. Free.
Folder: *Coalfield Way* (Sunderland City Council) 1997. 5pp; A4/3. £1.50 (+ 50p p&p).
Folder: *Stephenson Trail* (Sunderland City Council) 1997. 5pp; A4/3. £1.50 (+ 50p p&p).

Green Chain Walk   209

Gtr London   *64 km / 40 miles*

The Green Chain Walk provides a link between the River Thames and many of the open spaces in South-East London. The walk, which can also be started from the Thames Barrier or Erith riverside, caters for several variations of route in achieving the link as it passes through Oxleas Wood and Mottingham to terminate at either Crystal Palace or Chislehurst. Though there is inevitably some street walking, there is a surprising amount of woodland, grassland, park and garden.

Start:	Thamesmead, Gtr London	TQ472813
Finish:	Crystal Palace, Gtr London	TQ343705
Landranger maps:	176, 177	✔
1 : 25,000 maps:	Ex 161, 162	
Waymark:	Named signs with logo	

Publications, badges and certificates:
Folder: *Explore South East London's Green Chain* (SE London Green Chain Project) 1999. Set of ten cards; A4/2. £3.50 (incs p&p) – cheques payable to Greenwich Council.
Leaflet: *Explore South East London's Green Chain* (SE London Green Chain Project). A4/3. Free.

Green London Way   210

Gtr London   *148 km / 93 miles*

An urban walk through London suburbs utilising rivers, canals, disused railway lines, alley ways, parks, commons, woods, and heaths. It descends to the Lea Valley, and thence to East Ham, crossing the river at Woolwich and passing Shooters Hill, Crystal Palace, Streatham Common, Richmond Park, Kew and following a brief stretch along the River Brent, it rises to Harrow-on-the-Hill and Hampstead.

Start and Finish:	Finsbury Park, Gtr London	TQ315869
Landranger maps:	176, 177	
1 : 25,000 maps:	Ex 161, 162, 173, 174	

Publications, badges and certificates:
Paperback: *Green London Way* by Bob Gilbert (Lawrence and Wishart Ltd) 1991. ISBN 0853157464. 195pp; 155 x 234. £10.99 (incs p&p).

Greensand Ridge Walk 211

Beds, Bucks, Cambs   *64 km / 40 miles*

A route taking in woods and farmland along the dissected Greensand Ridge passing Woburn Abbey and Ampthill Park where it connects with the John Bunyan Trail. At Leighton Buzzard, the Two Ridges Link (8 miles and included on OS mapping) provides a link via the Grand Union Canal to Ivinghoe Beacon and the Ridgeway National Trail/Icknield Way Path. At Gaminglay the waymarked Clopton Way (11 miles and on OS mapping) goes on to Wimpole Hall from whence the waymarked Wimpole Way (11 miles and on OS mapping) takes the walker to Cambridge. The Seven Parishes Millennium Circular Walk (14 miles) is a route using part of the Greensand Ridge Walk. The waymarked Marston Vale Timberland Trail (14 miles) is a circular route coincident with the Greensand Ridge Walk between Ampthill Park and Lidlington. See Cross Bucks Way, Kingfisher Way, Leighton – Linslade Loop, North Bedfordshire Heritage Trail and Oxbridge Walk.

Start:	Leighton Buzzard, Beds	SP915251
Finish:	Gamlingay, Cambs	TL226533
Landranger maps:	152, 153, 165	✔
1 : 25,000 maps:	Ex 192, 193, 208	
Waymark:	Letters GRW and deer emblem	

Publications, badges and certificates:
Leaflet: *Greensand Ridge Walk* (Greensand Trust). A4/3. Free (+ SAE).
Leaflet: *Two Ridges Link* (Buckinghamshire County Council). A4/3. Free (+ SAE).
Leaflet: *Clopton Way* (Cambridgeshire County Council) 1990. A4/3. £0.40 (+ 50p p&p).
Leaflet: *Wimpole Way* (Cambridgeshire County Council) 1993. A4/3. £0.40 (+ 50p p&p).
Leaflet: *Seven Parishes Millennium Circular Walk* (Seven Parishes) 2000. A4/2. Free (+ stamp).
Leaflet: *The Marston Vale Timberland Trail* (Forest of Marston Vale) 2000. A4/3. Free (+ SAE).

Greensand Way 212

Kent, Surrey   *173 km / 107 miles*

The Way follows the Greensand ridge across Surrey and Kent. It passes the Devil's Punch Bowl and crosses Hascombe Hill and Winterfold Heath before descending to Dorking. In Kent it crosses Toys and Ide Hills, descends to Sevenoaks Weald and crosses the Medway Valley to Yalding. Then ascending the ridge it passes through villages, orchards and hop gardens and views over the Weald are achieved. The ridge becomes indistinct beyond Great Chart but the route crosses a rolling landscape of farmland and woodland. There are a number of link routes with the North Downs Way National Trail. A further link is provided by the Reigate and

Banstead Millennium Trail (18 miles) which is a route between Banstead Downs and Horley. The Way meets the Saxon Shore Way at Hamstreet near to the Royal Military Canal. See Ashford on Foot, Haslemere Circular Walk, Lapwing Walk, Socratic Trail, Tandridge Border Path, Wealdway and Vanguard Way.

Start:	Haslemere, Surrey	SU905328
Finish:	Hamstreet, Kent	TR002334
Landranger maps:	186, 187, 188, 189	✔
1 : 25,000 maps:	Ex 125, 133, 134, 136, 137, 145, 146, 147, 148	
Waymark:	Letters GW in Surrey; oast-house in Kent	

Publications, badges and certificates:
Booklet: *Along and Around the Greensand Way* by Bea Cowan (Kent County Council) 1997. ISBN 1873010915. 129pp; 210 x 215. £6.00 (post free).
Booklet: *Along and Around the Greensand Way* by Bea Cowan (Surrey County Council) 1997. ISBN 1899706356. 129pp; 210 x 215. £6.00 (post free).
Booklet: *The Greensand Way in Surrey* (Surrey County Council) 1989. ISBN 0946840415. 47pp; A5. £2.50 (post free).
Leaflets: *Reigate and Banstead Borough Council Millennium Trail* (Reigate and Banstead Borough Council) 2000. 8 leaflets; A4/3. Free.

Gritstone Edge Walk 213
Derbys, S Yorks 43 km / 27 miles

Linear walk running generally downhill along the eastern edge system of the Peak District, taking in Derwent, Stanage, Burbage, Froggatt, Baslow and Chatsworth Edges.

Start:	Flouch Inn, S Yorks	SE197016
Finish:	Baslow, Derbys	SK256725
Landranger maps:	110, 119	
1 : 25,000 maps:	OL 1, 24	

Publications, badges and certificates:
Booklet: *Peak District End to End Walks* by John Merrill (Walk & Write Ltd). ISBN 0907496393. 52pp; A5. £3.95 (+ 75p p&p).
Badge and certificate: (Walk & Write Ltd). £3.50 (incs p&p).

Gritstone Trail 214
Cheshire, Staffs 56 km / 35 miles

The Trail follows the gritstone edge providing views of the Peak District and Cheshire Plain with much of the upland walking above 1,000ft. The route takes in Lyme Park, Sponds Hill, Tegg's Nose Country Park, Croker Hill and Mow Cop. At Lyme Park the Trail connects with the Ladybrook Interest Trail Walk (10 miles and on OS mapping). It links with the Staffordshire Way near to Rushton Spencer and the South Cheshire Way at Mow Cop. See Dane Valley Way. See also E-Routes (E2).

Start:	Lyme Park, Disley, Cheshire	SJ972842
Finish:	Kidsgrove, Staffs	SJ837542

Landranger maps:	109, 118	✔
1 : 25,000 maps:	Ex 257, 267, 276	
Waymark:	Black bootmark & yellow letter G	

Publications, badges and certificates:
Paperback: *Gritstone Trail and Mow Cop Trail* by Carl Rogers (Mara Publications) 1995. ISBN 0952240947. 68pp; 135 x 210. £4.25.
Leaflet: *Gritstone Trail* (Cheshire County Council) 2001. A2/3. Free (+ 9 x 6 SAE) – includes details of incorporated Mow Cop Trail.
Booklet: *Guide to the Ladybrook Interest Trail* (Bill Shercliffe). 24pp; A5. £1.50 (+ 50p p&p).

Hadrian's Wall Path National Trail   215
Cumbria, Northumb, Tyne & Wear   130 km / 81 miles

Approved for National Trail status, the route will not be officially opened until 2003. For the present, footpaths are being created where none currently exist in order to provide a line as close to the Wall remains as is possible, but avoiding interference with it. Access to these new paths is being provided on an ongoing basis, but until such time as the footpath-creation project is complete a total crossing is only possible by resorting to existing paths/minor roads. There are real future concerns for this World Heritage Site and in consequence a 'User Code of Respect' has been developed to include recommendations for keeping to signed paths, avoiding interference with the remains and using promoted circular walks especially in wet winter conditions. Just the one circular walks pack is currently available, with others to be published for the Cumbria area in due course. The Keelman's Way between Wylam and Bill Quay (14 miles) is a cyclist/pedestrian route to the south of the River Tyne with links to the National Trail which is north of the river. The part of the Trail within the Tyneside area is known locally as Hadrian's Way. See Cumbria Coastal Way, Lake to Lake Walk, Pennine Way National Trail and Reiver's Way.

Start:	Wallsend, Tyne & Wear	NZ304660
Finish:	Bowness-on-Solway, Cumbria	NY225628
Landranger maps:	85, 86, 87, 88	
1 : 25,000 maps:	Ex 315, 316 OL 43	
Path website:	www.hadrians-wall.org.uk	

Publications, badges and certificates:
Softback: *Hadrian's Wall Path National Trail* (Official Guide) by Anthony Burton (Aurum Press). Details TBA 2002/3.
Paperback: *Hadrian's Wall: Vol 1: The Wall Walk* by Mark Richards (Cicerone Press) 1993. ISBN 1852841281. 224pp; 116 x 176. £7.99.
Booklet: *Hadrian's Wall Path National Trail Accommodation Guide* (Hadrian's Wall Information Line). Free.
Leaflet: *Hadrian's Wall Path National Trail – User Information* (Hadrian's Wall Path National Trail Office). Details TBA 2002.
Certificate: (Hadrian's Wall Path National Trail Office). Details TBA 2003.
Folder: *Circular Walks around Hadrian's Wall* (Northumberland County Council). 5 leaflets; 170 x 220. £3.95 (incs p&p).
Leaflet: *Keelman's Way* (Gateshead Council). 120 x 250. Free.

Haematite Trail 216
Cumbria *29 km / 18 miles*

The Trail was devised to explore some of the remains of the iron mining industry which brought about the industrial expansion of Furness and the subsequent emergence of Barrow. In its heyday the Furness mining industry was an equivalent to the American Gold Rush and provided some of the richest iron ore worked in Britain. The route passes Newton, Little Urswick, Lindal, Marton and Askam.

Start and Finish:	Barrow-in-Furness, Cumbria	SD190688
Landranger maps:	96	
1 : 25,000 maps:	OL 6	
Waymark:	Pithead logo and named posts	

Publications, badges and certificates:
Leaflet: *The Haematite Trail* (Barrow Tourist Information Centre). A4/3. Free.

Hambleton Hillside Mosaic Walk 217
N Yorks *58 km / 36 miles*

A route on the western edge of the North York Moors, passing along cliff tops and through woodlands and villages. Along the route are 23 mosaics made by local people which display the distinct aspects of the area.

Start and Finish:	Sutton Bank, N Yorks	SE516831
Landranger maps:	100	
1 : 25,000 maps:	OL 26	

Publications, badges and certificates:
Booklet: *The Hambleton Hillside Mosaic Walk* (North York Moors National Park). ISBN 0907480691. 28pp; A5. £3.95 (+ 95p p&p).

Hambleton Hobble 218
N Yorks *52 km / 32 miles*

A strenuous route with 2,500ft of ascent based on Black Hambleton, to the west of the North York Moors National Park. It passes through the villages of Osmotherley, Hawnby and Boltby.

Start and Finish:	Osmotherley, N Yorks	SE461985
Landranger maps:	100	
1 : 25,000 maps:	OL 26	

Publications, badges and certificates:
Leaflet: *Hambleton Hobble* (Lyke Wake Club). £0.25 (+ 9 x 4 SAE).
Badge: (Lyke Wake Club). £1.50 (+ SAE).

Hangers Way 219
Hants *34 km / 21 miles*

Named after the series of steep-sided hills, the Hampshire Hangers, the route is through wooded and grassed areas and the village of Selborne to Queen Elizabeth

Country Park, where it meets with the South Downs Way National Trail, and links to the Staunton Way which proceeds to the coast at Langstone Harbour.

Start:	Alton, Hants	SU723397
Finish:	Queen Elizabeth Country Park, Hants	SU718182
Landranger maps:	186, 197	✔
1 : 25,000 maps:	Ex 120, 133, 144	
Waymark:	Green and white discs with tree on hill	

Publications, badges and certificates:
Leaflet: *Hangers Way* (Hampshire County Council). A4/3. Free (+ SAE).

Hanslope Circular Ride   220
Milton K   *32 km / 20 miles*

A bridle route to the north of Milton Keynes, the Ride runs through open countryside centred on the village of Hanslope, with its distinctive spire, and gives extensive views over the Ouse and Tove Valleys.

Start and Finish:	Great Linford, Milton K	SP846424
Landranger maps:	152	✔
1 : 25,000 maps:	Ex 192, 207	
Waymark:	Named standard discs and posts	

Publications, badges and certificates:
Leaflet: *Hanslope Circular Ride* (Milton Keynes Council). Free (+ SAE).

Harcamlow Way   221
Cambs, Essex, Herts   *227 km / 141 miles*

A figure-of-eight walk, mainly on tracks and green lanes passing many places of historic interest, crossing low hills, woods and arable land via Standon and Manuden to meet the cross-over point at Newport. It continues through Saffron Walden and over the low Bartlow Hills to Horseheath and the Fleam Dyke, to enter Cambridge, the return route passing through Melbourn and Chrishall to Newport, continuing via Debden, Thaxted, Takeley and Hatfield Forest. The waymarked Five Parishes Millennium Boundary Walk (15 miles) is a circular route using part of the Harcamlow Way at Tilty.

Start and Finish:	Harlow, Essex	TL445113
Landranger maps:	153, 154, 166, 167	✔
1 : 25,000 maps:	Ex 174, 183, 194, 195, 208, 209, 210, 226	

Publications, badges and certificates:
Booklet: *Harcamlow Way* by Fred Matthews and Harry Bitten (Essex County Council) 1980. 52pp; A5. £2.50 (incs p&p).
Booklet: *Five Parishes Millennium Boundary Walk* (Five Parishes Walks) 2000. 8pp; A5. 50p (+ SAE).

Harden Hike   222

W Yorks   *40 km / 25 miles*

Using a mix of woodland, fields and moorland paths/tracks, the walk makes a complete circuit of Rombald's Moor, giving extensive views of Airedale and Wharfedale.

Start and Finish:	Golden Fleece Inn, Harden, W Yorks	SE085384
Landranger maps:	104	
1 : 25,000 maps:	Ex 288, 297	

Publications, badges and certificates:
Looseleaf: *Harden Hike* (Peter Bashforth). Free (+ 9 x 4 SAE).
Badge and certificate: (Peter Bashforth). £1.25 (+ SAE) & £0.25 (+ 9 x 6 SAE).

Hardy Way   223

Dorset, Wilts   *343 km / 214 miles*

The Way explores Thomas Hardy's Wessex and visits many Hardy locations beginning at his birthplace near Dorchester and takes in the Piddle and Frome valleys, an outstanding stretch of coast between Lulworth Cove and the Encombe Valley, to Corfe Castle and Dorchester, ending in Stinsford churchyard where his heart lies buried. Between Beaminster and West Bay through Bridport, the Way is mainly coincident with the waymarked Brit Valley Way (8 miles). See Dorset Jubilee Trail.

Start:	Higher Bockhampton, Nr Dorchester,	
	Dorset	SY728925
Finish:	Stinsford Church, Dorset	SY712910
Landranger maps:	183, 184, 193, 194, 195	
1 : 25,000 maps:	Ex 117, 118, 129 OL 15	
Waymark:	Named signs	

Publications, badges and certificates:
Paperback: *The Hardy Way – A 19th Century Pilgrimage* by Margaret Marande (Dorset Publishing Co) 1995. ISBN 0948699531. 208pp; 210 x 148. £9.95 (+ £1.55 p&p).
Leaflet: *The Hardy Way* (Dorset County Council) 1997. A4/3. Free (+ 9 x 4 SAE).
Folder: *Brit Valley Way & Circular Walks* (Dorset County Council). 8 route cards; 152 x 215. £3.95 (+ 9 x 6 SAE).

Harrogate Ringway   224

N Yorks   *34 km / 21 miles*

A trail encircling the spa town at a radius of 3-4 miles, mostly on attractive country paths. Can be divided into shorter stages or linked with Knaresborough Round to form a 36 mile route. See Rezzy Rush.

Start and Finish:	Pannal, N Yorks	SE307514
Landranger maps:	104	✔
1 : 25,000 maps:	Ex 297	
Waymark:	Named signposts	

Publications, badges and certificates:
Folder: *Harrogate Ringway* (Harrogate Borough Council) 1997. 6pp; A4/3. £2.50.
Leaflet: *Harrogate Ringway* (RA Harrogate Group). 4pp; A5. £0.30 (+ 9 x 4 SAE).
Badge: (Joan Clack). £1.50 (+ SAE).

Haslemere Circular Walk   225

Hants, Surrey, W Sussex   *36 km / 22 miles*

A circuit around Haslemere, with a large proportion of the route crossing National Trust woodland heathland, including Gibbet Hill, Blackdown, Marley Common, Waggoners Wells and the Devil's Punch Bowl. The walk intersects with the Greensand Way. Another link to the Greensand Way is provided by the Four Stations Way (11½ miles) from Haslemere to Godalming.

Start and Finish:	Devil's Punchbowl, Surrey	SU890358
Landranger maps:	186	
1 : 25,000 maps:	Ex 133	

Publications, badges and certificates:
Looseleaf: *Haslemere Circular Walk* by Elizabeth Pamplin (Elizabeth Pamplin). 3pp; A4. Free (+ SAE).
Route cards: *Four Stations Way* (RA Godalming and Haslemere) 2000. 2 cards; A4/2. £2.00 (incs p+p).

Haworth-Hebden Bridge Walk   226

W Yorks   *30 km / 19 miles*

Basically a 14.5 miles circular taking in Leeshaw Reservoir, Hardcastle Crags, Walshaw Dean Reservoirs, Top Withins and Bronte Bridge, but with extensions into Haworth (1.5 miles) and/or Hebden Bridge (3 miles) catered for.

Start:	Haworth, W Yorks	SE032370
Finish:	Hebden Bridge, W Yorks	SD993272
Landranger maps:	103, 104	✔
1 : 25,000 maps:	OL 21	
Waymark:	Named posts	

Publications, badges and certificates:
Leaflet: *Two Walks Linking Haworth and Hebden Bridge* (Hebden Bridge Tourist Information Centre). A4/3. £0.45 (+ 30p p&p).

Heart of Bowland Walk   227

Lancs, N Yorks   *29 km / 18 miles*

A varied circuit of moorland, steep-sided valleys, rivers and forests in the picturesque Forest of Bowland.

Start and Finish:	Slaidburn, Lancs	SD714523
Landranger maps:	103	
1 : 25,000 maps:	OL 41	

Publications, badges and certificates:
Looseleaf: *Heart of Bowland Challenge Walk* (LDWA West Lancashire Group). Free (+ 9 x 4 SAE).
Badge and certificate: (LDWA West Lancashire Group). £1.50 (+ A4 SAE).

Heart of England Way 228
Glos, Staffs, W Midlands, Warks 161 km / 100 miles

The Way follows a curving route through gently undulating farmland and lowland heath, woodland and riverside paths. It takes in Cannock Chase, Lichfield, Kingsbury Water Park, the Arden countryside (see Arden Way), the Avon Valley and the northern aspects of the Cotswolds to Chipping Campden, Swell and Lower Slaughter. At Bourton-on-the-Water it connects with the Cotswold Ring and Oxfordshire Way. The waymarked Avon Valley Walk (30 miles and included on OS mapping) provides a link from Stratford-upon-Avon to the Way at Bidford-on-Avon. Other connections include the Staffordshire Way on Cannock Chase, Centenary Way (Warwickshire) at Kingsbury Water Park, Grand Union Canal at Kingswood, Midland Link at Baddesley Clinton, Beacon Way on Gentleshaw Common and Cotswold Way at Chipping Norton. The waymarked Trans Solihull Link (15 miles) links the North Worcestershire Path with the Heart of England Way. See Cotswold Round and Walk, Coventry and Gloucestershire Ways and Warwickshire Villages Trail. See also E-Routes (E2).

Start:	Milford, Staffs	SJ975212
Finish:	Bourton-on-the-Water, Glos	SP170209
Landranger maps:	127, 128, 139, 140, 150, 151, 163	✔
1 : 25,000 maps:	Ex 205, 220, 221, 232, 244 OL 45	
Waymark:	Named green and white discs with oak trees	
User group:	Heart of England Way Association	

Publications, badges and certificates:
Paperback: *The Heart of England Way* by Richard Sale (Aurum Press) 1998. ISBN 1854105388. 144pp; 210 x 130. £12.99.
Paperback: *Heart of England Way* by John Roberts (Walkways) 2000. ISBN 0947708405. 124pp; A5. £6.95.
Paperback: *Heart of England Way* by Roger Noyce (Sigma Leisure) 1999. ISBN 1850586942. 144pp; 210 x 180. £6.95.
Booklet: *Heart of England Way – Chipping Camden to Bourton-on-the-Water* produced by Cotswold Wardens (Cotswold District Council) 1992. 22pp; A5. £1.25 (+ 33p p&p).
Leaflet: *Heart of England Way* (Heart of England Way Association). A4/3. Free (+ 9 x 4 SAE).
Looseleaf: *Heart of England Way Accommodation List* (Walkways). Free (+ SAE).
Leaflet: *Avon Valley Walk* (Stratford-upon-Avon District Council) 1993. A4/3. Free (+ SAE).
Badge and certificate: (Heart of England Way Association). £1.25 (+ SAE) & £1.00 (+ SAE).

Hebden Valleys Heritage Trek 229
West Yorks 32 km / 20 miles

A roller-coaster route contrasting the high moors and secluded valleys encircling Hebden Bridge and visting High Town, Hardcastle Crags, Jumble Hole Clough, Stoodley Pike, Broadhead Nature Reserve and the Rochdale Canal towpath. The

South Pennines Twin Challenge comprises the Hebden Valley Heritage Trek and the Manorlands Meander.

Start and Finish:	Hebden Bridge Tourist Information	
	Centre, West Yorks	SD992272
Landranger maps:	103, 104	
1 : 25,000 maps:	OL 21	

Publications, badges and certificates:
Booklet: *Hebden Valleys Heritage Trek* (Tony Wimbush). £2.00 (+ 60p p&p) – cheques payable to W. A. Wimbush.
Badge & certificate: (Tony Wimbush). Details from Tony Wimbush.

Helm Wind Walk   230
Cumbria   *32 km / 20 miles*

The Walk takes its name from the notorious Helm Wind which often rages fiercely on the summit of Cross Fell, at 2,960ft the highest point on the route. Care should be taken when attempting the Walk, especially in poor weather conditions.

Start and Finish:	Garrigill, Cumbria	NY744417
Landranger maps:	87, 91	
1 : 25,000 maps:	OL 31	

Publications, badges and certificates:
Looseleaf: *Helm Wind Walk* (LDWA Cumbria Group). Free (+ 9 x 4 SAE).
Badge and certificate: (LDWA Cumbria Group). £1.50 (+ SAE) & £0.50 (+ SAE).

Hereward Way   231
Cambs, Lincs, Norfolk, Northants,   *166 km / 103 miles*
Peterboro, Rutland, Suffolk

The Way links the Viking Way (at Oakham) with the Peddars Way near to Knettishall Heath. It passes through Stamford, Peterborough and Ely to reach the Brecklands heaths and forests at Brandon and Thetford. There are areas of flat open fenland. The Torpel Way (11 miles from Peterborough to Stamford and included on OS mapping) provides an alternative option between those two locations – the route is to the north of the Hereward Way. See also St Edmund Way. See also E-Routes (E2).

Start:	Oakham, Rutland	SK861088
Finish:	Harling Road Station, Norfolk	TL978879
Landranger maps:	141, 142, 143, 144	✔
1 : 25,000 maps:	Ex 226, 227, 228, 229, 230, 234, 235	
Waymark:	Tiger face, named posts in Rutland; double sword logo in Cambs	

Publications, badges and certificates:
Leaflet: *Hereward Way – Oakham to Stamford* (Oakham TIC). A4/3. £0.50 (+ 9 x 4 SAE) – cheques payable to Anglian Water Services.

Leaflet: *Hereward Way – Peterborough to Ely* (Cambridgeshire County Council) 2001. A5.
£0.30 (+ A5 SAE).
Booklet: *Country Walks around Peterborough – Volume 1* (includes Torpel Way) (Peterborough
City Council). £2.50 (+ 9 x 6 SAE).

Herriot Way   232
N Yorks   *88 km / 55 miles*

A route taking in many of the locations referred to in the James Herriot book and
based on the Youth Hostels at Aysgarth, Grinton, Keld and Hawes.

Start and Finish:	Aysgarth Falls Youth Hostel, N Yorks	SE012885
Landranger maps:	92, 98	
1 : 25,000 maps:	OL 30	

Publications, badges and certificates:
Booklet: *The Herriot Way* (Norman F. Scholes) 1997. ISBN 0953035700. 40pp; A5. £3.00 (incs
p&p).
Booklet: *Booking Bureau – Youth Hostels* (YHA Northern Region) Annual. 20pp; A5. Free.

Hertfordshire Chain Walk   233
Cambs, Gtr London, Herts   *138 km / 86 miles*

A chain of linking circular walks which stretch from near Crews Hill Station in the
London Borough of Enfield to Ashwell Station in Cambridgeshire. Though each walk
is complete in itself, they can be combined to provide a walk from London to Cam-
bridgeshire and back. The route runs in a generally northerly direction, passing
Cuffley, Little Berkhamstead, Hertingfordbury, Watton at Stone, Cottered and
Therfield.

Start and Finish:	Whitewebbs Park, Gtr London	TQ329998
Landranger maps:	153, 154, 166, 176, 177	✔
1 : 25,000 maps:	Ex 173, 174, 182, 193, 194	
User group:	East Herts Footpath Society	

Publications, badges and certificates:
Paperback: *Hertfordshire Chain Walk* by East Herts Footpath Society (East Herts Footpath
Society) 1994. ISBN 094855536X. 80pp; A5. £4.00 (+ 66p p&p).

Hertfordshire Way   234
Herts   *267 km / 166 miles*

The Way provides a route around one of the smallest counties visiting such as
Codicote, St Albans, Tring, King's Langley, Cuffley and Bishop's Stortford with
contrasting scenery and history.

Start and Finish:	Royston, Herts	TL293338
Landranger maps:	153, 154, 165, 166, 167	✔
1 : 25,000 maps:	Ex 174, 181, 182, 193, 194, 195, 209	

Waymark:	Name/head of deer
User group:	Friends of the Hertfordshire Way

Publications, badges and certificates:
Paperback: *The Hertfordshire Way* (Friends of the Hertfordshire Way) 1998. ISBN 0948555416. 104pp; 135 x 215. £5.50 (+ 80p p&p).
Certificate: (Friends of the Hertfordshire Way). £2.50 (+ A5 SAE).

High Hunsley Circuit   235

E Yorks   *39 km / 24 miles*

A route which takes in wooded valleys and a number of villages. It is coincident with sections of the Wolds Way National Trail and Beverley 20.

Start and Finish:	Walkington, E Yorks	SE999368
Landranger maps:	106, 107	✔
1 : 25,000 maps:	Ex 293	
Waymark:	Named signs	

Publications, badges and certificates:
Leaflet: *High Hunsley Circular* (RA Beverley Group). A4. Free (+ 9 x 4 SAE).
Badge: (RA Beverley Group). £1.00 (+ 6 x 4 SAE).

High Peak 60   236

Derbys   *96 km / 60 miles*

A walk designed by the New Mills Group to celebrate the RA Diamond Jubilee. The landscape varies from farmland and river valleys to bleak exposed moorland, with a number of steep ascents. The publication also includes details of a number of short circular walks in the Peak District, an 18 miles long extension to the High Peak 60 and see the Ten Church Challenge.

Start and Finish:	New Mills, Derbys	SK999855
Landranger maps:	110, 119	
1 : 25,000 maps:	OL 1, 24	

Publications, badges and certificates:
Paperback: *High Peak Hikes* by David Frith (Sigma Leisure) 1996. ISBN 1850584591. 180pp; A5. £6.95.

High Peak Way   237

Derbys, S Yorks   *45 km / 28 miles*

A walk including 6,500ft of ascent over moorland, through Hope, Hathersage and along the Great Ridge between Mam Tor and Lose Hill. The route is not recommended in adverse weather conditions.

Start:	Chinley, Derbys	SK038826
Finish:	Padley, Derbys	SK251788
Landranger maps:	109, 110, 119	
1 : 25,000 maps:	OL 1, 24	

Publications, badges and certificates:
Looseleaf: *The High Peak Way* (Alan S. Edwards). 20pp. Free (+ A5 SAE).
Badge and certificate: (Alan S. Edwards). £2.25 (incs p&p).

High Street Stroll 238
Cumbria   *48 km / 30 miles*

A scenic high-level route over the mountains of the central and eastern Lake District, avoiding tourist spots and visiting Harter Fell, Nabs Moor, Swindale, Mardale and High Street.

Start and Finish:	Ambleside, Cumbria	NY376045
Landranger maps:	90	
1 : 25,000 maps:	OL 5, 7	

Publications, badges and certificates:
Looseleaf: *High Street Stroll* (Joyce Sidebottom). Free (+ 9 x 4 SAE).
Badge and certificate: (Joyce Sidebottom). £2.50 (+ 9 x 7 SAE).

High Weald Landscape Trail 239
E Sussex, Kent, W Sussex   *145 km / 90 miles*

A walking route through the unique landscape of the High Weald, the centre of the 16th Century iron industry and still the most wooded area of England. The Trail takes in hop gardens, orchards, villages and historic gardens.

Start:	Horsham, W Sussex	TQ179309
Finish:	Rye, E Sussex	TQ918205
Landranger maps:	187, 188, 189, 198, 199	✔
1 : 25,000 maps:	Ex 125, 134, 135, 136	
Waymark:	Green named signs and discs with tree & church	

Publications, badges and certificates:
Leaflet: *The High Weald: Landscape Heritage Trails in West Sussex* (West Sussex County Council) 1997. A5. Free.
Booklet: *Along and Around the High Weald Landscape Trail* (Kent County Council) 1999. ISBN 0953601307. 113pp; 212 x 212. £8.00 post free.
Video: *High Weald Landscape Trail* (Promo-video Publications). 53 minutes. £12.50 (+ £1.00 p&p).

Hillingdon Trail 240
Gtr London   *32 km / 20 miles*

This route spans the London Borough of Hillingdon from Cranford Park in the south to Springwell Lock on the Grand Union Canal in the north. The Celandine Route (12 miles) along the River Pinn from Pinner provides another link to the Grand Union Canal Walk at the junction of the Slough Arm. See London LOOP.

Start:	Cranford Park, Gtr London	TQ103782
Finish:	Springwell Lock, Gtr London	TQ043929
Landranger maps:	176	✔

1 : 25,000 maps:	Ex 161, 172, 173
Waymark:	Fingerposts and trail logo

Publications, badges and certificates:
Folder: *The Hillingdon Trail* (Hillingdon LB) 1994. 6pp; A5. £2.00 (+ 50p p&p).
Leaflet: *The Celandine Route* (Hillingdon LB) 2000. A4/3. Free.

Holme Valley Circular Walk 241

W Yorks   *39 km / 24 miles*

A walk along the heights around the Holme Valley, it takes in Castle Hill, the villages of Farnley Tyas, Thurstonland, Hepworth, Netherthong and Honley. There is a variety of scenery including many viewpoints. The Holme Valley Hills and Hamlets Walk (9 miles) which is included on OS mapping but for which there is no available publication, incorporates a route linking Holmfirth and Netherthong with various sites of interest and in parts is coincident with the Holme Valley Circular Walk. The Holme Valley Circular Challenge Walk (24 miles) involves almost 4000ft of ascent and in parts is coincident with the main route.

Start and Finish:	Berry Brow, W Yorks	SE136137
Landranger maps:	110	✔
1 : 25,000 maps:	Ex 288 OL 1	

Publications, badges and certificates:
Paperback: *Holme Valley Circular Walk* by E. S. Boocock (Holmfirth Tourist Information Centre). 32pp; 135 x 200. £2.25 (+ 50p p&p).
Looseleaf: *Holme Valley Circular Challenge Walk* (Norman F. Scholes). Free (+ 9 x 4 SAE).
Badge and certificate: for Holme Valley Circular Challenge Walk (Norman F. Scholes). £1.00 (+ 9 x 4 SAE).

Hovingham Hobble 242

N Yorks   *37 km / 23 miles*

An undulating route through the Howardian Hills with views of Castle Howard House and passing unusual sites and bridges of interest. In parts the Hobble is coincident with the Centenary (North Yorkshire) and Ebor Ways.

Start and Finish:	Hovingham, N Yorks	SE667756
Landranger maps:	100	
1 : 25,000 maps:	Ex 300	

Publications, badges and certificates:
Looseleaf: *Hovingham Hobble* (Ben Booth). 4pp; A5. Free (+ 9 x 4 SAE).
Badge and certificate: (Ben Booth). £2.00 (+ 9 x 6 SAE).

Howden 20 243

E Yorks   *32 km / 20 miles*

From Howden the walk heads west along the bank of the River Ouse, and north across flat farmland and along the Derwent valley via Asselby and Wressle to Bubwith, from where it meanders southwards over farmland back to Howden.

Start and Finish:	Howden, E Yorks	SE748283
Landranger maps:	105, 106	✔
1 : 25,000 maps:	Ex 291	
Waymark:	Standard arrows with H20	

Publications, badges and certificates:
Looseleaf: *Howden 20* (Goole Rambling Club). Free (+ 9 x 4 SAE).
Badge and certificate: (Goole Rambling Club). £0.50 (+ 6 x 4 SAE).

Howdenshire Way   244

E Yorks   *26 km / 16 miles*

A route around the market town of Howden, the route passes from Eastrington to
Saltmarshe and then along the River Ouse to Boothferry where it turns to Asselby
and Newsholme.

Start and Finish:	Eastrington, E Yorks	SE786298
Landranger maps:	105	
1 : 25,000 maps:	Ex 291	
Waymark:	Standard arrows with white spot	

Publications, badges and certificates:
Looseleaf: *The Howdenshire Way* (Don Sweeting). 5pp; A4. Free (+ 9 x 4 SAE).
Badge and certificate (Don Sweeting). £1.20 (+ 6 x 4 SAE).

Humber Bridge Link Walk   245

E Yorks, N Lincs   *55 km / 34 miles*

Comprises two circuits based on Hessle and the Humber Bridge. The northern
circuit, coincident initially with the Wolds Way National Trail and Beverley 20,
follows the Humber Estuary to the west, then visiting Welton, Waudby and North
Ferriby. The southern circuit crosses the Humber Bridge to reach the northern
Lincolnshire Wolds passing through Barton upon Humber, where it links with the
Viking Way, and South Ferriby to return along the shore of the Humber.

Start and Finish:	Hessle, E Yorks	TA035256
Landranger maps:	106, 107, 112	
1 : 25,000 maps:	Ex 281, 293	

Publications, badges and certificates:
Looseleaf: *Humber Bridge Link Walk* (LDWA East Yorkshire Group). 2pp; A4. Free (+ 9 x 4 SAE).
Badge and certificate: (LDWA East Yorkshire Group). £2.00 (+ 9 x 6 SAE).

Hyndburn Clog   246

Lancs   *50 km / 31 miles*

A route originally created and promoted by the local Ramblers' Association Group
but now adopted by Hyndburn Borough Council, it circumvents Accrington, passing
through pastures, moorland villages and close to reservoirs. The booklet
publication includes details of two other routes which take advantage of parts of

the main Clog route. They are the Canal Clog (20 miles), using part of the towpath of the Leeds to Liverpool Canal, and the Moorland Heights Clog (20 miles).

Start and Finish:	Stanhill Village, Lancs	SD723277
Landranger maps:	103	
1 : 25,000 maps:	Ex 287	
Waymark:	Clog logo	

Publications, badges and certificates:
Booklet: *The Hyndburn Clog* (Hyndburn Borough Council). 22pp; A5. £1.50 (+ 9 x 6 SAE).
Leaflet: Hyndburn Clog (RA North East Lancashire Area). A5. £0.20 (+ 9 x 6 SAE).
Badge and certificate: (RA North East Lancashire Area). £1.00 (+ SAE) & £0.50 (+ SAE) – cheques payable to RA Hyndburn Group.

Iceni Way   247
Norfolk, Suffolk   *129 km / 80 miles*

A route from Breckland to the Coast. It starts at the meeting point of Peddars Way with the Angles Way and goes to Thetford. It then goes to Brandon (some of this section is coincident with the Little Ouse Path, a 10 mile path included on OS mapping) and continues along the Little Ouse to join the Great Ouse at Brandon Creek and, in part using the Fen Rivers Way, proceeds to King's Lynn. From here an inland route via Sandringham is taken to the coast near Snettisham and then the coast is followed to link up with the Norfolk Coast Path at Hunstanton. There are also links with the Icknield and Nar Valley Ways.

Start:	Knettishall Heath, Suffolk	TL944807
Finish:	Hunstanton, Norfolk	TF672412
Landranger maps:	132, 144	
1 : 25,000 maps:	Ex 228, 229, 236, 250	

Publications, badges and certificates:
Booklet: *The Iceni Way* (RA Norfolk Area) 1998. ISBN 1901184145. 28pp; A5. £2.10 (+ 30p p&p).
Leaflet: *Little Ouse Path* (Brecks Countryside Project). A4/3. £0.40 (incs p&p).

Icknield Way Path   248
Beds, Bucks, Cambs, Essex, Herts,
Luton, Suffolk   *169 km / 105 miles*

From the Ridgeway and using green lanes, farm and forestry tracks the Way follows, as far as is possible, the group of prehistoric trackways which form the Icknield Way along the chalk spine from the Chilterns to Norfolk. Many sights of archaeological interest are passed on the route through Luton, Baldock, Royston, Great Chesterford and Icklingham meeting the Peddars Way at the finish. An alternative route exists avoiding Dunstable and Luton. The Icknield Way Association Guide includes details of a link to Thetford from West Stow. See St Edmund Way, John Bunyan Trail, Greensand Ridge Walk, Kingfisher Way, Stour Valley Path (East Anglia), Lea Valley Walk, Cromer to the M11, Daffodil Dawdle and Icknield Way Trail. See also E-Routes (E2).

Start:	Ivinghoe Beacon, Bucks	SP960168
Finish:	Knettishall Heath, Suffolk	TL944807
Landranger maps:	144, 153, 154, 155, 165, 166	✔
1 : 25,000 maps:	Ex 181, 182, 193, 194, 195, 208, 209, 210, 226, 229, 230	
Waymark:	Named disc with neolithic flint axe emblem	
User group:	Icknield Way Association	

Publications, badges and certificates:

Paperback: *Icknield Way Path* (Icknield Way Association) 1998. ISBN 0952181916. 80pp; 210 x 148. £4.50.

Leaflet: *The Icknield Way – Walkers Route* (Cambridgeshire County Council). A4/3. Free (+ SAE).

Booklet: *Accommodation List* (Icknield Way Association). £1.00 (+ SAE).

Badge: (Icknield Way Association). £1.30 (+ SAE).

Icknield Way Trail 249

Beds, Bucks, Cambs, Essex, Herts, Luton, Suffolk   *169 km / 105 miles*

This is a multi-user route currently under development for walkers, riders and cyclists providing a bridleway link between the Peddars Way and the Ridgeway and based on the Icknield Way Path. Currently the southern end of the route (23 miles) is complete between Bledlow Cross (where it links with the Swan's Way) and Pitstone Hill (near to Ivinghoe Beacon) on the Ridgeway National Trail. This section passes Princes Risborough, Wendover and Wiggington. The Wimpole Books publication comes with supplements relating to new sections of the route. Though not named on OS maps it is largely coincident with the Icknield Way Path and is not shown separately from 248 in the Map Section.

Start:	Knettishall Heath, Suffolk	TL944807
Finish:	Pitstone Hill, Bucks	SP994154
Landranger maps:	144, 153, 154, 155, 165, 166	
1 : 25,000 maps:	Ex 181, 182, 193, 194, 195, 208, 209, 210, 226, 229, 230	
Waymark:	'Riders' Route' named signs on the southern section (see description)	

Publications, badges and certificates:

Leaflet: *The Icknield Way* (Buckinghamshire County Council). A4/3. Free (+ SAE).

Leaflet: *The Icknield Way Trail* (North Chilterns Trust) 2001. Free (+ SAE). Details TBA.

Paperback: *The Icknield Way Path* by Elizabeth Barrett (Wimpole Books). ISBN 0951601121. 48pp; A5. £4.50 (incs p&p).

Imber Range Perimeter Path 250

Wilts   *48 km / 30 miles*

This route is around the perimeter of a military training firing range on Salisbury Plain mainly following the escarpment above Westbury White Horse and passing several Iron Age hill forts. Warning notices must be adhered to.

Start and Finish:	Westbury, Wilts	ST893510
Landranger maps:	183, 184	✔

1 : 25,000 maps:	Ex 130, 143
Waymark:	Name of route with cannon logo

Publications, badges and certificates:
Looseleaf: *Imber Range Path* (Richard Archard). Free (+ 9 x 6 SAE).

Inn Way...to the Lake District   251

Cumbria   *145 km / 90 miles*

A walk taking in the attractions of the Lake District including such as Rydal Water, Braithwaite, Boot and Coniston. Forty four traditional inns are passed along the route.

Start and Finish:	Ambleside, Cumbria	NY376045
Landranger maps:	89, 90, 96, 97	
1 : 25,000 maps:	OL 4, 6, 7	

Publications, badges and certificates:
Paperback: *The Inn Way...to the Lake District* by Mark Reid (Inn Way Publications). ISBN 190200101X. 184pp; A5. £7.95 (+ £1.00 p&p).
Badge and certificate: (Inn Way Publications). £2.50 & £2.00 (both incs p&p).

Inn Way...to the North York Moors   252

N Yorks   *144 km / 89 miles*

A route visiting Hutton-le-Hole, Levisham, Egton Bridge, Rosedale Abbey and Hawnby passing 30 traditional inns on the way.

Start and Finish:	Helmsley, N Yorks	SE613838
Landranger maps:	94, 100	
1 : 25,000 maps:	OL 26, 27	

Publications, badges and certificates:
Paperback: *The Inn Way...to the North York Moors* by Mark Reid (Inn Way Publications). ISBN 1902001044. 185pp; A5. £7.95 (+ £1.00 p&p).
Badge and certificate: (Inn Way Publications). £2.50 & £2.00 (incs p&p).

Inn Way...to the Yorkshire Dales   253

N Yorks   *122 km / 76 miles*

A walk taking in many Yorkshire Dales attractions, catering for overnight stops at Buckden, Askrigg, Reeth, West Burton, Kettlewell and Grassington. Twenty-six traditional English inns are passed along the Way.

Start and Finish:	Grassington, N Yorks	SE003641
Landranger maps:	98	
1 : 25,000 maps:	OL 2, 13	

Publications, badges and certificates:
Paperback: *The Inn Way* by Mark Reid (Inn Way Publications) 1997. ISBN 1901214052. 136pp; A5. £7.95 (+ £1.00 p&p).
Badge and certificate: (Inn Way Publications). £2.50 & £2.00 (incs p&p).

DETAILS OF ROUTES

Ippikin's Way 254

Shrops *43 km / 27 miles*

Named after a 'robber-knight' the route visits Hughley and Wilderhope and passes over Caer Caradoc Hill, The Lawley, Wenlock Edge and Helmeth Hill.

Start and Finish:	Church Stretton, Shrops	SO456935
Landranger maps:	137	
1 : 25,000 maps:	Ex 217	
Waymark:	Named discs with chain design	

Publications, badges and certificates:
Folder: *Ippikins Way* (Shrewsbury and Atcham Borough Council). 3 leaflets; A3/3. £1.00 (+ 50p p&p) – cheques payable to SABC.

Ipswich Outer Ring 255

Suffolk *35 km / 22 miles*

A walk around Ipswich of fields and woods and passing Martlesham Creek. Road walking is kept to a minimum. The Walk is partly coincident with the Fynn Valley Walk (9 miles and named on OS mapping) and is the outer ring of a network of parish walks.

Start and Finish:	Brendon Drive, Ipswich	TM208448
Landranger maps:	169	
1 : 25,000 maps:	Ex 197	

Publications, badges and certificates:
Folder: *Parish Walks by Kesgrave Parish Council – the Outer Ring and other walks* (Suffolk County Council) 1999. Map and 9 leaflets; A5. £1.70 (+ 50p p&p).
Leaflet: *Fynn Valley Walk* (Suffolk County Council). A4/3. £0.20 (+ 9 x 4 SAE).

Irwell Sculpture Trail 256

Gtr Man, Lancs *48 km / 30 miles*

The Trail links the centre of Manchester with the moors above Bacup and makes use of a former railway line and follows the former Bolton – Bury Canal and through Bury, Ramsbottom and Rawtenstall to the finish where it links with the Rossendale Way. Since 1987, various sculptures have been sited along the Trail, the intention being that, on completion, there will be 50 in place.

Start:	Salford Quays, Gtr Man	SJ833976
Finish:	Deerplay, Lancs	SD866264
Landranger maps:	103, 109	✔
1 : 25,000 maps:	Ex 277 OL 21	
Waymark:	Dragonfly	

Publications, badges and certificates:
Folder: *The Irwell Sculpture Trail* (Rossendale Borough Council). 12 leaflets. £1.00 (+ 50p p&p).

Isaac's Tea Trail   257

Northumberland   *58 km / 36 miles*

Named after a character of yesteryear, this route is based on the Youth Hostel at Ninebanks and takes in Allendale, Nenthead and Alston. It passes a number of Methodist Chapels and other places associated with the Holden family, Isaac having worked as a travelling tea seller and money raiser.

Start and Finish:	Ninebanks Youth Hostel, Northumbria	NY771574
Landranger maps:	87	
1 : 25,000 maps:	OL 31, 43	

Publications, badges and certificates:
Booklet: *Isaac's Tea Trail* (Ninebanks Youth Hostel). 28pp; A5. £2.00 (+ 9 x 6 SAE).

Isle of Man Coast Path   258

IoM   *145 km / 90 miles*

The path circuits the island and, with a few exceptions, stays close to the shoreline and along the clifftops which provide spectacular views, and nesting sites for a rich variety of birdlife. Contrasting sections follow roads and promenades through the harbour and resort towns. See Millennium Way – Isle of Man.

Start and Finish:	Douglas, IoM	SC379754
Landranger maps:	95	✔
1 : 25,000 maps:	See publications for IoM North & South maps	
Waymark:	White gull and lettering on blue background	

Publications, badges and certificates:
Paperback: *Isle of Man Coastal Walk: Raad ny Foillan* by Aileen Evans (Cicerone Press) 1999. ISBN 1852842776. 152pp; 116 x 176. £7.99.
Booklet: *Walking the Isle of Man Coastal Path* by John Merrill (Walk & Write Ltd). ISBN 1874754535. 56pp; A5. £4.25 (+ 75p p&p).
Looseleaf: *Raad ny Foillan (Coastal Path)/Bayr ny Skeddan (Herring Road) & Accommodation List* (Isle of Man Department of Tourism & Leisure). 1pp; A4. Free.
Maps: *Isle of Man: North & South – 1:25000* (Isle of Man Department of Tourism & Leisure) 1995. £6.00 (+ 50p p&p).
Badge and certificate: (Walk & Write Ltd). £3.50 (incs p&p).

Isle of Wight Coast Path   259

IoW   *104 km / 65 miles*

The coastal path encircles the island and, with the exception of detours to the west of Thorness Bay and round the Osborne Crown Property at Osborne Bay, stays close to the coast. It is a very varied walk over chalk and sandstone cliffs, through popular holiday resorts and the less crowded inlets, bays, marshes and saltings. Coastal links from north (Cowes) to south (St Catherine's Lighthouse) and from east (Bembridge) to the Needles (west) add further route options. The Isle of Wight Permanent Trail starts and finishes at Shanklin Railway Station. See E-Routes (E9).

Start and Finish:	Cowes, IoW	SZ500956
Landranger maps:	196	✔
1 : 25,000 maps:	OL 29	
Waymark:	Named signs	

Publications, badges and certificates:
Paperback: *Isle of Wight Coastal Path Notebook* by Russell & Suzanne Mills (Ottakars) 1993. ISBN 0953578917. 63pp; A5. £4.99 (+ £1.00 p&p).
Booklet: *The Complete Isle of Wight Coastal Footpath* by Brian Smailes (Challenge Publications). ISBN 1903568080. 42pp; A5. £3.75 (incs p&p).
Paperback: *A Walker's Guide to the Isle of Wight* by Martin Collins & Norman Birch (Cicerone Press). ISBN 1852842210. 216pp. £9.99.
Booklet: *The Isle of Wight Coast Path* by John Merrill (Walk & Write Ltd). ISBN 0907496687. 56pp; A5. £4.95 (+ 75p p&p).
Website: (Isle of Wight Tourism). www.islandbreaks.co.uk.
Paperback: *Isle of Wight – North to South and East to West* by Brian Smailes (Challenge Publications) 2002. ISBN 1903568072. £3.75 (incs p&p).
Looseleaf: *Isle of Wight Permanent Trail* (Rother Valley Eagles Walking Club). 8pp; A4. £2.50 (incs p&p).
Badge or medal: (Rother Valley Eagles Walking Club). £2.50 (incs p&p).
Badge and certificate: (Walk & Write Ltd). £3.50 (incs p&p).

Itchen Way   260
Hants   *43 km / 27 miles*

Following the River Itchen from the mouth to the source this varied route leads from the chalk downland through Winchester to water meadows and nature reserves and the downs.

Start:	Southampton, Hants	SU435102
Finish:	New Cheriton, Hants	SU589273
Landranger maps:	185	✔
1 : 25,000 maps:	Ex 132 OL 22	
Waymark:	Named standard arrows	

Publications, badges and certificates:
No publications: on OS mapping.

Ivanhoe Way   261
Leics   *56 km / 35 miles*

A route around the north-western area of the county including Charnwood Forest. The castle at Ashby and the surrounding countryside were the setting for the novel of the same name. The route links with the Leicestershire Round at Bagwith/Shakerstone.

Start and Finish:	Ashby-de-la-Zouch, Leics	SK361165
Landranger maps:	128, 129, 140	✔
1 : 25,000 maps:	Ex 232, 233, 245	
Waymark:	Named signs	

Publications, badges and certificates:
Leaflet: *Ivanhoe Way* (Leicestershire County Council) 2000. A5. £1.00.

Jack Mytton Way   262

Shrops   *116 km / 72 miles*

From the northern edge of Wyre Forest, the Way follows a disused railway to Highley
and the Severn Valley and goes across rolling farmland to Much Wenlock where it
then follows the escarpment of Wenlock Edge and descends to Church Stretton. It
climbs to the Long Mynd via the Cardingmill Valley, to reach Plowden and Clun
Forest. It runs for a stretch alongside Offa's Dyke before finishing on the
Shropshire/Powys border.

Start:	Billingsley, Shrops	SO715835
Finish:	Llanfair Waterdine, Shrops	SO246760
Landranger maps:	127, 137, 138, 148	✔
1 : 25,000 maps:	Ex 201, 216, 217, 218, 242	
Waymark:	Horseshoe motif with horse and rider	

Publications, badges and certificates:
Booklet: *Jack Mytton Way* by Ian R. Jones (Ian R. Jones) 1995. 22pp; A5. £1.00 (+ 30p p&p).
Folder: *The Jack Mytton Way* (Shropshire County Council). 13 laminated cards; A5. £4.99 (+
£1.00 p&p).
Leaflet: *Jack Mytton Way: Shropshire's Long Distance Bridleway* (Shropshire County Council)
2001. Free.

John Bunyan Trail   263

Beds, Herts   *121 km / 75 miles*

The Trail was created by the Bedfordshire Group to celebrate the RA Diamond
Jubilee and is dedicated to the memory of John Bunyan, the Puritan Evangelist and
author of the book 'Pilgrim's Progress'. The route passes through a number of
attractive villages and scenic countryside, taking in many places of historic interest
connected with Bunyan. There are links with the Greensand Ridge Walk, Icknield
Way Path and North Bedfordshire Heritage Trail. The waymarked Clay Way ($11\frac{1}{2}$
miles) which follows the West Bedfordshire Clay Ridge is partly coincident with the
Trail at Cranfield.

Start and Finish:	Sundon Hills Country Park, Beds	TL047286
Landranger maps:	153, 166	✔
1 : 25,000 maps:	Ex 193, 208	
Waymark:	Circular disc with name and silhouette of head	

Publications, badges and certificates:
Leaflet: *The John Bunyan Trail – Section One* (G. J. Edwards). A4/3. £0.60 (+ 31p SAE).
Leaflet: *The John Bunyan Trail – Section Two* (G. J. Edwards). A4/3. £0.60 (+ 31p SAE).
Leaflet: *The Clay Way* (Forest of Marston Vale) 2002. A5. Price to be announced.

Jorvic Way   264

N Yorks   *104 km / 65 miles*

A low-level route around Greater York, the Way passes the sites of the former
Healaugh Priory and the Battle of Marston Moor, Moor Monkton – the confluence

of the Rivers Nidd and Ouse, and the Moorlands Nature Reserve. Many villages are incorporated into the walk, with 24 pubs providing ample opportunities for refreshment. It is coincident in part with the Ainsty Bounds Walk.

Start and Finish:	Tadcaster, N Yorks	SE488435
Landranger maps:	105	
1 : 25,000 maps:	Ex 290	
Waymark:	Named signs	

Publications, badges and certificates:
Folder: *Walking in the Countryside around York* (Yorkshire Footpath Trust). ISBN 189897800X. 13pp; 210 x 147. £3.45 (incs p&p).
Certificate: (Yorkshire Footpath Trust). Free (+ 9 x 6 SAE).

Jurassic Way 265

Lincs, Northants, Oxon, Rutland   *142 km / 88 miles*

The Way follows the band of Jurassic Limestone that runs along the northern boundary of Northamptonshire going first along the Oxford Canal and then via Middleton Cheney and Woodford Halse to Braunston on the Grand Union Canal. Here it turns to pass between Market Harborough and Corby, following the Welland Valley to Rockingham with its castle.

Start:	Banbury, Oxon	SP462402
Finish:	Stamford, Lincs	TF041075
Landranger maps:	140, 141, 151, 152	✔
1 : 25,000 maps:	Ex 191, 206, 222, 223, 224, 234	
Waymark:	Ammonite logo	

Publications, badges and certificates:
Folder: Jurassic Way (Northamptonshire County Council) 1994. 3 leaflets; A4/3. £1.95 (+ 30p p&p).

Kennet and Avon Walk 266

Bath NES, Bristol, N Somers, Reading,   *135 km / 84 miles*
W Berks, Wilts

A route linking the Thames at Reading with the west coast and also the Thames Path to the Cotswold Way National Trails, following the canal through Thatcham, Hungerford, Pewsey, Devizes, Bradford-on-Avon, Bath and Bristol where advantage is then taken of the Avon Walkway (30 miles and included on OS mapping) to the finish. See White Horse Trail.

Start:	Reading	SU731738
Finish:	Pill, N Somers	ST525759
Landranger maps:	172, 173, 174, 175	
1 : 25,000 maps:	Ex 154, 155, 156, 157, 158, 159	
Waymark:	AW logo on Avon Walkway section	

Publications, badges and certificates:
Paperback: *Exploring the Kennet and Avon Canal* By Nigel Vile (Countryside Books) 1992. ISBN
1853061247. 96pp; 210 x 150. £4.95 (+ £1.00 p&p).
Paperback: *The Kennet & Avon Walk* by Ray Quinlan – revised edition (Cicerone Press) 2002.
Details TBA.
Leaflet: *Explore the Kennet & Avon Canal Country* (British Waterways – Kennet & Avon) 2001.
A5. Free (+ A5 SAE).
Leaflet: *Places to Eat & Stay in Kennet & Avon Canal Country* (British Waterways – Kennet &
Avon) Annual. A5. Free (+ A5 SAE).
Stripmap (folded): *Kennet & Avon Canal* (GEOprojects) 1997. ISBN 0863510418. 135 x 213.
£4.75 (+ 50p p&p).

Kett's Country Walk   267

Norfolk   *32 km / 20 miles*

A walk based on the 16th century activities of Robert Kett, taking in a number of
churches along a meandering route. By using the Norwich Riverside Walk (no
publication) a link can be achieved to Marriott's Way. See Tas Valley Way.

Start:	Cringleford, Norfolk	TG200059
Finish:	Wymondham, Norfolk	TM109012
Landranger maps:	134, 144	
1 : 25,000 maps:	Ex 237	

Publications, badges and certificates:
Booklet: *Kett's Country* (Norfolk County Council) 1997. 12pp; A5. £0.70 (+ SAE).

Kielder Walks   268

Northumberland   *34 km / 21 miles*

These comprise the 'Bundle & Go to Kielder Stane' (12 miles) and the 'Devil's Lapful
& Three Pikes' (9 miles), both based on Kielder Castle. The first is through forest
and over fells including the use of a former railway line and the other provides
views of Bakethin and Kielder Water. In effect a figure-of-eight route is achieved
with a total ascent of 2868ft. A third walk in the series, the 'Bloody Bush', has
closed on a permanent basis.

Start and Finish:	Kielder Castle, Northumberland	NY633935
Landranger maps:	80	
1 : 25,000 maps:	OL 42	

Publications, badges and certificates:
Leaflet: *No 2 – Bundle & Go to Kielder Stane* (Forest Enterprise Northumberland). A4/3. £0.50
(+ 9 x 6 SAE).
Leaflet: *No 3 – Devil's Lapful & Three Pikes* (Forest Enterprise Northumberland). A4/3. £0.50
(+ 9 x 4 SAE).

Kinder Dozen Challenge 269

Derbyshire *39 km / 24 miles*

A demanding challenge involving 10,000ft of ascent, circumnavigating Kinder Scout and ascending it on 12 occasions visiting such as Grindslow Knoll, Crowden Tower, Edale Cross, Crookstone Knoll, Druid's Stone and Ringing Roger.

Start and Finish:	Edale, Derbys	SK123860
Landranger maps:	110	
1 : 25,000 maps:	OL 1	

Publications, badges and certificates:
Booklet: *Kinder Dozen* (Ken Jones). 12pp; A5. Free (+ 9 x 6 SAE).
Certificate: (Ken Jones). Free (+ 9 x 6 strengthened SAE).

King Alfred's Way 270

Hants, Oxon, W Berks *112 km / 70 miles*

The Way links places connected with the Saxon King. Starting at the Wessex capital it passes through Wantage where he was born and finishes where he established a seat of learning which eventually became the University. The route includes riverside path, Watership Down, canal towpath, the Berkshire Downs and Abingdon.

Start:	Winchester, Hants	SU485293
Finish:	Oxford, Oxon	SP513062
Landranger maps:	164, 174, 185	
1 : 25,000 maps:	Ex 132, 144, 158, 170, 180	

Publications, badges and certificates:
Booklet: *King Alfred's Way* (Peter Radburn) 1998. 32pp; A5. £2.00 (+ 40p p&p).

Kingfisher Way 271

Beds, Herts *34 km / 21 miles*

The Way follows the course of the River Ivel from the source at Ivel Springs to where it meets the River Great Ouse, passing through the towns and villages of the Ivel Valley. The route links the Icknield Way path at Baldock with the Greensand Ridge Walk. The waymarked Navigator's Way (7 miles) based on Shefford and making use of the disused River Ivel Navigation, can be linked to the Kingfisher Way at Langford.

Start:	Baldock, Herts	TL248342
Finish:	Tempsford, Beds	TL162535
Landranger maps:	153	
1 : 25,000 maps:	Ex 193, 208	
Waymark:	Name and/or Kingfisher profile in blue	

Publications, badges and certificates:
Folder: *The Kingfisher Way* (Ivel Valley Countryside Project). 4 leaflets. Free (+ 9 x 4 SAE).
Leaflet: *The Navigator's Way* (Ivel Valley Countryside Project). Free (+ 9 x 4 SAE).

King's Way   272
Hants   *72 km / 45 miles*
A walk devised by the Hampshire Area RA in memory of Allan King, one of their early members. The route links the old Roman strongholds of Portchester and Winchester.

Start:	Portchester, Hants	SU625044
Finish:	Winchester, Hants	SU487293
Landranger maps:	185, 196	✔
1 : 25,000 maps:	Ex 119, 132	

Publications, badges and certificates:
Booklet: *King's Way* (RA Hampshire Area) 1995. ISBN 086146091X. 48pp; A5. £3.25 (+ 50p p&p).

Kinver Clamber   273
Worcs   *32 km / 20 miles*
From the edge of the Black Country, this walk uses forestry tracks, canal paths, open field-paths and ridge paths. It passes Enville with its Hall, Kinver Edge with its rock dwellings, Caunsall and Whittingham. It picks up the Roman Road to return to Stourbridge.

Start and Finish:	Stourbridge, Worcs	SO882840
Landranger maps:	138, 139	
1 : 25,000 maps:	Ex 219	

Publications, badges and certificates:
Looseleaf: *Kinver Clamber* (Eric Perks). 4pp; A4. Free (+ 9 x 6 SAE).
Badge and certificate: (Eric Perks). £2.00 (+ SAE) & £1.00 (+ 9 x 6 SAE).

Kirkby Moor Round & Burney   274
Cumbria   *29 km / 18 miles*
A route visiting High Bank House Moor, Winnow, Gray Crags, Cocklakes, Shooting House Hill, Burney Trig and Beckside Hall.

Start and Finish:	Kirkby Community Centre, Cumbria	SD232822
Landranger maps:	96	
1 : 25,000 maps:	OL 6	

Publications, badges and certificates:
Looseleaf: *Kirkby Moor Round & Burney* (Brian Richmond). Free (+ 9 x 4 SAE).
Badge & certificate: (Brian Richmond). £1.00 (+ SAE).

Kirklees Way   275
W Yorks   *118 km / 73 miles*
The Way presents a large circle around Huddersfield and mixes the exposed moorland tops with the industrial towns in the valleys crossing the Spen Valley to

Oakwell Hall, Dewsbury, Clayton West and the Holme Valley to Marsden. The publication incorporates information on completing the route as a whole. See Brighouse Boundary Walk and Colne Valley Circular Walk.

Start and Finish:	Scholes, W Yorks	SE167259
Landranger maps:	104,110	✔
1 : 25,000 maps:	Ex 288, 299 OL 21	
Waymark:	Named discs and blue letter K	

Publications, badges and certificates:
Booklet: *A Stroller's Guide to Walks along the Kirklees Way* by C. Dexter Ellis (Holmfirth Tourist Information Centre) 1991. 40pp; A5. £3.50 (incs p&p).

Knaresborough Round   276

N Yorks   *32 km / 20 miles*

A route passing through the Nidd Gorge and a succession of villages to the north and east of this historic town. It can be divided into two stages or linked with the Harrogate Ringway to form a 36-mile route.

Start and Finish:	Knaresborough, N Yorks	SE350565
Landranger maps:	99, 104, 105	✔
1 : 25,000 maps:	Ex 288, 289	
Waymark:	Named signposts	

Publications, badges and certificates:
Leaflet: *Knaresborough Round* (RA Harrogate Group). 4pp; A5. £0.30 (+ SAE).
Badge: (Joan Clack). £1.50 (+ SAE).

Lady Anne's Way   277

N Yorks, Cumbria   *161 km / 100 miles*

Lady Ann Clifford was born at Skipton Castle in 1590, the last in line of the great Clifford family. This walk is based on some of the routes taken by her whilst visiting the many important buildings of her estate. From the castle, the valleys of Wharfedale and Wensleydale are explored before traversing the high-level Lady Anne's Highway at Abbotside Fells, to Mallerstang and the Eden Valley, passing the castles of Pendragon, Brough and Brougham Castle, where she died.

Start:	Skipton, N Yorks	SD990519
Finish:	Penrith, Cumbria	NY515305
Landranger maps:	90, 91, 98, 103, 104	
1 : 25,000 maps:	OL 2, 5, 19, 30	

Publications, badges and certificates:
Paperback: *Lady Anne's Way* by Sheila Gordon (Hillside Publications) 1995. ISBN 1870141350. 96pp; 115 x 175. £5.99 (+ 60p p&p).
Badge: (Sheila Gordon). £2.25 (post free).

Lake to Lake Walk 278

Cumbria, Durham, Northumberland   *267 km / 166 miles*

From Lakeland the route takes a line through Appleby and Brough to the Pennines then strikes north through Middleton in Teesdale, Allenheads, Allendale and Bellingham, crossing Hadrian's Wall near to Chester's Fort. In effect, the route links Lake Windermere with Kielder Water.

Start:	Bowness, Cumbria	SD403967
Finish:	Falstone, Northumbria	NY725875
Landranger maps:	80, 87, 90, 91, 92, 97	
1 : 25,000 maps:	OL 5, 7, 31, 42, 43	

Publications, badges and certificates:
Paperback: *The Lake to Lake Walk* by Alistair Wallace (MC Publications). ISBN 1841040061. 156pp; 150 x 210. £7.50 (+ £1.00 p&p).

Lakeland Challenge Walk 279

Cumbria   *29 km / 18 miles*

A tough 6,000ft ascent of ten Lakeland peaks in a circular walk from Langdale, firstly via Stickle Tarn and the Langdale Pikes to Esk Hause, followed by the ascent of Scafell Pike, returning via Bowfell, Crinkle Crags and Pike of Blisco.

Start and Finish:	Dungeon Ghyll, Cumbria	NY295066
Landranger maps:	89, 90	
1 : 25,000 maps:	OL 4, 6	

Publications, badges and certificates:
Booklet: *Lakeland Challenge Walk* by John Merrill (Walk & Write Ltd). ISBN 0907496504. 32pp; A5. £3.95 (+ 75p p&p).
Badge and certificate: (Walk & Write Ltd). £3.50 (incs p&p).

Lakeland Heritage Trail 280

Cumbria   *27 km / 17 miles*

A route designed to be completed in stages, following paths and fells, and visiting Grange in Borrowdale, Castle Crag, Ashness Bridge and Surprise View.

Start and Finish:	Moot Hall, Keswick, Cumbria	NY266235
Landranger maps:	89	
1 : 25,000 maps:	OL 4	

Publications, badges and certificates:
Looseleaf: *Lakeland Heritage Trail* (Tony Wimbush). Free (+ 9 x 4 SAE).
Badge and certificate: (Tony Wimbush). £2.50 & £0.50 (+ 9 x 4 SAE) – proceeds go to charity.

Lakeland Mountain Heritage Trail 281

Cumbria   *40 km / 25 miles*

A strenuous circuit of the Derwent Fells including Causey Pike, Cragg Hill, Buttermere, Robinson and Hindscarth, with 8000ft of ascent. The route provides an enlarged and high level alternative to the Lakeland Heritage Trail.

Start and Finish:	Keswick Moot Hall, Cumbria	NY266235
Landranger maps:	89	
1 : 25,000 maps:	OL 4	

Publications, badges and certificates:
Looseleaf: *Lakeland Mountain Heritage Trail* (Tony Wimbush). Free (+ 9 x 4 SAE).
Badge & certificate: (Tony Wimbush). £2.50 & £0.50 (+ 9 x 4 SAE) – proceeds go to charity.

Lakeland Top Ten   282
Cumbria   *91 km / 57 miles*

A route taking in 30,100ft of ascent in reaching the ten highest tops of the Lake
District, a challenge not to be under-estimated.

Start and Finish:	Thirlmere Bridge End, Cumbria	NY315192
Landranger maps:	89, 90	
1 : 25,000 maps:	OL 4, 5, 6	

Publications, badges and certificates:
Paperback: *The Lakeland Top Ten* by Brian Smailes (Challenge Publications) 1997. ISBN
0952690039. 72pp; 125 x 185. £6.50 (incs p&p).
Badge and certificate: (Challenge Publications). £3.30 & £0.55 (incs p&p).

Lakeland Tour   283
Cumbria   *167 km / 104 miles*

A route taking in Patterdale, Derwentwater, Ennerdale, Eskdale, Borrowdale and
Dunnerdale. The publication describes the main (high level) route, and also
includes a low level alternative (98 miles).

Start:	Staveley, Cumbria	SD469982
Finish:	Ambleside, Cumbria	NY376045
Landranger maps:	89, 90, 97	
1 : 25,000 maps:	OL 4, 5, 6, 7	

Publications, badges and certificates:
Paperback: A Walking Tour of Lakeland (Paul Buttle) 1997. ISBN 0951934511. 96pp; 198 x 128.
£2.00 (incs p&p).

Lakes & Tarns – Eastern Lakeland   284
Cumbria   *43 km / 27 miles*

A route devised to take advantage of the youth hostels at Windermere, Patterdale
and Grasmere, passing through remote valleys and over high passes.

Start and Finish:	Windermere Youth Hostel, Cumbria	SD405013
Landranger maps:	90	
1 : 25,000 maps:	OL 5, 7	

Publications, badges and certificates:
Booklet: *Lakes and Tarns of Eastern Lakeland* by Martin Hanks (YHA Northern Region). 16pp;
A5. £1.95 (incs p&p).
Booklet: *Booking Bureau – Youth Hostels* (YHA Northern Region) Annual. 20pp;
A5. Free.

Lambourn Valley Way   285

Oxon, W Berks   *35 km / 22 miles*

The Way runs from the Berkshire Downs near the Uffington White Horse to Newbury
along the valley of the River Lambourn connecting the Ridgeway with the Kennet
valley. The route passes through the villages of Lambourn, East Garston, Great
Shefford and Boxford.

Start:	Uffington Castle, Oxon	SU300863
Finish:	Newbury, W Berks	SU471671
Landranger maps:	174	✔
1 : 25,000 maps:	Ex 158, 170	
Waymark:	Named discs and posts	

Publications, badges and certificates:
Leaflet: *Lambourn Valley Way* (West Berkshire District Council) 2001. A4/3. Free (+ SAE).

Lancashire Coastal Way   286

Lancs   *106 km / 66 miles*

As the name suggests, a route along the coast but with the odd diversion where
necessary.

Start:	Silverdale, Lancs	SD461749
Finish:	Freckleton, Lancs	SD437297
Landranger maps:	97, 102	✔
1 : 25,000 maps:	Ex 286, 296 OL 41	
Waymark:	Gull & wave logo	

Publications, badges and certificates:
Leaflet: *Lancashire Coastal Way* (Lancashire County Council). A5. Free.

Lancashire Trail   287

Gtr Man, Lancs, Merseyside, N Yorks   *113 km / 70 miles*

A route linking industrial Lancashire with the Pennine Way National Trail, the
Lancashire Trail passes Billinge, Abbey Lakes, the viewpoints of Ashurst Beacon
and Harrock Hill, Coppull Moor, Blackrod and Rivington Pike. A relatively low-lying
section follows via Abbey village and Mellor before reaching Whalley and the climb
to Pendle Hill, from where the route descends to Barley. Link routes from the
centres of Wigan, Bolton and Burnley, to and from the Ribble Way at Sawley, and to
the Sandstone Trail are described.

Start:	St Helens, Merseyside	SJ512956
Finish:	Thornton-in-Craven, N Yorks	SD906484
Landranger maps:	102, 103, 108, 109	
1 : 25,000 maps:	Ex 275, 276, 287 OL 21	

Publications, badges and certificates:
Paperback: *The Lancashire Trail* by Brian Smailes (Challenge Publications) 2002. ISBN 1903568100. 125 x 185. Details TBA.

Lancashire-Lakeland Link 288
Lancs, Cumbria   *114 km / 71 miles*

The route takes in canal towpaths, former railway lines, parkland and riverside, providing easy access to castles, pele towers and mansions. The route links with the Dales Way at Burneside.

Start:	Preston, Lancs	SD542297
Finish:	Windermere, Cumbria	SD414986
Landranger maps:	97, 102	
1 : 25,000 maps:	Ex 286 OL 7, 41	

Publications, badges and certificates:
Paperback: *The Lancashire-Lakeland Link* (Jack Jowett) 1994. ISBN 1873888600. 96pp; 122 x 182. £4.99 (+ 50p p&p).

Lancaster Canal 289
Cumbria, Lancs   *91 km / 57 miles*

A towpath walk from the Ribble across the Fylde and through Lancaster and Carnforth to the Lake District.

Start:	Preston, Lancs	SD526303
Finish:	Kendal, Cumbria	SD520931
Landranger maps:	97, 102	
1 : 25,000 maps:	Ex 286 OL 7, 41	

Publications, badges and certificates:
Paperback: *A Walker's Guide to the Lancaster Canal* by Robert Swain (Cicerone Press) 1990. ISBN 1852840552. 124pp; 116 x 176. £5.99.
Leaflet: *The Lancaster Canal* (Lancaster to Kendal) (South Lakeland District Council). 12pp; A4/3. Free (+ 9 x 4 SAE).

Land's End Round 290
Cornwall   *80 km / 50 miles*

A walk combining coastal scenery with an attractive rural link to create a challenging circuit. Starting from the south Cornish coast, the route crosses the county to the north coast at St Ives. The South West Coast Path National Trail is then followed around Land's End back to Mousehole.

Start and Finish:	Mousehole, Cornwall	SW470264
Landranger maps:	203	
1 : 25,000 maps:	Ex 102	

Publications, badges and certificates:
Looseleaf: *The Land's End Round* (Dave and Anne Carrivick). 3pp; A4. Free (+ 9 x 4 SAE).
Certificate: (Dave and Anne Carrivick). £1.00 (post free).

Land's End to John O'Groats 291

Numerous 1368 km / 850 miles

There is no set route for this, one of the ultimate walking challenges in the UK and whatever the chosen route, it will not be less than 850 miles. There are inherent dangers in using lanes/roads but there are various established long distance routes of which advantage can be taken to avoid such hazards. A publication from Andrew McCloy (listed) describes a walk around the coast of England & Wales (approx 2970 miles/4780 km) which provides additional alternatives in reaching the border with Scotland.

Start:	Land's End, Cornwall	SW343251
Finish:	John O'Groats, Highland	ND379734
Landranger maps:	Numerous	
1 : 25,000 maps:	Numerous	

Publications, badges and certificates:
Paperback: *The Land's End to John O'Groats Walk* by Andrew McCloy (Cordee Ltd) 2001. ISBN 1871890594. £10.99.
Booklet: *Land's End to John O'Groats – the Golden Journey – How you can walk it* (Alan Profitt). 66pp; A4. £8.00 (incs p&p).
Paperback: *John O'Groats to Land's End – A Walkers, Cyclists and Motorists Guide* by Brian Smailes (Challenge Publications) 1999. ISBN 0952690047. 90pp; 125 x 185. £7.50 (incs p&p).
Paperback: *Coastwalk: Walking the Coastline of England & Wales* (Andrew McCloy) 1997. ISBN 0340657405. 266pp; 128 x 198. £7.99 (incs p&p).

Land's End Trail 292

Cornwall, Devon, Somers, Wilts 480 km / 298 miles

A route from the Ridgeway at Avebury connecting with other long distance routes as it takes an inland, generally high-level line through the South West peninsula. It provides an alternative option to those routes often used in linking Land's End with England's central ways. Route not included in Map Section. See also Celtic Way.

Start:	Avebury, Wilts	SU909696
Finish:	Land's End, Cornwall	SW343251
Landranger maps:	173, 180, 181, 182, 183, 185, 191, 200, 201, 203, 204	
1 : 25,000 maps:	Ex 102, 104, 106, 108, 109, 113, 127, 128, 130, 140,	
	141, 142, 143, 157 OL 9, 28	
Waymark:	Yellow chevron – sparingly and not on moorland	
	(Dartmoor, Exmoor, Bodmin, Penwith)	

Publications, badges and certificates:
Looseleaf: *The Land's End Trail – South to North* (R. Preston) 1998. 29pp; A4. £4.00 (incs p&p).
Looseleaf: *The Land's End Trail – North to South* (R. Preston) 1998. 25pp; A4. £4.00 (incs p&p).
Booklet: *The Land's End Trail – Accommodation Guide* (R. Preston) Annual. 11pp; A4. £1.00
(incs p&p).

Landsker Borderlands Trail · 293

Carms, Pembrokes   *96 km / 60 miles*

Landsker is an old Norse word for frontier. The route explores the rural area on the Pembrokeshire/Carmarthenshire border from Llanboidy and Efailwen in the north via Canaston Bridge on the Daugleddau to Landshipping and Lawrenny in the south, returning via Reynalton and Ludchurch. See South of the Landsker Trail.

Start and Finish:	Canaston Bridge, Pembrokes	SN067152
Landranger maps:	145, 157, 158	✔
1 : 25,000 maps:	Ex 177, 185 OL 35, 36	
Waymark:	Named disc with Celtic design for logo	

Publications, badges and certificates:
Booklet: *The Landsker Borderlands Trail* (SPARC) 2001. 28pp; A5. Free (incs p&p).

Langbaurgh Loop · 294

Cleveland   *61 km / 38 miles*

The route is along sandy coastland paths, high cliff edges, rich agricultural land, high rugged moors thick with heather, dense pine forests and ancient woods. Parts of the route are over little-used footpaths and rights of way, and some knowledge of map reading is required.

Start and Finish:	Saltburn-by-the-Sea, Cleveland	NZ668216
Landranger maps:	93, 94	
1 : 25,000 maps:	OL 26, 27	
Waymark:	Ellipse and callipers	

Publications, badges and certificates:
Leaflet: *Langbaurgh Loop* (Langbaurgh Loop Recorder). A4/3. Free (+ 9 x 4 SAE).
Badge and certificate: (Langbaurgh Loop Recorder). £2.50 (+ SAE).

Lapwing Walk · 295

Kent   *53 km / 33 miles*

The walk provides optional distance routes and includes use of parts of the North Downs Way (between Hollingbourne and Dunn Street) and the Greensand Way (between Hothfield and Sutton Valence) thus providing a link between the two. Leeds Castle is included in the route.

Start and Finish:	Hollingbourne, Kent	TQ845554
Landranger maps:	188, 189	
1 : 25,000 maps:	Ex 137, 148	

| Waymark: | North Downs Way/Greensand Way/Shepherd Neame |
| | – name and logo |

Publications, badges and certificates:
Booklet: *The Lapwing Walk* (Kent County Council). ISBN 1901509192. 18pp; A5. £2.00 (post free).

Lea Valley Walk   296

Beds, Essex, Gtr London, Herts, Luton   *87 km / 54 miles*

A route on riverside paths, linking the Icknield Way Path with Dunstable Downs and London Docklands, following the course of the river, which is variously spelt Lee and Lea. It incorporates the Lee Navigation towpath, the Upper Lea Valley Walk, and the Cole Green Way west of Hertford. It passes the numerous reservoirs that line the valley through North London. At Hoddesdon, the Stort Navigation branches off to Harlow and Bishop's Stortford. The Beane Valley Walk (14 miles) from Walkern, near Stevenage, provides a route south to Hertford where it can be linked to the Lea Valley Walk. The Pymmes Brook Trail (10 miles and included on OS mapping) provides a link from Monken Hadley Common through Palmer's Green to the Lea Valley Walk at Pickett's Lock. The listed stripmap shows the Walk from Hertford to Bow Locks only. See Grand Union Canal Walk.

Start:	Leagrave, Beds	TL061249
Finish:	East India Dock, Gtr London	TQ382828
Landranger maps:	166, 176, 177	✔
1 : 25,000 maps:	Ex 162, 173, 174, 182, 193, 194	
Waymark:	Named discs with swan logo	

Publications, badges and certificates:
Paperback: *The Lea Valley Walk* by Leigh Hatts published by Cicerone Press (Lee Valley Park Authority) 2001. ISBN 1852843136. 128pp; 174 x 117. £7.99 (+ £1.00 p&p).
Leaflet: *The Rivers Lee & Stort* (British Waterways – Enfield). A5. Free (+ SAE).
Stripmap (folded): *Lee and Stort Navigations* (GEOprojects) 2000. ISBN 0863511317. 135 x 213. £4.00 (+ 50p p&p).
Leaflet: *Beane Valley Walk* (Hertfordshire County Council). A4/3. Free (+ SAE).
Leaflet: *Pymmes Brook Trail* (Barnet Council). A4/3. Free (+ SAE).

Lead Mining Trail   297

Durham   *38 km / 24 miles*

A convoluted walk through the Durham moors and valleys, visiting lead mining sites, using the tracks of the old packhorse trails.

Start:	Cowshill, Durham	NY856407
Finish:	Edmundbyers, Durham	NZ018501
Landranger maps:	87	
1 : 25,000 maps:	Ex 308	
Waymark:	Named posts	

Publications, badges and certificates:
Folder: *Lead Mining Trail* (Durham County Council) 1996. 3 leaflets; 125 x 210. £2.25 (+ 50p p&p).

Leadon Valley Walks 298

Herefs, Glos *112 km / 70 miles*

The 'Secret River' publication comprises fourteen walks, all but one of which are circular and most of which are linked, providing ways of traversing the Leadon Valley from the source of the river to its confluence with the Severn. The publication is so named as this river avoids towns and even villages of any size. At Dymock three additional circular walks are met. These are Poets' Paths I and II (both 8 miles) and the Dymock Daffodil Way (10 miles).

Start:	Evesbatch, Herefs	SO675481
Finish:	Over, Glos	SO817199
Landranger maps:	149, 150, 162	
1 : 25,000 maps:	Ex 179, 190, 202 OL 14	

Publications, badges and certificates:
Paperback (spiral bound): *Secret River* by Roy and Pat Palmer (Green Branch Press) 1998. ISBN 0952603128. 76pp; 152 x 210. £6.95 (post free).
Leaflet: *Poets' Path I* by Windcross Public Paths Group (Ledbury TIC) 1998. A6. 50p (+ 75p p&p) – cheques payable to Herefordshire Council.
Leaflet: *Poets' Path II* by Windcross Public Paths Group (Ledbury TIC) 1994. A6. 50p (+ 75p p&p) – cheques payable to Herefordshire Council.
Leaflet: *Dymock Daffodil Way* by Windcross Public Paths Group (Ledbury TIC). A6. 50p (+ 75p p&p) – cheques payable to Herefordshire Council.

Lecale Way 299

Down *48 km / 30 miles*

One of the official Waymarked Ways in Northern Ireland, the Way follows the footsteps of St Partick from his landing place on the shores of Strangford Lough – the largest sea lough in the British Isles – around the rocky coastline of the Irish Sea. Within the Lecale AONB there are views not only of Strangford Lough but of the Mourne Mountains and the Murlough Bay.

Start:	Raholf, Down	J535474
Finish:	Newcastle, Down	J375305
Landranger maps:	OS(NI) 21, 29	✔
1 : 25,000 maps:	Not applicable in NI	
Waymark:	Route name/walker outline on blue background	

Publications, badges and certificates:
Leaflet: *An Illustrated Guide to the Lecale Way* (Down District Council). £0.50 (+ 9 x 6 SAE).

Leeds and Liverpool Canal Walk 300

Gtr Man, Lancs, Merseyside, N Yorks, *203 km / 127 miles*
W Yorks

This cross-Pennine canal is the longest in Britain, taking 46 years to complete, and despite it linking many industrialised towns and cities there is a wide variety of scenery on offer. It crosses the Pennine watershed near to Barnoldswick where there is a link with the Pennine Way National Trail.

Start:	Leeds, W Yorks	SE293351
Finish:	Liverpool Stanley Dock, Merseyside	SJ343921
Landranger maps:	103, 104, 108, 109	
1 : 25,000 maps:	Ex 275, 276, 287, 288, 289, 297 OL 2, 21	

Publications, badges and certificates:
Stripmap (folded): *Leeds and Liverpool Canal* (GEOprojects) 2001. ISBN 0863511325. 135 x 213. £4.75.

Leeds Country Way   301

W Yorks   *96 km / 60 miles*

Curently the route makes use of rights of way in the Leeds and Wakefield city areas but by 2002 amendments to the route are to be made to contain the whole Way within the Leeds area, visiting such as the Harewood Estate and Barwick-in-Elmet.

Start and Finish:	Golden Acre Park, W Yorks	SE267417
Landranger maps:	104, 105	✔
1 : 25,000 maps:	Ex 288, 289, 297	
Waymark:	Yellow owl and letters LCW on olive green plaque	

Publications, badges and certificates:
Leaflets: *Leeds Country Way* (Leeds City Council). Details TBA in 2002.

Leicester Line Canal Walk   302

Derbys, Leicester, Leics, Northants, Notts   *126 km / 78 miles*

This walk comprises a trail along the towpaths of the Grand Union Canal Leicester Line, the River Soar Navigation and the Erewash Canal. It leaves the main Grand Union Canal at Norton Junction, goes through Leicester and Loughborough, crosses the Trent and Mersey Canal at Trent Lock and ends at Langley Mill. See also Grand Union Canal Walk and Trent & Mersey Canal Walk.

Start:	Norton Junction, Northants	SP602657
Finish:	Langley Mill, Derbys	SK453475
Landranger maps:	129, 140, 141, 152	
1 : 25,000 maps:	Ex 222, 223, 233, 245, 246, 260	

Publications, badges and certificates:
Stripmap (folded): *Grand Union Canal map 4: Leicester Line, Soar Navigation and Erewash Canal* (GEOprojects) 2001. ISBN 0863511449. 135 x 213. £4.75 (+ 50p p&p).

Leicestershire Jubilee Way   303

Leics, Lincs   *25 km / 16 miles*

The Way, devised to mark the Queen's Silver Jubilee, connects Melton Mowbray with the Viking Way at Woolsthorpe by following a meandering course across pasture and woodland and past old ironstone workings near Eaton before climbing through woods to Belvoir castle from where there are fine views over the Vale of

Belvoir. A 6 mile extension at the southern end of the Way will bring the route to the Leicestershire Round. The waymarked Mowbray Way (8 miles and included on OS mapping) from Scalford on the Jubilee Way provides a second link to the Viking Way at Buckminster.

Start:	Melton Mowbray, Leics	SK756191
Finish:	Woolsthorpe, Lincs	SK846387
Landranger maps:	129, 130	✔
1 : 25,000 maps:	Ex 246, 247, 260	
Waymark:	Orb, yellow on brown	

Publications, badges and certificates:
Leaflet: *Leicestershire Jubilee Way* (Leicestershire County Council). A4/3. £0.30.
Leaflet: *Mowbray Way* (Leicestershire County Council) 1994. A5. £0.40.

Leicestershire Round 304

Leics, Rutland   *163 km / 101 miles*

The Round is within easy reach of the market towns of Oakham, Melton Mowbray, Loughborough, Hinkley and Lutterworth and passes through some of the most beautiful and historically interesting parts of the county including Burrough Hill, Foxton Locks, High Cross, Bosworth battlefield and Charnwood Forest. There are links with the Charnwood Round and Ivanhoe Way. See Leicestershire Jubilee Way.

Start and Finish:	Burrough Hill, Leics	SK766115
Landranger maps:	129, 140, 141	✔
1 : 25,000 maps:	Ex 222, 223, 232, 233, 234, 245, 246	
Waymark:	Circle of brown arrows on standard waymarks	

Publications, badges and certificates:
Paperback: *The Leicestershire Round* (Leicestershire Footpath Association) 1996. ISBN 0850223903. 126pp; 176 x 115. £5.00 – cheques payable to Leicestershire Footpath Association.
Badge: (Leicestershire Footpath Association). £2.50 (+ SAE).

Leighton – Linslade Loop 305

Beds   *32 km / 20 miles*

A walk encircling Leighton Buzzard through woods, villages, fields and along a towpath. The walk connects with the Grand Union Canal Walk, the Oxbridge Walk and the Greensand Ridge Walk.

Start and Finish:	Heath and Reach	SP920294
Landranger maps:	165	
1 : 25,000 maps:	Ex 192	

Publications, badges and certificates:
Booklet: *Leighton Buzzard Millennium Walks* (RA Leighton Buzzard) 2000. 34pp; 296 x 140. Free (+ 1st class stamp).

Leland Trail 306
Somers *45 km / 28 miles*

A route through the rolling hills of Somerset from near Stourhead to near Stoke-sub-Hamdon following the route traversed by John Leland during his 16th century survey of Britain. It connects with the Liberty Trail at Ham Hill. See River Parrett Trail.

Start:	Alfred's Tower, Somers	ST745352
Finish:	Ham Hill, Somers	ST478172
Landranger maps:	183, 193	✔
1 : 25,000 maps:	Ex 129, 142	
Waymark:	Bust of John Leland	

Publications, badges and certificates:
Folder: *Leland Trail* (South Somerset District Council) 1997. 14pp; A5. £4.25 (+ 75p p&p).
Leaflet: *An Introduction to the Leland Trail* (South Somerset District Council) 1997. 210 x 150. Free (+ SAE).

Liberty Trail 307
Dorset, Somers *45 km / 28 miles*

Linking the Leland Trail with the South West Coast Path National Trail this route follows the footsteps of people who, in 1685, walked to join the protestant Monmouth rebellion at Lyme taking in Crewkerne and Forde Abbey. For the last stretch through Dorset into Lyme Regis via the Iron Age hillforts of Lamberts and Coneys Castles it is coincident with the Wessex Ridgeway. See River Parrett Trail.

Start:	Ham Hill, Somers	ST478172
Finish:	Lyme Regis, Dorset	SY347922
Landranger maps:	193	✔
1 : 25,000 maps:	Ex 116, 129	
Waymark:	Named signs	

Publications, badges and certificates:
Folder: *The Liberty Trail* (South Somerset District Council) 1996. A5. £4.25 (+ 75p p&p).

Limestone Dale Walk 308
Derbys, S Yorks *39 km / 24 miles*

A route through the limestone dales of the White Peak, via Cunning, Woo, Deep and Horseshoe Dales to Earl Sterndale, and then Dovedale to Hartington, Milldale and Mapleton.

Start:	Buxton, Derbys	SK060735
Finish:	Ashbourne, Derbys	SK178469
Landranger maps:	119, 128	
1 : 25,000 maps:	OL 24	

Publications, badges and certificates:
Booklet: *Peak District End to End Walks* by John Merrill (Walk & Write Ltd). ISBN 0907496393.
52pp; A5. £3.95 (+ 75p p&p).
Badge and certificate: (Walk & Write Ltd). £3.50 (incs p&p).

Limestone Link (Cotswolds to Mendips) 309
Bath NES, S Glos, Somers   *58 km / 36 miles*

A route from the Cotswold Way National Trail at Cold Ashton through St Catherine's valley, along the Kennet and Avon Canal to Dundas Aqueduct and then to the Mendip escarpment past Burrington Combe and Dolebury Warren to the finish where it links with the West Mendip Way (Mendip Ways).

Start:	Cold Ashton, S Glos	ST751728
Finish:	Shipham, Somerset	ST443572
Landranger maps:	172, 182	✔
1 : 25,000 maps:	Ex 141, 142, 155	
Waymark:	Ammonite logo	

Publications, badges and certificates:
Booklet: *The Limestone Link* (Yatton Ramblers) 1995. ISBN 0951134248. 66pp; A5. £3.30 (incs p&p).

Limestone Link (Cumbria) 310
Cumbria   *21 km / 13 miles*

The Link runs across the limestone country of South Cumbria with its nationally important flora, through the low wooded hills of the Arnside area, across the flat open mosses between Hale and Holme, and over the rocky fells of Clawthorpe and Hutton Roof.

Start:	Arnside, Cumbria	SD461788
Finish:	Kirkby Lonsdale, Cumbria	SD611789
Landranger maps:	97	✔
1 : 25,000 maps:	OL 2, 7	
Waymark:	Named discs	

Publications, badges and certificates:
Leaflet: *The Limestone Link* (South Lakeland District Council) 1994. 12pp; A4/3. Free (+ 9 x 4 SAE).

Limestone Loop 311
Derbys   *63 km / 39 miles*

A route devised to take advantage of the youth hostels at Buxton, Hartington, Youlegreave, and Bakewell, also visiting Hollinclough, Crowdicote and Monyash. There is a described alternative distance route of 27 miles.

Start and Finish:	Buxton Youth Hostel, Derbys	SK062722
Landranger maps:	119	
1 : 25,000 maps:	OL 24	

Publications, badges and certificates:
Booklet: *Limestone Loop* by Martyn Hanks (YHA Northern Region). 16pp; A5. £1.95 (incs p&p).
Booklet: *Booking Bureau – Youth Hostels* (YHA Northern Region) Annual. 20pp; A5. Free.

Limestone Way   312

Derbys, Staffs   *80 km / 50 miles*

The original route was extended with the former finish point of Matlock now the end of a spur to the main Way with a second link created to Ashbourne. Many of the more well-known locations of the Peak District are accommodated such as Monyash, Miller's Dale and Robin Hood's Stride. A connection with the Pennine Way National Trail can easily be achieved from Castleton and at Rocester it connects with the Staffordshire Way.

Start:	Castleton, Derbys	SK150829
Finish:	Rocester, Staffs	SK108392
Landranger maps:	110, 119, 128	✔
1 : 25,000 maps:	Ex 259 OL 1, 24	
Waymark:	Derby ram	

Publications, badges and certificates:
Paperback: *Walking the Limestone Way* by R. & E. Haydock and B. & D. Allen (Scarthin Books) 1997. ISBN 0907758924. 80pp; A5. £5.95 (+ 60p p&p).
Leaflet: *The Limestone Way – The Northern Section – Castleton to Matlock* (Derbyshire Dales District Council). A3/3. Free (+ 9 x 4 SAE).
Leaflet: *The Limestone Way – The Southern Section – Matlock to Rocester* (Derbyshire Dales District Council). A3/3. Free (+ 9 x 4 SAE).

Limey Way   313

Derbys   *64 km / 40 miles*

A meandering traverse of the limestone countryside of the White Peak area visiting twenty dales including Cave Dale, Monsal Dale, Deep Dale, Lathkill Dale and Dove Dale. See Cal-Der-Went Walk.

Start:	Castleton, Derbys	SK151828
Finish:	Thorpe, Derbys	SK157505
Landranger maps:	110, 119	
1 : 25,000 maps:	OL 24	

Publications, badges and certificates:
Booklet: *Limey Way* by J. N. Merrill (Walk & Write Ltd). ISBN 0907496830. 48pp; A5. £3.95 (+ 75p p&p).
Badge and certificate: (Walk & Write Ltd). £3.50 (incs p&p).

Lindsey Loop   314

Lincs   *153 km / 95 miles*

A figure-of eight loop, devised by the Lincoln Group of the RA, over the rounded chalk hills of the Lincolnshire Wolds and lowland farmland. It links the six market towns of Market Rasen, Spilsby, Alford, Caistor, Horncastle and Louth and is divided into eight sections. See Towers Way.

Start and Finish:	Market Rasen, Lincs	TF111897
Landranger maps:	113, 121, 122	
1 : 25,000 maps:	Ex 273, 274, 282, 283, 284	

Publications, badges and certificates:
Folder: *Lindsey Loop* (Brett Collier). ISBN 1901184137. 60pp; A5. £4.95 (+ 65p p&p).
Badge: (Brett Collier). £1.25 (+ SAE).

Little John Challenge Walk 315

Notts *45 km / 28 miles*

A walk through Sherwood Forest, the heart of Robin Hood country, which includes forests, gorges, meandering rivers and historic houses, and passes Church Warsop, Cuckney, Cresswell Crags, Clumber Park, Bothamsall and Ollerton.

Start and Finish:	Edwinstone, Notts	SK626669
Landranger maps:	120	
1 : 25,000 maps:	Ex 270	

Publications, badges and certificates:
Booklet: *The Little John Challenge Walk* by John Merrill (Walk & Write Ltd). ISBN 0907496466. 32pp; A5. £3.95 (+75p p&p).
Badge and certificate: (Walk & Write Ltd). £3.50 (incs p&p).

Llangollen Canal Walk 316

Cheshire, Denbighs, Wrexham *82 km / 51 miles*

This canal towpath walk initially follows the Shropshire Union Canal to Hurleston Junction where access is gained to the Llangollen Canal. Passing Whitchurch, Ellesmere, and the junction with the Montgomery Canal, it continues beyond Chirk, Trevor and Llangollen.

Start:	Nantwich, Cheshire	SJ650524
Finish:	Horseshoe Falls, Llangollen, Denbighs	SJ203434
Landranger maps:	117, 118, 125	
1 : 25,000 maps:	Ex 256, 257	

Publications, badges and certificates:
Booklet: *A Walker's Guide to the Llangollen Canal* by John N. Merrill (Walk & Write Ltd). ISBN 1841730173. 56pp; A5. £4.95 (+ 75p p&p).
Leaflet: *Llangollen Canal* (British Waterways – Border Counties). A5. Free.
Stripmap (folded): *Llangollen & Montgomery Canals* (GEOprojects) 1997. ISBN 0863510337. 135 x 213. £4.75 (+ 50p p&p).
Badge and certificate: (Walk & Write Ltd). £3.50 (incs p&p).

Lleyn Peninsula Coastal Path 317

Gwynedd *145 km / 90 miles*

Although the route is obliged to turn inland on occasions, the sea is rarely out of sight. South to Bardsey much of the ancient Pilgrim's Route is followed encountering many small churches on the way, and from Llanwnda to Penygroes part of the Lon Eifion route (12 miles from Caernarfon to Bryncir) is followed. Between Pwllheli and Portmadoc the village of Llanystumdwy, childhood home of David Lloyd George, is visited. At Portmadoc the Path links to the Meirionnydd Coast Walk. The route of the second listed publication starts at Clynnog Fawr rather than at Caernarfon. Some of this route is on busy roads and advice is given to use wheeled transport for these sections.

Start:	Caernarfon Castle	SH477626
Finish:	High Street, Portmadoc	SH570385
Landranger maps:	114, 123	
1 : 25,000 maps:	Ex 253, 254, 263	

Publications, badges and certificates:
Paperback: *The Lleyn Peninsula Coast Path* by John Cantrell (Cicerone Press) 1997. ISBN 1852842520. 160pp; 115 x 175. £8.99.
Leaflet: *Lleyn Pilgrims' Trail* by Gwynedd County Council (Pwllheli TIC). A5. Free (+ SAE).
Leaflet: *Gwynedd Recreational Routes – Lon Eifion and other routes* (Pwllheli TIC) 1997. A4/3. Free (+ SAE).

Loaves & Fishes Walk   318
N Yorks   *37 km / 23 miles*

A route over limestone country in and around the Ribble Valley visiting Stainforth, The Jubilee Cave and Langscar Gate which takes its name from the two hills along the way, the Sugar Loaf and Rye Loaf, and the leaping salmon at Stainforth Foss.

Start and Finish:	Settle, N Yorks	SD821635
Landranger maps:	98	
1 : 25,000 maps:	OL 2	

Publications, badges and certificates:
Looseleaf: *Loaves & Fishes Walk* (Ian Parker). 1pp. Free (+ 9 x 4 SAE).
Badge and certificate: (Ian Parker). £2.00 & 50p (+ 9 x 6 SAE).

Lochaber Walks   319
Highlands   *Various km / Various miles*

A series of ten walks of distances between 7 and 17 miles some of which can be connected. The various start points include Drimnin, Strontian, Polloch, Kinlochan and Glenfinnan.

Start:	Various
Finish:	Various
Landranger maps:	40, 41, 47, 49
1 : 25,000 maps:	Ex 374, 384, 390, 392 & others TBA 2002
Waymark:	Named posts

Publications, badges and certificates:
Leaflets: *Lochaber Walks* (Scottish Rights of Way and Access Society). 8 leaflets; A4/3. Free with two 1st class stamps.

London Countryway · 320

Bucks, Essex, Herts, Kent, Surrey, Thurrock,   *331 km / 206 miles*
Windsor M

A complete circuit around Greater London, between 13 to 31 miles from the centre and coming to within 1 mile of the boundary at the closest. The Way is over the woodlands and heathlands of Surrey and Berkshire, along canal towpaths to Windsor, from where the river Thames is followed to Maidenhead and Marlow. Here it turns to the Chiltern hills to West Wycombe and Great Missenden, and then follows a meandering route to Kings Langley, St Albans, Broxbourne, the Lea valley, Epping Forest and Theydon Bois. The route continues to Brentwood, over the Essex fens to cross the Thames via the Tilbury to Gravesend Ferry, before heading south and then west along the sandstone and chalk hills of Kent and Surrey. See Middlesex Greenway.

Start and Finish:	Box Hill, Surrey	TQ173513
Landranger maps:	165, 166, 167, 175, 176, 177, 186, 187, 188	
1 : 25,000 maps:	Ex 145, 146, 147, 160, 163, 172, 174, 175, 181, 182	

Publications, badges and certificates:
Looseleaf: *London Countryway Route Description* (Keith Chesterton) 1977. 32pp; A5. £1.50 (incs p&p). A revised edition of the former Constable book is being prepared.

London LOOP 321

Bucks, Essex, Gtr London, Herts, Surrey   *232 km / 144 miles*

A route introduced by the London Walking Forum which is a group comprising among others, representatives from all London Boroughs. Starting at the Thames at Erith and finishing on the opposite bank at Coldharbour the LOOP (London Outer Orbital Path) provides a green route through numerous woods, commons and parks. Paths alongside the Grand Union Canal and London rivers such as the Colne, Crane, Cray, Darent and Ingrebourne are used. The Thames Path National Trail is crossed at Kingston upon Thames and many other paths including the Vanguard Way, Three Forests Way and Hillingdon Trail are met along the route. The Dollis Valley Greenwalk (10 miles and included on OS mapping) provides a link between the London LOOP and the Capital Ring. The waymarked Watling Chase Timberland Trail (10 miles) from Elstree to Hatfield is coincident with the LOOP at its start. From Hatfield there is a described link to St Albans. Individual leaflets for the sections not included in the South London pack are available free from London Boroughs. Not all were published at the time of going to press. Check with the London Walking Forum website for availability.

Start:	Erith Riverside	TQ514782
Finish:	Coldharbour Point	TQ520788
Landranger maps:	176 ,177, 187	✔
1 : 25,000 maps:	Ex 146, 147, 160, 161, 162, 172, 173, 174, 175	
Waymark:	Named discs with Hovering Kestrel	
Path website:	www.londonwalking.com	

Publications, badges and certificates:
Softback: *The London LOOP* by David Sharp (Aurum Press) 2001. ISBN 1854107593. 168pp;
210 x 130. £12.99.
Leaflets: *LOOP Walks South London* (Downlands Project) 1999. ISBN 0953599108. 8 leaflets;
A4/3. £6.00 (+ 51p SAE). See description for availability of leaflets.
Leaflet: *Dollis Valley Greenwalk* (Barnet Council). A4/3. Free (+ SAE).
Leaflet: *Watling Chase Timberland Trail* (Watling Chase Community Forest) 2002. Free (+ SAE)
– other details to be announced.

Longshaw Limber   322

Derbys   *48 km / 30 miles*

A high level route taking in Stanage Edge, Win Hill, Curbar Edge and White Edge.

Start and Finish:	Longshaw, Derbys	SK267801
Landranger maps:	110, 119	
1 : 25,000 maps:	OL 1, 24	
Path website:	www.paulpugh.co.uk/longshawlimber	

Publications, badges and certificates:
Booklet: *The Longshaw Limber* (Paul Pugh). A5. Free (+ 9 x 6 SAE).
Badge and certificate: (Paul Pugh). £2.50 (+ 9 x 6 SAE).

Lower Dales Three Hostels Walk   323

N Yorks   *51 km / 32 miles*

A route based on the youth hostels at Kettlewell, Linton and Malham taking in
some of the finest scenery in this popular part of the Yorkshire Dales National Park.

Start and Finish:	Kettlewell, N Yorks	SD971724
Landranger maps:	98	
1 : 25,000 maps:	OL 2, 30	

Publications, badges and certificates:
Booklet: *Lower Dales Three Hostels Walk* by Martyn Hanks (YHA Northern Region). 16pp; A4.
£1.95 (incs p&p).
Booklet: *Booking Bureau – Youth Hostels* (YHA Northern Region) Annual. 20pp; A5. Free.

Lune Valley Ramble   324

Lancs   *27 km / 17 miles*

A route following the course of the River Lune passing close to Aughton, Arkholme,
Newton and Whittington.

Start:	Lancaster Railway Station, Lancs	SD473617
Finish:	Kirkby Lonsdale, Lancs	SD615783
Landranger maps:	97	✔
1 : 25,000 maps:	OL 2, 41	
Waymark:	Named signposts	

Publications, badges and certificates:
Booklet: *Lune Valley Ramble* (Lancaster City Council). 12pp; A5. Free (+ SAE).

Lunesdale Walk 325

Lancashire *59 km / 37 miles*

From Carnforth the Lancaster Canal is followed to Capernwray, where the route traces a figure-of-eight line through Swarthdale, Melling, Roeburndale, Hornby, Arkholme and back to Capernwray and the finish. The crossing-over point is at Loyn Bridge on the River Lune near to Hornby. The Carnforth Canal Walks publication describes three short circular walks between Carnforth and Capernway providing alternative routes between those locations.

Start and Finish:	Carnforth Railway Station, Lancs	SD497708
Landranger maps:	97	
1 : 25,000 maps:	OL 41	
Waymark:	Named signs	

Publications, badges and certificates:
Booklet: *The Lunesdale Walk* (Lancaster City Council). 20pp; A5. Free.
Booklet: *Carnforth Canal Walks* (Lancaster City Council). 16pp; A5. Free.

Lyke Wake Walk 326

N Yorks *63 km / 39 miles*

This classic route was pioneered by the late Bill Cowley in 1955 when much of the route was undefined and whilst this is not now the case, the route provides a strenuous challenge. In the early stages it is coincident in parts with the Cleveland Way National Trail and the Coast to Coast route. It has suffered from over-use and subsequent erosion. In an effort to ease the use of the route the Shepherd's Round (40 miles) was devised to provide a strenuous circular challenge from Scarth Nick.

Start:	Scarth Wood Moor, Osmotherley, N Yorks	SE469994
Finish:	Ravenscar, N Yorks	NZ971012
Landranger maps:	93, 94, 99	
1 : 25,000 maps:	OL 26, 27	
Path website:	www.lykewakewalk.co.uk	

Publications, badges and certificates:
Paperback: *Lyke Wake Walk – The Official Guide* by Paul Sherwood (Dalesman Publishing Co Ltd) 2001. ISBN 1855681919. 48pp; 120 x 185. £2.99 (+ 50p p&p from Lyke Wake Club).
Paperback: *The Novices Guide to Completing the Lyke Wake Walk* by Brian Smailes (Challenge Publications). ISBN 0952690012. 125 x 185. £3.25 (incs p&p).
Paperback: *The Lyke Wake Walk in Quarter Mile Steps* by Jim Goodman (Minerva Press) 1997. ISBN 1861063687. 54pp; A5. £9.99.
Leaflet: *Shepherd's Round* (Lyke Wake Club). A4/3. £0.25 (+ 9 x 4 SAE).
Badge and certificate: *Lyke Wake Walk* (Lyke Wake Club). £1.50 (+ SAE) & £0.50 (+ SAE).
Badge: Shepherd's Round (Lyke Wake Club). £1.50 (+ SAE).

Macclesfield & Peak Forest Canals 327

Cheshire, Derbys, Gtr Man, Lancs, Staffs *42 km / 26 miles*

Linking with the Trent & Mersey Canal at Kidsgrove, the Macclesfield Canal takes a line through Congleton, Macclesfield and Bollington. At Marple, it links with the

Peak Forest Canal which runs for 14 miles between Whaley Bridge and Ashton Under Lyne.

Start:	Kidsgrove, Staffs	SJ834545
Finish:	Marple, Gtr Man	SJ960875
Landranger maps:	109, 110, 118	
1 : 25,000 maps:	Ex 268, 277 OL 1, 24	

Publications, badges and certificates:
Stripmap (folded): *Macclesfield & Peak Forest Canals* (GEOprojects) 2001. ISBN 0863511406. 135 x 213. £4.00.

Macmillan Way   328

Dorset, Glos, Leics, Lincs, Northants, Oxon,   467 km / 290 miles
Rutland, Somers, Warks, Wilts

A route devised to raise funds for the Macmillan Cancer Relief and to which all proceeds are donated. It runs along sea banks and river banks, across the Lincolnshire fens via Stamford, eventually to Abbotsbury on the Dorset Coast. It provides a link with the Viking Way at Oakham, the Thames Path National Trail near Thames Head and with the South West Coast Path National Trail at the finish. See Macmillan Way West, Cotswold Round and Dorset Jubilee and Warwickshire Villages Trails.

Start:	Boston, Lincs	TF327442
Finish:	Abbotsbury, Dorset	SY560845
Landranger maps:	130, 131, 141, 142, 151, 152, 162, 163,	
	172, 173, 183, 194	✔
1 : 25,000 maps:	Ex 117, 129, 142, 143, 156, 168, 179, 191, 206, 207,	
	223, 234, 235, 249, 261 OL 15, 45	
Waymark:	Green bow, walk name and the words – Across	
	Country for Cancer Care (both directions)	
User group:	Macmillan Way Association	

Publications, badges and certificates:
Paperback: *The Macmillan Way* by Peter Titchmarsh (Macmillan Way Association) 2000. ISBN 0952685124. 128pp; 134 x 215. £9.00 (incs p&p).
Booklet: *South to North Supplement* by Peter Titchmarsh (Macmillan Way Association) 2000. 26pp; A4. £4.50 (incs p&p).
Leaflet: *The Macmillan Way* (Macmillan Way Association). A4/3. Free.
Booklet: *The Macmillan Way Planner & Accommodation Guide – Boston to Abbotsbury* by Peter Titchmarsh (Macmillan Way Association). 12pp; A4. £2.75 (incs p&p).
Badge and certificate: (Macmillan Way Association). £2.50 & Free (+ SAE).

Macmillan Way West   329

Somers, Devon   164 km / 102 miles

A branch of the main Macmillan Way. All proceeds are donated to Macmillan Cancer Relief. From the main Macmillan Way at Castle Cary it goes across the Somerset Levels and along the Quantocks and can be linked with the South West Coast Path

National Trail at Minehead. It then crosses Exmoor and follows the Tarka Trail to Barnstaple, again linking with the South West Coast Path.

Start:	Castle Cary, Somers	ST640323
Finish:	Barnstaple, Devon	SS558328
Landranger maps:	180, 181, 182, 183, 193	
1 : 25,000 maps:	Ex 128, 129, 140, 141, 142 OL 9	
Waymark:	Green bow, walk name and the words – Across Country for Cancer Care (both directions)	
User group:	Macmillan Way Association	

Publications, badges and certificates:
Booklet: *Macmillan Way West* (Macmillan Way Association) 2001. ISBN 0952685132. 56pp; A5. £6.25 (incs p&p).
Booklet: *Macmillan Way West Planner* (Macmillan Way Association). 8pp; A4. £2.25 (incs p&p).
Leaflet: *Macmillan Way West* (Macmillan Way Association). A4/3. Free.
Badge and certificate: (Macmillan Way Association). £2.50 & free (+ SAE).

Maelor Way   330
Cheshire, Wrexham, Shrops   38 km / 24 miles

The Way links the Sandstone Trail, South Cheshire Way, Marches Way and Shropshire Way at Grindley Brook, to the Offa's Dyke Path National Trail at Chirk. It crosses farmland to Hanmer Mere and Overton, then follows woodland trails alongside the Rivers Dee and Ceiriog to Chirk.

Start:	Grindley Brook, Cheshire	SJ522433
Finish:	Bronygarth, Shrops	SJ263375
Landranger maps:	117, 126	✔
1 : 25,000 maps:	Ex 240, 256, 257	
Waymark:	MW monogram as arrow	

Publications, badges and certificates:
Paperback: *Guide to the Maelor Way* by Gordon Emery (Gordon Emery) 1991. ISBN 1872265987. 126pp; A5. £7.95 (incs p&p). Annual update (Free + SAE).
Leaflet: *The Maelor Way* (Wrexham County Borough Council) 1997. A4/3. Free.

Maltby Circular Walk   331
South Yorks   24 km / 15 miles

Based on the area to the south of Maltby, the walk visits Hooton Levitt, Laughten-en-le-Morthern, Letwell and Firbeck. It passes through ancient woodlands, limestone gorges and historical heritage of the area.

Start and Finish:	Roche Abbey, South Yorks	SK545898
Landranger maps:	111	
1 : 25,000 maps:	Ex 279	

Publications, badges and certificates:
Leaflet: *Maltby Area Circular Walk* (Rotherham Tourist Information Centre). A4/3. Free.

Malvern Hills Challenge Walk   332

Herefs, Worcs   *32 km / 20 miles*

Involving 3,000ft of ascent, this walk around the Malvern Hills heads south via Little Malvern on the lower slopes and returns north along the ridge.

Start and Finish:	Old Wyche, Malvern, Worcs	SO773442
Landranger maps:	150	
1 : 25,000 maps:	Ex 190	

Publications, badges and certificates:
Booklet: *The Malvern Hills Challenge Walk* by John Merrill (Walk & Write Ltd). ISBN 0907496954. 32pp; A5. £3.95 (+ 75p p&p).
Badge and certificate: (Walk & Write Ltd). £3.50 (incs p&p).

Malvern Link   333

Worcs   *72 km / 44 miles*

This route links the North Worcestershire Path with the Worcestershire Way, with a blend of fieldpaths, country lanes, woodland, parkland, canal and riverside scenery.

Start:	Forhill, Worcs	SP055755
Finish:	The Gullet, Worcs	SO756380
Landranger maps:	139, 150	
1 : 25,000 maps:	Ex 190, 204, 220	

Publications, badges and certificates:
Looseleaf: *Malvern Link* by Dave Irons (Dave Irons) 2001. 9pp; A4. £1.50 (incs p&p).

Manorlands Meander   334

West Yorks   *29 km / 18 miles*

A contrasting route of moor and valley over Penistone Hill, through Oxenhope and passing the Hewenden reservoir and railway viaduct and the waterfalls of Goitstock. It is part of the South Pennine Twin Challenge – see Hebden Valleys Heritage Trek. Proceeds from sales are donated to the Manorlands Hospice.

Start and Finish:	Haworth Tourist Information	
	Centre, West Yorks	SD030372
Landranger maps:	104	
1 : 25,000 maps:	OL 21	

Publications, badges and certificates:
Booklet: *Manorlands Meander* (Tony Wimbush). £2.00 (+ 60p p&p) – cheques payable to W. A. Wimbush.
Badge & certificate: (Tony Wimbush). Details from Tony Wimbush.

Mansell Way 335

Essex   *32 km / 20 miles*

The Way is dedicated to the memory of Dennis Mansell, photographer, journalist and hill walker. Using a short section of the Flitch Way (see Forest Way), this walk, never more than three miles from the centre of Braintree, visits the valleys through which the Rivers Pant, Blackwater and Brain flow.

Start and Finish:	Braintree, Essex	TL761228
Landranger maps:	167	
1 : 25,000 maps:	Ex 195	

Publications, badges and certificates:
Booklet: *The Mansell Way* by Edgar Eastall and John Spratling (Braintree & District Outdoor Pursuits) 1993. 18pp; A5. £1.00 (+ A5 SAE).

Marches Way 336

Caerphilly, Cardiff, Cheshire, Herefs,   *329 km / 204 miles*
Mons, Newport, Shrops, Torfaen

A route through the borderland between England and Wales linking the two Roman forts, Chester and Caerleon, which guarded the Welsh border. It takes in towns and villages such as Wem, Shrewsbury, Leominster, Abergavenny and Pontypool, mainly following the course of the Whitchurch – Newport railway lines. See Maelor Way.

Start:	Chester, Cheshire	SJ413670
Finish:	Cardiff	ST180765
Landranger maps:	117, 126, 138, 149, 161, 171	✔
1 : 25,000 maps:	Ex 151, 152, 166, 189, 202, 203, 217, 241, 257, 266	
	OL 13	
Waymark:	Named discs in Cheshire only	

Publications, badges and certificates:
No publications: on OS mapping.

Marriott's Way 337

Norfolk   *34 km / 21 miles*

A peaceful and secluded walk along a former railway line near to the River Wensum. At Hellesdon it can be linked with the Norwich Riverside Walk (5 miles; no publication), and at Aylsham to the Bure Valley Walk (9 miles and included on OS mapping; no publication) which, alongside the Bure Valley Railway, follows the River Bure through Coltishall to Wroxham. The Bickling Hall link path (1 mile; no publication), near Cawston can be used to connect with the Weavers Way. See Kett's Country Walk.

Start:	Hellesdon Bridge, Norfolk	TG198000
Finish:	Aylsham, Norfolk	TG195265
Landranger maps:	133, 134	✔

1 : 25,000 maps:	Ex 237, 238, 252	
Waymark:	Brown and cream coloured logo	

Publications, badges and certificates:
Leaflet: *Marriott's Way* (Norfolk County Council) 1996. A4/3. Free (+ SAE).

Medway Valley Walk 338

Kent, Medway *45 km / 28 miles*

A valley walk in west Kent, with interesting landscape, natural history and archaeology. It passes through a varied landscape of downland, woodland, orchards, hop gardens, meadows and farmland, lakes and marshland, unspoilt villages and historic towns. Links are made with the Greensand Way, North Downs Way, Saxon Shore Way and Wealdway. The Len Valley Walk (12 miles) connects with the Medway Valley Walk at Maidstone and following the course of the River Len also connects with the Stour Valley Walk (Kent) at Lenham, thus creating a waymarked 80 mile route between Tonbridge and the sea at Sandwich. The start of the walk is linked by the waymarked Eden Valley Walk (15 miles and on OS mapping) to the Vanguard Way at Haxted.

Start:	Tonbridge, Kent	TQ590465
Finish:	Rochester, Medway	TQ741688
Landranger maps:	178, 188	✔
1 : 25,000 maps:	Ex 136, 147, 148, 163	
Waymark:	Kingfisher logo & walk name	

Publications, badges and certificates:
Booklet: *Medway Valley Walk* by Kev Reynolds (Kent County Council). ISBN 1873010524. 92pp; 210 x 210. £5.00 (post free).
Booklet: *The Len Valley Walk* (Maidstone Borough Council). 24pp; A5. £3.00 (incs p&p).
Booklet: *Eden Valley Walk* (Kent County Council) 1991. ISBN 1873010060. 28pp; 210 x 210. £2.95 (post free).

Meirionnydd Coast Walk 339

Gwynedd *116 km / 72 miles*

This is a walk by standing stones, stone circles and holy wells. The end of the Dyfi Valley Way is passed near the start of the Walk and the Cambrian Way is met briefly at Barmouth Railway Bridge where pedestrians pay a toll. Barmouth and Harlech are visited and the walk links with the Lleyn Peninsula Coastal Path at its end. See Dyfi Valley Way.

Start:	Aberdyfi Railway Station	SN607961
Finish:	Portmadoc Railway Station	SH566392
Landranger maps:	124, 135	
1 : 25,000 maps:	OL 18, 23	

Publications, badges and certificates:
Paperback: *A Meirionnydd Coast Walk* by Laurence Main (Gwasg Carreg Gwalch) 2001. ISBN 0863816665. 115pp; 123 x 184. £4.50 (+ £1.00 p&p).

Mendip Ways 340

Somers, N Somers *79 km / 49 miles*

Comprising the West Mendip (30 miles) and the East Mendip (19 miles) Ways, there was involvement in their creation by Rotary Club members. The route of the West passes close to Cheddar Gorge and takes in Wookey Hole, that of the East passing Shepton Mallet. See Limestone Link (Cotswolds to Mendips).

Start:	Uphill, N Somers	ST315585
Finish:	Frome, Somers	ST777481
Landranger maps:	172, 182, 183	✔
1 : 25,000 maps:	Ex 141, 142, 153	
Waymark:	Mendip Way West – Rotary International logo;	
	Mendip Way East – Ash key logo	

Publications, badges and certificates:
Paperback: *Uphill to Frome* by David Wright (David Wright) 2000. ISBN 0953923703. 72pp; A5. £8.00 (incs p&p).
Booklet: *West Mendip Way* (official guide) by Andrew Eddy (Frome Tourist Information Centre) 1998. ISBN 0951036831. 50pp; A5. £3.50 (+ SAE).

Mid Suffolk Footpath 341

Suffolk *32 km / 20 miles*

The footpath broadly follows the valleys of the rivers Dove and Gipping via Eye, Thorndon and Mendlesham. The start of the walk connects with the Angles Way whilst at the end of the route is the waymarked Gipping Valley River Path (17 miles and on OS mapping) which takes the walker on to Ipswich.

Start:	Hoxne, Suffolk	TM184782
Finish:	Stowmarket Greens Meadow, Suffolk	TM042599
Landranger maps:	155, 156	✔
1 : 25,000 maps:	Ex 211, 230	
Waymark:	Named discs with poppy logo	

Publications, badges and certificates:
Folder: *The Mid Suffolk Footpath* (Mid Suffolk District Council) 1998. 5 leaflets; 229 x 127. £1.50 (incs p&p).
Leaflet: *Discover the Gipping Valley* (Suffolk County Council). A5. Free (+ SAE).

Middlesex Greenway 342

Essex, Gtr London, Surrey *69 km / 43 miles*

A route across almost the whole of the territorial county passing West Drayton, Uxbridge, Ruislip, Pinner, Mill Hill, Finchley and Enfield. It was designed to heighten public awareness of the former county and to help safeguard the Green Belt. There is a described link to the London Countryway. The publication comes with an update sheet describing minor route changes since 1990.

Start:	Staines, Surrey	TQ032725
Finish:	Waltham Abbey, Essex	TL376005
Landranger maps:	166, 176, 177	
1 : 25,000 maps:	Ex 160, 172, 173, 174	

Publications, badges and certificates:
Looseleaf: *The Middlesex Greenway* by Stephen J. Collins (Stephen J. Collins) 1990. 16pp; A4.
£1.00 (+ A4 SAE) – includes update sheet.

Middlewich Challenge Walk 343

Cheshire *35 km / 22 miles*

A figure-of-eight route taking in the Middlewich Canal which links the Trent &
Mersey and Shropshire Union Canals.

Start and Finish:	Church Minshull, Cheshire	SJ667606
Landranger maps:	118	
1 : 25,000 maps:	Ex 257, 267	

Publications, badges and certificates:
Booklet: *The Middlewich Challenge Walk* by John Merrill (Walk & Write Ltd). ISBN 1874754623.
32pp; A5. £3.95 (+ 75p p&p).
Badge and certificate: (Walk & Write Ltd). £3.50 (incs p&p).

Midshires Way 344

Bucks, Derbys, Gtr Man, Leics, Northants, *362 km / 225 miles*
Notts, Milton K

The Way, designed for multi-use, links the Ridgeway National Trail with the Trans
Pennine Trail. For the most part it follows bridleways and quiet lanes with, wherever
possible, alternative waymarked footpath routes provided for walkers. In
Derbyshire particularly, the bridleway development for other users has yet to be
completed. The Brampton Valley Way (14 miles) is used between Boughton
Crossing near Northampton and Little Bowden Crossing near Market Harborough.
From Whaley Bridge in Derbyshire to Compstall in Greater Manchester the route is
coincident with the Goyt Way (10 miles, no publication; see also E-Routes – E2).
After this, part of the Etherow-Goyt Valley Way is used to the finish. All three Ways
are named on OS mapping. See Etherow-Goyt Valley Way.

Start:	Bledlow, Bucks	SP770012
Finish:	Stockport, Gtr Man	SJ893903
Landranger maps:	109, 110, 119, 128, 129, 141, 152, 165	✔
1 : 25,000 maps:	Ex 181, 192, 207, 223, 233, 245, 246, 259, 260, 269	
	OL 1, 24	
Waymark:	Named discs with letters MW in linked acorn form	

Publications, badges and certificates:
Folder: *The Midshires Way* (Derbyshire County Council) 1994. 12pp; A5. £3.00 (+ 50p p&p) –
county sections from each Council: check price/availability with them.
Leaflet: *Brampton Valley Way* (Northamptonshire County Council) 1993. A4/3. £0.75 (+ 20p
p&p).

Millennium Way – Bradford　　　345

W Yorks　　　　　　　　　　　　　　　　*72 km / 45 miles*

A route within the Bradford Metropolitan boundary which visits many sites of interest
including Bronte Falls, Whitewells and Shipley Glen and also taking in Denholme,
Oxenhope and Silsden as it passes through woodland, farmland and moorland.

Start and Finish:	Bracken Hall, Shipley, W Yorks	SE132390
Landranger maps:	104	
1 : 25,000 maps:	Ex 288, 297 OL 21	
Waymark:	Named finger posts; named discs; yellow / blue arrows and 'MW'	

Publications, badges and certificates:
Booklet: *Bradford's Millennium Way* (Bradford Millennium Way Project). 24pp; A5. £1.99 (+ 9
x 6 SAE).

Millennium Way – Isle of Man　　　346

IoM　　　　　　　　　　　　　　　　*45 km / 28 miles*

Developed to celebrate the Manx Millennium, the 1000th anniversary of the
establishment of Tynwald, the Island's Parliament, the route is based on the Royal
Way, an ancient high-level route between Ramsey and the former capital,
Castletown. The Way crosses the island, climbing to open heather moorland on the
western slopes of Snaefell to reach the Way's highest point at 1,500ft. From here it
descends to Crosby and follows lowland paths, roads and the banks of the
Silverburn river through Ballasalla to the medieval castle of Rushen. From
Castletown the waymarked Herring Road/Bayr ny Skeddan (14 miles), which is also
included on OS mapping, provides a link to Peel. See Isle of Man Coast Path.

Start:	Sky Hill, IoM	SC432945
Finish:	Castletown, IoM	SC265675
Landranger maps:	95	✔
1 : 25,000 maps:	See publications for IoM North & South maps	
Waymark:	Stylized Legs of Man	

Publications, badges and certificates:
Paperback: *Isle of Man Coastal Walk: Raad ny Foillan* by Aileen Evans (Cicerone Press) 1999.
ISBN 1852842776. 152pp; 116 x 176. £7.99 – includes details of Isle of Man Millennium Way.
Looseleaf: *Millennium Way* (Isle of Man Department of Tourism & Leisure). Free.
Looseleaf: *Raad ny Foillan (Coastal Path) & Bayr ny Skeddan (Herring Road) and
Accommodation List* (Isle of Man Department of Tourism & Leisure). Free.
Maps: *Isle of Man: North & South – 1:25000* (Isle of Man Department of Tourism & Leisure)
1995. £6.00 (+ 50p p&p).

Millennium Way – Staffordshire　　　347

Staffordshire　　　　　　　　　　　　*56 km / 35 miles*

Spanning the width of the county, the route makes use of the Stafford – Newport
Greenway, farmland paths and canal towpaths as it passes through or close to

Stafford, Colwich, Rugeley, Yoxall and Barton Under Needwood. There is an intention to extend the route from Newport to Outwoods.

Start:	Outwoods, Staffs	SJ786187
Finish:	Burton upon Trent, Staffs	SK234234
Landranger maps:	127, 128	
1 : 25,000 maps:	Ex 242, 244, 245	
Waymark:	Red arrowhead on white background with rope knot and WMM	

Publications, badges and certificates:
Booklet (spiral bound): *The Way for the Millennium* (Staffordshire County Council). 52pp; A5. £3.50 (+ 50p p&p).
Leaflet: *The Staffordshire Way and Millennium Way – information/accommodation guide* (Staffordshire County Council). A5/4. Free (+ 9 x 6 SAE).

Millennium Way – York   348

N Yorks   *37 km / 23 miles*

The Way links the historic open strays of York crossing Hob Moor, Knavesmire, Fulford Ings, Walmgate Stray, Monk Stray, Bootham Stray and Clifton Ings providing opportunity to view the lesser known historic sites of interest in the City. The River Ouse is crossed by way of the Millennium Bridge.

Start and Finish:	Lendal Bridge, York, N Yorks	SE599519
Landranger maps:	105	
1 : 25,000 maps:	Ex 291	
Waymark:	Named fingerposts	

Publications, badges and certificates:
Folder: *Millennium Way* (York City Council). 6 leaflets; A5. £2.95 (+ 9 x 6 SAE).
Badge: (York City Council). £1.50 (+ 9 x 4 SAE).

Milton Keynes Boundary Walk   349

Bucks, Milton K   *96 km / 60 miles*

A route around the town boundary through the valleys of the Rivers Tove and Ouse. The landscape includes canal towpath, forest and thatched cottages. There is a link with the Swan's Way at Salcey Forest.

Start and Finish:	Stony Stratford, Bucks	SP788396
Landranger maps:	152, 153, 165	✔
1 : 25,000 maps:	Ex 192, 207, 208	

Publications, badges and certificates:
No publications: on OS mapping.

Mini-Alps   350

Worcs   *32 km / 20 miles*

The route takes in Worcestershire Beacon, Old Hollow, Whithams Hill, Hatfield Coppice and Herefordshire Beacon where it follows the ridge path.

Start and Finish:	Old Wyche, Malvern, Worcs	SO773442
Landranger maps:	150	
1 : 25,000 maps:	Ex 190	

Publications, badges and certificates:
Looseleaf: *Mini-Alps* (Eric Perks). 4pp; A4. Free (+ 9 x 6 SAE).
Badge and certificate: (Eric Perks). £2.00 (+ SAE) & £1.00 (+ 9 x 6 SAE).

Minster Way 351

E Yorks, N Yorks   *80 km / 50 miles*

The Way, linking the two famous medieval Minsters at Beverley and York, crosses farmland and the chalk hills of the Yorkshire Wolds. It follows the Wolds Way National Trail across Sylvan Dale before diverting to Millington, Bishop Wilton and Stamford Bridge. Here the River Derwent is followed before the Plain of York is crossed on field and woodland paths to meet and follow the River Ouse to the centre of York.

Start:	Beverley, E Yorks	TA038393
Finish:	York, N Yorks	SE603522
Landranger maps:	105, 106, 107	✔
1 : 25,000 maps:	Ex 290, 293, 294	
Waymark:	Letters MW on standard waymarks plus named signposts	

Publications, badges and certificates:
Booklet: *The Minster Way* (Ray Wallis). 46pp; A5. £4.00 (+ 55p p&p).
Badge: (Ray Wallis). £1.50 (+ SAE).

Monarch's Way 352

Bath NES, Brighton H, Bristol, Devon,   *981 km / 610 miles*
Dorset, E Sussex, Glos, Hants, N Somers,
S Glos, Shrops, Somers, Staffs, Warks, Wilts,
W Midlands, Worcs, W Sussex

The Way is based on the route taken by Charles II during his escape after the battle of Worcester in 1651, taking in Boscobel (**the** Royal Oak Tree), Stratford upon Avon, the Cotswolds, Mendips and the South Coast from Charmouth to Shoreham. The route takes in many historic buildings, features of interest and antiquity, with connections to numerous other long distance routes. In South Gloucestershire five of the thirteen Circular Rides in South Gloucestershire are encountered. These routes range from 8½ to 23½ miles and total 208 miles.

Start:	Worcester, Worcs	SO852544
Finish:	Shoreham-by-Sea, W Sussex	TQ237046
Landranger maps:	127, 138, 139, 150, 151, 163, 172, 173, 182, 183, 184, 185, 193, 194, 196, 197, 198	✔
1 : 25,000 maps:	Ex 116, 117, 119, 120, 121, 122, 129, 130, 132, 141, 142, 143, 154, 155, 167, 168, 204, 205, 218, 220, 221, 242, 244	

Waymark:	Name and crown in oak tree surmounted by ship
User group:	Monarch's Way Association

Publications, badges and certificates:
Paperback: *The Monarch's Way Book 1: Worcester to Stratford-upon-Avon* by Trevor Antill (Meridian Books) 1995. ISBN 1869922271. 112pp; 229 x 145. £5.95 (+ £1.00 p&p).
Paperback: *The Monarch's Way Book 2: Stratford-upon-Avon to Charmouth* by Trevor Antill (Meridian Books) 1995. ISBN 186992228X. 136pp; 229 x 145. £6.95 (+ £1.00 p&p).
Paperback: *The Monarch's Way Book 3: Charmouth to Shoreham* by Trevor Antill (Meridian Books) 1996. ISBN 1869922298. 136pp; 229 x 145. £6.95 (+ £1.00 p&p).
Certificates: (Monarch's Way Association). Free (+ 9 x 6 SAE) – available for each book section.
Leaflet: *The Monarch's Way Accommodation List* (B&B) (Monarch's Way Association) 1996. Free (+ SAE).
Leaflet: *The Monarch's Way Accommodation List* (camping) (Monarch's Way Association) 1996. Free (+ SAE).
Folder: *Circular Rides in South Gloucestershire* (South Gloucestershire Council) 2001. 13 leaflets; A4/3.

Montgomery Canal 353

Powys, Shrops 56 km / 35 miles

This partially restored canal runs from a junction with the busy Llangollen Canal to Newtown. The northern section crosses the North Shropshire Plain and the southern section goes through the Severn valley. Restoration is complete on about half of the canal.

Start:	Frankton Junction, Shrops	SJ371318
Finish:	Newtown, Powys	SO135925
Landranger maps:	126, 136	
1 : 25,000 maps:	Ex 215, 216, 240	

Publications, badges and certificates:
Leaflet: *Montgomery Canal* (Powys County Council). A4/3. £0.10 (+ SAE).
Leaflet: *Exploring the Montgomery Canal* (British Waterways – Border Counties). A5. Free.
Stripmap (folded): *Llangollen and Montgomery Canals* (GEOprojects) 1997. ISBN 0863510337. 135 x 213. £4.75 (+ 50p p&p).

Mortimer Trail 354

Herefs, Shrops 48 km / 30 miles

The Trail starts in Shropshire, but soon enters Herefordshire. It crosses the rivers Teme, Lugg and Arrow taking in the Mary Knoll Valley, the High Vinnals, Orleton Common, Croft Ambrey and Wapley hill fort and visits a number of villages on the route.

Start:	Ludlow, Shrops	SO510746
Finish:	Kington, Herefs	SO295567
Landranger maps:	137, 138, 148, 149	✔
1 : 25,000 maps:	Ex 201, 203	
Waymark:	Green/brown/yellow named disc with crown & shield logo	

Publications, badges and certificates:
Booklet: *The Mortimer Trail – Official Route Guide* (Leominster TIC) 2002. 48pp; 210 x 117. Cost TBA – cheques payable to Herefordshire County Council.
Booklet: *The Mortimer Trail* by Ian R. Jones (Ian R. Jones) 1997. 18pp; A5. £1.00 (+ 30p p&p).
Booklet: *The Mortimer Trail – Accommodation and Travel Guide* (Leominster TIC) 2002. A5. Cost TBA – cheques payable to Herefordshire County Council.

Moyle Way   355

Moyle   *32 km / 20 miles*

One of the official Waymarked Ways in Northern Ireland, the Way starts on the coast, heads around the forested slopes of Knocklayd and follows the River Glenshesk upstream. An ascent of Slieveanorra is followed by the boggy shoulder of Trostan. It connects with the Causeway Coast Path at Ballycastle.

Start:	Ballycastle, Moyle	J114407
Finish:	Glenariff, Moyle	J200208
Landranger maps:	(OSNI) 5, 9	
1 : 25,000 maps:	Not applicable in NI	
Waymark:	Route name/walker outline on blue background	

Publications, badges and certificates:
Leaflet: *The Moyle Way* (Moyle District Council). £0.50 (+ 9 x 6 SAE).

Mynydd Hiraethog & Denbigh Moors Footpath   356

Denbighs, Conwy   *64 km / 40 miles*

A walk through rural Wales taking in undulating moorland, riverside and forest paths as well as pastureland. See Clwydian Way.

Start:	Pentrefoelas, Conwy	SH874514
Finish:	Llanrhaedr, Denbighs	SJ082635
Landranger maps:	116	
1 : 25,000 maps:	Ex 264 OL 18	
Waymark:	Named discs with wall and tree design	

Publications, badges and certificates:
Looseleaf in plastic wallet: *Mynydd Hiraethog & Denbigh Moors Footpath Network* (Conwy County Borough or Denbighshire County Councils) 2000. ISBN 1840470046. 28pp; A5. £3.00 (+ B5 or larger SAE + 33/41p stamp) – cheques payable to relevant council.

Myrtle Meander   357

W Yorks   *40 km / 25 miles*

To the south of Bingley, the walk combines rarely used paths with more popular routes. Places visited include Egypt, World's End, Queensbury and Haworth.

Start and Finish:	Myrtle Park School, Bingley, W Yorks	SE108387
Landranger maps:	104	
1 : 25,000 maps:	Ex 288 OL 21	

Publications, badges and certificates:
Looseleaf: *Myrtle Meander* (Peter Bashforth). Free (+ 9 x 4 SAE).
Badge and certificate: (Peter Bashforth). £1.75 (+ SAE) & £0.25 (+ 9 x 6 SAE).

Nar Valley Way   358

Norfolk   *54 km / 34 miles*

A route contained almost entirely within the watershed of the River Nar, visiting
many attractive villages and historical sites. The walk links with the Peddars Way at
Castle Acre. An extension from Gressenhall into East Dereham is included. See also
Cromer to the M11, Iceni Way and Peddars Way.

Start:	King's Lynn, Norfolk	TF616198
Finish:	Gressenhall, Norfolk	TF975169
Landranger maps:	132, 143	✔
1 : 25,000 maps:	Ex 236, 238, 250	
Waymark:	Named signposts & white named discs	

Publications, badges and certificates:
Booklet: *Nar Valley Way* by C. Andrews & D. Dear (Pathway Publishing) 1999. ISBN
095266285X. 36pp; A5. £2.50 (incs p&p).
Leaflet: *Nar Valley Way* (Norfolk County Council). A5. £0.70 (+ SAE).

Navigation Way   359

W Midlands   *161 km / 100 miles*

A meandering towpath walk which passes through a mixture of urban and rural
areas and follows sections of the many canals in the area. The first loop follows the
towpaths of the Birmingham and Fazeley, Grand Union, Stratford-upon-Avon, and
Worcester and Birmingham Canals, returning to Gas Street Basin, with the second
loop along towpaths of parts of the Birmingham, Dudley, Stourbridge, Staffordshire
and Worcestershire, and Tame Valley Canals. The final section is along the Rushall
and Wyrley and Essington canals.

Start:	Birmingham, Gas Street Basin,	
	W Midlands	SP062867
Finish:	Chasewater, W Midlands	SK040070
Landranger maps:	138, 139	
1 : 25,000 maps:	Ex 219, 220	

Publications, badges and certificates:
Paperback: *The Navigation Way* by Peter Groves and Trevor Antill (Meridian Books) 1998. ISBN
1869922352. A5. £5.95.

Nene Way   360

Cambs, Lincs, Northants, Peterboro   *177 km / 110 miles*

A route along the Nene Valley including canalised riverbank passing through Northampton, Wellingborough, Oundle, Peterborough and Wisbech. At Badby the waymarked Knightley Way (12 miles and included on OS mapping) visits Foxley, Farthingstone and Fawsley Park to end at Greens Norton at the end of the Grafton Way (see North Bucks Way). At Sutton Bridge there is a link with the Peter Scott Walk (10 miles and on OS mapping). See also Fen Rivers Way.

Start:	Badby, Northants	SP560587
Finish:	Sutton Bridge, Lincs	TF482210
Landranger maps:	131, 141, 142, 143, 152, 153	✔
1 : 25,000 maps:	Ex 207, 223, 224, 227, 234, 235, 249	
Waymark:	Named signposts	

Publications, badges and certificates:

Folder: *Nene Way: A Northamptonshire County Path* (Northamptonshire County Council) 1990. A5. £3.00 (+ 40p p&p).
Leaflet: *Nene Way: A Cambridgeshire Country Walk* (Cambridgeshire County Council). A5. £0.30 (+ 50p p&p).
Leaflet: *Nene Way: A Peterborough Country Walk* (Peterborough City Council). A5. Free (+ 9 x 6 SAE).
Leaflet: *Knightley Way* (Northamptonshire County Council) 1998. A5. £0.75 (+ 20p p&p).

Nev Cole Way   361

Lincs   *93 km / 58 miles*

The way passes from the Jurassic scarp overlooking the River Trent, via the south bank of the Humber to Immingham and Grimsby. Here it turns inland into the gently sloping Lincolnshire Wolds, passing through several villages to Nettleton which provides a link with the Viking Way and which could be used to return north to Barton-upon-Humber. See Towers Way.

Start:	Burton upon Stather, Lincs	SE870178
Finish:	Nettleton, Lincs	TA112001
Landranger maps:	112, 113	
1 : 25,000 maps:	Ex 281, 284	
Waymark:	Named discs	

Publications, badges and certificates:

Booklet: *Nev Cole Way* (Wanderlust Rambling Club) 1991. ISBN 0951109227. 40pp; 147 x 206. £1.75 (+ 50p SAE).
Badge and certificate: (Wanderlust Rambling Club). £2.75 (+ SAE) & £0.75 (+ 9 x 4 SAE).

New Five Trig Points Walk   362

Gtr Man, W Yorks   *29 km / 18 miles*

The circuit along lanes, tracks and footpaths over the Pennine moors, and in parts coincident with the Pennine Way National Trail, was designed as a companion walk to the Saddleworth Five Trig Points Walk. It visits the trig points on Bishop Park, Tame Scout, Blackstone Edge, White Hill and Standedge.

Start and Finish:	Delph, Gtr Man	SD985079
Landranger maps:	109, 110	
1 : 25,000 maps:	OL 1, 21	

Publications, badges and certificates:
Looseleaf: *The New Five Trig Points Walk* (Carole E. Engel). A4. Free (+ 9 x 4 SAE).
Badge and certificate: (Carole E. Engel). £1.50 (+ SAE) & £0.20 (+ 9 x 6 SAE).

New River Path · 363

Herts, Gtr London *43 km / 27 miles*

A walk along the New River which is a man made channel dug in the early 17th century to bring clean water into London. In 1985 the New River was threatened with closure and the New River Action Group led those urging Thames Water to preserve the route as a long distance path. It is an important resource for leisure and wildlife. The walk is still under development and improvements are in progress. Waymarking south of Stoke Newington (where the river now ends) as close as possible to the erstwhile route to Sadlers Wells will be completed in 2002.

Start:	South bank of River Lea near Hertford	TL340138
Finish:	New River Head, Rosebery Avenue,	
	Islington	TQ314827
Landranger maps:	166, 176	
1 : 25,000 maps:	Ex 173, 174	
Waymark:	Named fingerposts (Hertford to Stoke Newington only)	
User group:	New River Action Group	

Publications, badges and certificates:
Paperback: *Exploring the New River – Hertford to Stoke Newington* by Michael Essex Lopresti (Brewin Books Ltd) 1997. ISBN 1858580684. 148 x 209. £8.95 (+ 90p p&p).
Booklet: *An historical walk along the New River – Stoke Newington to Islington* by Mary Cosh (Islington Archaeology & History Society) 2001. ISBN 0950753270. 32pp; A5. £5.00 (incs p&p).
Leaflet: *The New River Path in Hertfordshire* (Thames Water). A4/3. Free, post free.
Leaflet: *A Walker's Guide to the New River* (New River Action Group) 2002. A4/3. Details TBA.

Newlands Way 364

Cleveland, N Yorks, W Yorks *338 km / 210 miles*

A route devised on behalf of Newlands School, Middlesbrough with profits from sales donated to a Religious Order for work in developing countries. Six abbeys are visited as the Way takes in Ilkley, Thirsk, Osmotherley, Robin Hood's Bay and Whitby. A large portion of the Cleveland Way National Trail is used in the latter stages.

Start:	Kirkstall Abbey, Leeds	SE258362
Finish:	Middlesbrough, Cleveland	NZ499168
Landranger maps:	93, 99, 100, 104	
1 : 25,000 maps:	Ex 288, 289, 306 OL 26, 27, 30	

Publications, badges and certificates:
Booklet: *The Newlands Way* by C. M. J. Wright (Newlands School FCJ). ISBN 0953603016.
128pp; 150 x 105. £5.00 (+ 80p p&p).

Newmarket Circular Walk 365
Cambs, Suffolk *42 km / 26 miles*

A route around the town visiting neighbouring villages, the Race Course and Devil's Ditch. There are also routes of 6 and 12 miles.

Start and Finish:	Newmarket, Suffolk	TL638639
Landranger maps:	154	
1 : 25,000 maps:	Ex 210	

Publications, badges and certificates:
Looseleaf: *Newmarket Circular Walks* (HavAC Walkers). 6pp. £1.50.
Badge and certificate: (HavAC Walkers). £2.00 and free, each on completion.

Newry Canal Way 366
Armagh, Craigavon, Newry & Mourne *32 km / 20 miles*

One of the official Waymarked Ways in Northern Ireland, the Way follows the towpath of the now disused canal that was the first summit-level canal in the United Kingdom. It passes 13 lock gates and the villages of Scarva, Poyntzpass and Jerrettspass.

Start:	Portadown, Craigavon	J014538
Finish:	Newry, Newry & Mourne	J077295
Landranger maps:	OS(NI) 20, 29	✔
1 : 25,000 maps:	Not applicable in NI	
Waymark:	Route name/walker outline on blue background	

Publications, badges and certificates:
Leaflet: *An Illustrated Guide to the Newry Canal Way* (Newry & Mourne District Council). £0.50 (+ 9 x 6 SAE).

Newtondale Trail 367
N Yorks *32 km / 20 miles*

This walk links together the terminal stations of the North York Moors Railway, following Newton Dale northwards from Pickering across the moors to Grosmont, some sections close to the Railway and others following forest tracks and crossing the open moors high above the valley. The waymarked Newtondale Horse Trail describes a 35 miles long circular route along bridleways, starting and finishing in Pickering, basically providing alternative routes to and from Grosmont.

Start:	Pickering, N Yorks	SE797842
Finish:	Grosmont, N Yorks	NZ828053
Landranger maps:	94, 100	
1 : 25,000 maps:	OL 27	

Publications, badges and certificates:
Leaflet: *Newtondale Trail – Pickering to Grosmont/'Train Time Table'* (Peter Greenwood). A4/3.
Free (+ 9 x 4 SAE).
Leaflet: *Newtondale Trail – Grosmont to Pickering/'Train Time Table'* (Peter Greenwood). A4/3.
Free (+ 9 x 4 SAE).
Badge and certificate: (Peter Greenwood). £2.50 (+ 9 x 6 SAE).
Booklet: *Newtondale Horse Trail* (North York Moors National Park). ISBN 0907480527. 32pp;
120 x 170. £3.95 (+ 95p p&p).

Nidd Vale Circuit   368

N Yorks   *42 km / 26 miles*

Based mainly on Nidderdale, the route takes in the high moors to the River Cover
and Caldbergh passing close to Roundhill Reservoir. Proceeds from the sale of
badges and certificates are donated to a local hospice.

Start and Finish:	Lofthouse, N Yorks	SE101737
Landranger maps:	99	
1 : 25,000 maps:	Ex 298	

Publications, badges and certificates:
Looseleaf: *Nidd Vale Circuit* (Simon Townson). Free (+ 9 x 4 SAE).
Badge and certificate: (Simon Townson). £2.00 (+ 13 x 9 SAE).

Nidd Valley Link   369

N Yorks   *45 km / 28 miles*

A route connecting the Nidderdale Way at Hampsthwaite with the confluence of the
rivers Nidd and Ouse near to Nun Monkton, from where a link can be made into the
centre of York by way of the banks of the River Ouse (8 miles).

Start:	Hampsthwaite, N Yorks	SE259587
Finish:	Nidd-Ouse Confluence, N Yorks	SE513578
Landranger maps:	104, 105	
1 : 25,000 maps:	Ex 289, 290, 297	

Publications, badges and certificates:
Looseleaf: *Nidd Valley Link* (John Eckersley) 1997. 3pp; A4. £1.00 (incs p&p).
Certificate: (John Eckersley). £1.00 (incs p&p).

Nidderdale Way   370

N Yorks   *85 km / 53 miles*

A long-established route from the lowland pastures to the open fells near the
source of the River Nidd. The Way follows the northern side of the dale passing the
gritstone outcrops of Brimham Rocks high above the dale, and the old lead mill at
Smelthouses, before following paths close to the Nidd from Pateley Bridge to
Lofthouse. Here the Way loops round the head of the valley to Scar House
Reservoir. The route returns along the south side of the dale, looping away from the
Nidd to visit Merryfield Mines and Heyshaw Moor. See the Nidd Valley Link.

Start and Finish:	Hampsthwaite, N Yorks	SE259587
Landranger maps:	99, 104	✔
1 : 25,000 maps:	Ex 296, 297 OL 30	
Waymark:	Named signposts	

Publications, badges and certificates:
Paperback: *Nidderdale Way* by Paul Hannon (Hillside Publications) 1998. ISBN 1870141644.
48pp; 175 x 115. £3.50 (+ 35p p&p).
Folder: *Nidderdale Way* by J. K. E. Piggin (Yorkshire Footpath Trust). ISBN 1898978026. 14
cards; 204 x 117. £3.45 (incs p&p).
Certificate: (Yorkshire Footpath Trust). Free (+ 9 x 6 SAE).

North Bedfordshire Heritage Trail 371

Beds   *113 km / 70 miles*

The Trail passes through 23 villages including Bromham, Odell, Riseley, Wilden and
Sandy, two country parks and by 30 public houses. It connects with the Greensand
Ridge Walk at Sandy, Old Warden and Everton and also with the John Bunyan Trail
at Bromham Mill. The Skylark Ride (20 miles) is a circular route also connected.

Start and Finish:	St Paul's Square, Bedford	TL049497
Landranger maps:	153	
1 : 25,000 maps:	Ex 208	
Waymark:	Named signs – at road junctions only	

Publications, badges and certificates:
Leaflet: *North Bedfordshire Heritage Trail* (G. J. Edwards). A4/3. Free (+ 9 x 4 SAE).
Leaflet: *The Skylark Ride* (Ivel Valley Countryside Project) 2000. A4/3. Free (+ SAE).

North Bowland Traverse 372

Lancs, N Yorks   *50 km / 31 miles*

A low-level walk through the countryside of the Bowland Forest, crossing farmland
and meadowland. Although it is a fairly easy walk, it is best to go well-prepared, as
much of the route is well away from any good roads and conditions can change
rapidly. It links with the Witches Way at Slaidburn.

Start:	Slaidburn, Lancs	SD714523
Finish:	Stainforth, N Yorks	SD821673
Landranger maps:	97, 98, 103	
1 : 25,000 maps:	OL 41	

Publications, badges and certificates:
Looseleaf: *North Bowland Traverse* (David Johnson). Free (+ 9 x 4 SAE).
Badge and certificate: (David Johnson). £1.50 (+ 6 x 4 SAE).

North Bucks Way 373

Bucks, Milton K   *56 km / 35 miles*

A walk from the Ridgeway at Chequers Nature Reserve to the county boundary at
Pulpit Hill Nature Reserve crossing the Vale of Aylesbury and taking in a number of

villages. It connects with the Cross Bucks Way at Addington. At Wolverton the waymarked Grafton Way (13 miles and on OS mapping) leads to Greens Norton to join with the Knightley Way (see Nene Way). The Tramway Trail (6 miles) provides an alternative connection between Quainton and Waddesdon, the route taking to the Brill Tramway and the grounds of Waddesdon Manor. The Ouse Valley Walk (13 miles) follows the River Great Ouse between Buckingham and Milton Keynes and connects with the North Bucks Way at Iron Viaduct. See Aylesbury Ring and Oxfordshire Way.

Start:	Great Kimble, Milton K	SP830053
Finish:	Wolverton, Bucks	SP807413
Landranger maps:	152, 165	✔
1 : 25,000 maps:	Ex 181, 192	
Waymark:	Named discs	

Publications, badges and certificates:
Leaflet: *North Bucks Way* (Buckinghamshire County Council). A4/3. Free (+ SAE).
Leaflet: *Grafton Way* (Northamptonshire County Council) 1984. A5. £0.25 (+ 20p p&p).
Leaflet: *The Tramway Trail* (Buckinghamshire County Council). A4/3. Free (+ SAE).
Leaflet: *The Ouse Valley Walk* (Buckinghamshire County Council). A4/3. Free (+ SAE).

North Cotswold Diamond Way 374
Glos *96 km / 60 miles*

A route devised by the North Cotswold Group of the RA to commemorate the Association's Diamond Jubilee. A roughly diamond shaped walk visiting many small villages using quiet footpaths. A new publication will be available in 2002 – details TBA.

Start and Finish:	Moreton-in-Marsh, Glos	SP204325
Landranger maps:	150, 151, 163	✔
1 : 25,000 maps:	Ex 205 OL 45	
Waymark:	Blue diamond	

Publications, badges and certificates:
Softback: *North Cotswold Diamond Way* by Elizabeth Bell (RA Gloucestershire Area) 1995. ISBN 0900613912. A5. £3.50 (+ 50p).

North Downs Way National Trail 375
Kent, Surrey *250 km / 156 miles*

The North Downs Way National Trail broadly follows the historic Pilgrims Way along the Downs to Canterbury. The first 14 miles are over sandy countryside to the south. The Downs are first reached at Newlands Corner, east of Guildford and from there on the Trail mainly follows the crest of the southern escarpment of the North Downs or footpaths and tracks along their lower slopes. There are views over the Weald to the South Downs and several steepish ascents where the ridge is cut by valleys, notably those of the Mole at Box Hill, the Darent at Otford, the Medway at Rochester, and the Stour near Wye. Generally the route provides comparatively easy walking through woods, over chalk grassland and, especially in Kent, through orchards and farmland. At Boughton Lees there is a choice of routes. The direct one goes through Wye, over the Downs to Folkestone and along the cliffs to Dover. The alternative follows hills to the west of the river Stour and passes through orchards and the picturesque village of Chilham to Canterbury. From the cathedral city it heads south-east via Barham Downs, Shepherdswell and Waldershare Park to Dover. The waymarked circular Kingfisher Walk (14 miles) includes use of the North Downs Way (from Otford to Cotman's Ash) and the Darent Valley Path (from Eynsford to Otford), the middle section being through pasture and woodland. The waymarked Thames Down Link (15 miles and on OS mapping) connects the Thames Path at Kingston with the North Downs Way near Westhumble along a green corridor through Maldon Manor, Horton Country Park, the Commons of Epsom and Ashstead, and Mickleham Downs. See Ashford on Foot, Downs Link, Lapwing Walk, Medway Valley Walk, Skylark Walk, Socratic Trail, Tandridge Border Path and Wealdway. The Wey-South Path then Wey Navigation (15 miles) link Guildford to the Thames Path at Weybridge. See also E-Routes (E2).

Start:	Farnham, Surrey	SU844468
Finish:	Dover, Kent	TR308399
Landranger maps:	177, 178, 179, 186, 187, 188, 189	✔
1 : 25,000 maps:	Ex 137, 138, 145, 146, 147, 148, 149, 150, 163	
Waymark:	National Trail Acorn	
Path website:	www.nationaltrails.gov.uk	

Publications, badges and certificates:
Softback: *North Downs Way* (Official Guide) by Neil Curtis and Jim Walker (Aurum Press) 2000. ISBN 1854106740. 168pp; 210 x 130. £10.99.
Paperback: *The North Downs Way* by Kev Reynolds (Cicerone Press) 2001. ISBN 1852843160. 128pp; 174 x 116. £8.00.
Booklet: *North Downs Way: A Practical Handbook* (Kent County Council) 1997. ISBN 1873010990. 110pp; 210 x 100. £2.95 post free.
Leaflets (sectional): (North Downs Way National Trail Manager) 2001. 7 leaflets. Free.
Booklet: *Accommodation Information* (North Downs Way National Trail Manager) 2002. Details TBA.
Stripmap (folded): *North Downs Way* (West) (Harvey Maps) 2001. ISBN 1851373675. 240 x 115. £8.95 (+ 80p p&p).
Leaflet: *The Kingfisher Walk* (Kent County Council). A5. £1.00 post free.

North to South Surrey Walk 376

Slough, Surrey   *66 km / 41 miles*

This route, pioneered by the Surrey group of the LDWA, crosses Surrey's varied countryside from north to south passing Runnymede Memorial and going through Windsor Park and Chobham Common and over Gibbet Hill.

Start:	Colnbrook, Slough	TQ030771
Finish:	Haslemere Edge, Surrey	SU914312
Landranger maps:	176, 186	
1 : 25,000 maps:	Ex 133, 145, 160	

Publications, badges and certificates:
Looseleaf: *North-South Surrey* (Keith Chesterton) 1997. 2pp; A4. Free (+ SAE).

North Turton Trail 377
Lancs   *21 km / 13 miles*

The Trail makes use of woodland, moorland and passes the reservoirs of Turton & Entwistle and Wayoh. The distance can be extended to not less than 16 miles by adding the connecting circular walk around Jumbles Reservoir, the Jumbles Reservoir Trail (4 miles).

Start and Finish:	Edgworth, Lancs	SD741166
Landranger maps:	103, 109	
1 : 25,000 maps:	Ex 287	

Publications, badges and certificates:
Leaflet: *The North Turton Trail* (West Pennine Moors Ranger & Information Service). A3/4. £0.25 (+ 9 x 4 SAE).
Folder: *Jumbles/Turton & Entwistle/Wayoh Reservoir Trails* (West Pennine Moors Ranger & Information Service). 3 laminated cards; A5. £0.25 each (+ 9 x 6 SAE).

North Wales Path 378
Conwy, Denbighs, Gwynedd   *96 km / 60 miles*

The path is only partly coastal and significant stretches explore the hilly hinterland but with the larger resorts accessible. It links with the Offa's Dyke Path National Trail at Prestatyn. See Clwydian Way.

Start:	Bangor, Gwynedd	SH592720
Finish:	Prestatyn, Denbighs	SJ081838
Landranger maps:	114, 115, 116	✔
1 : 25,000 maps:	Ex 263, 264, 265 OL 17	
Waymark:	Named discs with stylised hills and sea	

Publications, badges and certificates:
Paperback: *The North Wales Path & Ten Selected Walks* by David Slater & Dave Worrall (Gwasg Carreg Gwalch) 1999. ISBN 0863815464. 120pp; 183 x 123. £4.50 (+ £1.00 p&p).
Folder: *North Wales Path* (Conwy County Borough Council) 1997. 16pp; A5. £3.00 (+ B5/larger SAE with 33p/41p stamp).

North Western Fells 379
Cumbria   *80 km / 50 miles*

A route visiting all the peaks described in the book, North Western Fells (A. Wainwright) and which involves 18,000ft of ascent.

Start and Finish:	Rannerdale Knotts, Cumbria	NY162182
Landranger maps:	89	
1 : 25,000 maps:	OL 4	

Publications, badges and certificates:
Looseleaf: *North Western Fells* (A. G. Foot). Free (+ 9 x 4 SAE).
Certificate: (A. G. Foot). £1.50 (incs p&p).

North Wolds Walk — 380

E Yorks   *32 km / 20 miles*

An undulating route across the chalk hills and valleys of the Yorkshire Wolds passing through the villages of Millington, Great Givendale, Bishop Wilton, Kirby Underdale and Thixendale.

Start and Finish:	Millington Road End, E Yorks	SE836567
Landranger maps:	100, 106	
1 : 25,000 maps:	Ex 294, 300	

Publications, badges and certificates:
Looseleaf: *North Wolds Walk* (Ron Watson). A4. Free (+ 9 x 4 SAE).
Badge: (Ron Watson). £1.50 (+ SAE).

North Worcestershire Hills Marathon — 381

Worcs   *42 km / 26 miles*

The route passes through Burcot, Linthurst and Lickey Beacon to the Clent Hills, and returns via Belbroughton, Pepper Wood, Dodford, Park Gate and Sanders Park.

Start and Finish:	Bromsgrove, Worcs	SO960707
Landranger maps:	139	
1 : 25,000 maps:	Ex 219	

Publications, badges and certificates:
Looseleaf: *North Worcestershire Hills Marathon* (Dave Irons) 1994. 6pp; A4. £1.00 (incs p&p).

North Worcestershire Path & Midland Link — 382

Warks, Worcs   *74 km / 46 miles*

The North Worcestershire Path links four country parks in the north-east of the County providing contrasting views of Birmingham and the Black Country in the north and the Vale of Worcester and Severn Valley to the south. The 'official' North Worcestershire Path, shown on OS mapping, terminates at Major's Green with the Midland Link (not on OS maps) commencing at Forhill, then visiting Earlswood, Tanworth in Arden, Kingswood, where a link is achieved with the Heart of England Way, Wroxhall and Kenilworth where it connects with the Centenary Way (Warwickshire). The route meets with the Worcestershire and Staffordshire Ways at Kinver Edge. The waymarked Trans Solihull Link (15 miles) starts from the North Worcestershire Path at Solihull Lodge, crosses the Solihull Way and joins the Heart of England Way near Balsall Common. It also joins the Coventry Way and ends at Meriden. See also Birmingham Greenway, Birmingham and Aberystwyth Walk and Malvern Link.

Start:	Kinver Edge, Worcs	SO829822
Finish:	Kenilworth, Warks	SP280724
Landranger maps:	138, 139, 140	✔ (not Link)
1 : 25,000 maps:	Ex 218, 219, 220	
Waymark:	Coloured arrows – pine cone logo (North Worcestershire Path); green oak leaf (Midland Link)	

Publications, badges and certificates:
Softback: *The North Worcestershire Path and Midland Link* by John Roberts (Walkways). ISBN 0947708347. 76pp; A5. £5.75 (incs p&p).
Paperback: *North Worcestershire Path Guide* (Worcestershire County Council) 1997. 38pp. £4.50.
Leaflet: *North Worcestershire Path* (Worcestershire County Council) 1992. A4/3. Free.
Looseleaf & Leafet: *Trans Solihull Link* (Solihull Metropolitan Borough Council) 1999. 4pp A4 & A4/3. Free (+ 9 x 4 SAE).

North York Moors Challenge Walk 383

N Yorks   *40 km / 25 miles*

A strenuous walk in the North York Moors National Park which includes high moorland.

Start and Finish:	Goathland, N Yorks	NZ838014
Landranger maps:	94	
1 : 25,000 maps:	OL 27	

Publications, badges and certificates:
Booklet: *North Yorkshire Moors Challenge Walk* by John Merrill (Walk & Write Ltd). ISBN 0907496369. 32pp; A5. £3.95 (+ 75p p&p).
Badge and certificate: (Walk & Write Ltd). £3.50 (incs p&p).

North York Moors Tour 384

N Yorks   *158 km / 98 miles*

From the start on the Esk Valley Railway, the route goes to Danby Rigg, Rosedale Abbey, Osmotherley, the Hambleton Drove Road and Rievaulx Abbey. It then goes to Kirkbymoorside, Hutton-le-Hole, the Cawthorn Roman camps, Levisham and Hole of Horcum to the finish at Goathland, where the North Yorkshire Moors Railway can connect the walker with the Esk Valley Railway.

Start:	Danby, N Yorks	NZ707084
Finish:	Goathland, N Yorks	NZ838014
Landranger maps:	93, 94, 99, 100	
1 : 25,000 maps:	OL 26, 27	

Publications, badges and certificates:
Paperback: *Footpath Touring: North York Moors* by Ken Ward (Footpath Touring) 1985. ISBN 0711704260. 64pp; 221 x 114. £4.00.

North York Moors Wobble 385

N Yorks   *51 km / 32 miles*

A route taking in Rudland Rigg, Farndale, Rosedale Abbey, Rosedale Moor, Cropton, Appleton-le-Moors and Hutton-le-Hole, aimed at raising funds for a locally based search and rescue team.

Start and Finish:	Gillamoor, N Yorks	SE684801
Landranger maps:	100	
1 : 25,000 maps:	OL 26, 27	

Publications, badges and certificates:
Booklet: *North York Moors Wobble* (George Davies). 12pp. £5.00 (+ A4 SAE).
Certificate: (George Davies). Free (+ 9 x 4 SAE).

Northumbrian Coastline   386

Northumb, Tyne & Wear   *96 km / 60 miles*

A coastal route with many interesting features including Berwick fortifications, Holy Island, Bamburgh Castle, Farne Islands, Dunstanburgh Castle, Warkworth Castle and Tynemouth Castle and Priory. The route links with the St Cuthbert's Way. The 'Exploring the Northumberland Coast' publication comprises six shorter trails based on Berwick-upon-Tweed, Holy Island, Bamburgh, Craster, Alnmouth and Warkworth which cater for alternative routes off the coastline.

Start:	Berwick-upon-Tweed, Northumb	NT994534
Finish:	North Shields, Tyne & Wear	NZ356678
Landranger maps:	75, 81, 88	
1 : 25,000 maps:	Ex 316, 325, 332, 340, 346	

Publications, badges and certificates:
Paperback: *Northumbrian Coastline* by Ian Smith (Sandhill Press Ltd). ISBN 0946098328. 175 x 125. £4.95 (+ 65p p&p).
Folder: *Exploring the Northumberland Coast* (Northumberland County Council). 6 leaflets. £2.50 (incs p&p).

Nuneaton Rotary Walk   387

Leics, Warks   *34 km / 21 miles*

A route around Nuneaton, devised by, and intended to raise funds for, the Nuneaton Rotary Club, visiting Chapel End, Bermuda and the Lime Kilns linking with the Heart of England Way to the west. In the publication are described two shorter routes and an alternative section along the Ashby Canal.

Start and Finish:	Sandon Park, Warks	SP358932
Landranger maps:	140	
1 : 25,000 maps:	Ex 221, 232	
Waymark:	Rotary International Wheel logo	

Publications, badges and certificates:
Leaflet: *The Nuneaton Rotary Walk* by Bob Bacon and Chris Mountford (Rotary Club of Nuneaton) 1999. A4/3. £1.00 (incs p&p).
Certificate: (Rotary Club of Nuneaton). £1.00 (incs p&p).

Offa's Dyke Path National Trail   388

Denbighs, Flints, Glos, Worcs, Mons,   *284 km / 177 miles*
Powys, Shrops, Wrexham

For over sixty miles the route of this National Trail runs along or close to the 8th century dyke passing many other historical sites. The Trail meanders along the east side of the Wye Valley to Monmouth, crosses lowland farmland to Pandy and Hatterrall Ridge which is followed to Hay-on-Wye. The Radnorshire Hills are crossed to Knighton as is the hill country of Clun. The next part of the route is across the plain of Montgomery, along the Severn Valley and across the Vale of Llangollen to the Clwydian Hills. The waymarked Three Castles Walk (Mons) (19 miles and on OS mapping) is a circular walk from Offa's Dyke visiting Skenfrith, White and Grosmont castles. See Clwydian Way, Ceiriog Trail, Gloucestershire Way, Wysis Way, Maelor Way, North Wales Path, Offa's Hyke, Wild Edric's Way and Glyndwr's Way/Llwybr Glyndwr National Trail.

Start:	Sedbury Cliff, Glos	ST552927
Finish:	Prestatyn, Denbighs	SJ081838
Landranger maps:	116, 117, 126, 137, 148, 161, 162, 172	✔
1 : 25,000 maps:	Ex 167, 201, 216, 240, 256, 264, 265 OL 13, 14	
Waymark:	National Trail Acorn	
User group:	Offa's Dyke Association	

Publications, badges and certificates:
Softback: *Offa's Dyke Path South* (Official Guide) by Ernie and Kathy Kay and Mark Richards (Aurum Press) 2000. ISBN 1854106716. 144pp; 210 x 130. £10.99.
Softback: *Offa's Dyke Path North* (Official Guide) by Ernie and Kathy Kay and Mark Richards (Aurum Press) 1995. ISBN 1854103229. 144pp; 210 x 130. £10.99.
Paperback: *Walking Offa's Dyke Path* by David Hunter (Cicerone Press) 1995. ISBN 1852841605. 224pp; 115 x 175. £8.99.
Paperback: *Langton's Guide to the Offa's Dyke Path* by Andrew Durham (Andrew Durham) 1996. ISBN 1899242023. 224pp; 210 x 130. £12.99 (incs p&p).
Paperback: *Offa's Dyke Circular Walks – Southern* (Sigma Leisure) 2000. ISBN 1850587256. 150pp. £7.95.
Paperback: *Offa's Dyke Circular Walks – Northern* (Sigma Leisure) 2001. ISBN 1850587264. 160pp. £7.95.
Leaflet: *The Offa's Dyke Path/Llwybr Clawdd Offa* produced by Countryside Council for Wales (Offa's Dyke Association) 1999. A4/3. Free (+ SAE).
Booklet: *Offa's Dyke Path Accommodation Guide* (Offa's Dyke Association) Annual. A6. £3.50 (+ 30p).
Looseleaf: *Backpackers and Camping List* (Offa's Dyke Association) Annual. £1.20 (+ 24p p&p).
Route Notes: *Offa's Dyke Path – South to North* (Offa's Dyke Association) 2000. £2.00 (+ 40p p&p).
Route notes: *Offa's Dyke Path – North to South* (Offa's Dyke Association) 2000. £2.00 (+ 40p p&p).
Folder: *Strip Maps of Offa's Dyke Path* by Ian Dormor (Offa's Dyke Association) 1998. 10pp. £5.00 (+ £1.00 p&p).
Leaflets: *Circular Walks, Offa's Dyke Path* produced by Countryside Council for Wales (Offa's Dyke Association). 4 leaflets; A4/3. Free (+ SAE).
Leaflets: *Beyond the Offa's Dyke Path – circular walks* (Denbighshire County Council). 9 leaflets; A4/3. Free (+ SAE).
Book (ring bound): *Three Castles Walk* (Monmouthshire County Council) 1998. 32pp; 150 x 210. £3.95 (+ 50p p&p) – includes annual accommodation guide.
Badge: (Offa's Dyke Association). £2.85 (+ 57p p&p).
Certificate: (Offa's Dyke Association). £2.50 (+ 50p p&p).

Offa's Hyke   389
Denbighs, Flints   *32 km / 20 miles*

A walk on and around the Clwydian Hills providing distant views. It is coincident with parts of the Offa's Dyke Path National Trail. Profits from the sale of badges/certificates go to Hope House Childrens Hospice.

Start and Finish:	Bwlch Penbarra, Denbighs	SJ161605
Landranger maps:	116	
1 : 25,000 maps:	Ex 265	

Publications, badges and certificates:
Looseleaf: *Offa's Hyke* (Michael Skuse). 1pp; A4. Free (+ SAE).
Badge and certificate: (Michael Skuse). £1.50 (+ SAE) & £0.50 (+ SAE).

Old Crown Round   390
Cumbria   *29 km / 18 miles*

A challenge walk over the tops of Skiddaw, Blencathra, Carrock Fell and Great Cockup, which can be achieved in any order. Navigational skills would be appropriate in certain weather conditions.

Start and Finish:	Hesket Newmarket, Cumbria	NY343386
Landranger maps:	90	
1 : 25,000 maps:	OL 4, 5	

Publications, badges and certificates:
Looseleaf: *The Old Crown Round* (Mick Cooper or Old Crown Inn). 1pp. Free (+ 9 x 4 SAE).
Badge and certificate: (Mick Cooper or Old Crown Inn). £1.50 for both (+ 9 x 4 SAE).

Old Sarum Challenge   391
Wilts   *40 km / 25 miles*

A route from Amesbury over chalk downland linking Old Sarum and intervening villages.

Start and Finish:	Amesbury Sports Centre, Wilts	SU161418
Landranger maps:	184	
1 : 25,000 maps:	Ex 130	

Publications, badges and certificates:
Looseleaf: *Old Sarum Challenge* (Judith Archard). Free (+ 9 x 4 SAE).
Badge (cloth): (Judith Archard). £1.00 (plus SAE).

Oldham Way   392
Gtr Man   *64 km / 40 miles*

A walk around the borough, where the landscape varies from moorland to urban canal. It starts at Dove Stone Reservoir near Greenfield, and continues over Saddleworth Moor to Diggle and Castleshaw Moor to Denshaw. It then skirts the north of Shaw and Royton to meet the Rochdale Canal at Chadderton Hall Park. It follows the canal south through Chadderton to Failsworth, after which it joins the Medlock Valley to Daisy Nook and Park Bridge before climbing over Hartshead Pike to Quick. See also E-Routes (E2).

Start and Finish:	Dove Stone Reservoir, Gtr Man	SE002036
Landranger maps:	109, 110	✓
1 : 25,000 maps:	Ex 277 OL 1, 21	
Waymark:	Owl	

Publications, badges and certificates:
Folder: *The Oldham Way* (Oldham Metropolitan Borough Council). 9 leaflets; A4/3. £1.99.

Ouse Valley Way 393
Beds, Cambs   *66 km / 41 miles*

The Way follows the River Great Ouse through Willington where there is an ancient Danish Camp, Great Barford, Eaton Socon, St Neots, Godmanchester and St Ives with significant areas of meadowland and elevated bank views from north of Holywell.

Start:	County Bridge, Bedford	TL046495
Finish:	Earith, Cambs	TL394746
Landranger maps:	142, 143, 153, 154	✓
1 : 25,000 maps:	Ex 208, 225	
Waymark:	Named discs with two swans on water (Beds); Standard waymarks with swan, water and tree logo (Cambs)	

Publications, badges and certificates:
Leaflet pack: *The Ouse Valley Way – Bedford to St Neots* (Ivel Valley Countryside Project) 2001. 3 leaflets; A4/3. Free (+ SAE).
Folder: *Ouse Valley Way – Eaton Socon to Earith* (Huntingdonshire District Council) 2000. 7 leaflets; A4/3. £3.00 (post free).
Certificate: (Huntingdonshire District Council at Countryside Services). Free (+ A4 SAE).

Ox Drove Way 394
Hants   *40 km / 25 miles*

The Ox Drove itself is part of an old cross-country route on the Downs to the northeast of Winchester called the Lunway, a name recalled in the Lunways Inn at Itchen Wood. This bridle route forms a figure of eight using the Ox Drove and passing Preston Down, Bentworth, Upper Wield, and Old Alresford.

Start and Finish:	Abbotstone Down, Hants	SU585361
Landranger maps:	185	✓
1 : 25,000 maps:	Ex 132, 144	
Waymark:	White arrows with green ox logo	

Publications, badges and certificates:
Leaflet: *The Ox Drove Way* (Hampshire County Council). A4/3. Free (+ SAE).

Oxbridge Walk 395

Beds, Bucks, Cambs, Oxon *185 km / 115 miles*

A route connecting the famous University cities of Oxford and Cambridge and making use of the Cross Bucks Way, Thame Valley Walk, Greensand Ridge Walk and Clopton Way. See Leighton – Linslade Loop.

Start:	Head of River Pub, Oxford, Oxon	SP055514
Finish:	The Backs, Cambridge	TL586445
Landranger maps:	153, 154, 164, 165	
1 : 25,000 maps:	Ex 180, 181, 192, 193, 208, 209	

Publications, badges and certificates:
Paperback: *An Oxbridge Walk* by James A. Lyons (Cicerone Press) 1995. ISBN 1852841664. 168pp; 180 x 120. £7.99. (2002 – out of print.)

Oxford Canal Walk 396

Northants, Oxon, W Midlands, Warks *133 km / 83 miles*

A walk connecting the cathedral cities of Oxford and Coventry using the continuous canal towpath, passing 43 locks, many bridges, one tunnel and crossing only one road. See Jurassic Way. See also E-Routes (E2).

Start:	Coventry, W Midlands	SP370840
Finish:	Oxford, Oxon	SP516060
Landranger maps:	140, 151, 152, 164	✔
1 : 25,000 maps:	Ex 180, 191, 206, 221, 222	
Waymark:	Multi-coloured diamond	

Publications, badges and certificates:
Leaflet: *Exploring the Oxford Canal* (British Waterways – Tring) 1996. A5. Free (+ SAE).
Leaflet: *The Oxford Canal Walk* (British Waterways – Tring) 1995. A4/3. Free.
Stripmap (folded): *The Oxford Canal Map* (GEOprojects) 1999. ISBN 0863510035. 135 x 213. £4.75 (+ 50p p&p).

Oxfordshire Way 397

Glos, Oxon *104 km / 65 miles*

The Way, a traverse of Oxfordshire from the Cotswolds to the Chilterns, links the Heart of England Way with the Thames Path National Trail across the rolling limestone countryside of the Cotswold Hills, passing through Shipton-under-Wychwood, Charlbury and other villages before crossing Otmoor to Studley, north of Oxford. Here it turns to Tetsworth and Pyrton, and crosses the open farmland and woods of the chalk hills of the Chilterns to reach the Thames. The waymarked Wardens' Way and Windrush Way (both 14 miles and on OS mapping) provide low and high level routes respectively from Bourton-on-the-Water to the Cotswold Way at Winchcombe. The waymarked Thame Valley Walk (15 miles and on OS mapping) which starts near Aylesbury ends at Albury on the Oxfordshire Way forming connections with the North Bucks Way and the Aylesbury Ring. See Chiltern Way, Cross Bucks Way and Gloucestershire Way. See also E-Routes (E2).

Start:	Bourton-on-the-Water, Glos	SP170209
Finish:	Henley-on-Thames, Oxon	SU757833
Landranger maps:	163, 164, 165, 175	✔
1 : 25,000 maps:	Ex 171, 180, 191, OL 45	
Waymark:	Letters OW on standard waymarks	

Publications, badges and certificates:

Paperback (spiral bound): *The Oxfordshire Way – A Walker's Guide* by Faith Cooke and Keith Wheal (Oxfordshire County Council) 1999. ISBN 1900478013. 90pp; A5. £5.99 (+ 80p p&p).

Looseleaf: *Oxfordshire Way – Accommodation list and refreshment information* (Oxfordshire County Council). Free.

Paperback: *Warden's Way and Windrush Way produced by Cotswold Wardens* (Cotswold District Council) 1991. 32pp; A5. £1.50 (+ 33p p&p).

Leaflet: *Thame Valley Walk* (Aylesbury Valley District Council). A4/3. Free (+ SAE).

Pathfinder Long Distance Walk   398

Cambs   *74 km / 46 miles*

Devised to perpetuate the name of the Royal Air Force Pathfinder Force, the route links the historic RAF Pathfinder stations at Wyton, Graveley, Oakington and Warboys, using rights of way through gentle countryside and passing many wartime memorials.

Start and Finish:	RAF Wyton, Cambs	TL282739
Landranger maps:	142, 153, 154	✔
1 : 25,000 maps:	Ex 225, 227	
Waymark:	Circular disc with silhouette of Mosquito aircraft	
Path website:	www.bwf-ivv.org.uk/pathfind.htm	

Publications, badges and certificates:

Paperback: *A Walker's Guide to the Pathfinder Long Distance Walk* by Gavin Sugden and published by J&KH Publishing (Pathfinder Long Distance Walk) 2001. ISBN 1900511711. 140pp; 115 x 180. £10.00 (incs p&p) – includes certificate.

Leaflet: *Pathfinder Long Distance Walk* (Huntingdonshire District Council). A4/3. Free (+ 9 x 6 SAE).

Badge: (Art of Embroidery). £6.99 (+ SAE).

Peak District High Level Route   399

Derbys, S Yorks, Staffs   *147 km / 91 miles*

This route around the Peak National Park is particularly strenuous taking in the limestone plateau to Dovedale, the Roaches, Shining Tor, Chinley Churn, the southern edge of Kinder to the Ladybower reservoir and the whole of the eastern gritstone edges from Stanage to Beeley before following the Derwent Valley to the finish.

Start and Finish:	Matlock, Derbys	SK298603
Landranger maps:	110, 119	
1 : 25,000 maps:	OL 1, 24	

Publications, badges and certificates:
Booklet: *The Peak District High Level Route* by John Merrill (Walk & Write Ltd). ISBN 0907496555. 60pp; A5. £4.50 (+ 75p p&p).
Badge and certificate: (Walk & Write Ltd). £3.50 (incs p&p).

Peakland Way 400

Derbys *156 km / 97 miles*

This route through the National Park visits Ilam, Longnor, Blackwell, Mam Tor, Kinder Scout, Snake Pass and Tissington where it joins the Tissington Trail. See White Peak Trails.

Start and Finish:	Ashbourne, Derbys	SK178469
Landranger maps:	110, 119	
1 : 25,000 maps:	Ex 259 OL 1, 24	

Publications, badges and certificates:
Booklet: *The Peakland Way* by John Merrill (Walk & Write Ltd). ISBN 0907496849. 64pp; A5. £4.50 (+ 75p p&p).
Badge and certificate: (Walk & Write Ltd). £3.50 (incs p&p).

Peddars Way & Norfolk Coast Path National Trail 401

Norfolk, Suffolk *150 km / 94 miles*

The first part of this National Trail follows tracks, footpaths and minor roads along, or as near as possible to, the Peddars Way (a Romanised section of the prehistoric Icknield Way, the extant sections of which are a scheduled ancient monument). From the wooded, sandy Breckland, it passes Castle Acre (linking with the Nar Valley Way) and the ruins of the priory and castle to reach the North Norfolk coast at Holme-next-the-Sea. Here a short section of the Norfolk Coast Path leads west to Hunstanton, while the main Trail heads east along or near to the shoreline over low cliffs, sand dunes, coastal defences enclosing marshes and mud flats, passing woodland, bird sanctuaries and harbours. Near to Great Hockham, the Great Eastern Pingo Trail (8 miles) provides a circular route through a SSSI in the Thompson Common area. See also Angles Way/Weavers Way, Iceni Way, Cromer to the M11 and Hereward Way/Icknield Way Path and Trail.

Start:	Knettishall Heath, Suffolk	TL944807
Finish:	Cromer, Norfolk	TG215420
Landranger maps:	132, 133, 134, 144	✔
1 : 25,000 maps:	Ex 229, 230, 236, 250, 251, 252	
Waymark:	National Trail Acorn	
Path website:	www.trails.f2s.com/Peddars.htm	

Publications, badges and certificates:
Softback: *Peddars Way and Norfolk Coast Path* (Official Guide) by Bruce Robinson (Aurum Press) 1996. ISBN 185410408X. 144pp; 210 x 130. £10.99.
Paperback: *Langton's Guide to the Peddars Way and Norfolk Coast Path* by Andrew Durham (Andrew Durham) 1994. ISBN 1899242007. 128pp; 210 x 130. £6.95 (incs p&p).

Paperback: *East Anglian Trackways* (includes Peddars Way) by Elizabeth Barrett (Wimpole Books) 1991. ISBN 0951601105. 129pp; A5. £7.95 (incs p&p).

Booklet: *Walking the Peddars Way and North Norfolk Coast Path with Weavers Way – including accommodation list* (RA Norfolk Area) 2001. ISBN 1901184463. 28pp; A5. £2.70 (+ 30p p&p).

Leaflet: *Peddars Way and Norfolk Coast Path* (Countryside Agency Publications) 2000. A4/3. Free.

Leaflet: *The Great Eastern Pingo Trail* (Diss Tourist Information Centre). A5. Free (+ SAE).

Badge: (RA Norfolk Area). £2.00 (incs p&p).

Pembrokeshire Coast Path National Trail   402

Ceredigion, Pembrokes   *299 km / 186 miles*

With the exception of the Milford Haven Waterway and three MOD establishments the route of this challenging National Trail follows the coastline around the county of Pembrokeshire and the Pembrokeshire Coast National Park. Apart from the resort of Tenby only small settlements and relatively few obtrusive holiday developments are encountered. The scenery provides an ever-changing contrast between the softer sedimentary rocks of the south coast, with its fine beaches, and the more resistant rocks of the rugged northern coast. The area is rich in prehistoric remains and is noted for its sea birds and seals. See South of the Landsker Trail.

Start:	St Dogmaels, Pembrokes	SN163469
Finish:	Amroth, Pembrokes	SN172072
Landranger maps:	145, 157, 158	✔
1 : 25,000 maps:	Ex 198 OL 35, 36	
Waymark:	National Trail Acorn	

Publications, badges and certificates:

Softback: *Pembrokeshire Coast Path* (Official Guide) by Brian John (Aurum Press) 1997. ISBN 1854104594. 168pp; 210 x 130. £10.99.

Paperback: *The Pembrokeshire Coastal Path* by Dennis R. Kelsall (Cicerone Press) 1996. ISBN 1852841869. 200pp; 115 x 175. £9.99.

Paperback: *Walking the Pembrokeshire Coast Path* by Patrick Stark (Gomer Press) 1995. ISBN 0863836860. 84pp; A5. £3.75 (+ 50p p&p).

Booklet: *The Pembrokeshire Coast Path* by John Merrill (Walk & Write Ltd). ISBN 0907496695. 84pp; A5. £4.95 (+ 75p p&p).

Leaflet: *Llwybr Arfordir Sir Benfro/The Pembrokeshire Coast Path* produced by Countryside Council for Wales (Pembrokeshire Coast National Park) 1999. A4/3. Free (+ SAE).

Leaflet: *Coast Path Accommodation Guide* (Pembrokeshire Coast National Park). £2.50 (+ 41p p&p).

Folder (full set): *Coast Path Cards* (Pembrokeshire Coast National Park). 10pp. £4.00 (+ 72p p&p).

Leaflet: *Coast Path Mileage Chart* (Pembrokeshire Coast National Park). £0.20 (+ 41p p&p).

Video: *Pembrokeshire Coast Path* (Pembrokeshire Coast National Park). £12.99 (+ £1.50 p&p).

Booklet: *Booking Bureau – Youth Hostels* (YHA Northern Region) Annual. 20pp. Free.

Badge: (Pembrokeshire Coast National Park). £1.35 (+ 26p p&p).

Certificate: available on proof of completion (Pembrokeshire Coast National Park). Record card free (+ 41p p&p).

Badge and certificate: (Walk & Write Ltd). £3.50 (incs p&p).

Pendle and Ribble Round 403

Lancs *32 km / 20 miles*

A route crossing Pendle Hill and visiting Downham before returning by riverside and farm paths.

Start and Finish:	Whalley, Lancs	SD732362
Landranger maps:	103	
1 : 25,000 maps:	Ex 287 OL 41	

Publications, badges and certificates:
Booklet: *Bronte Round/Pendle and Ribble Round* by Derek Magnall (Norman Thomas) 1994. 36pp; A5. £1.85 (incs p&p).
Badge and certificate: (Norman Thomas). £2.00 (+ SAE).

Pendle Way 404

Lancs *72 km / 45 miles*

A route through contrasting scenery, ranging from moorland to river valleys visiting Barnoldswick, Thornton-in-Craven, Wycoller, Reedley, Newchurch and Pendle Hill. The latter part of the route has associations with the Pendle Witches. See Bronte Way, Burnley Way and Clitheroe 60K.

Start and Finish:	Barrowford, Lancs	SD863398
Landranger maps:	103	✔
1 : 25,000 maps:	Ex 287 OL 21, 41	
Waymark:	Black witch	

Publications, badges and certificates:
Paperback: Pendle Way by Paul Hannon (Hillside Publications) 1997. ISBN 1870141571. 48pp; 175 x 115. £3.50 (+ 35p p&p).
Folder: *The Pendle Way* (Pendle Borough Council) 2001. 8 leaflets; A4/3. £3.00 (+ 50p p&p).

Penistone Boundary Walk 405

S Yorks *25 km / 16 miles*

A route around the boundary of the town, the lowest point at 140m and the highest at 355m. The route is crossed by the Trans Pennine Trail and also by the main Barnsley – Huddersfield railway line which caters for easy access.

Start and Finish:	Cubley Hall, Penistone, S Yorks	SE246016
Landranger maps:	110	✔
1 : 25,000 maps:	OL 1	
Waymark:	Head profile of Penistone Sheep	

Publications, badges and certificates:
Leaflet: *The Penistone Boundary Walk* (Penistone Town Council). A3/4. Free (+ 9 x 4 SAE).
Badge (metal, lapel): (Penistone Town Council). £1.00 (+ SAE).

Penistone Loop-D-Loop 406

S Yorks *77 km / 48 miles*

Comprising four walks of between 9 and 15 miles taking the form of a 'D', each of which links with the next and through Flouch, Penistone and Wortley with use made of sections of the Trans Pennine Trail.

Start and Finish:	Dunford Bridge, S Yorks	SE157025
Landranger maps:	110	
1 : 25,000 maps:	OL 1	

Publications, badges and certificates:
Looseleaf: *Penistone Loop-D-Loop* (Allen Pestell). 4pp; A4. £0.50 (+ 9 x 6 SAE).

Pennine Bridleway 407

Cumbria, Derbys, Lancs, N Yorks, W Yorks *335 km / 208 miles*

This proposed multi-use National Trail will follow a route through varied countryside. Already approved between Carsington Reservoir and Kirkby Stephen, consideration is being given to an extension from Kirkby Stephen to Byrness, a total distance of 348 miles. The first section, due to open in spring 2002, is the Mary Towneley Loop, a 44 miles long circuit in the South Pennines. Feeder routes to the Loop from Bolton and Keighley and a third from Penistone to Diggle are also incorporated within the project. The approved route is expected to be completed by 2004.

Start:	Carsington Reservoir, Derbys	SK249530
Finish:	Fat Lamb Inn, Kirkby Stephen, Cumbria	NY739023
Landranger maps:	91, 98, 103, 109, 110, 119	
1 : 25,000 maps:	OL 1, 2, 19, 21, 24	

Publications, badges and certificates:
Leaflet: *Pennine Bridleway* (Countryside Agency Publications) 1995. A4/3. Free.
Leaflet: *Mary Towneley Loop* (Countryside Agency Publications). Details TBA.

Pennine Way National Trail 408

Borders, Cumbria, Derbys, Durham, *404 km / 251 miles*
Gtr Man, N Yorks, Northum, W Yorks

This first National Trail was formally opened after a 30-year campaign led by Tom Stephenson of the RA. It follows the central upland spine of England from Derbyshire to the Scottish Borders, crossing a wide variety of terrain. The Way crosses the expanse of the gritstone moorlands of the Kinder Plateau, the Bronte country and the predominantly limestone areas of the Yorkshire Dales National Park which is traversed via Malham, Pen-y-ghent, Great Shunner Fell and Keld. The Way descends from the high fells to reach the River Tees which is followed past High Force and Cauldron Snout waterfalls then crossing the fells to High Cup, Great Dunfell and Cross Fell then descending to Alston to reach the Northumberland National Park and Hadrian's Wall. The Wall is followed to Housesteads Fort before turning north across the Kielder Forest to Redesdale and the uplands of the Cheviot Hills. The English-Scottish border fence is then followed before gradually descending to Kirk Yetholm, where it can be linked with the St Cuthbert's Way. At Alston the Way links with the South Tyne Trail (10 miles), providing a low level alternative up the valley towards Hadrian's Wall. A register is maintained at the Pen-y-ghent Café, Horton-in-Ribblesdale for signature/comments from those involved in walking the Way. Practical advice on attempting the Pennine Way is available from the Pennine Way Association (9 x 4 SAE required). See Abbott's Hike, Airedale Way, Bog Dodgers Way, Cuckoo Walk, Dales Way, Dam Long Walk, Falklands Way, Hadrian's Wall Path National Trail, Lancashire Trail, Leeds and Liverpool Canal Walk, Limestone Way, New Five Trig Points Walk, Ribble Way, Ribskip Challenge, Saddleworth Five Trig Points Walk, St Cuthbert's Way, Swale Way, Teesdale Way, Ten Reservoirs Walk, Tidewater Way, Tyne – Estuary to Source and Tyne Valley Train Trails. See also E-Routes (E2).

Start:	Edale, Derbys	SK125858
Finish:	Kirk Yetholm, Borders	NT827282
Landranger maps:	74, 75, 80, 86, 87, 91, 92, 98, 103, 109, 110	✔
1 : 25,000 maps:	OL 1, 2 16, 19, 21, 24, 30, 31, 42, 43	
Waymark:	National Trail Acorn	
User group:	Pennine Way Association	
Path website:	www.pennineway.demon.co.uk/frames.htm	

Publications, badges and certificates:

Softback: *Pennine Way North* (Official Guide) by Tony Hopkins (Aurum Press) 2000. ISBN 1854106724. 168pp; 210 x 130. £10.99.

Softback: *Pennine Way South* (Official Guide) by Tony Hopkins (Aurum Press) 1995. ISBN 1854103210. 210 x 130. £10.99.

Softback: *Guide to the Pennine Way* by Christopher John Wright (Constable and Robinson Ltd) 1991. ISBN 0094706409. 240pp; 171 x 114. £10.95.

Paperback: *The Pennine Way* by Martin Collins (Cicerone Press) 1998. ISBN 1852842628. 144pp; 116 x 176. £6.99.

Stripmap: *The Pennine Way, Part One: South – Edale to Teesdale, Map and Guide* (Footprint). ISBN 1871149012. £3.50.

Stripmap: *The Pennine Way, Part Two: North – Teesdale to Kirk Yetholm, Map and Guide* (Footprint). ISBN 1871149029. £3.50.

Booklet: *Pennine Way Association Accommodation and Camping Guide* (Pennine Way Association) Annual. £1.50 (incs p&p).

Leaflet: *The Pennine Way – Accommodation and Service* (Pennine Way Project Officer). A3/6. Free (+ 9 x 4 SAE).

Booklet: *Booking Bureau – Youth Hostels* (YHA Northern Region) Annual. 20pp; A5. Free.

Leaflet: *The Pennine Way* (Countryside Agency Publications). A4/3. Free.

Looseleaf: *Places of Worship on or along the Pennine Way* (S. E. Chandler). 4pp; A4. Free (+ 2 x 2nd class stamps).

Certificate: produced by Pennine Way Project (Peak National Park Information Centre). £4.50 (incs p&p).

Completion Memento: Selection of sketches (John Needham). £2.50.

Badge (enamel) & certificate: (Pennine Way Association). £2.00 (strong SAE) & £2.50 (incs p&p).

Badge and certificate: (Walk & Write Ltd). £3.50 (incs p&p).

Leaflet: *South Tyne Trail* (Northumberland County Council) 1997. A4/3. Free (+ SAE).

Pennington Round 409

Cumbria *40 km / 25 miles*

A walk over moorland countryside visiting the John Barrow monument overlooking the delightful market town of Ulverston. It is partly coincident with the Cumbria Way.

Start and Finish:	Beckside, Cumbria	SD235822
Landranger maps:	96	
1 : 25,000 maps:	OL 6	

Publications, badges and certificates:
Looseleaf: *The Pennington Round* (Brian Richmond). Free (+ 9 x 4 SAE).
Badge and certificate: (Brian Richmond). £1.00 (+ SAE).

Pilgrims' Trail 410

Hants, Portsmouth *45 km / 28 miles*

The Trail forms part of a longer route between Winchester and Mont Saint Michel in Normandy, France. It follows a route dating from medieval times when pilgrims visited Winchester Cathedral from the country, and abroad, to worship at the shrine of St Swithun, a former teacher of the young Alfred the Great. In Hampshire, the Trail follows the course of a Roman Road to Bishop's Waltham and from there via Kingsmead to the finish.

Start:	Winchester Cathedral, Hants	SU480300
Finish:	Ferry Port, Portsmouth	SU639018
Landranger maps:	185, 196	
1 : 25,000 maps:	Ex 119, 132	
Waymark:	Silhouette of Mont Saint Michel/sea shell/walking stick	

Publications, badges and certificates:
Folder: *Pilgrims Trail* (Hampshire County Council). 4 leaflets; A4/3. £2.99 (+ 35p p&p).

Pioneers Round 411

Gtr Man, Lancs *32 km / 20 miles*

A route devised to mark the 150th anniversary of the Co-operative Movement, starts from Toad Lane, the birthplace of the movement and takes in Healey Dell, Watergrove Reservoir, Hollingworth Lake, Milnrow and the Rochdale Canal.

Start and Finish:	Rochdale, Gtr Man	SD896136
Landranger maps:	109	
1 : 25,000 maps:	Ex 287 OL 21	

Publications, badges and certificates:
Booklet: *The Pioneers Round* by Derek Magnall (Rochdale Pioneers Museum) 1994. 34pp; A5. £1.85 (incs p&p).
Badge and certificate: (Rochdale Pioneers Museum). £2.00 (+ SAE).

Plogsland Round   412

Lincs, Notts   *76 km / 47 miles*

A walk around the city of Lincoln with the cathedral in view for much of the route. It links many villages following paths and green lanes across the flat, drained arable land and along the banks of the River Witham. Details are included for starting and finishing the route at Lincoln Youth Hostel.

Start and Finish:	Fiskerton, Lincs	TF058715
Landranger maps:	121	
1 : 25,000 maps:	Ex 271, 272	

Publications, badges and certificates:
Paperback: *The Plogsland Round* (Brett Collier). ISBN 1901184412. 40pp; A5. £5.50 (+ 65p p&p).
Badge: (Brett Collier). £1.25 (+ SAE).

Poppyline Marathon   413

Norfolk   *42 km / 26 miles*

An undulating route in North Norfolk partly coincident with the Norfolk Coast Path. The area was formerly traversed by the North Norfolk Railway known locally as the Poppyline. There is also an option for an 18 mile route.

Start and Finish:	Sheringham, Norfolk	TG159430
Landranger maps:	133	
1 : 25,000 maps:	Ex 251, 252	

Publications, badges and certificates:
Looseleaf: *Poppyline Marathon* (Bobbie Sauerzapf) 1997. 2pp; A4. Free (+ SAE).
Badge and certificate: (Bobbie Sauerzapf). £1.50 (+ A4 SAE).

Post Horn Trail   414

Lancs, N Yorks   *177 km / 110 miles*

Following the line of an ancient route, the Yorkshire plains are crossed to the moors of Blubberhouses then the route continues to the limestone Craven Hills and finishes along the Lune Valley.

Start:	York, N Yorks	SE602522
Finish:	Lancaster, Lancs	SD474618
Landranger maps:	97, 98, 99, 104, 105	
1 : 25,000 maps:	Ex 289, 290, 297, 298 OL 2, 41	

Publications, badges and certificates:
Paperback: *The Post Horn Trail* by Sheila Gordon (TBA 2002). Full details TBA 2002.

Pride of the Peak Walk 415
Derbys *48 km / 30 miles*

This route takes in a wide variety of scenery including limestone dales, gritstone edges, woodland, a number of villages and historical features such as Monsal Viaduct, Crossbrook Mill and Chatsworth House. There is 3,700ft of ascent.

Start and Finish:	Bakewell, Derbys	SK217685
Landranger maps:	119	
1 : 25,000 maps:	OL 24	

Publications, badges and certificates:
Booklet: *Pride of the Peak Walk* by Alan S. Edwards (Alan S. Edwards) 1991. 30pp; A5. £2.55 (incs p&p).
Badge and certificate: (Alan S. Edwards). £2.25 (incs p&p).

Purbeck Plodder Challenges 416
Dorset, IoW, Wilts *Various km / Various miles*

A series of challenge walks devised on behalf of the Purbeck Plodders Walking Club comprising: the Hardy Hobble (27 miles) – Hardy Monument to Corfe Castle; A Ridge Too Far (22 miles) – Maiden Newton circular; West Dorset Enigma (19 miles) – Litton Cheney circular; Day Return to Charmouth (18 miles) – circular; Purbeck Steam Package (24 miles) – Swanage to Corfe Castle; Cross Wight Traverse (29 miles) – Isle of Wight coast to coast; Inter-City Challenge (20 miles) – Wool to Weymouth; Majesty of the Wiltshire Downs (18 miles) – Broad Chalke circular; Locus Classicus (26 miles) – Bradbury Rings to Salisbury; and the Tesrod Elddod (33 miles) – Weymouth to Swanage. All are included in one publication.

Start:	Various	Various
Finish:	Various	Various
Landranger maps:	184, 193, 194, 195, 196	
1 : 25,000 maps:	Ex 116, 117, 118, 130 OL 15, 22, 29	

Publications, badges and certificates:
Booklet (spiral bound): *A Ridge Too Far* (Garth H. Gunn). 40pp; A5. £5.95 (incs p&p).

Purbeck Way 417
Dorset *39 km / 24 miles*

A route through varied scenery including riverside, heathland, woodland and downland, taking in Corfe Castle, the Purbeck hills and the dramatic Dorset coast. The Purbeck Way West (12½ miles and waymarked) leads from the Purbeck Way at Wareham to Coombe Keynes with a loop to Lulworth. Both link with the Wareham Forest Way at Wareham. See Stour Valley Way (Dorset).

Start:	Wareham, Dorset	SY922870
Finish:	Swanage, Dorset	SY035785
Landranger maps:	195	✔
1 : 25,000 maps:	OL 15	
Waymark:	Name and cliff scene logo	

Publications, badges and certificates:
Leaflet: *The Purbeck Way* (Purbeck Information & Heritage Centre). A5. £0.40 (+ SAE).
Leaflet: *The Purbeck Way West* (Purbeck Information & Heritage Centre). A5. £0.40 (+ SAE).

Quantock Way 418

Somers *53 km / 33 miles*

The Way visits Kingston St Mary, Timbercombe, Bicknoller Combe, West Quantoxhead and Watchet in crossing the ridge hills to the coast. Alternative routes beyond Bicknoller Combe and through the Brendon Hills are included, extending the total distance to over 40 miles.

Start:	Taunton, Somers	ST231254
Finish:	Minehead, Somers	SS979462
Landranger maps:	181, 182, 193	
1 : 25,000 maps:	Ex 128, 140 OL 9	

Publications, badges and certificates:
Booklet: *The Quantock Way* by John N. Merrill (Walk & Write Ltd). ISBN 1841730041. 60pp; A5. £4.95 (+ 75p p&p).
Badge and certificate: (Walk & Write Ltd). £3.50 (incs p&p).

Ramblers Route 419

Bracknell For, Wokingham *42 km / 26 miles*

A figure-of-eight route allowing for circuits of 19 or 13 miles through farmland, heaths, coniferous forests and visiting several country parks.

Start and Finish:	The Look Out, Bracknell For	SU875661
Landranger maps:	175	
1 : 25,000 maps:	Ex 160	
Waymark:	Black arrow on named white disc	

Publications, badges and certificates:
Leaflet: *Bracknell Forest Ramblers Route* (Bracknell Tourist Information Centre). A4/3. Free.

Ramsbottom Round 420

Lancs *32 km / 20 miles*

A route around Ramsbottom over moorland, riverside and farm paths taking in the Irwell Valley, Irwell Vale and Summerseat.

Start and Finish:	Ramsbottom, Lancs	SD792168
Landranger maps:	103, 109	
1 : 25,000 maps:	Ex 287	

Publications, badges and certificates:
Booklet: *Ramsbottom Round/Spanners Round* (Norman Thomas) 1992. 36pp; A5. £1.85 (incs p&p).
Badge and certificate: (Norman Thomas). £2.00 (+ SAE).

Red Kite Trail 421

Ceredigion, Powys   *118 km / 74 miles*

A route taking in Tregaron, Rhayader and Pumpsaint traversing the southern Cambrian Mountains, the home of the red kite and other birds of prey. Good navigational skills are required and the route between the four towns is self-devised.

Start and Finish:	Neuadd Arms Hotel, Llanwrtyd Wells,	SN879467
Landranger maps:	146, 147	
1 : 25,000 maps:	Ex 186, 187, 199, 200	
Path website:	www.bwf-ivv.org.uk/redkite.htm	

Publications, badges and certificates:
Looseleaf: *Red Kite Trail* (Llanwrtyd Wells Walking Club). A4/3. Free (+ SAE).
Badge and certificate: (Llanwrtyd Wells Walking Club). £2.00 (+ A4 SAE) & free.

Reiver's Way 422

Northumb   *242 km / 150 miles*

A meandering route across Northumberland, starting in the Tyne Valley passing the finest remains of Hadrian's Wall, and then heading northwest to Rothbury, over the Cheviots to Wooler, and finishing with the coast path from Budle Bay to Alnmouth.

Start:	Corbridge Station, Northumb	NZ989635
Finish:	Alnmouth, Northumb	NU248108
Landranger maps:	75, 80, 81, 87	
1 : 25,000 maps:	Ex 332, 340 OL 16, 42, 43	

Publications, badges and certificates:
Paperback: *The Reiver's Way* by James Roberts (Cicerone Press) 1993. ISBN 1852841303. 112pp; 116 x 176. £6.99.

Rezzy Rush 423

N Yorks   *64 km / 40 miles*

A route visiting the four reservoirs in the Washburn Valley, four in Oak Beck Valley and two in the Harrogate area. It is coincident in parts with the Harrogate – Dales Way link and the Harrogate Ringway and use is made of Yorkshire Water permissive and waymarked paths. The publication also caters for completion in a series of circular walks. Proceeds from sales are donated to charitable causes.

Start and Finish:	Valley Gardens, Harrogate, N Yorks	SE298554
Landranger maps:	104	
1 : 25,000 maps:	Ex 297	

Publications, badges and certificates:
Looseleaf: *Rezzy Rush* (John Eckersley). 6pp. £2.00 (incs p&p).
Certificate: (John Eckersley). £1.00 (incs p&p).

Rhymney Valley Ridgeway Walk   424

Caerphilly   *45 km / 28 miles*

A route winding its way across the hills encircling the unique and often spectacular scenery of the Rhymney Valley. The walk follows quiet countryside paths and lanes, where steep beech woodlands merge into panoramic mountain tops. Mynydd Machen is the highest point. It links with the Taff-Ely Ridgeway Walk at Caerphilly Common, and in the east is partly coincident with the Sirhowy Valley Walk. The Northern Rhymney Valley Ridgeway Walk (12 miles) links with the main circular walk at Gelligaer and finishes at Bryn Bach Park. See Capital Walk – Cardiff and St Illtyd's Walk.

Start and Finish:	Gelligaer, Caerphilly	ST137969
Landranger maps:	161, 171	✔
1 : 25,000 maps:	Ex 151, 152, 166	
Waymark:	Ridgeway Walk logo and standard arrows	

Publications, badges and certificates:
Leaflet: *Rhymney Valley Ridgeway Walk* (Caerphilly Mountain Countryside Service) 1993. A4/3. Free.
Leaflet: *Northern Rhymney Valley Ridgeway Walk* (Caerphilly County Borough Council). A4/3. Free.

Ribble Way   425

Lancs, N Yorks   *118 km / 73 miles*

The Way follows the valley of the River Ribble from the mouth to the source near to the Pennine Way National Trail on Gayle Moor. From the tidal marshes, the route passes Preston, Ribchester, Clitheroe, with views of Pendle Hill, Settle and Horton-in-Ribblesdale. At Horton, the Pen-y-ghent Café maintains a register for signature/comments by those taking part in the walk. See Clitheroe 60K, Lancashire Trail and Ribskip Challenge.

Start:	Longton, Lancs	SD458255
Finish:	Gayle Moor, N Yorks	SD813832
Landranger maps:	98, 102, 103	✔
1 : 25,000 maps:	Ex 287 OL 2, 21, 30, 41	
Waymark:	Blue and white letters RW/wave logo	

Publications, badges and certificates:
Softback: *The Ribble Way* by Gladys Sellers (Cicerone Press) 1993. ISBN 1852841079. 102pp; 116 x 176. £5.99.
Booklet: *A Walkers Guide to the Ribble Way* by Kevin Petrie and Allan Aspden (Kevin Petrie) 2001. 32pp; A5. £2.20 (+ 9 x 6 SAE).

Ribskip Challenge   426

N Yorks   *53 km / 33 miles*

The walk utilises the Settle – Carlisle Railway and whilst there are occasions when it takes to the routes of the Pennine Way National Trail, the Three Peaks Walk

(Yorkshire) and the Ribble Way, the route is generally along lesser used paths including visits to Pen-y-ghent, Attermire Scar, Otterburn and Gargrave.

Start:	Ribblehead Railway Station, N Yorks	SD766790
Finish:	Skipton Railway Station, N Yorks	SD989515
Landranger maps:	98, 104	
1 : 25,000 maps:	OL 2	

Publications, badges and certificates:
Looseleaf: *The Ribskip Challenge* (Edwin and Julia Tum). 5pp; A4. Free (+ 9 x 4 SAE).
Badge and certificate: (Edwin and Julia Tum). £3.00 (+ 9 x 4 SAE).

Ridgeway National Trail 427

Bucks, Herts, Oxon, Swindon, W Berks, Wilts   *136 km / 85 miles*

The western part of this National Trail largely follows the route of a prehistoric ridge track along the crest of the North Wessex Downs and passes many historic sites, including Barbury, Liddington, Uffington and Segsbury Castles (hill forts), Wayland's Smithy (long barrow) and Uffington White Horse. Much of the Trail is along a broad track which can be rutted. At Streatley the route crosses and then follows the River Thames for 5 miles before heading east into the Chiltern Hills, mainly along the north-western escarpment. The walking on the eastern half is more varied, along tracks and paths, across open downland, and through farm and woodland, passing Nuffield, Watlington, Chinnor, Princes Risborough (see Swan's Way), Wendover and Tring. At Wendover the waymarked Chiltern Link (8 miles and on OS mapping) leads to Chesham (see Colne Valley Way, Colne Valley Trail & Ebury Way). The Ridgeway is linked at Ivinghoe Beacon with the Greensand Ridge Walk by the Two Ridges Link (8 miles and included on OS mapping) and where it also connects with the Icknield Way Path. The Ashridge Estate Boundary Trail (16 miles) is a waymarked circular route coincident with the east end of the Ridgeway. See Wessex Ridgeway, Icknield Way Path and Trail, Land's End Trail, Midshires Way, d'Arcy Dalton Way, North and South Bucks Ways, Chiltern Way and Dorset Jubilee Trail.

Start:	Overton Hill, Wilts	SU118681
Finish:	Ivinghoe Beacon, Bucks	SP960168
Landranger maps:	165, 173, 174, 175	✔
1 : 25,000 maps:	Ex 157, 170, 171, 181	
Waymark:	National Trail Acorn	
User group:	Friends of Ridgeway	
Path website:	www.nationaltrails.gov.uk	

Publications, badges and certificates:
Softback: *The Ridgeway* (Official Guide) by Neil Curtis (Aurum Press) 1997. ISBN 1854102680. 144pp; 210 x 130. £10.99.
Paperback: *The Ridgeway Companion* (Ridgeway National Trail Officer). 96pp; 210 x 147. £3.95 (+ £1.05 p&p).
Paperback: *Exploring the Ridgeway* by Alan Charles (Countryside Books) 2000. ISBN 1853060097. 96pp; A5. £5.95 (+ £1.00 p&p).
Paperback: *The Ridgeway* by Ray Quinlan (Cicerone Press) 2002. ISBN 1852843462. Details TBA.

Booklet: *The Ridgeway Public Transport Guide* (Ridgeway National Trail Officer) Annual. 36pp; A5. Free (+ 9 x 6 31p SAE).
Leaflet: *The Ridgeway National Trail* (Ridgeway National Trail Officer). A5. Free.
Stripmap (folded): *The Ridgeway* (Harvey Maps) 1999. ISBN 1851373144. 240 x 115. £8.95 (+ 80p p&p).
Stripmap: *The Ridgeway Map and Guide* (Footprint). ISBN 1871149037. £3.50.
Leaflet: *The Chiltern Link* (Buckinghamshire County Council). A4/3. Free (+ SAE).
Leaflet: *Two Ridges Link* (Buckinghamshire County Council). A4/3. Free (+ SAE).
Leaflet: *The Ashridge Estate Boundary Trail* (Ashridge Estate Visitors Centre). A5. £1.00 (+ SAE) – cheques payable to National Trust.
Badge: (Ridgeway National Trail Officer). £1.40 (+ SAE).

Ring of Gullion Way   428

Newry & Mourne   *53 km / 33 miles*

One of the official Waymarked Ways in Northern Ireland, this route follows the natural geological formation known as a ring-dyke through the Ring of Gullion AONB with abundant views of Slieve Gullion, the ring-dyke, Carlingford Lough and the Mourne Mountains. Use is made of forestry and grass tracks, and rugged open hillsides.

Start:	Newry, Newry & Mourne	J095235
Finish:	Derrymore House, Bessbrook, Newry & Mourne	J055277
Landranger maps:	OS(NI) 29	✔
1 : 25,000 maps:	Not applicable in NI	
Waymark:	Route name/walker outline on blue background	

Publications, badges and certificates:
Leaflet: *An Illustrated Guide to the Ring of Gullion Way* (Newry & Mourne District Council). £0.50 (+ 9 x 6 SAE).

Ripon Rowel   429

N Yorks   *80 km / 50 miles*

A route around the ancient city of Ripon, visiting villages, sites of special and historical significance, wooded valleys, rivers, lakes and streams.

Start and Finish:	Ripon, N Yorks	SE319705
Landranger maps:	99	✔
1 : 25,000 maps:	Ex 298, 299	
Waymark:	Rowel logo – circular part of a spur	

Publications, badges and certificates:
Booklet: *The Ripon Rowel Walk* by Les Taylor (RA Ripon Group) 1996. 70pp; 210 x 145. £4.95 (+ 55p p&p).
Badge: (RA Ripon Group). £1.50 (+ SAE).

River Axe Walk · 430
Devon, Dorset, Somers **45 km / 28 miles**

A walk following the course of the River Axe from source to sea as closely as possible, using minor roads only where necessary. The former Cistercian Monastery of Forde Abbey is passed on the way and alternative routes are described at Axminster.

Start:	Beaminster, Dorset	ST480013
Finish:	Axmouth Harbour, Devon	SY256897
Landranger maps:	193	
1 : 25,000 maps:	Ex 116	

Publications, badges and certificates:
Booklet: *River Axe Walk* by Richard Easterbrook and Geoff Broadhurst (Easterhurst Publications Ltd) 2000. ISBN 0953827208. 56pp; A5. £3.95 (+ 45p p&p).

River Otter Walk · 431
Devon, Somers **55 km / 34 miles**

A walk following the course of the River Otter from its source at Otterhead Lakes to the sea as closely as possible, using minor roads only where necessary.

Start:	Churchinford, Somers	ST213126
Finish:	Budleigh Salterton, Devon	SY072820
Landranger maps:	192, 193	
1 : 25,000 maps:	Ex 115, 116, 128	

Publications, badges and certificates:
Booklet: *River Otter Walk* by Richard Easterbrook and Geoff Broadhurst (Easterhurst Publications Ltd) 2001. 56pp; A5. £3.95 (+ 45p p&p).

River Parrett Trail · 432
Dorset, Somers **80 km / 50 miles**

A route which follows the River Parrett from source to mouth winding through the Somerset Levels, moors, ecologically sensitive areas and some of England's richest pasture land where there is an abundance of history and wildlife. The Trail crosses the Liberty Trail near Haselbury and Ham Hill, where it also meets up with the Leland Trail.

Start:	Chedington, Dorset	ST490059
Finish:	Steart, Somers	ST281469
Landranger maps:	182, 193, 194	✔
1 : 25,000 maps:	Ex 117, 128, 129, 140	
Waymark:	Disc with curved line depicting river	
Path website:	www.riverparrett-trail.org.uk	

Publications, badges and certificates:
Booklet: *The River Parrett Trail* (South Somerset District Council). ISBN 1899983309. 26pp; 215 x 165. £5.95 (+ 85p p&p).
Leaflet: *River Parrett Trail* (South Somerset District Council) 2000. A4/3. Free.

River Teign Walk 433
Devon *64 km / 40 miles*

A walk following as closely as possible the course of the River Teign from its source on Dartmoor to the sea, using minor roads only where necessary. The end of the walk is on the tidal foreshore.

Start:	Fernworthy Reservoir, Devon	SX670838
Finish:	Shaldon, Devon	SX935722
Landranger maps:	191, 202	
1 : 25,000 maps:	Ex 110 OL 28	

Publications, badges and certificates:
Booklet: *River Teign Walk* by Richard Easterbrook and Geoff Broadhurst (Easterhurst Publications Ltd) 2002. A5. Details TBA.

Rivers Way 434
Derbys, Staffs *69 km / 43 miles*

A meandering route through the Peak District National Park, the Way links the five principal rivers – The Noe, Derwent, Wye, Dove and Manifold – and passes the villages of Hope, Grindleford, Baslow, Bakewell, Flagg, Hartington and Wetton. See Cal-Der-Went Walk.

Start:	Edale, Derbys	SK124853
Finish:	Ilam, Derbys	SK135509
Landranger maps:	119	
1 : 25,000 maps:	OL 1, 24	

Publications, badges and certificates:
Booklet: *The Rivers Way* by John Merrill (Walk & Write Ltd). ISBN 0907496415. 36pp; A5. £3.95 (+ 75p p&p).
Badge and certificate: (Walk & Write Ltd). £3.50 (incs p&p).

Riversides Way 435
Herefordshire, Shropshire, Powys *115 km / 72 miles*

A walk in the Welsh Marches centered on Aymestrey and taking in the valleys and hills of the rivers Teme and Lugg.

Start and Finish:	Aymestrey, Herefs	SO425650
Landranger maps:	137	
1 : 25,000 maps:	Ex 201, 203	

Publications, badges and certificates:
Paperback: *The Riversides Way* by David Milton (Meridian Books) 2001. ISBN 1869922433. 160pp; 145 x 230. £8.95 (+ £1.00 p&p).

Roach Valley Way 436

Essex *37 km / 23 miles*

A route around south-east Essex which takes in a variety of landscapes including the ancient woodlands of Hockley and the coastal margins of the Roach and Crouch estuaries. See Southend Millennium Walk.

Start and Finish:	Rochford, Essex	TQ873905
Landranger maps:	168, 178	✔
1 : 25,000 maps:	Ex 175, 176	
Waymark:	Blue/yellow river scene & name	

Publications, badges and certificates:
Booklet: *Roach Valley Way* (Essex County Council) 1997. ISBN 1852811498. 16pp; A5. £2.50.

Robin Hood Way 437

Notts *169 km / 105 miles*

The Way features areas of Nottingham associated with the legendary figure of Robin Hood and his exploits, crossing lowland farmland and heathland, and visiting the great houses and parks of the Dukeries and forests, including Sherwood Forest.

Start:	Nottingham, Notts	SK569392
Finish:	Edwinstowe, Notts	SK626669
Landranger maps:	120, 129	✔
1 : 25,000 maps:	Ex 260, 270, 271	
Waymark:	Bow and arrow, green on white	

Publications, badges and certificates:
Paperback: *The Robin Hood Walks* by Nottingham Wayfarers (Nottinghamshire County Council) 1994. ISBN 1871890020. 156pp; 192 x 133. £4.95 (+ 35p p&p).

Rochdale Way 438

Lancs *72 km / 45 miles*

A route around the Borough of Rochdale over moorland and through wooded valleys and passing historic urban sites. Blackstone Edge, Healey Dell, Knowl Hill, Queens Park, Tandle Hill and Piethorne Valley are visited along the Way.

Start and Finish:	Hollingworth Lake Visitor Centre, Littleborough	SK938151
Landranger maps:	109	✔
1 : 25,000 maps:	Ex 277 OL 21	

Publications, badges and certificates:
Paperback: *The Rochdale Way* (Hollingworth Lake Visitor Centre). 34pp; A5. £2.50 (+ 9 x 6 SAE + 2 x 2nd class stamps).

Rosedale Circuit   439
N Yorks   *59 km / 37 miles*

A route through Rosedale, Farndale, Bransdale, Westerdale, Danby Dale, Great Fryup Dale and Glaisdale, which includes many points of natural and historical interest, with moorland tracks and grassy dales. This is a strenuous route with 4,000ft of ascent.

Start and Finish:	Rosedale Abbey, N Yorks	SE723959
Landranger maps:	94, 100	
1 : 25,000 maps:	OL 26, 27	
Waymark:	Letters RC for most of the way	

Publications, badges and certificates:
Leaflet: *Rosedale Circuit* (Kim Peacock). A4. Free (+ 9 x 4 SAE).
Badge and certificate: (Kim Peacock). £1.30 (+ 9 x 6 SAE).

Rossendale Way   440
Lancs   *72 km / 45 miles*

A high-level route around Bacup, Rawtenstall, Haslingden and Whitworth in the Rossendale Valley, crossing the open moors and farmland of the South Pennines which roughly follows the Rossendale Borough boundary. Although easy to follow, it does need care in poor conditions. The Weighver's Way (9 miles) is a linear route from Hollingworth Lake, Littleborough, which connects with the Rossendale Way at Healey Dell. See Burnley Way, Crowthorn Rose and Irwell Sculpture Trail.

Start and Finish:	Sharneyford, Lancs	SD889246
Landranger maps:	103, 109	✔
1 : 25,000 maps:	Ex 287, OL 21	
Waymark:	Letters RW	

Publications, badges and certificates:
Folder: *Rossendale Way* (Rossendale Borough Council). 8pp; A4/3. £2.00 (+ 50p p&p).
Leaflet: *The Weighver's Way* (Hollingworth Lake Visitor Centre). A4/3. £0.40 (+ 9 x 4 SAE) – cheques payable to Rochdale Borough Council.

Rother Valley Walks   441
Hants, W Sussex   *166 km / 103 miles*

There are fourteen linked circular walks providing many options of traversing the Rother Valley. The scenery is varied and interesting and road walking has been kept to a minimum.

Start:	Selborne, Hants	SU742336
Finish:	Pulborough, W Sussex	TQ043187
Landranger maps:	186, 197	
1 : 25,000 maps:	Ex 120, 121, 133	

Publications, badges and certificates:
Booklet: *Rother Valley Walks* (Sussex Downs Conservation Board) 2000. 34pp; A5. £2.50 (incs p&p).

Rotherham Round Walk   442

S Yorks   *40 km / 25 miles*

This route takes in parkland, woods, lakes and the architectural monuments of Wentworth, followed by the steelworks of Parkgate, Wickersley and back into the town centre. Proceeds from sales donated to local charities.

Start and Finish:	Rotherham, S Yorks	SK428928
Landranger maps:	111	✔
1 : 25,000 maps:	Ex 278, 279	
Waymark:	Named discs with Chantry Bridge logo	
Path website:	www.rotherhamrotary.org.uk	

Publications, badges and certificates:
Leaflet: *Rotherham Roundwalk* (Rotherham Tourist Information Centre). A4/3. Free.
Looseleaf: *Route map* (Ratcliffe's Stationers). £1.00 (+ 9 x 4 SAE).
Badge and certificate: (Ratcliffe's Stationers). £1.90 & £1.00 (+ 9 x 4 SAE).

Round Preston Walk   443

Lancs   *37 km / 23 miles*

Created by the RA, this route around the town takes in the River Ribble (partly coincident with the Ribble Way), Grimsargh, Broughton, Woodplumpton and Lea.

Start and Finish:	Penwortham Bridge, Lancs	SD527288
Landranger maps:	102	
1 : 25,000 maps:	Ex 286	
Waymark:	Preston Guild logo (cross-bearing lamb)	
Path website:	http://members.aol.com/prestonra	

Publications, badges and certificates:
Booklet: *The Round Preston Walk* (RA Preston Group) 1991. 32pp. £1.80 (incs p&p).

Round the Reservoirs   444

Derbyshire   *48 km / 30 miles*

A tour around the reservoirs of the eastern part of the Dark Peak. Combining the tranquility and wilderness of many little-frequented reservoirs, the route includes a high-level crossing over Howden via Cut Gate to finish along the Derwent Valley.

Start and Finish:	Fairholmes Visitor Centre, Derbyshire	SK173894
Landranger maps:	110	
1 : 25,000 maps:	OL 1	

Publications, badges and certificates:
Booklet: *Round the Reservoirs* (Ken Jones). A5. Free (+ 9 x 6 SAE).
Certificate: (Ken Jones). Free (+ 9 x 6 strengthened SAE).

Royal Military Canal Path   445

E Sussex, Kent   *43 km / 27 miles*

The Royal Military Canal Path mainly follows a canal-side path, which fringes the
northern edge of Romney Marsh and which was built in the early 19th century as a
defence against a possible invasion by Napoleon. The Canal is a Scheduled Ancient
Monument and a SSSI. In addition to its historical and archaeological interest it is
a valuable wetland habitat for a variety of species of flora and fauna. Links are
made with the Saxon Shore Way at various points.

Start:	Pett Level, E Sussex	TQ888134
Finish:	Seabrook, Kent	TR188349
Landranger maps:	179, 189, 199	✔
1 : 25,000 maps:	Ex 124, 125, 137, 138	
Waymark:	Reeds and canal	

Publications, badges and certificates:
No publications: on OS mapping.

Royal Shrovetide Challenge Walks   446

Derbys   *31 km / 19 miles*

A route named after the annual game of football played in the area each Shrove
Tuesday when locals from either side of Henmore Beck attempt to score against the
other, the goals being placed 3 miles apart at Sturston and Clifton. As well as
visiting the location of each goal, the route takes in Nether Sturston, Madge Hill,
Tissington, Thorpe and Mayfield. The route publications includes details of a
second challenge walk of 11 miles, partly coincident with the longer one and also
visiting Sturston and Clifton.

Start and Finish:	Ashbourne, Derbys	SK184464
Landranger maps:	119, 128	
1 : 25,000 maps:	Ex 259 OL 24	
Waymark:	Orange discs on longer route, green on shorter;	
	orange/green on coincident parts	

Publications, badges and certificates:
Paperback (spiral/laminated): *Royal Shrovetide Challenge Walks* (Mike Warner). 41pp; A5.
£5.00 (incs p&p).
Complete package: including guidebook, badges and certificates for both routes (Mike
Warner). £7.50 (incs p&p).
Badge and certificate: (Mike Warner). £2.00 & £1.00 (post free) – available for each walk.

Rutland Round 447

Rutland *104 km / 65 miles*

A round of the County of Rutland with the route remaining within the county boundary and in parts actually along it. Braunston, Uppingham, Barrowden, Empingham and Thistleton are visited along the way with a deliberate diversion to Rutland Water included.

Start and Finish:	Rutland County Museum, Oakham,	
	Rutland	SK863085
Landranger maps:	130, 141	
1 : 25,000 maps:	Ex 234, 247	
Waymark:	Green and yellow coloured signs displaying name, acorn and CPRE	

Publications, badges and certificates:
Paperback: *The Rutland Round* by John Williams (Cordee Ltd). ISBN 1871890446. 40pp; 210 x 138. £4.99.

Rutland Water Challenge Walk 448

Rutland *38 km / 24 miles*

A route around the largest man-made reservoir in Europe.

Start and Finish:	Rutland Water, Rutland	SK935083
Landranger maps:	141	
1 : 25,000 maps:	Ex 234	

Publications, badges and certificates:
Booklet: *The Rutland Water* Challenge Walk by John Merrill (Walk & Write Ltd). ISBN 0907496881. 36pp; A5. £3.95 (+ 75p p&p).
Badge and certificate: (Walk & Write Ltd). £3.50 (incs p&p).

Saddleworth Five Trig Points Walk 449

Gtr Man *32 km / 20 miles*

A tough high level circuit over open moorland and across peat groughs, with parts of the Walk being coincident with the Pennine Way National Trail and other routes in this area. As its name suggests, the route links five trig points on the Saddleworth Moors, namely Alphin Pike, Featherbed Moss, Black Hill, West Nab and Broadstone Hill. Navigational skills recommended. See New Five Trig Points Walk.

Start and Finish:	Greenfield, Gtr Man	SE002040
Landranger maps:	109, 110	
1 : 25,000 maps:	OL 1	

Publications, badges and certificates:
Looseleaf: *Saddleworth Five Trig Points Walk* (Carole E. Engel). A4. Free (+ 9 x 4 SAE).
Badge and certificate: (Carole E. Engel). £1.50 (+ SAE) & £0.20 (+ 9 x 6 SAE).

Saddleworth Skyline 450

Gtr Man   *45 km / 28 miles*

A mainly high-level route linking the tops of Saddleworth over moorland, hills and valleys.

Start and Finish:	Dovestones Reservoir, Gtr Man	SE013034
Landranger maps:	109, 110	
1 : 25,000 maps:	OL 1	

Publications, badges and certificates:
Looseleaf: *The Saddleworth Skyline* (Sam R. Taylor). Free (+ 9 x 4 SAE).
Badge and certificate: (Sam R. Taylor). £1.80 & £0.20 (+ SAE's).

Saints' Way/Forth an Syns 451

Cornwall   *47 km / 29 miles*

The Way follows the route thought to have been taken by the ancient Cornish and Welsh Saints across mid-Cornwall through valleys, woodland, moors and villages. From the north coast, it crosses St Breock Downs to reach Helman Tor Gate where there are options through either St Blazey or Milltown to the south coast. At Padstow the Camel Trail (19 miles and named on OS mapping), using two sections of disused railway line, goes via Boscarne Junction to Bodmin and also from Boscarne Junction to Poley's Bridge. See Smugglers' Way.

Start:	Padstow, Cornwall	SW920754
Finish:	Fowey, Cornwall	SX127522
Landranger maps:	200, 204	✔
1 : 25,000 maps:	Ex 106, 107, 109	
Waymark:	Celtic Cross	

Publications, badges and certificates:
Folder: *The Saints' Way: Forth an Syns* (Cornwall County Council) 1999. 12 laminated cards; A5. £3.99 (post free) – includes accommodation leaflet.
Leaflet: *The Saints' Way* (Cornwall County Council). Free.
Booklet: *Look at the Camel Trail* by Anita Dunstan (Kernow Scopes) 1999. 32pp; A5. £2.95 (+ 9 x 6 SAE & 54p stamp).
Leaflet: *The Camel Trail* by Anita Dunstan (Kernow Scopes) 2000. A4/3. £0.10 (+ 9 x 4 SAE).

Salisbury Country Way 452

Hants, Wilts   *96 km / 60 miles*

A route around Salisbury across varied downland, ancient woodlands and a number of chalk stream valleys following age-old tracks. Public transport access into Salisbury is available at a number of points as is refreshment, there being 20 public houses along the way.

Start and Finish:	Stonehenge, Wilts	SU122423
Landranger maps:	184	
1 : 25,000 maps:	Ex 118, 130, 131 OL 22	

Publications, badges and certificates:
Booklet: *Salisbury Country Way* (Bill Brown) 1998. 24pp; A5. £2.95 (incs p&p).
Certificate: (Bill Brown). Free (+ A5 SAE).

Salt & Sails Trail 453
Cheshire *32 km / 20 miles*

A route following the Weaver Navigation from the River Mersey and passing a number of locks and the Anderton Lift.

Start:	Weston Point, Cheshire	SJ813804
Finish:	Winsford, Cheshire	SJ655663
Landranger maps:	117, 118	
1 : 25,000 maps:	Ex 267, 268	

Publications, badges and certificates:
Booklet: *The Salt & Sails Trail* by David Burkhill-Howarth (Walk & Write Ltd). ISBN 1874754586. A5. £4.50 (+ 75p p&p).
Badge and certificate: (Walk & Write Ltd). £3.50 (incs p&p).

Salter's Way 454
Cheshire *38 km / 24 miles*

The Way follows an old salt track across lowland Cheshire from the salt area around Northwich to the moors above Macclesfield. It passes still-working brine pumps, as well as such varied features as Jodrell Bank and the raised lowland bog of Danes Moss.

Start:	Broken Cross, Cheshire	SJ682732
Finish:	Salterford, Cheshire	SJ983763
Landranger maps:	118	
1 : 25,000 maps:	Ex 267, 268 OL 24	

Publications, badges and certificates:
Booklet: *The Salter's Way* by John Merrill (Walk & Write Ltd). ISBN 0907496970. 32pp; A5. £4.50 (+ 75p p&p).
Badge and certificate: (Walk & Write Ltd). £3.50 (incs p&p).

Samaritan Way 455
Cleveland, N Yorks *64 km / 40 miles*

A strenuous high-level route across the North York Moors National Park, crossing Commondale, Great Fryup Dale, Glaisdale and Farndale Moors to return via Westerdale, Baysdale and part of the Cleveland Way National Trail.

Start and Finish:	Guisborough, Cleveland	NZ615160
Landranger maps:	93, 94, 100	
1 : 25,000 maps:	OL 26, 27	

Publications, badges and certificates:
Looseleaf: *Samaritan Way* (Richard Pinkney). Free (+ 9 x 4 SAE).
Badge and certificate: (Richard Pinkney). £2.25 & £0.25 (+SAE's).

Sandstone Trail 456

Cheshire, Shrops *51 km / 32 miles*

The Trail follows the dissected central Cheshire sandstone ridge rising to heights of over 700ft and taking in Delamere Plain, Beeston Gap, the wooded Peckforton Hills and Bickerton Hills, to the Shropshire Union Canal where it links with the South Cheshire Way. See also Cheshire Ways, Lancashire Trail and Maelor Way.

Start:	Frodsham (Beacon Hill), Cheshire	SJ517767
Finish:	Whitchurch, Shrops	SJ527413
Landranger maps:	117	✔
1 : 25,000 maps:	Ex 257, 267	
Waymark:	Black bootmark and yellow letter S	

Publications, badges and certificates:
Booklet: *Sandstone Trail* by Ruth Rogers (Mara Publications) 1995. ISBN 0952240920. 68pp; A5. £4.99.
Booklet: *Longer Trails in Vale Royal* by Carl Rogers (Vale Royal Borough Council) 1993. 76pp; A5. £1.95.
Leaflet: *Sandstone Trail* (Cheshire County Council). A2/3. Free (+ 9 x 6 SAE).

Sarn Helen 457

Carms, Ceredigion, Conwy, Gwynedd *258 km / 160 miles*

Sarn Helen is the name of this Roman route through West Wales, connecting various Roman remains. In places the old road is clearly visible, but in others it is a matter of conjecture. From the Roman fort at Caerhun the route heads along the edge of Snowdonia to the Swallow Falls, Dolwyddelan, skirts Ffestiniog to Trawsfynydd, and continues to Dolgellau and Machynlleth. After crossing the Rheidol valley, the route becomes less wild and more agricultural to Bronant, Lampeter, and Carmarthen, albeit moorland at 1,200 ft is crossed in the Pencader area. Navigational skills would be appropriate on the northern part of the route.

Start:	Caerhun, Conwy	SH775704
Finish:	Carmarthen, Carms	SN400210
Landranger maps:	115, 124, 135, 146, 159	
1 : 25,000 maps:	Ex 177, 185, 186, 199, 213 OL 17, 18	

Publications, badges and certificates:
Paperback: *Sarn Helen: Walking a Roman Road Through Wales* by Arthur Rylance and John Cantrell (Cicerone Press) 1992. ISBN 185284101X. 248pp; 116 x 176. £8.99.

Sarum Way 458

Wilts *50 km / 31 miles*

A route around Salisbury with links to the Avon Valley Path, Clarendon Way and Monarch's Way with visits made to South Newton, Alderbury and Charlton and other villages.

Start and Finish:	Lower Woodford, Wilts	SU126353
Landranger maps:	184	
1 : 25,000 maps:	Ex 130	
Waymark:	Cathedral silhouette	

Publications, badges and certificates:
Booklet: *The Sarum Way* (RA South Wiltshire Group). 25pp; A5. £2.50 (+ 50p p&p).

Saxon Shore Way   459
E Sussex, Kent, Medway   *262 km / 163 miles*

The Way around the ancient coastline offers a diversity of scenery, from wide expanses of marshland bordering the Thames and Medway estuaries to the White Cliffs of Dover. There are views over Romney Marsh from the escarpment that marks the ancient coastline between Folkestone and Rye and from the cliffs of the High Weald at Hastings. Here the Romans invaded Britain and, later, built the Saxon Shore forts to defend the island against a new wave of invaders, and St Augustine landed to bring the Gospel to the Anglo-Saxon Kingdom which would later fall to the Normans who, in their turn, erected great fortresses like Dover Castle to defend their conquests. Two walks also included on OS mapping are the Swale Heritage Trail – from Murston to Goodnestone (11 miles) which caters for circular walks of up to 20 miles when incorporated with the Saxon Shore route between Murston and Faversham and the shorter waymarked Wantsum Walks which can be incorporated with the Way to provide extended circular routes. At Rye the route connects with the 1066 Country Walk. See E-Routes (E2). See Greensand Way, Medway Valley Walk, Royal Military Canal Path, Thanet Coastal Path and Wealdway. The waymarked Maritime Heritage Trail (total 32 miles) is a series of four connecting circular walks between Hastings and Rye and based on Hastings (7 miles), Fairlight (8 miles), Winchelsea (10 miles) and Rye (7 miles) so providing alternative routes for the 20 miles between the two towns.

Start:	Gravesend, Kent	TQ647745
Finish:	Hastings, E Sussex	TQ825094
Landranger maps:	177, 178, 179, 189, 199	✔
1 : 25,000 maps:	Ex 124, 125, 137, 138, 148, 149, 150, 162, 163	
Waymark:	Red Viking helmet	

Publications, badges and certificates:
Paperback: *The Saxon Shore Way* by Bea Cowan (Aurum Press) 1996. ISBN 185410392X. 168pp; 210 x 130. £10.99.
Booklet: *Swale Heritage Trail* (Kent County Council) 1995. ISBN 1873010508. 28pp; 210 x 148. £2.45 post free.
Folder: *Wantsum Walks – Coatal Walks in Kent* (Kent County Council) 1995. ISBN 1873010001. 3 leaflets; A4/3. £2.45 post free.
Folder: *Rye Bay Countryside Pack* – includes Maritime Heritage Trail produced by East Sussex County Council (Rye Bay Countryside Service). A5. £1.50 (incs p&p) – 5 route cards and 9 leaflets. Cheques payable to E Sussex County Council.

Scarborough Rock Challenge 460

N Yorks *42 km / 26 miles*

A route supported by the East Yorkshire Group of the LDWA taking in the coast, Oliver's Mount, Hackness, Burniston and Scalby.

Start and Finish:	Peasholm Park, Scarborough, N Yorks	TA035897
Landranger maps:	101	
1 : 25,000 maps:	OL 27	

Publications, badges and certificates:
Looseleaf: *Scarborough Rock Challenge Walk* (Mike Ellis). A4. Free (+ 9 x 4 SAE).
Badge: (Mike Ellis). £1.00 (+ SAE).

Seahorse Saunter 461

N Yorks *69 km / 43 miles*

The route crosses the North York Moors to the old Nordic settlement of Whitby. Following a mixture of field paths, bridleways and paved packhorse ways, the Saunter passes through farmland, open moors and wooded valleys, with 5000ft of ascent. Most of the route is easy to follow, but in poor weather conditions navigational skills are appropriate.

Start:	Kilburn White Horse, N Yorks	SE515814
Finish:	Whitby, N Yorks	NZ901113
Landranger maps:	94, 100	
1 : 25,000 maps:	OL 26, 27	

Publications, badges and certificates:
Leaflet: *Seahorse Saunter* (Simon Townson). A4. Free (+ 9 x 4 SAE).
Badge and certificate: (Simon Townson). £2.00 (+ 10 x 8 SAE).

Sefton Coastal Footpath 462

Merseyside *34 km / 21 miles*

From the northern outskirts of Liverpool the route through dunes, marshes and the towns of Southport and Crosby passes the Ainsdale Nature and Formby National Trust Reserves.

Start:	Waterloo Station, Merseyside	SJ321981
Finish:	Crossens, Merseyside	SD374205
Landranger maps:	102, 108	✔
1 : 25,000 maps:	Ex 266, 275	
Waymark:	Natterjack toad logo	

Publications, badges and certificates:
Booklet: *Walks on the Sefton Coast* by John Houston (Sefton Metropolitan Borough Council) 1994. 26pp; 250 x 225. £2.50 (incs p&p).

Settle Scramble   463

N Yorks   *40 km / 25 miles*

A route taking in Fountain's Fell, Helwith Bridge and Feizor.

Start and Finish:	Settle, N Yorks	SD821632
Landranger maps:	98	
1 : 25,000 maps:	OL 2	

Publications, badges and certificates:

Looseleaf: *Settle Scramble* (Ian Parker). A4. Free (+ 9 x 4 SAE).
Badge and certificate: (Ian Parker). £2.00 & £0.50 (+ 9 x 6 SAE).

Severn Way   464

Glos, Powys, S Glos, Shrops, Worcs   *338 km / 210 miles*

A route along the entire Severn Valley from the source to the sea. Starting on the
wild Plynlimon plateau in Mid-Wales, the route takes in Hafren Forest, Llanidloes,
Newtown, Welshpool, Shrewsbury and Ironbridge before heading south through
Worcester, Tewkesbury and Gloucester to the finish. A link into Bristol is available.
See Gloucestershire Way, Wye Valley Walk, Staffordshire and Worcestershire Canal
Walk, Worcester & Birmingham Canal Walk, Three Choirs Way and Telford and
Wrekin Walks.

Start:	Plynlimon, Powys	SN822899
Finish:	Severn Beach, Glos	ST540847
Landranger maps:	126, 127, 135, 137, 138, 150, 162, 172	✔
1 : 25,000 maps:	Ex 154, 167, 179, 190, 204, 214, 215, 216,	
	218, 219, 240, 241 OL 14	
Waymark:	Severn Trow logo and named posts	
Path website:	www.severnway.com/home/home.html	

Publications, badges and certificates:

Paperback (spiral bound): *Severn Way – the Longest Riverside Walk in Britain* (Official Guide)
produced by Severn Way Partnership (Environment Agency) 1999. ISBN 1902999002. 103pp;
A5. £6.95 (incs p&p).
Paperback (spiral bound): *Guide to Severn Way East Bank* by S. H. Gidman (Gloucestershire
County Council) 1989. ISBN 0904950735. 56pp; A5. £3.50 (incs p&p).

Sheffield Country Walk   465

Derbys, S Yorks   *85 km / 53 miles*

This varied route around the outskirts of the city passes many sites and buildings
of archaeological, historical and industrial interest. It follows woodland and
riverside paths, crossing undulating farmland and the open gritstone moorlands.

Start and Finish:	Eckington, Derbys	SK434798
Landranger maps:	110, 111, 120	
1 : 25,000 maps:	Ex 269, 278 OL 1, 24	
Waymark:	Yellow arrows and sheaf symbols	

DETAILS OF ROUTES

Publications, badges and certificates:
Booklet: *Sheffield Country Walk* by John Harker (RA Sheffield) 1996. £2.00 (incs p&p).

Sheffield Way   466
Derbys, S Yorks   *72 km / 45 miles*

A similar route to the Sheffield Country Way but is shorter by deliberately keeping to a tighter circuit mostly within the City boundary. Starting near the M1 it follows a route soon into woodlands and moors bordering the Peak District followed by Stanage, Totley and Coal Aston. See Dronfield 2000 Rotary Walk.

Start and Finish:	Tinsley, S Yorks	SK399912
Landranger maps:	110, 111, 119, 120	
1 : 25,000 maps:	Ex 269, 278 OL 1, 24	

Publications, badges and certificates:
Looseleaf: *Sheffield Way* by Peter Price (RA Sheffield). 52pp; A4. £2.50 (incs p&p).

Shetland Walks   467
Shetland   *Various km / Various miles*

These comprise a series of long distance routes along the coastlines of the islands of Shetland, namely Yell (101 miles), Unst (63 miles), Fetlar (31 miles), Westside (162 miles) and South Mainland (78 miles).

Start:	Various	Various
Finish:	Various	Various
Landranger maps:	1, 2, 3, 4	
1 : 25,000 maps:	Ex TBA 2002	

Publications, badges and certificates:
Paperback: *Walking the Coastline of Shetland: 1 – Yell* by Peter Guy (Shetland Times Ltd). ISBN 1898852189. 96pp; A5. £6.95 (+ £1.05 p&p).
Paperback: *Walking the Coastline of Shetland: 2 – Unst* by Peter Guy (Shetland Times Ltd). Details TBA 2002.
Paperback: *Walking the Coastline of Shetland: 3 – Island of Fetlar* by Peter Guy (Shetland Times Ltd). ISBN 0951584510. 70pp; A5. £4.99 (+ 60p p&p).
Paperback: *Walking the Coastline of Shetland: 5 – Westside* by Peter Guy (Shetland Times Ltd). ISBN 1898852065. 96pp; A5. £6.95 (+ £1.05 p&p).
Paperback: *Walking the Coastline of Shetland: 6 – South Mainland* by Peter Guy (Shetland Times Ltd). ISBN 1898852642. 112pp; A5. £8.99 (+ £1.35 p&p).

Shieldsman Walk   468
Tyne & Wear   *53 km / 33 miles*

A route along the coast and through the countryside of Tyneside with an historic theme, crossing the Tyne by pedestrian tunnel and ferry.

Start and Finish:	South Shields, Tyne & Wear	NZ370676
Landranger maps:	88	
1 : 25,000 maps:	Ex 316	

Publications, badges and certificates:
Leaflet: *Shieldsman Walk* (David Kidd). A4. Free (+ SAE).
Certificate: (David Kidd). Free (+ A4 SAE).

Shrewsbury to Holywell Walk 469

Cheshire, Denbighs, Flints, Shrops   *129 km / 80 miles*

A route claimed to have been taken by Guy Fawkes, and several kings of England, from Shrewsbury Abbey to St Winifride's Well. The route is of many contrasts as it takes in Wem, Whitchurch, Malpas, Rossett and Nont.

Start:	Shrewsbury, Shrops	SJ499116
Finish:	Holywell, Flints	SJ188763
Landranger maps:	116, 117, 126	
1 : 25,000 maps:	Ex 241, 256, 257, 265	

Publications, badges and certificates:
Booklet (Spiral bound): *Following Kings and Gunpowder Plotters* by Raymond Roberts (Clwydian Walks) 1998. ISBN 1874462410. 40pp; A5. £2.00 (incs p&p).

Shropshire Peaks Walk 470

Shrops   *160 km / 99 miles*

A walk taking in the main peaks of South Shropshire including Hopesay Hill, Bury Ditches, Hergan, Linley Hill, Stiperstones, Long Mynd, Caer Caradoc, the Lawley, Wenlock Edge, Brown Clee and Titterstone Clee and passing through the villages of Craven Arms, Clun, Bishop's Castle, Bridges, Church Stretton and Much Wenlock. The route utilises some parts of the Shropshire Way.

Start and Finish:	Ludlow, Shrops	SO510746
Landranger maps:	127, 137, 138	
1 : 25,000 maps:	Ex 203, 216, 217, 242	

Publications, badges and certificates:
Booklet: *The Shropshire Peaks Walk* by Ian R. Jones (Ian R. Jones) 1996. 42pp; A5. £1.80 (+ 30p p&p).

Shropshire Union Canal 471

Cheshire, Staffs, W Midlands   *60 km / 37 miles*

The Birmingham and Liverpool Junction Canal opened in 1835 and later, forming part of the Shropshire Union, was Thomas Telford's last great engineering challenge. The route passes through rural Shropshire via Gnosall, Norbury, Market Drayton and Audlem to Nantwich. The canal itself continues via Chester to Ellesmere Port. See Sandstone Trail.

Start:	Autherley Junction, W Midlands	SJ902020
Finish:	Nantwich, Cheshire	SJ640530
Landranger maps:	118, 127	
1 : 25,000 maps:	Ex 219, 242, 243, 257	

Publications, badges and certificates:
Leaflet: *The Shropshire Union Canal* (British Waterways – Chester) 1996. A5. Free (+ 9 x 4 SAE).
Paperback: *A Towpath Guide to the Birmingham and Liverpool Canal* by Jonathan Morris (Management Update Ltd) 1991. ISBN 0946679436. 117pp; 214 x 135. £5.99 (+ £1.00 p&p).
Stripmap (folded): *Shropshire Union Canal* (GEOprojects) 1996. ISBN 0863510329. 135 x 213. £4.75.

Shropshire Way   472
Shrops   *224 km / 139 miles*

A varied route crossing lowland farmland and many of the notable hills of Shropshire. It passes through Shrewsbury, Clun and Ludlow (the most southerly point), and on the return takes in the Clee Hills, Wenlock Edge, Ironbridge and the Wrekin. An 11 mile spur runs north from Wem to meet the Sandstone Trail, the Marches, Maelor and South Cheshire Ways at Grindley Brook. See Wild Edric's Way. The Wenlock Edge Ridge Walk (16 miles) goes between Craven Arms and the Shropshire Way at Much Wenlock whilst the Kerry Ridgeway (16 miles on OS mapping) runs between Bishop's Castle on the Shropshire Way and Kerry Hill in Powys. See also Shropshire Peaks Walk.

Start and Finish:	Wem, Shrops	SJ513289
Landranger maps:	117, 126, 127, 137, 138, 148	✔
1 : 25,000 maps:	Ex 201, 203, 216, 217, 241, 242, 257	
Waymark:	Buzzard	

Publications, badges and certificates:
Paperback: *The Shropshire Way and Wild Edric's Way* by Terry Marsh and Julie Meech (Cicerone Press) 1999. ISBN 1852842814. 192pp; 115 x 176. £9.99.
Paperback: *Rambler's Guide to the Shropshire Way* by R. W. Moore and I. R. Jones (Management Update Ltd) 1997. ISBN 0946679444. 70pp; A5. £5.99 (+ £1.00 p&p).
Booklet: *Wenlock Edge* by Ian R. Jones (Ian R. Jones) 1998. 18pp; A5. £1.50 (incs p&p).
Booklet: *Kerry Ridgeway* (Powys County Council). 14pp; A5. £1.50 (+ 30p p&p).

Sidmouth Saunter   473
Devon   *40 km / 25 miles*

A circuit combining coastal footpath and picturesque East Devon scenery. There is also a 13-mile route.

Start and Finish:	The Ham, Sidmouth, Devon	ST128872
Landranger maps:	192	
1 : 25,000 maps:	Ex 115	

Publications, badges and certificates:
Looseleaf: *Sidmouth Saunter* (Terry Bound). 3pp; A4. Free (+ SAE).
Badge and certificate: (Terry Bound). £1.20 (+ SAE) & free (+ A4 SAE).

Sirhowy Valley Walk   474

Blaenau G, Caerphilly, Newport   *42 km / 26 miles*

A challenging route from the built-up fringes of Newport to the mountain ridges of
Mynydd Machen and Mynydd Manmoel. It passes lowland and upland farms,
woodlands and riverside parks, many sites of historical interest, including an Iron
Age hill fort, an old mill and a canal centre, before finishing near Tredegar. The Walk
links with the waymarked Ebbw Valley Walk (16 miles from Wattsville to Ebbw Vale
and on OS mapping) near Cwm. The circular waymarked Raven Walk (12 miles and
included on OS mapping) uses some of the Sirhowy Valley Walk near Ynysddu. See
Rhymney Valley Ridgeway Walk.

Start:	Newport	ST310879
Finish:	Tredegar, Blaenau G	SO151105
Landranger maps:	161, 171	✔
1 : 25,000 maps:	Ex 152, 166 OL 13	
Waymark:	Letter S on standard waymarks	

Publications, badges and certificates:
Folder: *The Sirhowy Valley Walk* (Caerphilly County Borough Council). 14pp; 175 x 240.
£2.75.
Booklet: *The Ebbw Valley Walk* (Caerphilly County Borough Council) 1996. 24pp; 98 x 210.
£1.25.
Booklet: *The Raven Walk* by Islwyn Access Network (Caerphilly County Borough Council) 1995.
10pp; A5. £1.00.
Badge: for Raven Walk (Caerphilly County Borough Council). Free on completion, details in
booklet.

Skipton-Settle Link   475

N Yorks   *32 km / 20 miles*

A walk linking two North Craven market towns and visiting the trig points on Sharp
Haw and Weets, through moorland, field and fells.

Start:	Aireville Park, Skipton, N Yorks	SD979518
Finish:	Settle, N Yorks	SD821632
Landranger maps:	98, 103	
1 : 25,000 maps:	OL 2	

Publications, badges and certificates:
Looseleaf: *Skipton-Settle Link* (Ian Parker). A4. Free (+ 9 x 4 SAE).
Badge and certificate: (Ian Parker). £2.00 & £0.50 (+ 9 x 6 SAE).

Sky to Sea   476

Bridgend, Glamorgan, Rhondda CT   *56 km / 35 miles*

A route taking in the spectacular countryside of the West Glamorgan Heritage
Coast. There are links with the many other long distance routes in South Wales.

Start:	Dare Valley Country Park, Rhondda CT	SN983026
Finish:	Gileston, Glamorgan	SS956675
Landranger maps:	170	
1 : 25,000 maps:	Ex 151, 166	
Waymark:	Blue cloud & waves logo	

Publications, badges and certificates:
Leaflet: *Sky to Sea – over the Bwlch* (Groundwork Bridgend). A4/3. Free (+ SAE).
Leaflet: *Sky to Sea – Through the Vale* (Groundwork Bridgend). A4/3. Free (+ SAE).

Skye Trail 477

Highlands *120 km / 75 miles*

A route along a south to north line along the longest length of the island visiting both east and west coasts and traversing mountain and moorland regions.

Start:	Armadale, Highlands	NG038639
Finish:	Dantulm, Highlands	NG742401
Landranger maps:	23, 32	
1 : 25,000 maps:	Ex TBA 2002; OL 8	

Publications, badges and certificates:
Book: *A Long Walk on the Isle of Skye* by David Paterson (Peak Publishing Ltd). ISBN 0952190850. 144pp; 260 x 225. £14.95 (+ £2.00 p&p).

Skylark Walk 478

Kent *84 km / 52 miles*

The walk provides optional distance routes based on the North Downs Way and the Elham Valley Way, allowing for visits to such as Chilham, Wye, Etchinghill, Elham, Dover and Sheperdswell.

Start and Finish:	Canterbury, Kent	TR150578
Landranger maps:	179	
1 : 25,000 maps:	Ex 137, 138, 149, 150	
Waymark:	North Downs Way/Elham Valley Way	

Publications, badges and certificates:
Booklet: *The Skylark Walk* (Kent County Council). ISBN 1901509206. 30pp; A5. £3.00 (post free).

Sliabh Beagh Way 479

Dungannon & Tyrone, Fermanagh, Monaghan *48 km / 30 miles*

One of the official Waymarked Ways in Northern Ireland, this route passes by lakes and through valleys, crossing the Sliabh Beagh Mountain near to the summit. Use is made of forest tracks, country lanes and rugged open countryside. It connects with the Carleton Trail at Clogher.

Start:	St Partrick's Chair and Well, Clogher,	
	Dungannon	H598495
Finish:	Donagh, Fermanagh	H397298
Landranger maps:	OS(NI) 18, 19, 27	✔
1 : 25,000 maps:	Not applicable in NI	
Waymark:	Route name/walker outline on blue background	

Publications, badges and certificates:
Leaflet: *An Illustrated Guide to the Sliabh Beagh Way* (Dungannon & Tyrone Borough Council).
£0.50 (+ 9 x 6 SAE).

Smugglers Route   480

Cumbria   *45 km / 28 miles*

Although not truly based on the activities of smuggling, certain locations along the route do have such history. There are additional sites of interest along the way including Roman settlements, old churches and nature reserves. Initially the coastline to Allonby is followed then to Hayton, Aspatria and Mealsgate.

Start and Finish:	Maryport, Cumbria	NY038361
Landranger maps:	85, 89	
1 : 25,000 maps:	OL 4	

Publications, badges and certificates:
Paperback: *The Smugglers Route* by Ben Brinnicombe (Solway Rural Initiative Limited) 2000.
ISBN 0953441016. 90pp; A5. £6.00 (+ 50p p&p).

Smugglers' Way   481

Cornwall   *59 km / 37 miles*

A route across Bodmin Moor visiting such as Jamaica Inn, Dobwalls, Herodsfoot and Sowden's Bridge. For the actual crossing of the Moor navigational skills would be essential. The walk can be combined with the South West Coast Path National Trail (north and south) and the Saints Way to provide a 100 mile circular route.

Start:	Boscastle, Cornwall	SX095988
Finish:	Looe, Cornwall	SX255537
Landranger maps:	190, 201	
1 : 25,000 maps:	Ex 107, 109, 111	

Publications, badges and certificates:
Booklet: *The Smugglers' Way* by Frank Squibb (Frank Squibb) 1997. 32pp; A5. £2.30 (incs p&p) – accommodation and public transport information free on request with booklet.
Certificate: for Smugglers' Way (Frank Squibb). £2.00 (+ stamp).
Certificate: for Saints and Smugglers' 100 (Frank Squibb). £2.00 (+ stamp).

Snowdon Challenge Walk   482

Gwynedd   *48 km / 30 miles*

With 5,000ft of ascent to the top of Snowdon and back this is a tough walk. From Caernarfon Bay it climbs via Penygroes and the Ranger Path and then descends via the Rhyd-ddu path.

Start and Finish:	Pontllyfni, Gwynedd	SH435526
Landranger maps:	115	
1 : 25,000 maps:	OL 17	

Publications, badges and certificates:
Booklet: *Snowdon Challenge Walk* by John Merrill (Walk & Write Ltd). ISBN 0907496792. 40pp; A5. £3.95 (+ 75p p&p).
Badge and certificate: (Walk & Write Ltd). £3.50 (incs p&p).

Snowdonia 24hr Circuit   483

Conwy, Gwynedd   *72 km / 45 miles*

A tough rollercoaster-type circuit of approximately 16,500ft of ascent which includes the Snowdon Horseshoe, Glyders, Carneddau and Moel Siabod massifs.

Start and Finish:	Capel Curig, Conwy	SH721583
Landranger maps:	115	
1 : 25,000 maps:	OL 17	

Publications, badges and certificates:
Looseleaf: *Snowdonia 24hr Circuit* (Ed Dalton). 1pp; foolscap. Free (+ 9 x 4 SAE).
Certificate: (Ed Dalton). Free (+ 9 x 6 SAE).

Snowdonia Challenges   484

Conwy, Gwynedd   *Various km / Various miles*

These comprise three routes: the Heart of Snowdonia Circuit (50 miles) which is a 24 hour challenge walk traversing the 24 traditionally accepted 2,000ft summits (20,000ft of ascent), the Snowdonia Five Ranges Round (40 miles) which visits the highest summit in each of the principal mountain ranges of Central Snowdonia (12,500ft of ascent) and the Welsh 1000m Peaks Marathon (26 miles) which takes in Snowdon, Garnedd Ugain, Carnedd Llewelyn and Carnedd Dafydd (9,050ft of ascent).

Start:	Various	Various
Finish:	Various	Various
Landranger maps:	115	
1 : 25,000 maps:	OL 17, 18	

Publications, badges and certificates:
Looseleaf: *Three Snowdonia Challenge Walks* (Dave Irons) 1994. 14pp; A4. £2.00 (incs p&p).
Certificate: (Dave Irons). Free (+ A4 SAE).

Snowdonia Panoramic Walk   485

Gwynedd   *48 km / 30 miles*

A high-level strenuous walk with about 12,500ft of ascent over ridge paths of
Snowdonia, taking in the summits of Carnedd Llewellyn (Carneddau) and
Snowdon, and finishing over the seven peaks of the Nantlle Ridge.

Start:	Aber, Gwynedd	SH662720
Finish:	Nebo, Gwynedd	SH479505
Landranger maps:	115	
1 : 25,000 maps:	OL 17	

Publications, badges and certificates:
Booklet: *Snowdonia Panoramic Walk* (Ed Dalton) 1987. 8pp; A4. £1.50 (+ 9 x 6 SAE).
Badge and certificate: (Ed Dalton). £2.00 (incs p&p).

Snowdonia Round   486

Conwy   *103 km / 64 miles*

A youth hostel based route visiting the hostels at Idwal Cottage, Pen-y-Pass, Bryn
Gwynant and Lledr Valley taking in Drum, Glyder Fawr, Snowdon and Dulwyddelan.
Use of public transport between Conwy and Aber and Llanrwst back to Conwy is
suggested in the publication.

Start and Finish:	Conwy Youth Hostel, Conwy	SH772664
Landranger maps:	115	
1 : 25,000 maps:	OL 17	

Publications, badges and certificates:
Looseleaf: *Snowdonia Round Route Notes* (YHA Northern Region). £1.00 (incs p&p).
Booklet: *Booking Bureau – Youth Hostels* (YHA Northern Region) Annual. 20pp;
A5. Free.

Socratic Trail   487

Brighton H, E Sussex, Gtr London,   *76 km / 47 miles*
Surrey, W Sussex

The Trail follows paths and country lanes with little traffic across rolling Surrey hills
and the Sussex Weald making use of short stretches of the North Downs Way,
Greensand Way, Sussex Border Path and the South Downs Way, with panoramic
views along the journey to the sea. The walk has been adopted by Croydon LB as
its Millennium Trail.

Start:	Old Coulsdon, Gtr London	TQ312582
Finish:	Brighton	TQ333034
Landranger maps:	177, 187, 198	
1 : 25,000 maps:	Ex 122, 135, 146	

Publications, badges and certificates:
Folder: *The Socratic Trail Guide* (Maurice Hencke) 2000. 30pp; A5. £1.50 (+ 33p SAE).

Solent Way   488

Hants, Portsmouth, Soton   *96 km / 60 miles*

The route crosses coastal marshes to Lymington before going inland and past the heaths, woods and villages of the New Forest, Bucklers Hard and Beaulieu to reach Hythe on the Test Estuary. The ferry is taken to Southampton from where it follows the Solent shoreline, crossing the River Hamble to reach Portsmouth via the Gosport ferry. It continues along the historic waterfront of Portsmouth and Southsea and passes the coastal marshes and quays around Langstone Harbour. See Staunton Way and Wayfarer's Walk. See E-Routes (E9).

Start:	Milford-on-Sea, Hants	SZ292918
Finish:	Emsworth, Hants	SU753055
Landranger maps:	196, 197	✔
1 : 25,000 maps:	Ex 119, 120 OL 22	
Waymark:	Discs with tern logo	

Publications, badges and certificates:
Leaflet: *The Solent Way* (Hampshire County Council). A4/3. Free (+ SAE).

Solihull Way   489

W Midlands, Warks   *32 km / 20 miles*

Using farmland, open spaces and parks as much as possible the longest variation of this route by-passes the city centre. (Less rural alternatives reduce the total distance to a minimum of 17 miles.) The waymarked Trans Solihull Link (15 miles) is crossed near the southern end (see North Worcestershire Path/Heart of England Way). At Meriden Park, towards the north end of the route, the River Cole is crossed and the walks of the Cole Valley. These comprise the Cole Valley Way (7 miles) with a described link to the waymarked Millstream Way (3 miles) forming a route along the river from the M6 to Slade Lane in Birmingham.

Start:	Earlswood Lakes, Warks	SP116740
Finish:	Castle Bromwich, W Midlands	SP143898
Landranger maps:	139	✔
1 : 25,000 maps:	Ex 232	
Waymark:	Coat of arms	

Publications, badges and certificates:
Looseleaf & Leaflet: *A Solihull Way* (Solihull Metropolitan Borough Council House). 10pp & A4/3. Free (+ 9 x 4 SAE).
Booklet: *Cole Valley Walking Guide* (Project Kingfisher). 22pp; A5. Free (+ 9 x 6 SAE).
Leaflet: *The Millstream Way* (Millstream Project) 1996. A4/3. Free.

South Bucks Way   490
Bucks   *37 km / 23 miles*

From the Ridgeway the route descends through woodland to the source of the River Misbourne which it follows through Amersham to Denham where it joins the River Colne and ends on the towpath of the Grand Union Canal. See Chiltern Way and Heritage Trail.

Start:	Coombe Hill, Bucks	SP849067
Finish:	Denham, Bucks	TQ053862
Landranger maps:	165, 175, 176	✔
1 : 25,000 maps:	Ex 172, 181	
Waymark:	Standard waymark with name	

Publications, badges and certificates:
Leaflet: *South Bucks Way* (Buckinghamshire County Council). A4/3. Free (+ SAE).

South Cheshire Way   491
Cheshire, Shrops   *50 km / 31 miles*

A route linking the Sandstone Trail with the Staffordshire Way running through lowland farmland, passing Crewe and Alsager, before climbing to the finish. See also the Dane Valley Way, Gritstone Trail and Maelor Way.

Start:	Grindley Brook, Shrops	SJ522433
Finish:	Mow Cop, Cheshire	SJ856573
Landranger maps:	117, 118	✔
1 : 25,000 maps:	Ex 257, 258	
Waymark:	Letters SCW on standard waymarks	

Publications, badges and certificates:
Booklet: *Guide to the South Cheshire Way* by Justin McCarthy (Mid Cheshire Footpath Society) 1988. 20pp; 145 x 203. £0.75 (+ 9 x 6 SAE).

South Downs Way National Trail   492
E Sussex, Hants, W Sussex   *161 km / 100 miles*

This National Trail follows the northern escarpment of the chalk Downs from where there are extensive views across the Weald to the north and over the rounded hills and dry valleys to the sea in the south. There are several steep ascents when crossing the valleys of the Rivers Cuckmere at Alfriston, Ouse at Southease, Adur south of Bramber and Arun at Amberley. It visits Jevington and passes Iron Age hillforts and barrows. There is an alternative path running along the cliff tops to Beachy Head and the Seven Sisters turning inland at Cuckmere Haven along the Cuckmere Valley to rejoin the Way at Alfriston where there is a connection to the 1066 Country Walk. See Arun Way, Downs Link, Hangers Way, Socratic Trail, Staunton Way, Vanguard Way, Wealdway, Wey-South Path and Brighton Way. The Jubilee Way (East Sussex) (12 miles circular route) uses some of the South Downs

Way at Eastbourne and that part of it not on the South Downs Way is waymarked with a crown symbol. A publication is no longer available. See E-Routes (E9).

Start:	Eastbourne (Holywell), E Sussex	TV600972
Finish:	Winchester, Hants	SU483293
Landranger maps:	185, 197, 198, 199	✔
1 : 25,000 maps:	Ex 119, 120, 121, 122, 123, 132	
Waymark:	National Trail Acorn	
Path website:	www.nationaltrails.gov.uk	

Publications, badges and certificates:
Softback: *South Downs Way* (Official Guide) by Paul Millmore (Aurum Press) 1995. ISBN 1854104071. 168pp; 210 x 130. £10.99.
Paperback: *Along the South Downs Way to Winchester* (Includes accommodation guide) (Society of Sussex Downsmen) 2000. £6.33 (incs p&p).
Paperback: *The South Downs Way* by Kev Reynolds (Cicerone Press) 2001. ISBN 1852843241. 112pp; 174 x 116. £8.00.
Booklet: *Accommodation Guide to the South Downs Way* (South Downs Way National Trail Officer). £2.50.
Stripmap (folded): *South Downs Way* (Harvey Maps) 2000. ISBN 1851372423. 240 x 115. £8.95 (+ 80p p&p).

South of the Landsker Trail — 493

Pembrokes — *97 km / 60 miles*

The walk uses footpaths, bridleways and quiet roads, passing through farmland, woodland and small villages of the inland area of South Pembrokeshire, taking in a 20-mile section of the Pembrokeshire Coast Path National Trail along spectacular cliffs. The Trail also links with the Landsker Borderlands Trail.

Start and Finish:	Narberth, Pembrokes	SN121147
Landranger maps:	158	
1 : 25,000 maps:	OL 36	
Waymark:	Green Celtic knot symbol and name	

Publications, badges and certificates:
Leaflet: Details TBA (SPARC) 2002.

South Pennine Ring — 494

Lancs, W Yorks — *112 km / 70 miles*

A route following the towpaths, wherever possible, of the Rochdale, Ashton, Huddersfield Narrow, Huddersfield Broad and Calder & Bebble Canals with detailed alternative walking routes included for those walker-prohibited sections such as the Standedge Tunnel. Hebden Bridge, Todmorden, Rochdale, Ashton under Lyme, Stalybridge and Huddersfield are visited along the way.

Start and Finish:	Sowerby Bridge, West Yorks	SE062236
Landranger maps:	103, 104, 109, 110	
1 : 25,000 maps:	Ex 277, 288 OL 1, 21	

Publications, badges and certificates:
Paperback: *The South Pennine Ring* by John Lower (Hallamshire Press) 1998. ISBN 1874718377. 128pp; A5. £7.95.
Stripmap (folded): *Huddersfield Broad & Narrow Canals* (GEOprojects) 2001. ISBN 0863511457. 135 x 213. £4.00.

South Pennine Walks 495

Lancs, West Yorks   *Various km / Various miles*

This is a series of routes comprising:
Crompton Circuit (11 miles). A circuit through varied countryside around the town of Shaw visiting Low and High Crompton, Jubilee, Boothstead Edge, Crompton Moor and Fullwood.
Station to Station Walk (8.5 miles). Follows ancient packhorse routes including Rapes Highway and, in effect, links the Pennine Edge of Rochdale and Littleborough with the Colne Valley, passing Hollingworth Lake and the Piethorne and Readycon Dean Reservoirs.
Standedge Trail (12 miles). A circular from Marsden over Warcock Hill to Diggle returning by way of Dry Bridge, Dean Heads and the Redbrook and Tunnel End Reservoirs.

Start:	Various	Various
Finish:	Various	Various
Landranger maps:	109, 110	✔
1 : 25,000 maps:	Ex 277, 278 OL 1, 21	

Publications, badges and certificates:
No publications: routes on OS mapping.

South West Coast Path National Trail 496

Cornwall, Devon, Dorset, Plymouth,   *1014 km / 630 miles*
Somers, Torbay

Our longest National Trail gives the opportunity to enjoy some of Britain's finest coastal landscapes. These are extremely varied, from rugged and remote clifftops to sheltered estuaries, busy harbours and resorts. Moorland stretches contrast with plateaux incised by steep coastal valleys and intimate coves with long pebbly or sandy beaches. South Cornwall and Devon offer spectacular 'drowned' estuaries while in East Devon and Dorset there are extensive 'undercliffs' resulting from landslips. Ferries operate across most of the larger estuaries but some offer a reduced service or cease altogether out of the holiday season. Details are available in the South West Coast Paths Association Annual Guide. East of Lulworth army ranges restrict access at certain times (for details telephone 24 hour answering service 01929 462721 x4819). The St Michael's Way (12 miles), which is included on OS mapping, links Lelant (north coast of Cornwall) with Penzance/Marazion/St Michael's Mount on the south coast and can be extended into a much longer circular route when combined with the National Trail. The circular waymarked Dart Valley Trail (17 miles and on OS mapping) connects to the National Trail having the ferry between Dartmouth and Kingswear in common. It also links to the national rail network at Totnes. The Templer Way (18 miles and on OS mapping), which is waymarked except on open moorland, goes between Haytor Quarry and the National Trail at Teignmouth, using the ferry from Shaldon to Teignmouth. See Channel to Channel (Devon – Somerset), Dorset Jubilee Trail, East Devon Way, Land's End Round, Macmillan Way (and West), Smugglers' Way and Two Counties Way. See E-Routes (E9).

Start:	Minehead, Somers	SS972467
Finish:	South Haven Point, Dorset	SZ036866
Landranger maps:	180, 181, 190, 192, 193, 194, 195, 200,	
	201, 202, 203, 204	✔
1 : 25,000 maps:	Ex 102, 103, 104, 105, 106, 107, 108, 109,	
	110, 111, 114, 115, 116, 126, 139	
	OL 9, 15, 20	
Waymark:	National Trail Acorn	
User group:	South West Coast Path Association	

Publications, badges and certificates:

Softback: *South West Coast Path: Minehead to Padstow* (Official Guide) by Roland Tarr (Aurum Press) 1995. ISBN 1854104152. 168pp; 210 x 130. £10.99.

Softback: *South West Coast Path: Padstow to Falmouth* (Official Guide) by John Macadam (Aurum Press) 2000. ISBN 1854106732. 144pp; 210 x 130. £10.99.

Softback: *South West Coast Path: Falmouth to Exmouth* (Official Guide) by Brian Le Messurier (Aurum Press) 2001. ISBN 1854107682. 168pp; 210 x 130. £12.99.

Softback: *South West Coast Path: Exmouth to Poole* (Official Guide) by Roland Tarr (Aurum Press) 1995. ISBN 185410389X. 168pp; 210 x 130. £10.99.

Softback: *The Complete Guide to the South West Coast Path* (South West Coast Path Association) Annual. £6.00 (+ £1.00 p&p).

Paperback: *The South West Way Vol 1: Minehead to Penzance* by Martin Collins (Cicerone Press) 1989. ISBN 1852840250. 184pp; 116 x 176. £8.99.

Paperback: *The South West Way Vol 2: Penzance to Poole* by Martin Collins (Cicerone Press) 1989. ISBN 1852840269. 198pp; 116 x 176. £8.99.

Softback: *Walk the Cornish Coastal Path* by John H. N. Mason (Collins) 1999. ISBN 0004489292. 214 x 148. £5.99 (+ £1.00 p&p).

Booklet: *Plymouth's Waterfront Walkway* (Plymouth City Council) 2000. 32pp; A5. £2.50 (+ 50p p&p).

Booklet: *The South West Coast Path through Torbay* (Torbay Coast & Countryside Enterprises Ltd). 35pp; A5. £2.50 (+ 50p p&p).

Booklet: *Beneath the Skin of the Lizard – seven short National Trail based walks* (Lizard Peninsula Countryside Service) 2000. ISBN 1898166099. 35pp; A5. £3.75 (+ 90p p&p) – cheques payable to Cornwall County Council.

Booklet: *St Michael's Way* (Cornwall County Council) Temporarily out of print – details TBA.

Leaflet: *Dart Valley Trail* (Devon County Council). 3 leaflets; A4/3. £2.40 – quote ref. DP42.

Leaflet: *Templer Way* (Devon County Council). £0.25 (incs p&p) – quote ref. DP38.

Badge (cloth): (South West Coast Path Association). £2.95 (incs p&p).

Certificate: (South West Coast Path Association). £2.50 (incs p&p).

Southam Circular Way   497

Warks   *34 km / 21 miles*

A route around the town of Southam initially along the River Stowe to Ufton, passing Stoney Thorpe Hall, Harbury, Bishop's Itchington, Ladbroke and Napton-on-the-Hill. The Way then joins the Oxford Canal and Grand Union Canal, finally passing through Bascote.

Start and Finish:	Southam, Warks	SP419619
Landranger maps:	151	
1 : 25,000 maps:	Ex 206, 221, 222	

Publications, badges and certificates:
Leaflet: *Southam Circular Way* (RA Southam & District Group) 2001. A4/3. Free (+ SAE).

Southend Millennium Walk   498

Essex, Southend   *37 km / 23 miles*

A circular walk of coast and countryside. The walk links with the Roach Valley Way.

Start and Finish:	Southend Leisure Centre	TQ898875
Landranger maps:	178	
1 : 25,000 maps:	Ex 175	
Waymark:	Named discs	

Publications, badges and certificates:
Booklet: *The Ramblers' Millennium Walk Around Southend-on-Sea* by David Hitchman (Southend Borough Council) 2000. 16pp; A5. £1.00 (+ A5 or larger SAE).

Southern Upland Way   499

Borders, Dumfries & Gall, S Lanark   *343 km / 213 miles*

This official Long Distance Route provides a varied path through sparsely populated terrain, generally avoiding the high tops but with the highest point at The Merrick (843m). Across the Rhinns of Galloway and Glen Trool Forest Park to Sanquhar, the open, heather-clad Lowther Hills, it reaches St Mary's Loch near Broad Law. From here the Way passes through Melrose (where it can be linked with the St Cuthbert's Way), Lauder and over the foot hills of the Lammermuir Hills to reach the east coast. See also E-Routes (E2).

Start:	Portpatrick, Dum & Gall	NW998542
Finish:	Cockburnspath, Borders	NT774709
Landranger maps:	67, 71, 73, 74, 76, 77, 78, 79, 82	✔
1 : 25,000 maps:	Ex 309, 310, 320, 322, 328, 329, 330, 345, 346	
	OL 32, 44	
Waymark:	Thistle within hexagon	
Path website:	www.dumgal.gov.uk/Services/Depts/ei/SouthernUpland Way/intro2.htm	

Publications, badges and certificates:
Paperback: *The Southern Upland Way and Map* (Official Guide) by Roger Smith (Mercat Press) 1994. ISBN 0114951705. 212pp; 220 x 135. £14.99.
Paperback: *The Southern Upland Way* by Anthony Burton (Aurum Press) 1997. ISBN 1854104551. 168pp; 210 x 130. £12.99.
Leaflet: *The Southern Upland Way* (Dumfries and Galloway Council). A4/3. Free (+ 9 x 4 SAE).
Leaflet: *The Southern Upland Way – Accommodation List* (Dumfries and Galloway Council) Annual. A4/3. Free (+ 9 x 4 SAE).
Leaflets: *The Southern Upland Way – various wildlife/history etc* (Dumfries and Galloway Council) 1997. A4/3. Free (+ 9 x 4 SAE).
Freesheet: *Southern Upland Wayfarer* (Famedram Publishing Ltd) Annual. Free (+ A5 SAE).
Certificate: (Dumfries and Galloway Council). Free.

Spanners Round 500

Gtr Man, Lancs   *32 km / 20 miles*

A circuit across open moorland and along riverside and farmland paths, linking three reservoirs of the old Bolton Water Authority with three reservoirs of the former Irwell Valley Water Board (now all controlled by North West Water).

Start and Finish:	Jumbles Reservoir, Gtr Man	SD736139
Landranger maps:	103, 109	
1 : 25,000 maps:	Ex 287 OL 21	

Publications, badges and certificates:
Booklet: *Ramsbottom Round/Spanners Round* (Norman Thomas) 1992. 36pp; A5. £1.85 (incs p&p).
Badge and certificate: (Norman Thomas). £2.00 (+ SAE).

Spen Way Heritage Trail 501

W Yorks   *34 km / 21 miles*

A circuit of the former borough of Spenborough and the Spen, a tributary of the River Calder, the Way concentrates on the history of this old textile manufacturing area, visiting Scholes, East Bierley and Gomersal through a varied mixture of urban areas, parkland and farmland. See Brighouse Boundary Walk.

Start and Finish:	Cleckheaton, W Yorks	SE246199
Landranger maps:	104	✔
1 : 25,000 maps:	Ex 288	
Waymark:	Letters HT on standard waymarks	

Publications, badges and certificates:
Booklet: *Spen Way Heritage Trail* (Rotary Club of Cleckheaton & District). 16pp; A5. £2.00 (+ 9 x 6 SAE).
Badge: (Rotary Club of Cleckheaton & District). Details from Rotary Club.

Speyside Way 502

Highland, Moray *104 km / 65 miles*

One of the officially designated Long Distance Routes in Scotland, it links the Moray Coast with Aviemore in Strathspey but with spurs added to Dufftown (4 miles) and Tomintoul (15 miles). Although it generally offers easy walking on level ground, the extension into Tomintoul contains two climbs up to 1,800ft. Numerous whisky distilleries are sited along the route.

Start:	Buckie, Moray	NJ418655
Finish:	Aviemore, Highland	NH892125
Landranger maps:	28, 35, 36	✔
1 : 25,000 maps:	TBA 2002	
Waymark:	Thistle within hexagon	
Path website:	www.moray.org/area/speyway/webpages/swhome.htm	

Publications, badges and certificates:
Paperback (spiral/laminated): *The Speyside Way & Map* by Jacquetta Megarry and Jim Strachan (Rucksack Readers) 2000. ISBN 1898481083. 70pp; A5. £9.99.
Paperback: *Speyside Way* by Sandy Anton (Cicerone Press). ISBN 1852843314. Details TBA 2002.
Leaflet: *Speyside Way Accommodation & General Information Guide* (Speyside Way Ranger Service). A4/3. Free (+ SAE).
Stripmap: *Speyside Way* (Harvey Maps). ISBN 1851373373. £8.95 (+ 80p p&p).

St Cuthbert's Way 503

Borders, Northumb *100 km / 62 miles*

The Way was inspired by the life of St Cuthbert, who began his ministry at Melrose in 650 AD, eventually becoming the Bishop of Lindisfarne. The route provides a link over the Cheviot Hills between the Southern Upland Way (at Melrose) and the Pennine Way National Trail (at Kirk Yetholm) with the Northumbrian Coastline path. See also E-Routes (E2).

Start:	Melrose Abbey, Borders	NT548341
Finish:	Lindisfarne, Northumb	NU126418
Landranger maps:	73, 74, 75	✔
1 : 25,000 maps:	Ex 340 OL 16, 44	
Waymark:	Celtic Cross	
Path website:	www.northumberland.gov.uk/VG/ldwscw.html	

Publications, badges and certificates:
Paperback: *St Cuthbert's Way – The Official Guide* by Roger Smith & Ron Shaw (Mercat Press) 1997. ISBN 0114957622. 96pp; 220 x 135. £9.99.
Paperback: *St Cuthbert's Way – a Pilgrims' Guide* by Mary Low (Wild Goose Publications). ISBN 1901557227. 222pp; A5. £9.99 – not a guide book: complements 'Official Guide' with history/other information.
Paperback: *St Cuthbert's Way* by Roger Noyce (Sigma Leisure) 1999. ISBN 1850586934. 82pp; 210 x 180. £4.95.
Stripmap: *St Cuthbert's Way* (Harvey Maps). ISBN 1851372474. £7.95 (+ 80p).
Leaflet: *St Cuthbert's Way – Accommodation List and Facilities* (Jedburgh Tourist Information Centre) Annual. Free (+ SAE).

Leaflet: *St Cuthbert's Way – Melrose to Lindisfarne* (Jedburgh Tourist Information Centre) 1996. A4/4. Free (+ SAE).
Leaflet: *Booking facility – serviced accommodation* (Jedburgh Tourist Information Centre). Free.
Certificate: (Berwick-upon-Tweed Tourist Information Centre). £1.00 (+ SAE).
Badge: (Jedburgh Tourist Information Centre). £2.00 (+ SAE).

St Edmund Way   504

Essex, Suffolk   *142 km / 88 miles*

A route across Suffolk, using the Stour Valley Path (East Anglia) to Sudbury and Long Melford and then going via Lavenham and Little Welnetham to Bury St Edmunds along the waymarked Lark Valley Path (13 miles and included on OS mapping) to the Icknield Way Path at West Stow before striking over the Brecks to Thetford and the Hereward Way.

Start:	Manningtree, Essex	TM094322
Finish:	Brandon, Suffolk	TL784866
Landranger maps:	144, 155, 168, 169	✔
1 : 25,000 maps:	Ex 184, 196, 211, 229	

Publications, badges and certificates:
Paperback: *The St Edmund Way – A Walk Across Suffolk* (J. & J. Andrews) 1994. 66pp; 208 x 146. £3.75 (+ 50p p&p).
Leaflet: *Lark Valley Path* (Brecks Countryside Project) 1997. A4/3. £0.20 (+SAE).

St Illtyd's Walk   505

Carms, Neath PT, Swansea   *103 km / 64 miles*

From the sands this is a walk across varied terrain, canals, woodlands and gentle hills crossing the rivers Loughor, Tawe, Neath and Afan. The Walk links with the Coed Morgannwg Way at Margam giving access to the Rhymney Valley Ridgeway Walk and Taff Trail.

Start:	Pembrey, Carms	SN405008
Finish:	Margam, Neath PT	SS814852
Landranger maps:	159, 160, 170	✔
1 : 25,000 maps:	Ex 164, 165, 166, 178 OL 12	
Waymark:	Black turreted tower	

Publications, badges and certificates:
Booklet: *St Illtyd's Walk* by G. Colin Davies (Carmarthenshire County Council). ISBN 0953002706. 30pp; A5. £2.20 (+ 30p p&p).

St Peter's Way   506

Essex   *72 km / 45 miles*

The Way is across the open agricultural land of Essex passing Hanningfield Reservoir and inlets of the Blackwater Estuary and reaching the coast to the east of Tillingham, then following the sea wall from where there are extensive views across the Essex marshes.

Start:	Chipping Ongar, Essex	TL551036
Finish:	St Peter's Flat, Essex	TM032082
Landranger maps:	167, 168, 177	✔
1 : 25,000 maps:	Ex 175, 176, 183	
Waymark:	Red discs	

Publications, badges and certificates:
Booklet: *The St Peter's Way* by Fred Matthews and Harry Bitten (Essex County Council) 1990. 24pp; A5. £1.20.

Staffordshire and Worcestershire Canal Walk   507
Staffs, W Midlands, Worcs   *74 km / 46 miles*

A towpath walk linking the Severn Way in the south to the Trent and Mersey Canal Walk to the east of Stafford. The canal passes through Kidderminster and Wolverhampton.

Start:	Stourport on Severn, Worcs	SO810710
Finish:	Great Haywood Junction, Staffs	SJ995230
Landranger maps:	127, 138, 139	
1 : 25,000 maps:	Ex 218, 219, 244	

Publications, badges and certificates:
Leaflet: *Exploring the Staffordshire & Worcestershire Canal* (British Waterways – Stafford). A5. Free.
Stripmap (folded): *Staffordshire & Worcestershire Canal* (GEOprojects) 1999. ISBN 0863511147. 135 x 213. £4.75 (+ 50p p&p).

Staffordshire Moorlands Challenge Walk   508
Staffs   *38 km / 24 miles*

A walk from the Churnet Valley, involving 2,000ft of ascent, the route takes in Froghall Wharf, the Weaver Hills, Ordley Dale, Alton and Ousal Dale.

Start and Finish:	Oakamoor, Staffs	SK053448
Landranger maps:	128	
1 : 25,000 maps:	Ex 259	

Publications, badges and certificates:
Booklet: *Staffordshire Moorlands Challenge Walk* by John Merrill (Walk & Write Ltd). ISBN 0907496679. 32pp; A5. £3.95 (+ 75p p&p).
Badge and certificate: (Walk & Write Ltd). £3.50 (incs p&p).

Staffordshire Way   509
Cheshire, Derbys, Staffs   *153 km / 95 miles*

The route initially is along Congleton Edge to The Cloud, where it links with the southern end of the Gritstone Trail, and continues along the towpath of the Caldon Canal, through the Churnet Valley (see Churnet Valley Challenge Walk) and follows the River Dove to Uttoxeter. The Trent and Mersey Canal is then followed to Shugborough Hall with Cannock Chase and Highgate Common visited before reaching Kinver Edge where it connects with the Worcestershire Way and North Worcestershire Path. See also Birmingham and Aberystwyth Walk, Carpet Baggers 50, Dane Valley Way, Limestone Way and South Cheshire Way. See also E-Routes (E2).

Start:	Mow Cop, Cheshire	SJ856573
Finish:	Kingsford Country Park, Worc	SO829822
Landranger maps:	118, 119, 127, 128, 138, 139	✔
1 : 25,000 maps:	Ex 218, 219, 242, 244, 258, 259 OL 24	
Waymark:	Staffordshire knot	

Publications, badges and certificates:
Softback: *The Staffordshire Way – Official Guide* (Staffordshire County Council). 102pp; A5. £5.00 (+ 40p p&p).
Leaflet: *The Staffordshire Way & Millennium Way* – information/accommodation guide (Staffordshire County Council). A5/4. Free (+ 9 x 6 SAE).

Staunton Way 510

Hants   *21 km / 13 miles*

The Way connects with the Hangers Way and South Downs Way National Trail at Queen Elizabeth Country Park and roughly follows the Hampshire/Sussex border through Chalton and Finchdean, then follows a stream through Havant to Langstone Harbour where it connects with the Solent Way and Wayfarer's Walk. It is partly coincident with the Sussex Border Path. See E-Routes (E9).

Start:	Queen Elizabeth Country Park, Hants	SU718182
Finish:	Broadmarsh, Hants	SZ700057
Landranger maps:	197	✔
1 : 25,000 maps:	Ex 120	
Waymark:	Brown deer's head on standard arrows	

Publications, badges and certificates:
Leaflet: *Staunton Way* (Hampshire County Council) 1993. A4/3. Free (+ SAE).

Stepping Over Stone 511

Cumbria   *21 km / 13 miles*

From Kirkby Stephen, the end of the Yoredale Way and a crossing point for the Coast to Coast Walk, this route uses minor roads, tracks and footpaths in visiting Winton, Soulby, Crosby Garrett, Smardale, and Waitby.

Start and Finish:	Kirkby Stephen, Cumbria	NY775087
Landranger maps:	91	
1 : 25,000 maps:	OL 19	

Publications, badges and certificates:
Leaflet: *Stepping Over Stone* (Kirkby Stephen Tourist Information Centre). A4 extended/5. Free (+ 9 x 4 SAE).

Stort Valley Way   512

Essex, Herts   *45 km / 28 miles*

A route around Harlow, the River Stort Navigation is followed to Sawbridgeworth from where the villages of Sheering, Matching, Magdalen Laver and Epping Green are visited.

Start and Finish:	Roydon, Essex	TL406105
Landranger maps:	166, 167	✔
1 : 25,000 maps:	Ex 174	
Waymark:	Green and yellow named discs with dragonfly	

Publications, badges and certificates:
Leaflet: *Stort Valley Way* (Epping Forest Countrycare) 1996. A4/3. Free (+ SAE).

Stour and Orwell Walk   513

Suffolk   *67 km / 42 miles*

The walk is an extension to the Suffolk Coast and Heaths Path and follows the coast, estuaries and heaths to Cattawade providing links with the Essex Way (at Manningtree) and the Stour Valley Path (East Anglia) (at Cattawade).

Start:	Felixstowe, Suffolk	TM324363
Finish:	Cattawade, Suffolk	TM101333
Landranger maps:	169	
1 : 25,000 maps:	Ex 197	
Waymark:	Named signs	

Publications, badges and certificates:
Folder: *The Stour and Orwell Walk* by Annette Lea (Suffolk Coast and Heaths Project). 7 cards. £4.00 (+ 70p p&p) – includes accommodation list. Cheques payable to Suffolk County Council. Certificate: (Suffolk Coast and Heaths Project). £2.00 – cheques payable to Suffolk County Council.

Stour Valley Path (East Anglia)   514

Cambs, Essex, Suffolk   *96 km / 60 miles*

The Path follows the river valley downstream and links the Icknield Way path, which it crosses at Stetchworth, with Sudbury and the Essex Way at Manningtree passing through some of the most attractive country in East Anglia, including Constable country towards the end around East Bergholt. The waymarked Bury to Clare Walk (18 miles and on OS mapping) provides a link from the Path at Clare Castle to Bury St Edmunds (see St Edmund Way). See Daffodil Dawdle, Suffolk Coast and Heaths Path, Stour & Orwell Walk and Three Footpaths Walk. See also E-Routes (E2).

Start:	Newmarket, Suffolk	TL646636
Finish:	Cattawade, Suffolk	TM101332
Landranger maps:	154, 155, 168, 169	✔
1 : 25,000 maps:	Ex 196, 197, 210	

Waymark:	Named discs and posts with stylised river and dragonfly logo

Publications, badges and certificates:
Folder: *Stour Valley Path* (Suffolk County Council) 2001. 10 route cards; A5. £3.50 (incs p&p) – with accommodation and public transport details.
Leaflet: *Bury to Clare Walk* (St Edmundsbury Borough Council). A5. £0.20 (post free).

Stour Valley Walk (Kent)   515

Kent   *82 km / 51 miles*

A walk along the valley of the River Stour from the source, passing through a varied landscape, and taking in downland, woodland, orchards, hop gardens, lakes, dykes and marshland, unspoilt villages and historic towns. The remainder of the route traces the old Saxon shoreline of the Wantsum Channel to the important Roman site at Richborough, thence to the ancient Cinque Port of Sandwich. See Ashford on Foot and Medway Valley Walk.

Start:	Lenham, Kent	TR899522
Finish:	Pegwell Bay, Kent	TR347625
Landranger maps:	179, 189	✔
1 : 25,000 maps:	Ex 137, 148, 149, 150	
Waymark:	Head of grey heron	

Publications, badges and certificates:
Booklet: *Stour Valley Walk* (Kent County Council) 1995. ISBN 1873010516. 120pp; 210 x 210. £5.00 (post free).

Stour Valley Way (Dorset)   516

Bournemouth, Dorset, Poole, Wilts   *97 km / 60 miles*

This newly developed route follows the course of the River Stour as it winds through the Dorset countryside. The older Green Fields publication describes one route from Christchurch to the source of the river in Wiltshire. The newer Green Fields publication will describe the revised route. The waymarked Wareham Forest Way, which is included on OS mapping, connects at Sturminster Marshall and provides a 12-mile route to Wareham. The waymarked Ferndown, Stour and Forest Trail (10 miles circular and also included on OS mapping) links with the Way near to West Parley. The waymarked Castleman Trailway (17 miles and on OS mapping) goes between Ringwood and Upton Park and crosses the Way at Wimborne Minster.

Start:	Christchurch, Dorset	SZ160925
Finish:	Stourhead, Wilts	ST768345
Landranger maps:	183, 194, 195	✔
1 : 25,000 maps:	Ex 118, 129, 142 OL 22	
Waymark:	Name & kingfisher logo	

Publications, badges and certificates:
Paperback: *The Stour Valley Path* by Edward R. Griffiths (Green Fields Books) 1997. ISBN 0951937677. 168pp; A5. £5.95 (+ £1.00 p&p).

Paperback: *The Stour Valley Way* by Edward R. Griffiths (Green Fields Books) 2002. ISBN 0953033821. A5. £5.95 (+ £1.00 p&p).
Leaflet: *Wareham Forest Way* (Greenlink). A5. Free (+ SAE).
Leaflet: *Ferndown, Stour and Forest Trail* (Dorset County Council). A4/3. Free (+ 9 x 4 SAE).
Leaflet: *The Castleman Tramway* (Avon Heath Country Park) 1994. A5. Free.

Stratford-upon-Avon Canal Walk   517

W Midlands, Warks   *42 km / 26 miles*

A towpath walk linking the River Avon in the south to the Worcester & Birmingham Canal at King's Norton.

Start:	Stratford-upon-Avon, Warks	SP204548
Finish:	King's Norton Stop Lock, W Midlands	SP054794
Landranger maps:	139, 151	
1 : 25,000 maps:	Ex 205, 220	

Publications, badges and certificates:
Leaflet: *Exploring the Stratford-upon-Avon Canal* (British Waterways – Sawley) 1999. A5. Free (+ SAE).

Suffolk Coast and Heaths Path   518

Suffolk   *80 km / 50 miles*

The Path follows rights of way and permissive paths along the Suffolk Heritage Coast on river and sea walls and across marsh, heath, foreshore and low cliffs via the foot ferry to Bawdsey. It then follows the river wall along the large shingle spit of Orford Ness to meet the River Alde at Snape Maltings and regain the coast at the festival town of Aldeburgh and from there it follows the coast to Lowestoft Harbour. At Felixstowe, it connects with the Stour and Orwell Walk to provide links to the Stour Valley Path (East Anglia) and Essex Way at Manningtree.

Start:	Felixstowe, Suffolk	TM324364
Finish:	Lowestoft, Suffolk	TM548926
Landranger maps:	134, 156, 168, 169	✔
1 : 25,000 maps:	Ex 197, 212, 231 OL 40	
Waymark:	Small named yellow and purple markers	

Publications, badges and certificates:
Folder: *The Suffolk Coast and Heaths Path* (Suffolk Coast and Heaths Project) 2000. 10pp (+ booklet); A5. £4.00 (+ 70p p&p) – cheques payable to Suffolk County Council (includes the transport booklet).

Suffolk Way   519

Suffolk   *175 km / 109 miles*

The Suffolk Way is a rural route across the county from Constable country via the Box Valley to Lavenham with its ancient timber-framed buildings. It crosses the high Suffolk landscape to Halesworth, where it turns beside the River Blyth to the coast at Walberswick which it follows to Lowestoft.

Start:	Flatford, Suffolk	TM075333
Finish:	Lowestoft, Suffolk	TM548926
Landranger maps:	134, 155, 156, 169	
1 : 25,000 maps:	Ex 196, 197, 211, 212, 230, 231 OL 40	

Publications, badges and certificates:
Booklet: *Suffolk Way* by Ian St John (Ian St John) 1999. ISBN 0952088010. 95pp; A5. £6.95 (+ 90p p&p).

Sussex Border Path   520
E Sussex, Hants, Kent, Surrey, W Sussex   *216 km / 135 miles*

The route follows paths approximating to the Sussex border with Hampshire, Surrey and Kent, first making a 9-mile circuit around Thorney Island and then crossing the South Downs to South Harting and Liphook before heading to Gospel Green, Rudgwick, Gatwick and East Grinstead. Here the waymarked Mid Sussex Link (33 miles and on OS mapping) branches off along the line of the administrative boundary between East and West Sussex. The main Border Path heads through Ashurst, Wadhurst and Bodiam. Details of the Mid Sussex Link are included in the publication as well as details of completing the route in a series of single day walks. The waymarked Worth Way (7 miles and on OS mapping) is partly coincident with the Path as is the waymarked Forest Way (10 miles and on OS mapping) and the link between them at East Grinstead. See Brighton Way, Staunton Way, Socratic Trail, Sussex Diamond Way, Tandridge Border Path and Wealdway.

Start:	Emsworth, Hants	SU753055
Finish:	Rye, E Sussex	TQ918205
Landranger maps:	186, 187, 188, 189, 197, 198, 199	✔
1 : 25,000 maps:	Ex 120, 122, 125, 133, 134, 135, 136, 146, 147	
Waymark:	Martlet on green plaques or wooden signposts	

Publications, badges and certificates:
Softback: *The Sussex Border Path* by John Allen (Sigma Leisure) 1999. ISBN 1850586772. 114pp; A5. £6.95.
Leaflet: *The Worth Way* (West Sussex County Council) 1997. A4/3. Free (+ SAE).
Leaflet: *The Forest Way* (East Sussex County Council). A4/3. Free (+ SAE).

Sussex Diamond Way   521
E Sussex, W Sussex   *97 km / 60 miles*

A gently undulating route in the Low Weald passing through farmland, heath and woodland. At Heathfield the start of the waymarked Cuckoo Trail (11 miles and on OS mapping) is met which follows the line of a disused railway to Polegate. There are also links to the Wey-South Path, the Downs Link, Sussex Border Path, Wealdway and Vanguard Way.

Start:	Midhurst, W Sussex	SU885213
Finish:	Heathfield, E Sussex	TQ578213
Landranger maps:	197, 198, 199	
1 : 25,000 maps:	Ex 133, 134, 135	

Publications, badges and certificates:
Booklet: *The Sussex Diamond Way* (RA Sussex Area). ISBN 0953200604. 46pp; A5. £3.00 (+ 50p p&p).
Leaflet: *The Cuckoo Trail* (Wealden District Council) 2000. A4/3. Free (post free).

Swale Way   522
Cumbria, N Yorks   *124 km / 77 miles*

A route tracing the River Swale from the confluence with the Ure near Boroughbridge to the source at the head of Swaledale near Keld. Because of a lack of rights of way, the route does not slavishly follow the river, in some places diverging to visit the market towns of Thirsk and Richmond. En route the Pennine Way National Trail, Coast to Coast walk and Yoredale Way are encountered.

Start:	Boroughbridge, N Yorks	SE396660
Finish:	Kirkby Stephen, Cumbria	NY758988
Landranger maps:	91, 92, 99	
1 : 25,000 maps:	Ex 299, 302, 304 OL 19, 30	

Publications, badges and certificates:
Booklet: *The Swale Way* by John Brock (Richmondshire District Council) 1996. 16pp; A5. £1.30 (incs p&p) – cheques payable to Richmondshire District Council.

Swan's Way   523
Bucks, Milton K, Northants, Oxon   *104 km / 65 miles*

From the Northants border the route crosses the Vale of Aylesbury to meet the Ridgeway near Princes Risborough and then follows the chalk slopes of the Chilterns to the Thames at Goring. There is a link with the Cross Bucks Way at Swanbourne. The Judge's Ride (16 miles), coincident for short sections with the Swan's Way and the Ridgeway, provides a link to such as Stoke Row, the location of the Maharajah's Well. See Three Shires Way, Milton Keynes Boundary Walk and Icknield Way Trail.

Start:	Salcey Forest, Milton K	SP811514
Finish:	Goring-on-Thames, Oxon	SU601808
Landranger maps:	152, 164, 165, 174, 175	✔
1 : 25,000 maps:	Ex 171, 181, 192, 207	
Waymark:	Swan's head in horseshoe	

Publications, badges and certificates:
Leaflet: *Swan's Way* (Buckinghamshire County Council). A4/3. Free (+ SAE).
Leaflet: *Judge's Ride* (Oxfordshire County Council). A4/3. £0.50.

Sweet Pea Challenge Walk   524
Shrops   *43 km / 27 miles*

A route from the birthplace of the sweet pea through Grinshilland Prees, and along the Llangollen Canal.

Start and Finish:	Wem, Shrops	SJ514289
Landranger maps:	126	
1 : 25,000 maps:	Ex 241	

Publications, badges and certificates:

Booklet: *Sweet Pea Challenge Walk* by John N. Merrill (Walk & Write Ltd). ISBN 1874754497. 44pp; A5. £3.95 (+ 75p p&p).

Badge and certificate: (Walk & Write Ltd). £3.50 (incs p&p).

Taff Trail 525

Cardiff, Merthyr T, Powys, Rhondda CT 88 km / 55 miles

The Taff Trail for walkers and cyclists is mostly on converted railway lines also using former canals and forestry tracks. It runs along the Taff valley to Llandaff, Pontypridd and Merthyr Tydfil. From here the main route circles to the east of the Brecon Beacons via Talybont and Pencelli to Brecon. An alternative route via Neuadd reservoir caters for a circular between Merthyr and Brecon. At Gethin Woodland Park near Merthyr the Trail links with the Coed Morgannwg Way. See Capital Walk – Cardiff and St Illtyd's Walk.

Start:	Cardiff	ST182759
Finish:	Brecon, Powys	SO043286
Landranger maps:	160, 161, 170, 171	✔
1 : 25,000 maps:	Ex 151, 166 OL 12, 13	
Waymark:	Stylised viaduct in yellow arrow on black background	

Publications, badges and certificates:

Leaflets: *The Taff Trail* (Merthyr Tydfil TIC). 6 leaflet set; A5. £1.95 (incs p&p) – cheques payable to TSWW.

Leaflet: *The Taff Trail for Walkers and Cyclists* (Merthyr Tydfil TIC) 1995. 4pp; A4/3. Free (post free).

Taff-Ely Ridgeway Walk 526

Caerphilly, Rhondda CT, Cardiff 34 km / 21 miles

The Walk is a mixture of footpaths, bridleways and lanes following the line of hills running from Mynydd Maendy in the west, to Caerphilly Common in the east. The route passes through forests taking in ancient hill forts. There are links with the Rhymney Valley Ridgeway Walk at Caerphilly Common, the Taff Trail near to Taffs Well and the waymarked Ogwr Ridgeway Walk (13 miles and on OS mapping) at the start, which joins the Coed Morgannwg Way. There is currently no publication for the Ogwr Ridgeway Walk. See also Capital Walk – Cardiff.

Start:	Mynydd Maendy, Rhondda CT	ST977861
Finish:	Caerphilly Common, Caerphilly	ST153856
Landranger maps:	170, 171	✔
1 : 25,000 maps:	Ex 151	
Waymark:	Yellow/black disc with hills motif	

Publications, badges and certificates:
Leaflet: *Taff Ely Ridgeway Walk/Ffordd y Bryniau* (Caerphilly Mountain Countryside Service). A4/3. Free.

Taith Torfaen 527

Blaenau G, Caerphilly, Mons, Torfaen   *80 km / 50 miles*

The Taith Torfaen consists of two 25 miles loops, both from Pontypool, forming a figure-of-eight which can be completed as one or two walks. The northern loop goes through the Brecon Beacons National Park to reach the Blorenge Mountain with extensive views over Abergavenny and returns via Coity Mountain. The southern loop goes via Twmbarlwm and Mynydd Machen with panoramic views across the Bristol Channel. It returns via the Islwyn and Torfaen Hills.

Start and Finish:	Pontypool Leisure Centre, Torfaen	SO285006
Landranger maps:	161, 171	
1 : 25,000 maps:	Ex 152 OL 13	

Publications, badges and certificates:
Looseleaf: *Taith Torfaen* (Gerry Jackson). 6pp; A4. Free (+ 9 x 6 SAE).
Badge and certificate: (Gerry Jackson). £2.00 & £0.50 (+ SAE's).

Tamar Valley Discovery Trail 528

Cornwall, Devon   *48 km / 30 miles*

A walking route along the valley of the River Tamar through Bere Ferrers, Bere Alston, Gunnislake and Milton Abbot and crossing two rivers at Lopwell Dam (by foot) and Calstock (by train or ferry). The Trail links with West Devon Way and Two Castles Trail to form a circuit of approximately 100 miles.

Start:	Tamerton Foliot, Devon	SX470611
Finish:	Launceston, Cornwall	SX333847
Landranger maps:	201	
1 : 25,000 maps:	Ex 108, 112	
Waymark:	Outline of apple	

Publications, badges and certificates:
Folder: *Tamar Valley Discovery Trail* (Devon County Council). 9 leaflets. £3.40 (incs p&p) – quote ref. DP19.

Tame Valley Way 529

Gtr Man   *40 km / 25 miles*

The Way runs from central Stockport to Reddish Vale and Hyde from where canal towpaths are followed through Ashton-under-Lyne, Stalybridge and Mossley. From Uppermill, the route leaves the canal, following riverside paths to Delph and Denshaw. In spite of being through densely populated areas, the route is through much woodland.

Start:	Stockport, Gtr Man	SJ893903
Finish:	Denshaw, Gtr Man	SD975105
Landranger maps:	109	✔
1 : 25,000 maps:	Ex 277 OL 1, 21	

Publications, badges and certificates:
Folder: *The Tame Valley* (Tameside Countryside Warden Service). 10 leaflets; A4/3. £2.60 (incs p&p).

Tameside Trail 530

Gtr Man *64 km / 40 miles*

A walk along the Etherow Valley and Tame Valley to Stockport, where it turns through Audenshaw and Droylsden and picks up the Medlock Valley to Park Bridge. From Mossley it returns via the Swineshaw Valley and Hollingworth. See also E-Routes (E2).

Start and Finish:	Broadbottom, Gtr Man	SJ996936
Landranger maps:	109, 110	✔
1 : 25,000 maps:	OL 1	
Waymark:	Named discs	

Publications, badges and certificates:
Folder: *The Tameside Trail* (Tameside Countryside Warden Service) 1994. ISBN 1871324114. 27pp; A5. £3.00 (incs p&p).

Tandridge Border Path 531

E Sussex, Gtr London, Kent, Surrey, W Sussex *80 km / 50 miles*

This walk follows the boundary of Tandridge District with Kent, Sussex and Greater London, linking the villages and hamlets of East Surrey. It meets the Sussex Border Path, and the North Downs Way National Trail and Greensand and Vanguard Ways.

Start and Finish:	Tatsfield Village Green, Surrey	TQ413568
Landranger maps:	187	
1 : 25,000 maps:	Ex 146, 147	
Waymark:	Named green and white discs	

Publications, badges and certificates:
Booklet: *Tandridge Border Path* (Per-Rambulations). A5. Free (+ 41p SAE).

Tarka Trail 532

Devon, Somers *291 km / 181 miles*

The Trail traces the journeys of Tarka the Otter, taking in locations featured in the book. In effect, the Trail comprises two routes based on Barnstaple. The northern section takes an easterly line to and over Exmoor to the sea, then follows the coast line through Braunton to the start. The southern section is through Bideford and Great Torrington to Okehampton and Sticklepath, returning north and terminating at Eggesford where advantage can be taken of a rail link back to Barnstaple. The Taw-Teign Link (6 miles) can be used to connect Sticklepath with Chagford Bridge on the Two Moors Way. A second link, by way of the Little Dart Ridge & Valley Walk (11 miles and included on OS mapping) is available in connecting Eggesford with Witheridge which is also on the Two Moors Way. See Dartmoor and West Devon Ways and Macmillan Way West.

Start and Finish:	Barnstaple, Devon	SS558331
Landranger maps:	180, 190, 191	✔
1 : 25,000 maps:	Ex 113, 126, 127, 139 OL 9, 28	
Waymark:	Otter pawmark	

Publications, badges and certificates:
Paperback: *Tarka Trail – A Walker's Guide* (Devon County Council) 1995. ISBN 0861148770. 88pp; 150 x 230. £4.95 (incs p&p) – quote ref. DP32.
Leaflet: *An Explorers Guide to the Tarka Trail* (Devon County Council). A4/3. £0.60 (incs p&p) – quote ref. DP06.
Leaflet: *Tarka Country Guide & Accommodation List* (Devon County Council). 24pp. £0.60.
Leaflet: *The Taw-Teign Link* (Devon County Council). 6pp; A4. £0.25 (incs p&p) – quote ref. DP36.
Leaflet: *Little Dart Ridge & Valley Walk* (Devon County Council). 12pp; A4. £0.25 (incs p&p) – quote ref. DP35.

Tas Valley Way 533
Norfolk 42 km / 26 miles

The Way goes through Intwood, Swardeston, Mulbarton and Hapton and then follows the course of the River Tas to the source near to New Buckenham. The route continues to Attleborough where advantage can be taken of local services. In all 16 churches and towns or villages are visited along the route. At Cringleford there are links with the Ketts Country Walk and Yare Valley Walk (7 miles), the latter following the valley of the River Yare and returning along the wooded southern slopes.

Start:	Cringleford, Norfolk	TG200059
Finish:	Attleborough, Norfolk	TM045952
Landranger maps:	134, 144	
1 : 25,000 maps:	Ex 237	
Waymark:	Named discs	

Publications, badges and certificates:
Booklet: *Tas Valley Way* (Norfolk County Council). 16pp; A5. £0.70 (+ 9 x 6 SAE).
Leaflet: *Yare Valley Walk* (Norwich Fringe Project). A4/3. Free (+ 9 x 4 SAE).

Teesdale Way 534
Cleveland, Cumbria, Durham 161 km / 100 miles

The Way largely follows the banks of the River Tees. From Dufton it connects with the Pennine Way National Trail, visiting High Cup Nick, Cauldron Snout and High Force before passing through Barnard Castle and the south of Darlington to the North-East coast at Middlesbrough. From Middlesbrough Dock, the Tees Link

(11 miles), which is waymarked and included on OS mapping, provides a connection to the Cleveland Way National Trail at High Cliff Nab. See also E-Routes (E2).

Start:	Dufton, Cumbria	NY691250
Finish:	Middlesbrough, Cleveland	NZ557280
Landranger maps:	91, 92, 93	✔
1 : 25,000 maps:	Ex 304, 306 OL 26, 31	
Waymark:	Named discs with dipper logo in Durham and fish in Cleveland	

Publications, badges and certificates:
Paperback: *The Teesdale Way* by Martin Collins (Cicerone Press) 1995. ISBN 1852841982. 112pp; 115 x 176. £7.99.
Leaflet: *Teesdale Way – Piercebridge to Hurworth Place* (Darlington Borough Council). A4/3. Free (+ 9 x 4 SAE).
Leaflet: *Teesdale Way – Hurworth Place to Low Middleton* (Darlington Borough Council). A4/3. Free (+ 9 x 4 SAE).
Leaflet: *The Tees Link* (Tees Forest Project). A3/2. Free (+ 9 x 6 SAE).

Telford and Wrekin Walks 535
Telford W   *Various km / Various miles*

These three interlinked walks use the open spaces and countryside of the area. The Hutchison Way (18½ miles) goes from Wellington via Telford to Newport. The Silkin Way (14 miles) winds from Bratton to Coalport along dry canal beds and abandoned railway lines. The Ironbridge Way (10 miles) starts at Leegomery to end at Ironbridge. Both Coalport and Ironbridge are on the Severn Way.

Start:	Various	Various
Finish:	Various	Various
Landranger maps:	127	
1 : 25,000 maps:	Ex 242	
Waymark:	Discs with named walks	

Publications, badges and certificates:
Leaflet: *The Hutchison Way* (Telford & Wrekin Countryside Service). A4/3. Free (+ SAE).
Leaflet: *The Silkin Way* (Telford & Wrekin Countryside Service). A4/3. Free (+ SAE).
Leaflet: *The Ironbridge Way* (Telford & Wrekin Countryside Service). A4/3. Free (+ SAE).

Ten Church Challenge 536
Derbys   *34 km / 21 miles*

A circuit of ten chapels around the Black Brook, Goyt and Todd Brook valleys of the High Peak. See High Peak 60.

Start and Finish:	Whaley Bridge, Derbys	SK012811
Landranger maps:	110, 119	
1 : 25,000 maps:	OL 1, 24	

Publications, badges and certificates:
Paperback: *High Peak Hikes* by David Frith (Sigma Leisure) 1996. ISBN 1850584591. 180pp; A5. £6.95.
Certificate: (David Frith). 9 x 6 SAE & two 2nd class stamps.

Ten Reservoirs Walk   537

Derbys, Gtr Man   *35 km / 22 miles*

A tough circuit over the Saddleworth Moors, linking with the Pennine Way National Trail and several walks in this area. It visits Yeoman Hey, Greenfield, Black Moss, Swellands, Blakeley, Wessenden, Wessenden Head, Torside and Chew Reservoirs.

Start and Finish:	Dovestone Reservoir, Gtr Man	SE014034
Landranger maps:	110	
1 : 25,000 maps:	OL 1	

Publications, badges and certificates:
Looseleaf: *The Ten Reservoirs Walk* (Carole E. Engel). A4. Free (+ 9 x 4 SAE).
Badge and certificate: (Carole E. Engel). £1.50 & £0.20 (+ 9 x 6 SAE).

Tennyson Twenty   538

Lincs   *32 km / 20 miles*

The route circles the village of Sommersby, birthplace of Alfred Lord Tennyson, Victorian Poet Laureate, through the Lincolnshire Wolds passing small isolated villages and deserted hamlets as well as nature reserves.

Start and Finish:	Hagworthingham, Lincs	TF344696
Landranger maps:	122	
1 : 25,000 maps:	Ex 273, 274	

Publications, badges and certificates:
Looseleaf: *Tennyson Twenty* (Martyn Bishop). Free (+ 9 x 4 SAE).
Badge and certificate: (Martyn Bishop). £1.50 (+ SAE).

Test Way   539

Hants, W Berks, Wilts   *74 km / 46 miles*

The Way follows the Test Valley from the outskirts of Southampton over lowland farmland and woodland paths continuing along a disused railway line past Romsey, Mottisfont Abbey, Stockbridge, Wherwell and St Mary Bourne, before gradually climbing to Inkpen Beacon on the crest of the chalk downs to meet with the Wayfarer's Walk.

Start:	Totton, Hants	SU360140
Finish:	Inkpen Beacon, W Berks	SU365622
Landranger maps:	174, 185, 196	✔
1 : 25,000 maps:	Ex 131, 144, 159 OL 22	
Waymark:	Green letters TW on white background	

Publications, badges and certificates:
Leaflet: *Test & Clarendon Way* (Hampshire County Council) 1986. A4/3. Free (+ SAE).

Thames Path National Trail 540

Bucks, Glos, Gtr London, Oxon, Reading, 294 km / 184 miles
Slough, Surrey, Swindon, W Berks, Wilts,
Windsor M, Wokingham

This National Trail, unique insofar as it is the only one mainly following a river, was officially opened in 1996. From the source the Trail meanders through Cricklade, Lechlade, Oxford, Abingdon, Windsor, Reading, Henley, Marlow and Maidenhead passing Windsor Castle and the palaces of Hampton Court and Kew, and Richmond. There is extensive public transport availability along the route by way of rail, bus and river boat. The waymarked Thames Path Extension (10 miles) downstream from the Thames Barrier to Crayford Ness links to the London LOOP at Erith. The waymarked Thames Down Link (15 miles and on OS mapping) provides a link from Kingston upon Thames to Westhumble on the North Downs Way National Trail. The waymarked Beeches Way (16 miles and on OS mapping) makes a link with the Grand Union Canal at West Drayton. See Colne Valley Way, Colne Valley Trail & Ebury Way, Kennet and Avon Walk, Macmillan Way, Oxfordshire Way, Vanguard Way, Wey-South Path/Wey Navigation and Wysis Way. See also E-Routes (E2).

Start:	Thames Source near Kemble, Glos	ST981994
Finish:	Thames Barrier, Gtr London	TQ417794
Landranger maps:	163, 164, 174, 175, 176, 177	✔
1 : 25,000 maps:	Ex 160, 161, 162, 168, 169, 170, 171, 172, 173, 180	
	OL 45	
Waymark:	National Trail Acorn	
Path website:	www.nationaltrails.gov.uk	

Publications, badges and certificates:
Softback: *The Thames Path* (Official Guide) by David Sharp (Aurum Press) 1996. ISBN 1854104063. 168pp; 210 x 130. £12.99.
Paperback: *The Thames Path National Trail Companion* (Thames Path National Trail Officer) 2001. ISBN 0953520722. 134pp; A5. £4.95 (+ 90p p&p).
Paperback: *The Thames Path* (describes route from London Barrier to source) by Leigh Hatts (Cicerone Press) 1998. ISBN 1852842709. 184pp; 176 x 116. £7.99.
Booklet: *The Thames Path Public Transport Guide* (Thames Path National Trail Officer) Annual. A5. Free (+ 9 x 6 31p SAE).
Leaflet: *The Thames Path National Trail* (Thames Path National Trail Officer). Free.
Leaflet: *Camping Beside the River Thames* (Environment Agency – Thames Region). A4/3. Free.
Stripmap (folded): *Thames, the river and the path* (GEOprojects) 1996. ISBN 086351037X. 135 x 213. £4.75 (+ 50p p&p).
Leaflet: *The Thames Down Link* (Lower Mole Project) 2001. A4/3. Free (+ SAE).
Leaflet: *The Beeches Way* (Buckinghamshire County Council). A4/3. Free (+ SAE).

Thanet Coastal Path   541

Kent   *32 km / 20 miles*

A route as close as is possible to the coast passing through Margate, Broadstairs and Ramsgate. The Path links with the Saxon Shore Way (and Wantsum Walks) at the start and there are plans to add a second link to the Saxon Shore Way at the finish.

Start:	Near Reculver, Kent	TR243694
Finish:	Stonelees Nature Reserve, Kent	TR337625
Landranger maps:	179	✔
1 : 25,000 maps:	Ex 150	
Waymark:	Named logo with bird/fish/sandcastle	

Publications, badges and certificates:
Leaflet: *Thanet Coastal Path* (Ramsgate Tourist Information Centre) 2001. A4/3. Free (+ SAE).

Thirlmere Round   542

Cumbria   *35 km / 22 miles*

A strenuous high level walk around Thirlmere visiting High Seat, Calf Crag, Gibson Knott and Helvellyn.

Start and Finish:	Grasmere, Cumbria	NY339072
Landranger maps:	96, 97	
1 : 25,000 maps:	OL 7	

Publications, badges and certificates:
Looseleaf: *The Thirlmere Round* (Brian Richmond). Free (+ 9 x 4 SAE).
Certificate: (Brian Richmond). £0.30 (+ SAE).

Thirlmere Way   543

Cumbria, Gtr Man, Lancs   *209 km / 130 miles*

The Way provides a meandering link from the Greater Manchester conurbation through Lancashire to Cumbria visiting Hulton, Abbey Village, Longridge, Dolphinholme, Caton, Kirkby Lonsdale, Kendal, Windermere and Grasmere.

Start:	Heaton Park, Gtr Man	SD834044
Finish:	Thirlmere, Cumbria	NY310190
Landranger maps:	90, 97, 102, 109	
1 : 25,000 maps:	Ex 277, 287 OL 2, 5, 7, 41	

Publications, badges and certificates:
Softback: *The Thirlmere Way* by Tim Cappelli (Sigma Leisure) 1992. ISBN 1850582882. 124pp; A5. £6.95.

Three Castles Path (England) 544

Bracknell For, Hants, Windsor M **96 km / 60 miles**

This route was inspired by the 13th century journeys of King John via the Castle built by him near Odiham. The route takes in Windsor Great Park to Ascot, the Crown Estate south of Bracknell, the Blackwater Valley, the Basingstoke canal and the River Itchen from Itchen Abbas to Winchester Castle Hall.

Start:	Windsor Castle	SU968770
Finish:	Winchester Castle Hall, Hants	SU483293
Landranger maps:	175, 176, 185, 186	✔
1 : 25,000 maps:	Ex 132, 144, 159, 160	

Publications, badges and certificates:

Booklet: *The Three Castles Path* by David Bounds (RA East Berkshire Group) 1998. ISBN 1874258082. 48pp; 128 x 210. £2.95 (+ 70p p&p) – cheques payable to East Berks RA Publications.
Looseleaf: *Accommodation List* by Dave Ramm (Bracknell Tourist Information Centre). 1pp; A4. Free (+ 9 x 4 SAE).
Postcards: Three Castles Path – 12 scenes (RA East Berkshire Group). £1.50 (incs p&p) – cheques payable to East Berks RA Publications.

Three Choirs Way 545

Glos, Herefs, Worcs **161 km / 100 miles**

A route between Gloucester, Hereford and Worcester through countryside of hopyards, vineyards and orchard with a theme linking the walk to the ancient music festivals still celebrated annually in the three Cathedrals. The rivers Severn, Wye, Teme and Lugg are crossed as are the Marcle and Malvern Ridges and the Suckley Hills. The Way connects with the Worcestershire, Gloucestershire, Wysis and Severn Ways and the Wye Valley Walk.

Start and Finish:	Gloucester	SO830190
Landranger maps:	149, 150, 162	
1 : 25,000 maps:	Ex 179, 189, 190 OL 14	

Publications, badges and certificates:

Paperback: *The Three Choirs Way* by Gerry Stewart (Countryside Matters) 1999. ISBN 0952787024. 108pp; A5. £5.95 (post free).

Three Counties Challenge Walk 546

Cheshire, Derbys, Staffs **45 km / 28 miles**

A tough moorland route straddling the borders of Cheshire, Staffordshire and Derbyshire in the Peak District running via The Roaches, Shutlingsloe, Tegg's Nose, Shining Edge and Three Shires Head.

Start and Finish:	Tittesworth Reservoir, Staffs	SJ994605
Landranger maps:	118, 119	
1 : 25,000 maps:	OL 24	

Publications, badges and certificates:
Booklet: *Three Counties Challenge Walk* by John Merrill (Walk & Write Ltd). ISBN 1874754152.
32pp; A5. £3.95 (+ 75p p&p).
Badge and certificate: (Walk & Write Ltd). £3.50 (incs p&p).

Three Crags Walk 547

N Yorks, W Yorks   *25 km / 16 miles*

A route passing the crags of Almscliff, Caley and Cow & Calf.

Start:	Weeton Station, N Yorks	SE276476
Finish:	Cow & Calf, Ilkley, W Yorks	SE130467
Landranger maps:	104	
1 : 25,000 maps:	Ex 297	

Publications, badges and certificates:
Looseleaf: *Three Crags Walk* (Peter Bayer). £0.50 (+ A5 SAE).
Badge: (Peter Bayer). £2.00 (+ SAE).

Three Feathers Walks 548

Derbys, N Yorks, S Yorks   *Various km / Various miles*

A series of three circular walks, each set in a different National Park and based on: Kettlewell, Yorkshire Dales (34 miles); Kilburn, North York Moors (30 miles); Yorkshire Bridge, Peak District (28 miles). To qualify for a badge, the routes must be completed within a calendar year. All are arduous and should be planned accordingly.

Start and Finish:	Various	Various
Landranger maps:	98, 100, 110	
1 : 25,000 maps:	OL 1, 2, 26, 30	

Publications, badges and certificates:
Looseleaf: *Three Feathers Walks* (Keith Bown). A4. Free (+ 9 x 4 SAE).
Badge: (Keith Bown). £2.50 (+ SAE).

Three Footpaths Walk 549

Essex   *40 km / 25 miles*

Based on the village of Chappel, the site of the 1066ft long viaduct which was built between 1847 and 1849, the Walk takes advantage of parts of the Essex Way, the Stour Valley Path and the Essex Country to Coast Walk.

Start and Finish:	Chappel, Essex	TL894283
Landranger maps:	155, 168	
1 : 25,000 maps:	Ex 184, 195, 196	

Publications, badges and certificates:
Booklet: *The Three Footpaths Walk* (John Edwards Footpath Guides). 12pp; A5. £1.25 (incs p&p).
Certificate: (John Edwards Footpath Guides). £1.00 (incs p&p).

Three Forests Way 550

Essex, Herts   *96 km / 60 miles*

A route devised by the West Essex Group of the RA to commemorate Queen Elizabeth's Silver Jubilee. It links three Essex forests, although only eight miles of the Way are through them. The Way visits Hatfield Forest and via White Roding, the Roding valley and Abridge, the Hainault Forest and via Loughton, Epping Forest. The Stort Valley is followed back to the finish. See also London LOOP.

Start and Finish:	Harlow, Essex	TL445113
Landranger maps:	166, 167, 177	✔
1 : 25,000 maps:	Ex 174, 175, 183, 194, 195	

Publications, badges and certificates:
Booklet: *Three Forests Way* by Fred Matthews and Harry Bitten (Essex County Council) 1986. 24pp; A5. £1.00.

Three Moors Walk 551

N Yorks, W Yorks   *48 km / 30 miles*

A walk taking in The Chevin, Rombalds Moor and Round Hill (Langbar/Middleton Moor), it includes some of the more obscure paths, hence offering a navigational challenge.

Start and Finish:	Otley, W Yorks	SE204455
Landranger maps:	104	
1 : 25,000 maps:	Ex 297	

Publications, badges and certificates:
Looseleaf: *Three Moors Walk* (Peter Bayer). £0.50 (+ A5 SAE).
Badge: (Peter Bayer). £2.00 (+ SAE).

Three Peaks of Cheviot Walk 552

Northumb   *48 km / 30 miles*

This upland walk over rough terrain, involving 5,700ft of ascent and requiring good navigational skills, links the Schil, Windy Gyle and Hedgehope. The walk is open April – September with no completions recorded outside this period.

Start and Finish:	Hawsen Burn, Northumb	NT954225
Landranger maps:	74, 80, 81	
1 : 25,000 maps:	OL 16	
Path website:	www.blencathra.demon.co.uk.nldwa	

Publications, badges and certificates:
Looseleaf: *Three Peaks of Cheviot* (LDWA Northumbria Group). A4. Free (+ 9 x 4 SAE).
Certificate: (LDWA Northumbria Group). £0.20 (+ 9 x 6 SAE).

Three Peaks of Great Britain · 553

Caernarfon, Cumbria, Highland · *42 km / 26 miles*

A challenge which is not truly in keeping with other walks/challenges in this directory and included to draw attention to relevant matters. It is a misnomer that the challenge of climbing the highest peaks of Scotland, England and Wales, Ben Nevis, Scafell and Snowdon respectively, has to be completed within 24 hours. Heed should always be taken of the inconvenience often caused to the residents in the affected areas and of the real dangers for vehicle occupants when travelling between the peak bases. The listed publication provides details of suggested routes to the mountain tops as well as road routes between them and safety advice.

Start:	Car Park, Glen Nevis Youth Hostel, Highland	NN128718
Finish:	Car Park, Pen-y-pass Youth Hostel, Caernarfon	SH647556
Landranger maps:	41, 90, 115	
1 : 25,000 maps:	OL 4, 6, 17, 38	

Publications, badges and certificates:
Paperback: *The National 3 Peaks Walk* by Brian Smailes (Challenge Publications) 1999. ISBN 0952690071. 72pp; 125 x 185. £6.50 (incs p&p).
Badge and certificate: (Challenge Publications). £3.30 & £0.60 (both inc p&p).

Three Peaks Walk (Yorkshire) · 554

N Yorks · *39 km / 24 miles*

The classic walk, taking in the peaks of Pen-y-ghent (2,278ft), Whernside (2,416ft) and Ingleborough (2,376ft) and involving over 5,000ft of ascent. It has suffered from path erosion. The Three Peaks of Yorkshire Club, based at the Pen-y-ghent Café, operates a limited clocking-in safety service – advance notice required particularly for groups. Full details of it and the Club on application (01729 860333). Completers may be invited to join the Club. See also Ribskip Challenge.

Start and Finish:	Horton in Ribblesdale, N Yorks	SD809725
Landranger maps:	98	
1 : 25,000 maps:	OL 2	

Publications, badges and certificates:
Paperback: *The Yorkshire 3 Peaks Walk* by Brian Smailes (Challenge Publications) 2001. ISBN 1903568013. 43pp; 125 x 185. £3.75 (incs p&p) – includes loose sketch map.
Leaflet: *The Three Peaks Yorkshire Dales – A Hill-Walker's Map and Guide* by Altos Design Ltd (Pen-y-ghent Café) 1997. A4/3. £3.95 (+ 9 x 6 SAE).
Leaflet: *Three Peaks – Footpath Map & Guide* by Arthur Gemmell (Pen-y-ghent Café) 1993. ISBN 0906886627. A4/8. £1.30 (+ SAE).
Leaflet: *Pen-y-ghent Café Safety Service* (Pen-y-ghent Café). A4/3. Free (+ 9 x 4 SAE).
Stripmap: *Yorkshire Dales Three Peaks* (Harvey Maps). ISBN 1851372997. £7.95 (+ 80p p&p).
Badge: (Pen-y-ghent Café). Details from Pen-y-ghent Café.

Three Ridings on Foot 555

Cleveland, E Yorks, N Yorks, S Yorks,   *706 km / 438 miles*
W Yorks

A route tracing the border of Yorkshire on rights of way and permissive paths through the moors of the Pennines, the northern Yorkshire Dales, the North York Moors and the coastline.

Start and Finish:	Bawtry, S Yorks	SK652932
Landranger maps:	92, 93, 94, 98, 101, 103, 106, 107, 110, 111, 112	
1 : 25,000 maps:	Ex 278, 279, 291, 292, 293, 295, 301, 304	
	OL 1, 2, 19, 21, 26, 27, 30, 41	

Publications, badges and certificates:
Paperback: *Three Ridings on Foot* by A. & G. Birch and others (P3 Publications) 1996. 120pp; 200 x 103. £4.00 (incs p&p).

Three Rivers Walk 556

N Yorks, W Yorks   *40 km / 25 miles*

A walk from the Aire to the Wharfe at Ilkley and then via Denton to the River Washburn near Swinsty Hall before returning to the Wharfe at the finish.

Start and Finish:	Shipley, W Yorks	SE204455
Landranger maps:	104	
1 : 25,000 maps:	Ex 288, 297	

Publications, badges and certificates:
Looseleaf: *Three Rivers Walk* (Peter Bayer). £0.50 (+ A5 SAE).
Badge: (Peter Bayer). £2.00 (+ SAE).

Three Shires Way 557

Beds, Cambs, Milton K, Northants   *57 km / 35 miles*

A bridleway running through quiet rural landscape and remnants of ancient woodland. Linking with the Swan's Way at the start, it takes in the county boundaries of Bucks, Beds and Northants at Threeshire Wood. The Grafham Water Circular Ride (13 miles) can be added to the route at the finish.

Start:	Tathall End, Milton K	SP821467
Finish:	Grafham Water, Cambs	TL116691
Landranger maps:	152, 153	✔
1 : 25,000 maps:	Ex 192, 207, 224, 225	
Waymark:	Triple-linked horseshoes	

Publications, badges and certificates:
Leaflet: *Three Shires Way* (Cambridgeshire County Council) 1990. A4/3. Free (+ SAE).
Leaflet: *Grafham Water Circular Ride* (Cambridgeshire County Council) 1990. A5. Free (+ SAE).

Three Towers Circuit   558

Gtr Man, Lancs   *56 km / 35 miles*

Supported by the East Lancashire Group of the LDWA, a route through the West
Pennine Moors taking in the towers of Peel, Rivington and Darwen. Navigational
skills are appropriate.

Start and Finish:	Tottington, Gtr Man	SD776129
Landranger maps:	103, 109	
1 : 25,000 maps:	Ex 287	

Publications, badges and certificates:
Looseleaf: *Three Towers Circuit* (LDWA East Lancs). Free (+ 9 x 4 SAE).
Badge and certificate: (LDWA East Lancs). £0.90 & £0.10 (+ 9 x 6 SAE).

Tidewater Way   559

Lancs, N Yorks, W Yorks   *145 km / 90 miles*

A route connecting the tidal waters of the west coast with those of the east, thus
laying the claim to be a coast to coast walk. The Way follows the Rivers Lune and
Wenning, crossing the Pennine Way National Trail near Malham, the Dales Way in
Wharfedale and using parts of the Ebor Way. Part of the proceeds of sales are
donated to Christian Aid.

Start:	Skerton Weir, Lancaster, Lancs	SD482632
Finish:	Ulleskelf, N Yorks	SE525401
Landranger maps:	97, 98, 104, 105	
1 : 25,000 maps:	Ex 289, 290, 297 OL 2, 41	

Publications, badges and certificates:
Paperback: *Tidewater Way* by Tony Rablen (Mark Comer) 1996. ISBN 1871125278. 32pp; 210 x
148. £4.50 (+ 75p p&p) – cheques payable to Christian Aid.

Todmorden Centenary Way   560

W Yorks   *31 km / 19 miles*

A route around Todmorden created to commemorate the centenary of the granting
of Borough status, taking in moors, valleys, woods, reservoirs, villages and
poignant ruins.

Start and Finish:	Todmorden, W Yorks	SD936242
Landranger maps:	103, 109	✔
1 : 25,000 maps:	OL 21	
Waymark:	Named signs	

Publications, badges and certificates:
Folder: *Todmorden Centenary Way* (Hebden Bridge Tourist Information Centre) 1996. A5. £1.95
(+ 40p p&p).

Towers Way 561

Lincs *160 km / 100 miles*

A meandering route avoiding the Viking Way where possible and which links 40 churches. In addition to the Viking Way, there are connnections with the Wanderlust and Nev Cole Ways and the Lindsey Loop.

Start:	Barton Upon Humber, Lincs	TA032218
Finish:	Lincoln, Lincs	SK978719
Landranger maps:	112, 113, 121	
1 : 25,000 maps:	Ex 272, 281, 282, 284	

Publications, badges and certificates:
Type TBA: *The Towers Way* by Alan & Janet Nash and Tony Broad (RA Lincoln). Full details TBA 2002.

Traditional Hostels Lakes Walk 562

Cumbria *97 km / 60 miles*

This route was devised to connect the smaller traditional style youth hostels, namely Thirlmere, Carrock Fell, Skiddaw House, Cockermouth, Ennerdale, Black Sail and Honister House. An additional spur to the south of Honister allows for visits to three other hostels at Grasmere, Elterwater and Coniston, and adds about 20 miles to the walk.

Start and Finish:	Thirlmere Youth Hostel, Cumbria	NY318191
Landranger maps:	89, 90	
1 : 25,000 maps:	OL 4, 5	

Publications, badges and certificates:
Folder: *The Traditional Hostels Lakes Walk* by Martyn Hanks (YHA Northern Region) 1996. 16pp; A4. £1.95 (incs p&p).
Booklet: *Booking Bureau – Youth Hostels* (YHA Northern Region) Annual. 20pp; A5. Free.

Trans Pennine Trail 563

Cheshire, Derbys, E Yorks, Gtr Man, Lancs, *322 km / 200 miles*
Merseyside, N Yorks, S Yorks, W Yorks

A multi-user trail, braided in parts, following former railway lines, canal towpaths and other waterside routes, linking the urban areas of Hull, Doncaster, Barnsley, Greater Manchester and Merseyside. In spite of the urban nature of the Trail, there are long stretches of rural environment in the east and other extensive sections passing through attractive country in the Pennine and Manchester areas. There are spurs from the main Trail to York from Selby and, from Barnsley, to Wakefield/Leeds and Sheffield/Chesterfield. In parts the Trail makes us of other longer established and formally named paths including the Longdendale Trail, the Dove Valley Trail (each 9 miles) and, from the west of Warrington to Liverpool, the waymarked Mersey Way (30 miles and on OS mapping). The total length of the Trail and spurs is some 350 miles. The section from Hull to Liverpool forms part of the E8 European

Long Distance Path: see E-Routes. See East Riding Heritage Way, Etherow – Goyt Valley Way, Midshires Way, Penistone Loop-D-Loop and Penistone Boundary Walk.

Start:	Hornsea, E Yorks	TA208479
Finish:	Southport, Merseyside	SD338172
Landranger maps:	105, 106, 107, 108, 109, 110, 111	✔
1 : 25,000 maps:	Ex 266, 268, 269, 275, 276, 277, 278, 279, 281, 284, 285, 288, 289	
Waymark:	Named discs/posts with trail logo	
User group:	Friends of the Trans Pennine Trail	
Path website:	www.transpenninetrail.org.uk	

Publications, badges and certificates:

Illustrated map guide: *Trans Pennine Trail – Map 1 West – Southport to Penistone* (Trans Pennine Trail Officer). ISBN 0953227715. A2/4. £4.95 (+ £1.75 p&p).

Illustrated map guide: *Trans Pennine Trail – Map 2 Central – Penistone to Sprotborough* (Trans Pennine Trail Officer). ISBN 0953227723. A2/4. £4.95 (+ £1.75 p&p).

Illustrated map guide: *Trans Pennine Trail – Map 3 East – Sprotborough to Hornsea* (Trans Pennine Trail Officer). ISBN 0953227731. A2/4. £4.95 (+ £1.75 p&p).

Booklet: *Trans Pennine Trail Accommodation and Visitor Guide* (Trans Pennine Trail Officer). £4.95 (+ £1.75 p&p).

Package: (Trans Pennine Trail Officer). £17.80 (+ £2.15 p&p) – above four items (three Map Guides and Booklet).

Leaflets: *Trans Pennine Trail* (Trans Pennine Trail Officer). 3 leaflets; A4/3. Free (+ SAE) – covering each map area.

Folder: *Walk the Mersey Way* (Mersey Valley Partnership). A5+. Free (+ A4 SAE).

Trans Pennine Way 564

Lancs, N Yorks, W Yorks   *161 km / 100 miles*

The theme of this route is a connection of the extremities in traversing the Pennines. Although none of the route is within the Yorkshire Dales National Park, it links the Forest of Bowland and Nidderdale AONB's as it takes a line through Pendle Country, Haworth, Ilkley Moor, Washburn Valley, Pateley Bridge and the area of Brimham Rocks.

Start:	Garstang, Lancs	SD496460
Finish:	Ripon, N Yorks	SE308711
Landranger maps:	99, 102, 103, 104	
1 : 25,000 maps:	Ex 287, 297, 298 OL 21, 41	

Publications, badges and certificates:

Paperback: *Trans Pennine Way* by Paul Hannon (Hillside Publications) 1999. ISBN 1870141660. 104pp; 175 x 115. £6.99 (+ 70p p&p).

Trans-Dales Trail – 1 565

N Yorks   *97 km / 60 miles*

A route crossing Ribblesdale, Littondale, Wharfedale and Nidderdale, followed by opportunities to visit the rock formations at Brimham Rocks, the historic grandeur of Fountains Abbey, and the valley of the River Skell.

Start:	Ingleton, N Yorks	SD695730
Finish:	Ripon, N Yorks	SE319705
Landranger maps:	98, 99	
1 : 25,000 maps:	Ex 298 OL 2, 30	

Publications, badges and certificates:
Paperback: *Trans-Dales Trail 1* (Arnold Underwood) 1997. ISBN 0952977109. 40pp; A5. £2.50 (incs p&p).

Trans-Dales Trail – 2   566
Durham, N Yorks   *97 km / 60 miles*

A route initially through some of the quieter dales, Arkengarthdale and Swaledale, before visiting the more popular villages of Askrigg, Buckden, Malham and Gargrave, then continuing over wild moors and deep valleys, finishing along a canal towpath.

Start:	Greta Bridge, Durham	NZ086132
Finish:	Skipton, N Yorks	SD992521
Landranger maps:	92, 98, 103	
1 : 25,000 maps:	OL 2, 30	

Publications, badges and certificates:
Paperback: *Trans-Dales Trail 2* (Arnold Underwood) 1997. ISBN 0952977117. 52pp; A5. £2.50 (incs p&p).

Trans-Dales Trail – 3   567
Cumbria, N Yorks   *91 km / 57 miles*

The Trail initially takes to Mallerstang and Garsdale Head before following Wensleydale to Thornton Rust. Visits are then made to Thoralby, Carlton-in-Coverdale, Middlesmoor in Nidderdale before again taking to the high moors to the finish.

Start:	Kirkby Stephen Railway Station, Cumbria	NY761067
Finish:	Masham, N Yorks	SE225807
Landranger maps:	92, 98, 103	
1 : 25,000 maps:	Ex 298 OL 10, 30	

Publications, badges and certificates:
Paperback: *Trans Dales Trail 3* (Arnold Underwood) 1999. ISBN 0952977125. 42pp; A5. £2.50 (incs p&p).

Trent & Mersey Canal Walk   568
Cheshire, Staffs, Derbys   *161 km / 100 miles*

Initially following the Bridgewater Canal from the River Mersey to Preston Brook, the route then takes to the Trent & Mersey Canal which if follows for 92 miles to Derwents Mouth on the River Trent, passing sites of interest such as Anderton's Lift. A total of 75 locks and 230 bridges are also passed with an overall ascent of 350ft.

See Leicester Line Canal Walk, Macclesfield & Peak Forest Canals, Staffordshire and Worcestershire Canal Walk and Coventry Canal Walk.

Start:	Runcorn, Cheshire	SJ504823
Finish:	Shardlow, Derbys	SK458308
Landranger maps:	108, 117, 118, 127, 128, 129	
1 : 25,000 maps:	Ex 243, 244, 245, 258, 260, 267, 268	

Publications, badges and certificates:
Booklet: *Walking the Trent & Mersey Canal* by John N. Merrill (Walk & Write Ltd). ISBN 1874754195. 68pp; A5. £4.95 (+ 75p p&p).
Stripmap (folded): *The Trent & Mersey Canal – Map 1 – Preston Brook to Fradley Junction* (GEOprojects) 1999. ISBN 0863510469. 135 x 213. £4.75.
Stripmap (folded): *The Trent & Mersey Canal – Map 2 – Great Haywood Junction to Cromwell Lock* (GEOprojects) 1999. ISBN 0863510493. 135 x 213. £4.75.
Badge and certificate: (Walk & Write Ltd). £3.50 (incs p&p).

Trent Valley Way   569
Derbys, Notts   *135 km / 84 miles*

Devised to celebrate the Centenary of Nottinghamshire County Council, the Way follows the River Trent to the confluence with the Chesterfield Canal. Though sticking close to the river for the most part, it leaves occasionally, exploring various interesting features in the wider valley. The route passes through Nottingham and Newark, besides numerous smaller places with interesting churches, watermills and windmills.

Start:	Long Eaton, Derbys	SK507326
Finish:	West Stockwith, Notts	SK791949
Landranger maps:	112, 120, 121, 129	✔
1 : 25,000 maps:	Ex 260, 271, 280	
Waymark:	Wavy blue symbol	

Publications, badges and certificates:
No publications: on OS mapping.

Trollers Trot   570
N Yorks   *43 km / 27 miles*

A varied route in the Yorkshire Dales using footpaths over moorland, alongside riverbanks and through forests and fields. Part of the route passes over access land which on certain days (except Sundays) is closed to the public for grouse-shooting.

Start and Finish:	Bolton Abbey, N Yorks	SE072539
Landranger maps:	98	
1 : 25,000 maps:	OL 2	

Publications, badges and certificates:
Leaflet: *Trollers Trot* (John Sparshatt). A4. Free (+ 9 x 4 SAE).
Badge and certificate: (John Sparshatt). £2.00 (+ A4 SAE) – cheques payable to W Yorks LDWA.

Tunbridge Wells Circular Walk 571

E Sussex, Kent   *44 km / 28 miles*

Formerly named the High Weald Walk, this route explores the variety of countryside around Royal Tunbridge Wells on the borders of Kent and East Sussex and is within the High Weald AONB passing through a rolling landscape of ridges and valleys with a patchwork of small fields, hedges and broadleaved woodland. In addition to the long distance path there are four linked routes from the centre of Royal Tunbridge Wells. On OS maps the route is shown as the High Weald Walk.

Start and Finish:	Southborough Common, Kent	TQ575427
Landranger maps:	188	✔, see text
1 : 25,000 maps:	Ex 135, 136, 147	
Waymark:	Named squares with hill, path and trees	

Publications, badges and certificates:
Booklet: *Walk along and around the Tunbridge Wells Circular* (Kent High Weald Project) 2001. ISBN 1901509621. 58pp; 210 x 210. £5.00 (post free) – cheques payable to Kent County Council.
Video: *Tunbridge Wells Circular Walk* (Promo-video Publications). 35 minutes. £12.50 (+ £1.00 p&p).
Badge and certificate: (Kent High Weald Project). Free – if walk completed in three days or less. Details in guidebook.

Twin Valley 20 Walks 572

Lancs, W Yorks   *97 km / 60 miles*

Comprising two separate demanding circular walks, the Twin Valley 20 (Calderdale), is 33 miles long, based on Mytholmroyd, and the Twin Valley 20 (Rossendale) is 27 miles long, based on Stacksteads. Each circuit passes 10 trig points providing panoramic views over rural and urban landscapes. There is no set route to achieving the walks. Although full details of the locations of the trig points are provided, it is the decision of the walker as to what route to take.

Start:	Various	Various
Finish:	Various	Various
Landranger maps:	103, 104	
1 : 25,000 maps:	Ex 287 OL 21	

Publications, badges and certificates:
Looseleaf: *Twin Valley 20* (Anton Ciritis). A4. Free (+ 9 x 4 SAE).
Badge and certificate: (Anton Ciritis). £2.00 – on completion of both walks.

Two Beacons Challenge 573

N Yorks, W Yorks   *58 km / 36 miles*

Basically an extension of the Wharfedale Washburn Walk, also visiting Addingham Moor and Beamsley Beacon.

Start and Finish:	Menston, W Yorks	SE176432
Landranger maps:	104	
1 : 25,000 maps:	Ex 297	

Publications, badges and certificates:
Looseleaf: *Two Beacons Challenge* (Louise Mallinson). Free (+ 9 x 4 SAE).
Badge and certificate: (Louise Mallinson). £1.50 (+ SAE).

Two Castles Trail — 574

Cornwall, Devon   *38 km / 24 miles*

The Trail follows river valleys, ridge roads, open downland and woods on the edge of Dartmoor, linking the imposing Norman castles at Okehampton and Launceston. The Trail is coincident with the West Devon Way between Okehampton and Bridestowe. The Trail links with the Tamar Valley Discovery Trail and the West Devon Way to form a circuit of approximately 100 miles.

Start:	Okehampton, Devon	SX589952
Finish:	Launceston, Cornwall	SX331848
Landranger maps:	190, 191, 201	✔
1 : 25,000 maps:	Ex 112, 113 OL 28	
Waymark:	Named logo	

Publications, badges and certificates:
Folder: *Two Castles Trail* (including accommodation guide and route directions both ways) (Devon County Council) 1998. 4 leaflets. £2.40 (incs p&p) – quote ref. DP41.

Two Counties Way — 575

Devon, Somers   *90 km / 56 miles*

Passing through, or near to, Bradford on Tone, Wellington, Tiverton, Bickleigh, Exeter and Kenton, the route is coincident in short sections with the West Deane Way, Grand Western Canal walk and the Exe Valley Walk. In essence it provides a link from Taunton to the South West Coast Path National Trail.

Start:	Taunton, Somers	ST220249
Finish:	Starcross, Devon	SX973817
Landranger maps:	181, 192, 193	
1 : 25,000 maps:	Ex 110, 114, 128	
Waymark:	Named signs with coot logo	

Publications, badges and certificates:
Looseleaf: *The Two Counties Way* (Gary Broom). 10pp; A4. Free (+ 9 x 6 SAE) – donations appreciated.
Certificate: (Gary Broom). Free (+ 9 x 6 SAE).

Two Crosses Circuit · 576

Gtr Man, Lancs · *40 km / 25 miles*

Supported by the East Lancashire Group of the LDWA, a route through the West Pennine Moors taking in the Roman Cross at Affetside and the Pilgrim's Cross at Bull Hill passing Turton Tower and the Turton & Entwistle Reservoir. Some navigational skills are appropriate.

Start and Finish:	Tottington, Gtr Man	SD776129
Landranger maps:	109	
1 : 25,000 maps:	Ex 287	

Publications, badges and certificates:
Looseleaf: *Two Crosses Circuit* (LDWA East Lancs). Free (+ 9 x 4 SAE).
Badge and certificate: (LDWA East Lancs). £0.90 (+ SAE) & £0.10 (+ 9 x 6 SAE).

Two Moors Way · 577

Devon, Somers · *164 km / 102 miles*

A route across Dartmoor over exposed moorland to Teigncombe from where the River Teign is followed to Castle Drogo. The Exmoor National Park is reached at Tarr Steps and the Way then climbs to Exe Head and through Cheriton to the finish. Access to Ivybridge from the South Devon coast can be achieved by way of way-marked trails both included on OS mapping. These are the Erme-Plym Trail (10 miles) which provides a route from each of Plymouth and Wembury to Brixton and then a single route to Sequer's Bridge near Ermington. From here the Erme Valley Trail (3 miles) can be taken to Ivybridge. See Tarka Trail for links to the Two Moors Way.

Start:	Ivybridge, Devon	SX636563
Finish:	Lynmouth, Devon	SS721497
Landranger maps:	180, 181, 191, 202	✔
1 : 25,000 maps:	Ex 113, 114, 127 OL 9, 20, 28	
Waymark:	Named signs with coot logo	
User group:	Two Moors Way Association	

Publications, badges and certificates:
Paperback: *The Two Moors Way* by John Macadam (Aurum Press) 1997. ISBN 1854104586. 144pp; 210 x 130. £12.99.
Paperback: *The Two Moors Way* by James Roberts (Cicerone Press) 1994. ISBN 1852841591. 100pp. £5.99.
Paperback: *Two Moors Way* (Two Moors Way Association) 1996. ISBN 0900613432. 48pp; A5. £3.00 (+ 50p p&p).
Leaflet: *Two Moors Way* (Devon County Council). A4/3. £0.25 (incs p&p) – quote ref. DP34.
Looseleaf: *The Two Moors Way – Accommodation List* (Two Moors Way Association). 2pp; A5. £0.50 (+ 9 x 4 SAE).
Folder: *The Erme-Plym Trail* (Devon County Council). A4. £1.40 (incs p&p) – quote ref. DP40.
Folder: *The Erme Valley Trail* (Devon County Council). A4. £2.40 (incs p&p) – quote ref. DP39.
Badge and certificate: (Two Moors Way Association). Each £1.00 (+ SAE).

Two Rivers Way   578
Bath NES, N Somers   *32 km / 20 miles*

This route from Congresbury on the River Yeo to Keynsham on the River Avon, where the route meets the Avon Walkway (30 miles and included on OS mapping), passes through farmland and historic villages, such as Chew Stoke, Chew Magna and Compton Dando. The Three Peaks Circular Walk (17 miles and on OS mapping) which takes in the gentle tops of Maes Knoll, Knowle Hill and Blackberry Hill crosses the Way at Pensford and Chew Magna. See Community Forest Path.

Start:	Congresbury, N Somers	ST438639
Finish:	Keynsham, Bath NES	ST659690
Landranger maps:	172, 182	✔
1 : 25,000 maps:	Ex 154, 155	
Waymark:	Named discs with wave motif	

Publications, badges and certificates:
Booklet: *The Two Rivers Way* (Yatton Ramblers) 1992. ISBN 0951134264. 42pp; A5. £2.40 (incs p&p).
Leaflet: *2 Rivers Congresbury to Keynsham* (Bath & North East Somerset Council). A4/3. Free.
Leaflet: *Three Peaks Circular Walk* (Bath & North East Somerset Council). A4/3. Free (+ 9 x 4 SAE).

Tyne – Estuary to Source   579
Northumberland   *133 km / 83 miles*

A route following the Tyne Valley through North Shields, Newcastle, Hexham, Haltwhistle, Slaggyford, Alston and Garrigill. The publication caters for completing the route as a series of circular walks or a linear completion. There are links to the Pennine Way National Trail.

Start:	Tynemouth, Northumberland	NZ370698
Finish:	Tynehead, Cumbria	NY764380
Landranger maps:	87, 88, 91	
1 : 25,000 maps:	Ex 316 OL 31, 43	

Publications, badges and certificates:
Paperback: *Walking the Tyne* by J. B. Jonas (RA Northern Area) 2001. ISBN 1901184420. 64pp; A5. £4.00 (+ £1.00 p&p).

Tyne and Wear 20   580
Tyne & Wear   *34 km / 21 miles*

A route following tracks and riverside paths over undulating countryside visiting Blackhall Mill.

Start and Finish:	Newburn Bridge, Tyne & Wear	NZ165652
Landranger maps:	88	
1 : 25,000 maps:	Ex 308, 316	

Publications, badges and certificates:
Looseleaf: *Tyne and Wear 20* (J. Tinniswood). A4. Free (+ 9 x 4 SAE).
Badge and certificate: (J. Tinniswood). £1.00 (+ SAE).

Tyne Valley Train Trails 581

Northumberland   *69 km / 43 miles*

A series of shorter linear walks based on the Tyne Valley railway through the station towns/villages of Prudhoe, Stocksfield, Riding Mill, Corbridge, Hexham, Haydon Bridge and Bardon Mill, all of which can be linked to provide a linear route of at least 43 miles through woodlands and farmland, across open fells and along riverside paths. At Haltwhistle, the route links with the Pennine Way National Trail.

Start:	Wylam, Northumberland	NZ120642
Finish:	Haltwhistle, Northumberland	NY704637
Landranger maps:	86, 87, 88	
1 : 25,000 maps:	Ex 316 OL 43	

Publications, badges and certificates:
Folder: *Tyne Valley Train Trails – West* (Northumberland County Council). 6pp. £3.95.
Folder: *Tyne Valley Train Trails – East* (Northumberland County Council). 6pp. £3.95.

Tyne-Wear Trail 582

Durham, Tyne & Wear   *27 km / 17 miles*

A link between the Rivers Tyne and Wear passing through high moors and river valleys, and providing access to Beamish Museum. It connects with the Keelman's Way (14 miles) on the Tyne, and with the Great North Forest Trail at Causey Arch.

Start:	Newcastle, Tyne & Wear	NZ245638
Finish:	Chester-le-Street, Tyne & Wear	NZ272513
Landranger maps:	88	✔
1 : 25,000 maps:	Ex 308, 316	
Waymark:	Name/fish	

Publications, badges and certificates:
Leaflet: *Tyne-Wear Trail* (Great North Forest). A5. Free (+ 9 x 6 SAE).

Ulster Way 583

Numerous   *918 km / 570 miles*

The Ulster Way encircles the province and has links with trails in the Republic of Ireland including a 69-mile spur which traverses mountainous country in County Donegal. Most of the AONBs are visited with use made of paths, forestry tracks and minor lanes. However, in recent years maintenance has been neglected on some sections of the Way resulting in a number of access problems. The 'official' status previously afforded the route is to be reviewed with recommendations expected by the summer of 2002. For the present it is not being promoted by the various agencies involved.

Start and Finish:	Belfast Castle, Belfast	J290745
Landranger maps:	(OSNI) 4, 5, 7, 8, 9, 12, 13, 15, 17,	
	18, 19, 21, 26, 27, 29	✔
1 : 25,000 maps:	Not applicable in NI	
Waymark:	Walker with rucksack and stick/orange-coloured	
	arrows	

Publications, badges and certificates:
Paperback: *The Complete Ulster Way Walks* by Paddy Dillon (O'Brien Press Limited) 1999. ISBN 0862785898. 208pp; 198 x 130. £9.99.
Paperback: *Walking the Ulster Way: A Journal and a Guide* by Alan Warner (Appletree Press Ltd) 1989. ISBN 0862812275. 184pp; 209 x 148. £5.95.

Usk Valley Walk 584

Mons, Newport, Powys   *80 km / 50 miles*

The Walk follows the Usk valley upstream past the historic market town of Usk, via riverside, field and woodland paths and some minor roads to Abergavenny. Here it takes to the Monmouthshire and Brecon Canal towpath which it follows to Brecon. Mainly an easy waterside walk but there are two climbs, to the Kemeys Ridge north of Caerleon, and to Glanusk Park west of Crickhowell.

Start:	Caerleon, Newport	ST342902
Finish:	Brecon, Powys	SO043286
Landranger maps:	161, 171	✔
1 : 25,000 maps:	Ex 152 OL 13, 14	
Waymark:	Named yellow arrows	

Publications, badges and certificates:
Booklet: *Usk Valley Walk* (Monmouthshire County Council) 2001. Details TBA.

Vale Royal Round 585

Cheshire   *56 km / 35 miles*

The route uses part of the Trent and Mersey Canal towpath, the Whitgate Way and part of the Weaver Navigation and passes through or near to the Anderton Boat Lift, The Anderton Nature Park, Acton Bridge, Frodsham, Delamere, Winsford and Vale Royal Abbey.

Start and Finish:	Northwich Railway Station	SJ672739
Landranger maps:	117, 118	
1 : 25,000 maps:	Ex 267	

Publications, badges and certificates:
Leaflet: *Vale Royal Round* (Cheshire County Council). A3/4. Free (+ 9 x 4 SAE).

Vanguard Way 586

E Sussex, Gtr London, Kent, Surrey   106 km / 66 miles

The Way goes from the London suburbs to the sea connecting with the Wandle Trail and the London LOOP in Greater London and numerous other long distance paths including the North Downs, Greensand, Eden Valley and South Downs Ways. It passes the Selsdon Nature Reserve, the woods and heaths of Ashdown Forest, Alfriston and follows the coast through Seaford to the finish. The Wandle Trail (11 miles) provides a link to the Thames Path National Trail. See Sussex Diamond Way and Tandridge Border Path.

Start:	East Croydon, Gtr London	TQ329657
Finish:	Newhaven Harbour, E Sussex	TQ449009
Landranger maps:	176, 177, 187, 188, 198, 199	✔
1 : 25,000 maps:	Ex 122, 123, 135, 146, 147, 161	
Waymark:	Named discs	

Publications, badges and certificates:

Booklet: *Vanguard Way* (Vanguards Rambling Club) 1997. ISBN 095300760X. 68pp; A5. £2.95 (+ 45p p&p).

Paperback: *Wealdway and the Vanguard Way* by Kev Reynolds (Cicerone Press) 1987. ISBN 0902363859. 160pp; 116 x 176. £4.99.

Paperback: *The Wandle Guide* by the Wandle Group (Sutton London Borough). ISBN 0907335330. 78pp; 210 x 145. £4.95 (+ £1.50 p&p).

Leaflet: *Wandle Trail* (Wandle Industrial Museum). A4/3. £2.00 (+ 26p).

Badge: (Vanguards Rambling Club). £2.25 (+ SAE).

Vectis Trail 587

IoW   120 km / 75 miles

A route taking in the quieter parts of the island. There are seven other trails on the island which are all included on OS mapping and some of which are connecting. These are: Bembridge Trail (15 miles) – Shide to Bembridge; Nunwell Trail (10 miles) – Ryde St Johns to Sandown; Hamstead Trail (8 miles) – Brooke Bay to Hamstead Ledge; Shepherds Trail (10 miles) – Carisbrooke to Atherfield; Stenbury Trail (10 miles) – Blackwater to Week Down; Tennyson Trail (15 miles) – Carisbrooke to Alum Bay; Worsley Trail (15 miles) – Shanklin to Brightstone. See E-Routes (E9).

Start and Finish:	Yarmouth, IoW	SZ355897
Landranger maps:	196	
1 : 25,000 maps:	OL 29	

Publications, badges and certificates:

Paperback: *A Walker's Guide to the Isle of Wight* by Martin Collins & Norman Birch (Cicerone Press). ISBN 1852842210. 216pp. £9.99.

Paperback: *Vectis Trail* by Iris Evans and Barbara Aze (Barbara Aze). 32pp; 210 x 149. £2.00 (incs p&p).

Website: (Isle of Wight Tourism). www.islandbreaks.co.uk.

Vermuyden Way   588

Lincs   *32 km / 20 miles*

Supported by the Vermuyden Group of the LDWA, the Way follows an elongated circuit along the artificial water courses and low hills of the Isle of Axleholme, much of which was marshland prior to the intervention of Cornelius Vermuyden, a Dutch land drainage engineer of the 17th century.

Start and Finish:	Belton, N Lincs	SE782054
Landranger maps:	112	
1 : 25,000 maps:	Ex 280	
Waymark:	Stickers with letters VW	

Publications, badges and certificates:
Looseleaf: *Vermuyden Way* (LDWA Vermuyden Group). Free (+ 9 x 4 SAE).
Badge and certificate: (LDWA Vemuyden Group). £1.00 (+ 10 x 7 SAE).

Viking Way   589

Leics, Lincs   *237 km / 148 miles*

The Way is so named because it crosses an area which was occupied by Norse invaders. From the banks of the River Humber it crosses the Lincolnshire Wolds to Caistor, then along the Bain valley to Horncastle from where the Spa Trail is followed along the trackbed of a former railway to Woodhall Spa and along the Witham Valley, crossing flat fenland to Lincoln. Turning along the limestone escarpment of Lincoln Cliff and over Lincoln Heath, the route of the prehistoric Sewstern Lane is traced to reach Woolsthorpe Locks on the Grantham Canal. Another section of Sewstern Lane and other old tracks are followed to Thistleton from where the Way takes field-paths and lanes past Greetham, Exton and Rutland Water. At Oakham it links with the Macmillan Way and the Hereward Way. See Leicestershire Jubilee Way, Nev Cole Way, Humber Bridge Link Walk and Towers Way. See also E-Routes (E2).

Start:	Barton-upon-Humber, Lincs	TA028234
Finish:	Oakham, Leics	SK862088
Landranger maps:	106, 107, 112, 113, 121, 122, 130, 141	✔
1 : 25,000 maps:	Ex 234, 247, 272, 273, 281, 282, 284	
Waymark:	Viking helmet	

Publications, badges and certificates:
Paperback: *Viking Way* by John Stead (Cicerone Press) 1990. ISBN 1852840579. 172pp; 116 x 176. £5.99.
Paperback: *The Viking Way* (Lincolnshire County Council) 1997. ISBN 1872375251. 64pp; 125 x 206. Cost TBA 2002.
Looseleaf: *The Viking Way Factsheet* – Accommodation, Transport etc. (Lincolnshire County Council) Annual. 24pp; A4. Free.
Badge: (Brett Collier). £1.25 (+ SAE).

Wainwright Memorial Walk 590

Cumbria *164 km / 102 miles*

A route following that taken by Alfred Wainwright and three friends in 1931, visiting such as Patterdale, Scales, Keswick, the Buttermere Circuit and many others.

Start and Finish:	Windermere, Cumbria	SD407985
Landranger maps:	89, 90, 96, 97	
1 : 25,000 maps:	OL 4, 5, 6, 7	

Publications, badges and certificates:
Book: *The Wainwright Memorial Walk* by A. Wainwright (Michael Joseph). ISBN 0718136969. 192pp; 120 x 175. £10.99.

Walden Round 591

N Yorks *42 km / 26 miles*

A challenging route through Horsehouse to the head of Nidderdale, crossing Coverdale Beck into Waldendale, ascending Buckden Pike to then re-enter Wharfedale. There is a total ascent of 4,200 feet.

Start and Finish:	Kettlewell, N Yorks	SD969723
Landranger maps:	98	
1 : 25,000 maps:	OL 30	

Publications, badges and certificates:
Looseleaf: *Walden Round* (LDWA Nidderdale Group). 3pp; A4. Free (+ 9 x 4 SAE).
Badge and certificate: (LDWA Nidderdale Group). £2.00 (+ 9 x 6 SAE).

Wanderlust Way 592

Lincs *32 km / 20 miles*

This Way is an elongated circuit passing through attractive small villages and across the woods and farmland of the undulating Lincolnshire Wolds, from where there are views across the mouth of the Humber Estuary. See Towers Way.

Start and Finish:	Bradley Woods, Lincs	TA242059
Landranger maps:	113	
1 : 25,000 maps:	Ex 284	
Waymark:	Green and yellow letters WW	

Publications, badges and certificates:
Leaflet: *Wanderlust Way* (Alec Malkinson) 2001. A3/4. Free (+ 9 x 4 SAE).
Badge and certificate: (Alec Malkinson). £2.75 & £0.75 (+ 9 x 4 SAE).

Warwickshire Villages Trail 593

Warks *230 km / 143 miles*

The Trail links 71 villages, passing at least 48 churches and 37 village public houses. There are links with the Macmillan, Centenary (Warwickshire), Heart of England and Monarch's Ways.

Start:	Dunchurch, Warks	SP485712
Finish:	Hockley Heath, Warks	SP152725
Landranger maps:	139, 140, 150, 151	
1 : 25,000 maps:	Ex 191, 205, 206, 220, 222 OL 45	

Publications, badges and certificates:
Booklet: *The Warwickshire Villages Trail Route Guide* by Gerald Lawrence (Gerald Lawrence) 1998. ISBN 0953265005. 64pp; 150 x 210. £3.70 (+ 30p p&p).

Waveney Way   594
Suffolk   *116 km / 72 miles*

A walk around the boundary of Waveney District, coincident with Angles Way between Lowestoft and Bungay. This walk was completed in 2000 for the Waveney Ramblers silver anniversary. This is a gentle walk through varied landscape including stretches of the coast and the valleys of the Blyth and Waveney rivers.

Start and Finish:	Ness Point, Lowestoft, Suffolk	TM554931
Landranger maps:	134, 156	
1 : 25,000 maps:	Ex 231 OL 40	
Waymark:	Named discs with green directional arrow in white circle	

Publications, badges and certificates:
Booklet: *The Waveney Way* (RA Waveney) 2000. 24pp; A5. £2.10 (+ 40p p&p).
Leaflet: *Waveney Way* (Waveney District Council) 2002. A4/3. Free.

Wayfarer's Walk   595
Hants, W Berks   *114 km / 71 miles*

Initially coincident with the Solent Way, the Walk crosses the chalk ridge of Portsdown, the Meon Valley and goes through the villages of Hinton Amper and Drummer before climbing to become a ridgeway walk over Watership Down and Walbury Hill. See Staunton Way and Test Way.

Start:	Emsworth, Hants	SU753055
Finish:	Inkpen Beacon, W Berks	SU365622
Landranger maps:	174, 185, 196, 197	✔
1 : 25,000 maps:	Ex 119, 120, 132, 144, 158	
Waymark:	Green WW on white background	

Publications, badges and certificates:
Paperback: *Along and Around the Wayfarer's Walk* by Linda Herbst and others (Hampshire County Council) 1993. ISBN 0948176040. 96pp; 210 x 148. £4.95.
Leaflet: *The Wayfarer's Walk* (Hampshire County Council). A4/3. Free (+ SAE).

Wealdway   596
E Sussex, Kent   *132 km / 82 miles*

This route connects the Thames Estuary with the English Channel through the Weald of Kent and Sussex linking the North Downs Way at Trottiscliffe with the

South Downs Way near to Eastbourne. There are connections with other long distance routes including the Medway Valley Walk, Sussex Border Path and Diamond Way and the Greensand, Saxon Shore and Vanguard Ways.

Start:	Gordon Promenade, Gravesend, Kent	TQ654744
Finish:	Pier, Eastbourne, E Sussex	TQ620987
Landranger maps:	177, 178, 188, 198, 199	✔
1 : 25,000 maps:	Ex 123, 135, 136, 147, 148, 162, 163	
Waymark:	Letters WW on standard arrows	

Publications, badges and certificates:
Paperback: *Along and Around the Wealdway* by Helen Livingstone (East Sussex County Council and Kent County Council) 1999. ISBN 1873010931. 120pp; 200 x 208. £10.95 post free.
Paperback: *Wealdway and the Vanguard Way* by Kev Reynolds (Cicerone Press) 1987. ISBN 0902363859. 160pp; 116 x 176. £4.99.
Booklet: *Wealdway Accommodation Guide* by Geoffrey King (Dr Ben Perkins). ISBN 0951600613. 40pp; 148 x 105. £2.50 (incs p&p).
Video: *Wealdway* (Promo-video Publications). 40 minutes. £12.95 (+ £1.00 p&p).
Badge: (Dr Ben Perkins). £1.90 (incs p&p).

Weardale Way 597
Durham, Tyne & Wear 117 km / 73 miles

A route following the River Wear from the sea to the source keeping as close as is possible and visiting such as Lumley Castle, Durham, Barnard Castle and Stanhope. The River Wear Trail (10 miles and shown on OS mapping) is mainly coincident with the route between Roker and Fatfield.

Start:	Roker, Tyne & Wear	NZ408590
Finish:	Wearhead, Durham	NY858395
Landranger maps:	86, 87, 88, 91, 92, 93	✔
1 : 25,000 maps:	Ex 307, 308 OL 31	
Waymark:	Named signposts	

Publications, badges and certificates:
Paperback: *Walking the Great Rivers – The Weardale Way* by Alastair Wallace (Jema Publications) 1997. ISBN 1871468639. 85pp; A5. £5.99.
Leaflet: *River Wear Trail* (Sunderland City Council) 2000. A3/4. £1.50 (+ 50p p&p).

Weaver Valley Way 598
Cheshire 32 km / 20 miles

The Way follows the lower part of the Weaver Valley, in the main along the Weaver Navigation, and incorporates a detour to the Anderton Boat Lift. From Anderton, use can be made of the Anderton Nature Park and minor roads to re-access the Navigation at Northwich. There would seem to be no immediate plans to provide access to the canal between Anderton and Northwich. The publication includes reference to the Whitegate Way (7 miles) – Winsford to Cuddington.

Start:	Frodsham, Cheshire	SJ529784
Finish:	Bradford Lane Swing Bridge, Winsford, Cheshire	SJ656662
Landranger maps:	117, 118	
1 : 25,000 maps:	Ex 267	

Publications, badges and certificates:
Booklet: *Longer Trails in Vale Royal* by Carl Rogers (Vale Royal Borough Council) 1993. 76pp; A5. £1.95(incs p&p).
Leaflet: *Whitegate Way* (Cheshire County Council). A4/3. Free (+ 9 x 4 SAE).

Weavers Shuttle 599

Lancs *64 km / 40 miles*

The walk extends over open moorland and pastures in the Rossendale, Burnley and Pendle Districts and takes in many historical buildings and areas associated with the Industrial Revolution, Pendle witches and the Bronte Sisters. Items of interest range from an Iron Age clapper bridge to drovers' roads and canal towpaths. There is 5000ft of ascent.

Start and Finish:	Worsthorne, Lancs	SD876324
Landranger maps:	103	
1 : 25,000 maps:	OL 21	

Publications, badges and certificates:
Booklet: *Weavers Shuttle* (Max Tattersall). Free (+ 9 x 6 SAE).
Badge and certificate: (Max Tattersall). £1.00 (+ A4 SAE).

Weavers Way 600

Norfolk *90 km / 56 miles*

Use is made of public footpaths, disused railway line and some minor roads in passing through very varied scenery, from the mixed farmland and woodland of the north to the extensive, traditional grazing marshes of the Broadland river valleys. Notable landmarks to be seen along the Way include a number of fine flint churches, several large country houses, and a large number of windpumps. Parts of the Paston Way (18 miles and included on OS mapping) which visits 16 churches and villages over a meandering and convoluted route in north-east Norfolk can be used in linking Cromer with North Walsham. See Angles Way and Marriott's Way.

Start:	Cromer, Norfolk	TG215420
Finish:	Great Yarmouth, Norfolk	TG532076
Landranger maps:	133, 134	✔
1 : 25,000 maps:	Ex 252 OL 40	
Waymark:	Named boards	

Publications, badges and certificates:
Paperback: *Langton's Guide to the Weavers Way and Angles Way* by Andrew Durham (Andrew Durham) 1995. ISBN 1899242015. 144pp; 210 x 130. £6.95 (incs p&p).

Booklet: *Walking the Peddars Way & North Norfolk Coast Path with Weavers Way Guide* (RA Norfolk Area) 2001. ISBN 1901184463. 28pp; A5. £2.70 (+ 30p p&p) – includes accommodation list.
Leaflet: *Weavers' Way* (Norfolk County Council) 1997. A5. 70p (+ SAE).
Badge: (Norfolk County Council). Free – completed WW Challenge Card required.
Booklet: *The Paston Way* (Norfolk County Council) 1996. 12pp; A5. 70p (+ SAE).

Welsh 3000s   601

Conwy   *47 km / 29 miles*

This crossing of the 15 Snowdonian summits over 3,000ft, taking in the ranges of the Carneddau, the Glyders and the Snowdon Massif itself involves 12,000ft of ascent with much rough ground and some exposed scrambling. If that challenge is not enough the Welsh 3000s Double Crossing (28 summits) is also available.

Start:	Snowdon summit, Conwy	SH609544
Finish:	Foel Fras summit, Conwy	SH697682
Landranger maps:	115	
1 : 25,000 maps:	OL 17	

Publications, badges and certificates:
Paperback: *The Welsh Three Thousand Foot Challenges* by Ron Clayton and Ronald Turnbull (Grey Stone Books) 1997. ISBN 0951599666. 128pp; 175 x 115. £5.95.
Looseleaf: *Welsh 3000s Double Crossing* (Peter Travis). 3pp; A4. Free (+ 9 x 4 SAE).
Looseleaf: *Welsh 3000s Double Crossing* (Ed Dalton). 1pp; foolscap. Free (+ 9 x 4 SAE).
Certificates: (Peter Travis). Each £1.25 (incs p&p) – for single or double crossing.
Certificate (double crossing): (Ed Dalton). £2.00 (incs p&p).

Wessex Heights Walk   602

Dorset, Wilts   *124 km / 77 miles*

The walk was devised to use some of the less-walked paths over hills, passing several hill forts, with views across eastern Dorset and south Wiltshire. Road walking is kept to a minimum and Salisbury is included in the route.

Start:	Maiden Castle, Dorset	SY665887
Finish:	Old Sarum, Wilts	SU137328
Landranger maps:	184, 194	
1 : 25,000 maps:	Ex 117, 118, 130	

Publications, badges and certificates:
Softback: *Walking the Wessex Heights* (Marjorie Kerr). 64pp; A5. £3.00 (incs p&p).

Wessex Ridgeway   603

Devon, Dorset, Wilts   *221 km / 137 miles*

One of the links in a prehistoric route from The Wash to the South Devon Coast, this route basically extends the Ridgeway. Passed on the way, through Wiltshire, are the stone circles at Avebury, the Vale of Pewsey, the northern edge of Salisbury Plain, the Wylye Valley and Win Greene Hill. In Dorset Cranbourne Chase, Cerne Abbas with the 180ft high Cerne Giant and Pilsden Pen are visited before a short route through Devon leads to the finish in Dorset. At Marlborough a five mile link leads to the waymarked Wansdyke Path (14 miles and on OS mapping). The publication for this walk includes the Tan Hill Way (7 miles, waymarked and on OS mapping). See Dorset Jubilee Trail and Liberty Trail.

Start:	Marlborough, Wilts	SU187685
Finish:	Lyme Regis, Dorset	SY347922
Landranger maps:	173, 183, 184, 193, 194, 195	✔
1 : 25,000 maps:	Ex 116, 117, 118, 129, 130, 143, 157	
Waymark:	Wessex wyvern (Dorset only)	

Publications, badges and certificates:
Paperback: *The Wessex Ridgeway* by Anthony Burton (Aurum Press) 1999. ISBN 1854106139. 144pp; 210 x 130. £12.99.
Paperback: *Walk the Wessex Ridgeway in Wiltshire* by Brian Panton (RA Central Office – London) 1998. ISBN 1901184153. 64pp; 210 x 150. £4.50 (+ £1.50 p&p).
Paperback: *Walk the Wessex Ridgeway in Dorset* by Priscilla Houstoun (Dorset Publishing Co) 1994. ISBN 094869937X. 96pp; 215 x 160. £5.95 (+ £1.05 p&p).
Leaflet: *Walk the Wessex Ridgeway in Dorset* (Dorset County Council) 1994. A4/3. Free.
Folder: *The Wansdyke Path and the Tan Hill Way* (Kennet District Council). 7 leaflets. £2.00 (+ 50p p&p).

West Deane Way   604
Somers   *72 km / 45 miles*

Providing a variety of landscapes, including the flood plain and wooded valley of the River Tone and the Quantock Hills AONB, Appley, Waterrow, Wiveliscombe, Lydiard St Lawrence and Kingston St Mary are visited along the way. There are industrial remains, historic houses and gardens on or near to the route. It is coincident with the Somerset section of the Grand Western Canal walk between Greenham and Taunton. See Channel to Channel (Devon – Somerset) and Two Counties Way.

Start and Finish:	Taunton, Somers	ST220193
Landranger maps:	181, 193	✔
1 : 25,000 maps:	Ex 128, 140	
Waymark:	Named discs	

Publications, badges and certificates:
Softback (spiral bound): *West Deane Way* (Taunton Deane Borough Council) 1999. 57pp; A5. £5.00 (+ 50p p&p).

West Devon Way   605
Devon, Plymouth   *57 km / 35 miles*

The Way explores the rugged and spectacular countryside on the western fringe of the Dartmoor National Park, along the 18 miles between Okehampton, where it links with the Tarka Trail, and Tavistock. From there it continues a further 17 miles to Plymouth where it connects with the Erme-Plym Trail – see Two Moors Way. The Way links with the Tamar Discovery Trail and the Two Castles Trail to form a circuit of approximately 100 miles. See Dartmoor Way.

Start:	Okehampton, Devon	SX589953
Finish:	Plymouth	SX503529
Landranger maps:	191, 201	✔
1 : 25,000 maps:	Ex 108, 112, 113 OL 20, 28	
Waymark:	Stylised walker/church on hilltop	

Publications, badges and certificates:
Folder: *West Devon Way* (Devon County Council) 1999. 16pp; A5. £3.40 (incs p&p) – quote ref. DP16.

West Highland Way   606

Argyll, Bute, E Dunbarton, Highland, Stirling   153 km / 95 miles

Scotland's first official Long Distance Route crosses a variety of terrain which becomes more rugged as it moves northwards and between the major mountain groups. The Way follows the eastern side of Loch Lomond, crossing the slopes of Ben Lomond to Crianlarich and Bridge of Orchy, the western edge of Rannoch Moor and the entrances to Glen Etive and Glen Coe to reach Kinlochleven. The final section follows General Caulfield's military road over the slopes of the Mamores, crossing wild country with extensive views of the Ben Nevis range to reach Fort William. See Edinburgh to Glasgow Canals Walk and Great Glen Way. The book 'The Highland High Way' describes an alternative high level route.

Start:	Milngavie, E Dunbarton	NS555745
Finish:	Fort William, Highland	NN105742
Landranger maps:	41, 50, 56, 57, 64	✔
1 : 25,000 maps:	OL 38, 39	
Waymark:	Thistle within hexagon	
Path website:	www.west-highland-way.co.uk	

Publications, badges and certificates:
Paperback: *The West Highland Way & Map* (Official Guide) by Bob Aitken & Roger Smith (Mercat Press) 2000. ISBN 1841830046. 180pp. £14.99.
Paperback: *The West Highland Way* by Anthony Burton (Aurum Press) 1995. ISBN 1854103911. 144pp; 210 x 130. £12.99.
Paperback (spiral/laminated): *The West Highland Way & Map* by Jacquetta Megarry (Rucksack Readers) 2000. ISBN 1898481091. 70pp; A5. £9.99.
Paperback: *The West Highland Way* by Terry Marsh (Cicerone Press) 1997. ISBN 1852842350. 112pp. £6.99.
Hardback: *Guide to the West Highland Way* by Tom Hunter (Constable and Robinson Ltd) 1988. ISBN 0094690901. 192pp; 171 x 114. £9.95.
Hardback: *The Highland High Way* by Heather Connon and Paul Roper (Mainstream Publishing Co Ltd) 1996. ISBN 1851587918. 223pp; 220 x 127. £9.99.
Stripmap: *The West Highland Way Map and Guide* (Footprint). ISBN 1871149509. £4.50.
Stripmap: *The West Highland Way* (Harvey Maps). ISBN 1851372237. £8.95 (+ 80p p&p).

Booklet: *Walk the West Highland Way – Information & Accommodation List* (West Highland Way Ranger) Annual. Free (+ 9 x 4 SAE).
Freesheet: *West Highland Wayfarer* (Famedram Publishing Ltd). Free (+ A5 SAE).

West Island Way 607
Argyll & Bute   *48 km / 30 miles*

A route on the Isle of Bute embracing a variety of landscapes including seashore, moorland, farmland and forest. It passes St Blane's Chapel, the abandoned townships in Glen More and the outskirts of Rothesay. There is minimal road-walking.

Start:	Kilchattan Bay, Argyll & Bute	NS107546
Finish:	Kames Bay, Argyll & Bute	NS069674
Landranger maps:	63	
1 : 25,000 maps:	Ex 362	
Waymark:	Named signs	

Publications, badges and certificates:
Stripmap: *West Island Way – Map and Guide* (Footprint). ISBN 1871149517. £1.99 (+ 30p p&p).

Westmorland Way 608
Cumbria   *150 km / 94 miles*

A relatively low-level route across the historic county of Westmorland and the Lake District National Park, it follows footpaths, tracks and country lanes along river valleys and across farmland and the open fells via Shap, Pooley Bridge, Patterdale, Grasmere, Troutbeck and Kendal to reach Morecambe Bay. See Furness Way.

Start:	Appleby-in-Westmorland, Cumbria	NY683204
Finish:	Arnside, Cumbria	SD461788
Landranger maps:	90, 91, 97	
1 : 25,000 maps:	OL 5, 7, 31	

Publications, badges and certificates:
Paperback: *Westmorland Way* by Paul Hannon (Hillside Publications) 1998. ISBN 187014158X. 88pp; 175 x 115. £5.99 (+ 60p p&p).

Wey-South Path 609
Surrey, W Sussex   *58 km / 36 miles*

The Path follows the towpath of the Godalming Navigation along the River Wey to its confluence with the Wey & Arun Junction Canal crossing the North Downs Way National Trail near the start. Wherever possible the route follows the towpath, supplemented by paths, roads and disused railway, to reach and continue beside the Arun Navigation to the River Arun whence the path continues to meet the South Downs Way National Trail above Amberley. Several sections of the canals have been restored. See Arun Way and also Sussex Diamond Way. North from Millmead Lock, the Wey Navigation towpath (15 miles) reaches the Thames Path at Weybridge.

Start:	Millmead Lock, Guildford, Surrey	SU994494
Finish:	Near Amberley, W Sussex	TQ033125
Landranger maps:	186, 187, 197	✔
1 : 25,000 maps:	Ex 121, 134, 145	

Publications, badges and certificates:
Booklet: *The Wey-South Path* (W & A Enterprises Ltd) 1999. 68pp; A5. £5.50 (incs p&p).
Leaflet: *The Wey-South Path* (W & A Enterprises Ltd) 1997. A4/3. £1.20 (incs p&p).

Wharfedale Washburn Walk 610

N Yorks, W Yorks   *42 km / 26 miles*

A route visiting Otley Chevin, Pool, Lindley Wood and Ilkley. A 22-miles alternative is available. Proceeds from sales go to Martin House Hospice. See Two Beacons Challenge.

Start and Finish:	Menston, W Yorks	SE176432
Landranger maps:	104	
1 : 25,000 maps:	Ex 297	

Publications, badges and certificates:
Looseleaf: *Wharfedale Washburn Walk* (Louise Mallinson). Free (+ 9 x 4 SAE).
Badge and certificate: (Louise Mallinson). £1.50 (+ SAE).

Whicham Valley Five Trigs Walk 611

Cumbria   *32 km / 20 miles*

A mountain walk taking in Knott Hill, Blackcombe, Whitfell and Pike Stickle, for which map reading and compass skills are essential.

Start and Finish:	Duddon Bridge, Cumbria	SD199882
Landranger maps:	96, 97	
1 : 25,000 maps:	OL 6	

Publications, badges and certificates:
Looseleaf: The Whicham Valley Five Trigs Walk (Brian Richmond). Free (+ 9 x 4 SAE).
Badge: (Brian Richmond). £0.85 (+ SAE).

Whitby Way 612

N Yorks   *106 km / 66 miles*

The Way meanders through the Vale of York and over the North York Moors visiting many pilgrimage places of interest and taking in Crayke, Coxwold, Helmsley, Kirkby-moorside, Egton and Sleights. Ancient paved ways as well as moorland tracks and field paths form the route. Profits from sales are donated to Christian Aid.

Start:	York Minster, N Yorks	SE603522
Finish:	Whitby Abbey, N Yorks	NZ904113
Landranger maps:	94, 100, 105	
1 : 25,000 maps:	Ex 290, 299 OL 26, 27	

Publications, badges and certificates:
Booklet: *Whitby Way* by Leslie Stanbridge (Mark Comer). ISBN 1871125421. 36pp; A5. £4.50 (+ 75p p&p) – cheques payable to Christian Aid.

White Horse Trail   613

Wilts   *145 km / 90 miles*

A route created by Wiltshire County Council through Pewsey, Marlborough, Hackpen and Devizes providing views of the eight white horses which are cut into the turf of the chalk hillsides of Wiltshire. The route has been chosen to approach the horses from the best vantage points. As well as visiting many other historical locations use is made of part of the Kennet and Avon Canal.

Start and Finish:	Westbury White Horse, Wilts	ST899515
Landranger maps:	173, 183, 184	✔
1 : 25,000 maps:	Ex 130, 131, 143, 156, 157, 169	
Waymark:	White stylised horse on blue background	

Publications, badges and certificates:
Folder: *Wiltshire's White Horse Trail* (Salisbury District Council) 1999. 9 leaflets; A5. £6.00 (incs p&p).

White Peak Challenge Walk   614

Derbys   *40 km / 25 miles*

A strenuous challenge walk in the Peak National Park following the most rugged parts of the Peak and passing via Rowsley, Birchover, Youlgreave, Monyash, Flagg, Taddington and Great Longstone.

Start and Finish:	Bakewell, Derbys	SK217685
Landranger maps:	119	
1 : 25,000 maps:	OL 24	

Publications, badges and certificates:
Booklet: *White Peak Challenge Walk* by John Merrill (Walk & Write Ltd). ISBN 0907496776. 32pp; A5. £3.95 (+ 75p p&p).
Badge and certificate: (Walk & Write Ltd). £3.50 (incs p&p).

White Peak Rollercoaster   615

Derbys, Staffs   *38 km / 24 miles*

A circular walk set in the southern part of the Peak District National Park based on the Dove, Hamps and Manifold valleys. There is 4,500ft of ascent with many villages and varied scenery taken in.

Start and Finish:	Alstonefield, Staffs	SK131556
Landranger maps:	119	
1 : 25,000 maps:	OL 24	

Publications, badges and certificates:
Looseleaf: *White Peak Rollercoaster* (Alan S. Edwards). 4pp; A4. Free (+ 9 x 6 SAE).
Badge and certificate: (Alan S. Edwards). £2.25 (incs p&p).

White Peak Trails   616

Derbys, Staffs   *Various km / Various miles*

Former railway lines providing useful links with many other routes through the
White Peak area and which are open for use by walkers and cyclists. They are the
High Peak Trail (18 miles) Cromford – Dowlow; Tissington Trail (13 miles) Ashbourne
– Parsley Hay, where it connects with the High Peak Trail; Monsal Trail (9 miles) Wye
Dale – Coombs Viaduct, Bakewell; Manifold Trail (8 miles) Hulme End –
Waterhouses. No individual publication is available for the Manifold Trail. See
Peakland Way.

Start:	Various	Various
Finish:	Various	Various
Landranger maps:	119, 128	✔
1 : 25,000 maps:	OL 24	
Waymark:	Named posts	

Publications, badges and certificates:
Booklet: *Walking the High Peak Trail* by John Merrill (Walk & Write Ltd). ISBN 187475411X.
£3.95 (+ 75p p&p).
Booklet: *Walking the Tissington Trail* by John Merrill (Walk & Write Ltd). ISBN 1874754101.
£3.95 (+ 75p p&p).
Leaflet: *Tissington and High Peak Trails* (Peak District National Park) 1997. A4/3. Free (+ 9 x 4
SAE).
Booklet: *Walking the Monsal Trail & Derby Trails* by John Merrill (Walk & Write Ltd). ISBN
1874754179. £4.50 (+ 75p p&p).
Leaflet: *Monsal Trail* (Peak District National Park) 1996. A4/3. Free (+ 9 x 4 SAE).
Leaflet: *Peak National Park* (Peak District National Park) 1997. A4/3. Free (+ 9 x 4 SAE).
Badge and certificate: (Walk & Write Ltd). Each £3.50 (incs p&p) – individual badge and
certificate for each of High Peak, Tissington and Monsal Trails.

White Peak Way   617

Derbys   *129 km / 80 miles*

The walk, based on youth hostels, is a meandering circuit which visits many of the
limestone dales, including Dove Dale, Miller's Dale and Hay Dale and passes
Chatsworth House and Park, Haddon Hall and the Castleton Show Caves.

Start and Finish:	Bakewell, Derbys	SK217685
Landranger maps:	110, 119	
1 : 25,000 maps:	OL 1, 24	

Publications, badges and certificates:
Paperback: *The White Peak Way* by Robert Haslam (Cicerone Press) 1997. ISBN 1852840560.
96pp; 116 x 176. £4.99.
Booklet: *Booking Bureau – Youth Hostels* (YHA Northern Region) Annual. 20pp; A5. Free.

White Rose Walk   618

Cleveland, N Yorks   *50 km / 31 miles*

A route created by the Yorkshire Wayfarers in the late 60s and which originally provided alternative distances. It follows the course of the Cleveland Way National Trail
for much of the route taking in Sneck Yate, Thimbleby Moor, Sheepwash, Clay Bank
and Kildale, basically linking the landmarks of the White Horse and Roseberry
Topping.

Start:	White Horse, Kildale, N Yorks	SE514813
Finish:	Newton under Roseberry, Cleveland	NZ570128
Landranger maps:	93, 94, 100	
1 : 25,000 maps:	OL 26	

Publications, badges and certificates:
Looseleaf: *The White Rose Walk* (George E. Garbutt). 1pp; A4. Free (+ 9 x 4 SAE).
Badge and certificate: (George E. Garbutt). £1.10 & £0.20 (+ 9 x 4 SAE).

Wild Edric's Way   619

Shrops   *80 km / 50 miles*

Named after a Saxon Nobleman the route visits Bridges, Bishop's Castle, Clun and
Craven Arms. It is partly coincident with the Shropshire Way and Offa's Dyke Path.

Start:	Church Stretton, Shrops	SO456935
Finish:	Ludlow, Shrops	SO514752
Landranger maps:	137	
1 : 25,000 maps:	Ex 203, 216, 217	
Waymark:	Named discs with sword design	

Publications, badges and certificates:
Folder: *Wild Edric's Way* (Shrewsbury and Atcham Borough Council). 5 leaflets; A3/3. £1.50 (+
50p p&p) – cheques payable to SABC.
Paperback: *The Shropshire Way and Wild Edric's Way* by Terry Marsh and Julie Meech
(Cicerone Press) 1999. ISBN 1852842814. 192pp; 115 x 176. £9.99.

William Wordsworth Way   620

Cumbria   *290 km / 180 miles*

A route visiting in excess of 80 sites associated with William Wordsworth and
commencing with a visit to his birthplace. Also included are Keswick, Grasmere,
Hawkshead, Boot and Buttermere. Overall, there is 26,000 feet of ascent.

Start and Finish:	Cockermouth, Cumbria	NY120305
Landranger maps:	89, 90, 96, 97	
1 : 25,000 maps:	OL 4, 5, 6, 7	

Publications, badges and certificates:
Book: *The William Wordsworth Way* by Howard Beck (Mainstream Publishing Co Ltd). ISBN
1851589783. 192pp; 220 x 130. £9.99.

Wirral Shore Way 621

Cheshire, Merseyside *36 km / 22 miles*

From the historic city of Chester to the north western tip of the Wirral Peninsula the route of the Way is dictated by the old coastline of Wirral bordering the Dee Estuary, passing the remains of a Norman fortress used in the Edwardian wars against the Welsh, a line of dried out Elizabethan sea ports developed as Chester suffered a siltation, and a host of villages and seaside resorts. Along the Dee Estuary, the Way briefly links into the Wirral Way (12 miles) and from Hoylake, the Wirral Coastal Walk provides a 10 miles extension to Seacombe.

Start:	Chester Cathedral, Cheshire	SJ406665
Finish:	West Kirby, Merseyside	SJ204886
Landranger maps:	108, 117	✔
1 : 25,000 maps:	Ex 265, 266	

Publications, badges and certificates:
Booklet: *A Walker's Guide to the Wirral Shore Way* by Carl Rogers (Mara Publications). ISBN 0952240904. 48pp; 135 x 210. £3.95.
Leaflet: *Wirral Country Park – Wirral Way* (Thurstaston Visitor Centre). A5. £0.40 (+ 9 x 6 SAE).
Leaflet: *North Wirral Coastal Park – Wirral Coastal Walk* (Thurstaston Visitor Centre). A5. £0.20 (+ 9 x 6 SAE).

Witches Way 622

Lancs *50 km / 31 miles*

The Way heads from the heart of industrial Lancashire, over the moors between Blackburn and Accrington, and across lowland to Read before climbing to the summit of Pendle Hill, the setting for many of the tales of Lancashire witches. The Way descends to Downham and crosses the Ribble valley before going over Standridge Hill to Slaidburn. See North Bowland Traverse.

Start:	Rawtenstall, Lancs	SD809230
Finish:	Slaidburn, Lancs	SD712524
Landranger maps:	103	
1 : 25,000 maps:	Ex 287 OL 21, 41	

Publications, badges and certificates:
Looseleaf: *The Witches Way* (Jim Ashton) 1997. A4. Free (+ 9 x 4 SAE).
Badge and certificate: (Jim Ashton). £1.50 & £0.15 (+ SAE).

Witton Weavers Way 623

Lancs *51 km / 32 miles*

The Way is a network of four circular routes (named the Beamers, Reelers, Tacklers and Warpers Trails, respectively 6, 8, 11 and 9 miles), linked together to form a large loop to the west of Blackburn and Darwen. The route takes in Abbey Village, Darwen Moor and Jumbles Reservoir on the northern outskirts of Bolton. There is a link into Darwen itself. See Crowthorn Rose.

Start and Finish:	Witton Park, Lancs	SD659273
Landranger maps:	102, 103, 109	✔
1 : 25,000 maps:	Ex 287	
Waymark:	Mill logo on named standard markers	

Publications, badges and certificates:
Folder: *Witton Weavers Way: Blackburn & Darwen Borough-wide Walk* (Blackburn Borough Council) 1993. 4pp; A5. £2.00.

Wolds Way National Trail 624

E Yorks, N Yorks   *127 km / 79 miles*

This National Trail goes west along the River Humber and then north around the western edge of the Yorkshire Wolds, through woods and across arable land through Thixendale, and along the northern escarpment of the Wolds through dry valleys and sheep pasture to the coast and the Cleveland Way National Trail at Filey. See Centenary Way (North Yorkshire), East Riding Heritage Way, High Hunsley Circuit, Humber Bridge Link Walk, Minster Way. See also E-Routes (E2).

Start:	Hessle (Haven), E Yorks	TA035256
Finish:	Filey Brigg, N Yorks	TA126817
Landranger maps:	100, 101, 106, 107	✔
1 : 25,000 maps:	Ex 281, 300, 301	
Waymark:	National Trail Acorn	
Path website:	www.woldsway.gov.uk	

Publications, badges and certificates:
Softback: *Wolds Way* (Official Guide) by Roger Ratcliffe (Aurum Press) 1992. ISBN 1854101897. 210 x 130. £9.99.
Leaflet: *Wolds Way* (Countryside Agency Publications) 1992. A4/3. Free.
Booklet: *Wolds Way Accommodation and Information Guide* (North York Moors National Park) Annual. 30pp. £0.95 (+ 55p p&p).
Badge: (RA East Yorkshire & Derwent Area). £1.00 (+ SAE).

Worcester & Birmingham Canal Walk 625

W Midlands, Worcs   *48 km / 30 miles*

A towpath walk linking the Severn Way in the south to the Grand Union Canal Walk at Birmingham. See Stratford-upon-Avon Canal Walk.

Start:	Diglis Basin, Worcester	SO849538
Finish:	Gas Street Basin, Birmingham	SP062867
Landranger maps:	139, 150	
1 : 25,000 maps:	Ex 204, 220	

Publications, badges and certificates:
Leaflet: *Exploring the Worcester & Birmingham Canal* (British Waterways – Sawley) 1997. A5. Free (+ SAE).
Stripmap (folded): *Worcester & Birmingham Canal* (GEOprojects) 2001. ISBN 0863511465. 135 x 213. £4.00 (+ 50p p&p).

Worcestershire Way   626

Worcs   *77 km / 48 miles*

Starting on Kinver Edge, where it connects with the North Worcestershire Path and Staffordshire Way, the route takes a south-westerly direction to the River Severn passing to the east of Wye Forest to Bewdley. It continues over the hills of Abberley, Penny and Ankerdine before crossing the River Teme. The Suckley Hills on the northern end of the Malvern Hills are also crossed at Cowleigh. See also the Malvern Link and Gloucestershire and Three Choirs Ways.

Start:	Kingsford Country Park, Worc	SO829822
Finish:	Hollybush, Worc	SO763369
Landranger maps:	138, 149, 150	✔
1 : 25,000 maps:	Ex 190, 204, 218	
Waymark:	Coloured arrows with green pear logo	

Publications, badges and certificates:
Paperback: *The Worcestershire Way Walker's Guide* (Worcestershire County Council) 1996. ISBN 1853010197. 70pp; A5. £4.50 (incs p&p).

Wychavon Marathon   627

Worcs   *42 km / 26 miles*

An easy route of bridleways, field paths and woodland, visiting some of Worcestershire's most attractive villages. The route includes short sections of the Wychavon Way.

Start and Finish:	Pipers Hill, Worcs	SO957653
Landranger maps:	150	
1 : 25,000 maps:	Ex 204, 205	

Publications, badges and certificates:
Looseleaf: *Wychavon Marathon* by Dave Irons (Dave Irons) 2001. 12pp; A4. £1.50 (incs p&p).

Wychavon Way   628

Glos, Worcs   *67 km / 42 miles*

A link from the River Severn to the Cotswolds, the Way, opened to commemorate the Silver Jubilee in 1977, takes in Ombersley, Droitwich, The Lenches and Fladbury. Just after Netherton there is an optional detour via the summit of Bredon Hill, then on to Ashton under Hill, Gretton and the finish at Winchcombe on the Cotswold Way National Trail.

Start:	Holt Fleet, Worcs	SO824633
Finish:	Winchcombe, Glos	SP025283
Landranger maps:	150	✔
1 : 25,000 maps:	Ex 190, 204, 205 OL 45	
Waymark:	Crown symbol with letter W	

Publications, badges and certificates:
Paperback: *The Wychavon Way* (Wychavon District Council) 1993. ISBN 095080990X. 80pp; A5. £2.95 (+ 50p p&p).
Badge: (Wychavon District Council). £2.00 (incs p&p).

Wye to the Thames   629

Glos, Herefs, Oxon, Worcs   *192 km / 119 miles*

A route devised to encourage walkers to use the train when planning walks between Hereford and Oxford, it takes in Ledbury, Great Malvern, Evesham and Moreton-in-Marsh, and can be linked with several other routes.

Start:	Hereford, Herefs	SO515406
Finish:	Oxford, Oxon	SP503063
Landranger maps:	149, 150, 151, 163, 164	
1 : 25,000 maps:	Ex 189, 190, 204, 205, 180 OL 45	

Publications, badges and certificates:
Booklet: *From the Wye to the Thames* (Cotswold Line Promotion Group) 1996. ISBN 0952539705. 60pp; A5. £2.50 (incs p&p) – includes updated addendum sheet.

Wye Valley Walk   630

Glos, Herefs, Mons, Powys   *178 km / 111 miles*

A walk following the banks of the river for most of its length but including some hill climbing, it passes Lovers Leap and Tintern Abbey. Several vantage points are achieved before crossing over the Wye at Redbrook to continue along the riverside to Monmouth. The route then meanders on to pass English Bichnor, Welsh Bicknor and Goodrich Castle then leaves the Wye to go across country to Ross-on-Wye before reaching Hereford. Passing cider orchards, parkland and farmland, the Walk continues via Bredwardine, Merbach Hill, Hay-on-Wye, Builth Wells and Newbridge. In 2002 the route will be extended a further 21 miles towards the source of the River Wye on Plynlimon, meeting the Severn Way in Hafren Forest at SN857868 in 2002. A new publication will be released in Autumn 2002, details TBA. See Birmingham and Aberystwyth Walk, Gloucestershire Way and Three Choirs Way.

Start:	Chepstow, Mons	ST529924
Finish:	Rhayader, Powys	SN968679
Landranger maps:	136, 147, 148, 149, 160, 161, 162, 172	✔
1 : 25,000 maps:	Ex 167, 188, 189, 200, 201, 202 OL 13, 14	
Waymark:	Named arrows with yellow spot, & leaping salmon	

Publications, badges and certificates:
Paperback (spiral bound): *Wye Valley Walk – Official Route Guide* (Herefordshire, Monmouthshire, and Powys County Councils) 1996. ISBN 1853010200. 44pp; A5. £3.95 (incs p&p).
Paperback: *The Wye Valley Walk* by Anthony Burton (Aurum Press) 1998. ISBN 1854105329. 144pp; 210 x 130. £12.99.
Paperback: *Walking Down the Wye* by David Hunter (Cicerone Press) 1992. ISBN 1852841052. 192pp; 116 x 176. £6.99.

Leaflet: *Wye Valley Walk – Accommodation & Transport Guide* (Herefordshire, Monmouthshire, and Powys County Councils) Annual. A5. Free (+ 30p p&p).
Badge (cloth): (Powys County Council). £1.50 (+ 30p p&p).

Wylye Way — 631

Wilts   *50 km / 31 miles*

A walk along the River Wylye linking the great Wiltshire estates of Stourhead, Longleat and Wilton. The walk goes through a mixture of scenery including chalk downland and watermeadows. Numerous public houses feature in the guide.

Start:	Stourhead Visitor Car Park, Wilts	ST777340
Finish:	Wilton House Park, Wilts	SU104308
Landranger maps:	183, 184	
1 : 25,000 maps:	Ex 130, 142, 143	

Publications, badges and certificates:
Booklet: *The Wylye Way* by Bill Brown (Bill Brown) 2002. 24pp; A5. £2.95 (incs p&p).
Certificate: (Bill Brown). Free (+ A5 SAE).

Wyre Forest Alpine Walk — 632

Worcs   *32 km / 20 miles*

A demanding walk in the Wyre Forest area encircling the Severn Valley and always within sound of the Severn Valley Railway.

Start and Finish:	Bewdley, Worcs	SO788754
Landranger maps:	138	
1 : 25,000 maps:	Ex 218	

Publications, badges and certificates:
Looseleaf: *Wyre Forest Alpine Walk* (Eric Perks). 4pp; A4. Free (+ 9 x 6 SAE).
Badge and certificate: (Eric Perks). £2.00 (+ SAE) & £1.00 (+ 9 x 6 SAE).

Wyre Way — 633

Lancs   *66 km / 41 miles*

A walk exploring the history and wildlife of the Wyre estuary from the estuary mouth to the source. The Way comprises three routes: from Fleetwood to Knott End via Shard Bridge (16 miles), from Shard Bridge to Garstang (10 miles) and from Garstang to the finish (15 miles). The ferry between Fleetwood and Knott End is seasonal and the route is subject to flooding at Spring tides.

Start:	Fleetwood, Lancs	SD340480
Finish:	Abbeystead, Lancs	SD566542
Landranger maps:	102	✔
1 : 25,000 maps:	Ex 286, 296	
Waymark:	Named posts	

Publications, badges and certificates:
Leaflet: *The Wyre Way – Fleetwood to Knott End & Shard Bridge to Garstang* (Wyreside Ecology Centre) 1999. A5/8. Free (+ A5 SAE).
Leaflet: *The Wyre Way – Garstang to Marshaw/Tarnbrook* (Wyreside Ecology Centre) 1999. A5/8. Free (+ A5 SAE).
Badge and certificate: (Wyreside Ecology Centre). Details from Wyreside Ecology Centre.

Wysis Way 634

Glos, Mons   *88 km / 55 miles*

From Offa's Dyke Path National Trail at Monmouth to the beginning of the Thames Path National Trail high in Gloucestershire the Way crosses the distinctive areas of the Forest of Dean, Severn Vale and Cotswolds. See also Three Choirs Way.

Start:	Monmouth	SO510130
Finish:	Kemble, Glos	ST985975
Landranger maps:	162, 163	✔
1 : 25,000 maps:	Ex 168, 179	

Publications, badges and certificates:
Paperback: *The Wysis Way* by Gerry Stewart (Countryside Matters) 1997. ISBN 0952787016. 80pp; A5. £4.95 (incs p&p).

Yoredale Way 635

Cumbria, N Yorks   *163 km / 101 miles*

The Way follows the course of the River Ure from York to its source on Abbotside Common, 2,000ft above sea level near Kirkby Stephen. It passes through Boroughbridge, Ripon, Middleham, Aysgarth and Hardraw Falls before climbing to Ure Head and descending to follow the River Eden to Kirkby Stephen. See Stepping over Stone and Swale Way.

Start:	York, N Yorks	SE603522
Finish:	Kirkby Stephen, Cumbria	NY775087
Landranger maps:	91, 98, 99, 105	
1 : 25,000 maps:	Ex 290, 298, 299, 302 OL 19, 30	

Publications, badges and certificates:
Folder: *The Yoredale Way – a 100 mile walk from York to Kirkby Stephen* by J. K. E. Piggin (Yorkshire Footpath Trust). ISBN 1898978018. £3.45 (incs p&p).
Certificate: (Yorkshire Footpath Trust). Free (+ 9 x 6 SAE).

Yorkshire Dales Challenge Walk 636

N Yorks   *37 km / 23 miles*

A challenge walk through the National Park including much high moorland.

Start and Finish:	Kettlewell, N Yorks	SD971724
Landranger maps:	98	
1 : 25,000 maps:	OL 30	

Publications, badges and certificates:
Booklet: *Yorkshire Dales Challenge Walk* by John Merrill (Walk & Write Ltd). ISBN 0907496865. 32pp; A5. £3.95 (+ 75p p&p).
Badge and certificate: (Walk & Write Ltd). £3.50 (incs p&p).

Yorkshire Dales Top Ten 637

N Yorks   *129 km / 80 miles*

A challenging route which takes in the 10 highest peaks/fells in the Yorkshire Dales with over 22,000 feet of ascent. Included are: High Seat, Swarth Fell, Great Coum and Crag Hill as well as the better known peaks.

Start and Finish:	Hardraw, N Yorks	SD867913
Landranger maps:	98	
1 : 25,000 maps:	OL 2, 19, 30	

Publications, badges and certificates:
Paperback: *The Yorkshire Dales Top Ten* by Brian G. Smailes (Challenge Publications). ISBN 0952690055. 80pp; 125 x 185. £6.50 (incs p&p).

Yorkshire Square Walk 638

N Yorkshire   *39 km / 24 miles*

A walk devised by Mark Reid of 'Inn Way' routes to raise funds for the Marie Curie Cancer Care charity. It takes in Caldberg, West Scrafton, West Burton, Castle Bolton and Leyburn, providing extensive views of Wensleydale and the surrounding hills.

Start and Finish:	Middleham, N Yorkshire	SD127879
Landranger maps:	98, 99	
1 : 25,000 maps:	OL 30	

Publications, badges and certificates:
Looseleaf: *The Yorkshire Square Walk* by Mark Reid (Marie Curie Cancer Care). 2pp. £2.00 (+ 9 x 4 SAE).
Certificate: (Marie Curie Cancer Care). Cost included in publication price (+ SAE).

ROUTES BY DISTANCE

Path	km	miles	Path
Land's End to John O'Groats	1368	850	291
Celtic Way	1161	722	75
South West Coast Path National Trail	1014	630	496
Great English Walk	1003	623	206
Monarch's Way	981	610	352
Ulster Way	918	570	583
Three Ridings on Foot	706	438	555
Land's End Trail	480	298	292
Macmillan Way	467	290	328
Coast to Coast – Southern England	387/456	242/283	104
Southern Coast to Coast Walk	453	283	Index
Cambrian Way	441	274	63
Pennine Way National Trail	404	251	408
Channel to Channel Walk	390	247	Index
Around Norfolk Walk	363	227	Index
Midshires Way	362	225	344
Coast to Coast – Wales	Max 348	Max 216	105
Hardy Way	343	214	223
Southern Upland Way	343	213	499
Newlands Way	338	210	364
Ravenber	338	210	Index
Severn Way	338	210	464
Pennine Bridleway	335	208	407
Cotswold Round	333	207	114
London Countryway	331	206	320
Cape Wrath Trail	330	205	64
Marches Way	329	204	336
Trans Pennine Trail	322	200	563
Alternative Coast to Coast	309	192	Index
Coast to Coast	306	190	102
Pembrokeshire Coast Path National Trail	299	186	402
Thames Path National Trail	294	184	540
Tarka Trail	291	181	532
Famous Highland Drove Walk	290	180	184
William Wordsworth Way	290	180	620
Northern Coast to Coast	287	178	Index
Offa's Dyke Path National Trail	284	177	388
Cumbria Coastal Way	267	167	133
Hertfordshire Way	267	166	234
Lake to Lake Walk	267	166	278
Cromer to the M11	265	165	124
Saxon Shore Way	262	163	459
Westside	260	162	Index
Sarn Helen	258	160	457

Path	km	miles	Path
North Downs Way National Trail	250	156	375
Durham Round	250	155	166
Reiver's Way	242	150	422
Birmingham and Aberystwyth Walk	238	148	34
Blackpool to Bridlington (Aerospace Way)	238	148	Index
Viking Way	237	148	589
Grand Union Canal Walk	234	145	202
Around the Lakes	233	145	19
London LOOP	232	144	321
Warwickshire Villages Trail	230	143	593
Harcamlow Way	227	141	221
Shropshire Way	224	139	472
Wessex Ridgeway	221	137	603
Sussex Border Path	216	135	520
Glyndwr's Way/Llwybr Glyndwr National Trail	213	132	199
Thirlmere Way	209	130	543
Coast to Coast – Scotland	206	129	103
Elan Valley Way	206	128	174
Leeds and Liverpool Canal Walk	203	127	300
Anita's Mucking Ugley Ways Through Messing, Essex	200	125	16
Chiltern Way	200	125	93
Clwydian Way	196	122	100
Anglesey Coast Path	195	121	13
Wye to the Thames	192	119	629
Oxbridge Walk	185	115	395
Wye Valley Walk	178	111	630
Cleveland Way National Trail	177	110	97
Nene Way	177	110	360
Post Horn Trail	177	110	414
Suffolk Way	175	109	519
Dyfi Valley Way	174	108	167
Greensand Way	173	107	212
Abbott's Hike	172	107	5
Highland High Way	169	105	Index
Icknield Way Path	169	105	248
Icknield Way Trail	169	105	249
Robin Hood Way	169	105	437
Abbeys Amble	167	104	4
Lakeland Tour	167	104	283
Hereward Way	166	103	231
Rother Valley Walks	166	103	441
Macmillan Way West	164	102	329
Two Moors Way	164	102	577
Wainwright Memorial Walk	164	102	590
Cotswold Way National Trail	163	102	116
Leicestershire Round	163	101	304
Yoredale Way	163	101	635
Yell	162	101	Index
Bristol to Lynton Walk	161	100	54
Exmoor & Lorna Doone Tour	161	100	182

Path	km	miles	Path
Gloucestershire Way	161	100	198
Heart of England Way	161	100	228
Lady Anne's Way	161	100	277
Navigation Way	161	100	359
South Downs Way National Trail	161	100	492
Teesdale Way	161	100	534
Three Choirs Way	161	100	545
Trans Pennine Way	161	100	564
Trent & Mersey Canal Walk	161	100	568
Towers Way	160	100	561
Shropshire Peaks Walk	160	99	470
Centenary Way (Warwickshire)	158	98	79
North York Moors Tour	158	98	384
Cheshire Ring Canal Walk	158	97	88
Peakland Way	156	97	400
Bowland-Dales Traverse	153	95	49
Lindsey Loop	153	95	314
Staffordshire Way	153	95	509
West Highland Way	153	95	606
Peddars Way & Norfolk Coast Path National Trail	150	94	401
Westmorland Way	150	94	608
Green London Way	148	93	210
Cotswold Village Trail	148	92	115
Peak District High Level Route	147	91	399
Dorset Jubilee Trail	145	90	157
High Weald Landscape Trail	145	90	239
Inn Way...to the Lake District	145	90	251
Isle of Man Coast Path	145	90	258
Lleyn Peninsula Coastal Path	145	90	317
Tidewater Way	145	90	559
White Horse Trail	145	90	613
Inn Way...to the North York Moors	144	89	252
Brecon Beacons Traverse	142	88	51
Jurassic Way	142	88	265
St Edmund Way	142	88	504
Cross Cotswold Pathway	138	86	Index
Dartmoor Way	138	86	148
Hertfordshire Chain Walk	138	86	233
Ridgeway National Trail	136	85	427
East Riding Heritage Way	136	84	169
Kennet and Avon Walk	135	84	266
Trent Valley Way	135	84	569
Eskdale Way	134	83	177
Centenary Way (North Yorkshire)	133	83	78
Cotswolds Walk	133	83	117
Oxford Canal Walk	133	83	396
Tyne – Estuary to Source	133	83	579
Fife Coast Path	132	82	186
Wealdway	132	82	596
Dark Peak Boundary Walk	131	81	143

Path	km	miles	Path
Dales Way	130	81	137
Essex Way	130	81	179
Hadrian's Wall Path National Trail	130	81	215
Cumberland Way	129	80	132
Iceni Way	129	80	247
Shrewsbury to Holywell Walk	129	80	469
White Peak Way	129	80	617
Yorkshire Dales Top Ten	129	80	637
Wolds Way National Trail	127	79	624
Angles Way	126	78	12
Eden Way	126	78	172
Leicester Line Canal Walk	126	78	302
South Mainland	125	78	Index
Bromley Circular Walks	125	77	55
Swale Way	124	77	522
Wessex Heights Walk	124	77	602
Cranborne Chase Path	122	76	122
Inn Way...to the Yorkshire Dales	122	76	253
Furness Way	121	75	195
John Bunyan Trail	121	75	263
1 to 15 Link	120	75	1
Skye Trail	120	75	477
Vectis Trail	120	75	587
Barnsley Boundary Walk	119	74	25
Red Kite Trail	118	74	421
Kirklees Way	118	73	275
Ribble Way	118	73	425
Great Glen Way	117	73	207
Weardale Way	117	73	597
Capital Ring	116	72	65
Jack Mytton Way	116	72	262
Meirionnydd Coast Walk	116	72	339
Waveney Way	116	72	594
Riversides Way	115	72	435
Blackmore Vale Path	114	71	40
Lancashire-Lakeland Link	114	71	288
Wayfarer's Walk	114	71	595
Danum Trail	113	70	140
Lancashire Trail	113	70	287
North Bedfordshire Heritage Trail	113	70	371
Cumbria Way	112	70	134
Ebor Way	112	70	171
King Alfred's Way	112	70	270
Leadon Valley Walks	112	70	298
South Pennine Ring	112	70	494
Edinburgh to Glasgow Canals Walk	108	67	173
d'Arcy Dalton Way	107	67	141
Lancashire Coastal Way	106	66	286
Vanguard Way	106	66	586
Whitby Way	106	66	612

Path	km	miles	Path
Black Fen Waterway Trail	105	65	38
Borders Abbeys Way	105	65	46
Brown Fen Waterway Trail	105	65	58
Great North Forest Trail	105	65	208
Isle of Wight Coast Path	104	65	259
Jorvic Way	104	65	264
Oxfordshire Way	104	65	397
Rutland Round	104	65	447
Speyside Way	104	65	502
Swan's Way	104	65	523
Snowdonia Round	103	64	486
St Illtyd's Walk	103	64	505
Cateran Trail	101	63	71
Unst	101	63	Index
St Cuthbert's Way	100	62	503
Cardigan Bay Coast Walk	99	62	67
Black and White Village Trail	99	61	37
Donnington Way	99	61	156
South of the Landsker Trail	97	60	493
Stour Valley Way (Dorset)	97	60	516
Sussex Diamond Way	97	60	521
Traditional Hostels Lakes Walk	97	60	562
Trans-Dales Trail – 1	97	60	565
Trans-Dales Trail – 2	97	60	566
Twin Valley 20 Walks	97	60	572
High Peak 60	96	60	236
Landsker Borderlands Trail	96	60	293
Leeds Country Way	96	60	301
Milton Keynes Boundary Walk	96	60	349
North Cotswold Diamond Way	96	60	374
North Wales Path	96	60	378
Northumbrian Coastline	96	60	386
Salisbury Country Way	96	60	452
Solent Way	96	60	488
Stour Valley Path (East Anglia)	96	60	514
Three Castles Path (England)	96	60	544
Three Forests Way	96	60	550
Nev Cole Way	93	58	361
Durham Railway Paths	92	57	165
Lakeland Top Ten	91	57	282
Lancaster Canal	91	57	289
Trans-Dales Trail – 3	91	57	567
Two Counties Way	90	56	575
Weavers Way	90	56	600
Cotswold Ring	89	55	113
Herriot Way	88	55	232
Taff Trail	88	55	525
Wysis Way	88	55	634
Allerdale Ramble	87	54	9
Formartine and Buchan Way	87	54	190

Path	km	miles	Path
Lea Valley Walk	87	54	296
Chiltern Heritage Trail	85	53	92
Nidderdale Way	85	53	370
Sheffield Country Walk	85	53	465
Brighton Way	84	52	53
Skylark Walk	84	52	478
Llangollen Canal Walk	82	51	316
Stour Valley Walk (Kent)	82	51	515
Heart of Snowdonia Circuit	81	50	Index
Airedale Way	80	50	8
Calderdale Way	80	50	61
Carpet Baggers 50	80	50	70
Channel to Channel (Devon – Somerset)	80	50	84
Chesterfield Round	80	50	90
Dartmoor's Ancient Boundary Perambulation	80	50	149
Denby Way	80	50	151
Fen Rivers Way	80	50	185
Gallo Way Round	80	50	196
Land's End Round	80	50	290
Limestone Way	80	50	312
Minster Way	80	50	351
North Western Fells	80	50	379
Ripon Rowel	80	50	429
River Parrett Trail	80	50	432
Suffolk Coast and Heaths Path	80	50	518
Taith Torfaen	80	50	527
Tandridge Border Path	80	50	531
Usk Valley Walk	80	50	584
Wild Edric's Way	80	50	619
Dartmoor Ramble	79	49	147
Mendip Ways	79	49	340
Penistone Loop-D-Loop	77	48	406
Tabular Hills Link Walk	77	48	Index
Worcestershire Way	77	48	626
Cotswold Canals Walk	76	47	112
Plogsland Round	76	47	412
Socratic Trail	76	47	487
Centre of The Kingdom Walk	75	46	81
Beating the Bounds (Cheshire)	74	46	29
Cuckoo Way	74	46	131
North Worcestershire Path & Midland Link	74	46	382
Pathfinder Long Distance Walk	74	46	398
Staffordshire and Worcestershire Canal Walk	74	46	507
Test Way	74	46	539
Community Forest Path	72	45	109
Exe Valley Way	72	45	181
Falklands Way	72	45	183
Four Pikes Hike	72	45	193
King's Way	72	45	272
Millennium Way – Bradford	72	45	345

Path	km	miles	Path
Pendle Way	72	45	404
Rochdale Way	72	45	438
Rossendale Way	72	45	440
Sheffield Way	72	45	466
Snowdonia 24hr Circuit	72	45	483
St Peter's Way	72	45	506
West Deane Way	72	45	604
Malvern Link	72	44	333
Ainsty Bounds Walk	71	44	7
Mary Towneley Loop	70	44	Index
Middlesex Greenway	69	43	342
Rivers Way	69	43	434
Seahorse Saunter	69	43	461
Tyne Valley Train Trails	69	43	581
Stour and Orwell Walk	67	42	513
Wychavon Way	67	42	628
North to South Surrey Walk	66	41	376
Ouse Valley Way	66	41	393
Wyre Way	66	41	633
Around the Carneddau	64	40	18
Bronte Way	64	40	57
Burnley Way	64	40	60
Chalkland Way	64	40	83
Clyde Walkway	64	40	101
Coventry Way	64	40	119
Crowthorn Rose	64	40	128
Dane Valley Way	64	40	139
East Devon Way	64	40	168
Green Chain Walk	64	40	209
Greensand Ridge Walk	64	40	211
Limey Way	64	40	313
Mynydd Hiraethog & Denbigh Moors Footpath	64	40	356
Oldham Way	64	40	392
Rezzy Rush	64	40	423
River Teign Walk	64	40	433
Samaritan Way	64	40	455
Shepherd's Round	64	40	Index
Snowdonia Five Ranges Round	64	40	Index
Tameside Trail	64	40	530
Weavers Shuttle	64	40	599
Crowthorn Star	63	39	129
Limestone Loop	63	39	311
Lyke Wake Walk	63	39	326
Boudica's Way	61	38	47
Compo's Way	61	38	110
Coventry Canal Walk	61	38	118
Dam Long Walk	61	38	138
Langbaurgh Loop	61	38	294
South Pennines Twin Challenge	61	38	Index
Basingstoke Canal Walk	60	37	26

Path	km	miles	Path
Clitheroe 60K	60	37	98
Shropshire Union Canal	60	37	471
Capital Walk – Cardiff	59	37	66
Downs Link	59	37	158
Lunesdale Walk	59	37	325
Rosedale Circuit	59	37	439
Smugglers' Way	59	37	481
Bell Walk Major	58	36	30
Coed Morgannwg Way	58	36	106
Hambleton Hillside Mosaic Walk	58	36	217
Isaac's Tea Trail	58	36	257
Limestone Link (Cotswolds to Mendips)	58	36	309
Two Beacons Challenge	58	36	573
Wey-South Path	58	36	609
Three Shires Way	57	35	557
West Devon Way	57	35	605
Esk Valley Walk	56	35	176
Gritstone Trail	56	35	214
Ivanhoe Way	56	35	261
Millennium Way – Staffordshire	56	35	347
Montgomery Canal	56	35	353
Newtondale Horse Trail	56	35	Index
North Bucks Way	56	35	373
Sky to Sea	56	35	476
Three Towers Circuit	56	35	558
Vale Royal Round	56	35	585
Avon Valley Path	55	34	22
Bishop Bennet Way	55	34	36
Humber Bridge Link Walk	55	34	245
River Otter Walk	55	34	431
Three Feathers Walk (Kettlewell)	55	34	Index
Nar Valley Way	54	34	358
Causeway Coast Way	53	33	72
Charnwood Round	53	33	86
Cistercian Way	53	33	95
Cloud 7 Circuit	53	33	99
Doncastrian Way	53	33	155
Grantham Canal	53	33	204
Lapwing Walk	53	33	295
Mid Sussex Link	53	33	Index
Quantock Way	53	33	418
Ribskip Challenge	53	33	426
Ring of Gullion Way	53	33	428
Shieldsman Walk	53	33	468
Tesrod Eldodd	53	33	Index
Hambleton Hobble	52	32	218
Bradford Ring	51	32	50
Lower Dales Three Hostels Walk	51	32	323
Maritime Heritage Trail	51	32	Index
North York Moors Wobble	51	32	385

Path	km	miles	Path
Sandstone Trail	51	32	456
Witton Weavers Way	51	32	623
1066 Country Walk	50	31	2
Aylesbury Ring	50	31	23
Fetlar	50	31	Index
Hyndburn Clog	50	31	246
North Bowland Traverse	50	31	372
Sarum Way	50	31	458
South Cheshire Way	50	31	491
White Rose Walk	50	31	618
Witches Way	50	31	622
Wylye Way	50	31	631
Almscliff Amble	48	30	10
Avon Walkway	48	30	Index
Bilsdale Circuit	48	30	33
Cal-Der-Went Walk	48	30	62
Carleton Trail	48	30	68
Dearne Way	48	30	150
East Thriding Treble Ten	48	30	170
High Street Stroll	48	30	238
Imber Range Perimeter Path	48	30	250
Irwell Sculpture Trail	48	30	256
Lecale Way	48	30	299
Longshaw Limber	48	30	322
Mersey Way	48	30	Index
Mortimer Trail	48	30	354
Pride of the Peak Walk	48	30	415
Round the Reservoirs	48	30	444
Sliabh Beagh Way	48	30	479
Snowdon Challenge Walk	48	30	482
Snowdonia Panoramic Walk	48	30	485
Tamar Valley Discovery Trail	48	30	528
Three Feathers Walk (Kilburn)	48	30	Index
Three Moors Walk	48	30	551
Three Peaks of Cheviot Walk	48	30	552
West Island Way	48	30	607
West Mendip Way	48	30	Index
Worcester & Birmingham Canal Walk	48	30	625
Cross Wight Traverse	47	29	Index
Derbyshire Top Ten	47	29	153
Saints' Way/Forth an Syns	47	29	451
Welsh 3000s	47	29	601
Aiggin Stone Ramble	45	28	6
Back o' Skidda	45	28	24
Crewe and Nantwich Circular Walk	45	28	123
Derby Canal Ring	45	28	152
Essex Country to the Coast	45	28	178
Foss Walk	45	28	191
High Peak Way	45	28	237
Leland Trail	45	28	306

Path	km	miles	Path
Liberty Trail	45	28	307
Little John Challenge Walk	45	28	315
Medway Valley Walk	45	28	338
Millennium Way – Isle of Man	45	28	346
Nidd Valley Link	45	28	369
Pilgrims' Trail	45	28	410
Rhymney Valley Ridgeway Walk	45	28	424
River Axe Walk	45	28	430
Saddleworth Skyline	45	28	450
Smugglers Route	45	28	480
Stort Valley Way	45	28	512
Three Counties Challenge Walk	45	28	546
Three Feathers Walk (Yorkshire Bridge)	45	28	Index
Tunbridge Wells Circular Walk	44	28	571
Hardy Hobble	44	27	Index
Cavendish 27 Circuit	43	27	73
Crowthorn Crawl	43	27	127
Gritstone Edge Walk	43	27	213
Ippikin's Way	43	27	254
Itchen Way	43	27	260
Lakes & Tarns – Eastern Lakeland	43	27	284
New River Path	43	27	363
Royal Military Canal Path	43	27	445
Sweet Pea Challenge Walk	43	27	524
Trollers Trot	43	27	570
Arden Way	42	26	17
Daffodil Dawdle	42	26	135
Derwent Valley Skyline	42	26	154
Flower of Suffolk	42	26	187
Forest of Bowland Challenge Walk	42	26	188
Founders Footpaths	42	26	192
Glevum Way	42	26	197
Gordano Round	42	26	200
Locus Classicus	42	26	Index
Macclesfield & Peak Forest Canals	42	26	327
Newmarket Circular Walk	42	26	365
Nidd Vale Circuit	42	26	368
North Worcestershire Hills Marathon	42	26	381
Poppyline Marathon	42	26	413
Ramblers Route	42	26	419
Scarborough Rock Challenge	42	26	460
Sirhowy Valley Walk	42	26	474
Stratford-upon-Avon Canal Walk	42	26	517
Tas Valley Way	42	26	533
Three Peaks of Great Britain	42	26	553
Walden Round	42	26	591
Welsh 1000m Peaks Marathon	42	26	Index
Wharfedale Washburn Walk	42	26	610
Wychavon Marathon	42	26	627
Beacon Banks Challenge	40	25	27

Path	km	miles	Path
Beacon Way	40	25	28
Belvoir Witches Challenge Walk	40	25	31
Central Sperrins Way	40	25	80
Charnwood Forest Challenge Walk	40	25	85
Cheltenham Circular Footpath	40	25	87
Cheviot Hills 2,000ft Summits	40	25	91
Dales Traverse	40	25	136
Forest Way	40	25	189
Furness Five Trigs Walk	40	25	194
Harden Hike	40	25	222
Lakeland Mountain Heritage Trail	40	25	281
Myrtle Meander	40	25	357
North York Moors Challenge Walk	40	25	383
Old Sarum Challenge	40	25	391
Ox Drove Way	40	25	394
Pennington Round	40	25	409
Rotherham Round Walk	40	25	442
Settle Scramble	40	25	463
Sidmouth Saunter	40	25	473
Tame Valley Way	40	25	529
Three Footpaths Walk	40	25	549
Three Rivers Walk	40	25	556
Two Crosses Circuit	40	25	576
White Peak Challenge Walk	40	25	614
Churnet Valley Challenge Walk	39	24	94
Clarendon Way	39	24	96
High Hunsley Circuit	39	24	235
Holme Valley Circular Walk	39	24	241
Kinder Dozen Challenge	39	24	269
Limestone Dale Walk	39	24	308
Purbeck Steam Package	39	24	Index
Purbeck Way	39	24	417
Three Peaks Walk (Yorkshire)	39	24	554
Yorkshire Square Walk	39	24	638
Centenary Way (Derbyshire)	38	24	77
Cross Bucks Way	38	24	126
Dark Peak Challenge Walk	38	24	144
Grand Western Canal	38	24	203
Holme Valley Circular Challenge Walk	38	24	Index
Lead Mining Trail	38	24	297
Maelor Way	38	24	330
Rutland Water Challenge Walk	38	24	448
Salter's Way	38	24	454
Staffordshire Moorlands Challenge Walk	38	24	508
Two Castles Trail	38	24	574
White Peak Rollercoaster	38	24	615
Circular Rides in South Gloucestershire	14–38	8–23	Index
Birmingham Greenway	37	23	35
Black Mountains Traverse Challenge	37	23	39
Bog Dodgers Way	37	23	43

Path	km	miles	Path
Ceiriog Trail	37	23	74
Centenary Circle	37	23	76
Crake Valley Round	37	23	121
Dunford Round	37	23	162
Elham Valley Way	37	23	175
Hovingham Hobble	37	23	242
Hutton Hike	37	23	Index
Loaves & Fishes Walk	37	23	318
Millennium Way – York	37	23	348
Roach Valley Way	37	23	436
Round Preston Walk	37	23	443
South Bucks Way	37	23	490
Southend Millennium Walk	37	23	498
Yorkshire Dales Challenge Walk	37	23	636
Bollin Valley Way	36	22	44
Haslemere Circular Walk	36	22	225
Wirral Shore Way	36	22	621
Arun Way	35	22	20
Ashford on Foot	35	22	21
Chaddesley Chase	35	22	82
Coniston Water Circuit	35	22	111
Crooked Spire Walk	35	22	125
Delamere Way	35	22	Index
Ipswich Outer Ring	35	22	255
Lambourn Valley Way	35	22	285
Middlewich Challenge Walk	35	22	343
Ridge Too Far	35	22	Index
Ten Reservoirs Walk	35	22	537
Thirlmere Round	35	22	542
Anglezarke Amble	34	21	14
Burley Bridge Hike	34	21	59
Cotswold Link	34	21	Index
Gordon Way	34	21	201
Hangers Way	34	21	219
Harrogate Ringway	34	21	224
Kielder Walks	34	21	268
Kingfisher Way	34	21	271
Marriott's Way	34	21	337
Nuneaton Rotary Walk	34	21	387
Rudston Roam	34	21	Index
Sefton Coastal Footpath	34	21	462
Southam Circular Way	34	21	497
Spen Way Heritage Trail	34	21	501
Taff-Ely Ridgeway Walk	34	21	526
Ten Church Challenge	34	21	536
Tyne and Wear 20	34	21	580
Abberley Amble	32	20	3
Anglezarke Anguish	32	20	15
Beverley Twenty	32	20	Index
Bourne Blunder	32	20	48

Path	km	miles	Path
Bronte Round	32	20	56
Canal Clog	32	20	Index
Carneddau Challenge Walk	32	20	69
Colne Valley Way, Colne Valley Trail & Ebury Way	32	20	108
Dark Peak Stones	32	20	146
Duddon Horseshoe	32	20	160
Duddon Triangle Walk	32	20	161
Dunnerdale Horseshoe and Burney Challenge	32	20	163
Grasmere Skyline Classic Walk	32	20	205
Hanslope Circular Ride	32	20	220
Harrogate – Dales Way	32	20	Index
Headland Walk	32	20	Index
Hebden Valleys Heritage Trek	32	20	229
Helm Wind Walk	32	20	230
Hillingdon Trail	32	20	240
Howden 20	32	20	243
Inter-City Challenge	32	20	Index
Kett's Country Walk	32	20	267
Kinver Clamber	32	20	273
Knaresborough Round	32	20	276
Leighton – Linslade Loop	32	20	305
Malvern Hills Challenge Walk	32	20	332
Mansell Way	32	20	335
Mid Suffolk Footpath	32	20	341
Mini-Alps	32	20	350
Moorland Heights Clog	32	20	Index
Moyle Way	32	20	355
Newry Canal Way	32	20	366
Newtondale Trail	32	20	367
North Wolds Walk	32	20	380
Offa's Hyke	32	20	389
Pendle and Ribble Round	32	20	403
Pioneers Round	32	20	411
Ramsbottom Round	32	20	420
Saddleworth Five Trig Points Walk	32	20	449
Salt & Sails Trail	32	20	453
Skipton-Settle Link	32	20	475
Skylark Ride	32	20	Index
Solihull Way	32	20	489
Spanners Round	32	20	500
Tennyson Twenty	32	20	538
Thanet Coastal Path	32	20	541
Two Rivers Way	32	20	578
Vermuyden Way	32	20	588
Wanderlust Way	32	20	592
Weaver Valley Way	32	20	598
Whicham Valley Five Trigs Walk	32	20	611
Wyre Forest Alpine Walk	32	20	632
Darent Valley Path	31	19	142
Royal Shrovetide Challenge Walks	31	19	446

Path	km	miles	Path
Todmorden Centenary Way	31	19	560
West Dorset Enigma	31	19	Index
Blackwater Valley Footpath	30	19	41
Camel Trail	30	19	Index
Cown Edge Way	30	19	120
East Mendip Way	30	19	Index
Haworth-Hebden Bridge Walk	30	19	226
Leeds – Dales Way	30	19	Index
Three Castles Walk (Mons)	30	19	Index
Hutchinson Way	30	18½	Index
Brighouse Boundary Walk	29	18	52
Bury to Clare Walk	29	18	Index
Cuckoo Walk	29	18	130
Day Return to Charmouth	29	18	Index
Eddisbury Way	29	18	Index
Frome Valley Walkway	29	18	Index
Haematite Trail	29	18	216
Heart of Bowland Walk	29	18	227
High Peak Trail	29	18	Index
Kirkby Moor Round & Burney	29	18	274
Lakeland Challenge Walk	29	18	279
Majesty of the Wilshire Downs	29	18	Index
Manorlands Meander	29	18	334
New Five Trig Points Walk	29	18	362
Old Crown Round	29	18	390
Paston Way	29	18	Index
Reigate and Banstead Millennium Trail	29	18	Index
Templer Way	29	18	Index
Bonnie Prince Charlie Walk	28	17	45
Dark Peak Snake	28	17	145
Altrincham Circular	27	17	11
Castleman Trailway	27	17	Index
Dart Valley Trail	27	17	Index
Gipping Valley River Path	27	17	Index
Lakeland Heritage Trail	27	17	280
Lune Valley Ramble	27	17	324
Three Peaks Circular Walk (Avon)	27	17	Index
Tyne-Wear Trail	27	17	582
Ashridge Estate Boundary Trail	26	16	Index
Beating the Bounds (Essex)	26	16	Index
Blue Man Walk	26	16	42
Bristol & Bath Railway Path	26	16	Index
Ebbw Valley Walk	26	16	Index
Howdenshire Way	26	16	244
Jubilee Way (South Glucestershire)	26	16	Index
Judge's Ride	26	16	Index
Wenlock Edge Ridge Walk	26	16	Index
Beeches Way	25	16	Index
Kerry Ridgeway	25	16	Index
Leicestershire Jubilee Way	25	16	303

Path	km	miles	Path
Penistone Boundary Walk	25	16	405
Three Crags Walk	25	16	547
Bembridge Trail	24	15	Index
Berwickshire Coastal Path	24	15	32
Dronfield 2000 Rotary Walk	24	15	159
Eden Valley Walk	24	15	Index
Epping Forest Centenary Walk	24	15	Index
Etherow – Goyt Valley Way	24	15	180
Five Parishes Millennium Boundary Walk	24	15	Index
Flitch Way	24	15	Index
Maltby Circular Walk	24	15	331
Tennyson Trail	24	15	Index
Thame Valley Walk	24	15	Index
Thames Down Link	24	15	Index
Trans Solihull Link	24	15	Index
Ver-Colne Valley Walk	24	15	Index
Wey Navigation	24	15	Index
Worsley Trail	24	15	Index
Beane Valley Walk	23	14	Index
Brampton Valley Way	23	14	Index
Herring Road/Bayr ny Skeddan	23	14	Index
Keelman's Way	23	14	Index
Wansdyke Path	23	14	Index
Kingfisher Walk	22	14	Index
Marston Vale Timberland Trail	22	14	Index
Seven Parishes Millennium Circular Walk	22	14	Index
Silkin Way	22	14	Index
Upper Ceiriog Trail	22	14	Index
Wardens' Way	22	14	Index
Windrush Way	22	14	Index
Clyde Walkway	21	13	Index
Colne Valley Circular Walk	21	13	107
Grafham Water Circular Ride	21	13	Index
Grafton Way	21	13	Index
Lark Valley Path	21	13	Index
Limestone Link (Cumbria)	21	13	310
North Turton Trail	21	13	377
Ogwr Ridgeway Walk	21	13	Index
Ouse Valley Walk	21	13	Index
Ridley Round	21	13	Index
Staunton Way	21	13	510
Stepping Over Stone	21	13	511
Tissington Trail	21	13	Index
Purbeck Way West	20	12½	Index
Bundle & Go to Kielder Stane	19	12	Index
Celandine Route	19	12	Index
Jubilee Way (East Sussex)	19	12	Index
Knightley Way	19	12	Index
Lanchester Valley	19	12	Index
Len Valley Walk	19	12	Index

Path	km	miles	Path
Lon Eifion	19	12	Index
Northern Rhymney Valley Ridgeway Walk	19	12	Index
Raven Walk	19	12	Index
St Michael's Way	19	12	Index
Stanedge Trail	19	12	Index
Wareham Forest Way	19	12	Index
Wirral Way	19	12	Index
Four Stations Way	19	$11\frac{1}{2}$	Index
Brit Valley Way	18	11	Index
Clay Way	18	11	Index
Cleveland Street Walk	18	11	Index
Crompton Circuit	18	11	Index
Cuckoo Trail	18	11	Index
Durham Coastal Footpath	18	11	164
Little Dart Ridge & Valley Walk	18	11	Index
Longster Trail	18	11	Index
Swale Heritage Trail	18	11	Index
Tacklers Trail	18	11	Index
Torpel Way	18	11	Index
Wandle Trail	18	11	Index
Wimpole Way	18	11	Index
Worth Way (W Yorks)	18	11	Index
Clopton Way	17	11	Index
Derwent Valley Walk	17	11	Index
Tees Link	17	11	Index
Avon Valley Walk	16	10	Index
Bigod Way	16	10	Index
Chess Valley Walk	16	10	Index
Coalfield Way	16	10	Index
Dollis Valley Greenwalk	16	10	Index
Dymock Daffodil Way	16	10	Index
Erme-Plym Trail	16	10	Index
Ferndown, Stour and Forest Trail	16	10	Index
Forest Way (Sussex)	16	10	Index
Goyt Way	16	10	Index
Ironbridge Way	16	10	Index
Ladybrook Interest Trail	16	10	Index
Little Ouse Path	16	10	Index
Nunwell Trail	16	10	Index
Peter Scott Walk	16	10	Index
Pymmes Brook Trail	16	10	Index
River Wear Trail	16	10	Index
Shepherds Trail	16	10	Index
South Tyne Trail	16	10	Index
Stenbury Trail	16	10	Index
Stephenson Trail	16	10	Index
Thames Path Extension	16	10	Index
Watling Chase Timberland Trail	16	10	Index
Wirral Coastal Walk	16	10	Index

LIST OF ADDRESSES

A Coventry Way Association, c/o Bob Brandon, 11 Barons Croft, COVENTRY, CV3 5GQ – www.cbean.f9.co.uk

Abbott, Peter, 5 Hillstone Close, Greenmount, BURY, Lancashire, BL8 4EZ

Aberdeenshire County Council, Woodhill House, Westburn Road, ABERDEEN, AB51 5NL – www.aberdeenshire.gov.uk

Alexius Press, 114 Sandhurst Road, Kingsbury, LONDON, NW9 9LN

Andrews, J. & J., 6 Priory Close, Ingham, BURY ST EDMUNDS, Suffolk, IP31 1NN

Appletree Press Ltd, The Old Potato Station, 14 Howard Street South, BELFAST, BT7 1AP – www.appletree.ie

Archard, Judith, Amesbury Sports Centre, Holders Road, AMESBURY, Wilts, SP4 7ND – www.btinternet.com/~wwwalker/amesbury.walkers

Archard, Richard, 57 Countess Road, AMESBURY, Wiltshire, SP4 7AS – www.btinternet.com/~wwwalker/amesbury.walkers

Art of Embroidery, 3 Market Way, PETERBOROUGH, PE1 1ST

Ashburton Tourist Information Centre, Town Hall, North Street, ASHBURTON, Devon, TQ13 7QQ

Ashford Tourist Information Centre, 18 The Churchyard, ASHFORD, Kent, TN23 1QG – www.ashford.gov.uk

Ashridge Estate Visitors Centre, Moneybury Hill, Ringshall, BERKHAMSTEAD, Hertfordshire, HP4 1LX

Ashton, Jim, 19 Leslie Avenue, BURY, Lancashire, BL9 8DL

Aurum Press, 25 Bedford Avenue, LONDON, WC1B 3AT – www.aurumpress.co.uk

Avon Heath Country Park, Dorset County Council, Birch Road, St Ives, RINGWOOD, Dorset, BH24 2DA

Aylesbury Vale District Council, Countryside Service, Haydon Mill, Rabans Lane, AYLESBURY, Buckinghamshire, HP19 3ST

Aze, Barbara, Shalimar, Upper Hyde Farm Lane, SHANKLIN, IOW, PO37 7PS

Backpackers Press, 2 Rockview Cottages, MATLOCK BATH, DE4 3PG

Barnet Council, Leisure Services, Barnet LB, Barnet House, 1255 High Road, LONDON, N20 0EJ – www.barnet.gov.uk

Barrow Tourist Information Centre, Forum 28, Duke Street, BARROW IN FURNESS, Cumbria, LA14 1HU

Bashforth, Peter, 23 Effeningham Road, Harden, BINGLEY, West Yorkshire, BD16 1LQ

Basingstoke Canal Authority, Canal Centre, Mytchett Place Road, MYTCHETT, Surrey, GU16 6DD – www.basingstoke-canal.co.uk

Bath & North East Somerset Council, Transportation, Access and Waste Management, Floor 2 South, Riverside, Keynsham, BRISTOL, BS31 1LA

Battle Tourist Information Centre, 88 High Street, BATTLE, East Sussex, TN33 9AQ – www.1066country.com

Bayer, Peter, 12 Brooklands Lane, Menston, ILKLEY, West Yorkshire, LS29 6PJ

Bennachie Project, Bennachie Centre, Essons Car Park, Chapel Garioch, BY INVERURIE, Aberdeenshire, AB51 5HX

Berwick-upon-Tweed Tourist Information Centre, 106 Marygate, BERWICK-UPON-TWEED, Northumberland, TD15 1BN – www.berwickonline.org.uk

Bishop, Martyn, 32 Elmwood Avenue, BOSTON, Lincolnshire, PE21 7RU

Blackburn Borough Council, Tourist Information, King George's Hall, Northgate, BLACKBURN, Lancashire, BB2 1AA – www.blackburn.gov.uk/tourism/

Blackwater Valley Team, Ash Lock Cottage, Government Road, ALDERSHOT, Hampshire, GU11 2PS – www.blackwatervalleyservice.com

Bollin Valley Project, County Offices, Chapel Lane, WILMSLOW, Cheshire, SK9 1PU

Book Castle, 12 Church Street, DUNSTABLE, Beds, LU5 4RU – www.bookcastle.co.uk

Booth, Ben, 19 Rawcliffe Drive, Clifton, YORK, YO30 6NT

Bound, Terry, 3 Alpha Street, Heavitree, EXETER, Devon, EX1 2SP

Bown, Keith, Dale House, 35 Bawtry Road, Listerdale, ROTHERHAM, South Yorkshire, S66 0AR

Bracknell Tourist Information Centre, The Look Out, Nine Mile Ride, BRACKNELL, Berks, RG12 7QW

Bradford Millennium Way Project, 10 Laburnham Grove, Cross Roads, KEIGHLEY, West Yorkshire, BD22 9EP

Braintree & District Outdoor Pursuits, c/o 3 Beaufort Gardens, BRAINTREE, Essex, CM7 9JY

Brecks Countryside Project, Kings House, Kings Street, THETFORD, Norfolk, IP24 2AP – www.brecks.org

Brewin Books Ltd, Doric House, 56 Alcester Road, STUDLEY, Warks, B80 7LG – www.brewinbooks.com

British Aerospace Ltd, c/o Harry Cadman, Engineering Skill Centre, Greengate, Middleton, MANCHESTER, M24 1SA

British Heart Foundation, 1/1A Scheregate Steps, COLCHESTER, Essex, CO2 7AS

British Waterways, Customer Services, Willow Grange, Church Road, WATFORD, Hertfordshire, WD1 3QA – www.british-waterways.org

British Waterways – Border Counties, Border Counties Waterway Canal Offices, Birch, ELLESMERE, Shropshire, SY12 9AA – www.britishwaterways.co.uk

British Waterways – Chester, Wharfside, Tower Wharf, CHESTER, CH1 4EZ – www.britishwaterways.co.uk

British Waterways – Enfield, Enfield Lock, Ordnance Road, ENFIELD, Middlesex, EN3 6JG – www.britishwaterways.co.uk

British Waterways – Kennet & Avon, The Locks, Bath Road, DEVIZES, Wiltshire, SN10 1HB – www.britishwaterways.co.uk

British Waterways – Sawley, Sawley Marina, SAWLEY, Nottinghamshire, NG10 3AE – www.britishwaterways.co.uk

British Waterways – Stafford, Norbury Junction, Norbury, STAFFORD, ST20 0PN – www.britishwaterways.co.uk

British Waterways – Tring, Marsworth Junction, Watery Lane, Marsworth, TRING, Hertfordshire, HP23 4LZ – www.britishwaterways.co.uk

Bromley Countryside Ranger Service, High Elms Country Park, Shire Lane, FARNBOROUGH, Kent, BR6 7JH – www.bromley.gov.uk

Broom, Gary, 3 Ramshorn Close, Galmington, TAUNTON, Somerset, TA1 5DP

Brown, Bill, The Mill House, South Street, Wilton, SALISBURY, Wiltshire, SP2 0JX

Buckinghamshire County Council, Countryside Services, County Hall, AYLESBURY, Buckinghamshire, HP20 1UY – www.buckscc.gov.uk

Bungay Tourist Information Office, Broad Street, BUNGAY, Suffolk, NR35 1EE

Buttle, Paul, 18 Brewery Lane, KESWICK, Cumbria, CA12 5LJ

Caerphilly County Borough Council, Countryside & Landscape Services, Council Offices, Pontllanfraith, BLACKWOOD, NP12 2YW

Caerphilly Mountain Countryside Service, Taff Gorge Countryside Centre, Heol-y-Fforest, Tongwynlais, CARDIFF, CF15 7JR

Cambridgeshire County Council, Environment & Transport, Box ET1009, Shire Hall, Castle Hill, CAMBRIDGE, CB3 0AP

Carmarthenshire County Council, Visitor Centre, Pembrey Country Park, PEMBREY, Carms, SA16 0EJ

Carr, Geoffrey, Fern Cottage, Cardigan Lane, Manor Road, OSSETT, West Yorkshire, WF5 0LT

Carrivick, Dave and Anne, Elm View, Trispen, TRURO, Cornwall, TR4 9AZ

Cateran Trail Company Ltd, Boat Brae, BLAIRGOWRIE, Perthshire, PH10 7BH – www.caterantrail.com

Celtic Way Project – www.celticway.org

Challenge Publications, 7 Earlsmere Drive, Ardsley, BARNSLEY, South Yorkshire, S71 5HH – www.chall-pub.fsnet.co.uk

Chandler, S. E., Aisgill, 3 Aldham Croft, Totley, SHEFFIELD, S17 4GF

Chelmsford Borough Council, Technical Services Department, Civic Centre, CHELMSFORD, Essex, CM1 1JE – www.chelmsfordbc.gov.uk

Cheshire County Council, Public Rights of Way Section, Goldsmith House, Hamilton Place, CHESTER, CH1 1SE – www.cheshire.gov.uk

Chesterton, Keith, 'Firle', Chestnut Avenue, GUILDFORD, Surrey, GU2 4HD

Chiltern District Council, Council Offices, King George V Road, AMERSHAM, Buckinghamshire, HP6 5AW

Chiltern Society Mail Order Bookshop, Norman Joyce, 20 The Ridgeway, WATFORD, Herts, WD17 4TN – www.chilternsociety.org.uk

Chiltern Society Office, White Hill Centre, White Hill, CHESHAM, Bucks, HP5 1AG

Cicerone Press, 2 Police Square, MILNTHORPE, Cumbria, LA7 7PY – www.cicerone.co.uk

Ciritis, Anton, 80 Willowfield Crescent, HALIFAX, West Yorkshire, HX2 7JW

Clack, Joan, 40 Woodlands Grove, HARROGATE, North Yorkshire, HG2 7BG

Clwydian Walks, 38 Kelsterton Road, CONNAH'S QUAY, Flintshire, CH5 4BJ

Collier, Major Brett (retd), Chloris House, 208 Nettleham Road, LINCOLN, LN2 4DH

Collins, 137 Westerhill Road, GLASGOW, G64 2QT – www.fireandwater.com

Collins, Stephen J., 51 Russell Gardens, SIPSON, Middlesex, UB7 0LR

Colne Valley Society, c/o Mr P Kirkham, 16 Tommy Lane, Linthwaite, HUDDERSFIELD, West Yorkshire, HD7 5SQ

Comer, Mark, 171 Burton Stone Lane, YORK, YO30 6DG – www.cawalks.co.uk

Congleton Tourist Information Centre, Town Hall, CONGLETON, Cheshire, CW12 1BN

Constable and Robinson Ltd, 3 The Lanchesters, 162 Fulham Palace Road, LONDON, W6 9ER – www.constablerobinson.com

Conwy County Council, Countryside Service, Planning Department, Civic Offices, COLWYN BAY, LL29 8AR – www.conwy.gov.uk/countryside

Cooper, Mick, 10 Nab Wood Rise, SHIPLEY, W Yorkshire, BD18 4JA

Cordee Ltd, 3a De Montfort Street, LEICESTER, LE1 7HD – www.cordee.co.uk

Cornwall County Council, Transportation & Estates, County Hall, TRURO, Cornwall, TR1 3AY – www.cornwall.gov.uk

Cotswold District Council, Bourton-on-the-Water Tourist Information Centre, Victoria Street, BOURTON-ON-THE-WATER, Gloucestershire, GL54 2BU

Cotswold Line Promotion Group, c/o Derek J. Potter, Homerswood, Boon Street, Eckington, PERSHORE, Worcs, WR10 3BL

Countryside Agency Publications, PO Box 125, WETHERBY, West Yorkshire, LS23 7EP – www.countryside.gov.uk

Countryside Books, 2 Highfield Avenue, NEWBURY, Berkshire, RG14 5DS – www.countrysidebooks.co.uk

Countryside Council for Wales, Plas Penrhos, Penrhos Road, BANGOR, Gwynedd, LL57 2LQ

Countryside Matters, 15 Orchard Road, Alderton, TEWKESBURY, Gloucestershire, GL20 8NS – www.countryside-matters.co.uk

Coventry Way Association, A – *see* A Coventry Way Association

Cox, Vic, 36 Elwood Road, Bradway, SHEFFIELD, S17 4RH

Cumbria County Council, Rights of Way Section, Capitadbs, Viaduct Estate, CARLISLE, Cumbria, CA2 5BN

Dales Way Association, c/o David Smith, Dalegarth, Moorfield Road, ILKLEY, West Yorkshire, LS29 8BL

Dalesman Publishing Co Ltd, Stable Courtyard, Broughton Hall, SKIPTON, North Yorkshire, BD23 3AE – www.dalesman.co.uk

Dalton, Ed, Mountain View, Fachell, Hermon, BODORGAN, Anglesey, LL62 5LL

Darlington Borough Council, Rights of Way Section, Development & Environment, Town Hall, DARLINGTON, DL1 5QT

Dartmoor Towns Ltd – www.dartmoorway.org.uk

Davies, George, 33 Fir Tree Road, Fernhill Heath, WORCESTER, WR3 8RE

Davis, J. & M., PO Box 106, Kingswood, BRISTOL, BS15 1YP

Denbighshire County Council, Countryside Services, Loggerheads Country Park, near MOLD, Denbighshire, CL7 5LH – www.denbighshire.gov.uk

Denby, Peter, Outdoor Shop, Market Square, KIRKBY STEPHEN, Cumbria, CA17 4QT

Derbyshire County Council, Middleton Top Visitor Centre, Wirksworth, MATLOCK, Derbyshire, DE4 4LS

Derbyshire Dales District Council, c/o Tourist Information Centre, The Pavilion, MATLOCK BATH, Derbyshire, DE4 3NR – www.derbyshiredales.gov.uk

Derbyshire Footpaths Preservation Society, c/o Mrs E. W. Hodgkinson, 3 Crabtree Close, Allestree, DERBY, DE22 2SW

Devon County Council, Tourist Information Service, PO Box 55, BARNSTAPLE, Devon, EX32 8YR – www.devon.gov.uk

Diss Tourist Information Centre, Mere Street, DISS, Norfolk, IP22 3AG

Dorset County Council, Rights of Way Section, County Hall, DORCHESTER, Dorset, DT1 1XJ

Dorset Publishing Co, National School, North Street, WINCANTON, Somerset, BA9 9AT

Down District Council, c/o Down Tourist Information Centre, 53A Market Street, DOWNPATRICK, Northern Ireland, BT30 6LZ – www.downdistrictcouncil.gov.uk

Downlands Project, Highway House, 21 Chessington Road, West Ewell, EPSOM, Surrey, KT17 1TT

Drake, A. J., 2 Beech Lodge, 67 The Park, CHELTENHAM, Gloucestershire, GL50 2RX

Dronfield 2000 Rotary Walk, Mill House, Unstone, DRONFIELD, Derbyshire, S18 4DD

Dumfries and Galloway Council, Countryside Ranger Service, Environment and Infrastructure, Rae Street, DUMFRIES, DG1 2JD

Dungannon & Tyrone Borough Council, c/o Killymaddy Tourist Information Centre, 190 Ballygawley Road, DUNGANNON, Northern Ireland, BT70 1TF – www.dungannon.gov.uk

Durham County Council, Countryside Group, Environment & Technical Services Dept, County Hall, DURHAM, DH1 5UQ – www.durham.gov.uk

Durham, Andrew, Orchard House, 69 Common Road, Western Colville, CAMBRIDGE, CB1 5NS

East Herts Footpath Society, c/o Mark Westley, 38 Shephall Green, STEVENAGE, Hertfordshire, SG2 9XS

East Sussex County Council, Transport and Environment, Sackville House, Brooks Close, LEWES, E Sussex, BN7 1UE

Easterhurst Publications Ltd, 19 Wells Avenue, Feniton, HONITON, EX14 3DR

EastWest Mapping, Ballyredmund, Clonegal, ENNISCORTHY, Co Wexford – http://homepage.eircom.net/~eastwest

Eckersley, John, The Vicarage, School Lane, Heslington, YORK, YO10 5EE

Edwards, Alan S., 6 Brittain Road, Cheddleton, LEEK, Staffordshire, ST13 7EH

Edwards, G. J., 10 Howard Close, Haynes, BEDFORD, MK45 3QH

Ellis, Mike, 74 Nelson Road, HULL, East Yorkshire, HU5 5HN

Elvaston Castle Country Park, Borrowash Road, Elvaston, DERBY, DE72 3EP

Emery, Gordon, 27 Gladstone Road, CHESTER, CH1 4BZ

Engel, Carole E., 10 Brookfield, Penistone Road, Kirkburton, HUDDERSFIELD, West Yorkshire, HD8 0PE

Environment Agency, Hafren House, Welshpool Road, Shelton, SHREWSBURY, SY3 8BB

Environment Agency – Thames Region, Thames Regional Office, Kings Meadow House, Kings Meadow Road, READING, Berks, RG1 8DQ

Epping Forest Countrycare, Planning Services, Civic Offices, High Street, EPPING, Essex, CM16 4BZ

Epping Forest Information Centre, High Beach, LOUGHTON, Essex, IG10 4AF

Essex County Council, Public Rights of Way Team, Transportation and Operational Services, County Hall, CHELMSFORD, Essex, CM1 1QH – www.essexcc.gov.uk

European Ramblers Association, Generalsekretariat, Wilhelmshöher Allee 157–159, D-34121 Kassel, Germany – www.era-ewv-ferp.org

Famedram Publishing Ltd, P O Box 3, ELLON, AB41 9EA

Fen Rivers Way Association, c/o Mr D Mackay, 123 Birdwood Road, CAMBRIDGE, CB1 3TB

Fisher, Derek G., 8 Highcroft Road, NEWPORT, Mons, NP9 5EG

Five Parishes Walks, c/o Helen & Stuart Walker, The Brick House, BROXTED, Essex, CM6 2BU

Foot, A. G., Coombe House, Brithem Bottom, CULLOMPTON, Devon, EX15 1ND

Footpath Touring, Sea Chimneys, Southdown, BEER, Devon, EX12 3AE

Footprint, c/o Cordee Ltd, 3a De Montfort Street, LEICESTER, LE1 7HD

Forest Enterprise N Scotland, Forestry District Office, Strathoic, FORT AUGUSTUS, PH32 4BT

Forest Enterprise North Yorkshire, Outgang Road, PICKERING, North Yorkshire, YO18 7EL

Forest Enterprise Northumberland, Kielder Castle Forest Park Centre, Kielder, HEXHAM, Northumberland, NE48 1ER – www.kielder.org.uk

Forest of Avon, Ashton Court Visitors Centre, Ashton Court Estate, Long Ashton, BRISTOL, BS41 9JN – www.forestofavon.org.uk

Forest of Marston Vale, The Forest Centre, Station Road, MARSTON MORETAINE, Bedfordshire, MK43 0PR – www.marstonvale.org.uk

Friends of Ridgeway, c/o Ian Ritchie, The Limes, Oxford Street, RAMSBURY, Wiltshire, SN8 2PS – http://website.lineone.net/~friendsofridgeway/

Friends of the Hertfordshire Way, 53 Green Drift, ROYSTON, Herts, SG8 5BX – www.hertfordshireway.org.uk

Friends of the Trans Pennine Trail, c/o Richard Haynes, 32 Dalebrook Court, SHEFFIELD, S10 3PQ

Frith, David, 13 New Road, Whaley Bridge, HIGH PEAK, SK23 7JG

Frome Tourist Information Centre, The Round Tower, 2 Bridge Street, FROME, Somerset, BA11 1BB

Garbutt, George E., 17 Kingsclere, Huntington, YORK, YO32 9SF

Gateshead Council, Highways Dept, Development & Enterprise, Civic Centre, Regent Street, GATESHEAD, NE8 1HH

GEOprojects, 9-10 Southern Court, South Street, READING, Berkshire, RG1 4QS

Glasgow City Council, Land Services, Richmond Exchange, 20 Cadogan Street, GLASGOW, G2 7AD

Gloucestershire County Council, Tourism Office, Environment Department, Shire Hall, GLOUCESTER, GL1 2TH – www.gloscc.gov.uk

Gomer Press, Wind Street, LLANDYSUL, Ceredigion, SA44 4QL – www.gomer.co.uk

Goole Rambling Club, c/o Wendy Wales, 29 Mount Pleasant Road, GOOLE, East Yorkshire, DN14 6LH

Gordano Footpath Group, c/o Jim Dyer, 3 Harmony Drive, Portishead, BRISTOL, BS20 8DH

Gordon, Sheila, Haymeads, The Mains, Giggleswick, SETTLE, North Yorkshire, BD24 0AX

Great North Forest, Whickham Thorns, Market Lane, DUNSTON, NE11 9NX

Green Branch Press, Kencot Lodge, Kencot, LECHLADE, Gloucestershire, GL7 3QX

Green Fields Books, 13 Dalewood Avenue, Bear Cross, BOURNEMOUTH, Dorset, BH11 9NR

Greenlink, Avon Heath Country Park, Dorset County Council, Birch Road, St Ives, RINGWOOD, Dorset, BH24 2DA

Greensand Trust, The Forest Office, Haynes West End, BEDFORD, MK45 3QT – www.greensandridgewalk.com

Greenwood, Peter, 53 Wrenthorpe Road, WAKEFIELD, West Yorkshire, WF2 0LP

Grey Stone Books, c/o Cordee Ltd., 3a DeMonfort Street, LEICESTER, LE1 7HD

Griffiths, Margaret, 288 Turton Road, Bradshaw, BOLTON, Lancashire, BL2 3EF

Groundwork Bridgend, The Environment Centre, Maesteg Road, Tondu, BRIDGEND, CF32 9BT – www.bridgend.gov.uk

Groundwork Thames Valley, Colne Valley Park Centre, Denham Court Drive, Denham, UXBRIDGE, Middlesex, UB9 5PG

Guidepost, 4 Dale Road, Keyworth, NOTTINGHAM, NG12 5HS – www.guidepost.uk.com

Gunn, Garth H., Mam Tor, 60 Scarf Road, Cranford Heath, POOLE, Dorset, BH17 8QH

Gwasg Carreg Gwalch, 12 Lard yr Orsaf, Llanrwst, DYFFRYN, Conwy, LL26 0EH – www.carreg-gwalch.co.uk

Hadrian's Wall Information Line, The Railway Station, Station Road, HALTWHISTLE, NE49 0AH

Hadrian's Wall Path National Trail Office, The Countryside Agency, Cross House, Westgate Road, NEWCASTLE UPON TYNE, NE1 4XX

Hall, J. & Yeates, J., 2 Barnardo Road, EXETER, Devon, EX2 4NE

Hallamshire Press, 134 Archer Road, SHEFFIELD, S8 0JZ

Halsgrove Press, Halsgrove House, Lower Moor Way, Tiverton Business Park, TIVERTON, Devon, EX16 6SS – www.halsgrove.com

Hampshire County Council, Rights of Way Section, Arts, Countryside and Community Dept, Mottisfont Court, High Street, WINCHESTER, Hants, SO23 8ZF – www.hants.gov.uk

Harrogate Borough Council, c/o Tourist Information, Royal Baths Assembly Rooms, Crescent Road, HARROGATE, North Yorkshire, HG1 2RR

Harvey Maps, 12–22 Main Street, DOUNE, Perthshire, FK16 6BJ – www.harveymaps.co.uk

HavAC Walkers, c/o John Ling, 18 Orkney Close, HAVERHILL, Suffolk, CB9 0LS – www.bwf-ivv.org.uk/newmarke.htm

Haworth Tourist Information Centre, West Lane, HAWORTH, West Yorkshire, BD22 8EF

Heart of England Way Association, c/o 20 Throckmorton Road, ALCESTER, Warwickshire, B49 6QA – www.hoe-way.f2s.com

Hebden Bridge Tourist Information Centre, 1 Bridgegate, HEBDEN BRIDGE, HX7 8EX – www.calderdale.gov.uk

Hencke, Maurice, 25 Placehouse Lane, OLD COULSDON, Surrey, CR5 1LA

Herefordshire County Council, Hereford TIC, 1 King Street, HEREFORD, HR4 9BW

Hertfordshire County Council, Countryside Management Service (East), Little Samuels Farm, Widford Road, HUNSDON, Herts, SG12 8NN

Hertfordshire County Council (Hertford), Countryside Management Service, County Hall, Peggs Lane, HERTFORD, SG13 8DN

Hill, Richard, Cuckoo Cottage, Railwayside, South Clydach, ABERGAVENNY, Mons, NP7 0RD

Hillingdon LB, Central Library, 14/15 High Street, UXBRIDGE, Middlesex, UB8 1HD

Hillside Publications, 12 Broadlands, Shann Park, KEIGHLEY, West Yorkshire, BD20 6HX

Hollingworth Lake Visitor Centre, Rakewood Road, Littleborough, ROCHDALE, OL15 0AQ – www.rochdale.co.uk

Holmfirth Tourist Information Centre, 49-51 Huddersfield Road, HOLMFIRTH, West Yorkshire, HD7 1JP – www.holmfirthtic@kirkleesmc.gov.uk

Hood, Glen, 329 Kingston Road, Willerby, HULL, HU10 6PY

Hostelling International – Northern Ireland, 22 Donegal Road, BELFAST, BT12 5JN – www.hini.org.uk

Huntingdon District Council, Tourist Information Centre, Princes Street, HUNTINGDON, Cambridgeshire, PE29 3PH

Huntingdonshire District Council at Countryside Services, Pathfinder House, St Mary's Street, HUNTINGDON, Cambridgeshire, PE29 3TN

Hyndburn Borough Council, c/o Tourist Information Centre, Town Hall, Blackburn Road, ACCRINGTON, Lancashire, BB5 1LA

Icknield Way Association, c/o Mrs Chris James, 56 Back Street, ASHWELL, Herts, SG7 5PE – www.icknieldway.co.uk

Inn Way Publications, 102 Leeds Road, HARROGATE, North Yorkshire, HG2 8HB – www.innway.co.uk

Ireland All the Hostels, Flat 2A, Woodstock Road, Moseley, BIRMINGHAM, B13 9BN

Irish Tourist Board, 150 New Bond Street, LONDON, W1Y 0AQ – www.travel.ireland.ie

Irons, Dave, 57 Reservoir Road, Selly Oak, BIRMINGHAM, B29 6ST

Isle of Man Department of Tourism & Leisure, Tourist Information Centre, Sea Terminal Building, DOUGLAS, Isle of Man, IM1 2RG – www.gov.im/tourism

Isle of Wight Tourism, Westridge Centre, Brading Road, RYDE, Isle of Wight, PO33 1QS – www.islandbreaks.co.uk

Islington Archaeology & History Society, 8 Wynyatt Street, LONDON, EC1V 7HU

Ivel Valley Countryside Project, Biggleswade Library, Chestnut Avenue, BIGGLESWADE, Beds, SG18 0LL – www.ivelvalley.co.uk

Jackson, Gerry, 15 Edgehill, Llanfrechfa, CWMBRAN, Gwent, NP44 8UA

Jedburgh Tourist Information Centre, Murrays Green, JEDBURGH, Roxburghshire, TD8 6BE – www.scots-borders.co.uk

Jema Publications, 40 Ashley Lane, Moulton, NORTHAMPTON, NN3 7TJ

John Edwards Footpath Guides, 'Tryfan', 91 Colchester Road, White Colne, COLCHESTER, Essex, CO6 2PP

Johnson, David, The Hollies, Stainforth, SETTLE, North Yorkshire, BD24 9PQ

Jones, Glyn, Bing, KIRKINNER, Wigtownshire, DG8 9BZ

Jones, Ian R., 11 Alison Road, CHURCH STRETTON, Shropshire, SY6 7AT

Jones, Ken, Longview, 163 Long Line, SHEFFIELD, S11 7TX

Jowett, Jack, 58 Queens Walk, CLEVELEYS, Lancashire, FY5 1JW

Kennet District Council, Marlborough Tourist Information Centre, George Lane, MARLBOROUGH, Wilts, SN8 1EE

Kent County Council, Environmental Management Unit, Invicta House, County Hall, MAIDSTONE, Kent, ME14 1XX – www.kent.gov.uk/countrysideaccess

Kent High Weald Project, Council Offices, High Street, CRANBROOK, Kent, TN17 3EN – www.kenthighwealdproject.org

Kernow Scopes, The Camel Trail and Wildlife Shop, Eddystone Road, WADEBRIDGE, Cornwall, PL27 7AL – www.kernowscopes.co.uk

Kerr, Marjorie, 9 Heathlands Avenue, West Parley, WIMBORNE, Dorset, BH22 8RW

Kidd, David, (Shieldsman), 14 Froude Avenue, SOUTH SHIELDS, Tyne and Wear, NE34 9TB

Kimberley Publishing, 68 Kings Avenue, CHRISTCHURCH, Dorset, BH23 1NB

Kingdom of Fife, Forth Bridge Tourist Information Centre, c/o Queensferry Lodge Hotel, St Margaret's Head, NORTH QUEENSFERRY, KY11 1HP

Kirkby Stephen Tourist Information Centre, Market Street, KIRKBY STEPHEN, Cumbria, CA17 4QN – www.visiteden.co.uk

Kirkpatrick, Ian & Caroline, 6 Tor View, Horrabridge, YELVERTON, Devon, PL20 7RE – www.ian.kirkpatrick2.btinternet.co.uk

Kittiwake, 3 Glantwymyn Village Workshops, Cemmaes Road, NEAR MACHYNLLETH, Montgomeryshire, SY20 8LY – www.kittiwake-books.com

Lancashire County Council, Countryside Section, P O Box 9, Guild House, Cross Street, PRESTON, Lancashire, PR1 8RD – www.lancs.environment.com

Lancaster City Council, Lancaster Tourism, 29 Castle Hill, LANCASTER, LA1 1YN – www.lancaster.gov.uk

Langbaurgh Loop Recorder, Bywood, Victoria Terrace, SALTBURN-BY-THE-SEA, Cleveland, TS12 1JE

Lawrence and Wishart Ltd, 99a Wallis Road, LONDON, E9 5LN – www.l-w-bks.co.uk

Lawrence, Gerald, 21 Fenside Avenue, Styvechale, COVENTRY, CV3 5NF

LDWA Calderdale Group, c/o John Eggeling, Claremont South, Burnley Road, TODMORDEN, W Yorks, OL14 5LH

LDWA Cleveland Group, c/o Vince Thwaites, 22 Middleton Avenue, Thornaby, STOCKTON ON TEES, TS17 0HG

LDWA Cumbria Group, c/o David Hammond, 13 Broomy Hill, Aglionby, CARLISLE, Cumbria, CA4 8AF

LDWA East Lancs, c/o Peter Haslam, 7 Shetland Way, Radcliffe, MANCHESTER, M26 4UH

LDWA East Yorkshire Group, c/o Shirley Forster, Mill House, Ellerker, BROUGH, HU15 2DG

LDWA Membership Secretary, 63 Yockley Close, The Maultway, CAMBERLEY, Surrey, GU15 1QQ – www.ldwa.org.uk

LDWA Merchandise, 2 Sandy Lane, Beeston, NOTTINGHAM, NG9 3GS – www.ldwa.org.uk

LDWA Nidderdale Group, c/o Stuart Charlton, 21 Stonecrop, HARROGATE, HG3 2SQ

LDWA Northumbria Group, c/o Mike Rayner, 1 Corriedale Close, Pity Me, DURHAM, DH1 5GY

LDWA Vermuyden Group, c/o Frank Lawson, 74 Tatenhill Gardens, Cantley, DONCASTER, South Yorkshire, DN4 6TL

LDWA West Lancashire Group, c/o Robert Waller, 33 Hazelmere Road, Fulwood, PRESTON, Lancashire, PR2 9UL

Ledbury TIC, 3 The Homend, LEDBURY, Herefordshire, HR8 1BN

Lee Valley Park Authority, Lee Valley Park Information Centre, Abbey Gardens, WALTHAM ABBEY, Essex, EN9 1XQ – www.leevalleypark.org.uk

Leeds City Council, Leisure Services, The Town Hall, The Headrow, LEEDS, West Yorkshire, LS1 3AD

Leicestershire County Council, Environment Management, Department of Planning and Transportation, County Hall, Glenfield, LEICESTER, LE3 8RJ – www.leicestershire.gov.uk

Leicestershire Footpath Association, Gamekeepers Lodge, 11 London Road, GREAT GLEN, Leicestershire, LE8 0DJ

Leominster TIC, 1 Corn Square, LEOMINSTER, HR6 8LR

Lincolnshire County Council, Environmental Services, County Offices, Newland, LINCOLN, LN1 1DN

Lizard Peninsula Countryside Service, Unit 4, Higher Bochym, Cury Cross Lanes, HELSTON, Cornwall, TR12 7AZ

Llangollen Tourist Information Centre, Town Hall, Castle Street, LLANGOLLEN, Denbighshire, LL20 5PD – www.nwt.co.uk

Llanwrtyd Wells Walking Club, c/o Gordon Green, Neuadd Arms Hotel, LLANWRTYD WELLS, Powys, LD5 4RB

London Walking Forum, 3rd Floor, 31/33 Bondway, LONDON, SW8 1SJ – www.londonwalking.com

Lower Mole Project, 2 West Park Farmhouse, Horton Country Park, Horton Lane, EPSOM, Surrey, KT19 8PL – www.countryside-management.org.uk

Lyke Wake Club, P O Box 24, NORTHALLERTON, North Yorkshire, DL6 3HZ

Machynlleth Tourist Information Centre, Canolfan Owain Glyndwr's, Heol Maengwyn, MACHYNLLETH, Powys, SY20 8EE

Macmillan Way Association, St Mary's Barn, Pillerton Priors, WARWICK, CV35 0PG – www.macmillanway.org

Maidstone Borough Council, Planning Department, 13 Tonbridge Road, MAIDSTONE, Kent, ME16 8HG – www.digitalmaidstone.co.uk

Main, Laurence, 9 Mawddwy Cottages, Minllyn, Dinas Mawddwy, MACHYNLLETH, Powys, SY20 9LW

Mainstream Publishing Co Ltd, 7 Albany Street, EDINBURGH, EH1 3UG – www.mainstreampublishing.com

Malkinson, Alec, 2 Southern Walk, Scartho, GRIMSBY, DN33 2PG

Mallinson, Louise, 17 Prod Lane, BAILDON, West Yorkshire, BD17 5BN

Management Update Ltd, c/o Powney's Bookshop, 4–5 St Alkmund's Place, SHREWSBURY, Shropshire, SY1 1UJ – www.powneysbookshop.demon.co.uk

Map Shop, The, 15 High Street, UPTON UPON SEVERN, Worcestershire, WR8 0HJ – www.themapshop.co.uk

Mara Publications, 22 Crosland Terrace, Helsby, WARRINGTON, Cheshire, WA6 9LY

Marie Curie Cancer Care, West Yorkshire Fundraising Office, 2B Wood Lane, LEEDS, LS6 2AE

Maxiprint, Kettlestring Lane, Clifton Moor, YORK, YO3 4XF – www.maxiprint.co.uk

MC Publications, The Schoolhouse, New Road, CROOK, County Durham, DL15 8QX

McCloy, Andrew, Greystones Cottage, Bankside, YOULGREAVE, Derbys, DE45 1WD – www.owg.org.uk/andrew.mccloy

Mercat Press, 53 South Bridge, EDINBURGH, EH1 1YS – www.mercatpress.com

Meridian Books, 40 Hadzor Road, OLDBURY, West Midlands, B68 9LA

Mersey Valley Partnership, The Coach House, Norton Priory, Tudor Road, Manor Park, RUNCORN, WA7 1SX

Merthyr Tydfil TIC, 14a Glebeland Street, MERTHYR TYDFIL, CF47 8AU

Michael Joseph, 27 Wright's Lane, LONDON, W8 5TZ

Mid Cheshire Footpath Society, c/o Mrs Pauline Stott (Hon Sec), 17 Oakways, Appleton, WARRINGTON, WA4 5HD

Mid Suffolk District Council, Countryside Section, 131 High Street, NEEDHAM MARKET, Suffolk, IP6 8DL

Millstream Project, c/o Sarehole Mill, Colebank Road, Moseley, BIRMINGHAM, B13 OBD

Milton Keynes Council, Rights of Way Section, Landscape Division, Environmental Directorate, PO Box 113, Civic Offices, 1 Saxon Gate East, MILTON KEYNES, MK9 3HN – www.mkweb.co.uk/countryside

Minerva Press, 195 Knightsbridge, LONDON, SW7 1RE

Miway Publishing, PO Box 2, KESWICK, Cumbria, CA12 4GA

Monarch's Way Association, 15 Alison Road, Lapal, HALESOWEN, West Midlands, B62 0AT – www.monarchsway.50megs.com

Monmouthshire County Council, County Hall, CWMBRAN, Gwent, NP44 2XH

Moyle District Council, Ballycastle Tourist Information Centre, Sheskburn House, 7 Mary Street, BALLYCASTLE, BT54 6QH – www.moyle-council.org

Nash, Derek, 7 Crockford Drive, Four Oaks, SUTTON COLDFIELD, B75 5HH

National Map Centre, 22–24 Caxton Street, LONDON, SW1H 0QU – www.mapstore.co.uk and www.mapsnmc.co.uk

Neath & Port Talbot County Borough Council, Afan Argoed Countryside Centre, Afon Forest Park, PORT TALBOT, SA13 3HG

Needham, John, 23 Woodland Crescent, Hilton Park, PRESTWICH, M25 8WQ

New River Action Group, c/o Mrs Frances Mussett (Chairman), 24 Lavender Road, ENFIELD, EN2 0ST

Newlands School FCJ, Saltersgill Avenue, MIDDLESBROUGH, TS4 3JW

Newry & Mourne District Council, c/o Tourist Information Centre, Town Hall, NEWRY, Northern Ireland, BT35 6HR – www.south-armagh.com

Nightingale Publications, 23 Grange Road, BIDDULPH, Staffordshire Moorlands, ST8 7SB

Ninebanks Youth Hostel, Orchard House, Mohope, Ninebanks, HEXHAM, Northumberland, NE47 8DO – www.yhaninebanks.co.uk

Norfolk County Council, Planning & Transportation, County Hall, Martineau Lane, NORWICH, NR1 2SG – www.norfolk.gov.uk

North Chilterns Trust, c/o Three Valleys Water, Crescent Road, LUTON, Bedfordshire, LU2 0AD

North Downs Way National Trail Manager, Strategic Planning Department, Kent County Council, Invicta House, County Hall, MAIDSTONE, Kent, ME14 1XX

North York Moors Adventure Centre, Park House, Ingleby Cross, NORTHALLERTON, North Yorkshire, DL6 3PE – www.coast-to-coast.org.uk

North York Moors National Park, Information Service, The Old Vicarage, Bondgate, HELMSLEY, North Yorkshire, YO6 5BP – www.northyorkmoors-npa.gov.uk
Northamptonshire County Council, Countryside Services, P O Box 163, County Hall, NORTHAMPTON, NN1 1AX
Northern Map Distributors, 101 Broadfield Road, SHEFFIELD, S8 0XH
Northumberland County Council, Countryside Section, Technical Services, County Hall, MORPETH, Northumberland, NE61 2EF – www.northumberland.co.uk
Norwich Fringe Project, The Gate Lodge, The Training Workshop, Swanton Road, NORWICH, NR2 4LR – www.thefringe.fsnet.co.uk
Nottinghamshire County Council, Rights of Way Section, Trent Bridge House, Fox Road, West Bridgford, NOTTINGHAM, NG2 6BJ

Oakham TIC, Flores House, 34 High Street, OAKHAM, Rutland, LE15 6AL
O'Brien Press Limited, 20 Victoria Road, DUBLIN 6, Ireland – www.obrien.ie
Offa's Dyke Association, Offa's Dyke Centre, West Street, KNIGHTON, Powys, LD7 1EN – www.offa.demon.co.uk/offa.htm
Old Crown Inn, Hesket Newmarket, WIGTON, Cumbria, CA7 8JG
Oldham Metropolitan Borough Council, Countryside Service, Strinesdale Centre, Holgate Street, Waterhead, OLDHAM, OL4 2JW
Omagh District Council, c/o Omagh Tourist Information Centre, 1 Market Street, OMAGH, Northern Ireland, BT78 1EE – www.omagh.gov.uk
Ordnance Survey, Romsey Road, SOUTHAMPTON, SO16 4GU – www.ordnancesurvey.co.uk
Ottakars, 118 The High Street, NEWPORT, Isle of Wight, PO30 1TP
Oxfordshire County Council, Cultural Service, Countryside Service, Holton, OXFORD, OX33 1QQ – www.oxfordshire.gov.uk

P3 Publications, 13 Beaver Road, CARLISLE, Cumbria, CA2 7PS – www.p3publications.com
Pamplin, Elizabeth, Little Critchmere, Manor Crescent, HASLEMERE, Surrey, GU27 2PB
Parker, Ian, 4 Raikeswood Drive, SKIPTON, North Yorkshire, BD23 1LY
Pathfinder Long Distance Walk, PO Box 352, HUNTINGDON, PE28 2XS
Pathway Publishing, 16 Parkhill, Middleton, KING'S LYNN, Norfolk, PE32 1RJ
Peacock, Kim, 18 St Andrews Road, WHITBY, North Yorkshire, YO21 1LJ
Peak District National Park, Baslow Road, BAKEWELL, Derbyshire, DE45 1AE – www.peakdistrict.org.uk
Peak National Park Information Centre, Fieldhead, Edale, HOPE VALLEY, S33 7ZA
Peak Publishing Ltd, Camus Bhan, Invercoe, GLENCOE, Argyll, PH49 4HP
Pembrokeshire Coast National Park, Winch Lane, HAVERFORDWEST, Pembrokeshire, SA61 1PY – www.pembrokeshirecoast.org.uk
Pendle Borough Council, Town Hall, Market Street, NELSON, BB9 7LG – www.pendle.gov.uk
Penistone Town Council, Town Clerk's Office, St John's Community Centre, Church Street, PENISTONE, S36 9AR
Pennine Way Association, c/o Chris Sainty, 29 Springfield Park Avenue, CHELMSFORD, Essex, CM2 6EL
Pennine Way Project Officer, Countryside Agency, 4th Floor, Victoria Wharf, 4 The Embankment, Sovereign Street, LEEDS, LS1 4BA
Pentland Press Ltd, Hutton Close, Southchurch, BISHOP AUCKLAND, Durham, DL14 6XG – www.pentlandpress.co.uk
Pen-y-ghent Cafe, HORTON-IN-RIBBLESDALE, North Yorkshire, BD24 0HE
Perkins, Dr Ben, 11 Old London Road, BRIGHTON, Sussex, BN1 8XR

Perks, Eric, Selbhorne, 10 Cordle Marsh Road, BEWDLEY, Worcestershire, DY12 1EW

Per-Rambulations, c/o Larkshill, Cranston Road, EAST GRINSTEAD, West Sussex, RH19 3HL

Pestell, Allen, 8 Sledbrook Crescent, Crowedge, SHEFFIELD, S36 4HD

Peterborough City Council, Planning Services, Bridge House, Town Bridge, PETERBOROUGH, PE1 1HB

Petrie, Kevin, 2 Tillman Close, SETTLE, N Yorks, BD24 9RA

Pinkney, Richard, 11 Pine Road, Ormesby, MIDDLESBROUGH, TS7 9DH

Plymouth City Council, Plymouth TIC, 9 The Barbican, PLYMOUTH, PL1 2LS – www.plymouth.gov.uk

Powys County Council, Saint John's Offices, Fiveways, LLANDRINDOD WELLS, Powys, LD1 5ES – www.powys.gov.uk

Preston, R., The Chantry, Wilkes Walk, TRURO, Cornwall, TR1 2UF

Printability Publishing Ltd, 10/11 Lower Church Street, HARTLEPOOL, TS24 7DJ – www.atkinsonprint.co.uk/printability/index.htm

Pritchard-Jones, John, 2 Sycamore Close, Etwall, DERBY, DE65 6JS

Profitt, Alan, 199 Markfield, CROYDON, CR0 9HR

Project Kingfisher, Shard End Community Centre, Paddington Avenue, Shard End, BIRMINGHAM, B34 7RD

Promo-video Publications, PO Box 138, EAST GRINSTEAD, RH19 4ZD

Pugh, Paul, 34 Melbourn Road, SHEFFIELD, S10 1NS

Purbeck Information & Heritage Centre, Holy Trinity Church, South Street, WAREHAM, Dorset, BH20 4LU

Pwllheli TIC, Station Square, PWLLHELI, LL53 5HG

RA Beverley Group, c/o Dennis Parker, 11 Elmsall Drive, BEVERLEY, East Yorkshire, HU17 7HL

RA Cardiff, c/o Jim Hargreaves, 92 St Fagans Road, Fairwater, CARDIFF, CF5 3AN

RA Central Office – London, Second Floor, Camelford House, 87-90 Albert Embankment, LONDON, SE1 7TW – www.ramblers.org.uk

RA Chesterfield & NE Derbyshire, c/o Tony Hunt, 17a Loads Road, Holymoorside, CHESTERFIELD, S42 7ET

RA Doncaster, c/o Mrs M. Thompson, 31 Broomhill Drive, Cantley, DONCASTER, DN4 6QZ – www.donramblers@yahoo.co.uk

RA Dorset, c/o Mrs Susan Blake, 19 Shaston Crescent, DORCHESTER, Dorset, DT1 2EB

RA East Berkshire Group, P O Box 1357, MAIDENHEAD, Berks, SL6 7FP – www.RamblingforPleasure.co.uk

RA East Yorkshire & Derwent Area, c/o Mrs Sheila M. Smith, 65 Ormonde Avenue, Beresford Avenue, Beverley High Road, HULL, HU6 7LT

RA Gloucester, c/o John Street, The Knoll, Critty Craft Lane, Churchdown, GLOUCESTER, GL3 2LJ

RA Gloucestershire Area, c/o Geoff Smithdale, Tudor Cottage, Berrow, MALVERN, Worcestershire, WR13 6JJ

RA Godalming and Haslemere, c/o Kate Colley, 6 Hill Court, HASLEMERE, Surrey, GU27 2BD

RA Hampshire Area, c/o Peter Benham, 'Ashwood', Clubhouse Lane, Waltham Chase, SOUTHAMPTON, Hampshire, SO32 2NN

RA Harrogate Group, c/o Peter Goldsmith, 20 Pannal Ash Grove, HARROGATE, North Yorkshire, HG2 0HZ

RA Leighton Buzzard, c/o John Duxbury, 8 Carlton Grove, LEIGHTON BUZZARD, Bedfordshire, LU7 3BR

RA Lincoln, c/o Alan Nash, 19 Millfield Avenue, Saxilby, LINCOLN, LN1 2QN

RA Manchester Area, c/o Terry Perkins, 34 Grangethorpe Drive, Burnage, MANCHESTER, M19 2LG

RA New Forest Group, c/o Audrey Wilson, Clarendon, off West Road, Dibden Purlieu, SOUTHAMPTON, Hants, SO45 5RG

RA Norfolk Area, c/o Sheila Smith, Caldcleugh, Cake Street, Old Buckenham, ATTLEBOROUGH, Norfolk, NR17 1RU

RA North East Lancashire Area, c/o John Riley, 58 Westwood Street, ACCRINGTON, Lancashire, BB5 4BL

RA North Wales Area, c/o David Hollett, 69 Wethersfield Road, PRENTON, CH43 9YF

RA Northern Area, c/o Ann Key, 22 Highbury, Jesmond, NEWCASTLE UPON TYNE, NE2 3DY

RA Preston Group, c/o Andrew Manzie, 3 Ruthin Court, Dunbar Road, Ingol, PRESTON, PR2 3YE

RA Ripon Group, c/o Peter Sleightholme, 9 Melrose Road, Bishop Monkton, HARROGATE, North Yorkshire, HG3 3RH

RA Sheffield, c/o John Harker, 317 Prince of Wales Road, SHEFFIELD, S2 1FJ

RA South Wiltshire Group, c/o Mr P. Brown, 32 Hilltop Way, SALISBURY, Wiltshire, SP1 3QY – www.ramblers-wilts.org.uk

RA Southam and District Group, c/o Harry Green, 30 Warwick Road, SOUTHAM, Warwickshire, CV47 0HN

RA Sussex Area, 11 Old London Road, BRIGHTON, Sussex, BN1 8XR

RA Waveney, c/o Miss Brenda Le Grys, 1 Church Close, REDENHALL, Norfolk, IP20 9TS

RA West Riding Area, c/o Douglas Cossar, 27 Cookridge Avenue, LEEDS, West Yorkshire, LS16 7NA

Radburn, Peter, 31 Hillcrest Avenue, Chandler's Ford, EASTLEIGH, Hampshire, SO53 2JS

Ramsgate Tourist Information Centre, 17 Albert Court, York Street, RAMSGATE, Kent, CT11 9DN

Ratcliffe's Stationers, 31 Corporation Street, ROTHERHAM, S60 1NX

Reardon Publishing, 56 Upper Norwood Street, Leckhampton, CHELTENHAM, Gloucestershire, GL53 0DU – www.reardon.co.uk

Redcar & Cleveland Borough Council, Countryside Section, Redcar & Cleveland House, P O Box 86, Kirkleatham Street, REDCAR, TS10 1XX

Reigate and Banstead Borough Council, Town Hall, Castlefield Road, REIGATE, Surrey, RH2 0SH

Ribble Valley Borough Council, Tourist Information Centre, 12 & 14 Market Place, CLITHEROE, Lancs, BB7 2DA – www.ribblevalley.gov.uk

Richmond, Brian, 31 Dartmouth Street, BARROW-IN-FURNESS, Cumbria, LA14 3AS

Richmondshire District Council, Tourist Information Centre, Friary Gardens, Victoria Road, RICHMOND, North Yorkshire, DL10 4AJ – www.yorkshiredales.org.uk

Ridgeway National Trail Officer, Cultural Services, Holton, OXFORD, OX33 1QQ – www.nationaltrails.gov.uk

Rochdale Pioneers Museum, Toad Lane, ROCHDALE, OL12 0NU

Rossendale Borough Council, c/o Tourist Information Centre, 41-45 Kay Street, Rawtenstall, ROSSENDALE, Lancashire, BB4 7LS

Rotary Club of Cleckheaton & District, c/o 2 Turnsteads Avenue, CLECKHEATON, West Yorkshire, BD19 3AJ

Rotary Club of Nuneaton, c/o Chris Mountford, 242 The Long Shoot, NUNEATON, Warwickshire, CV11 6JN

Rother Valley Eagles Walking Club, c/o Lorne Johnson, 2 Ferndale, Broadacres, GUILDFORD, Surrey, GU3 3AX

Rotherham Tourist Information Centre, Central Library & Arts Centre, Walker Place, ROTHERHAM, S65 1JH – www.rotherham.gov.uk

Rucksack Readers, Landrick Lodge, DUNBLANE, FK15 0HY – www.rucsacs.com

Rye Bay Countryside Service, 111B High Street, RYE, East Sussex, TN31 7JF – www.ryebay.demon.co.uk

Salisbury District Council, Amesbury Tourist Information Centre, Redworth House, Flower Lane, AMESBURY, Wilts, SP4 7HG – www.wiltshiretourism.co.uk

Sandhill Press Ltd, 17 Castle Street, Warkworth, MORPETH, Northumberland, NE65 0UW – www.thebookhouse.demon.co.uk

Sauerzapf, Bobbie, 71b Plumstead Road, Thorpe End, NORWICH, Norfolk, NR13 5AJ – www.ldwa-norfolk-and-suffolk.org.uk

Sayer, Ann, 29 Twickenham Road, TEDDINGTON, Middlesex, TW11 8AQ

Scarthin Books, The Promenade, CROMFORD, Derbyshire, DE4 3QF – www.scarthinbooks.demon.co.uk

Scholes, Norman F., Danelea, Laburnum Avenue, Robin Hood's Bay, WHITBY, North Yorkshire, YO22 4RR

Scottish Rights of Way and Access Society, 24 Annandale Street, EDINBURGH, EH7 4AN – www.scotways.com

Scottish Youth Hostels Association, 7 Glebe Crescent, STIRLING, FK8 2JA – www.syha.org.uk

SE London Green Chain Project, PO Box 22119, LONDON, SE18 6WY – www.greenchain.com

Sefton Metropolitan Borough Council, Tourist Information Office, Lord Street, SOUTHPORT, PR8 1NY – www.visitsouthport.com

Seven Parishes, c/o David Arnold, 25 Salford Road, Aspley Guise, MILTON KEYNES, MK17 8HT

Shercliffe, Bill, 2 Hazel Drive, POYNTON, Cheshire, SK12 1PX

Shetland Times Ltd, 71/79 Commercial Street, LERWICK, Shetland, ZE1 0AJ – www.shetland-bookshop.co.uk

Shrewsbury and Atcham Borough Council, Shrewsbury Tourist Information Centre, The Music Hall, The Square, SHREWSBURY, SY1 1LH – www.shrewsbury.ws

Shropshire County Council, Countryside Service, The Shirehall, Abbey Foregate, SHREWSBURY, SY2 6ND – www.shropshire-cc.gov.uk

Sidebottom, Joyce, 8 Mill Lane, Horwich, BOLTON, BL6 6AT

Sigma Leisure, 1 South Oak Lane, WILMSLOW, Cheshire, SK9 6AR – www.sigmapress.co.uk

Skuse, Michael, Caenant Llangynhafal, RUTHIN, Denbighshire, LL15 1RU

Society of Sussex Downsmen, Publications Editor, 254 Victoria Drive, EASTBOURNE, East Sussex, BN20 8QT

Solihull Metropoliton Borough Council, c/o Tourist Information Centre, Central Library, Homer Road, Solihull, BIRMINGHAM, B91 3RG

Solihull Metropoliton Borough Council House, The Council House, PO Box 19, SOLIHULL, B91 3QT

Solway Rural Initiative Limited, Solway Coast Heritage Centre, Liddell St, SILLOTH ON SOLWAY, Cumbria, CA7 4DD

South Downs Way National Trail Officer, Queen Elizabeth Country Park, Gravel Hill, HORNDEAN, Hampshire, PO8 0QE

South Gloucestershire Council, Public Rights of Way Team, Civic Centre, High Street, Kingswood, BRISTOL, BS15 9TR

South Lakeland District Council, Cultural & Tourism Services Department, South Lakeland House, Lowther Street, KENDAL, Cumbria, LA9 4DL – www.lake-district-breaks.com

South Lanarkshire Council, Access Development Officer, Enterprise Resources, Montrose House, 154 Montrose Crescent, HAMILTON, ML3 6LL

South Norfolk Council, South Norfolk House, Swan Lane, LONG STRATTON, Norfolk, NR15 2XE – www.south-norfolk.gov.uk

South Somerset District Council, Petters House, Petters Way, YEOVIL, Somerset, BA20 1SH

South West Coast Path Association, Windlestraw, Penquit, Ermington, Nr IVYBRIDGE, Devon, PL21 0LU – www.swcp.org.uk

Southend Borough Council, Leisure Development Officer, Leisure Services Department, Civic Centre, Victoria Avenue, SOUTHEND ON SEA, SS2 6ER

Spalding Tourist Information Centre, Ayscoughfee Hall, Churchgate, SPALDING, PE11 2RA

SPARC, The Old School, Station Road, NARBETH, Pembrokeshire, SA67 7DU – www.southpembrokeshire-holidays.co.uk

Sparshatt, John, 30A Sandholme Drive, Burley in Wharfedale, ILKLEY, West Yorkshire, LS29 7RQ

Speyside Way Ranger Service, Boat o'Fiddich, CRAIGELLACHIE, AB38 9RQ

Squibb, Frank, 4 Bassett Place, FALMOUTH, Cornwall, TR11 2SS

St Edmundsbury Borough Council, c/o Bury St Edmunds Tourist Information Centre, 8 Angel Hill, BURY ST EDMUNDS, Suffolk, IP33 1UZ

St John, Ian, Old Hall, East Bergholt, COLCHESTER, Suffolk, CO7 6TG

Staffordshire County Council, Cultural & Corporate Services, Shire Hall, Market Street, STAFFORD, ST16 2LQ – www.staffordshire.co.uk

Stanfords, 12/14 Long Acre, LONDON, WC2E 9LP – www.stanfords.co.uk

Stile Publications, 16 Denton Road, Middleton, ILKLEY, West Yorkshire, LS29 0AA

Stilwell Publishing Limited, The Courtyard, 59 Charlotte Road, Shoreditch, LONDON, EC2A 3QW

Stockport Metropolitan Borough Council, Countryside Service, 4th Floor, Stopford House, Piccadilly, STOCKPORT, SK1 3XE

Stratford-upon-Avon District Council, Technical and Amenities Department, Elizabeth House, Church Street, STRATFORD-UPON-AVON, Warwickshire, CV37 6HX – www.stratford.gov.uk

Suffolk Coast and Heaths Project, Dock Lane, Melton, WOODBRIDGE, Suffolk, IP12 1PE

Suffolk County Council, Environment and Transport Department, St Edmund House, County Hall, IPSWICH, Suffolk, IP4 1LZ – www.suffolkcc.gov.uk

Sunderland City Council, c/o Tourist Information Centre, 50 Fawcett Street, SUNDERLAND, SR1 1RF – www.visitsunderland.com

Surrey County Council, Environment Department, County Hall, KINGSTON UPON THAMES, Surrey, KT1 2DY

Sussex Downs Conservation Board, Chanctonbury House, Church Street, STORRINGTON, West Sussex, RH20 4LT

Sutton London Borough, Leisure Stop, Central Library, St Nicholas Way, SUTTON, Surrey, SM1 1EA

Sweeting, Don, The Levels, Portington Road, Eastrington, GOOLE, DN14 7QE

Tameside Countryside Warden Service, Chief Wardens Office, Park Bridge Visitor Centre, The Stables, Park Bridge, ASHTON-UNDER-LYNE, OL6 8AQ – www.tameside.gov.uk

Tattersall, Max, 79 Ormerod Road, BURNLEY, Lancashire, BB11 2RU

Taunton Deane Borough Council, Leisure Services, The Deane House, Belvedere Road, TAUNTON, Somerset, TA1 1HE

Taylor, Sam R., 13 Dixon Street, Lees, OLDHAM, Lancashire, OL4 3NG

Tees Forest Project, Stewart Park, The Grove, MIDDLESBROUGH, TS7 8AR

Telford & Wrekin Countryside Service, Stirchley Grange, TELFORD, TF3 1DY

Thames Path National Trail Officer, Cultural Services, Holton, OXFORD, OX33 1QQ

Thames Water, Customer Services, PO Box 436, SWINDON, Wiltshire, SN38 6TU

Thomas, Norman, The Parsonage, off Ainsworth Avenue, Horwich, BOLTON, Lancashire, BL6 6LS

Three Rivers District Council, Planning Department, Three Rivers House, Northway, RICKMANSWORTH, Herts, WD3 1RL

Thurstaston Visitor Centre, Wirral Country Park, Station Road, Thurstaston, WIRRAL, Merseyside, L61 0HN – www.wirral.gov.uk/leisure/ranger

Tinniswood, J., 12 Beaconsfield Terrace, Chopwell, NEWCASTLE-UPON-TYNE, NE17 7JG

Torbay Coast & Countryside Enterprises Ltd, Cockington Court, Cockington, TORQUAY, Devon, TQ2 6XA

Townson, Simon, 15 First Avenue, Starbeck, HARROGATE, North Yorkshire, HG2 7PA

Trans Pennine Trail Officer, Trans Pennine Trail Office, Barnsley Metropolitan Borough Council, Central Offices, Kendray Street, BARNSLEY, S70 2TN – www.transpenninetrail.org.uk

Travis, Peter, 23 Kingsway East, Westlands, NEWCASTLE-UNDER-LYME, Staffordshire, ST5 3PY

Tum, Edwin and Julia, High Manley, Manley Street, BRIGHOUSE, West Yorkshire, HD6 1TE

Turner, Lawrence, 3 Ringwood Crescent, LEEDS, West Yorkshire, LS14 1AN

Turning The Tide, c/o Environmental and Technical Services Dept, County Hall, DURHAM, DH1 5UQ

Two Moors Way Association, c/o Joe Turner, Coppins, The Poplars, Pinhoe, EXETER, Devon, EX4 9HH

Underwood, Arnold, 41 The Orchards, LEVEN, East Yorkshire, HU17 5QA

Vale Royal Borough Council, Tourism Officer, Wyvern House, The Drumber, WINSFORD, Cheshire, CW7 1AH – www.valeroyal.gov.uk

Vanguards Rambling Club, c/o 109 Selsdon Park Road, SOUTH CROYDON, CR2 8JJ

Visitmap Limited, 28 Hartfield Road, FOREST ROW, East Sussex, RH18 5DY – www.visitmap.com

W & A Enterprises Ltd, c/o 24 Griffiths Avenue, LANCING, West Sussex, BN15 0HW – www.weyandarun.co.uk

Waendel Walkers Club, c/o Pete Holt, 5 Valley Rise, Desborough, KETTERING, Northants, NN14 2QR

Walk & Write Ltd, Unit 1, Molyneux Business Park, Whitworth Road, Darley Dale, MATLOCK, DERBYSHIRE, DE4 2JH – www.countrywalks.com

Walkways, 67 Cliffe Way, WARWICK, CV34 5JG

Wallis, Ray, 75 Ancaster Avenue, KINGSTON-UPON-HULL, HU5 4QR

Walsall Metropolitan Borough Council, Leisure Services, Darwall Street, WALSALL, West Midlands, WS1 1TZ – www.walsallcountryside.co.uk

Wanderlust Rambling Club, c/o Don Shaw, 5 Pelham Crescent, KEELBY, Lincolnshire, DN37 8EW

Wandle Industrial Museum, The Vestry Hall Annexe, London Road, MITCHAM, Surrey, CR4 3UD

Warner, Mike, Redland House, Clifton Cross, Clifton, ASHBOURNE, Derbyshire, DE6 2GJ

Warwickshire County Council, Information Centre, Kingsbury Water Park, Bodymoor Heath, SUTTON COLDFIELD, B76 0DY – www.warwickshire.gov.uk

Watling Chase Community Forest, Shenley Park, Radlett Lane, SHENLEY, Hertfordshire, WD7 9DW

Watson, Ron, 33 Sutherland Avenue, Endike Lane, HULL, HU6 7UG

Waveney District Council, Town Hall, High Street, LOWESTOFT, Suffolk, NR32 1HS

Wealden District Council, Sussex Country Information Centre, LOWER DICKER, East Sussex, BN27 4DT – www.wealden.gov.uk

West Berkshire District Council, Countryside and Environment, Council Offices, Faraday Road, NEWBURY, Berks, RG14 2AF

West Highland Way Ranger, Balmaha Visitor Centre, Balmaha, STIRLING, G63 0JQ

West Pennine Moors Ranger & Information Service, Great House Barn Information Centre, Rivington Lane, Horwich, BOLTON, BL6 7SB

West Sussex County Council, Planning Department, County Hall, Tower Street, CHICHESTER, West Sussex, PO19 1RL

Whitehead, Mrs Doreen, Butt House, Keld, RICHMOND, North Yorkshire, DL11 6LJ

Wild Goose Publications, Iona Community, Unit 16, Six Harmony Row, GLASGOW, G51 3BA – www.iona.org.uk

Wilkins, D. E., 21 Lane Ings, Marsden, HUDDERSFIELD, HD7 6JP

Willow Publishing, Willow Cottage, 36 Moss Lane, Timperley, ALTRINCHAM, Cheshire, WA15 6SZ

Wimbush, Tony, 10 Beaufort Grove, BRADFORD, BD2 4LJ

Wimpole Books, Pip's Peace, Kenton, STOWMARKET, Suffolk, IP14 6JS

Wintle, Anthony, 27 Belmont Grove, Rawdon, LEEDS, LS19 6AL

Worcestershire County Council, PO Box 373, County Hall, Spetchley Road, WORCESTER, WR5 2XG – www.worcestershire.gov.uk

Wrexham County Borough Council, Guildhall, WREXHAM, Clwyd, LL11 1AY

Wright, David, Inglenook Cottage, Rudge, FROME, Somerset, BA11 2QG

Wychavon District Council, Civic Centre, Queen Elizabeth Drive, PERSHORE, Worcestershire, WR10 1PT – www.wychavon.gov.uk

Wyreside Ecology Centre, Wyre Estuary Country Park, River Road, Stanah, THORNTON, Lancashire, FY5 5LR

Yatton Ramblers, c/o 92 Claverham Road, Yatton, BRISTOL, BS19 4LE

YHA Northern Region, PO Box 67, MATLOCK, Derbyshire, DE4 3YX – www.yha.org.uk

York City Council, PROW, 9 St Leonard's Place, YORK, YO1 7ET – www.york.gov.uk

Yorkshire Footpath Trust, 37 Hazel Garth, Stockton Lane, YORK, YO31 1HR – www.yorkshirefootpathtrust.org.uk

Young, Ken, 14 Wilton Orchard, TAUNTON, Somerset, TA1 3SA

Youth Hostels Association, PO Box 67, MATLOCK, Derbyshire, DE4 3YX – www.yha.org.uk

INDEX

MAP SECTION

CONTENTS

MAPS OF WAYMARKED ROUTES (plus a small selection of unwaymarked routes)

LIST OF UNWAYMARKED ROUTES

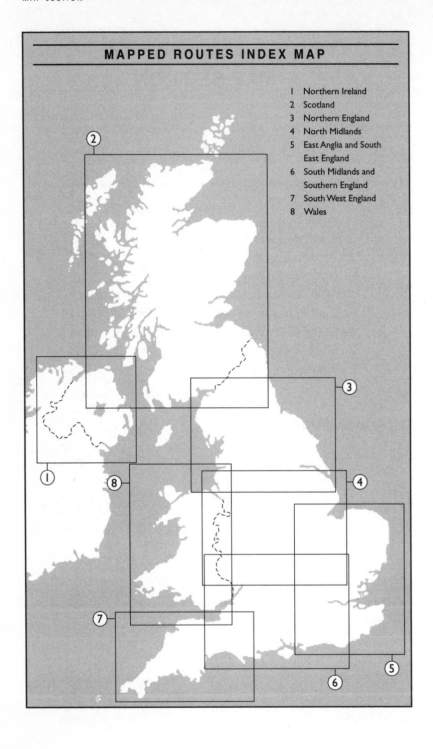

MAPPED ROUTES INDEX MAP

1 Northern Ireland
2 Scotland
3 Northern England
4 North Midlands
5 East Anglia and South
   East England
6 South Midlands and
   Southern England
7 South West England
8 Wales

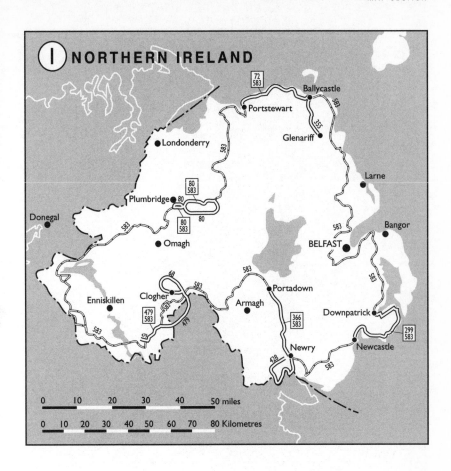

① NORTHERN IRELAND

Ballycastle
72
583
Portstewart
593
Glenariff
Londonderry
355
583
Larne
80
583
Plumbridge
80
80
583
80
Bangor
Donegal
583
583
Omagh
BELFAST
583
583
583
68
Portadown
583
Enniskillen
Clogher
Armagh
479
583
583
479
366
583
Downpatrick
479
299
583
583
Newry
Newcastle
478
583

0   10   20   30   40   50 miles

0   10 20 30 40 50 60 70   80 Kilometres

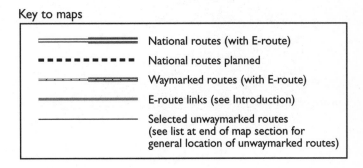

Key to maps

National routes (with E-route)

National routes planned

Waymarked routes (with E-route)

E-route links (see Introduction)

Selected unwaymarked routes
(see list at end of map section for
general location of unwaymarked routes)

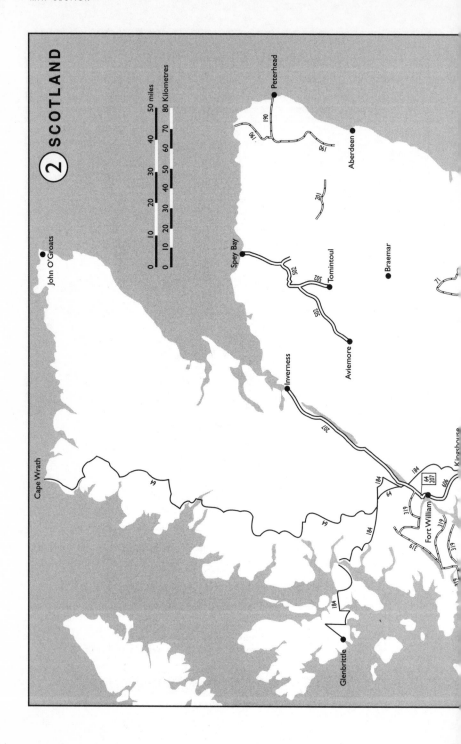

2 SCOTLAND

50 miles
80 Kilometres

John O'Groats
Cape Wrath
Peterhead
Aberdeen
Spey Bay
Tomintoul
Braemar
Aviemore
Inverness
Fort William
Kingshouse
Glenbrittle

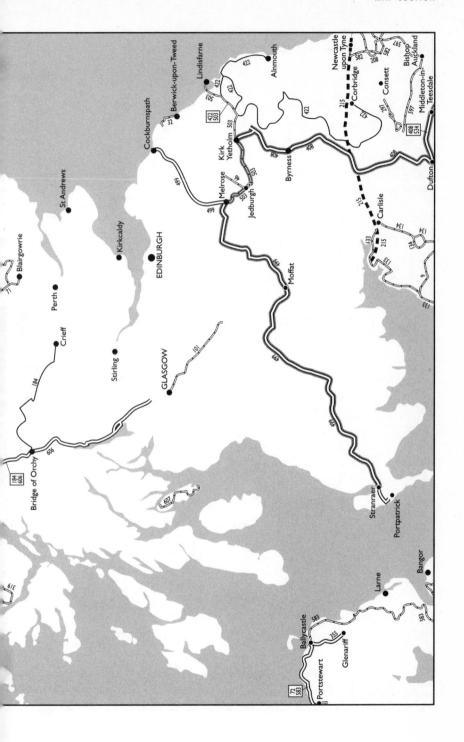

295

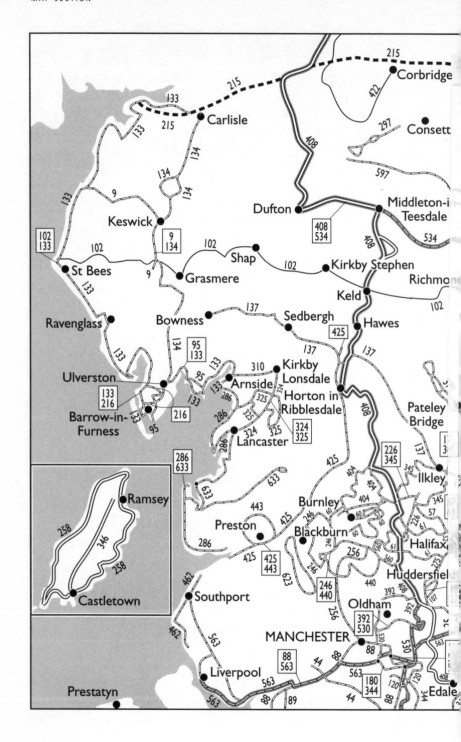

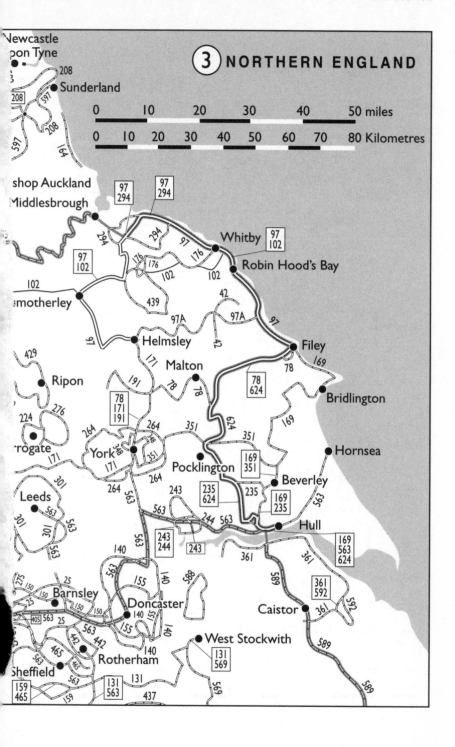

(3) NORTHERN ENGLAND

| 0 | 10 | 20 | 30 | 40 | 50 miles |

| 0 | 10 | 20 | 30 | 40 | 50 | 60 | 70 | 80 Kilometres |

Newcastle
upon Tyne
208
208 597 Sunderland
597 208
597 208
164

shop Auckland
Middlesbrough
97 294
294
294
97 176
176
176 176
97 102
102
102 102 42
emotherley
439
42
97A 97A
97
Helmsley 42
Filey
171 Malton 78 169
429
191 78
Ripon 78 624
224 276 78
171 78 624
264 171 191 351 624
rogate 264 264 624 351 169
York 348 169 Hornsea
171 348 351 351
171 Pocklington
264 235 Beverley
Leeds 264 624
301 563 243 235 169
301 563 235 563
563 301 563 244 563
140 243 Hull
301 243 169
Barnsley 140 244 361 563
275 150 155 588 624
25 150 140 589 361
25 150 405 563 155 361 361 592
563 25 465 442 140 Caistor 592 361
442 140
Sheffield Rotherham 131 589
131 563 569 West Stockwith 589
159 563 131 131
465 159 437 569

Whitby 97 102
Robin Hood's Bay
Bridlington
Doncaster

297

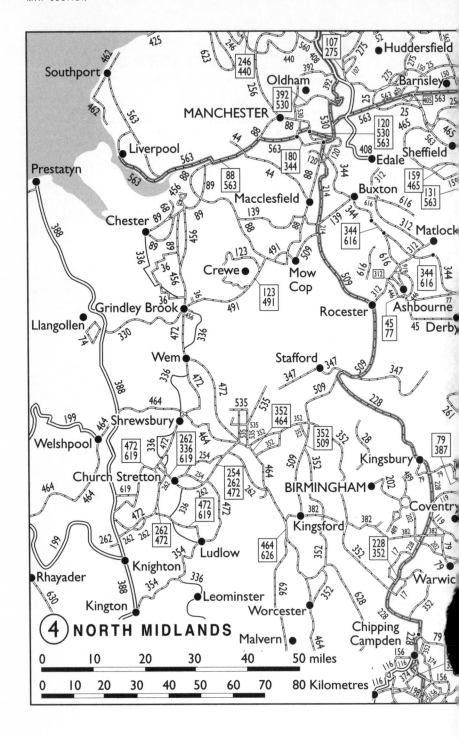

④ NORTH MIDLANDS

| 0 | 10 | 20 | 30 | 40 | 50 miles |

| 0 | 10 | 20 | 30 | 40 | 50 | 60 | 70 | 80 Kilometres |

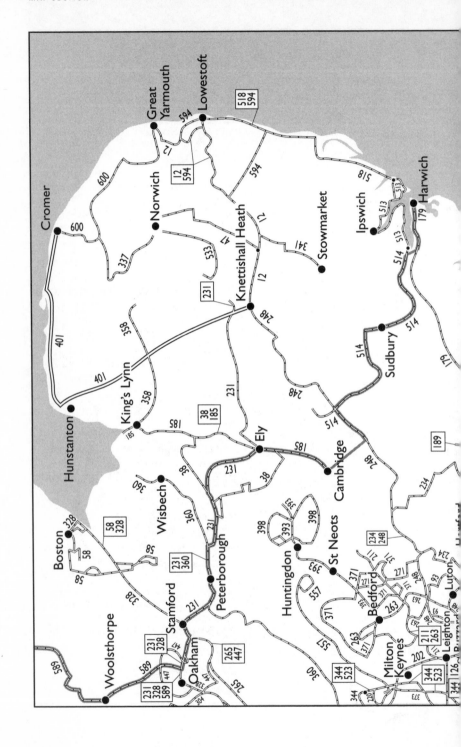

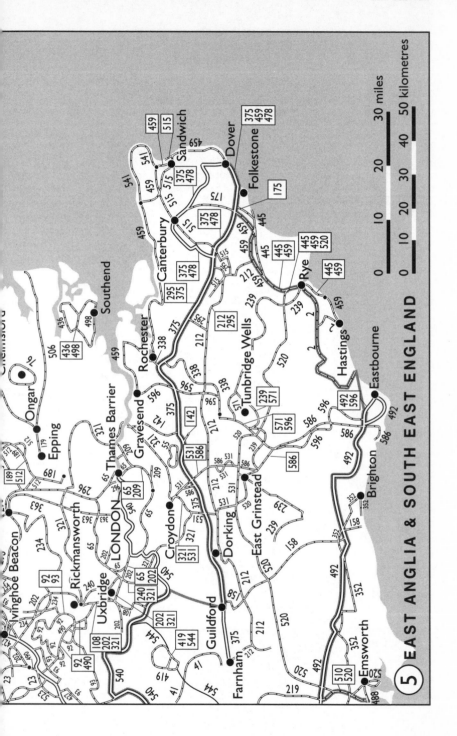

5 EAST ANGLIA & SOUTH EAST ENGLAND

30 miles

50 kilometres

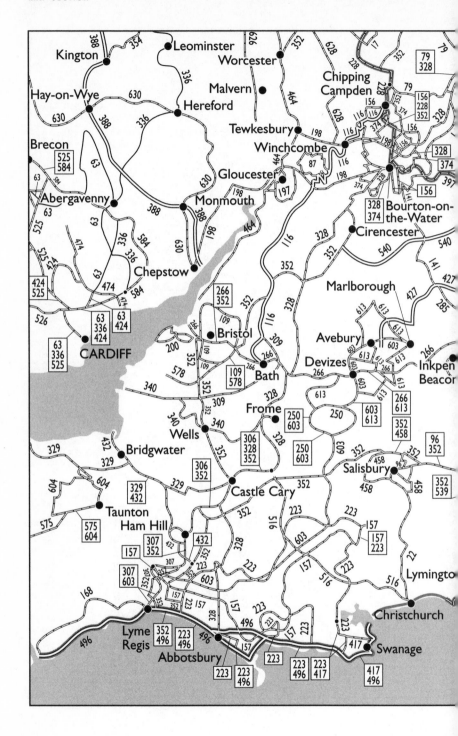

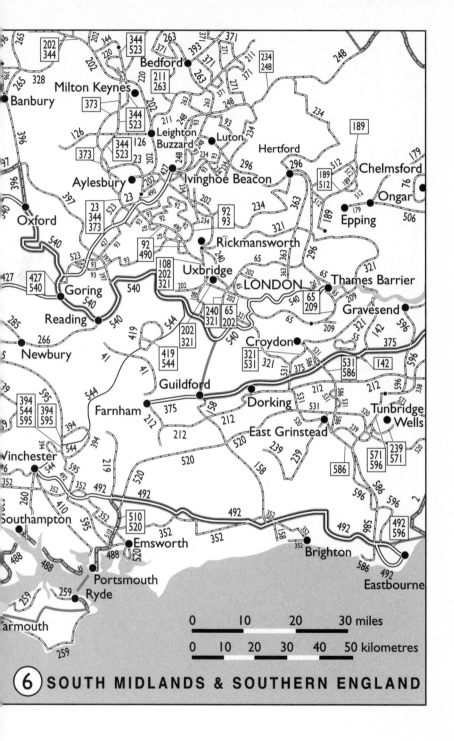

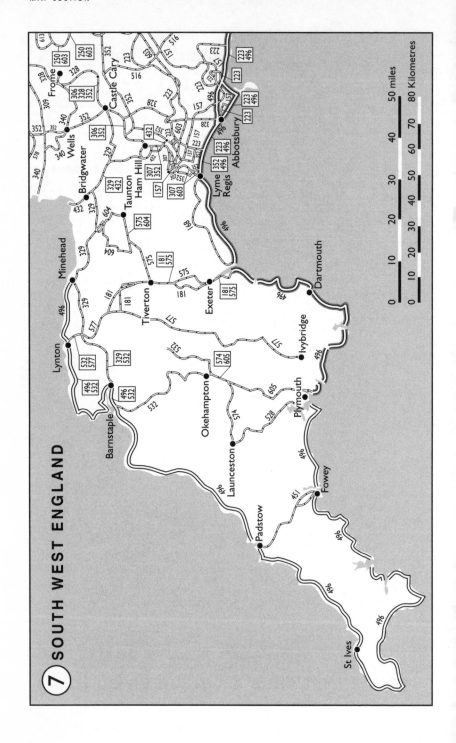

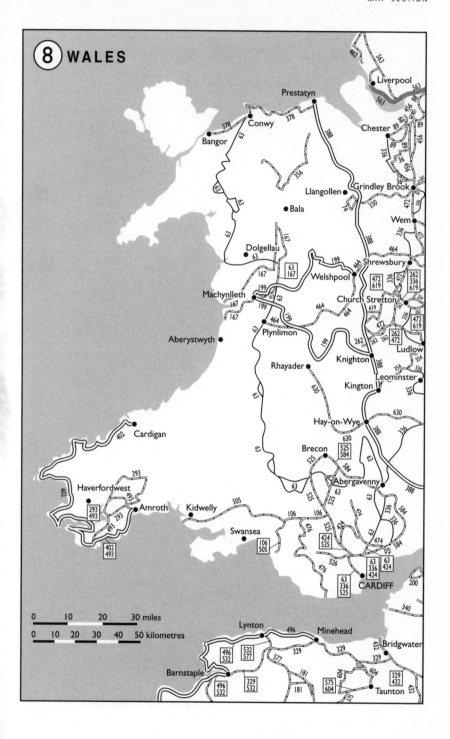

8 WALES

Liverpool

Prestatyn

Conwy

Bangor

Chester

Grindley Brook

Llangollen

Bala

Wem

Dolgellau

Shrewsbury

Welshpool

Machynlleth

Church Stretton

Plynlimon

Aberystwyth

Ludlow

Rhayader

Knighton

Leominster

Kington

Hay-on-Wye

Cardigan

Brecon

Abergavenny

Haverfordwest

Amroth

Kidwelly

Swansea

CARDIFF

| 0 | 10 | 20 | 30 miles |
| 0 | 10 | 20 | 30 | 40 | 50 kilometres |

Lynton

Minehead

Bridgwater

Barnstaple

Taunton

UNWAYMARKED ROUTES

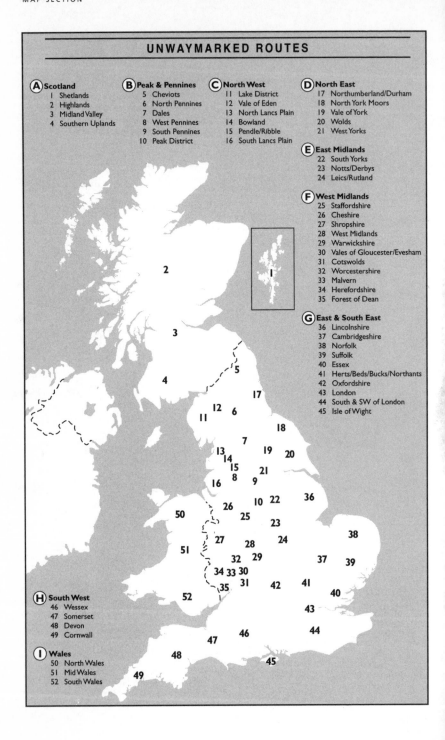

A Scotland
1 Shetlands
2 Highlands
3 Midland Valley
4 Southern Uplands

B Peak & Pennines
5 Cheviots
6 North Pennines
7 Dales
8 West Pennines
9 South Pennines
10 Peak District

C North West
11 Lake District
12 Vale of Eden
13 North Lancs Plain
14 Bowland
15 Pendle/Ribble
16 South Lancs Plain

D North East
17 Northumberland/Durham
18 North York Moors
19 Vale of York
20 Wolds
21 West Yorks

E East Midlands
22 South Yorks
23 Notts/Derbys
24 Leics/Rutland

F West Midlands
25 Staffordshire
26 Cheshire
27 Shropshire
28 West Midlands
29 Warwickshire
30 Vales of Gloucester/Evesham
31 Cotswolds
32 Worcestershire
33 Malvern
34 Herefordshire
35 Forest of Dean

G East & South East
36 Lincolnshire
37 Cambridgeshire
38 Norfolk
39 Suffolk
40 Essex
41 Herts/Beds/Bucks/Northants
42 Oxfordshire
43 London
44 South & SW of London
45 Isle of Wight

H South West
46 Wessex
47 Somerset
48 Devon
49 Cornwall

I Wales
50 North Wales
51 Mid Wales
52 South Wales

GEOGRAPHICAL GUIDE TO THE UNWAYMARKED ROUTES

Note: All unwaymarked routes are listed, including the small selection of important or strategic routes that are shown on the regional maps. The routes are split into a mixture of geographical and administrative areas. This is not particularly consistent but it is hoped that it will give an indication of the walking areas covered. A route may appear in more than one area. Where areas overlap, e.g. Dales and North Yorkshire, the geographical takes precedence over the administrative. Some old county names are included.

* indicates route shown in the map section

A   Scotland

1   Shetlands: *467*
2   Highlands: *64*, 103, 184*, 477, 553*
3   Midland Valley: *103, 173*, 186*
4   Southern Uplands: *196*

B   Peak & Pennines

5   Cheviots: *91, 268, 278, 422*, 552*
6   North Pennines: *206, 230, 257, 278, 422*, 579*
7   Dales: *4, 5, 8, 10, 49, 59, 73, 102*, 136, 183, 206, 222, 232, 253, 277, 287, 300, 318, 323, 364, 368, 369, 372, 407, 414, 423, 426, 463, 475, 522, 547, 548, 551, 554, 555, 556, 559, 564, 565, 566, 567, 570, 573, 591, 610, 635, 636, 637, 638*
8   West Pennines: *14, 15, 127, 128, 129, 193, 300, 377, 407, 411, 420, 438, 500, 558, 572, 576, 599, 622*
9   South Pennines: *6, 43, 50, 56, 62, 110, 151, 162, 193, 206, 229, 241, 334, 357, 362, 406, 407, 494, 495, 555, 564, 572*
10   Peak District: *30, 43, 62, 130, 138, 143, 144, 145, 146, 153, 154, 162, 206, 213, 236, 237, 269, 308, 311, 313, 322, 399, 400, 407, 415, 434, 444, 449, 450, 466, 494, 536, 537, 546, 548, 555, 614, 615, 617*

C   North West

11   Lake District: *5, 19, 24, 102*, 111, 121, 132, 160, 161, 163, 194, 195, 205, 238, 251, 274, 278, 279, 280, 281, 282, 283, 284, 288, 289, 379, 390, 409, 480, 542, 543, 553, 562, 590, 608, 611, 620*
12   Vale of Eden: *132, 172, 277, 278, 511, 608*
13   North Lancashire Plain: *288, 289, 414, 543, 559*
14   Bowland: *49, 81, 98, 188, 227, 372, 543, 564, 622*
15   Pendle/Ribble: *81, 98, 287, 403, 564, 622*
16   South Lancashire Plain: *287, 300, 494, 543*

D   North East

17   Northumberland and Durham: *165, 166, 206, 386, 422*, 468, 579, 580, 581*
18   North York Moors: *33, 102*, 177, 217, 218, 252, 326, 364, 367, 383, 384, 385, 455, 460, 461, 548, 555, 612, 618*
19   Vale of York: *7, 27, 102*, 217, 242, 364, 369, 414, 555, 559, 612, 635*
20   Wolds: *83, 170, 245, 380, 555*
21   West Yorkshire: *8, 50*

Continued...

E   East Midlands

22   South Yorks: *30, 331, 466, 555*
23   Notts and Derbys: *30, 90, 152, 204, 302, 315, 568*
24   Leics and Rutland: *31, 85, 86, 204, 302, 448*

F   West Midlands

25   Staffordshire: *34, 70, 94, 99, 118, 327, 471, 507, 508, 546, 568*
26   Cheshire: *11, 29, 99, 206, 316, 327, 336*, 343, 453, 454, 469, 471,*
     529, 568, 585, 598, 621
27   Shropshire: *34, 125, 174, 206, 336*, 353, 435, 469, 470, 524*
28   West Midlands: *34, 35, 359, 471, 507, 517, 625*
29   Warwickshire: *118, 497, 517, 593*
30   Vales of Evesham and Gloucester: *298, 545, 629, 634*
31   Cotswolds: *112, 113, 114, 115, 117, 629, 634*
32   Worcestershire: *3, 70, 82, 125, 174, 206, 273, 333, 381,*
     507, 545, 625, 627, 629, 632
33   Malverns: *206, 332, 350, 629*
34   Herefordshire: *34, 37, 39, 174, 298, 336*, 435, 545, 629*
35   Forest of Dean: *206, 634*

G   East and South East

36   Lincolnshire: *48, 204, 245, 314, 412, 538, 561*
37   Cambridgeshire: *1, 124, 135, 221, 365, 395*
38   Norfolk: *124, 247, 267, 413*
39   Suffolk: *1, 124, 187, 255, 365, 504, 519*
40   Essex: *16, 124, 178, 221, 320, 335, 549, 550*
41   Herts, Beds, Bucks & Northants: *1, 233, 302, 305, 320, 349, 395*
42   Oxfordshire: *114, 270, 395, 629*
43   London: *210, 342*
44   South and South West of London: *20, 21, 26, 53, 104, 192, 225,*
     272, 320, 376, 441, 487, 521, 544*, 609
45   Isle of Wight: *416, 587*

H   South West

46   Wessex: *40, 75, 104, 122, 270, 272, 292, 391, 416, 430, 452, 544*,*
     602, 631
47   Somerset: *54, 75, 84, 104, 203, 292, 418*
48   Devon: *54, 75, 84, 147, 148, 149, 182, 203, 292, 430, 431, 433, 473*
49   Cornwall: *75, 290, 292, 481*

I   Wales

50   North Wales: *13, 18, 63*, 69, 100, 105, 316, 317, 339, 389, 457, 469,*
     482, 483, 484, 485, 486, 553, 601
51   Mid Wales: *34, 63*, 67, 105, 174, 353, 421, 435, 457*
52   South Wales: *39, 51, 63*, 66, 75, 105, 336*, 457, 527*

Het parfum - *De reisgids*

Vertaald door Ger Boer

Oliver Mittelbach

Het parfum - *De reisgids*

2006 Prometheus Amsterdam

Jan. 2007

Oorspronkelijke titel *Auf den Spuren von Patrick Süskinds*
'Das Parfum'. Eine Reise zu Romanschauplätzen
© 2006 Oliver Mittelbach
© 2006 Nederlandse vertaling Uitgeverij Prometheus en Ger Boer
Omslagontwerp Marieke Oele
www.uitgeverijprometheus.nl
ISBN-10 90 446 0945 9
ISBN-13 978 90 446 0945 5

Inhoud

In het spoor van een moordenaar

De in 1985 verschenen roman *Das Parfum – Die Geschichte eines Mörders* behoort met een verkoopcijfer van ongeveer twaalf miljoen exemplaren tot de meest succesvolle Duits-talige romans aller tijden. Meer dan negen jaar achtereen kwam Patrick Süskinds boek voor op de bestsellerslijst van *Der Spiegel*, maar ook op soortgelijke lijsten in onder ande-re de vs, Groot-Brittannië, Frankrijk, Spanje, Italië en het Nederlandse taalgebied was het boek in vertaling lange tijd vertegenwoordigd.

Grenouille, de held van het verhaal, leeft en woont in een Parijs dat volstrekt verschilt van de stad die wij nu kennen. Zijn tijd is de achttiende eeuw en zijn milieu het stinkendste deel van een stad die volgens tijdgenoten in z'n geheel al ver-schrikkelijk stonk. Wij, moderne, hygiënische mensen, zou-

den er vermoedelijk niet overleven. Intrigerend is dat de meeste plekken waar de taferelen in de roman zich afspelen, er inderdaad precies zo uitzagen als Süskind ze beschrijft. Maar sinds de tijd van Grenouille is natuurlijk wel 250 jaar verlopen en veel van 'zijn' straten, pleinen en buurten zijn intussen sterk veranderd. Toch zijn er nog genoeg sporen van te vinden – voor wie weet waar hij moet zoeken.

Ontdek dat 'andere' Parijs! Ontdek bijvoorbeeld dat in de directe omgeving van het huidige Forum des Halles, naast de straat waar Grenouille geboren werd, in diens tijd het grootste kerkhof van de stad lag. Allang ontruimd natuurlijk, maar een bezoek aan de catacomben, waar de resten uit die en uit vele andere Parijse begraafplaatsen nu keurig geordend langs de wanden zijn opgestapeld, zet de verbeeldingskracht over die tijd zeker aan het werk.

Maar na de stank zoekt onze held Grenouille beter riekende oorden op en belandt hij in de Provence en aan de Côte d'Azur. En in de parfumstad Grasse kent men de roem van de roman *Het parfum* beter dan waar ook: wie hier de sporen van de bestseller wil volgen, kan zich melden voor een 'Parfumtoer', georganiseerd door het bureau voor vreemdelingenverkeer van de stad.

Het wereldwijde succes van de roman – hij werd in niet minder dan 42 talen vertaald – heeft uiteraard de belangstelling van de filmindustrie gewekt. Er zijn na het verschijnen van de roman bijna twee decennia voorbijgegaan voordat uiteindelijk de filmrechten werden verkocht, waarbij de keuze viel op de Duitse producer Bernd Eichinger. Wat volgde was een uitgebreide zoektocht naar plaatsen waar de historische scènes gedraaid konden worden. In Parijs zelf wa-

ren de producer en zijn team gauw uitgekeken – er was te veel veranderd. In Spanje echter, met name in Barcelona en zijn omgeving, vonden ze mooie, goed onderhouden straten en zelfs hele dorpen uit de Middeleeuwen en daaropvolgende perioden. Hier konden de belangrijke buitenopnames worden gemaakt, meestal onder enorme publieke belangstelling.

Lezer en liefhebber van *Het parfum*: wie de sporen van de roman achterna wil reizen, komt terecht op de mooiste plekjes van Frankrijk en Spanje, in de Provence en aan de Côte d'Azur, in Catalonië en in de wereldstad Barcelona – de prachtige decors van een literaire reis die volstrekt ontspannen ondernomen kan worden, zelfs door jonge meisjes… want Grenouille moordt niet meer.

VAN STANK NAAR GEURIGHEID

In het spoor van Patrick Süskinds roman in Parijs

In zijn roman Het parfum *plaatst Patrick Süskind de lezer in het Parijs van de achttiende eeuw. Het verhaal over de griezelige moordenaar Grenouille speelt zich er af tussen 1739 en 1789. Het Parijs waarin hij leeft wordt nog niet gekenmerkt door schitterende boulevards en luxe, maar eerder door nauwe steegjes, ruimtegebrek en een totaal gebrek aan hygiëne. Zijn milieu is dat van de armen en de wezen, de markten en de ambachtslieden.*

HET PARIJS VAN GRENOUILLE

In het begin van de achttiende eeuw was Parijs met zijn zevenhonderdduizend inwoners de grootste stad ter wereld. De Zonnekoning, Lodewijk XIV (1638-1715), was een mecenas voor kunst, literatuur en wetenschap en naar het voorbeeld van Rome liet hij Parijs verfraaien met indrukwekkende gebouwen, pleinen en parken. De hoofdstad van Frankrijk ontwikkelde zich zo tot het architectonische, stedenbouwkundige en culturele voorbeeld voor Europa.

Maar onder dit glanzende oppervlak zag het er heel anders uit. De feodale heffingen en pachtprijzen die op het platteland aan de grondbezitters en de kerk moesten worden betaald, maakten dat vele Franse boeren in abjecte armoede leefden. In de hoop daar een beter leven te kunnen vinden, ontvluchtten velen van hen het platteland en trokken naar de hoofdstad. Maar met dezelfde snelheid waarmee de menigte binnenstroomde kon Parijs zich niet uitbreiden: sinds het einde van de zestiende eeuw was het

◄ Een fraai stadhuisplein - waar vroeger heel wat hoofden rolden...

▲ Het schitterende uitzicht vanaf de Notre-Dame

inwoneraantal er verdubbeld. Hierdoor ontstonden over-bevolkte achterstandswijken waar de mensen onder ramp-zalige omstandigheden hun bestaan rekten. De heersende situatie met betrekking tot de hygiëne is voor ons niet meer voor te stellen.

In de slechts tweeëntwintig zinnen tellende tweede alinea van zijn roman gebruikt Patrick Süskind niet minder dan twintig keer een afleiding van het woord 'stinken'. Dat deze intensieve opsomming niet overdreven is, blijkt wel uit het verslag van de contemporaine schrijver Louis-Sébastien Mercier, die in zijn *Tableau de Paris* optekende:

> *Nauwe, slecht aangelegde straten, veel te hoge huizen die de vrije circulatie van lucht in de weg staan, slachthuizen, vis-markten, gierputten en begraafplaatsen – alles draagt bij aan de pestilentie van de atmosfeer, alles zuigt zich vol met schade-lijke partikels met als gevolg dat de lucht overal waar hij aan-eengesloten blijft hangen, vet en nauwelijks nog adembaar wordt. De buitenproportioneel hoge bebouwing onthoudt de bewoners van de onderste verdiepingen bovendien het licht, zelfs wanneer de zon op zijn hoogste punt staat. Er heerst altijd een vage schemering. (Mercier Bild, blz. 39 e.v.)*

Een behoorlijke riolering bestond in Grenouilles tijd nog niet. Daarvoor in de plaats was ieder gebouw uitgerust met een drekput. Het logische uitvloeisel daarvan was hoogst onsmakelijk.

Deze talloze latrines verspreiden een pestilente stank en maken vooral 's nachts, wanneer ze geleegd worden, hele wijken on-leefbaar. Reeds vele ongelukkigen die, door hun ellende ge-dwongen, het gevaarlijke en weerzinwekkende werk van put-jesschepper hebben opgenomen, zijn daarbij om het leven gekomen. Vaak zijn de putten ook nog slecht geconstrueerd, waardoor hun inhoud wegsijpelt naar nabijgelegen bronnen. Maar hierdoor niet in het minst gehinderd en zoals hij altijd al gedaan heeft haalt de bakker evengoed hier zijn water. Dat hij daarmee het belangrijkste voedingsmiddel van de bevolking ontegenzeggelijk besmet met allerlei ziektekiemen, valt niet te betwijfelen. Ook komt het wel voor dat de putjesscheppers voor het krieken van de dag de gier in een nabijgelegen afwaterings-greppel of trottoirgoot gooien om zich van hun stinkende last te ontdoen en zich er een vermoeiende tocht mee door de stad te besparen. Dan stroomt die afschuwelijke smurrie langzaam over de straten in de richting van de Seine, aan de oevers waar-van de waterdragers hun emmers vullen – met het water dat de geharde Parijzenaars moeten drinken, of ze dat willen of niet. (Mercier Bild, blz. 41 e.v.)

Dan was er nog de uitwaseming van de mensen. Sinds de zestiende eeuw was het baden en wassen verboden dankzij het bijgeloof dat de door het badwater zacht geworden huid ziektes kon opnemen. Ook de katholieke kerk, die zich op morele gronden tegen het baden in het openbaar verzette, droeg bij aan de stank. Zelfs de koning hield zich hieraan. Zo zou volgens de overlevering Lodewijk XIV in de jaren tussen 1647 en 1711 slechts één keer een bad genomen hebben. Hij had zweetvoeten die zo'n penetrante lucht moeten hebben verspreid dat zelfs de meest door de wol geverfde hovelingen die stank niet meer konden verdragen. Pas in de tweede helft van de zeventiende eeuw begon men er geleidelijk aan an-ders over te denken, waarmee Parijs een betere lucht kreeg.

HET HALLENDISTRICT

De protagonist van Süskinds roman, Jean-Baptiste Grenouille, wordt in juli 1738 achter een viskraam in de Rue aux Fers geboren. Zijn moeder wil hem stiekem laten creperen, maar Grenouille wenst te leven en maakt met een kreet zijn bestaan kenbaar.

De Rue aux Fers, de geboortegrond van Grenouille, zal men op een recente stadsplattegrond vergeefs zoeken omdat hij onder die naam niet meer bestaat. In 1864 werd deze doorgang tussen de Rue Saint-Denis en de Rue Baltard bij de Rue Berger getrokken.

Al in de Middeleeuwen was dit de plaats waar de belangrijkste markt van Parijs werd gehouden. Ook werden er in die tijd reeds kleine overdekte markten opgericht. In de loop van de eeuwen kwamen er steeds meer markten bij, steeds meer mensen van allerlei slag aantrekkend, waardoor deze handelsplek langzamerhand verpauperde tot een van de schimmigste en duisterste uithoeken van Parijs. Kort na zijn machtsovername in het midden van de negentiende eeuw gaf Napoleon III de architect Victor Baltard de opdracht het stadsgebied een nieuw aanzien te geven. Baltard ontwierp

▲ Het Hallenkwartier in de tijd van Grenouille

▲ Viskramen staan hier niet meer, maar een visje eten bij McDonald's kan nog wel

twaalf grote, gietijzeren markthallen waarvan elk voor een ambacht bestemd was. Tussen 1852 en 1870 werden er tien van gebouwd en ook toen al werden ze 'les Halles' genoemd. De twee laatste kwamen in 1936 tot stand. Meer dan honderd jaar drukten deze hallen van ijzer en glas hun stempel op het dagelijkse leven van Parijs. Napoleon III noemde de markt 'het Louvre van het volk' en de schrijver Emile Zola maakte er met zijn roman uit 1873 'Le Ventre de Paris' van, 'De Buik van Parijs'.

Na achthonderd jaar bestaan te hebben, moest de markt verdwijnen. De smalle straten konden de twintigste-eeuwse vrachtwagens voor aan- en afvoer niet meer aan. Chaotische opstoppingen waren aan de orde van de dag, het lawaai en de uitlaatgassen waren niet meer te harden. Tegen het einde van de jaren zestig werd de Parijse groothandelsmarkt naar een buitenplaats in de buurt van de luchthaven Orly verplaatst. Dit Rungis is ook vandaag nog het summum in kwaliteitsproducten voor het gastronomische Europa. In 1972 werden de oude Halles uiteindelijk gesloopt.

Alleen hal acht, waar ooit de markt van de poeliers heeft gestaan, bleef behouden als historisch monument. Hij werd tien kilometer ten oosten van Parijs herbouwd. De gemeente Nogent-sur-Marne heeft dit 'Pavillon Baltard' nu in ge-

▲ De laatste van 'Les Halles' staat in Nogent-sur-Marne

bruik als cultureel centrum. Op de zevenentwintighonderd vierkante meter van zijn vloeroppervlak vinden nu concerten, congressen, feesten en tentoonstellingen plaats. Bij het zien van dit mooie historische gebouw begrijpt men heel goed dat de sloop van de Halles in Parijs een storm van protest heeft doen opsteken.

Intussen gaapte midden in Parijs een reusachtige bouwput. Lang werd gediscussieerd en gepolemiseerd; plannen werden aangedragen en verworpen, tot in 1979 eindelijk het Forum des Halles tot stand kwam. Vier verdiepingen hoog steekt het grootste winkel- en cultuurcentrum van Parijs de lucht in. Er zijn bioscopen, theaters, restaurants, cafés en een zwembad.

Het terras voor de halfronde constructie van glas en metaal die aan de napoleontische Halles zouden moeten herinneren, verschaft uitzicht over het gehele complex en daarachter op de Saint Eustachekerk. Maar het eigenlijke leven speelt zich vooral onder de grond af. Daar bevinden zich op een vloeroppervlak van zo'n zeven hectare bijna tweehonderd winkels, waaronder vele boetieks. Het is een van de best lopende winkelcentra van Europa. Ook verder is het er een drukte van belang want onder het Forum bevindt zich bovendien een reusachtig metrostation dat dagelijks bijna een miljoen reizigers verwerkt.

Rondom dit centrum vind je tegenwoordig een bonte mengeling van zaken waaronder een massa boetieks, souvenirwinkeltjes en fastfoodrestaurants, een combinatie die voornamelijk toeristen aantrekt, maar ook veel jongeren uit de allochtone gemeenschappen in de voorsteden, voor wie het Forum des Halles het belangrijkste trefpunt in het centrum van Parijs is. Vooral 's nachts komen daklozen, zwervers en schimmige leden van de grotestadscultuur hier samen, wat de plek in die uren niet bepaald aantrekkelijk maakt.

In de stadspolitiek van Parijs is inmiddels het besef doorgedrongen dat er iets gedaan moest worden om de 'buik van Parijs' een nieuwe aantrekkelijkheid te verschaffen. Een hiervoor uitgeschreven prijsvraag voor architecten werd aan het einde van 2004 gewonnen door de Franse architect David Mangin. Zijn ontwerp voor de nieuwe omgeving van het Forum des Halles toont overwegend ruimte voor groenvoorzieningen, een aantal brede lanen en een glazen overkapping over een deel van het terrein. Het startschot voor deze werkzaamheden zou begin 2007 gegeven worden.

▲ Een constructie uit glas en metaal

PLACE DE GRÈVE

Grenouilles moeder werd als meervoudige kindermoordenares ter dood veroordeeld en op de Place de Grève onthoofd.

De Place de Grève is al bekend uit de twaalfde eeuw. Het plein strekt zich uit van de huidige Rue de Rivoli tot aan de haven bij de Seine-oever. Hier bevindt zich een kiezelstrand (Frans: grève) dat het plein zijn naam verleende. Maar in tegenstelling tot de plezierige associatie die het woord 'strand' algauw oproept, is de geschiedenis van het plein eerder huiveringwekkend. Hier rolden immers ontelbare hoofden. Tussen 1310 en 1830 vonden op dit plein vrijwel alle publieke terechtstellingen van Parijs plaats – en dat waren er niet weinig. Ook de eerste onthoofding met behulp van de guillotine werd hier, in 1792, verricht.

Grenouilles moeder heeft, relatief gezien, met haar snelle executie nog geluk gehad. Ze had ook terechtgesteld kunnen worden na een langdurige martelstraf. Levend verbranden, radbraken en vierendelen waren nauwelijks uitzonderingen.

▲ Op de Place de Grève was voldoende ruimte om de massaal op de terechtstellingen toestromende kijklustigen plaats te bieden

De gruwelijkste doodstraf die op dit plein werd uitgevoerd is waarschijnlijk die van Robert-François Damiens in 1757 geweest. Damiens had met een mes een aanslag gepleegd op de koning, die er evenwel met een lichte verwonding afkwam. De voorgeschreven straf voor een moordaanslag op de koning was dood door vierendeling. Maar voor het zover kwam werd de hand die het mes had vastgehouden eerst zo lang met gloeiende tangen bewerkt dat hij afviel. De reeds halfdode ongelukkige werd vervolgens tussen de paarden geketend, maar hoe hard die dieren ook trokken, ze slaagden er niet in het lichaam uiteen te rijten. Het mes van de beul kwam eraan te pas om het karwei af te maken.

De terechtstellingen waren voor grote menigten toegankelijk en die stroomden dan ook toe om ze bij te wonen:

> *Het gemene volk verlaat zijn werkplaatsen en winkels en schaart zich rond het schavot. Het wil met eigen ogen zien hoe de misdadiger de Grote Daad verricht, hoe hij op pijnlijke wijze en voor het oog van de toeschouwers zal sterven. (Mercier, p. 117)*

Vonden er geen executies plaats, dan verzamelden zich op de Place de Grève personen die geen werk hadden. Vermoedelijk komt daar de Franse term voor het staken vandaan: 'être en grève'.

Na de laatste terechtstelling in 1830 wilde men afrekenen met het bloederige verleden en werd het plein omgedoopt. De naam die gekozen werd, Place de l'Hôtel de Ville, lag voor de hand omdat hier inderdaad het stadhuis van Parijs staat, het Hôtel de Ville.

Het Hôtel de Ville is het centrale gemeentehuis voor de stad Parijs. Daarnaast heeft ieder arrondissement zijn eigen, kleinere gemeentehuis, de 'Mairie'.

Als eerste stadhuis werd aan de Place de Grève in de zestiende eeuw een gebouw in renaissancestijl opgetrokken. In de revolutie van de Parijse Commune viel dit echter in 1871 aan de vlammen ten prooi. Het nieuwe raadhuis, dat een in-

▲ Het stadhuis van Parijs, het Hôtel de Ville

drukwekkende voorgevel met talrijke torentjes en beeldhouwwerken kreeg, is met zijn lengte van meer dan 110 meter, 85 meter diepte en 48 meter hoogte twee keer zo groot als
het oude en geldt als grootste stadhuis van Europa. Een vir-
tuele rondleiding door het Hôtel de Ville kun je op internet
maken via www.vl.paris.fr/en/.

VOOR HET PUBLIEK:

Adres: Hôtel de Ville; Place de l'Hôtel de Ville.
Openingstijden voor publiek: maandag 10.30, maar de
vrijdag ervoor dient men de tijd telefonisch te verifiëren via
nummer 01 42 76 50 49. Ook voor individuele afspraken kun je
dit nummer bellen. De toegang is gratis.
Groepen kunnen voor een rondleiding een gids krijgen, maar
dienen zes weken van tevoren af te spreken.

CIMETIÈRE DES INNOCENTS

*In de onmiddellijke omgeving van Grenouilles
geboorteplek ligt het kerkhof Cimetière des Innocents,
de Begraafplaats der Onschuldigen. 29 jaren en 26
moorden later keert Grenouille er terug om zijn eigen
dood te vinden.*

Omgeven door de straten Rue aux Fers, Rue de la Ferronne-
rie, Rue de la Lingerie (tegenwoordig Passage des Lingeries
geheten) en Rue Saint-Denis, lag hier volgens Süskind in
zijn roman *Het parfum* de 'stinkendste stad van het hele koninkrijk' (vertaling Ronald Jonkers, p. 8). De Cimetière des
Innocents dankte zijn naam aan een nabijgelegen kerk die
aan de Onnozele Kinderen was gewijd. Tot het einde van de
achttiende eeuw was dit het grootste kerkhof binnen de muren van Parijs.

Reeds in de Gallo-Romeinse tijd werden op deze plek de doden bijgezet. Om de begraafplaats van de aangrenzende
markten te scheiden werd er in de twaalfde eeuw een muur
omheen gebouwd. De doden uit ongeveer twintig parochies
werden op de Cimetière des Innocents begraven, plus die uit

▲ Geen plek om er ontspannen rond te wandelen: de Cimetière des
Innocents in de achttiende eeuw

het ziekenhuis Hôpital Hôtel-Dieu. De snelgroeiende bevolking, epidemieën en hongersnoden maakten dat de ruimte op de begraafplaats al snel ontoereikend was. Om die ruimte te herwinnen werden vanaf de veertiende eeuw zogenaamde knekelhuizen opgericht. De doden werden eerst in de grond begraven omdat men meende dat de ontbinding daarin bijzonder snel verliep. Nadat de huur van het graf, de graftermijn, was verlopen, werden de botten opgegraven en in een knekelhuis opgestapeld. Louis-Sébastien Mercier beschrijft hoe akelig zo'n oord was:

Op de begraafplaats van de Onnozele Kinderen, waar vijftig-duizend doodskoppen bij elkaar liggen opgestapeld, gebeuren dikwijls wonderlijke dingen: een zo'n schedel beweegt en rolt uit zichzelf vooruit en toch lopen de mensen er gewoon langs. Het is een rat die zich in de schedel gedrongen heeft en er niet even gemakkelijk uit ontsnappen kan als hij erin gekropen is. Onder dit knekelpakhuis, dat zeker het afschuwelijkste in de ganse wereld is, leven de ratten tussen de menselijke gebeenten. Ze laten ze door elkaar vallen, omhoog komen en laten zo de indruk ontstaan dat dit volk van doden weer tot leven is geko-men. (Mercier, p. 218)

◄ De enige renaissance-fontein van Parijs

Maar de druk werd groot, de graftermijnen werden steeds korter – tot uiteindelijk ook de nog niet geheel ontbonden lijken weer werden opgegraven, wat in de wijde omgeving een beestachtige stank teweegbracht. De omwonenden protesteerden luidkeels, maar vooralsnog zonder resultaat. Pas nadat in 1779 in de direct aan het kerkhof gelegen Rue de la Lingerie verschillende bewoners in hun huis door het vrijgekomen, verstikkende methaangas om het leven waren gekomen, had ook de politiedirecteur van Parijs er genoeg van: in november 1780 vaardigde hij het bevel uit de Cimetière des Innocents voorgoed te sluiten. In dat jaar lag het maaiveld van de begraafplaats ongeveer tweeënhalve meter boven dat van de omringende straten.

Wat nu aan de orde kwam, was het vinden van een oplossing voor de reeds op het kerkhof liggende doden. Vanaf 1786 begon men de stoffelijke resten naar de in onbruik geraakte steengroeven onder de stad, de catacomben, te brengen. In totaal zouden de overblijfselen van meer dan twee miljoen opgegraven doden uit de Cimetière des Innocents in de catacomben een nieuwe rustplaats krijgen.

De stap van plek der doden naar die van levendigheid was radicaal: op het voormalige kerkhof werd eerst een levensmiddelenmarkt ingericht, de 'Marché des Innocents'. Maar in 1858 kwam men tot bezinning en werd er op die plaats een stadstuin ingericht. Het heet nu Place Joachim du Bellay, maar in de volksmond wordt er nog vaak aan gerefereerd als 'Place des Innocents'. Het is een populair trefpunt voor jongeren, waar alleen de fontein in renaissancestijl nog herinnert aan het weinig fraaie verleden.

Deze Fontaine des Innocents werd tussen 1547 en 1549 ontworpen door de architect Pierre Lescot. De sculpturen zijn van de hand van beeldhouwer Jean Goujon en stellen nimfen voor die water uit kruiken gieten. De fontein maakte ooit deel uit van een groter geheel dat op de hoek van de Rue aux Fers en de Rue Saint-Denis aan de kerk van Saint-Innocents gebouwd was. Toen de kerk, rond dezelfde tijd dat de begraafplaats werd opgeheven, werd gesloopt, verplaatste men in 1788 dit deel naar het heringerichte plein.

EXTRA EXCURSIE:
DE CATACOMBEN VAN PARIJS

Reeds in de Gallo-Romeinse tijd werd onder de drie heuvels Montparnasse, Montrouge en Montsouris naar bouwmateriaal gedolven. De mijngangen die daardoor ontstonden – men veronderstelt dat ongeveer 30 procent van het grondoppervlak van Parijs in feite ondermijnd is – hadden natuurlijk effect op de stabiliteit van de bodem: in 1774 stortte een deel van de tegenwoordige Place Denfert-Rochereau in. Waarmee de opengevallen ruimten te vullen om de bouwbodem zijn stabiliteit terug te geven? De creatieve stedenbouwkundigen van het Parijs uit de achttiende eeuw zagen daar nauwelijks een probleem in – er waren in de stad genoeg overvolle begraafplaatsen die nodig geruimd moesten worden. Aldus vervulden de nieuw gedolven catacomben een dubbele taak.

In april 1786 werden de zogenoemde Catacombes ingewijd. Twee jaar achtereen trokken iedere nacht priesters met dodenkarren door Parijs om de beenderen van de doden van de Cimetière des Innocents naar hun nieuwe verblijfplaats te brengen. Ook de andere begraafplaatsen die binnen de muren van de stad lagen, werden op deze wijze 'ontlast'. Bij deze verplaatste overblijfselen voegden zich al spoedig nieuwe lijken, die van de slachtoffers van de Franse Revolutie. En als er ergens 'egalité' heerst, dan is het wel hier: dich-

▲ Zou hier ook een botje van Grenouille tussen liggen?

◄ Een groteske liefdes-
verklaring

ters en hoeren, dienstmeisjes en straatrovers, madame Pompidour en Maximilian de Robespierre – zij allen liggen hier verenigd onder de aarde. Tot 1860, dus tot bijna een eeuw later, werden nog meer beenderen aan het Ossuarium toegevoegd. In totaal liggen in dit onderaardse labyrint de resten van ongeveer zes miljoen mensen.

Ongeveer tweehonderdduizend bezoekers leggen tegenwoordig jaarlijks het bijna twee kilometer lange skelettenparcours af. De enige officiële weg door de catacomben begint in het ten zuiden van het Quartier Latin gelegen Place Denfert-Rochereau. Een wenteltrap met 131 treden voert 20 meter de diepte in. Daar aangekomen loopt men eerst door een niet bepaald spectaculaire, donkere gang. Het is er zo vochtig dat het water van het gewelfdak druipt. Om de onwennige toerist enigszins het gevoel te geven dat hij zich kan oriënteren, dragen de wanden de straatnaambordjes die ook boven de grond aan de straten te zien zijn. Ten slotte komt men aan een deur die met zwart-witte pijlen is gemerkt. Erboven prijkt de waarschuwing die de bezoeker kan verwachten: 'Arrête! Ici c'est l'empire de la mort.' (Stop! Hier begint het Rijk der Doden.)

Al wat de ogen in het licht van de daartoe meegebrachte zaklantaarns kunnen zien, zijn beenderen. Netjes om en om

▲ Een uit knekels opgetrokken muur

gesorteerd – een laag botten en een laag schedels – liggen hier de resten opgestapeld die de wanden van de gangen vormen. Gedenkborden en houten kruizen vermelden uit welke begraafplaatsen de beenderen naar dit reusachtig ossuarium zijn gebracht en wanneer dat is gebeurd. In het begin had men de skeletten nog zonder veel omhaal door een schacht naar beneden gegooid, maar vanaf 1810 betoonde men de doden meer respect. Beenderen en schedels werden zorgvuldig gesorteerd en netjes opgestapeld. Zo liefdeloos als eerder alles door elkaar was gegooid, zo veel moeite getroostte men zich later met de ordening van de resten. Deze nieuwe rangschikking vertoont ook verrassende kanten in de vorm van bizarre, netjes verzorgde ornamenten: hier een kruis met een hart, daar gekruiste pijpbeenderen en verderop een fries van bekkenbeenderen. Macaber of artistiek? Ie-

VOOR HET PUBLIEK:

Adres: Catacombes de Paris; 1 Place Denfert-Rochereau, telefoon 01 43 22 47 63

Openingstijden: Dinsdag tot en met zondag van 10 tot en met 16 uur, maandag en sommige feestdagen gesloten.

Toegang: 5 euro, voor bezoekers van 14 tot 26 jaar 2,50 euro, voor kinderen tot en met 13 jaar gratis.

dere bezoeker moet dat maar voor zichzelf bepalen. Ook zijn er bordjes te zien met aforismen die betrekking hebben op de dood, zoals:

Waar is hij, de Dood? Altijd in de toekomst of in het verleden. Nauwelijks is hij tegenwoordig, is hij er niet meer.

Treurig was de beroemdheid die een man met de naam Philibert Aspairt in 1793 ten deel viel. Hij was in de meer dan driehonderd kilometer lange, onderaardse gangen de weg kwijtgeraakt en pas elf jaar later werd zijn geraamte gevonden. Alleen dankzij het feit dat hij in zijn zak een sleutel had gedragen, kon hij worden geïdentificeerd.

RUE SAINT-DENIS

De kleine Grenouille verhuist van de ene min naar de volgende omdat geen van hen hem langer dan een paar dagen wil en kan verdragen. Het kind, zeggen ze, is zo gulzig dat hij voor twee drinkt. Uiteindelijk wordt Grenouille aan de min Jeanne Bussie overgedragen. Zij woont in de Rue Saint-Denis.

▲ Parijs, stad der liefde (!)

◄ Een van de mooiste passages van Parijs: Passage du Grand Cerf

De Rue Saint-Denis, de straat waarin Grenouilles min Jeanne Bussie woonde, is een van de oudste van de stad en is allerminst zomaar een straat. In een ver verleden is hier heel wat spectaculairs te zien geweest. Zo reden de Franse koningen, met hun gevolg op weg naar de kroning in de kathedraal van Notre-Dame, op feestelijke wijze langs deze oude Romeinse straatweg. En was een koningsleven afgelopen, dan werd hij eveneens door de Rue Saint-Denis naar zijn begraafplaats in de noordelijk gelegen basiliek van Saint-Denis gedragen.

Maar die koninklijke glitter van toen is nu wel helemaal verdwenen. In het zuidelijke deel, bij het Forum des Halles, is de straat autovrij. Hier bevinden zich talloze cafés en spijkerbroekenwinkeltjes. Loop je in noordelijke richting, dan zie je de seksboetieks en peepshows talrijker worden. Daartussen staan in de deuropeningen van de hotels die hun kamers per uur verhuren de dames die van seks hun beroep hebben gemaakt op klanten te wachten; niet zelden is hun aan te zien dat ze al vele jaren in het vak zitten. Dit stuk straat is tegenwoordig de bekendste 'rosse buurt' van de stad, in de Franse media al uitgeroepen tot synoniem voor prostitutie. Nog verder naar het noorden verandert het beeld weer. Hier begint de wijk Le Sentier en die is het centrum van de Franse kledingindustrie. Maar wie denkt hier uitgebreid te kunnen shoppen, komt bedrogen uit: aardige boetieks zijn hier niet te vinden, alleen magazijnen van de groothandel.

Wat in deze straat beslist bezienswaardig is, zijn de passages. Er is bijvoorbeeld de elegante, onlangs gerenoveerde Passage du Grand Cerf uit 1835 en bij huisnummer 237 de nog oudere, uit 1799 stammende Passage du Caire met haar Egyptisch geïnspireerde inrichting. Ze is niet alleen de oudste nog gebruikte passage in Parijs, maar met haar overdekte lengte van 370 meter tevens de langste. De naam ('Passage van Caïro') is gekozen ter herinnering aan Napoleons roemruchte veldtocht naar de piramiden van Egypte die plaatsvond terwijl de doorgang werd gebouwd.

Aan het noordelijke uiteinde van de straat, waar de Rue Saint-Denis samenkomt met de Boulevard Saint-Denis, bevinden zich twee triomfbogen, de Porte Saint-Denis en de Porte Saint-Martin. Ze werden aan het einde van de zeventiende eeuw gebouwd ter ere van Lodewijk XIV ter herinnering aan diens overwinningen.

ACHTERGROND: *VONDELINGEN EN MINNEN*

Zoals overal in het Europa van de achttiende eeuw was ook in Parijs het te vondeling leggen van kinderen aan de orde van de dag, vooral als gevolg van armoede. Gelijke tred houdend met de bevolkingstoename vervielen hele lagen van de maatschappij tot verpaupering. Om in leven te kunnen blijven moesten man en vrouw beiden hard werken zodat voor het hebben van kinderen, vooral ook door het tijdrovende zogen, geen tijd was. Buitenechtelijke kinderen was dit lot vanzelfsprekend het vaakst beschoren. De moeder zag voor hun verzorging meestal geen mogelijkheden en bovendien maakte het hebben van een kind de kans om een echtgenoot te vinden wel heel erg klein.

De kroniekschrijver Mercier bericht over het enorme aantal te vondeling gelegde kinderen:

Over het algemeen worden zes- tot zevenduizend kinderen jaarlijks door hun ouders afgestaan om in vondelingentehuizen te worden opgenomen. En dat terwijl het aantal borelingen van de rest van de bevolking de veertien- tot vijftienduizend niet overschrijdt. (Mercier, p. 247)

Grenouille had het geluk niet naar een vondelingenhuis te zijn gebracht. De omstandigheden waren er dramatisch en door ziektes en honger overleefde het overgrote deel van de bewoners hun verblijf niet lang.

Hoeveel van deze zes- tot zevenduizend leven er na tien of twaalf jaar nog? Het is huiveringwekkend! Hoogstens honderdtachtig en dan overdrijven wij niet: het zijn betrouwbare bronnen die ons vertellen dat de dood (een dood die erbarmen heeft of juist meedogenloos is?) zich dergelijke enorme aantallen vondelingen toe-eigent. (Mercier, p. 247)

In andere landen was het niet veel beter: van de in totaal vijftienduizend zuigelingen die tussen 1755 en 1773 in het grootste vondelingenhuis van Toscane werden afgeleverd, haalden twee op de drie hun eerste verjaardag niet.

Het waren niet alleen vondelingen die aan een min werden overgedragen. Ook kinderen van ouders die hen zelf niet konden verzorgen kregen vaak een voedster. De registratie van de Parijse politieprefecten uit 1780 laat zien dat van de eenentwintigduizend kinderen die in dat jaar waren geboren, slechts duizend door de eigen moeder werden gezoogd, nog eens duizend door een huismin en de rest, het allergrootste deel, zegge negentienduizend, door voedsters die op het platteland leefden.

Het transport van de baby's naar het platteland was uitputtend en gevaarlijk. Opeengepakt in manden werden de kleintjes op karren of op de rug van ezels geladen en hotsend en botsend door de streek gereden. Een deel van hen stierf onderweg al.

Was het doel bereikt, dan werden de meeste baby's met vele andere in een kleine ruimte ondergebracht. Het zogen van twee of meer zuigelingen door een enkele min was gebruikelijk. Alleen op die manier kon de min genoeg geld verdienen om te kunnen leven.

EXTRA EXCURSIE: *CENTRE POMPIDOU*

Het Centre National d'Art et de Culture Georges Pompidou, kortweg Centre Pompidou, werd in 1977 geopend en kan nu met recht een symbolisch bouwwerk voor Parijs worden genoemd. Gemiddeld worden per dag 25.000 bezoekers geteld en dat is vijfmaal het aantal dat oorspronkelijk verwacht werd.

De initiator van het project was de toenmalige president van Frankrijk, Georges Pompidou (1911-1974), een bewonderaar van moderne kunst. Het was zijn bedoeling om midden in Parijs een groot centrum voor kunst en cultuur te laten verrijzen. Een prijsvraag voor architecten leverde 680 inzendingen uit de hele wereld op, waarvan die van het toen nog jonge architectenduo Renzo Piano en Richard Rogers werd gehonoreerd. Wat de twee voor ogen stond was een gebouw dat niet, zoals de meeste cultuurtempels, de bezoeker intimideerde. Het nieuwe centrum zou open en vernieuwend moeten zijn – en in die opzet zijn ze zeker geslaagd.

▲ Steigerwerk: nee! Architectuur: ja!

◀ Meer dan vijf miljoen
bezoekers lopen jaarlijks
het Centre Pompidou in
en uit

Toen op 31 januari 1977 de 160 meter lange constructie na
een bouwtijd van vijf jaar werd geopend, vroegen nogal wat
bezoekers zich af wanneer dan de 'steigers zouden worden
weggehaald'. Critici spraken van een 'olieraffinaderij in het
stadscentrum'. Een wonder is dat niet, want het Centre Pompidou is werkelijk buitenissig: niet alleen hebben de bouw-
meesters de dragende constructie van het gebouw aan de
buitenzijde geplaatst, ook de leidingen en andere utilitaire
voorzieningen bevinden zich daar, voorzien van een van
buiten zichtbare kleurcode. Leidingen voor lucht (aircondi-
tioning) zijn blauw, voor water groen en voor elektriciteit
geel. Liften en roltrappen zijn rood gemarkeerd, terwijl van
de laatste bijzonder is dat ze door plexiglazen tunnels voeren, waardoor ze in alle weersomstandigheden kunnen worden gebruikt. Met deze ongebruikelijke aanpak hebben de
architecten bereikt dat het weidse interieur van dit reusachtige gebouw nauwelijks verstoord wordt door pilaren, wat

voor exposities en voorstellingen een scala aan mogelijkheden biedt.

De grote toeloop van bezoekers liet aan het gebouw zware sporen achter en reeds na twintig jaar was een renovatie nodig, waarbij ook de binnenruimten opnieuw werden ingericht. Het museum voor moderne kunst kreeg eens zo veel plaats als het eerder had, de bibliotheek beslaat nu drie verdiepingen en heeft een eigen ingang gekregen. Twee jaar duurde de renovatie, waarna het vernieuwde kunst- en cultuurcentrum precies aan het begin van het millennium heropend kon worden.

In het museum voor moderne kunst (Musée National d'Art Moderne) is een van de belangrijkste collecties van werken uit de twintigste eeuw gehuisvest. Ze omvat bijna 53.000 kunstwerken, waarvan natuurlijk slechts een klein deel in de steeds wisselende tentoonstellingen geëxposeerd kan worden. Welke dat op een bepaald moment zijn, kan worden gevonden op de website van het museum. Veel disciplines in de kunst zijn in de verzameling vertegenwoordigd met schilderijen, beeldhouwwerken, plastieken, foto's, video-installaties, architectuur en designobjecten.

De tentoonstellingen bevinden zich op de vierde en de

vijfde verdieping; op de vierde zijn werken van na 1960 te zien en op de vijfde die uit de periode tussen 1905 en 1960, met werken van Matisse, Picasso, Braque, Dali, Kandinsky en vele anderen. De beide verdiepingen worden op het moment gerenoveerd, zodat telkens maar één kan worden bezocht. De heropening van het geheel is gepland voor 2007. De bovenste etage van het Centre Pompidou is gereserveerd voor bijzondere exposities. Maar ook is daar het Restaurant Georges gevestigd met een dakterras dat een prachtig uitzicht biedt op de wijk Beaubourg.

Een bijkomende reden van de hoge bezoekersaantallen van het Centre Pompidou is de Bibliothèque Publique d'Information, de grote openbare bibliotheek van Frankrijk. Deze is vrij toegankelijk, men heeft er een pasje noch een inschrijving voor nodig. Er zijn op drie verdiepingen achttienhonderd zitplaatsen waar gelezen kan worden, maar die zijn voortdurend bezet en voor de ingang staan dikwijls lange rijen wachtenden.

Het Centre Pompidou mag in zijn interieur dan veel aantrekkelijks bieden, toch komen veel bezoekers voor de sfeer die erbuiten, op het voorplein, te genieten valt. Het doel van de architecten is geweest naar het voorbeeld van de Piazza

▲ De indrukwekkende entreehal van het Centre Pompidou

▲ Ook buiten het cultuurpaleis kan men van kunst genieten

del Campo in Siena in het hart van de stad een openbare en levendige ruimte te scheppen. Vooral in de zomer is op deze 'piazza' van allerlei te beleven: kunstschilders, jongleurs, mimespelers, vuurspuwers en straatmuzikanten laten hun kunsten horen en zien – niet op georganiseerde wijze zoals binnen in het gebouw, maar spontaan en improviserend en niet zelden met de participatie van het publiek.

VOOR HET PUBLIEK:

Adres: Centre Pompidou, Place Georges Pompidou, telefoon 01 44 78 12 33

Openingstijden: Het Centre Pompidou is dagelijks, m.u.v. dinsdag, geopend van 11 tot 22 uur.

Museum en exposities: Dagelijks, m.u.v. dinsdag, van 11 tot 21 uur. Na 20 uur geen toegang meer.

Bibliotheek: maandag, woensdag, donderdag en vrijdag van 12 tot 22 uur; zaterdag, zondag en op feestdagen van 11 tot 22 uur.

Toegang (museum en exposities): 10 euro (met kortings-kaart 8 euro). Voor bezoekers onder de 18 jaar, werklozen en ge-handicapten is de toegang gratis. Op de eerste zondag van de maand is de toegang voor alle bezoekers gratis.

L'ÉGLISE SAINT-MERRI

Ook de min Jeanne Bussie weigert Grenouille nog verder te zogen. Ze stelt vast dat hij geen lichaamsgeur heeft en gelooft daarom dat hij van de duivel bezeten is. Het ligt dan voor de hand dat ze hem meteen het huis uit wil hebben en ze brengt hem naar pater Terrier van het klooster van Saint-Merri.

Volgens de legende kwam de abt St. Médéricus in de zevende eeuw vanuit Bourgondië naar Parijs, waar hij tot zijn dood in 700 als kluizenaar in een houten cel leefde. Op de plek waar die cel heeft gestaan, werd in 884 een kerk gebouwd die zijn naam kreeg, maar dan in afgekorte vorm: Saint-Merri. Sinds die tijd is hij de schutspatroon van de Parijse gebieden aan de rechteroever van de Seine. Het gebeente van de abt ligt in de crypte onder het noordelijke transept van de kerk van Saint-Merri.

In de loop der eeuwen is de kerk vele malen verbouwd om aan de behoefte van de zich voortdurend uitbreidende bevolking van het Hallendistrict te kunnen voldoen. Het laatgotische gebouw dat we tegenwoordig zien werd tussen 1500

▲ Contrastrijker kan bijna niet: een moderne fontein voor een ruïneus gebouw

► Een straatnaambord herinnert eraan dat hier vroeger het klooster van Saint-Merri stond

en 1552 helemaal nieuw gebouwd in de zogenaamde flamboyante stijl. Alleen een raam naar de Rue Saint-Martin is nog van de oude kerk overgebleven. In het interieur overheerst de barokarchitectuur. Het koor stamt uit het midden van de achttiende eeuw.

Ook deze kerk ontkwam niet aan de schade die de Franse Revolutie met zich meebracht. De artistieke beelden die aan de voorgevel stonden werden neergehaald en de kerk zelf werd in 1793 als zodanig gesloten om voortaan dienst te doen als kruitfabriek. Pas een halve eeuw later werd begonnen met de restauratie van het gebouw, waarbij ook de beelden aan de westelijke gevel werden herplaatst. Nadat hij weer in zijn oorspronkelijke gebruik was genomen, kreeg de kerk een employé die later beroemd zou worden: Camille Saint-Saëns, een van de belangrijkste Franse componisten uit de negentiende eeuw, werkte van 1853 tot 1857 als organist in de parochie van Saint-Merri.

Wat aan de met de Revolutie gepaard gaande vernielingen ontkwam, was de klok in de kleine toren aan de linkerzijde van de façade. Deze is in 1331 gegoten en is daarmee de oudste nog bestaande klok van Parijs.

VOOR HET PUBLIEK:

Adres: Église Saint-Merri, 78-76 Rue Saint-Martin, Rue de la Verrerie.

RUE DE CHARONNE

Grenouilles zwerftocht zet zich voort, want ook pater Terrier krijgt van hem al snel de griezels. En omdat een gevoel van akeligheid boven dat van christenplicht gaat, brengt de geestelijke de jongen naar madame Gaillard, die in het district Faubourg Saint-Antoine, aan het einde van de Rue de Charonne, woont. De pater belooft voor het levensonderhoud van de jongen te betalen en dus neemt zij hem onder haar hoede. Hij zal bij haar blijven tot hij acht jaar oud is.

In de Rue de Charonne, tegenover het klooster, stond het gesticht van de Notre Dame de Bon-Secours. Hier bezoekt Grenouille anderhalf jaar lang de fraterschool.

Het Quartier Faubourg Saint-Antoine ontleent zijn naam aan de in de twaalfde eeuw gevestigde abdij Saint-Antoine-des-Champs. In de vijftiende eeuw gaf de koning aan alle ambachtslieden die rond de abdij hun werk deden, vrijheid van gildeplicht. Deze omstandigheid trok veel ambachtslieden aan, vooral meubelmakers, schrijnwerkers en fineerwerkers die met nieuwe technieken experimenteerden, bijvoorbeeld het in hout inleggen van motieven. In de zeventiende en de achttiende eeuw groeide dit gebied in de omgeving van de Rue de Faubourg-Saint-Antoine uit tot het centrum van het Franse meubelmakersambacht.

Aan het einde van de twintigste eeuw voltrok zich in dit kwartier een verandering en werd het een nieuwe 'hippe' wijk. Veel kunstenaars vestigden zich in de buurt van de Bastille, gevolgd door uitbaters van restaurants, trendy bars en boetieks. De vroegere werkplaatsen van de ambachtslieden zijn opgeknapt en worden nu voor dikke prijzen als appartementen verkocht.

De Rue de Charonne splitst zich in noordoostelijke richting af van de Rue de Faubourg-Saint-Antoine en steekt tegenwoordig dwars door het 11de arrondissement tot aan de zuidzijde van de bekende begraafplaats Père Lachaise. In de achttiende eeuw bestond die omgeving nog uit tuinen, akkers en weiden. Madame Gaillard woont bijna aan het einde

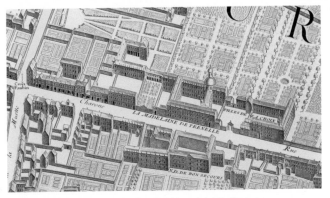

▲ Maar liefst drie kloosters stonden hier vlak bij elkaar

van de Rue de Charonne, in de buurt van het klooster Madeleine de Traisnel (in de roman *Trenelle*). Op oude stadskaarten wordt dit medio zeventiende eeuw gebouwde benedictijnenklooster nog genoemd; het moet zich bevonden hebben op de plaats van het huidige huisnummer 100. Nu staan hier kantoorgebouwen op de binnenplaats waarvan nog enkele geïsoleerde resten van het klooster te zien zijn.

Het benedictijnenklooster Notre Dame de Bon Secours stamt uit het jaar 1648 en bleef tijdens de Franse Revolutie gesloten. In 1802 begonnen twee ondernemers in de ruimtes de eerste katoenspinnerij van Frankrijk. Aan het begin van de twintigste eeuw werd eerst de kapel afgebroken en later, in de jaren zeventig van die eeuw, de complete voorgevel.

Ook het derde in de roman genoemde klooster bestaat niet meer, het dominicanenklooster van de Filles de la Croix uit 1641. Hier werkt in Süskinds roman de tuinmansknecht Jacques Lorreur, die af en toe bij madame Gaillard smerige karweitjes opknapt.

In 1904 werd dit klooster gesloten en twee jaar later gesloopt. De nieuwbouw die er in 1910 in de stijl van de 'belle époque' voor in de plaats kwam, werd benut als tehuis voor vrijgezelle mannen.

De meesten van hen werden voor de Eerste Wereldoorlog onder de wapenen geroepen en na de oorlog stond het gebouw eerst leeg. In 1926 werd het gekocht door het Leger des

Heils, dat hier, aan de Rue de Charonne 94, het 'Palais de la Femme' oprichtte, een toevluchtsoord voor meisjes en vrouwen in nood. Deze taak wordt er nog steeds vervuld, want jammer genoeg zijn thema's als armoede en misbruik in de eenentwintigste eeuw even actueel als destijds.

HÔTEL-DIEU

In 1799 wordt de oude en zieke Madame naar het Hôtel-Dieu gebracht – 'daar legde men haar neer in dezelfde, door honderden doodzieke mensen bevolkte zaal waarin ook haar man was gestorven...' (vertaling Ronald Jonkers, p. 33). Drie weken later sterft ook zij daar.

Het Hôtel-Dieu op het Ile de la Cité is het oudste ziekenhuis van Parijs en het op één na oudste van heel Frankrijk. Tegenwoordig is het een modern universiteitsziekenhuis met 350 bedden. Er werken vele artsen van wereldnaam. Maar zo is het niet altijd geweest.

Oorspronkelijk stond het Hôtel-Dieu ten zuiden van het huidige voorplein van de kathedraal van de Notre-Dame, waar nu het ruiterstandbeeld van Karel de Grote staat. Het ziekenhuis, het 'huis van God', werd al in 660 door bisschop Landry gesticht. Op zijn kosten werden de zieken uit de stad, maar ook pelgrims, er verzorgd. In Hôtel-Dieu was iedereen

◀ Het 'Huis van God'

▲ Het ziekenhuis bestaat nog altijd, zij het met een betere reputatie dan in Grenouilles tijd

welkom, ongeacht geslacht, leeftijd, herkomst of religie.

In de daaropvolgende eeuwen was de bevolkingstoename zo groot dat het Hôtel-Dieu steeds verder moest worden uitgebreid. Ofschoon het Ile de la Cité in de Middeleeuwen bijzonder dicht bebouwd was, werd daar toch steeds plaats voor gevonden. Maar toen die er uiteindelijk echt niet meer was, bouwde men gewoon een nieuwe brug over een aftakking van de Seine, de Pont-au-Double. Hierop werd een gebouw van twee verdiepingen neergezet waarin eveneens zieken konden worden ondergebracht. Het is nauwelijks verwonderlijk dat die brug te eniger tijd instortte. Evengoed werden met man en macht meteen nieuwe ziekenzalen op een nieuwe brug gebouwd. Zo bleef deze situatie tot 1847 bestaan.

Maar ook de dependance op de brug was spoedig overbevolkt; het Hôtel-Dieu barstte zowat uit zijn voegen. De meeste bedden moesten door drie, dikwijl ook vier of soms wel vijf patiënten gedeeld worden. Zieken werden bij stervenden of zelfs wel bij reeds overledenen in bed gelegd. Met de hygiëne was het erbarmelijk gesteld en het sterftecijfer lag dan ook op een voor moderne begrippen onvoorstelbare 20 procent. Hevige branden, waarvan de laatste in 1772 uitbrak, boden onvoorziene kansen om op andere plaatsen een groots opgezette nieuwbouw te doen verrijzen, maar deze mogelijkheden werden nooit benut; steeds opnieuw werd het ziekenhuis herbouwd en de situatie bleef even rampzalig als ze eerder ook al was. Wie het verslag van de kroniekschrijver Mercier leest, kan zich de angst van de arme madame Gaillard om hier aan haar einde te komen goed voorstellen:

> *Het Huis van God! Alles is onbarmhartig en bitter in dit oord en iedereen lijdt er. Patiënten met de meest uiteenlopende ziektes liggen er onder dezelfde deken, de geringste ongesteldheid verandert er in een vreselijke lijdensweg. (…) Het Hôtel-Dieu in Parijs voldoet aan alle voorwaarden om een bron van epidemieën te zijn. Zijn vochtige, zelden geluchte atmosfeer maakt dat wonden algauw gangreneus worden; wie langer blijft kan scheurbuik of schurft bijna niet ontlopen. De simpelste ziektes vertonen dankzij de onvermijdelijke, door de lucht aangevoerde besmetting algauw de ernstigste complicaties. Dezelfde oorzaak maakt dat onbeduidende wonden aan het hoofd of zelfs aan de benen in dit ziekenhuis dodelijk kunnen zijn. (Mercier, p. 256 e.v.)*

Pas zo'n honderd jaar later, in de lijn van de stedenbouwkundige metamorfose die de planoloog baron Georges-Eugène Haussmann tot stand bracht, werd uitkomst geboden. Haussmann, die de opdracht had gekregen het chaotische en overbevolkte Parijs met zijn vele nauwe straatjes en stegen om te bouwen tot een moderne metropool, maakte vele middeleeuwse gebouwen met de grond gelijk om plaats te maken voor brede boulevards en grootse paleizen. Ook het Ile de la Cité ontkwam niet aan zijn dadendrang.

Het huidige ziekenhuis werd tussen 1868 en 1878 gebouwd aan de andere kant van het voorplein van de Notre-Dame. Na de opening ervan werd het oude gebouw gesloopt.

VOOR HET PUBLIEK:

Adres: Hôtel-Dieu, 1 Place du Parvis Notre-Dame.

EXTRA EXCURSIE: *ILE DE LA CITÉ*

GESCHIEDENIS

Midden in de Seine ligt als een reusachtig schip het Ile de la Cité. Het wordt beschouwd als het historische en geografische centrum van Frankrijk. Toen in 52 v.Chr. de Romeinen het eiland bereikten, leefde er een Keltische stam, de Parisii. Na de nederzetting te hebben veroverd, stichtten de Romeinen er een stad die ze 'Lutetia' noemden. Liefhebbers van de Asterix-verhalen kennen deze naam als het machtscentrum in het bezette gebied van de Galliërs. De stad breidde zich al snel uit naar de linkeroever van de Seine, maar bleef politiek vooralsnog onbelangrijk. In het jaar 506 veroverde de Frankische koning Chlodovech (in het Frans gewoonlijk Clovis genoemd) de stad en maakte die tot hoofdstad van zijn rijk. In deze periode kreeg de stad de naam Paris. Het Ile de la Cité werd gekozen tot machtscentrum van de Franse koningen, evenals dat van de kerk en de justitie.

▲ Het Ile de la Cité ziet er bij zonsopgang op z'n mooist uit

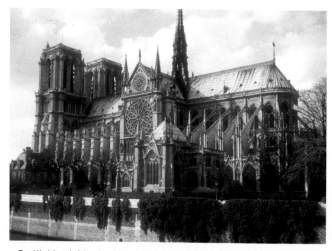

▲ De Klokkenluider had bepaald een mooie behuizing...

CATHÉDRALE DE NOTRE-DAME

Kerk en justitie bepalen – naast de dagelijkse stromen toeristen – ook vandaag de dag nog het beeld van het eiland. De kathedraal Notre-Dame de Paris is een van de drukst bezochte bezienswaardigheden van de stad: in 2005 zouden er ongeveer tien miljoen bezoekers zijn geweest. Het ligt dan ook voor de hand dat er vaak lange wachttijden zijn voor hen die de kerktoren willen beklimmen. Met een regelmaat van tien minuten mogen telkens twintig bezoekers naar boven en aan de hand van de lange rij wachtenden is wel ongeveer in te schatten hoe lang die oefening van geduld moet worden volgehouden. Maar het wachten en de klim naar boven zijn de moeite waard geweest: bij helder weer heb je vanaf zeventig meter hoogte een schitterend panorama over de daken van Parijs. Bovendien heb je hier van dichtbij zicht op de groteske gargouilles, de beroemde waterspuwers die over de stad waken.

Het interieur van de kathedraal imponeert meteen door zijn omvang: in deze grootste kerk van Parijs kunnen wel negenduizend kerkgangers een plaats vinden. Bijzonder waard om

► Het 13 meter hoge zuidelijke roosvenster

te worden bekeken zijn de reusachtige roosvensters. Dat in de westelijke gevel heeft een doorsnede van tien meter en is na meer dan zevenhonderd jaar nog ongeschonden. Het roosvenster op het zuiden is zelfs dertien meter groot.

De eerste steen voor deze gotische kathedraal werd in 1163 gelegd, waarna de afbouw bijna twee eeuwen in beslag nam. De imposante kathedraal heeft het decor gevormd voor veel belangrijke gebeurtenissen in de Franse geschiedenis: onder

▲ ...en zijn uitzicht was, samen met dat van de gargouilles, adembenemend

◄ Het geografische middelpunt van Frankrijk ligt op het Ile de la Cité in Parijs

meer vonden er plaats de kroning van Hendrik VI (1430), het cassatieproces van Jeanne d'Arc (1455) en het huwelijk van de jonge Maria Stuart met Frans II (1558). De Franse Revolutie spaarde de Notre-Dame evenmin als vele andere kerken. Omdat meteen erna weinig herstelwerkzaamheden werden uitgevoerd, begon het gebouw langzaam af te takelen. Pas nadat de romancier Victor Hugo de kerk had gekozen tot toneel van en beroemd had gemaakt met zijn in 1831 uitgegeven roman *Notre-Dame-de-Paris* (beter bekend als *De Klokkenluider van de Notre-Dame*), werd met een uitgebreid restauratieproject begonnen.

Tegenwoordig is er van het middeleeuwse hart van het eiland zoals dat door Victor Hugo in die roman beschreven

VOOR HET PUBLIEK:

Adres: Cathédrale de Notre-Dame de Paris; 6 Place du Parvis; telefoon 01 42 34 56 10.
Openingstijden: van 7.45 tot 19 uur. Tijdens godsdienstige plechtigheden (als eucharistievieringen) zijn enkele delen van de dom niet toegankelijk voor bezichtiging. De toegang is gratis.
Openingstijden van de toren: van april tot en met september dagelijks van 10 tot 18.30 uur, maar van juni tot en met augustus in de weekends tot 23 uur. Van oktober tot en met maart dagelijks van 10 tot 17.30 uur. Toegangsprijs: 7,50 euro. Van november tot en met maart op elke eerste zondag van de maand gratis.

werd, vrijwel niets meer te zien. Baron Haussmann, die aan het einde van de negentiende eeuw het plein voor de kathedraal aanlegde, moest daarvoor vele gebouwen, waaronder kerken, laten platgooien. Alleen de markeringen op het voorplein, de Place du Parvis, herinneren nog aan de wirwar van steegjes die zich hier vroeger bevond. Wie er een beetje zoeken voor overheeft, kan midden op het plein een in de grond ingelaten geelkoperen plaat vinden, het Point Zéro, uit welk zogenaamde nulpunt alle afstanden binnen de grenzen van Frankrijk afgemeten zijn.

SAINTE-CHAPELLE

De kathedraal Notre-Dame is niet de enige bezienswaardige kerk op het Ile de la Cité. De mogelijk mooiste kerk van Parijs, de Sainte-Chapelle, ligt ietwat verscholen in het uitgebreide complex van het paleis van justitie. Hij werd op last van koning Lodewijk ix rond het midden van de dertiende eeuw gebouwd om er de vermeende doornenkroon van Jezus Christus plus een splinter van het kruis in bij te zetten.

◄ Veel mensen vinden de Sainte-Chapelle de mooiste kerk van Parijs

▲ De gotische gewelven van de Sainte-Chapelle

Voor deze relikwieën had hij een prijs betaald die drie keer zo hoog was als die van de bouw van de kerk, compleet met de uit hout gesneden apostelbeelden.

Ongewoon is dat de kerk twee verdiepingen heeft. De onderste daarvan is voor het oog niet zo interessant, maar de bovenste daarentegen des te meer. Het gewicht van het met sterren bezaaide, gewelfde plafond lijkt niet door muren gedragen te worden, slechts door slanke steunpilaren en de vijftien meter hoge vensters van gebrandschilderd glas, die

◄ De glas-in-loodramen van de bovenkapel dienen niet alleen ter versiering, maar maken ook deel uit van de architectonische statica

VOOR HET PUBLIEK:

Adres: Sainte-Chapelle; 4 Boulevard du Palais; telefoon 01 53 40 60 80.

Openingstijden: van april tot en met september dagelijks van 9.30 tot 18 uur, van oktober tot en met maart van 9 tot 17 uur.

Toegangsprijs: 5,50 euro, met korting 3,50 euro. Een combi-kaartje voor de kerk en de Conciergerie kost 9 euro, met korting 6 euro. Van oktober tot en met maart op elke eerste zondag van de maand is de toegang gratis, evenals voor bezoekers onder de 18 jaar.

precies 1134 religieuze taferelen laten zien. Twee op de drie van deze glas-in-loodramen stammen nog uit de dertiende eeuw en wanneer de zon erop schijnt werpen ze een wondermooi licht in het interieur. Om de schoonheid van de grote roosvensters in haar volle glorie te aanschouwen is het aan te bevelen de kerk rond zonsondergang te bezoeken.

PALAIS DE JUSTICE

Op de plaats van het gebouwencomplex van het paleis van justitie met zijn machtige façade, die de gehele breedte van het Ile de la Cité beslaat, bevond zich in de Middeleeuwen het Palais de la Cité, het stadspaleis. Tot het midden van de veertiende eeuw was dit de residentie van de Franse koningen, daarna werd het door het Parijse parlement betrokken. In de daaropvolgende eeuwen werd het paleis verschillende keren door brand verwoest en telkens met bepaalde veranderingen weer opgebouwd.

Van het vroegere koningspaleis is weinig behouden gebleven. Ook de Conciergerie is een latere aanbouw die door Filips de Schone (1284-1314) als uitbreidende vleugel aan het paleis is toegevoegd. Zijn naam ontleent het gebouw aan 'concierge', in dit geval de rentmeester van de koninklijke gebouwen. De gotische zaal van de 'Gens d'Armes' (gewapende mannen, naamsoorsprong van 'gendarme', militair politieagent), de vroegere banketzaal van de koning, geeft nog een indruk van hoe schitterend het paleis destijds moet zijn geweest. De ruimte gaat door voor de oudste middeleeuwse zaal van Europa en is al indrukwekkend door haar maten: ze is vierenzestig meter diep en zevenentwintig meter breed, terwijl haar bogenplafond meer dan acht meter in de hoogte reikt.

In het jaar 1391 werd de Conciergerie omgebouwd tot gevangenis. Zoals in die tijd gebruikelijk, was de behandeling van een gevangene afhankelijk van zijn financiën, zijn maatschappelijke rang en zijn relaties. Wie geld had kon een eigen cel met een bed en een tafel kopen. De armsten moesten hun bestaan zien te rekken in donkere, benauwde kerkers met hoogstens wat stro – de best denkbare broedplaats voor de pest en andere epidemieën.

Gedurende de Franse Revolutie was de Conciergerie in gebruik als de beruchte staatsgevangenis waarin de ter dood veroordeelden op hun transport naar de guillotine wachtten. In de bovenverdieping heeft men de te bezichtigen cel nagebouwd waarin Marie-Antoinette van 2 augustus tot 16 oktober 1793 gevangen heeft gezeten. In de cel van de koningin staat niets dan een bed, een tafel en een stoel en slechts een kamerscherm onttrok haar aanwezigheid aan de ogen

▲ Het Palais de Justice en de Église Sainte-Chapelle zijn een bezoek meer dan waard

◄ De oudste publieksklok in Parijs

van de cipiers die haar dag en nacht bewaakten. In een aangrenzende cel zou later Maximilian de Robespierre de nacht voor zijn terechtstelling hebben doorgebracht.

Na het einde van het schrikbewind werd de Conciergerie gerestaureerd en in nieuw-gotische stijl verbouwd. Nog tot 1914 diende het gebouw als gevangenis, waarna het tot historisch monument werd verklaard en als museum werd ingericht. Aan het benedendeel van de hoektoren bevindt zich het oudste voor het publiek bestemde uurwerk van de stad. Deze klok werd in 1370 geplaatst en loopt nog steeds.

VOOR HET PUBLIEK:

Adres: Conciergerie; 1 Quai de l'Horloge; telefoon 01 53 40 60 93.

Openingstijden: van maart tot en met oktober dagelijks van 9.30 tot 18 uur. Van november tot en met februari dagelijks van 9 tot 17 uur.

Toegangsprijs: 6,50 euro, met korting 4,50 euro. Een combi-kaartje voor de Conciergerie en de kerk Sainte-Chapelle kost 9 euro, met korting 6 euro. Van oktober tot en met maart op elke eerste zondag van de maand is de toegang gratis, evenals voor bezoekers onder de 18 jaar.

RUE DE LA MORTELLERIE

Als de betalingen voor het onderhoud van Grenouille door pater Terrier worden gestaakt, is er ook een einde gekomen aan de zorgplicht van madame Gaillard. Zij verkoopt de achtjarige jongen aan leerlooier Grimal, die altijd behoefte heeft aan jeugdige helpers. Het leven dat Grenouille bij Grimal leidt is zwaar. Hij doet er een zware ziekte op, maar tegen de verwachting in sterft hij er niet aan.

Volgens oude registratieaantekeningen bestond er op deze plek al in de elfde eeuw een straat. Eerst heette deze Rue de la Foulerie en pas later Rue de la Mortellerie. Maar nadat in 1832 een zware cholera-epidemie alleen al in deze straat 300 slachtoffers had gemaakt, dienden de overlevende bewoners een petitie in om de straatnaam te veranderen opdat de onheilspellende eerste lettergreep 'mort' ('dood') zou verdwijnen. Sinds die tijd heet de straat Rue de l'Hôtel-de-Ville.

De Rue de la Mortellerie was in de tijd van Grenouille langer dan zijn huidige opvolger. Hij strekte zich uit van de Rue du Figuer tot aan het Hôtel de Ville. In 1837 werd een deel van de straat opgeofferd aan de uitbreiding van het Hôtel de Ville en later werden ook in het oostelijke deel enkele huizen gesloopt om plaats te maken voor de tuin van het Hôtel de Sens.

Tegenwoordig loopt de straat evenwijdig aan de verkeersdrukke Quai de l'Hôtel-de-Ville. Aan het huis met het nummer 95 is nog een inscriptie met de oude straatnaam te zien.

◄ Alleen de in de steen gehakte inscriptie herinnert aan de vroeger zo onheilspellende naam van deze straat...

PAVILLON DE FLORE EN PONT ROYAL

*In de schaduwen van het Pavillon de Flore staat
Grenouille een tijdje te kijken naar het vuurwerk dat ter
ere van een koninklijk jubileum wordt afgestoken.
Plotseling vangt hij in zijn neus een vleugje van een
nimmer eerder geroken, heerlijke geur op.*

Het Pavillon de Flore strekt zich uit langs de rechteroever
van de Seine en maakt tegenwoordig deel uit van het Musée
du Louvre. Het is in 1600 gebouwd toen Hendrik IV besloot
het voormalige stadskasteel van de Franse heersers, het Tuilerieënpaleis, naar het zuiden te verplaatsen en hem op die
manier op de Grande Galerie des Louvre te laten aansluiten.
In de daaropvolgende eeuwen kwam het paviljoen bij her-
haling weer in de belangstelling te staan. Tijdens de Franse
Revolutie werd het gebouw bestormd en Lodewijk XVI werd
er met zijn gezin gevangengenomen. Onder het Schrikbewind van Robespierre dat hierop volgde, vergaderde in het
Pavillon de Flore het 'Comité du Salut Public', zogenaamd
een comité voor het welzijn van de gemeenschap, maar in

▶ De trouwe bewakers
van de Leeuwenpoort
van het Louvre

▲ De Pont Royal, waar Grenouille voor het eerst de verleidelijke jon-
ge-meisjesgeur opsnuffelde

werkelijkheid het zenuwcentrum van dit terreurregime. Tijdens de opstand van de Parijse Commune in 1871 werd het
Tuilerieënpaleis in brand gestoken, waarna de ruïnes op last
van de Nationale Volksvergadering werden gesloopt. Slechts
het Pavillon de Flore en het ertegenover liggende Pavilon de
Marsan werden later als onderdeel van het Louvre herbouwd. De voorgevel van het Pavillon de Flore weerspiegelt
met zijn talrijke beelden, ornamenten en guirlandes aardig
de architectuur van zijn tijd.

Tegenwoordig worden op de eerste verdieping van dit
'bloemenpaviljoen' Spaanse en Italiaanse schilderijen uit de
zeventiende en achttiende eeuw tentoongesteld. De door
twee bronzen leeuwen bewaakte poort, de Porte des Lions, is
in 1998 geopend als tweede ingang van het museum. Als bezoeker is het een poging waard om hier naar binnen te komen, vooral wanneer bij de hoofdingang, de piramide, weer
eens een zeer lange rij wachtenden staat.

Aan het einde van deze vleugels van de hoofdgebouwen
van het Louvre ligt de Pont Royal, de 'koninklijke brug', die
zijn naam te danken heeft aan de zonnekoning, Lodewijk
XIV; hij heeft voor de brug betaald. De van vijf bogen voorziene brug is tussen 1685 en 1689 gebouwd en is lange tijd de
enige benedenstrooms van de Pont Neuf liggende oeverver-

binding van de Seine geweest. Hij verbond het toenmalige koningspaleis met Faubourg Saint Germain, dat toen nog een voorstad was.

De brug heeft opstanden, oorlogen, overstromingen en ook de dadendrang van baron Haussmann goed overleefd, want vrijwel ongeschonden ligt hij er al bijna driehonderd jaar. Alleen de markante bult, ook wel 'ezelsrug' genoemd, is rond het midden van de negentiende eeuw enigszins afgeplat.

VOOR HET PUBLIEK:

Adres: Pavillon de Flore, Musée du Louvre; 14 Quai François Mitterand.

RUE DES MARAIS

Grenouille volgt het spoor van de verleidelijk geur en komt al ruikend in een zijsteeg van de Rue de Seine terecht, de Rue des Marais. In een hofje ontdekt hij de bron van de geur. Dit moment zal zijn leven drastisch veranderen...

Het bestaan van de Rue des Marais wordt pas aan het begin van de zestiende eeuw genoemd. Sinds 1864 heeft hij de naam Rue Visconti, naar de Franse architect Louis Visconti (1791-1853), die onder meer het graf van Napoleon I in Les Invalides heeft ontworpen. De Rue Visconti is een dwarsverbinding tussen de ook in de roman voorkomende Rue de Seine en de Rue des Petit Augustins (tegenwoordig Rue Bonaparte geheten).

In deze straat hebben enkele beroemde mannen gewoond. De belangrijke toneelschrijver Jean Racine bracht de laatste zeven jaar van zijn leven door in het huis met het nummer 24. In huis 17, waarin zich nu een grote boekhandel bevindt, probeerde Honoré de Balzac tussen 1826 en 1828 een boekdrukkerij te exploiteren, wat echter op een misluk-

◄ Hoe nietig het straatje ook is, de naam van de Rue des Marais is verbonden met die van beroemdheden als Balzac en Christo

king uitdraaide en hem het faillissement bracht – wat misschien wel zo gelukkig was, want zo had hij tijd om te schrijven en als schrijver is hij wereldberoemd geworden. In hetzelfde huis heeft later de schilder Eugène Delacroix zijn atelier gehad. Bij welk huis de kleine binnenplaats hoort waar in de roman Grenouille het meisje met de mirabellen vindt, blijft onduidelijk.

Evenals in de tijd van de roman is de Rue des Marais een nauw straatje, zoals Süskind schrijft: 'amper een armlengte brede steeg' (vertaling Ronald Jonkers, p. 43). Dat is weliswaar nogal overdreven, maar de steeg is wel degelijk smal, op sommige plekken niet meer dan 3 1/2 meter breed. Deze engte was ook de reden waarom het actiekunstenaarsduo Christo en Jeanne-Claude het straatje heeft uitverkoren om er hun eerste monumentale project uit te voeren. In 1962 stapelden ze hier 240 lege olieflessen op tot een vier meter hoge, onpasseerbare muur. Ze noemden het kunstwerk *Het IJzeren Gordijn* – zijnde hun commentaar op de Muur in Berlijn. Anders dan nu werkten ze in die tijd nog niet samen

6ᵉ Arrᵗ

**RUE
VISCONTI**

1791 - 1853
ARCHITECTE AUTEUR DU TOMBEAU
DE NAPOLÉON 1ᴇʀ

RUË DES
MARAIS
20

▶ Een aardige service
voor de liefhebbers van
Het parfum – de oude
straatnaam is nog te le-
zen

met de autoriteiten en voor het project was dus geen toestemming gevraagd. Het duurde dan ook niet lang of de Parijse 'flics' verschenen ten tonele, kennelijk zonder veel artistiek gevoel over de verbouwing van de Rue Marais. Niet
langer dan ongeveer acht uur bleef het kunstwerk bestaan,
toen moesten Christo en Jeanne-Claude op bevel van de po-
litie het bouwsel afbreken en de straat ook verder toegankelijk maken.

Wie op zoek is naar kunst met een wat langere levensduur
kan tegenwoordig terecht in de van vele galeries voorziene
straten rondom de kunstacademie en aan de Rue Visconti.
Bijna een op de twee winkels is er een galerie waar je allerlei
soorten beeldende kunst, alsook kunstnijverheid kunt kopen.

RESTAURANT LA TOUR D'ARGENT

Nadat parfumeur Baldini ontdekt heeft hoe getalenteerd Grenouille is in het mengen van geurtjes, besluit hij de bijzondere jongen van Grimal te kopen. Onder het genot van een fles witte wijn beklinken de twee ondernemers de zaak. Overlopend van vreugde over de geslaagde transactie drinkt Grimal in zijn eentje verder, wat hem dezelfde avond nog het leven zal kosten. Stomdronken valt hij in de Seine en verdrinkt jammerlijk.

De La Tour d'Argent is het oudste restaurant van Parijs. Reeds in 1582 bevond zich op deze plaats een herberg die dezelfde naam voerde en die door de latere eigenaar in 1780 in een restaurant werd veranderd, waarvan de keuken ook toen al zeer goed moet zijn geweest. De La Tour d'Argent was zo in trek dat rijke gasten duels uitvochten om er een tafeltje te kunnen krijgen.

Het restaurant is gelegen op de zesde verdieping van een gebouw aan de linkeroever van de Seine. Het uitzicht over

◄ Dankzij slimme marketing werd zelfs de Engelse koningin ertoe gebracht hier de specialiteit van het huis, eend in geheime saus, te eten

het Ile de la Cité met de kathedraal Notre-Dame is van daaruit onovertroffen. Nauwelijks minder spectaculair dan de bovenetage is de wijnkelder, die meer op een wijnmuseum lijkt. Hier liggen 500.000 flessen opgeslagen, met als oudste een bordeaux uit het jaar 1858. Dat deze wijn vermoedelijk zijn beste jaren allang achter zich heeft liggen, vermag nauwelijks afbreuk te doen aan zijn historische waarde.

Nog altijd komen de gasten in La Tour d'Argent om de specialiteit van het huis te proeven: 'Caneton Tour d'Argent' – jonge eend in bloedsaus. Al sinds 1890 worden de eenden volgens geheime receptuur bereid en elk ervan krijgt een nummer mee. De gast krijgt ter herinnering een certificaat mee waarop dat nummer staat en in een gastenboek wordt bijgehouden wie de zoveelste eend heeft genuttigd. Zo weten we dat Franklin D. Roosevelt in 1929 eend nummer 112.151 heeft gegeten, de Engelse koningin Elizabeth II nummer 185.397 heeft opgepeuzeld en Paul McCartney eend nummer 692.048 soldaat heeft gemaakt. Restaurateurs die hun creaties zo handig op de markt weten te brengen, weten dat ze ook de hogere machten dank verschuldigd zijn: in april 2003 werd de nuttiging van de miljoenste eend gevierd met een groots vuurwerk – afgestoken op een daartoe passende plaats, namelijk boven de kathedraal Notre-Dame.

Men vraagt zich af in hoeverre La Tour d'Argent tegenwoordig alleen nog maar drijft op zijn legendarische naam. Critici verwijten het restaurant dat zijn keuken te traditioneel is. Deze mening wordt kennelijk gedeeld door de restaurantgids van Michelin. Na in 1996 al een van zijn drie sterren te zijn kwijtgeraakt, werd in de editie van 2006 ook de tweede afgepakt zodat het beroemde restaurant het voortaan met een enkele ster moet doen.

Maar evengoed moet degene die zich wil scharen in het prominente gezelschap van de eendeters en het certificaat daarvan aan zijn souvenirs wil toevoegen, enkele weken van tevoren een tafel reserveren en er geen been in zien ongeveer 300 euro in een menu voor twee personen te investeren. Daarentegen is het gevaar om, net als de leerlooier Grimaldi, na het bezoek stomdronken in de Seine terecht te komen,

niet bijster groot gezien de hier en daar astronomische be-
dragen die moeten worden neergeteld voor de alcoholische
rariteiten op de uitgebreide wijnkaart.

VOOR HET PUBLIEK:

Adres: La Tour d'Argent, 15-17 Quai de la Tournelle.
Telefoon: 01 43 54 23 31, fax 01 44 07 12 04.
Openingstijden: maandag gesloten, dinsdag alleen 's avonds
geopend.

PONT-AU-CHANGE

*Bij de parfumeur Baldini op de Pont-au-Change wordt
Grenouille ingewijd in de geheimen van de geurwinning,
destillatie en uiteindelijke fabricage van parfums en hij
ontvangt een gezellenbrevet. Grenouilles geniale
creaties leggen de verouderende Baldini bepaald geen
windeieren.*

De Pont-au-Change verbindt het Ile de la Cité met de rechteroever van de Seine. Tegenwoordig is de brug onderdeel
van de verkeersader die gevormd wordt door de Boulevard
de Sébastopol, aansluitend op de Boulevard Saint-Michel.

Reeds in 872 n.Chr. lag op deze plek een stenen brug die
eeuwenlang de enige overgang over de hoofdstroom van de
Seine vormde. En daarvoor al, in de Gallo-Romeinse tijd,
zou er een houten brug hebben gelegen. In 1441 beval koning
Lodewijk VII alle goudhandelaren en geldwisselaars zich op
de brug te vestigen. Uit die tijd dateert de naam 'Pont-au-
Change', ofwel 'Wisselbrug'. Geleidelijk aan verrezen op de
brug bouwsels die dienstdeden als wisselkantoor en vanaf
1516 werden er ook woningen gebouwd, bestaande uit kleine
kamers die ter weerszijden van de eigenlijke brug op palen
in de Seine stonden. Bruggen die op deze manier bebouwd
waren zag je in het historische Parijs overal over de Seine liggen. Pas de Pont Neuf werd niet bebouwd.

▲ Nog tot in de achttiende eeuw waren de meeste bruggen van Parijs dicht bebouwd

In oktober 1621 werd de Pont-au-Change getroffen door een grote brand die ook een honderdtal winkels in de as legde. Tussen 1639 en 1647 werd de brug herbouwd, nu met zeven bogen, en de meer dan honderd gebouwen die er ook weer werden opgetrokken, kregen nu vier verdiepingen. De brug was nu 32 meter breed en daarmee de breedste brug van de stad.

Maar het waren nu niet meer alleen goudhandelaren en geldwisselaars die zich op de Pont-au-Change vestigden; ook andere ondernemers als winkeliers in dure modeartikelen en zelfstandigen als kunsthandwerkers vonden er een plaats en ja, op de brug heeft wel degelijk een parfumeur een zaak geopend!

Süskind schrijft in zijn roman dat Baldini bij het instorten van zijn huis in 1756 om het leven kwam. Maar in werkelijkheid was het niet voor 1785 dat op de brug vijf huizen instortten. Deze gebeurtenis was de aanleiding tot de sloop van de daar overgebleven gebouwen, twee jaar later.

Op de oever van het Ile de la Cité staat de Conciergerie, ooit de beruchte staatsgevangenis. Tussen januari 1793 en mei 1795 werden hier meer dan 2700 personen ter dood veroordeeld. Voor veel van deze slachtoffers voerde de laatste gang over de Pont-au-Change – in de richting van de guillotine.

Toen baron Haussmann rond het midden van de negen-

◀ Voor wie anders dan voor Napoleon zou deze 'N' kunnen staan?

tiende eeuw van start ging met het ombouwen van Parijs tot een moderne metropool, vond hij dat de Pont-au-Change niet meer in dat nieuwe concept paste. De huidige brug werd tussen 1858 en 1860 gebouwd onder leiding van de architecten Vaudrey en De Lagalisserie. De napoleontische 'N' die iedere brugpijler versiert is het teken van die tijd.

EXTRA EXCURSIE: *PARFUMMUSEA IN PARIJS*

Wie niet in de gelegenheid is de voetsporen van Grenouille door de parfumstad Grasse te volgen, kan ook in Parijs terecht voor het opdoen van wetenswaardigheden over de parfumbereiding en dat nog gratis ook.

Het parfummuseum in de buurt van de Opéra de Paris wordt geleid door Fragonard, een parfummaker uit Grasse. In een mooi stadshuis uit 1860 wordt hier de bezoeker ingewijd in de drieduizend jaar oude geschiedenis van het parfum. In een verfijnde ambiance, waar antieke meubels en olieverfschilderijen de sfeer mede bepalen, staan prachtige flacons uit vele tijdperken uitgestald, evenals een keur aan toestellen die voor de parfumbereiding zijn gebruikt. Ook kan men er een idee krijgen over de voor parfums geschikte grondstoffen. Zo ziet men in een vitrine rariteiten als de

► Het parfummuseum in
de Rue Scribe

klierblaas van een bever, waaruit vroeger de geurstof casto-
reum, ook wel bevergeil genoemd, werd gewonnen. Het is
maar een geluk voor de bevers dat die geurstof tegenwoordig synthetisch vervaardigd kan worden.

Voor een tweede mogelijkheid om een vleugje parfumken-
nis op te snuiven ga je naar het museumtheater Capucines,
dat eveneens in handen van parfumeur Fragonard is. Dit in
1895 als theater gebouwde museum kreeg zijn huidige functie
in 1993. Hier wordt meer de nadruk gelegd op het werken met
het gereedschap dat voor het maken van parfum nodig is. Bijvoorbeeld is er een koperen destilleervat uit de negentiende
eeuw te zien, en daarnaast worden de destijds toegepaste technieken voor geurwinning aanschouwelijk gemaakt.

VOOR HET PUBLIEK:

Adres: Musée du Parfum Fragonard; 9 Rue Scribe; telefoon 01
47 42 04 56.
Openingstijden: maandag tot en met zaterdag van 9 tot 18
uur; zon- en feestdagen van 9.30 tot 16 uur.
Adres: Le Théâtre Musée des Capucines; 39 Boulevard des Capucines; telefoon 01 42 60 37 14.
Openingstijden: werkdagen van 9 tot 17.50 uur, feestdagen
van 9.30 tot 16 uur, op zondag gesloten.

TOERTIPS VOOR BOEKENWURMEN

Op eigen houtje:
parfumtoer door Parijs

De toer begint bij het **Forum des Halles**, dat met de metro goed bereikbaar is. We weerstaan de verleiding om het winkelcentrum binnen te gaan en daar een kijkje te nemen in de FNAC, de grootste boekwinkel van Frankrijk, maar laten het Forum achter ons en zetten meteen koers naar de **Fontaine des Innocents**. Waar nu de fontein staat, bevond zich ooit de grootste begraafplaats van Parijs, de Cimetière des Innocents. En dit is ook de plaats waar aan het slot van de roman Grenouille op een nacht wordt verslonden door een groep van pure liefde krankzinnig geworden misdadigers. Met dit gegeven in het achterhoofd smaakt de in de op de fontein uitkijkende McDonald's op te peuzelen hamburger meteen een stuk lekkerder…

◀ Het spiegelbeeld zoals dat van het terras van het Forum des Halles te zien is

▲ De 'Vuurvogel' naast het Centre Pompidou

Het Forum achter ons latend lopen we de tot in de achttiende eeuw nog Rue aux Fers geheten **Rue Berger** in en
steken we de **Rue Saint-Denis** over. De dames die in deze
straat rondhangen zijn beslist geen minnen en daarom lopen we stug door tot we na korte tijd het kunst- en cultuurcentrum **Centre Pompidou** in het oog krijgen. Voor een
rustpoos op het plein is het nog te vroeg, maar voor een blik
van verbazing over de gevel is het nooit te vroeg.

Een bezoek aan het Musée National d'Art Moderne is in
het kader van onze parfumtoer niet aan de orde en in plaats
daarvan wenden we onze schreden in zuidelijke richting
door de Rue Brismiche. Op de achtergrond zien we de mas-
sieve **Église Saint-Merri** al, maar eerst wijden we onze
aandacht aan de kleurrijke **Strawinskyfontein**. De bonte
figuren van de Franse kunstenares Niki de Saint Phale visu-
aliseren de werken van de Russische componist Igor Stra-
winsky.

De weg voert ons rondom de kerk. Mocht hij voor publiek geopend zijn, dan werpen we een blik in het barokke
interieur. Na weer in de Rue Saint-Martin te zijn uitgeko-
men, gaan we linksaf tot aan de Rue Rivoli, die we opnieuw
naar links ingaan en we volgen hem tot we aan een groot
plein komen. Dit is het voormalige Place de Grève, tegenwoordig **Place de l'Hôtel de Ville** genaamd. Na de prach-

▲ Destijds de plek voor terechtstellingen: de Place de Grève

tige gevel van het stadhuis uitvoerig te hebben bewonderd, vervolgen we onze weg in de richting van de Seine.

Aan de oever aangekomen zien we op het Ile de la Cité het breed uitgemeten gebouw van het **Hôtel-Dieu**. We steken de Seine over en wandelen langs zijn oever het ziekenhuis voorbij – in de geruststellende wetenschap dat de tegenwoordige situatie in het Hôtel-Dieu volstrekt niet te vergelijken is met die in de achttiende eeuw. De brug ter hoogte van het ziekenhuis is de Pont Notre-Dame en de daaropvolgende de **Pont au Change**. Enige verbeeldingskracht is nodig om je voor te stellen dat deze brug ooit met meerdere verdiepingen tellende huizen was volgebouwd.

Bij de opgang van de brug blijven we even staan, kijken naar links en bewonderen de oude klok in de gevel van de **Conciergerie**. Wie daar zin in heeft kan de Conciergerie ook vanbinnen bekijken en zich bijvoorbeeld verbazen over de cel waarin ooit Marie-Antoinette, wachtend op haar terechtstelling, gevangen heeft gezeten. Je kunt ook een combikaartje kopen waarmee je behalve tot de Conciergerie bovendien toegang krijgt tot de aangrenzende kerk van **Sainte-Chapelle** – wat beslist aan te bevelen is. Vervolgens slaan we de Rue de Lutece in, waar zich het **Métrostation Cité** bevindt. Alvorens de trappen van dit station af te dalen, slenteren we nog even over de mooie bloemenmarkt, een van de laatste van Parijs. Op zondag staat hier een vogel-tjesmarkt.

We nemen **Lijn 4** van de metro in de richting van de Porte d'Orleans en stappen op het derde station, **Saint-Germain-des-Prés**, weer uit. Nog altijd geldt het quartier Saint-Germain-des-Prés als dé wijk waar het literaire en in-tellectuele leven van Parijs zich afspeelt. Er zijn hier dan ook vele uitgevers, boekhandels en galeries, evenals de kunstaca-demie en uiteraard ontelbaar veel cafés. Het centrum van de buurt is ongetwijfeld het plein rondom de gelijknamige kerk, die overigens de oudste van Parijs is. Tussen de beide wereldoorlogen kwamen hier, met name in café Les Deux Margots en in café Flore, regelmatig de intellectuele kop-stukken uit die tijd bij elkaar, onder wie Jean-Paul Sartre, Si-mone de Beauvoir en Ernest Hemingway.

We gaan verder door de **Rue Bonaparte**, voorbij aan kleine galeries en deftige boetieks. We steken de Rue Jacob over en slaan vervolgens rechtsaf een kleine, onooglijke straat in. De markering aan het hoekhuis onthult ons dat we ons nu in de voormalige Rue des Marais bevinden, al heet die tegenwoordig **Rue Visconti**. Maar hoe we ook snuffe-len en snuiven, we kunnen er niet achter komen op welk binnenplaatsje Grenouille zijn eerste slachtoffer ontdekte.

We lopen de steeg door tot we aan het einde komen en

▲ Terrasjes nodigen, zeker in Parijs, uit tot het ontspannen gebruiken van een drankje

▲ Om mee naar huis te nemen: nostalgisch aandoende posters

slaan dan linksaf de **Rue de Seine** in. Vele galerie-etalages lopen we voorbij, steeds in de richting van de Seine. Rechts zien we het schitterende Institut de France, de Academie van Wetenschappen. Op de plek waar de Rue de Seine op de **Quai Malaquais** uitkomt, bevindt zich links, op nummer **13**, het huis waarin de Duitse natuuronderzoeker Alexander von Humboldt ooit woonde en zijn reisverslagen schreef.

Literair ingesteld als we zijn, zetten we onze tocht langs de Seine voort, want hier staan de boekhandelaren, de zogenaamde 'bouquinistes', met hun uitstallingen. Voor ons, boekenwurmen, is het natuurlijk verleidelijk om hier in de dozen te grasduinen naar mooie, oude of zeldzame boeken. Aan de overzijde van de Seine herkennen we de Denon-vleugel van het Louvre, aan welks einde zich het **Pavillon de Flore** bevindt, het doel van onze tocht.

Om naar Parijs te komen...

zijn er mogelijkheden te over: trein, vliegtuig, bus, eigen auto. Het vliegtuig biedt natuurlijk het snelste transport, maar de reis naar de luchthaven (zeker als je niet in de buurt woont), het inchecken, wachten op boarding enzovoort neemt veel van dat voordeel weg. Het kan zijn dat andere reisopties snellere en goedkopere mogelijkheden bieden, al zijn de zogenaamde 'price-fighters' onder de luchtvaartmaatschappijen op dat gebied bijna niet meer te kloppen.

Met de trein

Vanuit Nederland en België is het reizen met de trein aantrekkelijk: met de Thalys ben je in iets meer dan 4 uur van Amsterdam in Parijs. Andere opstapplaatsen zijn Schiphol, Den Haag, Rotterdam, Antwerpen en Brussel, vanuit welke stad de rest van de reis met een snelheid van 300 km/u wordt afgelegd. Vertrektijden en prijzen (vanaf 69 euro) zijn te vinden op www.thalys.nl.

Met de bus

De pendelbusdienst Eurolines rijdt iedere dag twee keer op Parijs. Opstapplaatsen in Nederland zijn Groningen, Utrecht, Amsterdam, Den Haag, Rotterdam, Breda, Eindhoven en Den Bosch. De reistijd van Amsterdam naar Parijs is een kleine 8 uur en een retourtje voor dit traject kost 79 euro. Kijk voor reistijden en speciale prijzen op www.eurolines.nl.

Met de auto

Wil je met je eigen auto naar Parijs gaan, dan moet je rekening houden met het feit dat op vrijwel alle Franse snelwegen tol wordt geheven. Vanaf de Belgische grens betaal je tot de Franse hoofdstad ongeveer 12,50 euro per personenauto. Mocht je een omweg via Metz willen maken, dan kosten de Franse autowegen erna ongeveer 32 euro.

Met het vliegtuig

Verscheidene luchtvaartmaatschappijen vliegen van Schiphol naar Parijs Charles de Gaulle. De meest frequente lijndiensten worden onderhouden door de KLM en Air France. Het is vaak mogelijk voordelige tickets te krijgen, bijvoorbeeld van andere vliegtuigmaatschappijen. De beste manier om daar achter te komen is internet te raadplegen; kijk bijvoorbeeld op www.atp.nl, www.cheaptickets.nl, www.vliegticketspecialist.nl of een van de vele andere bedrijven die zich na even googelen aanbieden.

De Franse hoofdstad beschikt over twee internationale luchthavens, waarvan de Aeroport Charles de Gaulle (CDG) de grootste is en in grootte tevens de derde van Europa, na London Heathrow en Frankfurt. Hij ligt op ongeveer zesentwintig kilometer ten noordoosten van het stadscentrum en is vooral aanvlieghaven voor de grotere lijnvliegtuigen.

De tweede luchthaven is die van Orly (ORY), die veertien kilometer ten zuiden van Parijs ligt. Hier starten en landen voornamelijk de vliegtuigen voor binnenlandse vluchten.

Vervoer van de luchthavens naar de stad

CHARLES DE GAULLE:

Taxiritten van de luchthavens de stad in zijn relatief duur; van Charles de Gaulle naar de binnenstad ongeveer 36 euro en van Orly ongeveer 25 euro – in beide gevallen vooropgesteld dat er geen files zijn! Aantrekkelijker geprijsd (en dikwijls nog sneller ook) is het openbaar vervoer. Vanaf Charles de Gaulle (station bij Terminal 2) biedt de metro de snelste manier om naar Gare du Nord, Châtelet-Les Halles en de volgende metrostations te reizen. De metrotreinen vertrekken tussen 5 uur en circa 24 uur om de 15 minuten; de prijs is ongeveer 8 euro. Lijn 2 van de busdienst van Air France rijdt vanaf 5.45 uur tot 23 uur om de 15 minuten van de luchthaven, Terminal 2, naar de Place d'Etoile. Wie in het zuiden van de stad moet zijn neemt bus 4 naar het station Montparnasse of Invalides. De bussen van deze lijn rijden van 7 uur tot 21.30 om de 15 minuten. Dan is er ook nog de

Roissybus die van 5.45 uur tot 23 uur om de 15-20 minuten naar l'Opéra rijdt en daarover 45 minuten doet. Voor deze rit betaal je circa 8,40 euro.

ORLY:

Er vinden vanuit Nederland en België geen vluchten op Parijs Orly plaats, maar mocht je er toch terechtkomen, dan is het goed te weten dat er vanaf het treinstation een RER-sneltreinverbinding met het centrum van Parijs bestaat en dat dit station vanaf de luchthaven te bereiken is met een shuttlebus.

Een uitgebreider dienstrooster van het openbaar vervoer is te vinden op de website van de beide Parijse luchthavens: www.adp.fr.

DE ZOEKTOCHT NAAR DE VOLMAAKTE GEUR

Grenouilles reis naar Frankrijks zuiden

In mei van het jaar 1756 verlaat Grenouille Parijs om in Grasse de kunst van de geurwinning te leren. Hij trekt te voet door het zuiden van Frankrijk.

HET CENTRAAL MASSIEF EN MONTPELLIER

Parijs achter zich latend, neemt Grenouille de weg naar Orléans. Maar bij het ruiken van de geuren van die stad besluit hij er met een grote boog omheen te lopen. Hij zet koers naar het oosten tot Château-sur-Loire, zwerft daarvandaan nog enkele kilometers verder en steekt bij Sully-sur-Loire de Loire over. Op zijn verdere weg naar het zuiden mijdt hij steden en dorpen, tot hij in augustus eindelijk de Auvergne en het Centraal Massief bereikt. Hier bevond zich 'de pool, namelijk het punt dat het verst van alle mensen lag van heel het koninkrijk' (vertaling Ronald Jonkers, p. 121), de top van de berg die Plomb du Cantal wordt genoemd.

Zo 'mensenver' als het Cantalmassief in Grenouilles tijd is geweest, is het nu allang niet meer. Dit indrukwekkende landschap in het zuiden van Frankrijk behoort met zijn doorsnede van ongeveer tachtig kilometer tot de grootste vulkaangebergten ter wereld en trekt tegenwoordig talloze toeristen. In de zomer komen de wandelaars, in de winter de skiërs en snowboarders. Vanuit het wintersportcentrum Super-Lorian kan men zich via een kabelbaan gemakkelijk naar de top van de Plomb du Cantal laten vervoeren om er

◄ Zoals de vogel hem ziet: de Plomb du Cantal

op 1850 meter hoogte te zoeken naar de grot waarin Grenouille zich had teruggetrokken om er zijn eenzame bestaan te leiden.

Grenouille brengt zeven jaar door in zijn hol, tot de schokkende waarheid tot hem doordringt dat hij zichzelf niet kan ruiken. Hij, die over zo'n buitengewone, uitgesproken reukzin beschikt, bezit geen eigen lichaamsgeur! In februari 1763 verlaat hij de berg en trekt naar het zuiden. In de omgeving van het stadje Pierrefort jaagt hij met zijn verwilderde uiterlijk de boeren de stuipen op het lijf. Men brengt hem voor de burgemeester, die op zijn beurt aan de leenheer van de stad, markies de la Taillade-Espinasse, verslag uitbracht over deze 'holenmens'.

De markies is een ontwikkeld man met open oog voor zowel de dingen die hem omringen als voor de mogelijke verbetering van die dingen. Zijn geestdriftige, wetenschappelijke geest is verrukt van de komst van Grenouille, die hij ziet als de belichaming en het bewijs van zijn theorie over het 'fluidum letale'. Hij neemt hem dan ook met groot enthousiasme op in zijn paleis in Montpellier.

◀ ...en wanneer hij embarkeerde was het niet in boten van dit snelle type

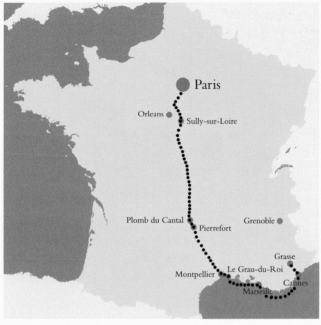

▲ Grenouille liet te voet vele kilometers achter zich...

Montpellier was in de achttiende eeuw in grootte de derde stad van Frankrijk. De plaatselijke universiteit, waar de markies Grenouille voor het voetlicht haalt, is een van de oudste van Frankrijk en 's lands eerste waar, in 1220, een medische faculteit was gevestigd. Ook tegenwoordig bepaalt het universitaire leven een groot deel van het stadsbeeld: met ongeveer 60.000 studenten aan drie universiteiten is Montpellier na Parijs en Toulouse nog altijd de derde universiteitsstad van Frankrijk.

In het begin van maart vervolgt Grenouille zijn weg. In het havenstadje Le Grau-du-Roi, vandaag de dag een populaire vakantiebestemming, embarkeert hij zich op een schip dat hem naar Marseille brengt. Hij vindt er een ander schip en vaart naar Cannes, waar hij aan land gaat om via de napoleontische straatweg landinwaarts te trekken, richting Grasse.

LAVENDELGEUR EN DEODORANT

Snuffeltoer door Grasse, wereldhoofdstad van het parfum

Zijn reisdoel wordt bereikt – Grenouille komt aan in de wereldhoofdstad van het parfum. Ruim twee jaar zou hij in Grasse blijven, om zich verder te bekwamen in het maken van parfums.

HOE HET PARFUM IN DE PROVENCE KWAM

Reeds in de Middeleeuwen werd Grasse erom geroemd een rijke en bedrijvige handelsstad te zijn. De oorsprong daarvan lag in het feit dat de waterrijkdom van de streek in de twaalfde eeuw ambachtslieden had aangetrokken, vooral leerlooiers. Ze vervaardigden geitenleer van bijzonder hoge kwaliteit en het duurde niet lang voordat het leer uit Grasse wijd en zijd beroemd was. Zo ontwikkelde dit ambacht zich tot de grootste economische drijfveer van de stad.

In de tijd van de Renaissance kwam een nieuwe mode uit Italië en Spanje ook in Frankrijk in zwang: geparfumeerde handschoenen, en de Grasser leerlooiers reageerden adequaat op deze trend. Daarbij ontdekten ze dat lavendel zich uitstekend leent tot het parfumeren van leer. Algauw parfumeerden zij dan ook niet alleen meer handschoenen, maar ook vesten, ceintuurs en tasjes met welriekende oliën. De aristocratie van heel Europa kocht nu haar leerwaren in Grasse en in het jaar 1614 stelde de koning voor dit nieuwe handwerk de meestertitel Handschoenenmaker-Parfumeur in.

De boeren in de omtrek begonnen op hun velden de par-

◄ De spitsloze kerktoren van Grasse

◄ Geurstoffen uit de hele wereld vinden hun weg naar Grasse

fumplanten te verbouwen. Het milde klimaat en de vruchtbare bodem van de Provence waren als het ware geschapen voor de cultivering van lavendel, rozen, tuberozen, jasmijn en sinaasappelboompjes. Er ontstond een levendige handel tussen de boeren en de parfumeurs en het belang van de parfumvervaardiging werd voor stad almaar groter. In 1724 maakten de gezamenlijke parfumeurs zich los van het gilde van de leerlooiers en gingen verder onder een eigen gilde.

Na de Franse Revolutie werd de belasting op lederwaren verhoogd. Daarbij kwam dat de omwonenden steeds vaker klaagden over de stankoverlast die de leerlooierijen in de stad veroorzaakten. Het aantal leerlooiers nam af, terwijl dat van de parfumeurs juist toenam. In 1845 waren er nog dertien leerlooierijen in Grasse; de laatste verdween ten slotte in 1914.

Al in de negentiende eeuw verdrong de parfumindustrie het leerlooiersambacht als belangrijkste bedrijfstak van de stad. Van de parfumeurs hadden velen zich intussen gespecialiseerd om de opgevoerde productie door de Parijse parfumeurs het hoofd te bieden; zij produceerden nu vooral geuressences voor die markt. De Industriële Revolutie bracht nieuwe productiemethoden met zich mee die meer ruimte vergden en de fabrieken werden nu vanuit de stad naar de omgeving verplaatst.

WASVERZACHTER EN ZEEP:
DE GEURINDUSTRIE VAN NU

Tot op de dag van vandaag is de geurwinning naast het toerisme de belangrijkste bron van inkomsten van de regio. Grasse afficheert zich met het nodige aplomb als 'wereldhoofdstad van de parfums'. Maar zoals men in de tijd van Grenouille met geur werkte en zoals men er nu mee omgaat verschilt van elkaar als de dag van de nacht. Doordat buitenlandse, meestal beduidend goedkopere grondstoffen op de markt kwamen en vooral door de kwalitatief steeds beter wordende synthetische geuressences werden de fabrikanten gedwongen zich aan te passen. Het merendeel van de ongeveer zestig bedrijven die in Grasse actief zijn, werkt tegenwoordig in opdracht van multinationals aan het mengen van geuren voor wasmiddelen en wasverzachters, voor douchegel en deodorants. Natuurlijke grondstoffen zijn daarvoor veel te duur. Andere bedrijven hebben zich gespecialiseerd in de productie van geurstoffen voor levensmiddelen.

Voor deze banale producten heeft men rozenblaadjes noch fraaie flacons meer nodig en zo is de moderne parfumindustrie een deel van haar luxueuze uitstraling kwijtgeraakt. Maar wat is erop tegen om je te laten meeslepen in

◄ De 'Parfumeur', het symbool van de stad

▲ Een van de laatste 'neuzen' van Grasse: Jacques Maurel, chef-par-fumeur van Galimard

nostalgie? Want de Provence en zijn geur zijn beslist nog steeds een bezoek waard en de geschiedenis van de parfum-bereiding wordt in Grasse liefdevol gecultiveerd en met graagte met de bezoeker gedeeld. En het spreekt vanzelf dat in bijna ieder winkeltje een stukje lavendelzeep of een geur-zakje op een nieuwe eigenaar wacht.

In de eenentwintigste eeuw hebben de scheikundigen het vaandel dus overgenomen van de kunstenaars en de schep-pende parfumtovenaars. Slechts drie 'neuzen' (in het jargon: parfumeurs) werken nog in de sector die deze Zuid-Franse

VOOR HET PUBLIEK:

Adressen: Molinard; 60 Boulevard Victor Hugo, 06130 Grasse; telefoon: 04 92 42 33 11, www.molinard.com.
Fragonard; Boulevard Fragonard; 06130 Grasse; telefoon: 04 93 36 44 65, www.fragonard.com.
Galimard; Route de Cannes; 06130 Grasse; telefoon: 04 93 70 36 22, www.galimard.com.
Openingstijden van alle drie de musea: dagelijks van 9 tot 18 uur.

▲ Een van de drie grote parfumerieën van Grasse: Molinard

stad in de hele wereld beroemd heeft gemaakt, die van de exquisiete, dure parfums.

De voormalige fabrieken van de drie grote parfumeurs Galimard, Molinard en Fragonard in de stad zijn allang omgebouwd tot musea. De bezoeker kan er veel wetenswaardigs opdoen over de grondstoffen en de verschillende procedés die voor de geurwinning werden toegepast. In fraaie vitrines staan historische flacons uit diverse epoques opgesteld. In al die musea worden gratis rondleidingen gehouden met uitleg in verscheidene talen.

ACHTERGROND:
GEURWORKSHOP – JE EIGEN PARFUM

Zou je, net als Grenouille, zelf wel eens je eigen, onweerstaanbare geurtje willen creëren, dan is deelname aan een geurworkshop zoals die bijvoorbeeld bij Molinard wordt gegeven, aan te bevelen. In een mooie, negentiende-eeuwse villa bevindt zich het zogenaamde 'tarinologieatelier' ('tarin' is jargon voor 'neus'). Onder leiding van 'tarinologe' Céline Reinard-Demets mag de geurbewuste toerist hier naar hartenlust mengen.

Na wat informatieve verkenningen op het gebied van de boven-, midden- en ondertoets van een parfum mogen de deelnemers hun gang gaan. Op schappen van carrouselkastjes staan meer dan tachtig verschillende essences klaar waaruit iedere deelnemer, na gesnuffeld te hebben, zijn of haar lievelingsluchtjes kiest. Dit is helemaal niet zo gemakkelijk, want later zal pas blijken of de verschillende aroma's ook werkelijk bij elkaar passend gekozen zijn – wat voor de bezitter van de ongeoefende neus een schier onmogelijke taak is, vooral wanneer men, zoals gebruikelijk, zeven of acht van die bruinglazen reservoirs heeft uitgekozen. De hele ruimte is plotseling vervuld van de meest uiteenlopende geuren, wat een nostalgische stemming oproept – en niet zelden een aantal niesbuien.

Voordat er gemengd gaat worden, komt Céline Reinard-Demets nog even naar de verzameling kijken. Met haar ervaring is een snelle snuffel genoeg om te concluderen of uit de gekozen essences wel of niet een welriekend mengsel zal ontstaan. Zo nodig ruilt ze nog wat bestanddelen om voordat ze helpt bij het vaststellen van de precieze verhouding van de componenten. Met plastic pipetten worden nu die voorgeschreven hoeveelheden uit de reservoirs opgezogen en naar een flesje overgebracht. Tot slot wordt het flesje licht

▲ De jonge-meisjesessence zullen we hier wel vergeefs zoeken...

▲ Een zeepfabriek in de achttiende eeuw

geschud en is het parfum klaar – zo individueel als maar mogelijk is.

Bij het afscheid ontvangt iedere deelnemer een diploma waarop het nummer van het zojuist samengestelde parfum vermeld staat. De formule ervan krijgt hetzelfde nummer en dit wordt in de archieven van Molinard opgeslagen, waardoor het mogelijk wordt dat de maker zijn of haar 'eigen parfum' later kan nabestellen.

VOOR HET PUBLIEK:

Adres: Molinard; 60 Boulevard Victor Hugo, 06130 Grasse; telefoon: 04 92 42 33 11.

De workshop duurt anderhalf uur en kost, inclusief een flacon van het eigen parfum, 40 euro per persoon.

Aanmelding vooraf wordt sterk aanbevolen.

PLACE AUX AIRES

*Na zijn aankomst in Grasse zoekt Grenouille het
leerlooiersdistrict op. Daar, in het stadscentrum ligt ook
de Place aux Aires, waar hij in een herberg eerst een
middagmaaltijd eet.*

De langgerekte Place aux Aires is het centrale plein van
Grasse. Het wordt omgeven door gerestaureerde herenhui-
zen en onder de colonnade die langs de zijde loopt bevinden
zich bedrijven en restaurants – een prima plek voor een kof-
fiepauze. Het hart van het plein wordt gekarakteriseerd
door een uit 1828 stammende, prachtige fontein met drie
boven elkaar geplaatste bekkens. Kleine neringdoenden zetten hier iedere morgen opnieuw hun kraampjes op om er
bloemen, fruit en andere producten uit de regio te verko-
pen. De marktklok stamt uit 1802.

Documenten uit de vijftiende eeuw vermelden het bestaan van het plein al. In die tijd werd hier het graan ge-
dorst, werden de korrels gedroogd en vervolgens verkocht.
In de periode waarin Grenouille naar Grasse komt is die situatie al veranderd want de Place aux Aires is met zijn zij-
straten dan het domein van de leerlooiers. In 1745 hadden

▲ Het is maar goed dat de Place aux Aires is 'drooggelegd'

alleen al in dit district zestig looiers met hun bedrijf emplooi gevonden. Het voor dit ambacht noodzakelijke water was ruim voorhanden: vanuit een bron in een berg stroomde een beek tot onder het midden van het plein. Kanalisatie hiervandaan had men niet nodig gevonden; het water stroomde simpelweg door de straatjes en steegjes, bijvoorbeeld door de Rue des Moulinets. Zoals de naam al aangeeft stonden daar destijds kleine watermolens, drie in getal, die door het van de Place aux Aires wegstromende water werden aangedreven.

Aan de noordzijde van het plein staat het mooie paleis van Maximin Isnard (1758-1825) met zijn prachtige smeedijzeren balkons. De naam van deze monsieur Isnard, een rijke leerlooier en koopman, heeft waarschijnlijk Patrick Süskind geïnspireerd om de in zijn roman voorkomende lakenkoopman, die per abuis zijn eigen huisknecht neerschoot, Misnard te noemen.

Achter het huisnummer 27 van de Place aux Aires bevindt zich tegenwoordig onder de galerij een boekwinkel. Maar eerder stond daar het Hôtel du Dauphin, lange tijd de enige herberg van de stad. Dit doet vermoeden dat dit de plek is waar Süskind zijn protagonist Grenouille zijn middagmaal laat gebruiken, ook al wordt de naam als zodanig niet in de roman genoemd. Daarentegen wordt wel concreet melding gemaakt van de naam van de stamkroeg van Druot, de gezel van madame Arnulfi, die bovendien met haar het bed deelt. Druot bezoekt regelmatig het etablissement Quatre Dauphins, dat in werkelijkheid in Grasse nooit bestaan heeft. Wel bevinden zich een plein en een hotel met die naam in Aix-aux-Provence, de stad waar Patrick Süskind een jaar lang heeft gestudeerd. Dit geeft grond aan het vermoeden dat Süskind door de namen ietwat te verdraaien een hommage heeft willen brengen aan zijn vroegere studiestad.

RUE DROITE

Tijdens zijn eerste omzwerving door de stegen van Grasse stuit Grenouille op de Rue Droite, de hoofdstraat van de stad. Hier woont de welgestelde Antoine Richis met zijn beeldschone dochter Laure. Haar geur maakt hem gek van verlangen hem te bezitten. Maar hij besluit daarmee te wachten tot het kind Laure een jonge vrouw is geworden.

De naam 'Rue Droite' is niet, zoals men wellicht kan vermoeden, afgeleid van 'droite' ('rechts'). In de Middeleeuwen heeft deze straat de bijnaam 'via diretta' gehad, ofwel 'directe weg' omdat hij inderdaad de kortste, meest rechtstreekse route tussen de zuidelijke en de noordelijke delen van de stad vormde.

Tegenwoordig is de voormalige Rue Droite in de oude binnenstad de belangrijkste promenade om te zien en gezien te worden. Talrijke parfumerieën, boetieks en vanzelfsprekend ook souvenirwinkeltjes maken de straat aantrekkelijk voor toeristen, maar ook voor mensen uit stad en streek. Hier en daar verandert de straat van naam: aan het begin, bij de zuidelijk gelegen Place du Cours, heet hij Rue

▲ De doorgang naar de oude binnenstad

▲ Destijds nog weelderiger dan tegenwoordig: het huis van Antoine Richis

Jean Ossola, verderop Rue Marcel Journet en alleen in het noordelijke eindtraject heeft hij nog zijn oorspronkelijke naam. Het paleisachtige huis waarin Süskind Antoine Richis laat wonen, staat aan het begin van de tegenwoordige Rue Jean Ossola. Het is het voormalige, uit de zestiende eeuw stammende Hôtel Luce met walnotenhouten deuren die fraai uitgesneden zijn. Ooit gebouwd voor een zekere familie Villeneuve, werd het gebouw in het begin van de negentiende eeuw eigendom van de familie Luce. In 1934 werden er na een grondige verbouwing twee afzonderlijke gebouwen van gemaakt.

Het huis met het nummer 14 is tegenwoordig in het bezit van de parfumfabrikant Fragonard, die er ook enkele kantoren heeft. Men zegt dat D'Artagnan, de befaamde musketier des konings, in de zeventiende eeuw hier gewoond heeft. Je vraagt je af of hij het meisje Laure misschien beter beschermd had kunnen hebben…

Een bordje aan de gevel van nummer 16 herinnert eraan dat dit gebouw ooit deel uitmaakte van Hôtel Villeneuve. Het huis is tegenwoordig in particuliere handen. De mooie tuin waarin Laure zich bevond toen Grenouille voor het eerst haar geur bespeurde, strekt zich van de achterzijde van

▲ Het was niet de geur van de bloemen die Grenouille de weg wees, het was de geur van Laure...

het gebouw uit tot aan de stadsmuur. De takken van de sinaasappelboom waarvan in de roman sprake is, kan men ook nu nog van de buitenkant van de stadsmuur daarbovenuit zien steken. Maar om in de tuin zelf te komen, moet men door het huis heen en dat is helaas niet toegankelijk voor publiek.

Voor het bedenken van namen heeft Patrick Süskind zich enige anagrammatische grapjes veroorloofd: zo zal men in de stadsarchieven van Grasse weliswaar vergeefs zoeken naar een zekere Antoine Richis, maar wel stuiten op een koopman die de naam Antoine *Chiris* droeg.

RUE DE LA LAUVE

Nog twee jaar heeft Grenouille de tijd om zijn kennis over de geurwinning te perfectioneren. Want dan zal naar zijn mening het meisje Laure gerijpt zijn tot vrouw. In het parfumatelier van madame Arnulfi krijgt hij een aanstelling als gezel. Hij bereidt er zich in alle rust voor op wat zijn meesterwerk moet worden.

De Rue de la Louve waarin Süskind het parfumatelier van madame Arnulfi plaatst, is de enige in de roman genoemde straat die in werkelijkheid niet bestaat of bestaan heeft. Wel is er een straat die Rue de la Lauve heet, een naam die is afgeleid van het Provençaalse woord 'laùvo', waarmee de vlakke stenen platen werden aangeduid die over de waterloop van de leerlooierijen werden gelegd.

Maar dat is ook ongeveer het meest interessante wat over de Rue de la Lauve gemeld kan worden. De steeg is een aftakking van het laatste deel van de Rue Droite en ligt in een niet bepaald aantrekkelijk deel van de noordelijke binnenstad. Het straatbeeld wordt overheerst door voormalige winkels waarvan ramen en deuren dichtgespijkerd zijn, slooppanden en muren die overdekt zijn met graffiti, terwijl aan de overkant een geasfalteerd sportterrein ligt. Zou hier ooit een parfumeur gewerkt hebben, dan is daar in ieder geval niets meer van te ruiken.

Süskind laat Grenouille zijn intrek nemen in een kleine hut in madame Arnulfi's olijfboomgaard achter een franciscanenklooster. De archieven bevestigen dat er ooit een klooster is geweest, gebouwd in de dertiende eeuw, maar overblijfselen ervan zal men vergeefs zoeken want op deze destijds gewijde plek staat nu een filiaal van de Franse supermarktketen Monoprix.

▲ Schrijffout of met een bedoeling anders gespeld? In de Rue de la Louve plaatst Süskind madame Arnulfi's atelier

ACHTERGROND: *DE PARFUMWINNING*

In hoofdstuk twintig van de roman *Het parfum* vraagt de doodziek te bed liggende Grenouille aan de parfumeur Baldini:

> *Zeg eens, Maître: zijn er nog andere methoden dan persen of destilleren om uit een voorwerp geur te winnen? (vertaling Ronald Jonkers, p. 106)*

Het antwoord van Baldini completeert de destijds bekende extractiemethoden:

> *Daarvan zijn er drie, mijn zoon: de* enfleurage à chaud, *de enfleurage à froid en de* enfleurage à l'huile. *Ze zijn in veel opzichten verheven boven het destilleren en men maakt er gebruik van voor de winning van de allerfijnste geuren: van jasmijn, van roos en van oranjebloesem. (vertaling Ronald Jonkers, p. 107)*

De **uitpersing** is een oude en eenvoudige techniek die wordt toegepast voor het winnen van citrusoliën. De schil van een sinaasappel, mandarijn, citroen of bergamotcitroen wordt ingesneden en vervolgens uitgeperst.

De **destillatie** is in de eerste plaats geschikt voor betrekkelijk ongevoelig plantaardig materiaal als hout en kruiden, maar ook voor bijvoorbeeld lavendel. Oorspronkelijk werd

◄ Bloesems in vet: de 'koude enfleurage'

▲ Destillatie met een koperen alambiek

zulk materiaal samen met water in een destilleerkolf, een zo-genoemde alambiek, op open vuur verhit. De waterdamp onttrekt aan de planten hun geurmoleculen en neemt ze mee naar boven. De daarbij ontstane condensdruppels liet men afkoelen en hieruit kon de essence worden gewonnen. Rond het midden van de negentiende eeuw werd deze methode ver-beterd: het gedroogde plantenmateriaal werd op een rooster over het kokende water gelegd, waardoor de waterdamp er-doorheen werd geleid. Dit proces kan minuten, maar ook da-gen duren, al naar gelang uit welk materiaal de olie gewonnen moest worden. Een half uur was voldoende voor het destille-ren van 450 kilo lavendel, terwijl eenzelfde hoeveelheid san-delhout tachtig tot honderd uur aan de damp blootgesteld moest worden om er een geurige essence aan te onttrekken.

Een veel delicatere manier dan destillatie is de extractie met vetten, de zogenaamde **enfleurage**. Bij de koude versie hiervan, de **enfleurage à froid**, worden glasplaten bestre-ken met geurloos, dierlijk vet. Op deze vetlaag legt men vers geplukte bloesems met de kelk naar boven. Het vet onttrekt aan de bloesems de geurstoffen en binnen enkele dagen zijn de aromatische substanties van de planten in het vet opge-nomen. Nu verwijdert men de 'uitgeputte' bloesems en ver-vangt ze door nieuwe, net zo vaak tot het vet verzadigd is

◄ Toestel voor de extrac-
tie met vluchtige oplos-
middelen

met de etherische oliën van de bloesem. Tot slot wordt het
vet-geurmengsel, de pommade, in bijna zuivere alcohol ge-
wassen. De geurstoffen treden in de alcohol over en het resultaat is de zogenoemde 'absolue d'enfleurage', een zeer fijne bloesemolie.

Een gelijkaardig proces wordt gevolgd bij de **enfleurage
à l'huile**: doeken van linnen of katoen worden doortrokken
met fijne olie waarop de bloesem worden gelegd. Nadat de
aroma's in de olie zijn getrokken, wordt de olie uit de doeken
geperst. Deze twee technieken lenen zich goed voor kwets-
bare bloesems als die van jasmijn, tuberoos en viooltjes – en
natuurlijk ook voor jonge vrouwen, want dat heeft Grenouille uit en te na bewezen!

In de warme enfleurage (**enfleurage à chaud**), ook wel
maceratie genoemd, worden de bloesems in tot 50 à 70 gra-
den verwarmd vet gestrooid en daarin uitgekookt. Ook bij
deze methode wordt de bloesemolie vervolgens met alcohol
uit het vet losgemaakt. Maceratie wordt toegepast op bloesems die pas bij hogere temperaturen hun geurstoffen afgeven – rozen, mimosa en oranjebloesems.

Enfleurage wordt tegenwoordig praktisch niet meer toegepast omdat de methode te tijdrovend en te duur is. Ervoor
in de plaats gekomen is de **extractie met vluchtige oplosmiddelen**, min of meer een ontwikkeling uit de enfleu-

rage. Bij extractie wordt het vet vervangen door geurloze oplosmiddelen als petroleumether of butaan. Voor een grote
productie wordt het oplosmiddel door de plantaardige of
dierlijke grondstof gepompt die in een trommel ronddraait
of op een fijnmazig rooster ligt. Het oplosmiddel onttrekt
uit de grondstof niet alleen de etherische oliën, maar ook
kleurstoffen en was. Dit proces wordt enkele malen her-
haald, waarna het nu verzadigde oplosmiddel wordt gedes-
tilleerd. Het resultaat van die destillatie is een vaste massa
die 'essence concrète' wordt genoemd. Vervolgens wordt
met behulp van alcohol de was afgescheiden, waarna de 'essence absolue' overblijft, de absoluut zuivere bloesemolie.
Deze methode, die aan het einde van de negentiende eeuw
in zwang raakte, is tegenwoordig de meest toegepaste. Met
deze methode konden voor het eerst ook de weerbarstige
geurstoffen van lelietjes-van-dalen worden gebonden.

FONTAINE DE LA FOUX

Grasse wordt geteisterd door een seriemoordenaar!
Nadat eerder al drie jonge vrouwen dood in de
bloemenvelden werden aangetroffen, wordt buiten de
stadspoort het lijk van een vierde slachtoffer, een
wasvrouw uit Sardinië, gevonden. Ze ligt bij een fontein,
de Fontaine de la Foux.

Aan het einde van de Boulevard du Jeu de Ballon bevindt
zich tegenwoordig een verkeersrotonde met in het midden
een stukje groenvoorziening. Dit is de plek waar ooit de
Fontaine de la Foux stond, nu nog in herinnering gebracht
door de naam van het plein, Place de la Foux – toneel van
een van Grenouilles vrouwenmoorden. Met de stad in de
rug een paar passen verder, meteen naast het kantoor voor
toeristische informatie, maakt een bord je attent op de bron
die het water voor de fontein leverde.

Tot aan het einde van de negentiende eeuw was de stad
voor zijn drinkwater geheel en al op de Source de la Foux
aangewezen. Deze bron was de uitloop van een zeer groot

▲ Een openbare wasplaats met bogengalerij

waterreservoir dat zich ongeveer tussen Cabris, Coussols, Grasse en Châteuneuf bevond. Een deel van dat water stroomde naar de fontein, maar het meeste naar openbare wasplaatsen. Vervolgens vloeide het water door waterlopen naar watermolens, fabrieken en velden.

◄ Wat het schaap ermee van doen heeft is onduidelijk, maar dit is de 'Fontaine de la Foux'

CATHÉDRALE NOTRE-DAME DU PUY

*Het moorden gaat door en de burgers van Grasse zijn
doodsbang. Hoogst persoonlijk spreekt de bisschop
vanaf de kansel van de kathedraal Notre-Dame du Puy
over de moordenaar een banvloek uit. Vooralsnog lijkt
die te werken...*

De op een rotsplateau staande Cathédrale Notre-Dame du
Puy is vanaf grote afstand al te zien, want ook zonder een ge-
weldige kerktoren domineert hij het stadsbeeld. Hij werd in
de dertiende eeuw gebouwd toen de bisschopszetel van An-
tibes naar Grasse werd verplaatst. De 160 centimeter dikke
zijmuren uit witte kalksteen getuigen er nog van dat de kerk
ooit deel uitmaakte van de verdedigingsgordel van de stad.
Uit die tijd is alleen de toren behouden gebleven, behalve
dan dat hij destijds eens zo hoog was. In de zeventiende en
achttiende eeuw is de kerk herhaaldelijk verbouwd en ver-
groot, maar toch is de romaanse bouwstijl nog te herken-

▶ De kathedraal uit de
dertiende eeuw

nen. Tijdens de Franse Revolutie werd de kerk als opslag-
plaats voor voedsel gebruikt.

In het hoge interieur met zijn kruisgewelven is het donker
en de stenen muren maken een grove indruk, ook al omdat
ze nauwelijks versieringen dragen. Maar in de zuidelijke zij-
beuk hangen drie vroege schilderijen van Rubens. Deze zijn
rond 1600 in opdracht van een katholieke kerk gemaakt,
maar daar geweigerd. Niet al te eervol voor de schilder werden ze vervolgens aan het ziekenhuis van Grasse overgedaan. Sinds 1972 worden ze in de kathedraal geëxposeerd.
Verder is het enige religieuze werk dat hier te zien is het

VOOR HET PUBLIEK:

Adres: Hôtel de Ville, Place du Petit Puy, 06131 Grasse.
Telefoon: 04 97 05 50 00
Openingstijden: van oktober tot en met juni: maandag tot en
met zaterdag van 9.30 tot 11.30 en van 15 tot 17.30 uur, zondag
gesloten. Van juli tot en met september: dagelijks van 9.30 tot
11.30 en van 15 tot 18.30 uur.

schilderij *De Voetwassing* van de hand van de in Grasse geboren schilder Jean-Honoré Fragonard.

Naast de kathedraal staat het voormalige bisschopspaleis, het huidige stadhuis, het Hôtel de Ville. Tussen de kathedraal en het stadhuis loopt een weg die naar het plein voert waarop de bewijsstukken werden uitgestald die in het bezit van de inmiddels gearresteerde Grenouille waren aangetroffen. Hiervandaan heb je een mooi uitzicht op het dal.

EXTRA EXCURSIE: *PARFUMMENU IN RESTAURANT LE GAZAN*

Bloesems hebben niet alleen een heerlijke geur – na op geraffineerde wijze te zijn bereid hebben ze ook een heerlijke smaak. Wie zich daarvan persoonlijk wil overtuigen, mag zich een bezoek aan restaurant Le Gazan niet onthouden. Dicht in de buurt van de kathedraal bieden Jacky en France Soler hun gasten een menu aan dat in gelijke mate de smaak- en geurzenuwen aanspreekt. De ruime verzameling stickers op de buitendeur doet het vermoeden rijzen dat dit sympa-

▲ Restaurant Le Gazan heeft zich gespecialiseerd in het koken met bloemen

VOOR HET PUBLIEK:

Adres: Restaurant Le Gazan; 3 Rue Gazan, 06130 Grasse, telefoon 04 93 36 22 88.
Openingstijden: in de zomer dagelijks 's middags en 's avonds. Zondag gesloten.
Prijs: het parfummenu kost ongeveer 25 euro.

thieke restaurateursechtpaar als het ware een abonnement heeft op aanbevelingen in Franse gastronomische gidsen.

Als aperitief wordt een glas champenoise met een scheutje mimosasiroop opgediend. Op de bodem van het glas laat een gedroogde mimosabloesem nog wat koolzuurbelletjes los. Na deze verfrissende dronk komt het voorgerecht, bestaande uit filets van zeebarbeel met een aromatische tapenade van olijven en tuinkruiden uit de Provence, ter tafel. De tussengang heet 'Petite Pause Provençale' en is een ongewone, zeer verfrissende combinatie van tijmsorbet en citroenijs. Dan volgt het hoofdgerecht: kwartel in een stevige, vol smakende saus, bereid met een gelei van rozenblaadjes, vergezeld van een met rozemarijn gearomatiseerde, gebakken appel. Als sluitstuk van de maaltijd serveert men een geurige crème brûlée met jasmijnaroma. Tongstrelend!

COURS HONORÉ CRESP

De in de kerker geworpen Grenouille wordt ter dood veroordeeld. Hij zal op de Cours Honoré Cresp op het kruis de marteldood moeten sterven. Alles is voor de terechtstelling in gereedheid gebracht. Maar slechts enkele druppels van zijn geheime parfummengsel zijn voldoende om de geplande executie in een massale seksorgie te doen omslaan.

▲ Uitzicht op het dal vanaf de Cours

Wie vanuit het zuiden naar het centrum van Grasse gaat,
komt onvermijdelijk langs de Cours Honoré Cresp. Als een
uit de berg gehouwen terras ligt het plein op 350 meter boven de zeespiegel, een adembenemend uitzicht over de tota-
le vallei van Grasse biedend en zelfs tot de Côte d'Azur met
de daarvoor liggende eilanden.

Er vinden op dit plein vandaag de dag natuurlijk geen terechtstellingen meer plaats, laat staan gangbangs zoals Süskind in zijn roman beschrijft. Wel evenementen van allerlei
aard en die trekken al evenveel bezoekers als het optreden
van Grenouille – bijvoorbeeld de Jasminade, het jasmijnfeest dat ieder jaar in het eerste weekend van augustus wordt
gehouden. Het bloemencorso, dat het hoogtepunt van het
feest vormt, trekt dan vanaf het plein met zijn rijkversierde
themawagens, vergezeld van allerlei folkloristische groepen,
door de straten van de stad. Vanaf de wagens strooien meisjes, onder wie de zojuist uitverkoren Jasmijnkoningin, bloemen over het publiek. Maar echte jasmijn is daar niet vaak
bij omdat die te duur is. De dochter van Antoine Richis,
Laure, heeft met al haar schoonheid nooit de kans gehad Jasmijnkoningin te worden, want het feest ter ere van de jasmijn bestaat pas sinds 1946.

Aan de lange zijde van het plein staat het mooie Palais de
Congrès uit de negentiende eeuw, dat tegenwoordig onder

◄ De fontein met de leeu-
wen in het midden van
het plein

meer het kantoor voor vreemdelingenverkeer onderdak
biedt. De in de roman voorkomende Charité, waarvan de
bewoners hun kamers moesten verlaten om de toeschouwers van de terechtstelling van dienst te zijn, bestaat niet
meer.

Het gebouw met de rode voorgevel aan het einde van het
plein, links van de doorgang naar de oude stad, omvat het
internationale parfumeriemuseum. Sinds 1989 worden hier
de bezoekers omstandig geïnformeerd over de geschiedenis
van de parfumbereiding. Sinds september 2005 zijn aan het
museum renovatie- en uitbreidingswerkzaamheden aan de
gang. Door twee aanpalende gebouwen bij het museum te
trekken wil men het vloeroppervlak van de tentoonstel-

VOOR HET PUBLIEK:

Adres: Musée International de la Parfumerie; 8 Place du Cours, 06130 Grasse.
Telefoon: 04 97 05 58 00.

lingsruimte, die tot nog toe vijftienhonderd vierkante meter bedroeg, verdubbelen. Volgens de plannen moet het werk rond het einde van 2007 klaar zijn. Gedeelten van de museumverzameling zijn tijdens de werkzaamheden te zien in het nabijgelegen museum voor kunst en geschiedenis van de Provence.

JETSET, KLOOSTERS EN MIMOSA

De Provence en de Côte d'Azur

DE BLOEMENVELDEN

Het lijk van het eerste meisje werd gevonden in een rozenveld tussen Grasse en het dorp Opio en de twee daaropvolgende in jasmijnvelden in de omgeving van Grasse.

De streek rond Grasse is ideaal voor de bloementeelt. De lichtelijk hellende velden zorgen voor een goede afvloeiing van het water, het vlakbij oprijzende gebergte beschermt ze tegen al te veel wind en in de bloeitijd schijnt vrijwel altijd de zon. In Grenouilles tijd was de omgeving van Grasse nog een zee van bloeiende bloemen. Maar dat is voorbij. Enerzijds was er de concurrentie, met name uit Noord-Afrika, die voor een enorme prijsdaling leidde omdat de inkopers van parfumproducenten een veel lagere prijs hoefden te betalen voor bloesems uit Egypte en Marokko, anderzijds werden vele parfums inmiddels uitsluitend vervaardigd uit synthetische geurstoffen, wat de vraag naar bloesems verder drukte.

Zo'n honderd jaar geleden waren in de regio nog vijfduizend bloementelers werkzaam, vandaag de dag zijn er nog precies dertig van overgebleven. Veel boeren hebben de moeizame arbeid rond de jasmijnteelt vaarwel gezegd en hebben delen van hun land voor goede prijzen verkocht aan vastgoedmakelaars, want de vraag naar bouwland voor huizen of villa's in het mooie Provençaalse landschap is alleen maar gestegen.

Er liggen nog enkele bloemenvelden langs de hoofd-

◄ Een van de mooiste dingen die de Provence te bieden heeft: bloeiende lavendelvelden in de zomer

◄ Handenarbeid is hier nog onontbeerlijk

wegen, dikwijls aan het oog onttrokken door schuttingen. Dergelijke velden zul je slechts door toeval kunnen zien. Voordat je dus vertwijfeld in de omgeving tussen Grasse en Opio gaat ronddwalen, kun je beter meteen naar Plascassier rijden. Op niet meer dan een paar kilometer van Grasse ligt daar het 'Domaine de Manon' en de eigenaar daarvan, Hubert Biancalana, is de enige bloementeler in de omgeving die rondleidingen door zijn bloemenvelden geeft. Welke bloemen je te zien krijgt hangt af van het seizoen: vanaf begin mei tot medio juni bloeien de rozen, van medio juli tot eind oktober verspreidt de jasmijn zijn geuren.

VOOR HET PUBLIEK:

Adres: Le Domaine de Manon; 36 Chemin du Servan, 06130 Grasse Plascassier.
Telefoon: 04 93 60 12 76 of 06 12 18 02 69.

ACHTERGROND:
PARFUMPLANTEN UIT DE PROVENCE

LAVENDEL

Lavendel is in de geschiedenis van het parfum de plant die het langst en het vaakst is gebruikt. Reeds in de antieke wereld was de lavendelplant bekend, al werd hij toen in de eerste plaats aangewend voor medicinale doeleinden. Lavendel is in zijn toepassing en zijn werkzaamheid zeer veelzijdig. Zijn rustgevende en slaapbevorderende werking is al heel lang bekend. Bovendien zou hij helpen tegen keelpijn, verkoudheid en migraine en ook wonden ontsmetten. De lavendelkussentjes die onze oma's op kastenplanken en in lades legden, verspreidden niet alleen een lekker luchtje, maar hielden ook de motten uit de buurt van het linnengoed. Zijn naam ontleent lavendel overigens aan het Latijnse 'lavare', wat 'wassen' betekent, want vele eeuwen wordt immers aan wasmiddelen en zeep lavendelgeur toegevoegd om het wasgoed de karakteristieke, frisse geur mee te geven.

Bijna iedereen kent wel die enorme lavendelvelden die zich in de midzomer in eindeloos lange banen over de Provençaalse vlakten uitstrekken en er zo fotogeniek bij liggen. Maar niet alles wat in de Provence blauwviolet bloeit, is ook echt lavendel. In de moderne industrie zou het een en ander allang in het honderd zijn gelopen als men lang geleden niet een voordeliger variant had ontwikkeld.

Zo bloeit er op vele van de Zuid-Franse velden *lavandin*, een hybride die beduidend winstgevender is dan de echte lavendel. Dit komt doordat het oogsten van deze nieuw ontwikkelde plant met landbouwmachines kan worden gedaan; de echte lavendel groeit op hogere percelen, dikwijls op rotsachtige grond, die met die machines niet of heel moeilijk bereikt kunnen worden. Hier moeten de planten ook tegenwoordig nog met de traditionele sikkel worden geoogst en de lonen van de arbeiders die dat zware werk doen, worden natuurlijk doorberekend, wat de prijs van lavendel veel hoger maakt dan die van lavandin. De echte lavendel vindt tegenwoordig vooral toepassing in parfums en geneesmiddelen, terwijl voor zeep, wasmiddelen, wasverzachters lavandin wordt gebruikt – evenals voor de vulling van de meeste 'lavendelzakjes' die toeristen als souvenir aan de Provence mee naar huis nemen.

Om een blik op de indrukwekkend mooie velden te kunnen werpen, moet je vanuit Grasse in westelijke richting rijden. De grootste velden van de Provence liggen op het Plateau de Valensole op ongeveer twee uur rijden. De bloeitijd ligt tussen medio juli en eind augustus, variërend met de soort plant, de omgeving en het weer. Een zeldzaamheid op de velden is tegenwoordig de koperen alambiek waarin men vroeger ter plekke de gedroogde lavendel destilleerde.

JASMIJN

De jasmijnstruik is rond het midden van de zestiende eeuw door de Moren en de Spaanse zeelieden naar Zuid-Frankrijk gebracht. In zijn land van herkomst, India, heeft hij ook de naam 'koningin van de nacht'. Het duurde niet lang voordat de jasmijn zich in de omgeving van Grasse verspreidde. In 1930 oogstte men achttienhonderd ton bloesems, maar sindsdien is de oogst gestaag afgenomen; in 1974 lag de opbrengst nog rond de 170 ton en in de laatste jaren komt men niet verder dan 27 ton.

De essence absolue van jasmijnbloesems is zo waardevol dat ze gerust met goud vergeleken kan worden. Een kilo jasmijnextract kost ongeveer vijftienduizend euro en voor die ene kilo moeten acht miljoen bloesems hun geur afgeven. De winning is bijzonder kostbaar: jasmijnbloesems moeten geplukt worden bij het aanbreken van de dag omdat hun geur in de zon snel aan intensiteit verliest. Tegen het middaguur zijn de meest afzienbare velden dan ook ontdaan van bloesems, terwijl ze de volgende dag alweer wit schitteren van de witte bloesems. Bij het oogsten kunnen geen machines gebruikt worden; iedere bloesem moet met de hand uit de struik worden geplukt.

Om de kostbare essence niet verloren te laten gaan moet de oogst heel snel worden verwerkt. Vroeger werden aan de bloesems de geurstoffen onttrokken door middel van enfleurage, maar tegenwoordig is het de techniek van extractie met vluchtige oplosmiddelen die wordt toegepast (zie 'Achtergrond: de parfumwinning').

Een paar van de beroemdste parfums van de wereld zou-

► Tegenwoordig niet zo vaak te zien: een veld met jasmijn

◄ Jasmijn is nu zijn gewicht in goud waard

den zonder de jasmijn uit Grasse niet hebben bestaan. Bijvoorbeeld het legendarische Joy van Jean Patou, dat vrijwel uitsluitend uit meiroos en jasmijn uit de omgeving van Grasse bestaat; bloesems uit andere regio's zouden het parfum een ander karakter gegeven hebben.

Grasse is dus ook tegenwoordig nog onafscheidelijk verbonden met jasmijn. Ter ere van deze bloem wordt jaarlijks in augustus het jasmijnfeest gevierd (zie ook het hoofdstuk 'Cours Honoré Cresp').

MEIROOS

De roos heeft als 'bloem der liefde' een heel oude geschiedenis. Reeds in het oude Griekenland gold hij als de bloem van Aphrodite, godin van liefde en schoonheid. Wij kennen de roos hoofdzakelijk als snijbloem en tuinplant, maar oorspronkelijk werd hij vooral gekweekt om zijn geur.

De in de omgeving van Grasse gecultiveerde meiroos werd tegen het einde van de zestiende eeuw in Holland gekweekt. Zijn weelderige, volle bloesems bezorgden hem de naam 'centifolia', de 'honderdbladige'. Om een liter rozenolie

◄ De meiroos is nog altijd een ingrediënt in Chanel No. 5, het beroemdste parfum ter wereld

◄ Rozengeur werd vroe-
ger door middel van des-
tillatie gewonnen

van eerste kwaliteit te winnen zijn wel vier ton rozenblaadjes nodig. De bloesems van de meiroos met hun intense geur
worden vroeg in de ochtend, wanneer ze net zijn ontloken,
met de hand geplukt. Hoe warmer het in de loop van de dag
wordt, des te minder wordt het oliegehalte en tegen de mid-
dag is er al eenderde van vervlogen. Voor het verwerken van
de bloemblaadjes heeft men niet meer dan een paar uur de
tijd omdat de intensiteit van de geur al heel snel verdwijnt.

De concurrent van de centifolia komt uit Bulgarije en
Turkije. In die landen wordt op grote schaal de Damascener
roos gekweekt. Hij heeft een heel andere geur, maar de prijs
van een kilo van zijn bloesems bedraagt slechts een kwart
van die van centifoliabloesems. Het is dan ook geen wonder
dat tegenwoordig in nog maar een enkel, zeer duur parfum
als de klassieker Chanel No. 5 het aroma van de echte meiroos kan worden geroken.

MIMOSA

Wie het in Zuid-Europa over 'mimosa' heeft, spreekt over de
bolvormige, goudgele bloesems, terwijl wij gewoonlijk denken aan de 'mimosa pudica', in de volksmond kruidje-roer-
mij-niet genoemd omdat hij bij de geringste aanraking zijn
blaadjes samenvouwt. De mimosa die voor ons van belang
is, behoort echter tot de acaciafamilie.

De hoofdstad van de mimosa is de kustplaats Mandelieu-

◄ Mimosa bloeit alleen in februari

La Napoule (zie ook het hoofdstuk La Napoule). In geen andere plaats aan de Côte d'Azur vind je zo veel mimosaboomkwekerijen als hier. Het uitgesproken milde klimaat, te danken aan het Massif de l'Estérel, dat het gebied tegen vorst en bijtende winden beschermt, is hiervan de belangrijkste reden. De bezoeker die in februari en maart komt kijken, mag een wonderschoon langs de berghellingen naar beneden glooiende bloesemzee verwachten. De schrale steengrond is dan met een kanariegeel, uit miljoenen geurige bloesems bestaand tapijt overdekt. Een rampzalige bosbrand vernietigde in 1970 een groot deel van de beplanting en een ongewoon strenge vorst richtte in het daaropvolgende jaar nog meer schade aan. De nieuwe aanplant kwam uiterst moeizaam op gang en ook vandaag nog is van de honderd mimosaplantages van vroeger nog slechts een achttal over.

In Mandelieu-La Napoule wordt sinds 1931 ieder jaar in februari het mimosafeest gevierd, waarin met bloemen versierde wagens door de straten van de stad rijden. Dit feest is aan de Côte d'Azur een der grootste evenementen van deze soort en jaarlijks komen er meer dan 75.000 bezoekers op af. Twaalf ton mimosa wordt ervoor gebruikt.

LA NAPOULE

Antoine Richis wil met een list zijn dochter Laure buiten het bereik van de meisjesmoordenaar brengen. Maar Grenouille 'doorziet' met zijn neus de bedoeling en wacht in de herberg van La Napoule aan de Zuid-Franse kust zijn laatste slachtoffer op.

Aan de Côte d'Azur, op slechts enkele kilometers van Cannes, ligt de badplaats La Napoule. In 1970 werd het dorp samengevoegd met Mandelieu, zodat het nu deel uitmaakt van de gemeente Mandelieu-La Napoule.

Vanaf de tijd van het Romeinse Rijk tot in de Middeleeuwen stond de streek van het huidige Mandelieu bekend als 'Avignet'. De stad en de vesting die ervoor stond werden meerdere keren door de Arabieren uit Noord-Afrika en Spanje aangevallen vanwege hun strategisch gunstige ligging voor verdere veroveringen in de Provence. Nadat de stad in 1387 met de grond gelijk was gemaakt, liet de graaf van Villeneuve hem weer opbouwen, deze keer dichter bij de kust en onder bescherming van het kasteel, dat extra versterkt werd. De naam Villeneuve luidt in het Grieks 'Neapolis' en daarvan is de huidige naam La Napoule afgeleid.

Door de eeuwen heen is het gebied opnieuw en opnieuw

▲ Een vesting aan het strand: het Château van La Napoule

▲ Deze route had Laure moeten nemen - in het plan van haar vader

geteisterd door oorlogen en epidemieën. Ook het Château de la Napoule is meermalen verwoest en even vaak weer opgebouwd. In het begin van de achttiende eeuw was het de hertog van Savoye die de streek verwoestte en het kasteel in puin achterliet, waarna het tweehonderd jaar zou duren voordat het weer werd opgebouwd. In de tijd dat Grenouille er was, bestond de bevolking van La Napoule uit nauwelijks meer dan honderd zielen, hoofdzakelijk landarbeiders.

Pas toen de Côte d'Azur zich rond het einde van de negentiende eeuw ontwikkelde tot geliefd reisdoel van welgestelde bezoekers uit alle windstreken, profiteerde ook La Napoule daarvan. Om het de verwende en kieskeurige gasten zoveel mogelijk naar de zin te maken, werd er flink geïnvesteerd in infrastructuur en ontspanningsmogelijkheden. Zo kwamen er de 'Old Course', het oudste golfterrein aan de Côte d'Azur, een paardenrenbaan en een poloveld, terwijl ook de jachthaven werd uitgebreid. In de belle époque was de mondaine badplaats zeer in trek, vooral bij aristocratische bezoekers.

In 1918 werd het middeleeuwse kasteel van La Napoule gekocht door de rijke Amerikaan Henry Clews (1876-1937). Zijn nieuw verworven bezitting bevond zich in een treurige staat en was nauwelijks meer dan een ruïne. De beide verdedigingstorens waren zwaar beschadigd, in de kapel huisden

▲ Zou dit bedoeld worden met 'iemand de oren wassen'?

schapen en een van de bijgebouwen was in gebruik als glas-fabriek. Henry en zijn vrouw Marie gingen meteen aan de slag met de restauratie, uitgaande van de voorstelling die zij hadden van hoe het er ooit uitgezien zou hebben. Terwijl Marie de rol van architecte speelde leefde Henry, die een groot bewonderaar van de kunstenaar Auguste Rodin was, zich uit als beeldhouwer. Overal zijn van zijn hand details te zien die hier en daar wat potsierlijk overkomen. Zo gluren in de zalen waarin het excentrieke echtpaar zich gedroeg als middeleeuwse vorsten en zich ook zo kleedde, vanachter de pilaren groteske gargouilles naar de bezoekers. En ook het beeld op de binnenplaats, getiteld *God of Humormystics*, ziet er zonderling uit.

De mooie tuin is aangelegd door Marie Clews in deels

VOOR HET PUBLIEK:

Adres: Château de la Napoule, 06210 Mandelieu-La Napoule, telefoon 04 93 49 95 05.

Openingstijden: van 7 februari tot en met 7 november dage-lijks van 10 tot 18 uur; van 8 november tot en met 6 februari op werkdagen van 14 tot 17 uur en in de weekends en op feestdagen van 10 tot 17 uur.

Toegangsprijs: 4,60 euro.

Franse en deels Engelse tuinarchitectuur; veel aandacht is gestoken in de vele van fonteinen voorziene rustplaatsen. Na de dood van haar man zette Marie Clews het restauratiewerk aan het kasteel voort. In 1951, acht jaar voor haar eigen overlijden, begon ze er een stichting ten bate van internationale kunstenaars.

ILE SAINT-HONORAT

Antoine Richis wil zijn dochter Laure buiten het bereik van de moordenaar brengen op het kloostereiland Ile Saint-Honorat. Maar plannen pakken niet altijd goed uit...

Een mooie gelegenheid om de zomerse hectiek van de Côte d'Azur te ontvluchten bieden de twee eilanden Ile Saint-Marguérite en Ile Saint-Honorat, die in de baai van Cannes liggen. Het Ile Saint-Honorat, dat de laatste vluchtplaats van het meisje Laure voor haar moordenaar had moeten worden, is met zijn oppervlakte van veertig hectare het kleinste van de twee. In nog geen uur tijd kun je het eiland gemakkelijk rondgaan. De mooie rondweg wordt geflankeerd door eucalyptus- en pijnbomen en voert langs zeven kapellen,

▲ Het Ile Saint-Honorat op idyllische wijze gefotografeerd

waarvan enkele nog uit de Middeleeuwen stammen. Het is hier waarachtig rustig; al wat je hoort is het sjirpen van de cicaden en het op het strand slaan van de golven.

In het begin van de vijfde eeuw stichtte de oorspronkelijk uit Trier komende heilige Honoratus op dit eiland een klooster dat zich in de loop van de tijd ontwikkelde tot een van de belangrijkste kloosters van West-Europa. In de achttiende eeuw woonden hier tot wel achtduizend monniken en tot het omvangrijke bezit van de orde behoorden ook landerijen op het vasteland. Dat deze rijkdom jaloezie en hebzucht wekte, zal geen verbazing wekken en het eiland werd dan ook verschillende keren door de Saracenen aangevallen en geplunderd. Rond het midden van de elfde eeuw bouwden de monniken een vesting om zich tegen deze aanvallen te beschermen, de Monastère Fortifié de Saint-Honorat. Dit indrukwekkende, aan de zuidelijke landtong van het eiland oprijzende verdedigingswerk werd tot in de veertiende eeuw verder uitgebreid. Toen het eiland in de vijftiende eeuw door piraten werd bezet, diende het bolwerk met zijn op verscheidene verdiepingen gebouwde bogengangen en zijn onderaardse waterreservoir als tijdelijk klooster. In 1635 en 1637 werden beide eilanden veroverd door de Spanjaarden. Uit deze tijd dateren de bij de kapellen geplaatste batterijen kanonnen waarmee de Spanjaarden de veiligheid van de eilanden verhoogden.

▲ Of Laure hier wel veilig zou zijn geweest, blijft de vraag...

◄ Het interieur van de citadel met zijn dubbele zuilengalerij

Na het einde van de Middeleeuwen verloor het klooster steeds meer van zijn betekenis. Rond 1800 woonde er op het eiland nog maar een handvol monniken, zodat het uiteindelijk opgegeven moest worden. Pas in 1869 kwamen de monniken van de cisterciënzerorde uit Sénanque op het eiland om de kloosterlijke traditie voort te zetten.

Vandaag de dag volgen in het klooster vijfentwintig monniken een eenvoudige en strenge levenswijze. De kerk uit de negentiende eeuw belichaamt het beginsel van de simpelheid die de cisterciënzers voorstaan: men vindt aan de kerk geen muurschilderingen, beelden of versieringen en ook het interieur is bijzonder sober gehouden.

In de abdij bevindt zich een winkeltje waar door de monniken vervaardigde producten, waaronder rode en witte wijn van op het eiland verbouwde druiven en verschillende likeuren, te koop zijn.

VOOR HET PUBLIEK:

De veerpont vertrekt uit Cannes, van de Quai des Iles. Afvaart voor heen- en terugreis ongeveer ieder uur; eerste afvaart om 8 uur; laatste thuisvaart om 18 uur.
Prijs voor een retour: volwassenen 11 euro, kinderen van 5 tot 10 jaar 5 euro, jonger dan 5 jaar gratis.
Telefoon: 04 92 98 71 38.

Op eigen houtje: parfumtoer door Grasse

Startpunt voor een wandeling door Grasse in het spoor van de roman *Het parfum* is de **Cours Honoré Cresp**, een groot plateau dat voor de oude stad ligt. Het is handig dat in het mooie, niet te missen gebouw van het Palais de Congrès een van de twee kantoren voor toeristeninformatie van Grasse gevestigd is. Je kunt je hier versterken met een gratis stadplattegrond. Het is voor ons dus een geluk dat Patrick Süskind in zijn roman dit op zich al bezienswaardige plein gekozen heeft om er zich belangrijke gebeurtenissen te laten afspelen. Het maakt dat de ongeveer anderhalf uur in beslag nemende route die wij voor onze wandeling door de oude stad volgen, maar weinig afwijkt van de route die in de stadsplattegrond is ingetekend. Om ons buiten deze route-planner te helpen bij de oriëntering, bevinden zich langs de route in de grond verzonken **messing platen** als herken-ningspunten.

Wij treden voor onze parfumwandeling door Grasse in de voetsporen van Grenouille door als eerste doel de Place aux Aires in het vroegere leerlooiersdistrict te kiezen. We dalen dus vanaf de Cours de trap af, steken de straat over en

◀ Het stadswapen van Grasse met schaap en bisschopsstaf

◀ Een van de paleisachtige woningen uit de bloeitijd van de
stad

dan zijn we al in de oude stad, op de voormalige Rue Droite,
die tegenwoordig de **Rue Jean Ossola** heet. Naar het huis
waarin Antoine Richis met zijn betoverende dochter Laure
heeft gewoond, zoeken we nog niet; in plaats daarvan slaan
we eerst linksaf de **Rue Admiral de Grasse** in.

Aan onze rechterhand ontwaren we de rode gevel van het
uit de zeventiende eeuw stammende Hôtel Court de Font-
michel. Het schitterende gebouw licht een tip van de sluier
op over de rijkdom die invloedrijke burgers in vroegere tijden moeten hebben genoten. We volgen de straat en komen
na enkele minuten aan op het trapeziumvormige **Place
aux Aires**.

▶ De bloemenmarkt op de Place
aux Aires

◀ Een van de vele fonteinen van Grasse

De aanblik van de vele, in het midden van het plein geplaatste stoelen en tafels die bij de omliggende cafés horen, maakt het bijna onmogelijk je voor te stellen dat hier ooit een open kanaal met stromend water geweest is. Anders dan Grenouille deed, zullen we hier niet het middagmaal gebruiken, maar na een korte inspectie van de Provençaalse markt die aan de noordzijde van het plein staat, linksaf de steeg in lopen.

Bij de kleine fontein beklimmen we de trap, waarna we de **Boulevard du Jeu de Ballon** bereiken. Zoals de naam al doet vermoeden amuseerde men zich hier vroeger met het balspel. Aan iets dergelijks zullen we ons nu niet wagen, want behalve dat we er geen tijd voor hebben zouden we ons de woede van de gemotoriseerde verkeersdeelnemers maar op de hals halen. We begeven ons dus maar bergopwaarts naar de eenvoudige rotonde. Precies daar, op de **Place de la Foux**, bevond zich in de achttiende eeuw de wasplaats waar in de roman een van de vermoorde meisjes werd aangetroffen. Een paar passen verderop zien we aan onze linkerhand het tweede kantoor waar toeristen informatie kunnen krijgen. Aan de gevel van het gebouw verwijst een bordje naar de **Source de la Foux**, lange tijd de enige bron die heel Grasse van water voorzag.

We lopen terug en slaan linksaf de aflopende **Rue Maximin Isnard** in. Of we nu achter het aan de linkerkant liggende filiaal van Monoprix zoeken naar de hut in madame Arnulfi's olijfboomgaard, dan wel in de troosteloze **Rue de la Lauve** naar de overblijfselen van haar parfumatelier, beide pogingen zijn vergeefs. We slaan dus maar rechtsaf de smalle straat in die ons naar de Rue de l'Oratoire leidt.

Aan het einde van de Rue d'Oratoire komen we opnieuw de **Rue Droite** tegen en hier gaan we rechts in. We laten ons niet afleiden door de vele winkeltjes die hier zijn, maar houden doelbewust vast aan ons voornemen de kathedraal te bekijken. Daartoe slaan we de eerste straat aan onze linkerhand, de Rue Mougins Roquefort, in om na enkele meters links een plein te bereiken dat een meer aandachtige beschouwing waard is, de **Place de la Poissonerie**, die overschaduwd wordt door een ietwat zonderlinge, groene baldakijn in Jugendstil. De gevels van de huizen op de achtergrond schitteren in de voor deze regio karakteristieke kleuren geel, oranje en rood. We beklimmen de trap naast de fontein met de bogen en komen aan de **Place du Petit Puy**. Voordat we de kathedraal binnengaan om zijn interieur te bewonderen, zijn we nieuwsgierig genoeg om eerst een smeedijzeren poort aan onze linkerhand binnen te gaan. We komen nu op een binnenplaats die wordt opgesierd door een mooiere fontein uit de negentiende eeuw. Deze binnenplaats hoort bij het **Hôtel de Ville**, het stadhuis van Grasse.

▶ De binnenstad van Grasse is populair bij toeristen en dagjesmensen

Nadat we de **kathedraal** van binnen en buiten bekeken hebben, genieten we vanaf de open ruimte achter de kathedraal van het mooie uitzicht op het landschap. Hiervandaan lopen we door de Rue Gazan weer naar de drukste winkelstraat van de oude stad, de **Rue Jean Ossola**. Achter de huidige huisnummers 14 en 16 bevindt zich de paleisachtige woning waarin Süskind in zijn roman Laure en haar vader Antoine Richis laat wonen. Helaas kunnen we de fraaie tuin niet bewonderen omdat het huis van een particuliere eigenaar is. En zo eindigt onze rondwandeling in het spoor van Jean-Baptiste Grenouille door Grasse.

Aansluitend zijn er natuurlijk legio mogelijkheden om op eigen houtje veel meer indrukken van de stad op te doen. Je kunt wandelen door de stegen van de binnenstad, een doolhofachtig gebied dat door de inwoners wel de 'casbah' wordt genoemd, je kunt een van de drie grote, nu als museum dienstdoende voormalige parfumfabrieken bezoeken, terwijl ook het genieten van het aromatische parfummenu in restaurant Le Gazan in de Rue Gazan tot de mogelijkheden behoort.

▶ Gevels in de kleuren van de Provence

▲ De entree van het stadhuis

Parfumrondleiding door Grasse

Het toeristenbureau van Grasse biedt een rondleiding, dus met gids, aan langs de plaatsen die in de roman *Het parfum* worden genoemd. De kunsthistoricus Laurent Poupeville leidt je met grote deskundigheid door de oude binnenstad en kent ook interessante plekjes en achtergronden die niet in de roman naar voren worden gehaald. De twee uur durende rondleiding, waarvoor reservering bij het toeristenbureau nodig is, wordt voorzien van commentaar in het Engels, Frans en Italiaans. Voor groepen is de prijs all-in: tot tien deelnemers circa 97 euro, vanaf elf deelnemers circa 107 euro en vanaf 21 deelnemers circa 120 euro.

VOOR HET PUBLIEK:

Office de Tourisme, Palais de Congrès, 22 Cours Honoré Cresp, 06130 Grasse.
Telefoon: 04 933 66666.

Om naar Grasse en de Côte d'Azur te komen...

Vanuit Nederland en België verdient het aanbeveling om te vliegen. De reis met de eigen auto is wel aantrekkelijk wanneer een bezoek aan de Provence en de Côte d'Azur deel uitmaakt van een rondreis door Frankrijk.

De luchthaven die zich het dichtst in de buurt bevindt is Nice Côte d'Azur International Airport (NCE). Hij ligt op ongeveer zeven kilometer ten westen van het centrum van Nice en is de belangrijkste luchthaven aan de Franse Middellandse-Zeekust, en de op één na grootste van heel Frankrijk.

Luchtvaartmaatschappijen die op Nice vliegen:

Vanaf Schiphol onder andere: KLM, Air France, Transavia, Lufthansa
Vanaf Brussel onder andere: Virgin Express

Voor eventuele voordeliger vluchten kun je op internet zoeken, bijvoorbeeld op de websites die genoemd werden onder 'Om naar Parijs te komen…'

Van de luchthaven naar Grasse:

Een busrit van de luchthaven naar Grasse neemt ongeveer een uur in beslag en kost circa 1,30 euro.

De halte van lijn 500 bevindt zich aan busperron 2 voor terminal 1. De vertrektijden kun je vinden op de website van de luchthaven van Nice, www.nice.aeroport.fr.

Met een huurauto ben je natuurlijk minder afhankelijk. De stad Grasse is weliswaar te voet heel goed te verkennen, maar de bloemenvelden en de heerlijke bergdorpen in het achterland, bijvoorbeeld Gourdon en St-Paul-de-Vence, zijn met het openbaar vervoer moeilijk te bereiken. Op de luchthaven hebben alle grote autoverhuurbedrijven een vestiging.

De luchthaven van Nice ligt meteen aan de snelweg. De snelste manier om in Grasse te komen voert via de A8 in de richting Cannes. Dit is een tolweg, maar het tolbedrag van 2,60 euro is goed besteed wanneer je gauw je doel wilt bereiken en bovendien omzeil je zo de op sommige stukken zeer drukke kustweg. Na ongeveer twintig kilometer zie je afrit 42, waar ook Grasse al wordt aangekondigd. De nu voor je liggende, nog vijftien kilometer verder naar Grasse voerende vierbaansweg RN 85 is eveneens snel afgelegd.

ROLL   SCENE

PERFUME

Prod.: Bernd Eichinger   *Const*

Director: Tom Tykwer   **B**

Camera: Frank Griebe

Date: 07.09.05   24   FPS

HET PARFUM

De film

EEN 'BOEK VAN DE EEUW' VOOR DE FILMINDUSTRIE

Meteen na de publicatie van de roman *Het parfum* in 1985 wist producent Bernd Eichinger dat hij dit verhaal ooit zou verfilmen. Hij was van mening dat hij hier een 'boek van de eeuw' in handen had. Maar de als publiciteitsschuw bekendstaande auteur Patrick Süskind hield vooralsnog de boot af. Hij zou voor de verfilming het liefst de om zijn perfectionisme beroemd geworden Amerikaanse regisseur Stanley Kubrick zien. Kubrick hield het boek echter voor onverfilmbaar zodat het er lang naar uitzag dat de geschiedenis het witte doek nooit zou halen. Pas na de dood van Kubrick in maart 1999 toonde Süskind enige bereidheid een andere regisseur de verantwoordelijkheid voor de film toe te vertrouwen. In januari 2001 was het dan eindelijk zover: Bernd Eichinger kocht de filmrechten voor naar schatting zo'n tien miljoen euro.

Eichinger behoort tot de belangrijkste producenten van Duitsland. Hij beschikt over ervaring in het verfilmen van literair werk en kan met *The Name of the Rose*, *The House of the Spirits* en *Smilla's Sense of Snow* bogen op internationaal succes. Het lag in zijn voornemen om met de verfilming van de roman *Het parfum* op deze successen voort te borduren.

Wat Eichinger nu moest doen was het zoeken naar een geschikte regisseur. Een tijd lang zag het ernaar uit dat zijn voorkeur uitging naar de Britse regisseur Ridley Scott, die na de filmklassiekers *Alien* (1979) en *Blade Runner* (1982) een poos weinig van zich had doen spreken maar in 2002 met de kaskrakende en Oscarwinnende spektakelfilm *Gladiator* een

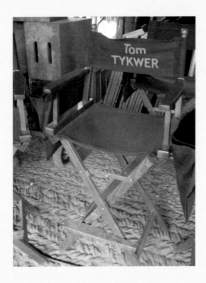

◄ De regisseursstoel

grandioze comeback had gemaakt. In het begin van 2004 viel zijn keuze echter op de Duitse regisseur Tom Tykwer (*Lola Rennt*, *Der Krieger und die Kaiserin*, *Heaven*). Eichinger maakte bekend dat hij in hem het meeste vertrouwen had om het karakter van het boek het best in beelden om te zetten.

De volgende stap was het kiezen van de hoofdrolspeler. Maar dit bleek moeilijker dan verwacht. Er werd onderhandeld met de Hollywood-sterren Leonardo Di Caprio en Or-

► Een scène waarin een 'vakgenote' van Grenouilles moeder voorkomt

▲ In deze hal werd Baldini's wereld nagebouwd

lando Bloom. Maar Di Caprio zag niets in de rol van Grenouille en de ster uit *The Lord of the Rings*, Orlando Bloom, werd door regisseur Tykwer ongeschikt bevonden. De eigenlijk voor 2004 geplande opnames moesten dus worden uitgesteld. Na een zoektocht die nog anderhalf jaar duurde, kwam aan het einde van 2004 een verrassing uit de bus: de in onze streken nog volstrekt onbekende Britse acteur Ben Whishaw zou de rol van Jean-Baptiste Grenouille spelen.

Een relatief onbekende hoofdrolspeler dus, en dat vroeg om bekende gezichten in de overige rollen. Voor de rol van Baldini werd voor Dustin Hoffman gekozen en voor die van Antoine Richis voor Alan Rickman, die in de Harry Potter-films de sinistere professor Snape gestalte geeft. Richis' roodharige dochter Laure wordt gespeeld door de tijdens de eerste opnamen vijftien jaar oude Britse actrice Rachel Hurd-Wood, die eerder als Wendy te zien was in de film *Peter Pan*. In de bijrollen vinden we onder anderen de actrices Corinna Harfouch als madame Arnulfi, Karoline Herfurth als Grenouilles eerste slachtoffer en Birgit Minichmayr als Grenouilles moeder.

Met het draaien van de duurste Duitse film aller tijden – men spreekt van een budget van zestig miljoen euro – werd begonnen in de zomer van 2005. Al met al waren er vijfenzeventig draaidagen gepland en de eerste daarvan, in juni, leverde opnamen in de bloeiende lavendelvelden van de Provence op. De eigenlijke speelfilmopnamen gingen medio juli van start en werden geschoten op het terrein van Bavaria Film in Geiselgasteig bij München, waar de zogenoemde Bayerische Filmhalle zich bevinden. Met zijn vloeroppervlak van drieduizend vierkante meter vormt deze ruimte de grootste filmstudio op het Europese vasteland. Hier werd het parfumatelier opgebouwd waarin Baldini met de hulp van Grenouille zijn geuren creëert. Alle scènes waarin Dustin Hoffman een rol speelt worden hier opgenomen.

In de 320.000 vierkante meter grote Bavaria Filmstadt kunnen bezoekers een rondleiding krijgen langs de filmsets van verschillende producties – bijvoorbeeld de decors van de Duitse soapopera *Marienhof*, de originele onderzeeboot uit Wolfgang Petersens met een Oscarnominatie bekroonde antioorlogsfilm *Das Boot*, het Gallische dorp en het Romeinse kamp, compleet met martelkamer, uit *Asterix en Obelix tegen de Galliërs* en nog verschillende andere, grotere en kleinere decorstraten. Het is jammer dat de decors van Baldini's atelier er niet worden getoond.

CATALONIË

Er was nog een belangrijke uitdaging die het team stond te wachten: het vinden van een passende locatie voor de buitenopnamen. Veel van de plaatsen van handeling in de roman bestaan in Parijs als zodanig niet meer. Zo staan er op de Pont au Change geen huizen met verdiepingen meer, noch verspreidt de Cimetière des Innocents een verpestende lijkenstank over de stad. En om te beginnen zijn er in het huidige Parijs nauwelijks nog straten waarin de aaneengesloten huizen een realistische achttiende-eeuwse indruk kunnen maken, zodat alleen met zeer intensief en zeer kostbaar gebruik van digitale technieken achteraf de gewenste sfeer zou kunnen worden ingemonteerd. En waarom zou er sowieso per se in de Franse hoofdstad gefilmd moeten worden? Het team reisde langs allerlei locaties in Europa en vond ten slotte in Noord-Spanje wat het zocht: pleinen, tuinen, gebouwen en zelfs hele straten met huizen die nog uit de Middeleeuwen leken te stammen.

Voordat het draaien kon beginnen, moesten de figuranten nog worden gecast. De audities daarvoor vonden tussen 11 en 29 juli 2005 in Barcelona plaats, en het bleek een enorme klus te zijn, niet alleen omdat er in totaal vijfduizend personen moesten worden gecast, maar vooral ook omdat zich onder hen ook echte ambachtslieden als slagers en glasblazers moesten bevinden, evenals jongleurs en andere straatartiesten. En de figuranten moesten daarbij nog aan bepaalde voorwaarden voldoen: zo waren zichtbare tattoos en piercings voor een ambachtsman of een dienstmeisje natuurlijk evenzeer uit den boze als onnatuurlijk geverfd haar of rastalokken. Verder ging de voorkeur uit naar mensen met een bleke huidskleur want een door de zon gebruinde huid kwam pas veel later in de mode. Midden in de zomer van het zonnige Spanje waren dergelijke personen niet zo gemakkelijk te vinden...

BARCELONA

De gotische wijk in de oude binnenstad

De Barri Gòtic, de gotische wijk in de binnenstad van Barcelona, biedt het ideale decor om het Parijs van de achttiende eeuw te ensceneren. Dit stadskwartier met zijn doolhofachtige stegen en kleinere en grotere pleinen is het oudste deel van Barcelona en een van de populairste bezienswaardigheden van de Catalaanse hoofdstad, al is het beslist geen openluchtmuseum; het is een levendige buurt met traditionele bedrijven, maar ook met trendy boetieks en bars waar men komt om te zien en gezien te worden.

◄ In de Barri Gòtic van Barcelona is het de moeite waard om naar verborgen details te zoeken

◀ Buiten de draaidagen is op deze straat geen spoor van de drek uit de film te vinden

De volgende stap was de autoriteiten van de stad over te halen hun toestemming te verlenen voor de filmopnamen, die de nodige overlast met zich zouden meebrengen. Om te beginnen moest het verkeer worden omgeleid. In principe is het stadsbestuur van Barcelona graag bereid om aan dergelijke grootschalige filmproducties mee te werken; het ziet niets liever dan dat de Catalaanse metropool ook op filmgebied op de kaart komt te staan. Maar toen duidelijk werd dat het filmteam veel meer noten op zijn zang had, moest er meer overredingskracht worden aangewend. Om de straten en gebouwen het aanzien van de achttiende eeuw te verlenen, dienden moderniteiten als straatlantaarns, lichtreclame en reclameslogans van bedrijven te worden verwijderd of achter decorstukken verstopt. Ook bestond er in het Parijs van de achttiende eeuw nog niet iets wat op een riool leek en dus moesten de straten tot enkelhoogte worden bedekt met modder en andere troep, terwijl ook de gevels van de huizen behoorlijk smerig dienden te worden gemaakt. In het boek spelen zich in dit soort omgevingen belangrijke scènes af en het spreekt dus vanzelf dat alles er zo authentiek mogelijk moest uitzien.

Een van de straten die Tom Tykwer in de gotische wijk had uitgekozen om er te filmen, was de Carrer de Ferran, een drukbezochte winkelstraat en zijstraat van de beroemde boulevard, de Ramblas. Het stadsbestuur ging uiteindelijk akkoord met het afzetten van en het filmen in die straat op een enkele, onverbiddelijke voorwaarde: het moest op een zondag in het begin van augustus 2005 gebeuren. In de ochtend van de daaropvolgende maandag moesten niet alleen de opnamen klaar zijn, maar moesten ook alle sporen van het werk spoorloos verdwenen zijn, de drek en alle andere viezigheid niet uitgezonderd. Tom Tykwer zei later in een interview met het tijdschrift *Stern* dat dit 'weekend er een van absolute waanzin is geweest' en dat is volkomen begrijpelijk.

Grenouilles eerste moord werd geheel en al in de Barri Gòtic in scène gezet. Op de Plaça Nova, voor de kathedraal, werd het vuurwerk afgestoken dat in Süskinds roman op de Pont Royal van Parijs plaatsvindt. De mirabellenverkoopster, Grenouilles eerste slachtoffer, loopt daarvandaan langs de Carrer del Bisbe, bewonderend nagestaard door omstanders. De fontein waarbij het 'ongeluk' gebeurt, staat op de Plaça de Sant Felip Neri. Op het rustige, ietwat verscholen liggende plein in de buurt van de kathedraal staat de gelijknamige barokkerk uit de achttiende eeuw, die sporen van inslagen draagt – natuurlijk niet van het filmen, maar littekens uit de tijd van de Spaanse Burgeroorlog.

Buiten de gotische wijk, in de buurt van de haven, ligt de Plaça de la Mercè. Op dit plein werd op 17 augustus 2005 de markt gereconstrueerd waar Grenouille ter wereld komt.

▲ De Plaça Nova voor de kathedraal

◄ Misschien het mooiste plein van Barcelona: de Plaça Reial

Plaça Reial

Andere taferelen werden gefilmd op de Plaça Reial, een van de mooiste pleinen van Barcelona. Het werd in het midden van de negentiende eeuw aangelegd en is omgeven door okerkleurige gebouwen met colonnades. Vele palmbomen en een centraal geplaatste fontein nodigen uit om er even te verwijlen. De lantaarns op het plein zijn ontworpen door de beroemde Catalaanse architect Antoni Gaudí.

Meteen aan dit plein, aan de Carrer Vidre, ligt de Herboristeria del Rei, waar planten en geneeskrachtige kruiden te koop zijn. Deze 'koninklijke kruidenhandel' werd in 1823 opgezet en is daarmee een van de oudste bedrijven van Barcelona. Voor de film werd de fraaie winkelruimte afgehuurd en met behulp van decorstukken geheel omgebouwd tot parfumerie. Een hele dag werd zowel binnen als buiten de winkel gefilmd. De scène waarin de hond aan Grenouille snuffelt, moest keer op keer worden overgedaan voordat hij naar wens op het celluloid stond.

Parc del Laberint d'Horta

Hoewel in het Zuid-Franse Grasse aan de architectonische voorwaarden voor de film beslist beter voldaan werd dan in Parijs, werden alle scènes die zich in Grasse afspelen, even-

▲ Bijna als Alice in Wonderland – alleen het witte konijn is er niet

eens in Spanje gedraaid; dit om budgettaire redenen. Voor het paleisachtige huis annex tuin van Antoine Richis werd gekozen voor het Parc del Laberint d'Horta, een voormalig landgoed in het ten noorden van Barcelona gelegen district Horta-Guinardó, dat tot het einde van de achttiende eeuw het eigendom was van markies Joan Antoni Desvalls. De tuin van de bezitting behoort nu met zijn overvloedig aanwezige beelden, keramiek en waterpartijen tot de mooiste parken van Barcelona. Zoals ook zijn Catalaanse naam al doet vermoeden is de belangrijkste attractie van het park de

► In de roman staat het huis van Antoine Richis in Grasse, maar in de film bevindt het zich in Barcelona

VOOR HET PUBLIEK:

Parc del Laberint d'Horta; Passeig Castanyers; Horta-Guinardó.
Telefoon: 93 41 32 400.
Openingstijden: dagelijks van 10 uur tot zonsondergang.
Toegangsprijs: volwassenen ca. 1,90 euro, kinderen ca. 1,25 euro. Op woensdag en zondag gratis toegang.

in het midden gelegen, door cipressen gevormde doolhof. Hier kwam de filmscène tot stand waarin Richis vanaf het terras van zijn paleis toekijkt hoe zijn dochter Laure 's nachts door het labyrint loopt. Ook in het helaas zeer vervallen paleis zelf zijn enkele scènes opgenomen, zoals bijvoorbeeld de feestelijkheden rond de zestiende verjaardag van Laure.

Het park is lange tijd particulier eigendom geweest van de erfgenamen van Desvalls, maar in 1971 heeft die familie het park aan de stad overgedragen. Tegenwoordig is het meer dan negen hectare grote landgoed als openluchtmuseum toegankelijk voor publiek.

Poble Espanyol

De meest spectaculaire en tegelijkertijd ook de moeilijkste scène is ongetwijfeld in Poble Espanyol opgenomen. Zoals we weten loopt de bedoelde terechtstelling van Grenouille op de Cour van Grasse uit op een massale seksuele orgie. In de dagen tussen 2 en 12 september 2005 lagen in de Poble Espanyol nu en dan tot wel 750 spiernaakte personen in innige koppeltjes, elkaar omarmend, kussend en strelend in een 'onvoorwaardelijke liefde' – een krankzinnig gezicht. In de roman is sprake van tienduizend mensen, en in de uiteindelijke film zullen er ook meer te zien zijn dan die in de Poble Espanyol aanwezig waren; de moderne computertechnieken hebben daarbij dan een handje geholpen. Het was voor de regisseur al moeilijk genoeg om het doen en laten van het voorhanden zijnde aantal figuranten in de hand te houden en naar wens in scène te zetten.

Om de choreografie soepel en geloofwaardig te laten ver-

▲ Massale seksuele uitspattingen hoeft men op dit plein niet te verwachten...

lopen werd de Spaanse theatergroep La Fura dels Baus te hulp geroepen. In een Barcelonese sportzaal leerden de amateurtoneelspelers, die in verschillende groepen waren ingedeeld, vooraf hoe hun bewegingen eruit moesten zien. Bij die lessen werden ook ontspanningsoefeningen gegeven – het is voor de meeste mensen immers niet de normaalste zaak van de wereld om in het zicht van honderden vreemden uit de kleren te gaan. Een belangrijke tip die gegeven

▲ Een dorp in de stad: de Poble Espanyol

VOOR HET PUBLIEK:

Adres: Poble Espanyol; Av. Marquès de Comillas 13; Barcelona.
Telefoon: 93 50 86 300.
Internet: www.poble-espanyol.com
Openingstijden: dagelijks vanaf 9 uur, maandag tot 20 uur, dinsdag tot en met donderdag tot 2 uur, vrijdag en zaterdag tot 4 uur. Zondag tot 24 uur.
Toegangsprijs: ca. 7,50 euro, met korting ca. 5,50 euro. Kinderen van 7 tot en met 12 jaar ca. 4 euro.
's Nachts kost de toegang ca. 4 euro.

werd om de scène niet te laten overkomen als een fragment uit een pornofilm: de acteurs moesten tijdens het lichamelijke contact hun ogen niet laten dwalen, maar elkaar recht in de ogen blijven kijken.

De locatie was voor de opnamen van deze lastige scène ideaal: niet alleen konden de gebouwen en de omgeving heel goed doorgaan voor die uit de achttiende eeuw, maar ook is de toegang tot de Poble Espanyol slechts mogelijk door een enkele poort, zodat het niet zo moeilijk was om kijklustigen op afstand te houden. Welke aantallen toeschouwers het tafereel met meer dan zevenhonderd naakte mensen op de been zou hebben gebracht is nauwelijks voor te stellen!

Maar de Poble Espanyol is van oorsprong natuurlijk niet gebouwd om er dit soort bacchanalen in scène te zetten. Dit 'Spaanse Dorp' in de stad strekt zich in de streek ten westen van de hellingen van de Montjuïc uit over een oppervlakte van bijna vijftig hectare. Het is gebouwd voor de Wereldtentoonstelling van 1929 en bedoeld om de Spaanse architectuur en Spaanse ambachten op een enkele plaats te laten zien. In totaal werden er 117 gebouwen neergezet, elk als voorbeeld van de architectuur van een bepaalde Spaanse regio, met tussen de gebouwen stegen en pleinen. Het voornemen was om het dorp na de tentoonstelling af te breken, maar het enthousiasme van de vele bezoekers heeft ertoe geleid dat het behouden bleef.

Evenals toen is het dorp nu een openluchtmuseum. Bezoekers van over de hele wereld komen hier om iets van de

Spaanse cultuur op te snuiven. Er zijn ongeveer veertig werkplaatsen en ateliers waar je er getuige van kunt zijn hoe de ambachtslieden hun arbeid verrichten, bijvoorbeeld als pottenbakker, goudsmid, schilder, glasblazer, poppenmaker of in een van de vele andere antieke handvaardigheden. Toch is de Poble Espanyol er niet alleen voor de toeristen; 's avonds en 's nachts is het met zijn bars en restaurants ook een trekpleister voor de stadsbewoners.

Martorell

De volgende plek waar de opnamen werden gemaakt was het ten westen van Barcelona gelegen Martorell. Hier werd een oude school in korte tijd omgebouwd tot weeshuis. Voor de casting van de figurantjes werd naarstig gezocht naar kinderen die zo mager mogelijk waren. Logisch natuurlijk, want het zou onaannemelijk zijn voor de weesjes van die tijd kinderen met flink wat vlees op de botten ten tonele te voeren.

DE PROVINCIE GIRONA
Blanes/Costa Brava

Medio september 2005 brachten de witte vrachtwagens het filmteam en zijn uitrusting verder naar het noorden, de provincie Girona in. De eerste stopplaats was Blanes aan de

◄ Behalve om er te filmen is Blanes ook zeer gewild om er vakantie te houden

Costa Brava. Deze vakantie- en vissersplaats ligt aan een baai met mooie stranden, maar is gelukkig minder ingericht op het massatoerisme dan het nabijgelegen, beruchte Lloret de Mar. In de binnenstad bevinden zich talrijke historische gebouwen, maar het team zocht voor zijn opnamewerk een andere locatie.

Op een rots, de haven overziend, staat El Convent, een voormalig klooster uit 1583. Dit fraai gerestaureerde, door pijnbomen omringde gebouw is tegenwoordig particulier eigendom, maar wordt regelmatig verhuurd, bijvoorbeeld voor bruiloften. Ook worden hier in juli en augustus van ieder jaar bekende muziekfestivals gehouden. Vanaf de rots heb je een schitterend uitzicht over de zee, maar in de film zul je daar niets van waarnemen; het gebouw wordt daarin voorgesteld als een parfumfabriek in Grasse – en hoe mooi die Provençaalse stad ook is, aan zee ligt hij niet.

Girona

Op zo'n honderd kilometer ten noordoosten van Barcelona ligt Girona, hoofdstad van de gelijknamige provincie. Van daaruit zijn de stranden van de Costa Brava in de zomer on-

▲ De Riu Onyar splitst de stad Girona in twee delen op

geveer even snel bereikbaar als in de winter de skipistes in de Pyreneeën. Zijn strategische ligging en zijn nabijheid van de Franse grens heeft ervoor gezorgd dat eeuwenlang om het bezit van Girona is gevochten. In de middeleeuwse binnenstad kun je ook vandaag nog sporen zien van eerdere veroveraars – vanaf de Romeinen, West-Goten, Moren en Franken tot aan de napoleontische troepen toe.

De historische binnenstad van Girona, de Barri Vell, behoort tot de best bewaarde van Spanje. In het centrum ligt de Call, ooit de joodse wijk van de stad en nog steeds een ware doolhof van stegen en steile trappen. Boven de binnenstad rijst de kathedraal op. Met de bouw ervan is in de elfde eeuw begonnen, maar omdat die zeshonderd jaar heeft geduurd, is het resultaat een mengelmoes van verschillende bouwstijlen. Een bijzonderheid is dat het interieur wordt gekenmerkt door zijn middenschip; dit is met zijn drieëntwintig meter breedte het breedste gotische schip ter wereld.

De wirwar van stegen in de binnenstad van Girona werd gebruikt voor de scènes die zich in Grasse afspelen. Om de Barri Vell er authentiek te laten uitzien was het zaak ook hier de nodige veranderingen aan te brengen: verkeerstekens en -lichten, afvoerpijpen en straatverlichting moesten uit het

▲ Langs de oever van de Onyar zijn fraaie huizen te zien

zicht worden verwijderd. Tijdens de opnamen, die van 19 tot 24 september 2005 plaatsvonden, werden vele straten en stegen afgesloten voor het verkeer, niet alleen voor voertuigen maar ook voor voetgangers – en dat was voor die laatste groep maar goed ook, want evenmin als in Barcelona werd de bestrating de ruimhartige bedekking met viezigheid onthouden.

Vanaf 29 september 2005 werd de middeleeuwse vesting in de buurt van de stad Cantallops, het Castillo de Requesens, het toneel van een aantal scènes. Vier dagen later trok de crew verder naar Besalú in een van de best bewaarde middeleeuwse omgevingen van Catalonië. Dit dorp is een 'conjunto histórico artistico', wat betekent dat het als geheel op

VOOR HET PUBLIEK:

Adres: Plaça Gala i Salvador Dalí 5, Figueres. Telefoon: 972 67 75 00. Internet: www.dali-estate.org.

Openingstijden: van oktober tot januari van 10.30 tot 17.45 uur. Maandag gesloten, behalve wanneer dit een feestdag is. Van juli t.e.m. september dagelijks (ook op maandag) van 9 tot 19.45 uur.

Toegangsprijs: ca. 10 euro, met korting ca. 7 euro. Kinderen tot 9 jaar hebben gratis toegang.

de lijst van beschermde monumenten staat. Karakteristiek voor het dorp is de indrukwekkende, van twee verdedigingstorens voorziene romaanse brug over de Rio Fluviá. Ook hier werden enkele scènes opgenomen.

Figueres

Figueres is een rustig provinciestadje dat op zo'n veertig kilometer ten noorden van Girona ligt. De bekendste inwoner die Figueres ooit gehad heeft is zonder enige twijfel de in 1904 hier geboren Salvador Dalí geweest. Aan hem is het te danken dat het stadje tegenwoordig het doel is van ontelbare dagjesmensen: het in de jaren tachtig door Dalí geconcipieerde 'teatre-museu' herbergt 's werelds grootste verzameling kunst van zijn hand. Aan de hand van de tentoongestelde werken is de artistieke loopbaan van dit extravagante genie precies na te gaan: van zijn eerste schetsen en tekeningen via de wereldberoemde surrealistische werken tot de kunstzinnige uitingen van zijn laatste levensjaren. Ook het op het dak met witte eieren van beton getooide museumgebouw zelf is een kunstwerk. Na zijn dood in 1989 werd Salvador Dalí in een crypte van het museum bijgezet zoals hij dat gewild had.

▲ Deze statige en stevige brug over de Rio Fluviá bewaakt Besalú al vanaf de twaalfde eeuw

◄ Al even excentriek als de naamgever is de archi-tectuur van het Dalímuse-um

Voor het filmteam meer van belang dan het Dalímuseum was het op ongeveer een kilometer afstand gelegen Castell de Sant Ferran. Deze omvangrijke vestingwerken zijn in 1753 aangelegd om de grens in de Pyreneeën te verdedigen tegen Franse aanvallen. Met zijn meer dan drie kilometer lange muur en een oppervlakte van tweeëndertig hectare wordt het Castell beschouwd als het grootste verdedigingsbolwerk van Europa. Nog in de twintigste eeuw werd het door mili-tairen bemand, terwijl de beroemdste rekruut die hier zijn dienstplicht heeft vervuld niemand minder was dan dezelf-de Salvador Dalí. Het monumentale bouwwerk heeft muren die hier en daar drie meter dik zijn, wachttorens, kilometers lange weergangen en waterputten en vormt dan ook een ge-liefd decor: *Het parfum* was al de derde film die er alleen al in 2005 werd opgenomen. Medio oktober werden hier de laatste scènes voor de film gedraaid.

VOOR HET PUBLIEK:

Adres: Castell de Sant Ferran, Calle de la Pujada al Castell, Figueres. Telefoon: 972 50 60 94.
Openingstijden: van 1 juli tot 15 september dagelijks van 10.30 tot 20 uur. In de rest van het jaar van 10.30 tot 15 uur.
Toegangsprijs: ca. 3 euro.

Tips voor boekenwurmen

Alle boekenwurmen die nog meer willen beleven van de historische achtergronden worden de volgende bronnen aanbevolen:

Het *Tableau de Paris* van Louis-Sébastien Mercier

Louis-Sébastien Mercier (1740-1814) is ongetwijfeld de belangrijkste kroniekschrijver van het Parijs van de achttiende eeuw. Ook is hij vermoedelijk de eerste 'journalist' geweest die over het dagelijkse leven in de grote stad schreef. Het twaalfdelige *Tableau de Paris* (1782-1788), waarin hij zijn impressies verzamelde, is in dat opzicht een uniek standaardwerk. In de meer dan duizend hoofdstukken van het werk doet hij verslag van zijn wandelingen door de stad en van zijn inkijkjes in onbekende hoeken ervan, daarbij een diepe belangstelling voor de meest uiteenlopende thema's aan de dag leggend.

Van het originele werk zijn verschillende hoofdstukken door Günther Metken in het Duits vertaald en als *Paris am Vorabend der Revolution* uitgegeven door Amadis Verlag Karlsruhe (1967). Uit deze verzameling zijn door de auteur de passages gekozen die in dit boek voor extra achtergrondinformatie zorgen. Ze zijn aangegeven met 'Mercier', gevolgd door de paginanummers. De met 'Mercier Bild' aangegeven fragmenten zijn afkomstig uit het boek *Mein Bild von Paris*, uitgegeven in 1979 door Insel-Verlag Leipzig. Deze boeken zijn alleen nog antiquarisch te vinden. Aangezien het werk van Mercier voor zover bekend niet in het Nederlands is vertaald, heeft de vertaler van deze reisgids voor de passages 'Mercier' en 'Mercier Bild' de Duitse vertalingen gebruikt.

Le miasme et la jonquille van Alain Corbin

De in 1936 geboren Alain Corbin is historicus en hoogleraar aan de universiteit Sorbonne in Parijs. Hij schreef talrijke boeken, vooral over onderwerpen uit de achttiende en negentiende eeuw. In zijn in 1982 uitgegeven boek *Le miasme et la jonquille* (in de Nederlandse vertaling uit 1982: *Pestdamp en bloesemgeur*) beschrijft hij gedetailleerd en uitgebreid de maatschappelijke geschiedenis van de geur. Wie dit boek leest, zal merken dat de uiteenzettingen van Alain Corbin de schrijver van *Das Parfum*, Patrick Süskind, zeker mede geïnspireerd hebben, bijvoorbeeld door de verklaringen over de 'fluïdaaltheorie'. Deze is ruim gedocumenteerd aan de hand van talrijke eigentijdse getuigenissen uit het Parijs van de achttiende eeuw en de milieus die Süskind beschrijft. Voor wie zich interesseert in historie en ontwikkeling van onze reukzin is *Le miasme et la jonquille* (in het Duits vertaald als *Pesthauch und Blütenduft*) zeker een aanrader. De Nederlandse vertaling, uitgegeven door SUN in Nijmegen, beleefde in 1986 een herdruk.

Plan de Turgot

Het Plan de Turgot is een van de mooiste stadsplattegronden van Parijs en dateert uit de achttiende eeuw. Het was de tijd vóór de grote verbouwingen onder Napoleon III en baron Haussmann, dus voor het aanzicht van de stad finaal veranderd werd. In zijn totaliteit bestaat het Plan de Turgot uit 21 bladen van groot formaat die aan elkaar gelegd kunnen worden en dan een plattegrond opleveren van ongeveer tweeënhalve bij drie meter. Duidelijk herkenbaar ingetekend zijn de afzonderlijke straten, huizen, kerken en zelfs tuinen en de losse bomen die daarin staan. In 1734 besliste de burgemeester van Parijs, Michel Etienne Turgot, dat er een nieuwe, gedetailleerde stadsplattegrond van zijn stad moest komen en hij droeg de kunstenaar Louis Bretez de taak op om stad en voorsteden compleet en natuurgetrouw in tekening te brengen. Deze opdracht nam twee jaar in beslag en nog eens drie jaren waren nodig om de drukplaten gereed te maken. Het Plan de Turgot verscheen dus niet eerder dan in 1739. De drukplaten maken momenteel deel uit van de verzameling van het Louvre.

Het is tegenwoordig bijna niet meer mogelijk om het boek met de 21 bladen te vinden. Wel zijn er, op kleiner formaat, posters te koop die een totaalaanzicht op de stad bieden, onder andere in de winkel van de Bibliothèque Historique in de Rue Mahler. Maar ook een paar minuten googelen levert resultaat op: wie zoekt op 'Plan de Turgot' kan bijvoorbeeld terechtkomen op de website van de universiteitsbibliotheek van Kyoto, die alle 21 bladen op monitorformaat laat zien.

SNUFFELREIS DOOR DE PROVENCE

Voor een reis in de voetsporen van Grenouille heeft men eigenlijk niet meer nodig dan deze gids. Maar wie dieper in deze boeiende en bloeiende materie wil duiken, zou kunnen overwegen om online een reis te boeken bij de Duitse specialist in dit soort kwalitatief hoogwaardige, individuele tochten. Geboden wordt een driedaagse reis naar de parfumstad Grasse, inclusief twee overnachtingen in een stijlvol Provençaals landhuis, een huurauto om de omgeving te verkennen, een rondleiding door de stad, een bezoek aan een parfumerie en het scheppen van een eigen, individueel parfum. Kosten: vanaf circa 504 euro per persoon.

Verdere informatie en boeken bij: www.itravel.de of telefonisch: (49)2215341090

Verantwoording

CITATEN:

Voor de citaten uit de roman *Das Parfum* heeft de vertaler van deze reisgids Ronald Jonkers' vertaling (*Het parfum. De geschiedenis van een moordenaar*, Prometheus, 46ste druk, 2005) gebruikt.

ILLUSTRATIES:

akg images/Hofbauer: blz. 23
Bavaria Film/Manfred Lämmerer: blz. 129
Créa3P: blz. 18
Philippe Dufour: blz. 74
Michael Engler: kaart blz. 77
Antonio Fernandez: blz. 139
Met vriendelijke toestemming van de Fundació Gala-Salvador Dalí: blz. 144, 145
Met vriendelijke toestemming van Galimard: blz. 11, 81
José Antonio Gómez: blz. 131, 132, 133, 134, 135 beneden
Manfred Kaczerowski: blz. 12, 37, 45, 47 boven, 50 boven, 52, 67
Eugenia Llano Vázquez: blz. 128 beneden
Philippe Migeat en Georges Méguerditchian/Centre Pompidou: blz. 33, 35, 36
Oliver Mittelbach: 9, 14, 17, 19, 22, 24, 26, 27, 28, 29, 30, 34, 39, 42, 43, 46, 47 beneden, 48, 50 boven, 53, 55, 56, 58, 59, 60, 64, 65, 66, 68, 69, 70, 78, 84, 85, 86, 88, 91, 92, 93, 96 boven, 96 beneden, 97, 99, 109 beneden, 110, 112, 113, 114, 115, 116, 120, 122, 123
Met vriendelijke toestemming van Molinard: blz. 76, 81, 85, 94
Ulrike Müller: blz. 11, 80, 101, 102, 118
Office de Tourisme Grasse: blz. 106, 109 boven, 108, 111, 119 boven, 119 beneden, 121
Josep M. Oliveras/Ajuntament de Girona: blz. 140/141, 142
Phototèque des Musées de la Ville de Paris: blz. 63

Poble Espanyol de Barcelona: blz. 137 boven, 137 beneden
Laurent Pouppeville: blz. 89, 90
Manel Raya/Parcs i Jardins de Barcelona: blz. 135 boven
Xavier Samsa Reilly: blz. 126, 128 boven
Hans Michael Sauer: blz. 104
Joan Ureña Vidal: blz. 143
Meike Ziemer: blz. 38, 54

Ook verkrijgbaar:

PATRICK SÜSKIND

Het
parfum

De geschiedenis van
een moordenaar

PROMETHEUS

ISBN 90 446 0878 9 / € 12,50